Alan J. Pakula

HIS FILMS AND HIS LIFE

Jared Brown

BACK STAGE BOOKS/NEW YORK

Also by Jared Brown

The Fabulous Lunts

Zero Mostel: A Biography

The Theatre in America During the Revolution

Senior Editor: Mark Glubke

Project Editor: Ross Plotkin

Cover Design: Bob O'Brien

Interior Design: Leah Lococo, Ltd.

Production Manager: Ellen Greene

First published in 2005 by Back Stage Books,

an imprint of Watson-Guptill Publications,

a division of VNU Business Media, Inc.

770 Broadway, New York, NY 10003

www.wgpub.com

The Cataloging-in-Publication data for this title is on file with the Library of Congress

LIBRARY OF CONGRESS CONTROL NUMBER

2005929533

ISBN: 0-8230-8799-9

Manufactured in the United States of America

First printing 2005

1 2 3 4 5 6 7 8 9 / 11 10 09 08 07 06 05

CONTENTS

Acknowledgments

A GREAT DEAL OF THE RESEARCH for this book was conducted by interviewing those who knew Alan J. Pakula best: his family, friends, and co-workers. To all those who gave me information I am most grateful. The complete list of those who were interviewed appears in the bibliography, but I offer particular thanks to Hannah Pakula, Robert Mulligan, Donald Laventhall, and Robert Redford, all of whom provided indispensable help.

I am indebted to Mark Glubke, my editor, whose insightful comments have helped produce a clearer and more focused manuscript. My thanks, too, to Mitchell Waters, whose efforts on behalf of the book went beyond the call of an agent's duty.

The American Film Institute generously gave me permission to quote extensively from two long sessions Alan Pakula spent answering questions from students (*The American Film Institute Seminar with Alan Pakula on November 20, 1974* and *The American Film Institute Seminar with Alan Pakula held May 27, 1976*)—and from *Filmmakers on Filmmaking*, edited by Joseph McBride, published by J. P. Tarcher, Inc. © 1983. Many other quotations are from an interview with Alan Pakula conducted by Annette Insdorf at Manhattan's 92nd Street "Y" in Dr. Insdorf's "Reel Pieces" series. I am extremely grateful to Annette Insdorf as well as to the American Film Institute. I have quoted from *Adventures in the Screen Trade* by William Goldman; copyright © 1983 by William Goldman; by permission of Warner Books, Inc.

Thanks also to the following: Debby Maisel, who made available irreplaceable family photographs; Christopher Murray, who gave me access to several photographs he took as well as others; Anna Boorstin, who provided a family photograph; Martin Starger, who permitted the use of the photos taken on the set of *Sophie's Choice*; Harry Clein, Donald Carveth, and Rudy Koppl, who permitted me to quote from articles they wrote; Robert J. Emery; the editors of *Sight and Sound* and *Film Comment*; Boaty Boatwright, who helped put me in touch with some people who were difficult to reach; Ned Brown and Jennifer Nahum; Donna Kail; and the members of the Faculty Development Committee at Illinois Wesleyan University, who awarded me a substantial grant in 2002, without whom this book would have taken several years longer to write.

As Daniel Okrent observed in the acknowledgments to his book *Nine Innings*, it is customary for authors to thank their spouses for their help in responding to and proofreading their books. Still, there is only one Judy Brown and, as her criticisms and suggestions were invariably helpful, she deserves far more than a standard acknowledgement and I can't thank her enough.

—JARED BROWN, May 2005, Bloomington, Illinois

Foreword

BY HARRISON FORD

I FIRST MET ALAN PAKULA in his office in New York, somewhere near the southwest edge of Central Park, on 54th Street, I think. The old, unpretentious building, with its creaky elevator, was the site of his small, but comfortable office. I remember that it felt like a psychiatrist's office.

The meeting, if I recall correctly, had something to do with *Sophie's Choice*. I was in awe of Alan but I felt very comfortable with him. He was a somewhat patrician figure but wonderfully democratic and easy to talk to.

As I got to know him better in later years, I came to understand some of what was special about Alan. He was very proud of his wife Hannah, a distinguished historian and successful writer. He was devoted to his stepchildren and other members of his extended family. He was involved in their lives, always aware of them, and took pains to spend time with them.

My interest in working with Alan had to do not only with the project he was about to make but with my admiration for his earlier films: particularly *Klute*, *The Parallax View*, *Starting Over* (I had read the script for it and had wanted the part Burt Reynolds played), and *All the President's Men*. They were extremely powerful and highly significant movies. And they still "play." That is, they seem neither dated nor awkward; rather, they are both immediate and involving. It's not simply his direction of them, but his point of view, the sincere and very deep ambition to plumb the human spirit and instinct in widely different forms of expression. He attempted to give his audiences the opportunity to think through how complicated life was and how characters that they might not imagine they had anything in common with had gone through experiences that might help them in their own lives.

As a director, Alan was among the best I ever worked with. Even while we were making *The Devil's Own*, his last picture and one in which circumstances made it nearly impossible to make a satisfactory film (Chapter Nineteen in this book describes those circumstances in considerable detail), he managed to turn it into a movie that I was proud of having been involved in. Normally, he would not have directed a film like *The Devil's Own*, he wasn't a director for hire, but we roped him into it. He took his greatest pleasure from directing (and often writing) films he developed or originated.

I enjoyed the work on *The Devil's Own* and on *Presumed Innocent* because of Alan's affection for actors and his respect for their processes. He understood what the costs were for actors in terms of being vulnerable—not only in portraying vulnerability, but the vulnerability that is at the core of nearly every actor. He respected the spirit and experiences of actors, and found ways to bring those qualities to the screen.

As with all the best directors, Alan worked differently with each actor, based upon how he felt the actor might best reach what's needed. With me his method was a simple one: he would give me a chance to present my ideas about the story, and through that process I would sometimes ask for certain changes in the lines I was to deliver. I'd say, "I think I can act that without the use of dialogue," and he was invariably supportive. Rather than forcing me to adjust to the script, he would make small adjustments for me and the other actors, adjustments that not only made us more comfortable but that I think resulted in better performances.

This book about Alan Pakula should help others who have ambitions to be filmmakers, especially those who, like Alan, might approach the process of moviemaking through writing or through an intellectual rather than a visceral method. They will find that although Alan's films were entertaining and emotional, they were achieved through intellect.

As it turned out, *The Devil's Own* was Alan's final movie. He was killed in a terrible accident in 1998. He had been hoping to make a film he had been working on for years about Franklin Delano Roosevelt. Certainly he would never again have made a cops-and-robbers story like *The Devil's Own*. After that experience, he was heading—it might be more accurate to say that he was fleeing—into more intellectual territory, the territory explored by nearly all his films.

More than anything else, what distinguished my experience with Alan Pakula was that he and I were in agreement on how to tell a story and develop a character; but, as well, we had similar taste. It's an elusive thing to define, but I think it came from the nature of his personality and his understanding of and empathy for other people. There's not a lot of "taste" going around these days in the film business. Today it seems that anything is allowable for effect, but, fortunately for a generation of filmgoers, Alan never thought that way. His films are the proof.

—HARRISON FORD
May 2005
Jackson Hole, Wyoming

Preface

"For me, Alan Pakula was one of the great American filmmakers, but if you
look at his films, they look so simple. The camera is not doing back-flips
and he's not afraid to hold a shot. You can argue that if you do your work
really well, no one should notice."

—TODD FIELD, director of <u>In the Bedroom</u>

In 1998, ALAN J. PAKULA was working on an adaptation for the
screen of Doris Kearns Goodwin's *No Ordinary Time*, an account of Franklin and
Eleanor Roosevelt during the Second World War. He had already spent more than
a year researching the project, and had accumulated more than five hundred pages
of notes. He had written approximately the first fifty pages of the screenplay. He
had spoken to Jane Alexander, inquiring informally if she would be interested in
playing Eleanor, a role she had acted years earlier in a two-part television series
called *Eleanor and Franklin*.

The project was immensely important to Pakula. One of America's finest
filmmakers, he had produced *To Kill a Mockingbird*, directed *Klute* and *All the President's
Men*, and wrote the screenplay for—as well as directed—*Sophie's Choice*. Among his
other best films were *Presumed Innocent*, *The Parallax View*, and *Starting Over*. His track
record as director, screenwriter and producer had won him the much sought-
after privilege of "final cut"—the right to determine precisely how his films would
be shown, without interference from film studios, financial contributors, or anyone else. He had achieved autonomy in casting, and had made bold choices, casting newcomers in leading roles and established performers against type: Gregory
Peck as a middle-aged father in *To Kill a Mockingbird*, his first departure from conventional leading-man roles; Jane Fonda in an intensely dramatic role in *Klute*,
although she was best known at the time as a cartoonish sex symbol in the *Barbarella*
movies; Paula Prentiss as a distinctly non-comic character in *The Parallax View*,
although she was thought of primarily as a comedienne; Jason Robards as the
dynamic Ben Bradlee in *All the President's Men*, although Robards had built his repu-

tation playing dysfunctional characters unable to cope with life's demands (only after *All the President's Men* did Robards become identified with tough, gritty characters); Burt Reynolds as the wry, laid-back protagonist of *Starting Over*, although Reynolds was best known for his smash 'em, crash 'em movies; and Kevin Kline in his first screen role as the paranoid schizophrenic Nathan Landau in *Sophie's Choice*, although Kline's most recent Broadway success had been in the buffoonish comic role of the Pirate King in *The Pirates of Penzance*.

But Pakula was seventy years old in 1998, and some in the film industry found it hard to believe that he could maintain his pace for long, even though the quality of his films remained consistently high and his enthusiasm for filmmaking hadn't waned for thirty years. However, as early as 1992, he had felt the need, against his best instincts, to make films of a less personal nature than the films for which he was renowned. Such movies as *Dream Lover* (1986), *Orphans* (1987), and *See You in the Morning* (1989) had all failed to resonate with large audiences and lost large sums of money. Any filmmaker depends upon public approval of his work—movie studios will not provide money for filmmakers who have shown they are consistently unable to attract an audience—and Pakula keenly felt the need to make some movies that would demonstrate significant box-office appeal, so that he could maintain his independence and afford once again to make the kinds of personal films he preferred.

Thus a series of subsequent films had been undertaken largely for their commercial appeal, in order to demonstrate that he had not lost his popular touch. He succeeded with *Presumed Innocent* in 1990 and attempted to do so again with 1992's *Consenting Adults*, but the film was unsuccessful both critically and with audiences. Perhaps the solution was one he had rarely employed before: to cast major stars in order to assure success. The strategy worked with *The Pelican Brief* (1993), as Julia Roberts and Denzel Washington gave a material boost to the box office. Indeed, the film had grossed more than $100 million—the only film Pakula ever made to earn so much money. But success came at a price. *The Pelican Brief* was regarded as a Julia Roberts movie, even though the line "An Alan J. Pakula Film" appeared before the credits. The director had, for the first time in his career, been involved in a film that was thought of primarily as a vehicle for a performer rather than the expression of a personal vision.[1]

At first he resisted when, in 1995, he was asked to make *The Devil's Own*, a project with a simplistic, violence-filled script that represented everything Pakula's films had avoided in the past. But the producers returned to him again and

---

[1] *One could argue that* All the President's Men *was perceived by the public primarily as a Robert Redford/Dustin Hoffman picture. However, Pakula's wish to direct the film was based primarily on his attitude toward the events that came to be known as "Watergate." Moreover, Pakula did not initially favor the casting of Redford and Hoffman (see Chapter Ten).*

again, finally offering him such an enormous amount of money that he was unable to turn it down. Again, he was hired primarily to burnish the careers of two star actors, but even the casting of Harrison Ford and Brad Pitt could not rescue *The Devil's Own* in 1997, a film that was beset with problems from the beginning, and that met with only lukewarm public support. Even more damaging, Pitt trashed the film to a *Newsweek* reporter before it was released; his angry outburst seemed to indicate that Pakula had allowed the production to spiral out of control.

Nonetheless, Pakula did yeoman work on *The Devil's Own*, turning out a film that was far better than anyone expected it to be. But, despite the result, and despite Brad Pitt's tacit apology, the damage to Pakula's reputation was significant. He longed to return to the sort of work he had done in the past, and nothing could represent that wish more than *No Ordinary Time*, a film that Pakula believed would prove to be one of his greatest achievements.

But *No Ordinary Time* was rife with risk. A film set in a period few audience members would have lived through. A film about the private and public lives of political figures. A literate approach to complex material despite audiences who had for many years expressed their preference for exploding heads, car chases, laser weapons, and other special effects. Still, if he were to retain his autonomy as a filmmaker, *No Ordinary Time* would have to be the instrument that would restore him to his position in the cinematic world. Thus, the prospective film assumed enormous importance to Pakula from every point of view. It was the kind of socially and psychologically relevant film for which he had become renowned: it would not depend upon conventional casting choices; it would deal with the sort of literate material about which he felt most strongly; and he himself would write the screenplay. If it did not ultimately achieve the commercial success of *The Pelican Brief*, well, that would be acceptable as long as it could earn those connected with it a reasonable profit. Pakula was convinced that it would.

On November 19, 1998, Pakula climbed into his black three-year-old Volvo station wagon to return from his office in Manhattan, where he had been working on the screenplay for *No Ordinary Time*, to his home in East Hampton, New York. Thirty-five miles into his trip on the Long Island Expressway, he was following at what seemed to be a safe distance behind another car. Just east of Exit 48, at 11:15 AM, the motorist in front of Pakula swerved to avoid a seven-foot-long metal pipe lying on the expressway. The car drove over the pipe, however, sending it hurtling through Pakula's windshield and into his head. The Volvo swerved into a fence. By 12:22 in the afternoon, doctors at North Shore University Hospital in Plainview had pronounced him dead. Where the metal pipe had come from remains a mystery; the likeliest theory is that it had fallen off a truck moments before the accident.

No Ordinary Time may yet be filmed—Pakula's associate, Donald Laventhall, is working to complete his screenplay—but it will inevitably be different than the version Pakula intended. The loss of the film, and its promise of greatness, is as unfortunate as the loss of Pakula's life was tragic.

* * *

Devotees of film have seen all of Alan J. Pakula's best-known movies. Even casual filmgoers will be familiar with *Klute*, *All the President's Men*, and *Sophie's Choice*. But there can be no denying that Pakula's name is unfamiliar to many. A conundrum: although Pakula was one of the most successful and admired filmmakers in the United States, few people know his name. Some speculation as to why that is true is in order.

Alan Pakula was not a self-promoter; his films spoke for themselves. Other directors are far more often in the public eye. Think of the most renowned directors in America during the past sixty years: Orson Welles, Alfred Hitchcock, Francis Coppola, and Martin Scorsese are representative examples. One glance at those names and an image of the director may spring to mind. They are (or were) dynamic individuals who, either by accident or by design, became every bit as famous as the stars who were featured in their films. The image would also include hearing the rhythms of the director's speech (remembered from appearances on television, either as a performer or in an interview or in another capacity). Immediate associations connect the director with the sort of films he makes or made: Scorsese's rat-a-tat, violent style, accompanying his well-known Catholic sense of guilt; Hitchcock's virtuosity with the camera and his brilliance at creating and maintaining suspense; Coppola's slow, superb accretion of detail and the characterization of unforgettable characters such as Michael Corleone and Colonel Kurtz. But Alan Pakula's style cannot be swiftly or easily summarized. Even a frequent filmgoer might well ask: Is there such a thing as a "Pakula style"?

Alan Pakula's films will be remembered not for their stylistic similarities to one another but for their differences. It seems virtually impossible that a single director could have been responsible for the tense drama of investigative reporting, *All the President's Men*, and the whimsical comedy *Starting Over*; or the anguished film about the horror of the Holocaust, *Sophie's Choice*, and the riveting portrait of the underbelly of society, *Klute*. Consider the portrait of young innocence in *The Sterile Cuckoo* in contrast to the wary, almost cynical view of American politics in *The Parallax View*; or the probing legal drama, *Presumed Innocent* as compared to the tender autobiographical comedy-drama, *See You in the Morning*. Each film demanded and received vastly different treatments. Is this a weakness? Only if one expects an artist to repeat his achievements again and again. Rather, the differences in Pakula's approaches to his films should be regarded as a strength—the strength of a highly accomplished artist refusing to impose any specific directorial approach on highly diverse cinematic material. Each film was treated as a unique entity, and each entity received a treatment that was most appropriate to expressing its central idea.

When one discusses those ideas, those themes, one is closer to identifying the unifying factor in Pakula's work. All of his films shared certain characteristics: the attempt to examine his characters with the utmost psychological complexity, and, in many cases, the hope to create a more just society, generally by probing the weaknesses of America's system of government and its most powerful institutions. *Klute* and *Sophie's Choice* represent the psychological films, whereas *All the President's Men*, *The Parallax View*, *Rollover*, *Presumed Innocent*, and *The Pelican Brief* represent the social films.

In Pakula's movies, all the conventional elements of style—camera movement and angles, displays of visual pyrotechnics—are subordinated to the telling of the story (frequently a story of social import). The story functions as a means of exploring and codifying the characters' psychology, for the characterizations in the social films are invariably drawn with great complexity. One does not find scenes of dazzling camera work, for every shot, every cut, every movement is designed to reinforce the filmmaker's purpose. This is not to say that Pakula's films are *without* visual style, simply that the style supports and reinforces the content. A careful viewing of any Pakula film reveals that every visual and aural element has been chosen with utmost care to unobtrusively forward the story and acquaint the audience more fully with the psychology of the characters. Only the most important visual images are presented. In other words, Pakula's style is characterized by restraint, in contrast to the styles of Welles and Scorsese, which may be said to be characterized by flamboyance.

Another reason why Pakula's films are not necessarily recognizable as "Alan J. Pakula Productions" is that Pakula never considered himself an *auteur*—the only artist of importance on a film. Of course, as director, he provided the overall conception for each picture and guided each to a conclusion with which he was satisfied. But he always gave full credit to his actors, screenwriters, cinematographers, editors, composers, et al. Film, he said, represented—more than any other art form—the art of collaboration. He permitted all those with whom he worked, including production assistants, sound men, cameramen, script supervisors, and others to contribute opinions regarding the progress of each film, and, if he agreed with their points of view, unhesitatingly used their suggestions. In the end, he maintained, every film was so thoroughly collaborative that he could not have said specifically what any of the artists, including himself, had contributed to the totality. Thus, a Pakula film does not bear the stamp of a Coppola film or a

Hitchcock film—or of any individual—but of Pakula *and* his many collaborators.

Pakula was, by nature, a modest man. He had no wish, and no need, to take credit for the contributions of others. Rather than say, "I created Jane Fonda's performance by doing thus-and-so," he would say, "Jane Fonda's insights, innate talent, and hard work were responsible for her brilliant performance." In fact, Jane Fonda's performance was less likely to be brilliant without the directorial guidance of Alan Pakula, but he would not have made such a claim. Thus, some moviegoers attribute the success of *Klute* to Jane Fonda, of *Sophie's Choice* to Meryl Streep, of *All the President's Men* to Jason Robards. Certainly, Fonda, Streep, and Robards (all of whom won Academy Awards for their efforts) gave brilliant performances, but would they have been so successful without the directorial help of Alan Pakula? When one realizes that they would not even have been *cast* had it not been for Pakula, the answer becomes apparent.

Some directors rule their domains with an iron hand, further affixing their signatures to their films, and there is no question that the public is fascinated by dictatorial and mercurial directors. By contrast, Pakula's approach was far more relaxed. One could not say that his system was democratic—all directors stand at the top of a pyramid made up of every other individual who works on the film— but it was surely benevolent.

For all these reasons, the name of Alan J. Pakula is little known—if at all—to most filmgoers. If, however, that prevents him from securing the audience he deserves, it can only be described as unfortunate, for the innovative and provocative films he has directed, produced, and occasionally written are known and appreciated by millions.

CHAPTER ONE

Beginnings

"It's important for filmmakers to know painting, literature, music, because
filmmaking is a marriage of all those arts in the twentieth century. A filmmaker can't simply be a director or a cinematographer anymore. If he
wants to be an artist he has to know everything."

—LEONARD ROSENMAN, composer for more than 100 films

SOON AFTER THE TWENTIETH CENTURY BEGAN, six-year-old
Paul Pakula was among eight children—seven boys and one girl—who came
to America from Tomaszow, a small town in Poland. Despite the fact that no one
in the family knew any English, and that they owned few possessions, Paul's
father eventually came to own a small grocery store on the Lower East Side of New
York City.

Paul grew up without any trace of a Polish accent. Eventually, after being mus-
tered out of the service in World War I, he and his brother Ben became co-own-
ers of a printing and advertising business, The Bryant Press on East 19th Street.
He met and fell in love with Jeanette Goldstein, an American-born woman whose
family also emigrated from Poland, and whose father had died soon after arriving
in his new country, leaving a family of four children, including two-year-old
Jeanette. William Goldstone, Jeanette's brother, who was about twelve years old,
took over the paternal role, and was, according to Goldstone's daughter Selma
Hirsh, "very protective of Jeanette, and very, very devoted."[2] In 1922, Selma was a
four-year-old flower girl at the wedding of Paul and Jeanette, both of whom were
in their mid-twenties.

Paul and Jeanette settled down on Loring Place in the Bronx, where their

---

[2] *William and Jeannette had different surnames because William legally changed his name to Goldstone. (Further complicating
matters: William and Jeannette's brother, Nat, changed his name to Golding.) As Selma Hirsh explained, Goldstein "was a name
that was given when my father's parents arrived at Ellis Island. They were handing out names to Jews, either 'Goldstein' or 'Levy,'
or whatever, and so my father never felt that that was a legitimate name, anyway."*

daughter, Felice, was born. Alan Jay followed three years later, on April 7, 1928. The printing business eventually allowed Paul to support his family in something approaching luxury. Although Alan's friend Alvin Sargent never met Paul, the accounts he heard from Alan when they were both in their twenties in California persuaded him that Alan's parents were "well-to-do and had sort of an elegant life." Their attainment of upper-middle-class comfort was the result of Paul's hard work. "My father worked day and night," Alan said, adding that Paul was "driven."

Paul may have suffered "some kind of breakdown" at some point—at least that is part of family lore, as told to me by Paul and Jeanette's granddaughter, Debby Maisel. "It was never really discussed," she said, "but there was always some kind of emotional instability about him."

Although Paul had achieved considerable success and always projected an ami-ability to the world—"when you would see him, he'd give you a warm embrace," Debby said—Alan's relationship with his family during his formative years was not always easy. Paul and Jeanette hoped that Alan would pursue a career in medicine (evidently because, as a very young child—"a good Jewish child," as he said—he told his parents that he wanted to be a doctor). However, he eventually realized that he had better correct that impression, "because I was terrified of blood and thought, my God, what's going to happen when they find me out and I faint in front of an operating table and my life is ruined and they realize their son is a fake?" When he finally summoned up the courage to tell his parents, Paul's temper flared.

Jeannette attempted to soften Paul's anger. Selma Hirsh observed that Jeanette "understood [Alan] more than his father. She was much more eager for him to go and find his way and do his thing, and forget about what Dad would like. She was very supportive of him. He was very close to her."

But Paul and Alan continued to see life differently. One point of conflict that arose was caused by the very different rhythms in Paul's and Alan's personalities. Paul was "very precise about everything, always punctual" a family member told me, whereas Alan was languid and invariably late. Paul would say, "You're meet-ing me at twelve today for lunch," and Alan would always arrive twenty or thirty minutes after the hour. "He never was in a hurry to do anything," which was a source of constant irritation for Paul.

Alan's languid, deliberate tempo was not simply a reaction against his father. It was his natural rhythm. He walked slowly, and, when he was old enough to get his driver's license, drove slowly. Alvin Sargent, his good friend in Los Angeles in the late 1940s, said, "He always moved carefully—watching, you know, observant, and very careful. If you wanted to be safe on the road, you drove with Alan. Alan drove as if he was holding eggs, it was just so smooth and slow. That's how he walked, too. He walked from one place to another with a v-e-r-y s-l-o-w pace, an almost unnaturally slow pace. I'd say, 'Come on, man, can we walk a little faster?'" But he might as well not have spoken, for "Alan *wasn't* going to walk a little faster." According to a family member, "even if he had to make a plane, he was always there at the last moment, and I heard that one time they held the plane for him."

Anyone outside the immediate family had a difficult time understanding Alan's difficult relationship with his father, for Paul was the soul of affability with others. His grandchildren were particularly fond of him. Rodd Baxter, Debby Maisel's brother and Paul's grandson, described Paul as "a very nice guy, very outgoing; everybody loved him." But Alan once confided to Debby that his mother and father "were wonderful grandparents but not such easy parents." Baxter recalls that "Alan would be amazed at what a great relationship my sister [Debby] and I had with [Paul and Jeanette] in terms of how close we were with them and how open they were with us," because his own relationship with his parents had at one time been prickly. Alan told Selma Hirsh that Paul and Jeanette "used to fight a lot when he was growing up, and he always had to comfort Felice, tell her not to worry, that he was sure it was going to turn out all right."

Still, it seems likely that Alan's relationship with his parents was no more stressful than that of any boy growing up in a home with a mother and father who hoped the best for him. In any case, he was fortunate to have had a close relationship with his sister, whom he "adored," according to Alan's future wife, Hannah. Alan and Felice comforted one another throughout their lives. "Alan used to say that my mother [Felice] had a lot of fears, a lot of insecurities and emotional issues," Debby Maisel said, "and that he had the same." Evidently Felice's anxieties never abated, but Alan, who underwent many years of psychotherapy when he lived in California, managed to put his fears to rest.

Selma Hirsh, Alan's cousin, eleven years older than he, knew Alan from the time of his birth. She was one of his first baby-sitters and later helped him with his homework. "Our families lived around the corner from one another and he was my favorite little cousin," she said. Later still, Selma became a confidante, and, when Alan was an adult, a good friend. She described his personality as a child: "He was a very sweet and very compassionate kid, and always with a delightful sense of humor. Not a competitive kid. Very friendly, very outgoing."

Selma recalled the time when Alan had reached the advanced age of eight and she was trying to teach him to use a two-wheel bicycle. But, as she said, Alan "was not very athletic" and "he would not let go of the training wheels. I said, 'You're nearly nine years old, and no nine-year-old goes around with training wheels.' But he didn't care—he went around with training wheels."

The Pakula family moved to Long Beach, a small town on Long Island, when Alan was four years old. Paul became active in the Long Beach community, and helped youngsters who had no money to go to school by starting a "Dad's club." Alan began his education at the primary school in Long Beach, continuing in the junior high school and high school. He proved to be intelligent, highly organized, and tenacious, qualities that enabled him to achieve excellent grades.

As early as seven years old, Alan had begun his lifelong infatuation with film. "As a child," he later said, "I would come home from the movies on Saturday night and I would draw on some of the characters I'd seen in the movies. They were usually war movies I created, in which I was the bugle boy in the First World War or the Civil War, and I would go off into battle and then I would proceed to save all the young men in the troop and I would die in the battlefield or come close to dying, and they'd all be running around saying, 'We had no idea how brave he was.' I used to lie awake at night continuing this series of adventures. . . . In a sense, in my own fantasy world I've been making films since I was seven or eight years old."

There were undoubtedly hundreds of movies that impressed Alan on those Saturday night excursions, but he later spoke specifically of *It Happened One Night*, *Mr. Smith Goes to Washington*, *The Big Parade*, *Lost In the Stars*, and *Meet Me in St. Louis* as significant influences.

When he was about thirteen, the Pakula family went to Hollywood on a vacation. Among other sights, the Pakulas toured Warner Bros. studios, where Paul Pakula's oldest friend was president of the cartoon division. Less than ten years later, Alan would make use of that relationship by accepting a position at Warners.

When Alan was fourteen, the family moved from Long Beach to 86th Street and Riverside Drive in Manhattan, where several legitimate theatres were within a bus ride's distance. On Sunday afternoons Alan would customarily wait in front of a theatre until the end of the first intermission, then file back into the theatre with the rest of the crowd to see the rest of the play.

By the time he was a teenager, his ambition was to become an actor. That dream lasted only until he was sixteen, however, for, after appearing in some high school and junior high school plays, he decided that his skill as an actor was too limited. Nevertheless, he had begun to believe that his destiny lay within the theatre or as a filmmaker.

This created a conflict at home. Paul's hope was that Alan would succeed him in the family's printing business. It was, in fact, more than a hope. "I wanted him in my business . . . *badly*," he said to John Culhane when Culhane interviewed him for the *New York Times* in 1982, "because he was the only [male] heir I had." But Alan, according to his own account, "had nothing but scorn for business."

In September 1942, however, Paul desperately hoped to deflect his son's growing interest in a career in the arts, and enrolled Alan in the Bronx High School of Science. Alan always wondered what he was doing there, especially because his father was friendly with the principal of the School of the Arts, a school Alan would have preferred to attend.[3] Moreover, the daily subway trip to and from 205th Street, where the High School of Science was located, was a long one from his home on Riverside Drive. Still, he did well there, maintaining his reputation as a first-rate student.

On the Bronx High School of Science transcript, "Medicine" is listed under Alan Pakula's "Vocational Plans." Whether or not that information came from Alan or Paul is unknown, but during his teenage years Alan seriously contemplated becoming a psychoanalyst, and, although he did not pursue that notion, his interest in psychology—which only grew over the years—was excellent preparation for his eventual career as a director. As he later said, "the resemblances between being a director working with a group of actors and a psychoanalyst are obvious."

Perhaps the most challenging aspect of the director's job is to understand the characters in his play or film intimately: not merely *what* they do but *why* they do it, what motivates their behavior. The director must understand subconscious as well as conscious motives. He or she must also discern why characters behave as they do in relation to other characters and must have the fullest possible understanding of his characters' inner lives. The more deeply a director can penetrate a character's psyche, the more he can offer the actor who will ultimately appear before a camera or an audience interpreting the character. Alan's interest in psychology not only sustained him at the Bronx High School of Science, but proved vitally important to his development as a director. Long after the choice had been made, he continued to refer to himself as "an analytic buff."[4]

His teachers listed history as his strongest subject, Latin as his weakest. They also listed model airplanes and chemistry as "Special Interests." He enrolled in as many non-science courses as he was permitted (Art Appreciation and Band, for example), but much of his time was spent studying biology and "General Science."

In September 1944, Paul and Jeanette transferred their son to the private Hill School in Pottstown, Pennsylvania, for his last year of secondary school. Paul hoped that Alan would attend Yale University, and he undoubtedly felt that a year's attendance at the posh Hill School would pave the way.

Alan's experience at Hill cannot have been easy. For one thing, as the youngest

---

[3] *Not until many years later, when Alan was in his sixties, did he question Paul directly, when the two of them and their wives were having dinner at a New York restaurant. "Dad," he said, "I really wish you'd tell me why, when I was obviously totally involved in the arts, why did you send me to the Bronx High School of Science?"*

Jeanette looked at her husband. "Paul, do you think we should tell him?"

Paul nodded. "Well, I guess maybe we should."

Jeanette's gaze settled on her son. "You know," she said, "it was your father's last hope that you'd be a doctor."

[4] *In college, his senior thesis was entitled "The Psychology of the Drama." His mother later proudly recalled that he received an A+.*

member of his class he was enrolled in the "accelerated program." More significantly, as his friend, Barbara Davis, recently told me: "Hill School was a very starchy place, and he was a Jewish kid from New York City. His parents were well-off, but they didn't lend him any cachet. It had to have been tough for him, being who he was: a New York Jew in what must have been an alien environment."

Indeed, at the Hill School he encountered anti-Semitism for the first time. He did not say how this was manifested, but he obviously surmounted that difficulty, for he became one of the most popular boys in his class. The school principal, in a recommendation written for Alan, called him "a fine, well-balanced youth, and there is very little, indeed, that one can say in reference to him of a negative character. He is extremely well-bred, and with him, good breeding is a thing that goes straight to the core. He is kindly, friendly, highly cooperative, and highly considerate of all his fellow humans. He is, in personality, attractive with very mature interests, which make a definite appeal to, and delight, older people who come in contact with him." The principal went on to praise Alan's study habits and his academic achievements. He ended by noting Alan's I. Q.: 133.

Alan recalled in 1982 that he took his Latin final exam on D-day in 1945, and, although passing the test was his immediate concern, "what I was worrying about [was that] men were dying in Normandy." But perhaps there was another, even more pressing anxiety behind his thoughts about dying soldiers. "Although I could intellectually talk about what was happening in the world, and I followed the news religiously," he said, "I think I was a very self-absorbed adolescent, worried about my own self-doubts, insecurities, and fantasies of what I wanted to be."

The Hill School yearbook makes no mention of his having participated in dramatic activities. Instead, Alan restricted his extracurricular activities to singing in the choir, and becoming a member of the "Pipe Club."[5]

The registrar of the Hill School recommended that Alan attend Harvard or Yale, although Alan's wish was to go to the University of Chicago. Later, he related how the decision was finally made:

Well, Harvard and Yale are pretty heady stuff and I desperately wanted to get to a politically liberal environment [at] Chicago. . . . My father really wanted me to go to Harvard or Yale, so I said, "All right," begrudgingly and very dramatically—I was a terribly dramatic adolescent. I said I would go to Yale, and I went there because I'd rooted for their football team over Harvard when I was eight years old, some totally irrational reason.

---

[5] Juniors and Seniors, according to an administrator of the Hill School, "were given smoking privileges at certain times of the day. It seems they had a 'clubhouse' of sorts on campus, which the club was responsible for maintaining. It seems this group also played cards, bridge and Canasta." The club has long since been disbanded.

But before leaving for Yale in the fall of 1945, Alan applied for and was given a summer apprenticeship with the Leland Hayward Theatrical Agency, an experience that he claimed changed his life forever. Nominally, he was an office boy, but part of his job was to deliver scripts in the afternoon. However, as he said in 1983, "I didn't. I would take them home at night, read them, and make notes about them for myself; then I'd go and deliver them in the morning. And that's when I realized I was hooked. That summer really changed my life."

After the heady experience of working at the Hayward Agency, Alan began his studies at Yale, culminating in a B.A. in Drama in 1948. He may initially have been disappointed that he did not go to the University of Chicago, but, as one whose interest in drama was becoming more passionate with each passing year, he must have known of the reputation of the Yale School of Drama, which by 1945 was well established as one of the two or three finest such programs in the United States. The opportunity to pursue his passion at such an institution could not have been too severe a disappointment.

The great majority of his classes were taken outside the School of Drama, as he attempted to learn as much about the history and culture of the Western world as possible in a four-year span. As a freshman he took courses in philosophy, zoology, English, government, and history; as a sophomore he was enrolled in literature classes, as well as courses in psychology, sociology, political science, and French; in his junior year he took two sociology classes and two literature classes, while continuing in French; and as a senior he took two semesters of architecture, history, philosophy, psychology, and political science.

At the end of four years he had received a truly well-rounded liberal arts education, one that would serve him well as a director, who needs to possess knowledge in a great many areas, for he may well direct a play or film demanding a knowledge of history or a familiarity with literature or philosophy. A knowledge of architecture is relevant to stage design and design for film. An acquaintance with sociology can only deepen the director's understanding of the social forces with which any play or film deals. Rather than narrow his focus to studies on dramatic art, then, he widened his knowledge of the world so that his understanding of dramatic art would be informed by all the subjects he studied in the classroom. In short, Alan Pakula's college career served, in the broadest way, as an apprenticeship for the career he would ultimately pursue.

In later years, Pakula was critical of technical programs focused entirely on cinema. "Don't just study films," he would say to students who asked him what sort of education they should pursue. "Get a B.A. Get involved in things. You're not going to make films about films." He always contended that a liberal arts background was a far better preparation for a prospective director than a concentration in film studies. And, as a human being, his interests were so wide (in politics, literature, and psychology, for example) that one who met him casually would not have known that he was a professional filmmaker, for he rarely talked about film.

Although he took classes in many subjects and in many departments at Yale (and, on an extracurricular basis, sang with the Yale Glee Club and directed radio plays for the Understudy Club), the class that most intrigued him was directing. The textbook for the class offered rules for every conceivable facet of directing. But Alan quickly learned that after "you learn all the rules, . . . you've got to go on your own. You've got to decide 'what's inside myself' and go with that." He determined to formulate his own methods, disregarding the "rules."

He directed his first play at Yale, Chekhov's *The Anniversary*, for the University Club. It was a thrilling experience for him, for he discovered that he had the ability to transmit his ideas to young actors and significantly improve their performances. "I had a great need to be a strong father figure to people and dispense wisdom at the age of seventeen," he later said. Directing gave him precisely those opportunities. "I was in love with the theatre," he said. "I'll never forget the moment after the first day of rehearsal when I felt that . . . the actors were finding things in themselves that they wouldn't have found without me and doing things, for better or worse, that they wouldn't have done without me. This sense of being a catalyst, this sense of power, was overpowering." After the rehearsal, he recalled "bounding through the campus with great, goat-like leaps, feeling I had found my . . . fulfillment, I had a calling." Or, as he put it on another occasion, he had found "God through the theatre."

He was also profoundly influenced by the productions he saw at New Haven's Shubert Theatre. "I would hang out in the balcony," he said. "I would sneak in, and I would watch Gar[son] Kanin [directing] dress rehearsals of *Born Yesterday*. I would watch Josh Logan [directing] a dress rehearsal of *Annie Get Your Gun*, and I was totally hooked."

And one night he saw *The Glass Menagerie*, featuring Laurette Taylor in a legendary performance as Amanda Wingfield. Pakula was overwhelmed. She wasn't *acting*, he thought, but *behaving*. It was what he would strive for in his work with actors.

The productions he saw at the Shubert and his experiences of directing convinced him that the theatre should be his life's work, and directing his specialty. But should it be the stage (as he originally thought) or the movies (as he came to believe)? In either case, a friend warned him that he would have difficulty convincing anyone to entrust him with a directorial position. He was only twenty when he graduated and he looked several years younger. His friend said, "Alan, nobody will trust you, you look too young." Indeed, his youthful appearance may have been the motivation for him to grow a mustache within a few years, then a beard some time later—and to keep it for the rest of his life.

After some deliberation, Alan was certain that he wanted to direct films. In order to fulfill his dream, he had to abandon the family printing business and go to Hollywood. Lacking money, he appealed to his parents. "You subsidize me for two years," he suggested, "and if I can't accomplish it in two years, that means I can't do it. If I can't make it, I'll come into your business." Surprisingly, perhaps, Paul agreed.

Armed with the subsidy from his father that he had negotiated, Alan went to California and—thanks to his father's friend, who asked him, "Would you be interested in working and seeing how the cartoon company works?"Alan got his first job in Hollywood. While working at Warners' cartoon division, "I didn't do anything," Pakula said. "They paid me almost nothing and my job was kind of close to cleaning up after the elephant. I worked below the secretary. I really was more of a kind of a not-so-glorified go-fer." He remained in the job for three months. In any case, it was a start in the movie business.

However, the job proved valuable in his later career, for, as he said, he "learned simple storytelling. I remember being in a story session and they would have all these cartoonists come in and critique the storyboard before they animated it. And one of the rules they had was that Bugs [Bunny], this very brash character, had to have some justification before he did all these brash, outrageous things. Usually a hunter or somebody else had to do something that was not strictly kosher, something that was endangering Bugs, and then, from that point on, having gained the audience's sympathy, Bugs could now be the underdog who becomes as outrageous and as brash as you want to make him. The whole essence of it was to first get the audience on your character's side and then you can do what you want to do. I found all of that fascinating."

Undoubtedly because working at Warners failed to give him the artistic satisfaction he was seeking, he became involved with the Circle Theatre, an amateur company in Los Angeles, where, in 1949, after stage-managing a number of productions, he directed Jean Anouilh's *Antigone*, a modernized version of the ancient Greek play by Sophocles. Fortunately, rehearsals were held at night, so he was able to continue his day job at Warners.

Alvin Sargent, then an aspiring actor, but now renowned as a screenwriter (he has written several scripts for Pakula, and won an Academy Award for his screenplay for *Julia*), was acting at the Circle Theatre at the same time Pakula was stage-managing and directing. Sargent vividly recalls Pakula in 1948, "wandering around in his seersucker Yale coat, with a pipe. And he always moved carefully—watching, you know, observant, and very careful." They became close friends, and remained close until Pakula's death.

Another actor at the Circle at the time was Sydney Chaplin, Charlie's son. Sydney was acting in Camus' *Caligula*, and, because the production was not going smoothly, Charlie Chaplin took over the directorial reins in the final week of rehearsals. Chaplin inadvertently gave Pakula a vivid lesson in how not to direct. Of course, Chaplin directed his own films and achieved brilliant results. At the Circle Theatre, however, he was dealing with young non-professional actors, who found it nearly impossible to meet Chaplin's demands. Pakula observed that the exasperated Chaplin's most frequent advice to his son was, "Relax, Sydney, relax." And then, as Pakula noted, "You'd see Sydney become tighter and tighter and tighter."

The performer playing Caligula was having a particularly difficult time in a scene, so Chaplin, as Pakula described it, "stepped in and showed him how *he* would play it. He looked into an imaginary mirror and began playing the mad emperor. The joyous yet hideous Pan character he created in front of your eyes was overwhelming. It was stunning. Then he said to the young actor, 'Now, you do it.' The actor, of course, was paralyzed." And so were the other actors, who feared that Chaplin would give them similar "coaching" that they could not possibly duplicate.

The lesson for Pakula was clear: the job of the director is to inspire the actor, to bring out the best the actor has to offer. But the process of doing so is not an imitative one; it involves a subtle transaction between director and actor in which the director draws from the actor's life experience, personality, observation, and empathy. Moreover, each actor is unique, and must be treated as an individual. A particular directorial method will work with one actor and fail with another. If the actor is unable to respond to the director's suggestion, the director is obliged to find another that will achieve results. Occasionally, the director can simply show the actor what to do and expect the actor to give a precise imitation; but that, for several reasons, is seldom successful. The actor is robbed of creativity and becomes no more than a puppet; therefore, he is likely to resent the director's approach and give a mechanical, uninspired performance. Or the actor, unable to understand *why* the director did what he did, will not be able to reproduce it with any sense of truth.

The example of Charlie Chaplin was one Pakula never forgot. When he began directing films he became known as an "actor's director," precisely because he evoked complex performances from his actors in subtle, creative ways. Eventually, as he said, he came to disdain "directors who use actors as puppets. They believe there is one conception for the film and everybody else is a puppet to carry out that conception. I believe the making of a film is a life process; no matter what the conception is to begin with, there will be changes in the making of the film. The film must come alive in spontaneous and surprising ways."

In 1949, when the two-year limit Alan had imposed on himself was only three weeks short of expiring, Paul, who was in Dallas on business, called his son in California. Alan could only tell his father about the one play he had directed at the Circle Theatre and his job at the cartoon department-signs of accomplishment, but far short of success. "Dad," he said, "I'm coming into your business. I'm coming home."

Paul was pleased, but, for reasons that even he didn't fully understand, replied, "Son, you *can't* come into my business." He told Alan that he didn't want a disgruntled partner who would forever regret his failure to break into the world of cinema. Only if Alan succeeded in his ambition, but later realized that filmmaking was not for him, did Paul want his son to return home. He offered to continue subsidizing Alan's life in California for an unspecified time. "I'll never forget when I hung that telephone up," Paul told John Culhane in 1982, "the tears just rolled down my cheeks. Here I wanted him in my business, and I'd said, 'Son, you can't come into my business.'" Alan theorized that "somewhere the insecure young man in himself must have related to the insecure young man in me." He quoted Paul as saying, "Do what you want and stay with what you want and don't worry about the failures and disappointments."

Alan added, "There may be two or three moments in the life of parenting that can make or break a child, and that was one of them for me."

If Alan had in any way resented his parents before this time, he was forever afterwards grateful to them. They developed a warm and loving relationship. Many years later, soon after his parents celebrated their sixtieth anniversary, Alan characterized his parents' union as "a close marriage as long as I've known it. My mother's very happily married to my father."

And, after Alan had become a successful director, Paul, entirely reconciled to Alan's decision not to join him in the family business, became his biggest fan. As Debby Maisel told me, "My grandparents lived on 62nd Street and Third Avenue, and there's a string of movie theatres right on Third Avenue. Whenever Alan's movies would show there, my grandfather would walk there and talk to the ticket takers to see how much money the movie was bringing in. Alan was the light of his life. He was the prince." As Selma Hirsh confirmed, "they got so they had a very good relationship in the very last years. Paul was very proud of him." Whatever tension may have existed between Alan and his parents when he was a child and a young adult vanished. "The Pakula family was really a very close family," Maisel said, and that closeness extended to Felice and to all the nieces, nephews, and cousins living in the New York area.

In 1949, released from his pledge to return home and grateful for the enormous weight that his father's remarks had lifted from his shoulders, Alan also recognized what a remarkable favor his father had done for him, and how much anguish it must have cost him. "Everything he said on the phone was against what he wanted to say, which was, 'Come home, come back, the business is waiting for you.' And," Alan marveled, "I felt it was not something he thought over for a second."

Shortly thereafter, Alan got the break he had been hoping for. Don Hartman, a writer/producer/director at MGM who had seen Pakula's production of *Antigone*, was impressed enough to offer Alan a position as his apprentice. His work involved reading scripts, much as he had done years before at the Hayward Agency. He also sought out potential script material and wrote synopses of the novels and short stories he read.

Hartman must have found Pakula to be a first-rate employee, for, when Hartman became head of production at Paramount in 1951, he asked Pakula to join him as his assistant.

Alan was only twenty-two and had only apprenticed under Hartman for eight months, but was comfortably established in an important job: assistant head of production at Paramount Pictures (although, as he acknowledged, "My salary didn't match my title"). Seldom is success in show business accomplished in so short a time. Most young people who aspire to succeed in the field, whether on stage or screen, allow themselves five to ten years—if they give themselves a deadline at all—during which they understand that progress is likely to be painfully slow. Members of Alan's family speak about his long, difficult period of struggle in Hollywood, but millions of aspiring directors—or actors or producers—would be delighted to become successful so quickly in the world's most competitive profession.

Being Hartman's assistant was no small matter. Lawrence Turman (later the producer of *The Graduate*), was a close friend of Pakula's at the time. Turman can't recall precisely what Alan's duties were, but his guess is probably accurate: "When you're assistant to a studio head, you can be secretary and general factotum and reader and advice-giver and fender-offer and everything—there's no one task. You do a lot of reading and evaluating scripts and giving opinions."

Indeed, Pakula commented on scripts submitted to the studio and wrote memoranda on every film Paramount made for nearly six years, recommending which screenplays should be filmed. Hartman relied on his judgment, for Pakula turned out to be an expert adviser. He did make one spectacular mistake, when he read the script for *Rear Window* and said, "It's not that much." Then, when he saw the dailies from Alfred Hitchcock's production, he realized his error. "I swallowed and learned that there are certain movie scripts that read very well and they don't really play very well, and there are certain scripts that don't read well at all, but they're not written to be read; they're meant to be made," he said.

During his years at Paramount he was able to observe some of the leading directors in America at work: Hitchcock, William Wyler, George Stevens, and Billy Wilder all made films at the studio while Pakula was assistant head of production. He frequently had the opportunity to watch the dailies—the raw footage of each day's shooting. "I sat in on major meetings," he said. "I saw Audrey Hepburn's original screen test for *Roman Holiday*, and was in on the meetings in which the major decision by six or seven grown men was on whether Audrey Hepburn's teeth [should] be straightened. . . . Wisely, they were not."

Most importantly, Pakula said, he "learned the difference between what you read in a script and what you see on film. And if I had any doubt about the importance of a director and the difference a director can make, I found it out then. Because you would see good scripts made by competent directors [become] good films; made by less competent directors, good scripts were made into bad films; and you would see scripts that seemed acceptable, but not extraordinary, made into extraordinary films by remarkable directors."

Alan's importance to the studio gradually increased. As his position evolved, he began working with screenwriters, helping them to sharpen their scripts. Before long, Hartman suggested that Pakula had within him the possibility of becoming the next Irving Thalberg—the legendary "boy wonder" who had run MGM (under Louis B. Mayer's aegis) from 1924 until his untimely death in 1936. From the outset, Pakula's hope was to become a director, but he proved to be such an invaluable assistant to Hartman that his boss thought of him only in terms of a potential production executive.

Larry Turman said that Pakula was "sort of a hidden workaholic, really a very hard-working, conscientious guy. Very disciplined about his work, and very ambitious, in the best sense of the word." Pakula gave some the impression of being "soft," Turman said, but "I always experienced him to have steel in his backbone."

Pakula told Frank Pierson, with whom (many years later) he co-wrote the screenplay for *Presumed Innocent*, that when he first came to Hollywood, "Everybody underestimated me because I looked like a Botticelli angel." Then he added, with a wicked smile, "Little did they know." As Pierson said, "There was a fierce determination in that guy. He was not going to be turned aside."

Throughout his tenure at Paramount, Pakula yearned to direct. But neither Don Hartman nor anyone else could see him in that role. The longer he worked as an executive, the more he was perceived as an executive. Someone at the studio told him that he would never be permitted to direct, because "You've never worked with actors. You probably wouldn't be good with actors." Pakula could only gnash his teeth, for his experiences directing *The Anniversary* and *Antigone* convinced him that he could skillfully evoke fine performances from the people on his stage.

It must have been apparent to his co-workers that Pakula was unhappy with his position. One day, an executive at Paramount told him, "You can work with writers, why don't you become a producer?" The idea excited Pakula, who thought it might have the additional benefit of leading to a directorial assignment.

In the mid-1950s, television was making serious inroads in the popularity of motion pictures. Indeed, the future of film as a mass medium seemed in doubt. As a producer, Pakula helped to make the sort of films that were able to attract audiences away from their television sets and back into the movie theatres—films about troubled individuals dealing with the sorts of problems, social and emotional, that were all but ignored on television.

In 1955, Pakula found a book he wanted to adapt for the screen and sought Hartman's approval to produce the film himself. Hartman, impressed by Pakula's enthusiasm for the project, agreed. Still a very young man, Alan Pakula embarked on a career as a film producer at the age of twenty-six.

CHAPTER TWO

Hollywood & New York:

Fear Strikes Out and Theatrical Ventures

"Once a director's on a set, there can only be one person working with those actors. I don't believe in producers who hang around sets. I would meet with Bob [Mulligan] at the end of the day, and we'd see dailies together and we'd discuss the work, but he was absolutely in charge of those actors—and that's the way it should be. You can't have two father figures at the same time."

—ALAN J. PAKULA

THE INSPIRATIONAL STORY that set Pakula on his way as a producer was *Fear Strikes Out*, an autobiography by Jim Piersall[6], an outfielder with the Boston Red Sox and several other American League teams, who suffered from periodic bouts of mental illness. Paramount bought *Fear Strikes Out* and assigned Pakula a one-million-dollar budget, inexpensive even for 1957.

The choice of material puzzled Pakula's old friend, Alvin Sargent. "Why he did that particular movie, I don't know," he said. "I don't think of Alan as a sports fan—not at all. I can't imagine him rooting at a baseball game." But what attracted Pakula to the material was not the baseball setting but his lifelong fascination with psychology.

Although the book only hinted at the pressures Piersall's father had imposed on his son, they became the centerpiece of a psychological drama. Pakula described his attitude toward *Fear Strikes Out* in a 1983 interview:

I at one time toyed with the idea of being a psychoanalyst. It would have meant going to that dreaded med school, but I thought seriously about it and I was very

---

[6]*Piersall's book was written in collaboration with Albert S. Hirshberg.*

interested in analysis, and when I read the book about Jimmy's breakdown, what fascinated me was that it dealt with a ballplayer . . . the all-American figure, and at that time, the fifties, there was much of Middle America who thought about mental breakdown and emotional illness in terms of neurasthenic, bohemian, artistic, sensitive types rather than recognizing that it is something that can happen to anyone . . . Plus, it dealt with a theme that has great interest to me, and that is, somebody trying to live through somebody else; in this case it was the father trying to live through the son, and it was a theme that fascinated me.

On another occasion, Pakula elaborated: "The central theme was a boy repressing all his ambivalent feelings toward a parent who had taken over his life, a boy who did not have the freedom to finally grow up and become his own man."

Casting the role of Jim Piersall would be crucial, Pakula knew, since the film would rise or fall on the basis of the actor's performance. Based on his viewing of some dailies from *Friendly Persuasion* (a 1956 film directed by William Wyler) Pakula had seen, he offered the role to Anthony Perkins, who was at that time a virtual unknown. Perkins, he said, possessed "a kind of mystery and darkness and sensitivity."

Since Paramount refused to entrust Pakula to direct the film, he sought a young director, "somebody from my generation," he said, "because I felt there would be a rapport and a collaboration that I wouldn't have otherwise." He considered several possibilities, one of whom was Robert Mulligan, then twenty-nine. Mulligan, a one-time theological student and a former Marine, had directed several successful television dramas. The two had never met, but Pakula, who had admired Mulligan's television work, arranged a half-hour meeting at Paramount— one of several conferences he held with potential directors. Mulligan made a favorable impression, but Pakula was not yet convinced that Mulligan, who had never directed a film, should be offered the job.

Meanwhile, the screenplay was being written by Ted Berkman and Raphael Blau. They turned Piersall's father into the single agent who destroyed Jim's mental health. Mr. Piersall was portrayed as so ambitious for his son to succeed that his constant goading eventually pushed Jim into a mental breakdown. Pakula, in his role as producer, actively participated in the development of the script.

During that time, Pakula watched a number of television shows on which Perkins appeared. As he watched, he became more and more concerned that he had made a casting mistake. "I was kind of shattered," he said, "because [Perkins] seemed very mannered and very stylized and self-conscious—and this was probably the insecurity of a young actor who was just starting out. I really got worried. And then several weeks later I saw Tony in a television play that Bob [Mulligan] directed . . . and Tony was just marvelous; all the mannerisms were gone, and it really was a dramatic change. [He had recovered] simplicity and honesty, and I thought it must be on account of the director."

The following day, during a meeting at Paramount, Pakula asked how Perkins would respond if Mulligan were to direct *Fear Strikes Out*. Perkins literally dropped to his knees, put his hands together in a praying position, and said, "Please, please, please." The next day Pakula flew to New York and offered Mulligan the job. Pakula then "took a very deep breath," Mulligan said, and spoke. "Well, the rest is simple," he said, bursting into laughter. "All we have to do now is make a really *great movie*."

As Mulligan recalled their meeting, "He [Pakula] was very young, very smart, and very articulate. He also had a wonderfully quick sense of humor which he often turned on himself. I liked him from the start."

Pakula established a rule for himself as producer that he never violated, either in the making of *Fear Strikes Out* or in the subsequent movies he produced and Mulligan directed: he would meet daily with Mulligan early in the morning and at the end of the day, but would absent himself from the set when filming was in progress. "Alan was never on the set during shooting," Mulligan confirmed. "It was his choice and not something I demanded. . . . But Alan knew he was welcome to visit whenever he wished. From time to time he'd drop by to walk a new set with me or welcome a new actor to the movie. Or just to say 'hello' at the start of the day. Once the camera was ready to roll, he'd wish me luck and leave. His visits were always calm and positive."

By no means did this mean that Pakula abrogated his duties as producer. He saw to all the duties customarily associated with the position: finding a studio willing to finance the films he and Mulligan worked on; working with the screenwriters to shape the scripts; selecting the films' cinematographers, editors, production designers, costume designers, et cetera; collaborating with the director on the casting; keeping a close eye on the budgets; providing the most congenial conditions for the artists to work effectively; responding critically to the dailies and offering the director suggestions; overseeing the release of the films; and, as he said, "protecting the film on release." As Mulligan made clear, Pakula's judgment was essential in the creation of *Fear Strikes Out* and every other film they made.

Pakula enumerated the most significant aspects of his professional relationship with Mulligan. "One of the things we agree on is that the most important thing you can do for an actor is to create the environment in which he feels free to do his best work. That's your job as the producer—and as the director, as well. To just say that there's a safe environment there. And [it's important] to go with your instincts. You both know why you're making this picture and what the values are and what the dangers are—and have an ease of communication and an honesty with each other." And, he added emphatically, "*have fun!*"

In the film, which was released early in 1957, Mr. Piersall, who longs for his athletically gifted son to become a major league baseball player, pushes Jim unmercifully with his harsh criticisms. Jim's enjoyment in baseball is gradually eroded, as his only desire becomes to please his father.

Jim is offered a contract by the Boston Red Sox and is sent to Scranton of the Eastern League, where he meets a young nurse, Mary, falls in love with her, and proposes. We see the beginnings of mental illness in a scene in which Jim, third in the league in hitting (his father's reaction is, "well, that isn't first"), is shown in a near-panic, confessing to Mary that he has no confidence in his hitting ability.

During his second minor-league season, we see that the pressure to make the majors is too much for Jim to cope with—particularly when the Red Sox's manager informs Jim that he will be playing shortstop in the big leagues, whereas he has always been an outfielder in the past. Jim suffers a near-breakdown, and tells Mary that he doesn't want to continue his baseball career. But Mary and Jim's father assure a distraught Jim that he will succeed.

At spring training and after the season begins, Jim behaves irrationally, getting into fights with teammates and with the manager, even coming to believe that Mary has turned against him. Finally, during a game, an out-of-control Piersall grabs a bat and swings it wildly at his teammates. Four policemen are required to remove the bat and hold him down. He is taken to a mental hospital, the victim of a complete breakdown. We see some attempts by a psychiatrist to treat Jim (including electroshock treatments, which are portrayed as therapeutic) but, for several months, all attempts at rehabilitation are unsuccessful.

Jim is seen in several scenes with the psychiatrist. At one point they are watching a baseball game on television in the psychiatrist's office when the doctor gently suggests that Jim's father may have pushed his son too hard to succeed. Jim lashes out angrily, yelling, "If it hadn't been for my father standing behind me and pushing me and driving me, I wouldn't be where I am today!" It is one of the most effective moments in the film, as Jim silently realizes the implications of his remark.

Later, when Jim's father tries to forcibly remove Jim from the hospital, the son stands up to his father for the first time. "All my life," he shouts, "I've been splitting my guts to please you, and I never could. No matter what I do, it's not enough. You're killing me!" For Jim, his outburst represents a breakthrough.

Later, released from the hospital, Jim is reunited with Mary and Mr. Piersall. Jim is seen in an angle which makes him appear to tower over his father, a visual demonstration that he no longer plays the subservient role in the relationship.

The last scene of the film shows Jim about to take the field for the Red Sox on the first day of the next season. Mary urges Jim not to play, and Jim admits that he's scared. But this is a different Jim: inwardly apprehensive, perhaps, but far calmer and more mature than we've ever seen him. He takes the field to the cheers of the crowd as the film ends.

One of the most effective features of the movie is Karl Malden's portrayal of Mr. Piersall. Although the father is portrayed as the obvious cause of Jim's difficulties, he is clearly tormented by his inability to achieve closeness with his son. He occasionally appears to be monstrous (as when he tries to force Jim to leave the hospital), but he is not a monster, rather a man who has too thoroughly sublimated his own dreams into his son's hoped-for success. Malden captures these qualities poignantly.

Perkins, too, skillfully delineates the progress of his illness and his recovery ("the breaking out of the chrysalis . . . of finding himself possessed, almost literally possessed, by his father," Pakula called it). If he seems to switch rather abruptly from good spirits to paranoid schizophrenia and then to robust mental health, it may be the fault of the script, which gives him little time to fully develop the transitions his character undergoes.

At the end of the film, the impression is conveyed that Jim is "cured" and in perfect mental health. In reality, Piersall's behavior continued to be erratic for many years afterward. This convenient Hollywood ending, along with heightening the relationship between father and son, are a few examples of the film's many departures from reality.

It is intriguing that the very qualities for which Mr. Piersall is criticized in the film—being overly critical of his son's accomplishments, pushing him too hard to succeed—are the very qualities that are most often praised in the fathers of sports heroes. They challenge their children to be better, always encouraging them to reach new heights.[7] However, in the film, Mr. Piersall's behavior is nearly always portrayed as destructive.

Viewing the film now, almost fifty years after it was made, the psychologizing (particularly the assigning of all blame for Jim's condition to his father) seems rather facile, the complete faith in psychoanalysis naïve, and Jim's full recovery improbable. In its time, however, it must have seemed both daring and sophisticated. Bosley Crowther, then perhaps the most influential film critic in the

---

[7]One remembers how Mickey Mantle wanted to quit baseball in his first minor league year because he found the competition daunting; when Mantle told his father his intentions, his father arrived to helped him pack his belongings, suggesting in no uncertain terms that his son was a quitter and that he had lost respect for him. As a result of this "tough love," Mantle continued his career, eventually becoming regarded as one of baseball's greatest players and a member of the Hall of Fame. Whenever Mantle told this story, the purpose was always to show how his father had salvaged his baseball career, and how grateful he was to him.

United States, wrote in the *New York Times* on March 21, 1957 that the picture "so improves upon an original autobiography of Mr. Piersall and a television drama based thereon that it is the initiation of a first-rate psychological film." Crowther praised Perkins's and Malden's performances as well as Mulligan's "vigorous" direction.

Other notices were equally enthusiastic. *Time* began its review, "*Fear Strikes Out* rolls Frank Merriwell and Sigmund Freud into a ball and then lines it out for a solid hit." It goes on to commend the film for not being "the history of an illness but the story of a human life; it does not attempt to acquaint the mind with theories and statistics but to educate the heart with compassion and understanding." Malden, Mulligan, screenwriters Berkman and Blau, and, especially, Perkins, were all singled out for praise. *Newsweek* was no less fervent. The movie "should do great business," it noted.

Shortly before the film was completed, Pakula proposed that he and Mulligan embark on a long-term partnership, with Pakula as producer and Mulligan as director. Mulligan needed little convincing: "During *Fear Strikes Out*, we found that we enjoyed working together. We trusted one another. We liked one another. We had become friends. At some point near the end of production, Alan brought up the idea and we shook hands on the spot. No lawyers. No agents. Just our word. We agreed that as soon as we found a project we both liked we'd do it together as equal partners."

Immediately after the release of *Fear Strikes Out*, however, Pakula returned to his duties as assistant head of production at Paramount, and Mulligan returned to directing live television. The notion of forming an organization of their own seemed impossible. As Mulligan said, "Neither of us had a dime to invest in buying scripts or setting up a production company—or anything like it. I had a young family to take care of and once *Fear Strikes Out* was completed, I had to get back to live TV, looking for more movies to direct and earning a living." But Pakula did not let the idea die. He met with writers to search for other projects he and Mulligan could make together, and, in the course of doing so, made contacts with literary agents on both coasts.

One such project about which both Pakula and Mulligan were wildly enthusiastic was an adaptation of Thomas Wolfe's *Look Homeward, Angel*, again to feature Anthony Perkins. "Alan was absolutely passionate about the project," Mulligan said, "and determined to make it happen. He was convinced we could make an important and classic American film." Unbeknownst to them, however, Ketti Frings had written a stage play based on the novel, and a production was scheduled to open on Broadway in late 1957. When Pakula found out, Mulligan said, "Alan took it particularly hard. It took him some time to let it go and move on."

The play *Look Homeward, Angel* opened in New York on November 28, 1957, with Anthony Perkins in the leading role of Eugene Gant.

Pakula sought other projects he could produce and Mulligan direct. At least for the present, Pakula accepted the repeated suggestions of Paramount executives that he should not attempt to direct. Later, however, he came to feel that "working with Bob set me back in directing several years because I enjoyed working with him, and we were having a good time, and I enjoyed the work." Consequently, he sublimated his directorial ambitions for twelve years.

Still, Pakula certainly enjoyed the relationship with Mulligan, and Mulligan felt similarly. "I do know laughter had a lot to do with it," he said, "and Alan was the source of most of it. There was also mutual trust and respect and a lasting bond of real work shared and enjoyed. And through it all there were laughs. I'm not given to easy laughter, but Alan could get to me every time. Whenever I took myself too seriously or my Bronx Irish temper flared at some front office executive, Alan would deflate it or deflect it with a quiet line. It worked every time."

* * *

In 1958, Pakula initiated a series of ventures into New York theatre. The plays he produced do not seem to have been unified thematically or structurally, each simply reflecting a desire to present a work that, for one reason or another, intrigued him. Perhaps because of this random approach—and because the plays he chose to present were all significantly flawed—his career as a Broadway producer was undistinguished.

Pakula's first production for the theatre was an original play called *Comes a Day*, directed by Mulligan. The play, by Speed Lamkin, was co-produced by Pakula and Cheryl Crawford, with a cast including Judith Anderson and George C. Scott. As Brooks Atkinson described in the *New York Times*, it was about "a girl who is in love with an attractive traveling salesman, although the family budget requires her to marry the richest young man in town. She agrees. But . . . the richest young man [Scott] is a sadist—sick, sick, sick. . . . [A]s the curtain comes down [the members of the family] resolve to lead better lives."

During an out-of-town tryout, one critic called the play "powerful and provocative with keen psychological insight and a brilliant cast." However, when *Comes a Day* opened at the Ambassador Theatre on Broadway on November 6, 1958, it received a chorus of negative reviews. Atkinson conceded that the play "has theatrical moments," but called it "uneven" and "baffling," and "a puzzling drama that looks like art every now and then" but "subsides into psychiatric melodrama." That the play should have a "psychiatric" side is not surprising, considering

Pakula's penchant for the psychological approach, but the play's descent into melodrama caused its rapid demise.

George C. Scott (who later received a Tony nomination for his performance) was the best-reviewed of the actors. *Theatre Arts* magazine called Scott (as the sadistic young man) "the most exciting actor to come along . . . since Marlon Brando." Brooks Atkinson characterized Mulligan's direction as "mechanical." The production, he said, had "the contrived style of a television show," which was perhaps true since Mulligan had never directed for the theatre before. In fact, although he attended Fordham University in New York City, he did not see a play on Broadway until he was in his late twenties or early thirties.

Pakula had talked Mulligan into accepting the directorial position. Years later, Mulligan said, "[Pakula] believed I could do it despite the fact that I had no training or experience in theatre—and no real sense of stagecraft." Mulligan called it "an exciting challenge and an intense learning experience," but said, "I knew, at the end, I wanted to make movies. Theatre was not my game."

Mulligan recalls that Pakula and Crawford worked well as producers, putting together a good cast and a knowledgeable staff. But it was not enough. *Comes a Day* closed after only twenty-eight performances.

The Pakula-Mulligan partnership was then put on hold until Pakula was ready to make another film. Meanwhile, Pakula still harbored ambitions to succeed on Broadway. Even before the production of *Comes a Day*, he had begun to prepare a production of *Laurette*, a play about Laurette Taylor, whose performance in *The Glass Menagerie* had impressed him so deeply when he was in college. In 1956 Pakula asked Horton Foote, whose work he also admired, to dramatize *Laurette*, but, Foote said, "I just didn't feel it would work. I think it's almost impossible because there's going to be that moment when you say, 'Let's see her act.' And there's so much built up about her great acting ability that I just didn't think it would work."

Eventually, the play, based on the memoir by Taylor's daughter, Marguerite Courtney, was dramatized by Stanley Young. Pakula's role in the preparation of the script was extensive. On June 4, 1957, for example, he wrote Young a thirty-page letter detailing his conception of the play, his suggestion for the plot structure and the characterizations. Many other memos followed as the script was being developed.

Pakula knew that whoever played the role of Laurette Taylor would be crucial to the success of the play. He considered Geraldine Page and Kim Stanley, among others, but his strong first choice was Judy Holliday, the brilliant comic performer who had triumphed in *Born Yesterday* and *Bells Are Ringing*. Beginning in January 1958, Pakula made repeated attempts to persuade

Holliday to accept the role. At last, in 1959, she agreed to play the role under José Quintero's direction.[8]

Other members of the cast included Jack Gwillim, Patrick O'Neal, Joan Hackett, and Nancy Marchand. One actor who was not cast—although Pakula wished to hire him—was a young Robert Redford. Quintero wanted another performer, however, and he prevailed. But Redford and Pakula would often meet again, and would work together on two occasions, one of them a highlight of their careers as well as of the American cinema.

"Luckily," Pakula said in 1975, "Bob does not hold grudges."

At first, *Laurette* appeared likely to win success. The advance sale for the Broadway run neared $500,000, "one of the largest advance sales for a straight play in the history of the theatre," Pakula wrote to his investors. And, even before rehearsals began, United Artists expressed interest in making a film of *Laurette*, for which Pakula worked up a budget of $1.5 million, a rather modest sum for a picture that would feature a large cast, many locations, numerous elaborate costumes, and two distinct time periods.

The stage production was scheduled to begin rehearsing in the Forty-sixth Street Theatre in New York on August 27, but, when Pakula tried to move in, he found that the cast of the musical *Tenderloin* was rehearsing in the theatre and refused to leave. Robert Griffith and Harold Prince, the producers of *Tenderloin*, insisted that they would remain until their show began its out-of-town tour on September 6. Pakula responded that he had a firm commitment from the theatre's owner to make the space available to *Laurette*, and that *Tenderloin* would have to find another rehearsal space. Griffith and Prince would not leave, they said, "unless the cops kick us out." They admitted that, at the time they booked the theatre, they were told that *Laurette* would move in on August 27, but insisted, in Prince's words, "We didn't take this seriously at the time."

Louis Lotito, who represented the theatre's owner, reacted scornfully. "Mr. Griffith and Mr. Prince asked me whether they could use the theatre for rehearsals. As a favor for a couple of nice guys, I graciously said 'Yes,' but told them they couldn't stay beyond August 27 because *Laurette* had been promised the theatre after that date. They're not even paying rent. This is like *The Man Who Came to Dinner*. We let them in and they want to stay forever. I never heard of anything like this." Pakula seemed stunned by the chain of events. Ultimately, confronted by Griffith and Prince's intractability, he agreed to move to another space.

When rehearsals began, the deficiencies of Stanley Young's script became

<hr>

[8] *Originally, Robert Mulligan was slated to direct Laurette, but his experience with* Comes a Day *was sufficiently discouraging that he withdrew. Quintero was signed on November 11, 1959.*

more and more apparent. Judy Holliday was particularly upset by those aspects of the dramatization that put greater emphasis on spectacle than on character development. While Pakula was in London, seeking to cast the role of Laurette Taylor's husband, a series of tense meetings involving Holliday, Young, and Quintero took place in New York. In a letter, Pakula assured Young and Quintero that he would take their side in any dispute with the star. "I have faith in your intuitions and instincts," he told them, adding that revisions on the play should be limited to three people: "Stanley, [Quintero], and myself p-e-r-i-o-d," specifically excluding Judy Holliday from the process.

Ultimately, Holliday's distress became so intense that, on two separate occasions, she refused to give an evening performance in New Haven unless Quintero agreed to cut certain scenes. Reluctantly, he did so. However, Quintero, Young, and Pakula became convinced that Holliday's insistence upon structuring the play as she wished represented an unconscionable example of star temperament.

Laurette opened in New Haven on September 26, 1960, in what was intended to be the first stop on a pre-Broadway tour. The reviews were discouraging. According to the *New Haven Evening Register*, "*Laurette* is a play in which nothing, for the moment, at least, is quite right. . . . Judy Holliday . . . must overcome—somehow—the episodic, pillar-to-post costume and cosmetic changes which the play demands through its too-rapid switch from scenes in actuality to scenes played in her memory." The criticism seemed to validate Holliday's concerns about the play's overemphasis on spectacle.

Even more discouraging was the review in the *New Haven Journal-Courier*, which said the play "droned on . . . stolidly and with great monotony, with little change in mood for the entire three long acts. Judy Holliday, . . . hampered by illness, gives a very subdued performance." Holliday's illness, more serious than initially feared, would soon force the closure of *Laurette*.

The production went on to Philadelphia, where, on October 6, the scheduled opening performance was canceled only ninety minutes before the curtain was due to rise. Two days later, Judy Holliday withdrew from *Laurette* because of what was announced as a throat ailment. She checked in to New York Hospital with a serious bronchial condition, the hospital indicating that she would undergo surgery. Despite the pressure from some of the investors to replace Holliday with another performer, Pakula, realizing that only the presence of a charismatic and well-known actress could attract the public, immediately announced that the "show will not open" as scheduled on October 27 at the Martin Beck Theatre in New York.

On October 18, surgeons operated on Judy Holliday. A two-hour operation at the Harkness Pavilion of the Columbia-Presbyterian Medical Center resulted in the removal of a non-malignant tumor from her throat. For the next two weeks

Holliday remained in the hospital, forbidden to speak. Although only the throat tumor was disclosed to the public, doctors had also discovered a malignant lump in her left breast, and a mastectomy was performed. She was released from the hospital on November 3, 1960.[9]

Fortunately for Pakula and for the investors, the producer had taken out an insurance policy for $100,000 with Lloyds of London against the possibility that illness might force Judy Holliday out of her role. Lloyds eventually paid the full amount, and the proceeds were distributed among the backers. However, the play still lost a good deal of money, including virtually all of Pakula's, who had spent four frustrating and "painful" (his word) years working on *Laurette*.

For a time, it seemed possible that a film version of *Laurette* would be made with Judy Garland in the title role. Pakula wrote to Marguerite Courtney in 1961, "I have been waiting to hear from [United Artists] regarding if she [Garland] is insurable." The many occasions on which Garland had behaved erratically had, by that time, caused most studios and producers to shun her, despite her uncontested greatness. "I must admit," Pakula continued, "that the idea of getting involved with another Judy and other insurance problems leaves me feeling a bit ambivalent. But they say Garland is in good shape and I do think that I have developed some pretty tough scar tissue during the last 'Judy' episode that might make some of the problems easier to face the next time." In any case, negotiations with United Artists broke off and no film of *Laurette* was ever made.

Thus, Pakula had nothing whatever to show for his involvement with *Laurette*. The experience was, from every point of view, a disaster. Nevertheless, Pakula, working from a modest apartment in Manhattan—he could no longer afford an office—continued to pursue a Broadway success.

Pakula's assistant did her best to organize Pakula's day ("Call Judy Holliday," "Call Gregory Peck," and "Make dental appointment," are some of the many notes that appeared on his daily list of things to do), but his chronic lateness was only one of the idiosyncrasies she had to contend with. On frequent occasions, he failed to return messages, with the result that the daily to-do lists grew progressively longer, each one including requests to *please* call so-and-so, who had been trying to reach the producer for days.

Later, another assistant took over his predecessor's duties. "I am slowly going out of my mind trying to get Alan to do things," he told her in a letter in August 1962. For example, he sent a memo to Pakula, saying, "Hate to bring this up at

---

[9]*Holliday never fully recovered her health. She did perform once again on Broadway, in a play called* Hot Spot *two years later, but died of throat cancer on July 7, 1965, an especially tragic event considering her age (she was forty-three), depriving the American theatre of a superb comic performer.*

this time, but the phone bill should be paid soon as well as quite a few other bills." But Pakula, though continuing to formulate plans for future plays and films, had no money to pay the phone bill. Clearly, working for Pakula could often be frustrating, primarily because of the producer's lack of organization and failure to attend to routine tasks. But Pakula was determined not to permit his inability to pay the bills on time to cut down on his level of activity.

Pakula plunged back into the theatrical maelstrom in 1962, when he and Joel Schenker co-produced *There Must Be a Pony!* The notion for the production began when Pakula saw Myrna Loy, who had been a film star for more than thirty years, in her stage debut in a summer stock production of *Marriage-Go-Round*. Loy performed the play at the Lakes Region Playhouse and later in other New England summer theatres. Pakula caught up with it in Westport, Connecticut, and, according to his friend and eventual agent, Boaty Boatwright, "decided that he wanted Myrna for his planned Broadway production of *There Must Be a Pony!*" Robert Mulligan confirmed that Pakula was "very excited about it and very taken with Myrna Loy."

The play, about a failing Hollywood actress who suffers an emotional collapse and tries to re-establish her career as well as a bond with her teenaged son, was adapted by James Kirkwood, Jr. from his own novel. Under the auspices of Pakula and Schenker, *There Must Be a Pony!* began playing summer stock in the summer of 1962 as a pre-Broadway tryout. Pakula's notion was to produce the play in such towns as Mineola, New York, Westport, Connecticut, and Millburn, New Jersey, rather than the larger cities (such as Philadelphia, New Haven, Washington, D.C., and Boston) usually chosen for pre-Broadway performances. In this way, the producers hoped to fine-tune the play and production away from the glare of media attention. Moreover, production expenses in summer stock were considerably lower than in the usual "out-of-town" tryout.

But problems bedeviled the project from the beginning. In Ogunquit, Maine, the production's first venue, the critics were hostile, both to the play and to its star. *Variety* reviewed *There Must Be a Pony!* when it played at the Falmouth Playhouse in Coonamesset, Massachusetts. Its critic wrote that the play "does not display enough quality to make its future prospects very bright. . . . Kirkwood has taken what might have been potentially absorbing theatre fare and marred it by inept dramaturgy." Kirkwood began replacing certain scenes with others, but the new scenes, Myrna Loy believed, were less effective than those they replaced.

Kirkwood, evidently believing that Loy was not doing justice to his play, recommended a cast change. Pakula's assistant suggested, however, that the problem lay with the play itself, and recommended that a play doctor be hired to revise Kirkland's script. But hiring a play doctor would have entailed considerable expense and Pakula calculated that the budget would not permit it—and he certainly had no money of his own to spend. "I have told Jim [Kirkwood] all of the financial facts of my personal life," Pakula wrote to his assistant in August, "which could conceivably [result] in my not continuing the project." He ended his note plaintively: "I had to explain that to my parents who are relying on me to get a job to get some money in." Paul and Jeannette, then living in some degree of luxury on Park Avenue, were growing tired of their son's failure to make a living despite his impressive credits as film studio executive and producer in Hollywood and on Broadway.

Alan, believing that a return to film offered the best chance to get his finances in order, continued to divide his time between *There Must Be a Pony!* and preparations to film a dramatization of Harper Lee's bestselling novel, *To Kill a Mockingbird.* To that end, he and Robert Mulligan met periodically in California even while *There Must Be a Pony!* continued to perform on the East Coast, with his assistant representing Pakula's interests.

Discussions about *To Kill a Mockingbird* were so encouraging that Pakula rapidly lost interest in *There Must Be a Pony!* After seven weeks of performances, Pakula's enthusiasm for the play had evaporated so thoroughly that he and Schenker informed the playwright and the cast that they were withdrawing from the production. They sold their interest in *There Must Be a Pony!* to another producer, who considered replacing Myrna Loy with Kim Stanley, although nothing came of that notion. The play continued in summer stock throughout the summer, closing before its scheduled opening at the Cort Theatre on Broadway.

Kirkwood tried to interest other producers in bringing *There Must Be a Pony!* to Broadway, but no production of the play was given until it was made as a television film with Elizabeth Taylor in 1986.

In time, Pakula became known for the loyalty he showed to the various projects with which he was associated. His withdrawal from *There Must Be a Pony!* in the midst of its tryout can be interpreted in one of two ways, one interpretation being that he behaved callously, the other that he acted shrewdly. Either his decision to sever his connection with the production and his desertion of Myrna Loy, whom he had invited to play the lead, provide evidence of a driven young man, flitting from one project to another without any apparent logic, seeking success at virtually any cost—and, since it must have been apparent that *There Must Be a Pony!* stood little chance of enhancing his career, he simply abandoned it. Or, alternatively, one might conclude that he wisely reached a decision not to expend more time and money on a project he realized had no chance to succeed.

However one interprets Pakula's actions, they seem out of character for a man who was afterwards held in high esteem for his loyalty to his actors and his integrity as an individual and as a producer (and, later, as a director). In any case, the disastrous results of *Comes a Day*, *Laurette*, and *There Must Be a Pony!* surely provided Pakula with valuable experience that he would later apply profitably to his work in film.

After withdrawing from *There Must Be a Pony!* in 1962, Pakula was not quite finished with the theatre—the next year he received billing as a co-producer of *Jennie*, a Broadway musical, although his involvement was minimal—but, after three failures and with his career in jeopardy, he decided to return to Los Angeles and devote the bulk of his time to film. The immediate result was one of the masterpieces of the American cinema.

CHAPTER THREE

To Kill a Mockingbird

"For me, producing a film means starting out with a passion, a conception, starting out with a piece of material you find or somebody else finds or a conception of film that interests you, and following that conception through with a very specific vision of what that film should be, and protecting that vision in every way, all the way through."

—ALAN PAKULA, 1973

Harper Lee began writing *To Kill a Mockingbird*, a novel of her youth growing up in Alabama during the Depression, in 1950, completing it in 1958. Although J. B. Lippincott accepted it for publication in 1960, the company was utterly unprepared for it to become wildly successful. The first printing was a mere five thousand copies.

Lee's novel, which focuses on two children from the Depression-era South who encounter evil for the first time in their lives but surmount the encounter and emerge more mature with the help of their father, eventually sold tens of millions of books. It remained on the *New York Times* bestseller list for nearly two years, and won the 1961 Pulitzer Prize for Harper Lee. One survey of American readers in the 1960s rated the book as second in sales only to the Bible.

The surprise was that no major studio purchased the rights to the book before it was published, a common practice in Hollywood. Several of them who had seen the book in galleys turned it down because they viewed it as a work lacking action, mystery, romance, and adventure. "A lot of the studios didn't bid on it," Robert Mulligan explained, "because they said, . . . 'You have this middle-aged lawyer with two kids, there's no romance, there's no violence—except off screen—there's no action. What is there? Where's the story?'" Pakula and Mulligan were therefore lucky that the novel remained unsold six weeks into its tenure on the bestseller list. When agent Isabel Halliburton suggested that Pakula read the book, he was enchanted and quickly secured an option on the rights—virtually snatching it away from Warner Bros., one of several companies that had begun to show interest in filming the novel.

When the partners tried to attract financing from a Hollywood studio, they were told that they would need to have a major star in the cast. Pakula took the novel to Gregory Peck, whom they saw as an ideal actor to portray the children's father, Atticus Finch, despite the fact that it would be quite unlike anything Peck had played before. After reading the book, Peck said, "I sensed it would be the role of my life," and accepted it immediately. "If you want me, I'm your boy," he told Pakula and Mulligan. On that basis, Peck's company, Brentwood Productions, financed the film and Universal agreed to distribute the picture.

Pakula and Mulligan were compelled to form a production company in order to sign contracts with Gregory Peck and with Universal. "Given the fact that we still didn't have any real money between us" Mulligan said, "it seemed ridiculous to be facing a maze of legal paper, much of it dealing with how Alan and I would handle our 'corporation profits.'" What was originally a simple partnership based on a handshake turned into a corporate entity, complete with an army of agents and lawyers. "One of us said something about 'funny money,'" Mulligan said. "That led to 'Monopoly,' then to 'Boardwalk.' It seemed a natural. We registered 'Boardwalk Productions' as our company name. Later on we named a subsidiary 'Park Place.'"

"This was only Pakula's and Mulligan's second film," the eventual screenwriter, Horton Foote said, "so they had relatively little clout, as they say. But Gregory, for some reason, in his divine wisdom, I've always felt, insisted in his contract that Pakula and Mulligan would have the final cut of the film. And Universal gave in to it."

For Peck, the role would mark a major departure from his customary film roles. For the first time, he would not be playing a romantic leading man, but a middle-aged, bespectacled father of two adolescent children. However, his acceptance of the role was based not only on the acting challenge it would offer him. "I felt a close identification with the characters, with the story, with the social problem, with the father and children. I somehow felt that it was something that I had to do," he said.

Pakula and Mulligan discussed the book for several weeks afterwards, "breaking it down and exploring ways of turning it into a movie," in Mulligan's words. But they knew that a professional writer would be needed for the screenplay. Mulligan had worked with playwright Horton Foote in television drama on several occasions, and, when Harper Lee declined to adapt her novel for film, Mulligan felt that Foote, a Southerner, would be an ideal choice to write the screenplay. Foote, who had written six plays (one of which, *The Trip to Bountiful*, became a successful film years later), was also a leading playwright for television, having written episodes of *Studio One*, *The Philco Television Playhouse*, and *The United States Steel Hour*.

Pakula, who knew Foote but had never worked with him, was immediately enthusiastic, and the partners approached the playwright. Foote hesitated. "I was busy on things of my own," he said, "and I really didn't want to adapt anything. So I put it aside and didn't pay any attention to it. Then my wife read it and she was very enthusiastic, and she said, 'You'd better get to that book right away.' I did like it, so I called Alan to say I was interested."

Still, Foote was uncertain that he could preserve the tone of the book, which was so essential to its success. Pakula suggested to him that the film should maintain the point of view of the children, and Foote's reservations immediately dissipated. Alan then took Harper Lee to meet with the screenwriter at Foote's home in Nyack, New York. They formed an immediate friendship, and Lee expressed her hearty approval of Foote as screenwriter.

"[Harper Lee] trusted us," Mulligan said, "that the book would not be emasculated in any way, or changed, that we would honor the book and be true to the book." In Nyack, Foote worked closely with Pakula as he wrote the script. Foote said that Pakula "was passionately devoted to the novel—passionately. We'd go over what I was doing, and he made one wonderful suggestion," Foote observed. "He said, 'Look, the novel goes over a series of years. I think it's more interesting if we confine it all to one year.' Now, why that meant so much to me I can't really tell you, but it did. That let me go into the architecture of the novel."

Pakula pointed out to Foote a review of the novel by R. P. Blackmuir, entitled "Scout in the Wilderness," which argued that the character of Scout was closely modeled upon Huckleberry Finn and Tom Sawyer. As Foote remarked, "I thought the comparison was wonderful and remarkable, and I don't know why, but it just opened the whole thing for me."

Pakula worked with Foote throughout the process, driving from New York City to Nyack nearly every day. "Often we'd discuss what I had done that day, and he often gave me notes," Foote said. "He was wonderful to work with. He had great respect for the process of writing. And he never tried to tamper with your vision. He simply tried to help you free it."

Mulligan noted, "Together Alan and Horton solved the problems of moving the novel to a film script. We were all determined from the outset to remain absolutely true to the spirit of Harper Lee's book. That is not an easy thing to do. Alan and Horton made it happen—and deserve full credit for it."

Mulligan is perhaps being too modest. At one point, when Pakula and Foote felt the screenplay was complete, they flew to Hollywood to show the script to Mulligan. The director said, "You know what your problem is: too often you lose the point of view of the children." Foote and Pakula realized that Mulligan's observation was accurate, and they embarked on another rewrite. Ultimately, Harper Lee called the screenplay "a masterful piece of craftsmanship."

The novel is "a memory of a time that is gone, and yet we all want to hold on to it," Foote said. "It isn't that it's a perfect world—it's an imperfect world, but it's a world that we recognize. Most of us have some distant feelings about childhood [and] as we get older we give it certain kind of talismans and meaning . . . and somehow this coalesces into something rather important."

Taking place in 1932, *To Kill a Mockingbird* revolves around Atticus Finch, a middle-aged lawyer and widower, and his two young children: Scout, his six-year-old daughter, and Jem, his eleven-year-old son. Atticus is as close to an ideal father as one could imagine: thoughtful, sensitive, supportive—and his relationship with his children is filled with warmth. One lesson, among many that he teaches them, is one that has been passed on from his own father: that it is a sin to kill a mockingbird, because mockingbirds are harmless creatures.

The only menacing figure in the children's world is their next-door neighbor, Boo Radley, whom they have never seen, but conceive of as a monster. When their friend Dill asks Jem to describe Boo, Jem replies, "Well, judging from his tracks, he's about six-and-a-half feet tall. He eats raw squirrels and all the cats he can snatch. There's a long, jagged scar that runs across his face. His teeth are yellow and rotten. His eyes are popped, and he drools most of the time." A good deal of the first hour of the film is devoted to building the children's picture of Boo.

Atticus is asked to defend a black man, Tom Robinson, who has been charged with raping and beating a white woman, Mayella Ewell. Because the town in which they live is segregated and determined to remain so, the white townspeople—particularly Mayella's father—resentfully accuse Atticus of siding with "the niggers" against "his own kind." The loss of the children's innocence begins to occur when Jem hears Mayella's father revile Atticus. "There's a lot of ugly things in the world, son," Atticus tells him. "I wish I could keep them all away from you. That's never possible."

On the day of the trial, the children sneak into the courthouse's balcony, where they sit with the black citizens of Maycomb, the main floor being reserved for whites. Atticus persuasively demonstrates that Robinson had no sexual relationship with Mayella—that any "relationship" was in her mind, as wish-fulfillment. But Tom dooms himself in an answer to a question from the prosecutor when he says, "I felt right sorry for her." For the white men on the jury—and for all the whites in the courtroom—it is the height of impudence for a black man to feel sorry for a white woman. The jury finds Robinson guilty.

Mayella's father, the brutal and bigoted Bob Ewell, despises Atticus and determines to harm his children as well. One evening, he attacks Jem, then Scout. But an unidentifiable figure stabs Ewell, killing him. The man, it is later revealed, is Boo Radley, making his first appearance in the film after the picture is nearly two hours old. Boo, whose reclusiveness, limited mental capacity, and extraordinary shyness has made him a frightening creature to the children, turns out to be their savior.

Atticus believes that Jem killed Ewell in self-defense. But the sheriff, who knows that Boo stabbed Ewell, insists that Ewell fell on his knife and "killed himself." Atticus, who then realizes that Boo was Ewell's killer, says nothing to the sheriff. Scout tells Atticus that arresting Boo "would be sort of like shooting a mockingbird."

Ultimately, the children's lives are changed because of the events depicted in the film. Mary Badham, who was chosen to play Scout, described the theme of the movie thirty-five years after the film was shot: "There's a lot of hope in this whole story, hope for a better future, an understanding that the children finally come to about the reality of the world and how they have to take what life gives them, somehow using these experiences to better not only their own lives, but the lives around them."

Beyond the focus on the children, the story describes the beginnings of the Civil Rights movement in the South. "The big danger in making a movie of *To Kill a Mockingbird*," Mulligan said, "is in thinking of this as a chance to jump on the segregation-integration soap box. The book does not make speeches. . . . It deals with bigotry, lack of understanding and rigid social patterns of a small southern town."

One of the first concerns that Pakula and Mulligan addressed was the visual style of the film. They were determined that it be shot in black-and-white, and managed to convince the Universal executives to use black-and-white stock.[10]

Casting the children required an extraordinary search. Mulligan said, "Let's find kids who are kids," not actors, because "kids lose their sense of childhood very quickly when they become professional actors at age seven or eight." A young Southern woman named Alice Lee "Boaty" Boatwright, who worked in the publicity department at Universal, saw Pakula at Sardi's one afternoon having lunch with Roddy McDowall. She knew McDowall, and asked to be introduced to Pakula. "Honey," she said to him, "I don't know what I'm doin' on this film, but I'm doin' somethin' on this film, 'cause it's the story of my life." As Boatwright said later, "He must have liked my enthusiasm and energy," for a few days afterwards, Pakula

---

[10]In 1998 Pakula said, "The tragedy is now it's almost impossible to get investors to allow you to use black-and-white because they say it [negatively] affects the ancillary rights" for foreign distribution and for video sales.

engaged Boatwright to conduct a search for children who could play the pivotal roles of Scout and Jem.

Boatwright began by seeing professional child actors in New York, but soon came to agree with Mulligan: "We realized very quickly that that was not going to be the tone we were looking for." So she began touring the South, staying with friends or in hotels and interviewing local children. All the little girls looked alike, she found, coming to the interview "with their mothers, [their hair in] lots of curls and looking like Shirley Temple," whereas she was looking for a tomboy. She began in Richmond, went to Winston-Salem, Raleigh, Dallas, New Orleans, Atlanta. By that time—three weeks into her search and after having seen more than five hundred children—she was overwhelmed. "You couldn't ask them to come in and read a scene," she said; "most of them were too young to do that." So she had to interview each child at length, an exhausting process. She called Pakula to say that she was on the verge of quitting.

But, with Pakula's encouragement, she continued until, in Birmingham, "I looked at this child and she was perfect, she was Scout, you just knew it." The girl, Mary Badham, was nine years old, but quite small for her age. Boatwright commented upon her size, and Mary answered, "Well, if you drank as much coffee and smoked as many corn silks as I do, you'd be little, too."

That was all Boatwright needed. She called Pakula. "I've found the child," she told him. "There's a little girl here that I cannot wait for you to see." And then, within a few days, she found Philip Alford, who, she realized with the same certainty, was perfect for the role of Jem. Badham had never acted before, but Alford, then thirteen, had been in a play or two at the local community theatre. Ironically, after a multistate search, the two young performers who were cast lived within four blocks of one another in Birmingham, and knew one another.

After Boatwright recommended Badham and Alford, Pakula went to Birmingham to meet the children. He then asked them to go to New York for screen tests. Rather than audition, they simply appeared before the camera while Mulligan asked them questions. "They both had a quality that I was looking for," Mulligan said. "They were bright. They were alive. They both seemed to have active imaginations." And, importantly, "they looked as if they could be brother and sister." They were cast in December 1961.

Mary Badham said during the filming that she had no plans to continue acting after *To Kill a Mockingbird*, and, indeed, she did not pursue a career in films. After performing in *This Property is Condemned* as Natalie Wood's sister, she chose what she called a "normal life." Philip Alford, on the other hand, did continue performing, appearing in *Shenandoah* and several other films. But *To Kill a Mockingbird* remained the high point of his career. He later returned to Birmingham, where he became the owner of a clothing store and a bar.

One of the children cast in the film did have professional experience. John Megna, nine years old at the time, had performed in the Broadway cast of *All the Way Home*. But, Pakula said, Megna was "a very unaffected kid, and he was not a movie kid." Megna played Dill, Scout's and Jem's friend, a character who was based on Truman Persons (who later called himself Truman Capote), a neighbor of Harper Lee's when they were children.

Philip Alford's father was not certain that he wanted his son to appear in the film. Hollywood had often proved a bad influence on child actors, he said. But he was gratified to discover that Philip's personality did not change during the shooting—and that his grades actually improved once he began attending school for a brief, concentrated time each day at the film studio.

Rehearsals took place on the sets—a great advantage for the actors, who could immerse themselves in the environment of the film. Directing the children required quite a different technique than working with adults. "You have to explain the scenes to children in terms they can understand," Mulligan said, "but you can't overdirect them. They're extremely natural, and you'll lose it if you start telling them what to do." His fundamental approach was to treat the children as children, creating an environment which would resemble their own backyard. The set, as Pakula noted, "in a way became [the children's] playground." They were permitted to "climb on the equipment as long as they didn't get in the way of the work," Mulligan said.

Moreover, Mulligan was "sensitive to the fact that they're going to get bored. . . . In order to keep focused within a scene—which is the toughest thing for kids to do and sustain—the only way that can happen is for them to be relaxed. But not to [rehearse scenes] over and over and over again. I learned very quickly to try to get something going in the rehearsal and then shoot it quickly, and not to go more than two or three takes on a scene."

Gregory Peck helped to put the children at ease. He invited them to his home on several occasions; he allowed them to wander in and out of his dressing room; he taught Alford how to play chess. Mulligan said, "I often saw Mary go up and just crawl in his lap in between takes."

The rehearsals lasted for two weeks. Mulligan said, "I staged pretty much from day one. Get 'em up and get 'em on their feet. I believe in that. I don't like to have actors sit around tables talking."

About the other actors who were selected, Pakula said, "We wanted to retain the sense of discovery, which was so important in the novel. We didn't want familiar faces that everyone in the audience would recognize. So, aside from Gregory Peck, we're using Broadway actors, who are not too well-known to motion picture audiences, and the completely unknown children." Prominent in the cast were Frank Overton, Rosemary Murphy, Brock Peters, Collin Wilcox, Paul Fix, and James Anderson—many of them actors with whom Mulligan or Foote had worked in television. Filmgoers would probably have had a difficult time identifying them in 1962 or, for that matter, in subsequent years. Horton Foote recommended an actor he had seen in live television to play Boo Radley. Pakula and Mulligan thus cast Robert Duvall, who made his film debut in *To Kill a Mockingbird*.

Boo Radley is characterized by his reclusiveness, mysteriousness, and almost pathological shyness. Duvall needed no help from the director in order to fully understand the character. Without telling Mulligan or Pakula, he altered his appearance for the film. "I'll never forget the first day I saw Bob Duvall walk out on the set in wardrobe, in full costume," Mulligan said. "He was standing way at the end of this soundstage, but in a pool of light. [He wore a] ragged shirt, baggy pants, and old, worn work shoes. He had dyed his hair white. He had stayed out of the sun so his skin was really pale. [He wore] no makeup. I took one look and I said, 'God almighty, that's Boo.'"

Near the end of the film, Scout, who has been terrified of Boo throughout the narrative, reaches out to him and murmurs, "Hey, Boo," signaling her acceptance of and gratitude for him. It is a touching moment, beautifully achieved, often cited as one of the most moving in film history. After Scout's remark, Duvall looks at her. "That's a lesson in screen acting," Peck said, "that he was able to convey so much in a glance—of shyness, of awkwardness, or some kind of deep affection for the child, of being exposed to people when he's a recluse—all those things he conveyed with the most subtle expression, and really it came from deep inside of Bob."

One actor whose name *would* have been recognized by the film's audience was uncredited. Kim Stanley read the narration (as an adult Scout, looking back at her childhood), primarily as a favor to Mulligan and Foote, with whom she had often worked on television. Stanley's voice established both the tone and the film's point of view. "That voice was so important," Mulligan said, "in pulling you in and [giving you] the sense of the South, and the sensibility."

Pakula and Mulligan were determined to reproduce a bygone era so thoroughly that members of the audience would be reminded of their childhoods. To that end, under the guidance of the production designer, Henry Bumstead, they oversaw the creation on Universal Studio's back lot of a dusty southern street, on which stood a series of houses. "We all went down to Monroeville, Alabama, Miss Lee's hometown," Mulligan said, "hoping that it could double for Maycomb, the town in the story. But it had changed radically since the Depression days of the novel." The Monroeville of 1961 was replete with "television antennas, neon signs, new storefronts," and no longer had the feel of a small town.

Bumstead found a small town in the San Fernando Valley that was scheduled for demolition to make way for a freeway. He rescued a number of the houses, moved them to the back lot of Universal Studios, "and there we were in Maycomb," Mulligan said. The set, built at a cost of $225,000, covered fifteen acres, contained more than thirty buildings, and was one of the largest to be built in Hollywood in many years.

So successful was Bumstead in creating "Maycomb" that for many years after *To Kill a Mockingbird* was released, people would tell Mulligan, "I know exactly where you shot that" or "I've been there" or "It's my uncle's town." Mulligan said, "They were very disappointed when I said, 'I'm sorry, but it was done at Universal Studios.'"

One structure, the courthouse in Monroeville, was reproduced almost exactly for the film. The set as a whole was very similar to the town described in the novel. "Harper Lee visited the set and was stunned," Mulligan related, "in that it looked so much like a Southern town, like her town."

During the scouting of Monroeville, Peck met Lee's father, Amasa Coleman Lee, who had been the model for Atticus Finch. The meeting was significant for Peck, for he found A. C. Lee an inspiring individual: courageous, courteous, humble, and wise. For his part, Lee was "amused," Peck said, "that his tomboy daughter grew up to be a Pulitzer Prize-winner. And he was even more amused by the Hollywood types who barged into his hometown."

Pakula and Mulligan agreed that, during the shooting, the cameras and other equipment should be as distant as possible from the children, and be moved closer slowly and unobtrusively. It worked. Many years after the film was released, Philip Alford said, "We weren't aware that they were setting up. As we rehearsed they would slowly move everything up, so that by the time we were ready to actually shoot, the camera's right here, the crew's right there, and the lights were ready to go and they'd just start rolling."

Peck recalled the first day of filming:

[We shot] a scene where Atticus was coming home from the courtroom, or his law office, and the kids were expecting him, and the boy took his briefcase and they walked on down the street talking over the events of the day. And during the shot, which was covered by a camera on a dolly track, I just glanced at Harper—she was walking along behind the moving camera—and I saw something shining on her cheek. We finished the scene. . . . I walked over to Harper and I said, "Are you crying? How do you feel?" And she said, "Gregory, you've got a little pot belly just like my daddy." I said, "That's great acting."

In an early scene in which Atticus puts Scout to bed, Gregory Peck and Mary Badham display a remarkable rapport. Mulligan said, "She did things in that scene that no director—and I mean nobody—could tell a kid to do. She was just so natural and so easy. And spontaneous. And it did, I think, affect Greg—and pulled him into the scene." Pakula added, "There's shyness in Greg and there's a freedom in Mary, and I think the combination together is very touching."

Amasa Coleman Lee died not long before filming began. Harper Lee gave her father's pocket watch to Gregory Peck. "I had noticed when I was in Monroeville," Peck said, "that he carried it in an old-fashioned way—put through a buttonhole in his vest—and he had a way of playing with it. And I stole that mannerism and I used it in the courtroom."

An old woman, played by Ruth White, was to be a principal character in the film. According to Pakula and Mulligan, White's performance was excellent, but nearly all of it had to be cut. The problem, as Pakula explained, was that "this film narratively builds up . . . to the courtroom [scene], and stopping for [another] sequence just stopped the drive to the courtroom and the narrative of the picture began to crumble. It really was like in some [stage] musicals, out-of-town they sometimes take out the best number because it stops the show. Well, this was one of those things, and it was so hard to do because the woman was a remarkable actress."

Brock Peters played the pivotal role of Tom Robinson, the gentle and kind black man who is wrongly accused of raping Mayella. Brought to trial, he is forced to defend himself before an all-white, all-male, all-bigoted jury. Knowing that he is almost certain to be found guilty, he nevertheless tries to clear his name. Peters became extraordinarily involved in the scene and his characterization. "The anger, the frustration, the isolation that one could experience, and often did experience, was an easy place for me to get to, to tap, to use in my performance," Peters said.

Mulligan frankly stated that "the only direction I gave Brock—well, it was no direction at all—I simply said, 'There is nothing I can tell you that you don't know about this man.'" Indeed, Mulligan had cast him immediately after they first sat down together to talk. Pakula felt that Peters had a "heroic dimension," a "star quality."

Of the interrogation scene in the courtroom, Peck said, "Brock gave me a problem, because when Brock started to tell his story of what really happened, he started to cry and tears ran right down his face, and I found that I couldn't look him in the eye, because I started to choke up. So I resorted to looking past him. It was the only way I could get through it because you didn't want to have the witness and the lawyer both crying at the same time."

Despite Peters' heartfelt performance, the day's shooting was almost ruined.

Peck said, "One thing I always had to do was keep a rein on my emotions, because Atticus was not a fellow to be demonstrative or let his emotions slop over," but the actor became more emotional during the scene than the director wished. Mulligan shouted, "Hold on, hold on," because, as he explained, "with all that adrenaline running—and here was the key moment—it's Atticus trying to save this man's life—all of those thoughts and all of that energy being funneled into those few moments on-screen could be too much."

The role of Mayella, who is attracted to Tom Robinson, was played by Collin Wilcox. Mayella possesses limited intelligence but a healthy set of hormones. Wilcox explained her character's attraction for Tom Robinson: "here is a very attractive, very dignified, very kind, soft-spoken man." When she accuses Robinson of raping her, "She knows she's lying [but] she's just trapped [on the witness stand] and that's her only defense. That's one of the reasons I went into this sort of bizarre body language—a trapped animal. She's trapped in life, trapped by her conditioning, trapped by her own hatred and prejudice—and the poverty in which she lives—and she'll never get out of it."

During the trial scene, Scout and Jem sneak into the courtroom and sit in the balcony, which is populated only by blacks, with all the whites seated on the lower floor. Segregation "was a social tragedy," Pakula said, "but a great gift for staging—having the kids sit with the blacks."

At the end of the trial, one of the most moving moments of the film occurs when all the whites leave the courtroom, but the blacks in the balcony remain. As Atticus packs his briefcase and prepares to leave, all the blacks come to their feet, and one of them tells Scout to stand up. When she gives him an inquiring look, he says, "Your father's passing."

James Anderson played Mayella's vicious, hate-filled father, Bob Ewell. Anderson was the actor who had played Caligula at the Circle Theatre and had been redirected by Charlie Chaplin. Pakula recommended him to Mulligan, but the director "had been warned that he would be trouble, because, talk about an angry young man, he was an angry young man." Anderson himself had "had a hard life," Mulligan said, and his background gave him insight into his character. "He was a very tough guy with a tendency not to show up on time, he'd be drinking and in bar fights and ending up in the drunk tank in downtown L.A. Alan and I decided to see him for the part for several reasons. He had been born and raised in the South—and he definitely looked like a mean, dangerous, and unpredictable man. His face was an unmistakable map of a hard life scarred with pain and sullen anger. That described Ewell perfectly." Anderson glared at Mulligan and growled, "I know that man." According to Mulligan, "he said it in such a way that I *knew* he knew this man, I mean there was absolutely no mistake."

Pakula lobbied for Anderson, whom he regarded as "a brilliant actor." Therefore, when Anderson came back to see Mulligan several days later, "I sat him down," Mulligan remembered recently, "and said, 'I want you to be in this movie, but you and I are going to have to have a clear understanding, and you're going to have to take my hand and shake it, . . . you have to promise me that you will be sober, that you will be on time, that you will not cause trouble for me or for anyone and that you will do honor to the script.' And he said, 'I understand,' and he put out his hand. I shook it—and he kept his word."

The casting of every role in *To Kill a Mockingbird* was given intense scrutiny by the producer and director. Pakula said: "I think that seventy-five percent of directing is casting—and I think that's being conservative. Maybe more like eighty-five percent. You can't create what's not there. And if you miscast, you can cut your losses, but that's about it."

At the end of each day of shooting, Pakula and Mulligan would watch the dailies together, then go to their office and discuss the progress of the film over drinks. They would "just kibitz and free-associate and just relax," according to Pakula, "and let the picture roll over us and just say, 'Where does this seem to be?'"

Pakula admired Mulligan's restraint in his directorial approach to the film. "Because it was such a well-loved novel it would have been easy to get pretentious with it," he said. But "there's a real discipline in the way Bob shot the film. Bob's use of camera movement is very controlled." Mulligan also limited his use of close-ups, so, Pakula said, "when you suddenly do go to a close-up, it has enormous power."

Gregory Peck felt that Pakula deserved a significant amount of the credit for *To Kill a Mockingbird*'s success. "Alan was younger than I," Peck said recently, "and, for that matter, younger than Bob. But one day, in the middle of the film, in a time that we were intensely involved, . . . tempers flared between [Mulligan] and me, and for a moment the picture was in real danger. And it was young Alan who came between us and steadied us down and saved the day and maybe the picture."

One of Pakula's responsibilities was to deal with the Universal studio heads, who did not fully understand the filmmakers' intentions. The executives "would see the dailies and at one point I got a comment, shortly after the picture had started shooting, with great concern that Greg did not look glamorous and that he was looking rather old in the film and did I think we should do something about the makeup and the hair and all? I don't think I even told Bob [Mulligan]," Pakula said, "because I thought it was absolutely ludicrous."

Peck's performance cannot be underestimated as one of the reasons for the film's astounding success. His name and reputation helped to attract a mass audience, as the studio had hoped, but he also gave a splendidly constructed performance that resonated with filmgoers everywhere. Pakula felt that Peck's performance reflected his character. "Gregory Peck," he said in the 1990s, "is the truest, noblest film star I've ever known."

Mulligan's directorial style throughout the film is deliberate and restrained. For example, during Atticus's summation, the director opted not to use reaction shots from the members of the jury. This was a considered decision, as Mulligan wanted Atticus's speech to be spoken to the film's audience, and reaction shots might have interfered with that concept. His use of understatement is evident in the treatment of Tom Robinson's killing at the hands of a prison guard. The audience does not see Robinson's death—and, for that matter, no act of violence is portrayed in the film. As Pakula said, "there could have been a temptation—and certainly today [1998] there would be—to [show] Tom Robinson being taken off to jail and see him running away and being shot," but that would have shifted the emphasis away from the major characters: the children.

One exception to Mulligan's judicious use of close-ups occurs during the trial scene. When Collin Wilcox as Mayella gives way to a hysterical outburst, she is photographed in close-up. Her performance is simply too large and too intense for such a shot, which calls attention to Wilcox's acting rather than to Mayella's character. A longer shot would have been a more judicious choice in this instance.

Pakula and Mulligan knew that audience members might become impatient watching *To Kill a Mockingbird*, especially if they were expecting an action-packed piece or a romantic story. Moreover, the film required an audience to listen carefully, for the film is more complex than one might suppose. The first hour, as Pakula pointed out, "is just building the children's world." Then, as the plot begins to develop, there is a long, slow build to the trial scene: two quite different story lines, one involving Boo Radley and another involving Tom Robinson. And that understates the case, for the Atticus-Scout-Jem story line is even more prominent than the others. "They do all come together at the very end," Pakula said, "but not until the very end. . . . I think we [he and Mulligan] were both very nervous: would the audience hold for all this? And yet it's what makes this film worth doing." Perhaps the fact that more than nine million people had read the novel by the time *To Kill a Mockingbird* came to the screen was a factor in the film's success, for many members of the audience were prepared for a leisurely pace.

Elmer Bernstein, who had composed the music for *Fear Strikes Out*, was hired to perform the same function for *To Kill a Mockingbird*.[11] This turned out to be a deci-

---

[11]*Bernstein had also written successful scores for* The Man with the Golden Arm *(1955),* The Ten Commandments *(1956),* The Sweet Smell of Success *(1957), and* The Story on Page One *(1960). Altogether, he composed the music for 250 films and television production before his death in 2004.*

sion of major importance, for Bernstein's haunting, evocative score was a significant element in the film's success. "It had to have an individual language," Bernstein said. "We were seeing an adult world . . . through the eyes of children. One approaches it in terms of what would address itself to children. What would children play on a piano, given a chance? What do children do when they go up to the piano? Very often they'll just play one note at a time." That notion was turned into a highly effective musical theme for the film.

Bernstein also created a musical motif with full orchestra for Boo Radley. Boo frightens Scout and Jem, Bernstein observed, but "children love to be scared. It's part of the adventure of life. And I got into that in a big way. The first time they go to the Boo Radley house the music's a bit over the top, almost. It's very Gothic, it's very big. That's part of a commentary on the way the kids feel about him." Pakula said that in creating "the mysterious world of children, Elmer Bernstein's score helped enormously. . . . I don't think you can [overestimate] what a score can do when it's properly done—and what Elmer contributed to this film."

Another element that proved to be decisive in creating the children's world was the title sequence designed by Stephen Frankfurt. Pakula and Mulligan asked him to design a sequence that would evoke "the mysterious world of childhood," and Frankfurt's effort, showing a child removing items from a cigar box, was perfect. "It caught the spirit of the movie perfectly and added a great deal to its success," Mulligan observed.

The last stage in post-production is the film laboratory's issuance of the final print. In the case of To Kill a Mockingbird, this resulted in a disastrous showing. The lab presented Pakula with a "print that was just gray and white instead of black and white," the producer said. He insisted that the lab start from the beginning. At last they produced an excellent print. However, before the film went into general release, Pakula showed the film in Washington to members of Congress and the Supreme Court.[12] Somehow, the lab sent the initial, rejected print. "And," said Pakula, "the whole film was just a study in grays. It had no visual resonance. It was one of the worst nights of my life." The moral, he concluded: "beware of labs." Pakula made sure that the gray-and-white print was never shown again.

Harper Lee was enchanted with the film Mulligan, Pakula, and Foote had adapted from her novel. "For me," she wrote, "Maycomb is there, its people are there: in two short hours one lives a childhood and lives it with Atticus Finch,

---

[12]Robert Mulligan cannot recall why the film was selected for this purpose, but is "sure Universal had a great deal to do" with it. "And," he said, "I assume both Gregory Peck and Lew Wasserman [the president of Universal Pictures], who were particularly active in Democratic Party activities, had some influence." Of course, the topical nature of the subject matter—racial relations in the South—might have been of particular interest to members of Congress, since a major bill on civil rights was being actively discussed. The Civil Rights Act was passed by both houses of Congress and signed by President Lyndon Johnson in 1964.

whose view of life was the heart of the novel . . . and the result is a film that has a life of its own as a work of art."

Pakula was equally pleased. The novel has "become as much a part of the American mythos as Huckleberry Finn and Tom Sawyer," he said. "It's a triumph of Harper, and I think the triumph of the film is [that] it did capture the soul of that book." And he was thrilled about the direction and the performances. "You don't feel like people are acting," he observed. "You feel a moment-to-moment honesty, where you don't see the director and the intention, and that for me is what really wonderful directing is all about."

Pakula was confronted more than once by people who felt the film was overly sentimental. "What a number of people resented," he felt, "and fortunately, they were not in the majority, was that it dealt with a childhood that most of us never had. Whatever the terrors, these were children who belonged somewhere. And in their first confrontation with evil they had a father figure who represented what most of us would like to have had and probably didn't. . . . So for people who have had rather more rootless childhoods, it seemed [sentimental]."

He also responded to those who felt that Atticus was an idealized character, too good to be true. "If you deal with a character and indicate a kind of simplicity and a kind of strength, and a capacity to love without self-dramatization and hysteria, it's questioned—possibly because we live in . . . an enormously doubting time. But there are certain people who are better adjusted, happier, and more giving and stronger than others."

To Kill a Mockingbird was released in February 1963. It comes as a surprise to read some of the contemporary reviews, for a movie that is now perceived as a classic was often reviewed negatively. Bosley Crowther's review of the film in the *New York Times* is an example. "There is so much feeling for children in the film that has been made from Harper Lee's bestselling novel, *To Kill a Mockingbird*," Crowther's notice began, "so much delightful observation of their spirit, energy, and charm . . . that it comes as a bit of a letdown at the end to realize that, for all the picture's feeling for children, it doesn't tell us very much of how they feel." The criticism seems odd, for it would be difficult to conceive of a film that is as successful at portraying the attitudes, maturation, and deep feelings of children.

Several other critics were no more enthusiastic than Bosley Crowther. Brendan Gill in the *New Yorker* described the film's "portentous airlessness" and claimed that Mulligan's pace "often approaches slow motion." *Newsweek* found much of the film "unsupportable," ending its review by saying, "we can no longer share the warmth of [Scout's] love."

On the other hand, a number of critics felt the power of *To Kill a Mockingbird* keenly. *Time*, for example, called it "one of the year's most moving and affecting pictures." But it was the filmgoers of America who validated the film most thoroughly, as they flocked to it in large numbers and left little doubt of its impact upon them. For Universal Studios, the film was successful on a financial level, as well—one of the "most profitable movies made" in 1962, according to the *New York Times*.

To Kill a Mockingbird won three Academy Awards: for Gregory Peck, for Horton Foote's screenplay, and for Henry Bumstead for his art direction. The film received five other nominations: for Mary Badham as best supporting actress, for Mulligan as best director, for Elmer Bernstein's musical score, for Russell Harlan's cinematography, and for best picture. The film also won the Golden Globe award for "Best Film Promoting International Understanding."

After viewing *To Kill a Mockingbird* again in 1998, Pakula said, "One of the things when I look at the film that I find amazing and that I find saddening about today is the leisure with which you could build a story and texture [in 1962] so you felt things were happening. It's so hard today, with the restlessness of an audience that has been besieged by images of MTV and every other area, now in their computers [and video games]—it's like some old roué who has experimented so much sexually that he needs greater and greater stimulation to arouse him—and it's like for an audience now, they've been just besieged with the kind of amusement-park rhythms and it's harder to take the kind of time to tell the story that one does in *To Kill a Mockingbird*—and it's a great loss in many ways."

When *To Kill a Mockingbird* opened in New York, Pakula flew there from California for the premiere. Because it was a picture about children, he invited his niece, Debby Maisel, then nine years old, to accompany him. "So he took me to Radio City Music Hall," Maisel recalled, "and I remember sitting with him, and I was fascinated by the whole thing and the whole experience that we had together. He didn't have children of his own, so I felt a tremendous bond with him."

Horton Foote's work with Pakula led to a lifelong friendship. "He was my best friend," Foote said. "I was devoted to him. We'd talk about many things: books, families, politics, the theatre—for Alan loved to talk, and I certainly loved to talk. And we found we agreed about most things. There were times, of course—life gets complicated—when I'd be on one coast and he'd be on the other coast, and we wouldn't see each other, but once we got together it was just like [we had never been apart]. I can't tell you how much I admired him. He was an enormous influence on my whole career. He was always interested in my work, he was supportive, he was helpful, and I could always turn to him. He was a rare friend."

CHAPTER FOUR

A Marriage and Two Divorces

"Alan was without question a creative collaborator. He often initiated projects but we'd move ahead only if we agreed to make it as a movie. Material came to us individually and as a company from all kinds of sources: agents, writers, friends. But it was Alan who actively worked the phones and read the galleys while I was shooting. There is no question Alan made a significant contribution on <u>every</u> film we made—and in every conceivable way. Alan had a direct hand in—or influenced—aesthetic choices and decisions throughout all our films."

—ROBERT MULLIGAN, 2002

FROM 1963 TO 1969 PAKULA WAS EXTRAORDINARILY BUSY professionally and experienced both great happiness and despair in his personal life. The films he produced were not particularly distinguished—perhaps because he was unable to make several that promised to be remarkable and that he wanted desperately to produce. But each film on which he collaborated with Robert Mulligan led him a bit closer to realizing his great ambition: to become a director.

One searches for a theme or vision that links all of the collaborations that Pakula produced and Robert Mulligan directed, but there was no such connective tissue. As Mulligan told me, "Alan and I never discussed making a certain kind of film. All we wanted to do was to make movies." Perhaps as a consequence, the partnership produced one thoroughly successful film, one disastrous effort, and five intriguing but flawed pictures. Alan Pakula's great contributions to American cinema would emerge in the films he went on to direct, most of which were linked by clearly discernible themes and concerns.

It is virtually impossible to isolate Pakula's specific contributions to the films he made with Mulligan. When I asked Mulligan if he could supply that information, he responded that Pakula's "creative contributions occurred not just in moments, but totally. Completely. From start to finish. In many ways. On every production. Alan initiated almost every film we made. He suggested the writers and worked closely with them to develop a screenplay, often without real assistance from me until a first draft was done. He was closely involved in the casting process, and was responsible for hiring talented people like Boaty Boatwright and Alixe Gordon to work with us on the casting. Alan often suggested production designers, film editors, and directors of photography for me to consider. His choices were always the very best in the field. He also concentrated real effort on the choice of a composer on every film and always had a strong choice or two in mind. We'd review scores together—and his preferences were always on the mark."

Mulligan was unable to say what Pakula had contributed to any particular film, because, he said, "We made our films *together*. I never felt that he did one thing and I did something else. We separated only when the shooting began. But even then Alan knew what I was doing, because I told him. There were no secrets, no mysteries. No ego territory fenced off between us. And we discussed the work every day. Nothing was left unsaid between us about the movie we were doing at any time."

On a personal level, Pakula's frenetic schedule, which carried him from one coast to the other and to Europe, had, for a long time, prevented him from committing to a woman. As he admitted, "There was a long period when I was avoiding marriage. I was going back and forth between New York and Los Angeles, and very often I'd get seriously involved with a woman in New York, and somehow there'd be a reason why I had to be in Los Angeles, and vice-versa." But that would change at last in the early 1960s.

Having just produced one of the best films in many years, *To Kill a Mockingbird*, scripts were submitted to Pakula and Mulligan in such profusion that "they needed to weed through it," as David Lange put it. Lange, who had recently graduated from Harvard, was a young man in Hollywood who often ran into Pakula at parties and "admired him tremendously." Pakula and Mulligan thought highly of Lange, as well, and, in 1963, asked him to become their story editor, reading the material that was submitted and seeking out other works, such as novels, that might be turned into a distinguished film. Lange recalls perusing *Publishers Weekly* and *Kirkus Reviews* every week, looking for promising material.

Many of the scripts sent to Lange were similar in one respect or another to *To Kill a Mockingbird*. "Everybody was sending in material about animals and children," Lange said recently. Mulligan was determined not to become noted as a "children's director," however, and made clear to Lange that he hoped to direct "something tougher."

But Lange was unable to influence the choice of material immediately, for, in late 1962, Pakula and Mulligan had already become involved with the preparation for, and shooting of, *Love with the Proper Stranger*. The film originated when the producer and director were discussing an idea for a new picture with screenwriter Arnold Schulman, a close friend of theirs. Schulman told them he was too busy to begin work on an original screenplay, but suggested that they might be interested in a script he had already written but which had never been produced. The script had to do with the experience of the children of Italian immigrants in the New York City of the 1960s—a subject that had long interested Mulligan. He and Pakula liked the screenplay and commissioned Schulman to make some revisions.

They presented their plans for *Love with the Proper Stranger* to Paramount Pictures. When they told Paramount that Natalie Wood and Steve McQueen, two of the most prominent actors in Hollywood, had agreed to star in the picture, the studio agreed to distribute the film.

Soon afterward, the screenplay complete, exterior shooting on *Love with the Proper Stranger* began in New York, then the interiors in Hollywood, where sets that resembled apartments in the Little Italy section of New York were built.

Steve McQueen played Rocky Papasano, a jazz musician, and Natalie Wood played Angie Rossini, an employee at Macy's. The two characters had become sexually involved for a single night a few months before the beginning of the movie, and Angie had become pregnant. As the film begins, Angie asks Rocky's help so that she can get an abortion. Between them, they raise enough money, but when she goes to a seedy apartment for the operation (the film pre-dates, by more than a decade, the Roe v. Wade decision legalizing abortion) and sees the indifference of the abortionist (who is not a doctor) and his assistant (not a nurse), both Rocky and Angie refuse to go through with the procedure. The scene is the most harrowing episode in what is basically a romantic comedy. It is also the finest scene in the film, suggesting that the rest of the picture will be on the same level. Unfortunately, it is not.

Rocky offers to marry Angie, but it is clear to her that his offer has been made grudgingly, and she defiantly refuses. She spends the rest of the film alternately showing contempt for Rocky and attempting to attract him. At one point she shouts at him, "You're dead! Dead!" Despite Angie's angry intensity, it is apparent to the audience that she is as drawn to Rocky as he is to her. In the next—and last—scene, Rocky shows up outside Macy's just as Angie is getting off work. He carries a sign, reading, "Better to be wed than dead"—presumably in reference to her outcry in the scene before. The film ends with the implication that Rocky and Angie will marry.

Even while *Love with the Proper Stranger* was in production, Pakula was thinking about his next films. As David Lange noted, "Alan liked to have two or three or four projects going on at once at that time." Consequently, he met with various actors who might be cast in a future picture. One of them was Hope Lange, David's sister, whom Pakula invited to his office to discuss appearing in a film he intended to produce. "He called me in," Hope Lange recalled in 2003. "He asked me if I'd be interested, and I was, very much, because I liked him so much. I liked him the minute I saw him. I loved his humor. And he was an immensely sensitive man. But I had some contractual agreement, so I couldn't do it." Three years younger than Pakula, she had achieved considerable success in Hollywood, appearing in *Bus Stop* in 1956, *Peyton Place* in 1958, *The Best of Everything* in 1959, and *A Pocketful of Miracles* in 1961. The following year she played Roxanne, opposite Christopher Plummer, in a televised version of *Cyrano de Bergerac*.

They met again later at a party given by their mutual friend, Katie Manulis. Pakula invited Lange out on several occasions and very soon fell deeply in love with her—so much so that he proposed marriage after a short time. "Alan became emotionally involved pretty quickly," David Lange said. Hope was equally attracted to him, but having recently divorced the actor Don Murray, was initially reluctant to remarry. However, when she saw how Pakula took to her children, Chris and Patty—and they to him—she began to change her mind. As David Lange said, "He was just wonderful with them. They were at an age when they needed a father, and he was just ideal."

Pakula was certainly mesmerized by Hope, but it hardly interfered with his frantic professional schedule. He and Mulligan took an option on Ray Bradbury's book of short stories, *The Martian Chronicles*, announcing on June 9, 1963 that they intended to turn the work into a film with a screenplay by Bradbury. Although other science-fiction films had been made, this was to be the first high-budget ($5 to $10 million) movie about outer space.

"Now that man has orbited the moon," Pakula said, "it is time for a serious movie to be made about outer space by a mature writer." Mulligan added that the film would be more than "piles of rocks and desert vistas in a strange light and with unusual musical effects." He conceded that "adventure is a part of such a movie, of course," but noted, "more important are the emotional, intellectual, and spiritual changes among the colonists from Earth, and the contrast of the cultures of Earth and Mars. This is a study of morality and a social issue against a background of science fiction as only Ray Bradbury can do it."

The film never got beyond the planning stage, however. Pakula and Mulligan met with Bradbury in his home office in Los Angeles, which, according to Mulligan, "was surprisingly small and crammed with bookcases from floor to ceiling that were filled with books, paperbacks, journals, small framed paintings, bright watercolors by Ray [Bradbury], various antique toys, assorted photos, and personal memorabilia. It was a visual, delightful circus."

Pakula became so fascinated by the objects in the room that he all but forgot the purpose of the visit. And Bradbury was all too eager to tell fascinating stories about each object. "Our script conference was completely forgotten," Mulligan said. "It was simply a case of Alan's compulsive curiosity meeting Bradbury's congenital and compelling storytelling."

Other meetings were somewhat more productive, but Bradbury gradually became more interested in other projects. Pakula and Mulligan were not particularly distressed, since, as Mulligan said, "we were involved with developing several other things." Eventually, the producer and director decided to let their option lapse on Bradbury's stories, and the film was never made. This was unfortunate, for *The Martian Chronicles*, a collection of brilliantly achieved stories, might well have made an exceptional film, just the sort that Pakula and Mulligan needed to solidify their reputations after *To Kill a Mockingbird*. But the proposed project was only one of many potentially exciting ventures that did not come to fruition during this period.

A theatrical enterprise that involved Pakula only peripherally occurred shortly afterwards. Mary Martin and her husband Richard Halliday originally held the option on Marguerite Courtney's biography of her mother, Laurette Taylor. Their interest was in creating a musical focusing on Taylor's early career, when she sang, danced, and performed in melodrama. However, they were unable to persuade a writer, producer, or director of the soundness of their approach, so they dropped the option, whereupon Pakula picked it up and produced the unsuccessful *Laurette*.

Three years after that production, in 1963, Pakula still held the rights to Courtney's biography. Martin, undiscouraged by the failure of *Laurette*, wanted another try at the material, so she had to negotiate with Pakula for the theatrical rights. A deal was struck: Martin would be allowed to adapt the book, but Pakula would be given a producer's credit in the billing.

When the production opened in New York City on October 17, 1963, at the Majestic Theatre, the billing stated: "Produced by Cheryl Crawford and Richard Halliday; Produced by arrangement with Alan J. Pakula." The critical reception was unenthusiastic, and *Jennie* ran for only eighty-two performances, a poor run for a Broadway musical—especially one which starred Mary Martin, a longtime favorite—closing on December 28.

Pakula invested some money in the $500,000 production but had no other involvement, for he was at work on a new film. Indirectly, however, he did benefit from the production of *Jennie*, for George Jenkins, after designing the sets, went on to serve as production designer for many of the films Pakula would later direct.

Only two days after *Jennie* opened in New York—on October 19, 1963—Pakula and Hope Lange were married at Martin and Katie Manulis's house before a small gathering of friends.

The Pakulas rebuilt a home on Bristol Street in Brentwood—"a wonderful old house that they redid all in their own tastes," according to Colleen Creedon, one of Lange's oldest friends. They went out rarely, but saw "lots of mutual friends, and had *lots* of parties," Creedon said. "Hope didn't like to go out as much as she liked to have people come to the house. I can remember the big dining room, it was always full of people, and there were always a lot of people outside, especially around the pool. People would drop in and they'd ask them to stay for dinner. It was very informal." Robert Redford also remembers attending a number of parties at the Pakulas' house, "parties with Roddy MacDowall, Mike Nichols, Natalie Wood—they always had pretty high-end attendance at their parties in Brentwood," he said.

Rodd Baxter, Pakula's nephew from New York, visited California when he was thirteen years old and observed Lange and Pakula together. "He was crazy about her," Baxter recalls. "You always got that sense. She was a gorgeous woman—breathtakingly beautiful. Men around her would melt." Alvin Sargent, Pakula's old friend, said, "He *really* loved her. She was the beautiful woman, the girl next door. I think he was proud of her." Redford said, "She had a very strong personality, very attractive, very engaging, and it seemed that Alan adored her."

In December 1963, *Love with the Proper Stranger* was released. For a film of that time, it was regarded as somewhat daring. Rocky and Angie's casual affair, Angie's pregnancy, and particularly the scene with the abortionist were all unconventional material for American movies. Pakula, in a 1972 interview, said, "I don't think that either Bob or myself saw it as a daring or advanced picture, although it's true that most films at that time didn't mention things like abortion—least of all a film that was essentially a romantic comedy. It really was an attempt at a modern version of a thirties kind of film: a love story of two very unlikely people." Thus, the romantic comedy undercut the realistic and daring elements of the film, turning what might have been a groundbreaking treatment of innovative material into a conventional love story.

Bosley Crowther's notice in the *New York Times* was particularly critical of Rocky—though it's not clear if he was unhappy with the way the role was written or performed. He found Natalie Wood appealing, but felt that she "deserves someone much more substantial and attractive than this lug of Mr. McQueen. She's a sweet and courageous little creature . . ."

Time liked the film with few qualifications: "This romantic comedy-drama succeeds in spite of itself, for it is brimful of enough warmth and hip humor to mask a decidedly rancid plot." The *New Yorker*'s Brendan Gill said, "about all that I can recommend . . . are Natalie Wood and Steve McQueen, who give performances of considerable vehemence and are pleasant people to watch."

The varied responses to the film are understandable, for those portions of it that are well-achieved are balanced, in about equal measure, by those that are not. *Love with the Proper Stranger* is generally tasteful and restrained, the musical score by Elmer Bernstein is up to his usual high standard, and Natalie Wood is appealing. But many of the other characters are little more than clichés. For example, Angie's family—her mother, stepfather, and brothers—are all conventionally "Italian"—fiery, emotional, protective. Rocky shares an apartment with a worldly nightclub stripper whose character, also a cliché, is never developed beyond her ability to deliver wisecracks. In addition, the ending seems rather contrived, since the prognosis for Angie and Rocky's marriage—a marriage of two highly volatile people who don't appear to have even begun working through their problems with one another—is, to say the least, highly questionable. Furthermore, Steve McQueen's mannerisms throughout the film are both distracting and unconvincing, and the picture never seems to find a style with which it is comfortable.

Pakula was fully aware of the stylistic problem. "The great danger of that film," he said, "was that it starts out rather dramatically and there is comedy along the way, and it gets to the abortion—which is a terrifying scene, really almost a horror scene—and then from that goes into almost straight romantic comedy. We were always concerned about the welding of this and the synthesis of it, and indeed whether it would ever work. It seemed to work for a lot of audiences, but we were always concerned about it."

An objective view of the film is that, despite an occasional charming moment, it evaded the significant issues it raised, thus undercutting any possibility that it might have become an important contribution to American cinema.

In 1964, Pakula persuaded United Artists to purchase the rights to John Cheever's bittersweet novels, *The Wapshot Chronicle* and *The Wapshot Scandal*, with the intention of blending them into a single film. Perhaps this would restore the Pakula-Mulligan team to the high ground they had occupied after *To Kill a Mockingbird*. They surely hoped so, believing that the project held the promise of a brilliant film, if a script as subtle as the novels could be written and if the leading roles could be cast with outstanding actors.

Pakula and Mulligan hoped that Cheever would write the screenplay. To that end, they met with the author at the Beverly Hills Hotel, where Cheever amazed his guests with his ability "to drink two large tumblers filled to the brim with vodka during a morning meeting in his room and then move on to several glasses of wine at an early lunch, while remaining absolutely sober and lucid," Mulligan said.

Although captivated by Cheever's elegant prose style, Pakula and Mulligan were baffled by the motivations for the activities of some of the characters.

Consequently, they asked Cheever why the characters behaved as they did. "Cheever smiled a bemused smile," Mulligan said, "then looked at us in a kind of wonder and said he didn't know the answer."

It soon became clear that, despite Cheever's literary brilliance, an experienced screenwriter would be needed to adapt the novels to the screen. Tad Mosel, an accomplished writer for television and the author of the sensitive 1963 Broadway play, *All the Way Home*, was recruited, and, with Pakula's assistance, produced what Mulligan called "a very workable first draft." The producer and director then focused on casting. Their first choices for the film's major characters, Leander and Honora, were Spencer Tracy and Katharine Hepburn, who, if they could be persuaded to accept the roles, would likely attract other important actors. And, as Mulligan said, he and Pakula would be able to "encourage [a major] studio to move the project into pre-production."

Pakula and Mulligan's agent drove them to Hepburn and Tracy's house in Los Angeles, where, as Mulligan recently recalled,

> Kate Hepburn greeted us at the front door. She led us through a hallway toward the rear of the house. It had the look of a New England cottage. There was Tracy, walking toward us. His hair was snow white. He looked older [than Mulligan had remembered], smaller, and a bit frail. But the familiar grin was there. His voice was strong and his handshake firm. As we were introduced, his eyes fixed directly on yours and remained there for what seemed a long moment. Alan and I said later, it wasn't so much Tracy looking at you but looking into you—and allowing you to do the same to him.

The meeting began, with "Hepburn in slacks and sweater, cross-legged on the floor, Tracy in a large armchair," Mulligan recalled. "Kate Hepburn started. Lots of questions—and comments. Typically edgy. Challenging Yankee flint behind every remark, and that sharp intelligence always at work. She felt her part was underwritten. We didn't. She wanted more scenes. We disagreed, and gave reasons. She argued her case. It soon became clear that she enjoyed verbal combat and didn't like to lose.

"Tracy seemed amused by all this," Mulligan continued, "and then interrupted her. It was done softly, with a smile. He called her 'Kathy.' He told her he was sure that we got the point, because she had been 'emphatic,' as usual. She smiled, turned to us, and said that as a peace offering she'd make some tea.

"Tracy then gave us his notes. It was a completely different experience. His questions and remarks were all carefully thought out and non-combative. They were specific, focused on character—on how Leander served the story in certain scenes and on how he related to other characters. He was interested in emotional detail. His copy was marked with tabs, and he suggested moments from the novel. Would we consider including them in the next draft? We agreed to do that. It was a wonderful demonstration of a real actor at the work of breaking down a script."

Tracy then asked Pakula and Mulligan if they knew that he and Hepburn had a "reputation for being difficult to deal with" and for "driving producers nuts." Pakula, without hesitation, said that he'd willingly take the risk if Hepburn and Tracy would agree to appear in the film. But Tracy, turning to Mulligan, said, "we often eat directors for breakfast," and suggested that Mulligan would be well-advised "to bring a whip and a chair to the set." Mulligan joked that he would strap on a gun, if necessary. Tracy fixed him with a look and said, "That might help. But don't bet on it." According to Mulligan, "I decided there was no response required and wisely kept my smart-ass Bronx-Irish mouth shut."

When the meeting ended, Hepburn drove Pakula and Mulligan back to the William Morris agency. As they began down the hill, Tracy waved goodbye from the front porch. Then, Mulligan recalled, Hepburn "said something Alan and I never forgot. She said, 'You know, there's a big difference between Spencer and me. For him the acting is easy and the living is hard. For me the acting is very hard but the living is easy.'"

Tracy and Hepburn agreed to appear in the film, but Pakula and Mulligan "just couldn't make a deal," David Lange, the story editor of Boardwalk Productions, remembers. Although United Artists paid for Mosel's screenplay, they refused to invest more money in the project. Lange believes that the problem derived from the filmmakers' wish to condense two books into a single film. "It was pretty spread out, and it became unfocused," he believed. "I think essentially what happened is that we were all so in love with Cheever and respected him so much that we couldn't make it our own." Thus, another opportunity was missed.

Pakula then turned his attention to bringing about a musical adaptation of *Great Expectations* for the stage, with songs by André and Dory Previn. Mulligan, who realized after *Comes a Day* that the stage was not his métier, was not involved. The Previns wrote what David Lange recalls as "gorgeous music," and Tad Mosel agreed to write the book, but, once again, the project never came about. Lange believes that Pakula simply "got involved in other things. Alan loved having a lot of projects," Lange said, and, in this case, his rather frenetic pursuit of every conceivable property he hoped to turn into a film or play was responsible for the jettisoning of what might have been a significant production.

Great Expectations was the last of Pakula's dreams of a Broadway success. Indeed, he never again worked in the theatre, although he professed interest on occasion. Years later, Placido Domingo asked him to stage an opera and the Gate Theatre in

Dublin asked him to direct one or more plays for them. Pakula was flattered at being asked and did not decline the offers immediately, but he never got around to them. He devoted the rest of his professional life exclusively to the cinema.

Unable to make the films and present the plays he most wanted to produce—*The Wapshot Chronicle*; *Look Homeward, Angel*; *The Martian Chronicles*; *Great Expectations*—Pakula settled for lesser material. It is clear in hindsight that many of the choices he made were unwise, for the films that resulted were undistinguished. But a producer must produce, and, rather than cease operations, Pakula opted to base his next several films on the best material he could find, even if it failed to rival the exceptional models that he had been unable to bring to fruition. One might think that the artists who made *To Kill a Mockingbird* would have had access to the most superb material, but, as David Lange recently said, "You would think. But it wasn't true. You're only as good as your last picture," and *Love with the Proper Stranger* had not achieved the same sort of success as *To Kill a Mockingbird*.

Still, Pakula had high hopes for *Baby the Rain Must Fall*, a picture adapted by Horton Foote from his own play, *The Traveling Lady*, which had been performed on the Broadway stage in 1954. According to Foote, "the character of Georgette [the traveling lady] was very attractive to Alan. He had great compassion for her and he was very sympathetic to her plight and moved by her." Foote and Pakula worked closely together to shape the screenplay, as they had done with *To Kill a Mockingbird*. "Alan was very anxious to 'open the film up,'" Foote said, "because he thought that a play is one form and that it doesn't necessarily work on the screen." As a result, they looked closely at the characters and the play, and, at Pakula's suggestion, decided to shift the focus from one of the male characters in the play to another.

Lee Remick was cast as Georgette, and Steve McQueen was assigned the male lead. Once again, Paramount was responsible for financing and distributing the film, which was released early in 1965.

Baby the Rain Must Fall focuses on Georgette, a young mother, who travels by bus with her four-year-old daughter Margaret Rose from Tyler to Columbus, Texas, to see Georgette's husband, Henry Thomas, a deeply troubled young man who has been serving time at a nearby prison for stabbing a man in a fight. When Georgette and her daughter arrive in Columbus, she tells Henry that she wrote to inform him that she would be coming, but Henry clearly is surprised by her appearance. This is only one of the many unexplained mysteries in the film. Did she actually write him a letter? Did he receive it and pretend otherwise? Did his foster mother intercept the letter and never show it to Henry?

The film's title derives from a song Henry sings with his string band at a dance. During that scene, we see Henry's violent side when he pulls out a knife and threatens to stab an antagonist but is subdued by two men.

After another violent incident, Henry is arrested but allowed by the sheriff to say goodbye to his wife and daughter. Later, Slim, Henry's best friend, drives Georgette and Mary Rose to "the valley"—the last of a procession of towns where this "traveling lady" and her daughter have lived. As the film ends, they pass Henry in the backseat of a police car. We are left with another series of unanswered questions: is Slim going to "the valley" with Georgette and Margaret Rose, or is he only giving them a ride? Will Henry and Georgette ever come together—or has Slim taken Henry's place?

Throughout the film, Henry shows no affection for his wife and daughter. He greets Georgette with a handshake when he first sees her.[13] One scene shows Henry and Georgette in bed together, but there is no physical contact between them. Nor is it at all clear if Henry has any feeling for Georgette; he tries to pick up a girl at the dance, for example, although Georgette is waiting at home for him. He never hugs or kisses his daughter. These aspects of his character suggest that Henry is the archetype of a remote man unable to get in touch with his feelings. If so, Steve McQueen was unable to convey Henry's character with sufficient clarity.

In many respects, *Baby the Rain Must Fall* is an ambitious and affecting film. As with nearly all Horton Foote's work, the dominant tone of the piece is melancholy and poignant. Lee Remick hits most of the right notes as a woman who wants so desperately to be happy that she seems able to convince herself (and others) that she *is* happy—although nothing she hopes for comes to pass. She drifts through one incident after another, suffering heartbreak and humiliation, but refusing to acknowledge them.

A comparison of the film with the play from which it was derived is instructive: *The Traveling Lady* makes clear that Slim falls in love with Georgette, and, at the end, when he is about to drive her to the valley, he plans to settle there as well. So the play ends on a note of romance and anticipated happiness, whereas the film's ending communicates a sad uncertainty.

The shift of emphasis in the film from Slim to Henry as the main character seems fully justified. Even though Henry is seen only briefly in the play and Slim's character is fully explored, Henry is the more intriguing character. And the mysteries and ambiguities in the film, which are, perhaps, the picture's most compelling feature, do not exist in the play.

When *Baby the Rain Must Fall* was released in January 1965, it received mixed reviews, at best. *Newsweek*'s critic, describing Henry as a "dismal dimwit," had nothing good to say about the film, and noted, "Why Georgette puts up with him

---

[13] *According to Horton Foote, this was not intended to suggest an emotional remoteness between Henry and Georgette; "that's simply a truthful statement about people of that class at that time," he said. "They were not demonstrative. They were shy with each other. Particularly country people. You'd often see them shaking hands."*

is never explained." The *New Yorker*'s Brendan Gill dubbed the picture "a spectacular failure" and found it "too simple for its own good."

Bosley Crowther's *New York Times* review made clear that he found the mysteries off-putting. He discussed "a major and totally neglected weakness" in the film: "why the object of the woman's deep affection is as badly mixed-up as he is and why the woman, who seems a sensible person, doesn't make a single move to straighten him out . . . leaves one sadly let down at the end." True enough, the characters' behavior and motivation are enigmatic, but that is perhaps the most impressive aspect of the film. Not everything in life is knowable, and the film seems to demonstrate that there are mysteries in life that cannot be fully understood or explained. Obviously, this approach runs the risk of leaving audiences unsatisfied, but it surely reflects reality in a way that certainty does not.[14]

One must concede, however, that there are several mysteries connected with the making of the film as well. Why, for instance, did Pakula and Mulligan cast as Margaret Rose a four-year-old child whose every line—and she has a good many—is unintelligible and who is unable to convey emotion with face or body? Couldn't they have cast a nine- or ten-year-old who would have been more expressive? Why was Steve McQueen's (or whoever's voice was used) singing so off-key and unmelodious? Was that intended to tell the audience something about Henry Thomas's lack of talent, or was it simply a case of a poorly cast singer? Why did the producer and director allow McQueen's dubbing of the songs to be so absurdly out of synch? Surely they did not want to call attention to the poor dubbing, but, as several critics pointed out, audiences could not restrain their laughter.

Despite these flaws, *Baby the Rain Must Fall* deserves more thoughtful analysis than it received from the critics in 1965. It is by no means a masterpiece—and it is a disappointing effort for those who made *To Kill a Mockingbird*—but it will intrigue filmgoers who have a taste for ambiguity.

By the time the film was released, some signs of strain were beginning to appear in Pakula's marriage. David Lange said, "There was a part of Alan that, with all his humor, needed things in order—to the point of being somewhat uptight. Hope was much looser than that, and sort of laughed when Alan would get upset about something." According to some of their mutual friends, Pakula wanted a traditional marriage (for the mid-1960s) in which he would go off to work each day with his wife there to greet him when he came home. And, indeed, she took a five-year hiatus from performing during their marriage, but, as a successful actress, was frustrated in her role as a housewife.

---

[14]When I discussed this interpretation of the film with Horton Foote, he observed that "we never consciously tried for ambiguity," and he never discussed the notion with Pakula or Mulligan. However, he did not deny that an atmosphere of ambiguity may have come to dominate the film.

One wonders if the growing tension in Pakula's marriage had something to do with the dismal failure of the next Park Place production, *Inside Daisy Clover*, financed and distributed by Warner Bros. in 1966. The film reunited Pakula and Mulligan with Natalie Wood, and presented Robert Redford in his film debut. If *To Kill a Mockingbird* is indisputably the finest film on which Pakula and Mulligan collaborated, *Inside Daisy Clover* is without doubt the least successful. Much of the film is so awkward and contrived it appears to be a parody—but, unfortunately, it is not.

Gavin Lambert, a friend of Pakula's and Mulligan's, adapted the screenplay from his own novel, and David Lange has no doubt that the friendship was the primary reason the producer and director sought to be involved. But friendship may have blinded them to the deficiencies of the project. Whatever the merits of the novel might be, the screen version is improbable, melodramatic, and—one searches in vain for a more descriptive word—silly.

The story of the movie, set in 1936, details the rise from rags to riches of Daisy (Natalie Wood) from the age of fifteen. She is first shown living with her mother (Ruth Gordon), whose behavior is so bizarre that it cannot simply be described as eccentric—rather, it borders on lunacy—in a rundown section of Los Angeles. Somehow, Daisy manages to record a song and send it to the head of a film studio (Christopher Plummer), who gives her a screen test, the results of which convince him that she is the stuff of which dreams are made. He resolves to transform the little urchin into a star.

Daisy falls in love with Wade Lewis (Redford), another star on the same lot. Eventually, Daisy—now known as America's Little Valentine—and Lewis are married, but he leaves her after their wedding night. The studio head arranges for a quick divorce. Soon after comes the one successful scene in the film: Daisy's breakdown while dubbing a song. The scene, done mostly in silence—as no sound can be heard from outside the dubbing booth—is both innovative and effective. However, this scene is followed by an outlandish attempt at farce when Daisy tries to kill herself by putting her head inside an oven, only to be repeatedly distracted by the ringing of the telephone or the doorbell. Then, for no apparent reason, Daisy reverts back to her happy-go-lucky self as she turns on the gas in the oven and the fire on a burner. She gaily walks down the beach as the house explodes behind her and the movie ends.

The score by André Previn, featuring two mediocre musical numbers (one of which is repeated again and again, each time with less impact), is but one of *Inside Daisy Clover*'s many problems. Every melodramatic twist of the plot (and there are many) is accompanied by highly melodramatic music. But one cannot place all the blame for the failure of the film on the music, for the screenplay and most of the performances are equally second-rate. Much of the dialogue—especially the lines written for Redford—is painfully stilted and awkward.

Perhaps the most interesting aspect of *Inside Daisy Clover* is the off-screen story of Robert Redford's participation. Before shooting began, Pakula saw Redford's performance in *Barefoot in the Park* on Broadway, then visited the actor in his dressing room to discuss his participation in *Inside Daisy Clover*. As Redford described the experience, he learned that

the character I would be playing was described as homosexual. When we talked it over and I read the screenplay, which I really liked, I said, "I don't think I'm the right guy to do this. But what would be more interesting to me is playing a bisexual character, because to me that is far more complex and interesting. That's a far more interesting character problem to work on, a guy who just took everything: men, women, children, animals, anything, just a total narcissist, constantly on the take, giving out charm in exchange for taking, taking, taking. Alan got really intrigued by that and then [Pakula and Mulligan] decided to go that way.

When the character was rewritten as bisexual, Redford agreed to make his first screen appearance in the picture. When filming was in progress, Redford's performance was predicated on the character's bisexuality. But he was in for an unpleasant surprise.

When I was in Louisiana doing *This Property is Condemned* they started to preview *Inside Daisy Clover,* and [a friend of mine] saw the preview, and apparently my character had come off very well with Natalie. The cards [filled out by the members of the audience at the preview] apparently suggested that the audience was more interested in Daisy and me [than in other aspects of the film], and they didn't want me to disappear. So it left Pakula and Mulligan in a quandary. So, according to what I was told, they decided that they had to really get rid of my character and make his disappearance more palpable, so the audience wouldn't want him back. So they made him a homosexual again. And they did it in the editing by looping a line in a conversation that Natalie has with the wife of the studio head. The wife is heard saying, "Don't you know he prefers young boys?" That was never in the script. I didn't know about this. Somebody who saw the preview told me about it and remarked about my playing a homosexual. I said, "No, I played a bisexual," and he said, "Well, that's not what the film says."

Redford was understandably angry about the alteration and about not being consulted, so, he said, "I called Alan and Bob and confronted them, and they admitted it. They came to my dressing room, they told me what had happened. They said, 'Look, we don't feel good about this, but we were kind of led this way by Warners; the picture was in a lot of trouble, and we made the decision. And it wasn't fair of us not to tell you.' They were very apologetic, and so all was forgiven—because of the way they handled it, particularly Alan. He was very dignified and stand-up about it. So that was the end of that."

When Pakula saw the film after its first preview, he told David Lange, "[I] overproduced it, [I] should have kept it smaller." He felt, according to Lange, that the failure of the picture "was his fault." Pakula's concept—that Hollywood can be a vicious and destructive force—"got in the way of a simple little story," Lange said. Since Pakula's Hollywood marriage was deteriorating even as the film was being made, it does not seem outlandish to suggest that the film's melodramatic touches might have derived, at least in part, from Pakula's anguish at his own domestic situation.

Mulligan had no reservations about the quality of the picture. He said as recently as 2003, "We had a good time making it. We both loved Gavin Lambert's book and enjoyed working on the screenplay with Gavin. And we were pleased with the result." Pakula evidently kept his reservations to himself.

Howard Thompson's review in the *New York Times* began, "There have been [few] pictures about Hollywood . . . as triumphantly, all-around bad as *Inside Daisy Clover*." Thompson went on to employ such adjectives as "dank," "verbose," "ploddingly cynical," "dull," "cold," "laughable," "null and void," and threw in such adverbs as "absurdly" and "inexplicably." Bosley Crowther's Sunday piece added "ridiculous," "fatuous," "discouraging," and "vulgar."

Brendan Gill's notice in the *New Yorker* was equally disdainful. "By the Hollywood standards of 1936—the time of the story—the picture would have been pretty bad, and by today's Hollywood standards it is still pretty bad, its weaknesses all the more embarrassing for being inadvertent."

The review in *Newsweek*, however, was quite favorable, the anonymous author calling the film "a wry and entertaining Hollywood fairy tale." He managed to find meaning and distinction in the picture, but his enthusiastic opinion stands virtually alone.

The partners immediately turned to the preparation and filming of *Up the Down Staircase*, a film released in August 1967, and a distinct improvement over *Inside Daisy Clover*, though hardly free of flaws. The movie, distributed by Warner Bros. and credited as a Park Place production, is as far removed from the tone and content of *Inside Daisy Clover* as can be imagined.

It concerns the unwieldy New York City school system and one teacher's attempt to circumvent its bureaucratic obstacles to reach her students and turn them into active, eager learners. Tad Mosel wrote the screenplay, adapted from Bel Kaufman's predominantly comic novel. But Mosel chose to emphasize the teacher's frustrations in a realistic manner rather than making the school system seem an amusing, though frustrating, institution. The filmmakers emphasized the gritty reality of teaching in a rundown New York City high school in the 1960s, and the various obstacles put in the way of the good teacher: the crumbling buildings, the boredom and surliness displayed by students and their parents, the defeatism of veteran teachers who long ago sublimated their idealism and were simply going along with the corrupt and inefficient system, the overcrowding, the stifling bureaucracy, the deadening monotony, and the overwhelming sense of irrelevance in the face of insurmountable social difficulties. At the end of the film, certainly, one finds it hard to believe that the idealism of Miss Barrett (the film's protagonist) will be able to survive for long—despite the film's best efforts to suggest otherwise.

Up the Down Staircase was shot in and around the public schools of New York. Its Calvin Coolidge High was an actual school building in Manhattan, its neighborhood a depressing slum. The students in the film were cast not with professional actors, but with New York adolescents, many of them from troubled families, so representative of their peer group that some of them reported to the set with switchblades.

Sylvia Barrett (Sandy Dennis), a young teacher in her first classroom assignment, becomes progressively more upset by the students' attitude toward her—generally hostile or apathetic, at first—and the administrators' lack of interest in facilitating good educational practices. The administrators' insistence on following bureaucratic procedure is shown as absurd, and some of the characters are portrayed stereotypically as routine-driven, unthinking, obtuse robots. Gradually, Sylvia does manage to inculcate at least a drop of enjoyment in learning in a few of her students. Although at one point she decides to quit the school and take a job where the classrooms will be less crowded, up-to-date textbooks will be available, and administrative attitudes will be more open to change, she eventually changes her mind.

The film details the frustrations of teaching in the big-city environment with great effectiveness but is far less convincing in persuading the viewer that an idealistic attitude can overcome those frustrations. When, in the film, Sylvia ultimately returns to her classroom, smilingly facing the obstacles that she knows will still be forthcoming, her decision seems arbitrary and unmotivated.

Up the Down Staircase contains some very effective scenes. The best of them is a sequence in which a shy, painfully awkward young student is driven to a suicide attempt because the teacher to whom she wrote a love letter responds with cruel indifference. The student comes to school early the next morning to see Miss Barrett, but Sylvia, occupied with her own thoughts, dismisses her, saying she'll speak to her at the end of the day. But before the meeting can occur, the girl jumps out of a window. Although the student survives, Sylvia blames herself. Meanwhile, the male teacher (Roy Poole) who is really responsible for the girl's despair remains indifferent and refuses to accept any responsibility.

The strength of this sequence is balanced by the odd decision on the part of the filmmakers never to show the girl again. Nor is she even referred to. The effect is to turn her anguish into a vignette rather than an incident in a series of events leading to a meaningful conclusion.

Some of the other scenes include a boy who mistakes Sylvia's interest in him as a desire for sex; a lesson she gives her class in *A Tale of Two Cities* which excites them, for the first time, in learning; and Sylvia's class staging a mock trial, which is portrayed as a triumph for her teaching methods but seems curiously unconvincing.

Certainly the film might have been more melodramatic than it is. Instead, although the events portrayed are frustrating at best and harrowing at worst, the treatment is somewhat restrained. The film is always interesting and sometimes arresting, but between its best moments are long stretches of repetition and scenes that strain credibility.

Up the Down Staircase was shown before its general release to several national educational organizations such as the National Congress of Parents and Teachers and the American Association of School Administrators, which conferred upon it the 1967 School Bell Award on May 15, 1967 in the hope that the public "would identify with the struggling, devoted, almost-but-not-quite defeated heroine. They cheered the message which seemed to say that the good teacher is at the heart of education and will triumph over all odds," summarized the *New York Times*. And the organizations seemed hopeful that *Up the Down Staircase*, with its idealistic young protagonist, would supplant the sensationalistic 1955 film *The Blackboard Jungle* as the public's image of the New York City school system.

Bosley Crowther was generally impressed by *Up the Down Staircase*, writing that the film revealed "the complex character and the commonplace personality outcroppings of a huge problem-area school in a city such as New York." He called the film "amusing" and "poignant," paying particular tribute to Tad Mosel's screenplay, and the performances of Eileen Heckart, Sorrell Booke, Roy Poole, Ruth White, first-time performer Ellen O'Mara (as the girl who attempts suicide), and, particularly, Sandy Dennis as Sylvia Barrett, "who walks away with the show." Crowther is critical of a few scenes, but, he says, "the flaws are few. For the most part, this is a beautifully balanced, fluid film with engrossing contemporary material."

Time's critic argued that "the film has no characters, only characteristics. Thus Sandy Dennis, as the teacher-heroine, is Trust, competing for the students' souls with the administrative assistant (Roy Poole), who is Distrust. Miss Schracter, an older teacher played beautifully and all too briefly by Ruth White, is Wisdom, while various students stand for sexuality, boastfulness, pride, and sensitivity." This seems a fair assessment, for the filmmakers, in their eagerness to portray the horrors of the school system and Sylvia's impassioned attempts to overcome them, appear not to have had the time or patience to develop genuinely individualized characters.

Stanley Kauffmann in the *New Republic* gave the picture short shrift. His critique of the acting ("particularly affectless") and the musical score by Fred Karlin ("condescendingly coy") can be accepted simply as his opinion, but his comment that "there's almost no sense of the New York milieu" makes it appear that he is writing about another film, for if *Up the Down Staircase* is distinguished by any characteristic, it is for its vivid portrayal of that city's environment.

Penelope Gilliat, the film critic for the *New Yorker*, argued that the notion of a gifted and inspired individual being able to bring about changes in a corrupt or immovable system is a peculiarly American belief, and essentially a mythical one. She also claimed that, in *Up the Down Staircase*, the idea is particularly meaningless, "because the script unwittingly makes [Miss Barrett's] class seem a lot more attractive when it is being bad than when it is being good. Once teacher's magic works, the classroom turns into a breeding ground for toadies." Gilliat's observation cannot be dismissed lightly, for the students' transition from antagonists to eager learners comes about so swiftly and so totally that it is indeed unconvincing.

But her larger point, that "the oldest of all American faith-healing religions" is the belief that "a complex ill can be cured by the simplicity of one individual" is not convincingly argued. Perhaps the notion that one good teacher can somehow overcome the barriers erected by the system and effect positive change in the lives of her students is naïve. Still, how else can deeply embedded attitudes begin to change? "One individual" may not be able to alter a system, but a collection of like-minded individuals can—and have, as history has demonstrated again and again.

By the time *Up the Down Staircase* was in general release, when David Lange visited his sister and Pakula, he was stunned by the palpable tension evident in their relationship. "I was amazed," he said. "The feeling I had whenever I had dinner with them was that Hope was drifting away from Alan somehow." Obviously unhappy, she eagerly accepted an offer to play the lead in a weekly television show, *The Ghost and Mrs. Muir*, in 1968. Her schedule severely disrupted Pakula's sense of domestic order. While she was appearing in the series, she would go to bed at six o'clock in the evening and arise early in the morning for the day's shooting. On those days, her husband rarely saw her at all. "She cared so much about her career," Martin Manulis said. "You could tell that the marriage was eventually going to break up."

Pakula showed little understanding of his wife's desire for a successful acting career. And, for her part, Hope Lange lamented that when Alan was working on his films, "I hardly saw him." David Lange felt that the marriage foundered because "it was essentially two stars. Alan was totally committed and totally focused. He loved his work, and Hope was also starring in a series. They were two busy people and Hope was not one to give in to Alan."

Larry Turman, Pakula's friend, never discussed the state of Alan's marriage with him, but said, "From the outside, it appeared rather golden. Hope was a beautiful woman; Alan was on a good trajectory in his career. And they had a very active, slightly glittering social life with people whose names you read in the paper. They had a lovely home, and I was surprised when the marriage broke up. I didn't see gleanings of that, ever."

"His marriage to Hope Lange was a wonderful thing in the beginning," Martin Manulis said. "But I think that before long they had great differences. Alan was a very intellectual man, and no one could ever say that about Hope Lange. She was a lovely person and a good person, but she simply had no intellectual qualities."

"Alan was always fired up," Colleen Creedon recalls. "He had a lot of energy. Hope had energy, too," but it was of a different sort. She could barely keep up with his constant barrage of ideas and his need for a well-regulated home life. He was, as Hope Lange told me in 2003, "a demanding, high-maintenance husband."

While his home life was deteriorating, Pakula did not lessen his involvement with film. He produced and Mulligan directed *The Stalking Moon*, a drama of the old West, released in January 1969 by National General Pictures (Gregory Peck's company). Peck brought the project to Pakula and Mulligan, proposing that he play the lead. Horton Foote was enlisted to write the screenplay, but Alvin Sargent revised his script so thoroughly that only Sargent received screen credit. When I asked Foote why Pakula and Mulligan didn't film his draft, he responded, simply, "They didn't like it. And I didn't agree with the changes they wanted to make so I just said, 'God bless you and go ahead.'"

Foote says that his separation from the film did not affect his friendship with Pakula, but they were careful to avoid the subject afterwards. "It was a difficult thing for me and I'm sure for Alan," Foote said. "We were close friends, and it's very difficult to reject a friend's work." Pakula offered to give Foote screen credit as co-author of the screenplay, but Foote said, "No, I don't think that's correct because I haven't contributed a single word to the film."

Alvin Sargent remembers that "Pakula and Mulligan needed a new script fast!" They must have been severely rushed for time, for they told Sargent that he needn't read Foote's version. Nor did Sargent have time to read the novel by Theodore V. Olsen that served as the film's source material. According to Sargent, "Alan and Bob made it clear that they liked Mr. Foote's script but needed another approach. They told me the story and I wrote on my own with their guidance."

As rewritten by Sargent, Sam Varner is the leading character, a soldier whose regiment comes stealthily upon an Indian encampment at the beginning of the film. They gather the Indians, survivors of an Apache massacre ten years before, together. Among them is a white woman, Sarah Carver, whose entire family was wiped out in the massacre. She holds an Indian boy, about nine years old, close to her. The following morning Varner takes Sarah and the boy to Hennessy—where everyone who has been waiting for the stagecoach has been slaughtered by Salvaje, the Apache Indian who committed the massacre in which Sarah's family met their deaths. Sarah tells Varner, "He [Salvaje] is not finished. He came for his son."

Varner offers Sarah a job at his ranch as a cook. With the boy, they take the train to New Mexico, where they eventually reach Varner's house, an isolated cabin in the wilderness. Nick Tana, an Indian friend who served in the U.S. army with Varner, comes to the ranch to report that Salvaje is on his way to New Mexico to look for his son. Varner relays this information to Sarah, who tells him that she was raped by Salvaje and is the mother of the Indian boy. Varner vows that he will kill Salvaje before Salvaje can inflict further damage. Sarah embraces him—but there is no hint of sexuality in the embrace, simply gratitude that she has finally found a protector. Ultimately, Salvaje appears, kills Nick Tana, and wounds Varner in the leg. After a long and savage struggle, Varner shoots Salvaje—again and again. Only after trying to strangle Varner does Salvaje collapse and die.

Several elements of *The Stalking Moon* are intriguing. Most significant, perhaps, is the fact that the film contains a minimum of dialogue. Perhaps ninety percent of the story is told in pictures, not words. During the last third of the movie, there are no more than four or five lines spoken. This puts a great premium on the actors' ability to communicate with facial expression, and both Gregory Peck as Varner and Eva Marie Saint as Sarah respond well to the challenge. The Indian boy, played by eleven-year-old Noland Clay, never speaks at all. Alvin Sargent was grateful that the emphasis was on the characters' behavior rather than language, for, given the brief time he was given to write the screenplay, it was virtually impossible to write a great deal of dialogue.

Salvaje, until he is finally killed at the very end, is relentless in his pursuit of his goals—so much so that he becomes a terrifying figure, evil personified. As in *Baby the Rain Must Fall*, the film contains moments of ambiguity, such as the two occasions when the boy runs to Salvaje, either to rejoin his father or to plead with him not to harm Sarah and Varner. Surely the ambiguity of his motivation is woven into the film intentionally, and was not—as some critics contended—a failure of the filmmakers to dot every "i" and cross every "t."

An element that works against the film's success is its excessive reliance on music. Many scenes are underscored from start to finish, and almost invariably, the music by Fred Karlin lessens the tension. Silence, or—when appropriate—the sound of the wind, would have been more effective than the nearly constant musical accompaniment. This is demonstrable, for when the music *does* stop, the tension increases palpably.

Although *Life* magazine said, "It has the simplicity and fascination of a myth dredged up from the unconscious," most of the critics were indifferent to the virtues of the film. Vincent Canby of the *New York Times* called *The Stalking Moon* "a beautiful movie [visually, but] one that just may be too tasteful for its own good." Westerns, he argued, are by tradition violent, excessive, vulgar, and sentimental. But Mulligan and Pakula "avoided these excesses and made, instead, a rather pious, unimaginative suspense film."

In a very long, very negative review for the *New Yorker*, Pauline Kael excoriated the film as racist, excessively violent, a "factory picture, with its conflicting intentions and its compromises and its sanctimonious think pieces about the future of America." Kael's review thus tenaciously fastened on racism, an aspect of the film that Pakula and Mulligan never intended (although this is not untypical of Pauline Kael, who, brilliant as her criticisms were, often told the reader more about Pauline Kael than about the movies she reviewed). It is worth noting that although Salvaje (whose name means "Savage") is clearly an unredeemed villain, the only other Indian characters—Nick Tana and Salvaje's son—are portrayed sympathetically, which would seem to discredit Kael's contention that *The Stalking Moon* is a viciously bigoted film.[15]

But the kindest possible assessment of *The Stalking Moon* is that it is little more than a well-intentioned but indifferent movie. As the final picture in the Pakula-Mulligan partnership, it is a distinct disappointment. If Pakula's domestic situation had been more satisfying, perhaps the film would have been better achieved. If the projects Pakula was most enthusiastic about had come to fruition, perhaps the pictures he produced between 1963 and 1969 would have been more distinguished. But one can only describe the films Pakula and Mulligan made after *To Kill a Mockingbird* as disappointing. Many of them contain virtues, but in none of them are the positive attributes great enough to overcome the deficiencies.

In hindsight, it seems evident that the Pakula-Mulligan collaboration was no longer capable of achieving excellence. The most sensible course was for them to go their separate ways, especially because Pakula's yearning to direct was becoming clearer with each passing film.

In a sense, the end of the Pakula-Mulligan partnership was like an amicable

---

[15]Pakula "would have loved to get a good review from Pauline Kael," David Lange said—referring to all the films he produced and directed. However, he never did.

divorce, but a split was inevitable, for Pakula realized that he would never recognize his ambition to direct as long as the partnership continued. "Alan told me very early on that he might like to direct someday," Mulligan said. "He talked about his work in the theatre program at Yale and how much he enjoyed that time in his life when he'd taken his first steps as a director. I told him that whenever he wanted to make the move he should go for it." But, picture after picture, Pakula had stayed off the set, leaving the direction to Mulligan. Now, however, at the age of forty, he felt he could wait no longer and informed his longtime colleague that the time had come for him to direct his first film.

The agreement to dissolve their partnership came with no acrimony. "Alan's decision was a reason to celebrate," Mulligan recently observed, "and we did. He was excited about what was coming. I was happy for him and offered whatever help he'd need at any time. Just as he'd done for me for so many years. When the time came, our partnership ended as it had begun—with a handshake."

It was a surprise to Mulligan that his partnership with Pakula lasted as long as it did. "Alan and I started out as complete strangers and total opposites in background, temperament, and many other ways," he said. "It was hardly predictable that we'd become partners in making films or enjoy a friendship that would last for so many years. It was certainly not something either of us could have anticipated. It just happened."

Mulligan went on to direct such films as *Summer of '42* and *Same Time, Next Year*, but never equaled the success of *To Kill a Mockingbird*.

* * *

To Pakula's complete surprise, Hope Lange asked for a separation in 1969, on their sixth anniversary, as they were on the way home from having dinner with Martin and Katie Manulis. "I don't think he was thrilled," she said wryly in 2003, but that is an understatement. According to those who knew him in 1969, he was devastated. "When they separated he was really brokenhearted," Alvin Sargent remembers. "I saw him in real pain about that. I don't know how quickly or how slowly the end of that relationship came, but I know it was awfully hard for him. I'd never seen him that broken." Colleen Creedon remembered him as "very despondent, very sad, very upset by it. He didn't want the divorce. It was Hope's idea."

Boaty Boatwright, who had worked with Pakula on *To Kill a Mockingbird* and later became his agent, said, "I think Alan was devastated when he and Hope split. Everybody was so surprised, probably no one more than Alan." Martin Manulis agreed. "It was a very difficult, very painful thing for him—especially with the separation and divorce played out in the press." Indeed, the press had taken an interest in the two of them from the time when Hedda Hopper, the famed gossip columnist, appeared uninvited at their wedding at the Manulis's house.

I asked Hope Lange why their marriage came to an end after a relatively short time. "Well," she said, "being married to Alan was a full-time career. He needed a lot of attention. He really liked to have me around when he was there, and he had *enormous* energy, and sometimes it was a little exhausting. I had two small children, and I was working [in *The Ghost and Mrs. Muir*] and I couldn't balance all those balloons in the air."

Pakula's pain only seemed to increase as time went on, leading him to seek psychiatric help. "You know, Alan didn't like any kind of failure," Boatwright noted. "And he had waited a long time to get married and he was very much in love with Hope, he loved being a father to her children, he loved all the nice things that came with" the marriage.

His cousin, Selma Hirsh, had a series of "intense [conversations] with him" after the separation, as she put it. "We came from very culturally conservative families, both of us, and I was the first one in the family to get a divorce. So he felt he had someone he could talk to." Alan told Selma that the marriage failed in part because Lange put her career before their relationship.

Pakula also believed that his wife had been having an affair during the time they were married. "I heard rumors," Larry Turman said, "uncorroborated, unsubstantiated, that Hope had had an affair with a prominent actor near the end of that marriage. And I guess the knowledge of that was sort of devastating and humiliating" for Pakula. According to one of Alan's relatives, who asked not to be identified, Pakula believed that his wife was sleeping with Frank Sinatra. Martin Manulis said that whenever her relationship with Sinatra began, "she separated right into Sinatra's arms." On the other hand, David Lange felt that his sister's relationship with Sinatra did not begin until after she and Pakula had separated. "Hope was not the type to fool around while she was married," he said. "She just wouldn't have. I'm sure Alan would have spoken to me about it if he believed that." He concluded, "If Hope had been unfaithful during the marriage, I would have known about it."

Whether or not Hope Lange was involved with other men when she and Pakula were married, she told me, before she died in December 2003, that "I have to sort of blame myself [for the failure of the marriage] if there's blame to be placed."

Lange's request was for a separation, but Pakula soon wanted a divorce. As David Lange said, "After two or three weeks of separation, he felt, 'To hell with it, I want a divorce, I want out of it.' He was going through great pain and obviously didn't feel there was any chance of a reconciliation."

Hope Lange recalled that Pakula "came over to the house one day and said he had met someone, and he was thinking he would marry her." The "someone" was

Hannah Cohn Boorstin, a widow with three children whose husband, Robert, had died of a heart attack in 1969 during a vacation in Greece.

"I think that Hope always thought she might come back to him," Martin Manulis said. "But I think by that time [after the separation but before the divorce] he didn't want her to come back." The divorce was finalized in 1971. With the help of psychoanalysis, Pakula moved on, though burdened by a sense of failure.

Despite Pakula's anguish, he and Lange remained friends after their divorce. Whenever he spoke about her to his friends, however, he always referred to her as "my first wife," never as "Hope." And when he was asked about her in a 1975 interview, all he could find to say was that she was "a talented woman." Peter Jennings, a friend and neighbor of Pakula's years later, after Pakula was married to Hannah Boorstin, said, "Alan used to talk about Hope Lange all the time. And I used to wonder a little bit about Alan's fairly constant references to her—almost invariably by way of saying, 'Hannah has eased my life, whereas my first wife made my life complicated.'"

If Pakula had mixed feelings about Hope Lange, he felt no such ambivalence toward her children, whom he loved when he and Hope were married and continued to love until he died. His close friend Barbara Davis commented, "He was always very responsible about his stepchildren from his first marriage—and in a genuine way. It wasn't just that he sent them expensive presents on birthdays and holidays, but that he really went on taking an interest in them after his marriage with their mother broke up. He was extraordinarily loyal. I think that was an important part of who he was."

Pakula's relationship with his stepchildren, which remained intensely close until his death, was perhaps the only positive result of the events of 1963-69, during which he went through a painful separation after a promising beginning to his marriage; produced a series of largely disappointing films; failed to bring to fruition several projects which held great promise; and ended his professional relationship with the man who had been his creative partner since he had begun producing. The entire period might be thought of as a setback both to his domestic happiness and to his career. But the eventual result could not have been more pleasant, for he met and eventually married the woman with whom he found complete happiness, and he embarked on a directing career that was responsible for some of the greatest films in American history.

CHAPTER FIVE

On His Own:
The Sterile Cuckoo

"One thing I think that characterizes Alan as an actor's director is that he
is in love with the process of directing—he loves the encounter with actors.
You can feel when the director can't wait to get into the editing room to
really make this movie and to get rid of these horrible egos and all the
distracting personalities and mess that is a film set. But Alan is so orderly
in his mind that being on the set isn't a burden to him. [And] his priority
on the set is the encounter with the actors."

—MERYL STREEP

EVER SINCE HE HAD DIRECTED *The Anniversary* at Yale, more than
twenty years before, Alan Pakula's greatest ambition was to direct actors. Despite his
success as a studio executive and as a producer, he never lost sight of his primary goal.
His collaborations with Robert Mulligan had brought him wealth, fame (within the
film community, at least), and a good deal of satisfaction. Still, he said, "I always
would go into a depression when those pictures started shooting," because he wanted so desperately to assume the director's role. "The only reason I had come out to
Hollywood in the first place," he said, plaintively, "was to work with actors."

Horton Foote had advised Pakula on more than one occasion to make the
transition to directing. As Foote said, Pakula "felt that it was a difficult step,
fraught with danger, but I encouraged him to go out and find something" to
direct. Still, Pakula remained cautious.

One morning, however, during the filming of *The Stalking Moon*, Pakula went to
Bloomingdale's department store. He ran into the film director Sidney Lumet,
who asked him, "What the hell are you doing here? Aren't you making a picture?"
Pakula said, "Yes, I'm producing, but I'm not needed on the set. Bob has everything under control." Then Lumet shook his head and said, with mock severity,

'While Bob is working his ass off shooting, you're in here buying shirts." Lumet intended his comment as a joke, not as a reprimand, but it forced Pakula to think critically about his indecision in taking the step to become a director. As he left the store, he said to himself, "It's about time I put up or shut up." He decided to put up. He called Nyack, New York, to tell Horton Foote of his resolve. Alvin Sargent, who had seen Pakula's directorial work years before at the Circle Theatre, wasn't surprised. "He *had* to be a director," he said. "I'm sure he was chafing at the bit, just waiting to do that."

Still another shopping excursion provided Pakula with the material he was looking for. While browsing in a bookstore in New York, he came across a novel by John Nichols entitled *The Sterile Cuckoo*. Impressed, and excited by its film possibilities, he optioned the book with his own money. His first thought was that the film, about young people in their college years, clumsily, painfully dealing with their insecurities, would be best served by a young director, and he began searching for one. "And then I thought, 'Wait a minute—I want it for myself! I thought that it's ridiculous to use a young director. Why don't I use a man who is not quite so young, but who is certainly inexperienced, meaning myself. I'm getting less and less young by the hour and by the day, and if I don't do it now, I'll never do it. And suddenly life came into focus again.'"[16]

He hired his old friend Alvin Sargent to write the screenplay, and the two of them worked on it together. Later, Sargent looked back fondly at his working relationship with Pakula. When they were working together on the script (Pakula critiquing Sargent's work and suggesting alternative approaches), Sargent said, "He danced around a lot. He was very silly. He just couldn't control himself. He got up, and he got an idea, and he started dancing, and his hands would go back and forth, and he'd be so excited, just truly, truly excited, happy with what he'd found, he'd struck gold—or, when we were working together, we struck gold, or I struck gold, or we both agreed on something that was going to work."

Once the script was complete, Pakula let it be known that any studio that wanted to distribute the film would have to accept him as director. Pakula retained the position of producer on *The Sterile Cuckoo*, so, as the head of Boardwalk Productions, he hired himself to direct. At roughly the same time, Liza Minnelli, who had only played one brief film role to that point, read the book. The main character, the

---

[16]*At least, that's Pakula's recollection. Mulligan remembered things differently. According to him, when Pakula selected* The Sterile Cuckoo, *"Alan would produce and I would direct, as always. We had preliminary meetings about writers to do the screenplay and interviewed young actresses to play the lead. But somewhere early in the process my interest flagged. I don't know why. As much as I liked John Nicols' book, my creative motor did not kick in. I do remember sensing that Alan had a better feel for the material than I did. We talked and, as I listened to Alan, it was obvious he had a real connection to the story and the young characters, and a strong vision about how to turn it into a film. The decision was made. This was Alan's movie. He was going to direct."*

voluble Pookie Adams, "got to me, her incredible imagination," Minnelli said. "She knew so little about the real world that, in an odd way, she could see it very clearly. She's like somebody who's been in prison for nineteen years; you don't want to go outside after that long. You prefer what you imagine it to be."

Minnelli's agent called Pakula to say that his client had read the book and loved the role of Pookie Adams. He asked the director to meet with Minnelli. They met, but Pakula didn't call back for several weeks. Instead, he interviewed other actresses, but, he said, he "just couldn't see it without Liza." Ultimately, he offered her the role.

In order to persuade an independent company to produce the film, he shot a screen test in 1969 with Liza Minnelli and Wendell Burton, whom he had decided to cast as Jerry Payne, despite the fact that Burton's acting experience was extremely limited. "It was," Pakula said, "the most overly directed piece of film I think in the history of celluloid." As a first-time director, Pakula "had them do everything you could possibly do in a lifetime in five minutes of film. They cried and they laughed and they were happy and they were unhappy and they were ecstatic and they were sui-cidal. Name it—every life experience—and they felt it in five minutes. Liza, being a really gutsy girl, did it all. The crew all applauded, I might add, during the middle of that test. There's a certain kind of virtuoso work that wakes people up when they're tired, and Liza got applause for the very things that were wrong with the test. It was *too* virtuoso and too show-offy. When the crew breaks into applause, it very often means you're over the top. It's very dramatic to the naked eye but the camera looks at it and says, too much, too much, too much, when you see it on film."

The result was a blatantly overdirected and overacted screen test. When he showed it to the production company he hoped would finance the picture, Pakula recalled that the spectators "were in a state of shock and nervousness, longing for escape. They said, 'We wonder if Liza is right for this,'" and indicated that they were no longer interested. A showing for a second company yielded the same result. Realizing at last that his direction had been responsible for the actors' overplaying, he hid the screen test in a drawer and never showed it again. Then, he said, "Paramount saw the script. Bob Evans was the head of Paramount, and he said, 'Who do you want to play it?' I said, 'Liza Minnelli,' and he said, 'We ought to test her.' He didn't know I had already made a test. I quickly thought, if I tell him I've tested her, he'll ask to see the test and the ball game is over. So I said, 'I don't need to test her, Bob. I know she's right for it. I've met with her and we've read it together.'" Ultimately, Paramount agreed—"with much trepidation," Pakula said—to put up the money for the project, to accept Liza Minnelli as Pookie and Wendell Burton as Jerry, and to distribute the film. Paramount's acceptance of Pakula's casting was unusual, for major studios generally insisted that well-known movie stars be cast in their films, a reasonable position since most movie-goers attend films on the basis of the actors playing the leading roles.

Once Evans agreed to make the movie, he remained in the background. "Evans never said anything about what I wanted to do," Pakula said. "He just said there are great dangers in using an inexperienced boy such as Wendell. But he didn't try to stop me. He just wanted me to know what his concerns were. He didn't even see the film until the rough cut."

"If anything," Pakula said, "working with [Liza Minnelli] in the test made me more enthusiastic because her range was as extraordinary as my lack of control in directing the test." Minnelli often asked Pakula if she could see the screen test. He said that he "waited until after we completed shooting, and [after seeing it] she looked at me afterwards and she said, 'Well, why did you hire me?' I said, 'No, the question is, why did I hire *me*?'"

But the most important lesson Pakula learned from the overdirected screen test—one that became a ruling principle for him—was this: "One of the rules of directing is . . . that a story is told as much as by what you don't see, what you don't show, as what you do show. If you show everything, nothing has importance." To a degree, he put that principle into practice in *The Sterile Cuckoo*, but his understated directorial style would become more pronounced and more assured with later films.

In the film, Pookie—insecure, unpopular with her college classmates, unloved at home—craves attention and goes to remarkable lengths to get it. But her desperate need for affection drives away precisely those she wishes to attract. She cannot restrain herself from behaving prankishly and making inappropriate remarks—often funny, but also demonstrating Pookie's vulnerability and self-destructiveness. She relentlessly pursues Jerry, a shy, conventional young man whom she meets on a bus as they travel to the colleges they are preparing to attend. Pookie claims that everyone else is a "weirdo," but her behavior is stranger than any Jerry has ever encountered. Despite their extreme differences—or perhaps because of them—Jerry eventually finds himself falling in love with Pookie, but, invariably, she embarrasses him with her outrageous behavior.

Both virgins at the film's outset, they sleep with one another in a motel room, in an amusing scene of halting, awkward innocence. The rest of the movie chronicles their deteriorating relationship, leading to an ambiguous ending, as in so many of the films Pakula was to direct. A melancholy Pookie and Jerry sit on a bench, waiting for a bus that will take Pookie to an unknown future (recalling the opening of the film, when Pookie shared a bench with her father). Pakula said, "Liza thought [Pookie] was going to be fine, and I thought that was important for her to feel. However, I didn't agree with her."

Missing from the film are details that would place it squarely in its social context. There is no mention of Vietnam, for example, or of the Civil Rights movement. But Pakula wanted to focus on two young people who are so engrossed in their own problems that they are virtually unaffected by the world around them. "It is a story of awakening," Pakula said. "Of joy and ecstasy and pain. It's a sense of nostalgia for that experience. It is the country of our youth."

Pakula led his actors through an intense three-week rehearsal period on the Lucille Ball soundstage at Paramount and another week on location at Hamilton College in upstate New York, treating the film "as if it were a play," he said. During the rehearsals, the actors and Pakula discussed the characters, their relationships to others (i.e., individuals, such as Pookie's father, who affect the characters but are given very little or no screen time, as well as other characters who appear in the film), their conscious and subconscious motivations for behaving as they do, and any other relevant items.

"By the time we got up to location, at Hamilton College," Minnelli said, Pakula "had Wendell Burton and me doing only improvisations. We would become the characters. We knew them that well." Many of the improvised scenes did not appear in the film, but, as Pakula said, "*could* have been part of the story." Each improvisation gave the actors a richer understanding of their roles and their relationship. And at least one scene that resulted from an improvisation was filmed. "The scene where Pookie introduces Jerry to the gravestones came out of [an improvised] rehearsal," Pakula said. "It grew out of the fact that she cannot function with real people." And another scene—one that was scripted—benefited from improvisation. "In the chapel," Pakula said, "I gave Liza the idea of the bridal march, but the way she walked down the aisle and what she did—waving idiotically at an imaginary relative—was all Liza."

The chapel scenes in *The Sterile Cuckoo* were not in the original script at all. Only when Pakula discovered that a chapel adjoined the motel in which Pookie and Jerry make love for the first time did he decide to include the chapel in the film. "Who would have thought that a chapel would be located next to a motel?" he asked. "But that's what we found on location. It seemed too good to be true."

Nudity, an element becoming commonplace in American films by 1969, is absent from *The Sterile Cuckoo*. "I wanted to protect" the actors, Pakula said. "When Jerry takes off Pookie's bra [in the motel room], I go in to her face. They are so young. It would be exploiting them. Liza said, 'I'll do it nude if you really want me to,' but I didn't want [any sense of] self-consciousness, undressing in front of fifty middle-aged men" on the crew. The scene in which Pookie, eager for the sexual encounter to begin ("Want to peel the tomato?" she asks) encourages Jerry—whose precise businesslike manner (neatly folding each piece of clothing and setting it on the table) allows him to delay the moment of decision as long as possible—is one of the most effective in the film. "I was warned by several people that the scene was running too long," Pakula said. "Actually, I hadn't planned to do it at that length. But if I had [sped] it up, it would have become farcical. I was dealing with their shyness, so I wanted to slow things down."

Minnelli knew that she had gotten inside Pookie—or vice-versa—when, one day,

Alan got me together with four college girls, there at Hamilton, who were going to play the girls in Pookie's dorm. He wanted us to get to know each other, just as ourselves, so each girl started talking about her background. The first girl said, 'Well, my mother collects antiques, my father's a minister,' and so on. So I thought, what am I gonna say? That I come from a show-business family, my mother [Judy Garland] was really a groovy chick, no matter what you read about her, my father [Vincente Minnelli] is a director? And they're not gonna know what I'm talking about. And at that moment, Pookie moved in. And when I had to talk, I told her background, just automatically. Alan said, 'Good, that's it.' He did lots of things like that, he let us take our time.

Several times during the filming, Minnelli—who "knew the script backwards and forwards before she ever started shooting—I've never seen an actress more prepared," said Pakula—would approach Pakula and ask, "Alan, can you just tell me the story of the picture?" Pakula, with infinite patience and no sense of being put upon, would take Minnelli to his trailer, sit her down,

and I said in the most simplistic, infantile terms, as you'd talk to a nine-year old child, "Once upon a time, there was a little girl, and she didn't have a mother, and she didn't know what it was like to be a woman, and she was obsessed with a death wish because her mother had died young. And she wanted somebody to love her. And she sat in the attic and wrote fantasies. And she didn't think her father loved her. Her father was very remote and lonely and she was lonely, but she hid it. And she was terrified of people"—you know, just very simple terms. "And she d be very, very funny so that people didn't make fun of her. And then she went to college and met this very quiet boy and she fell . . ." And I told the story just in that way, very quietly, and she said, "Thank you." That was very helpful to her. It had nothing to do with giving her some incredible subtext. And then we went back and she was marvelous in the scene.

Pakula and Minnelli discovered a unique way of communication that worked for them, but almost surely would not have functioned effectively with another combination of actor and director. Their relationship reinforced Pakula's conviction that every actor must be treated differently—"each one needs different things," he said—and that any attempt to use the same method with every actor would be certain to fail. That conviction led him to deal privately with each actor, taking the performer aside and whispering to him or her out of the hearing of others. "I don't like to be criticized in front of a lot of people watching," he said, "and I don't like to criticize people in front of others. It's something very private."

On one occasion, Minnelli was having trouble with a climactic scene and Pakula couldn't understand why. "And I talked. And the more trouble she was having, the more I talked. 'There's *this* in the scene, why don't you try *this*?' Finally, she said, 'Let's try it.' She was terrific." Pakula, uncertain what he had said that finally allowed Minnelli to play the scene effectively, asked, "What did I say?" She responded, "Oh, I didn't understand any of what you were saying. I just knew. There was a look in your eyes. Unconsciously, in your eyes, something was happening of what you wanted. I guess there was an image that I just held on to somehow."

Minnelli had finished playing the title role in *Tell Me That You Love Me, Junie Moon*, directed by Otto Preminger, only a month before *The Sterile Cuckoo* was released. "You get the impression with Otto," she said, "that you don't have time to ask questions, [so you] don't ask, and if you do it wrong, you get yelled at." Clearly, she preferred Pakula's gentle, patient, meticulous approach, with its emphasis on discovering the psychological truth of the character.

Wendell Burton's performance in the film is muted almost to the point of invisibility. He did attempt to play several scenes more boldly during the shooting, but, according to Pakula, those sequences "forced the film into big theatrical scenes which were wrong for the total picture," so they were cut. Ultimately, Pakula was perfectly satisfied with Burton's portrayal. "A straight romantic leading man would never get involved with Pookie," he said. "In real life, Wendell and Liza came from such different worlds that it seemed as if he were from Mars and she from Jupiter. That worked for the film. And Wendell gives the audience a point of view. She couldn't get her laughs if he didn't cue them."

Perhaps Pakula saw something of himself in the character of Jerry Payne. He too was soft-spoken, conservatively attired, and a bit shy. And, as Wendell was exploring a relationship with a woman for the first time in his life, Pakula was exploring his relationship with the responsibilities of the director.

The first morning of shooting was supposed to be an exterior scene, but a heavy rain forced a change. Rather than "doing some easy little transition scene to get the actors into it in a kind of unintimidating way, we wound up doing the only thing that we had any cover set for, which was Liza Minnelli's scene in the phone booth, which is the most bravura scene in the film." Pookie, who is afraid she's going to lose Jerry, breaks down during the conversation as Jerry tells her that he will not be able see her during spring vacation. In a single long take, she communicates hopefulness, joy, despair, and a range of other emotions. The choice of this scene turned out to be inspired, for Minnelli's subtly modulated performance—which she was able to give because of the long rehearsal time and the many hours of discussion about Pookie's character—set the tone for the rest of the picture. But, as Pakula freely admitted, the choice had been entirely an act of circumstance, and the fact that it worked out so well could not have been predicted.

Getting the shot required three attempts. "The first take was actually good enough to use," Pakula said. "It was stunning. She broke down, but I wanted her to fight it. On the second take she was exhausted, dry. After she went off alone for a few minutes, she did the third take perfectly. I figured if she could get that scene, it would give her confidence, and it would also give the crew confidence. I mean, here they were working with some kid who was Judy Garland's daughter and with me who had never directed before."

As the film was being shot, Pakula discovered "Liza has a great film face. You can use a medium shot instead of a close-up" without forfeiting subtlety of expression. "We made photographic tests, and with the lighting and the camera angle, we figured out how we wanted her to look. We could make her unattractive or . . . lyrical, depending on how Jerry subjectively sees her at that moment."

Pakula appreciated the subtleties of Minnelli's portrayal. "My concern was that she not give too much. She's got so much to give," he said. "I'd just tell her to put a lid on it, and she'd understand what I meant." He would prepare her for each scene by "going over the beats of the scene"—the emotional responses to stimuli that lead to behavior—"with her for an hour."

Pakula said, "There was one moment during the film [when] suddenly she lost her concentration. And we went through the take and it was strangely unconcentrated. I stopped it and I said, 'What is it? You lost it. What happened?' And she said, 'I did. You know what happened? I was suddenly thinking how happy I was, how happy it made me to do this work.' And it moved me, because that's what the work does for me as a director."

The Hamilton College location was only about an hour away from Syracuse University, where Pakula's nephew Rodd Baxter was attending school. Always wishing to please the members of his family, Pakula invited Baxter and some of his classmates to watch the filming, then—as an unplanned bonus—got them into the movie as extras. Baxter was grateful for the opportunity to appear in a film and happy with the day's pay, but, he fondly recalled, "The greatest thing was we got to eat catered food!"

Later, additional scenes were shot at Paramount in Los Angeles. Each morning, after the crew readied the set, Pakula would let the technicians go, so that he could rehearse the scenes to be shot that day with the actors. Then, as he explained, "once I've locked the scene in with the actors, I run it for the cameramen and the technical people. I talk about coverage. Then I work with the technical people only. The stand-ins come on, and I tell the actors to get off the set and do whatever they have to do, prepare makeup or whatever. When the technical people are ready, and we've lit the whole scene, we do the final rehearsals and we shoot." He quickly discovered his method to be so unconventional that it aroused considerable comment. "Thank God there were all these big pictures like *Darling Lili* and *Paint Your Wagon* being made when I did *The Sterile Cuckoo*," he said, "because somebody at Paramount said, 'You know, your technicians go wandering around the lot in the middle of the workday.'"

An occasional visitor to the set was the scenarist, Alvin Sargent. However, although Sargent wished he had been there more often, "this was Alan's first directorial effort, and I think he felt safer without me there," so his visits were infrequent.

Pakula said that directing *The Sterile Cuckoo* was "just constantly thrilling." He could have made the same statement at any point during his career, for directing never lost its appeal. But *The Sterile Cuckoo* always remained special to him. He later said that making the movie was "the only relaxed film I ever did."

The plot of *The Sterile Cuckoo*—a young man attempting to rescue a woman who is trapped by circumstances over which she has no control—is one that Pakula would repeat again and again, often without realizing, until long after the fact, that he had done so.

Working with actors—the aspect of directing that most excited Pakula at the time—is clearly the triumph of *The Sterile Cuckoo*. Many of the performances, particularly Minnelli's, are finely observed and sensitively played. However, as Pakula noted, "I found also that I was very involved with the camera and very involved with all of the crafts of film, and found myself on that tightrope of directing, which is trying to balance elements that are very often in conflict." Although he was working with gifted artists, many of whom had considerable experience, he was unable to achieve that balance very successfully in his first directorial effort. Inspiring the composer to write music that would suit the style of the film, deciding when to use it, supervising the editing, finding an appropriate visual style, trimming scenes where necessary, and expanding others that would have added materially to the audience's understanding of the characters all took a backseat to guiding the actors.

One should note, however, that Pakula's focus on the actors rather than on technical virtuosity in the film was a conscious decision. "Naturally I'm concerned with technical requirements," he said, "but I don't change the relationships [of the characters] to fit specific kinds of camera angles. My first directing notes were filled with tricks and theatrical angles which had nothing to do with the story. I finally decided I wanted a quality of understatement. I didn't want something to come between the audience and these two people."

After the film was released, "The critical reaction was by and large good, but mixed," Pakula said. "From the audience point of view in the States it was surprisingly successful. It grossed over $6 million." (In 1969, a $6 million gross was considered more than respectable.) "But with the exception of some countries in South America, and a fairly nice reception in Japan, it really didn't do well over the world. Nothing comparable to what it did in the States." Pakula thought that the title under which the film played in Britain—*Pookie*—probably harmed its box-office appeal there. "I never liked *The Sterile Cuckoo* as a title," he said, "but *Pookie* is worse."

Liza Minnelli was rewarded for her performance with an Academy Award nomination for "Best Actress." Minnelli said, "This is the most important thing about *Cuckoo*: that I did Pookie right; that people are understanding this marvelous, funny, tortured girl. . . . I thought I could make people comprehend this girl, and I did. And her story is told properly. To me, that's the success." Pookie Adams would become the first of many sensitively portrayed female characters in Pakula's films.

A review in *Motion Picture Exhibitor* praised the direction of the film as "delicate, understated, unobtrusive, . . . and brimming with sympathy." Vincent Canby of the *New York Times* found Liza Minnelli's performance enchanting, but disliked the film, which, he said, "aspires to an unconventional (by Hollywood standards) narrative honesty that is constantly undercut by conventional cinematic slickness. . . . Miss Minnelli comes on so strong," he wrote, "you fear she's going to wreck the film. It's quickly apparent, however, that it's the film that almost wrecks her."

Indeed, Pakula's first directorial effort is only intermittently successful. Among other things, he clearly overused the musical theme; as Canby pointed out, "the relentlessly sentimental background music . . . fills the sound track every time [Pookie and Jerry] wander through a meadow."

The Sterile Cuckoo is thus the work of a promising director, but not one fully in command of his craft. However, if it was, in a sense, apprentice work, Pakula's apprenticeship was remarkably brief, for the next film he directed would bring him worldwide recognition and respect from the public and his peers.

CHAPTER SIX

Klute

"The best of film for me, and the worst of film, is that it is such a collaborative process. You are dealing with [and] are dependent upon incredibly
different types of people. I pride myself on having specific conceptions
of a film when I decide to do it, and a specific vision of what I want that
film to be. But, unlike an author or a composer, I have now become dependent. I am working with a writer, I am working with the actors, I am working
with a set designer, I am working with the cameraman, I am working with
endless, endless numbers of people. It is enraging at times and it is also
the most exciting part of it at times. In the end, if the film is successful,
it is a synthesis of so many people that it is impossible to remember who
did what and when."

—ALAN J. PAKULA

IF THE MOST ACCOMPLISHED ASPECT of Pakula's direction of *The
Sterile Cuckoo* was its work with actors and its least satisfactory aspect was its handling
of such elements as music and cinematography, Pakula solved those problems with
his next film, *Klute*—and did so without neglecting his performers in any way. If
anything, the performances in *Klute* were so uniformly excellent that Pakula's reputation as an actor's director was enhanced.

Gaining control of the many diverse aspects of filmmaking and integrating
them with excellent performances came about partly because Pakula surrounded
himself with so many outstanding artists and craftsmen in *Klute*. Not only was he
grateful for their contributions, he worked with many of them again and again.
Gordon Willis, the cinematographer, collaborated with Pakula on five more films;
Michael Small, the composer, scored nine of Pakula's films; Jane Fonda, who
played the central character in *Klute*, acted for Pakula more frequently than any
other leading performer: three times; and George Jenkins served as production
designer or art director for nearly every film Pakula made.

The contribution made by these artists was balanced by Pakula's ability to stimulate their imaginations and heighten their artistry. As an example, in 1998, Michael Small was asked to explain his approach to scoring a film. He answered, "I try to come up with a concept that relates to the whole idea of the picture rather than trying to just underscore dramatically each little moment. I will say that my teacher in this regard is Alan Pakula, because when I did *Klute,* his expectation for the score was far beyond anything that I had attempted. He wanted the score to not only be a suspense score, but to underscore the psychology of the main character. Ever since that experience I always look for that extra voice that a score can add to a film."

Small's comment is not untypical. Throughout Pakula's career, he surrounded himself with consummate artists and expert technicians, and challenged them to attain greater heights than they had achieved in the past. He listened carefully to their points of view regarding any aspect of the film, and—whether an observation came from a script supervisor, a production assistant, or whomever—if the observation was a sound one, he applied it to the film. Dianne Dreyer, his script supervisor on *The Pelican Brief,* put it this way:

> From my initial interview with him and throughout my experience with him and of him, if he asked a question, he was interested in the answer. If an idea was good, he used it. If not, he had a wonderful way of dismissing it without hurting anyone's feelings, in large part due to the way in which he welcomed any and all collaborative voices. That's not to say he was easy to approach. His intelligence and his straight up-and-down manner were formidable qualities, but once you were in his employ it was clear that if you had something important to contribute, the door was open.

Before long, Pakula admitted that working with the actors in a film—though still supremely important to him—had become secondary to the collaboration with *everyone* on the set. His location manager for eight films, Celia Costas, said, "He loved the idea that he and 125 of his close friends were going to show up every morning and figure out all the problems. And he was very congenial and collegial in his approach. He liked to be surrounded by his cinematographer, his production designer, his costume designer, all of us. And he was very receptive to the potential problem-solving ideas of the people who worked on the film. And those ideas could come from the key grip or the gaffer or the prop man." I asked Costas if Pakula would replace a craftsperson if he or she failed to live up to Pakula's standards. Her answer: "In a heartbeat. This is part of being at the very top of your craft, and your level of taste. And that's important to all of us—for a director to keep us at the very top rung of our capability, and keep us on our toes. I loved to function on that level, where somebody assumes that I'm going to do absolutely the best job that I can. It makes me want to meet that expectation."

This process—of hiring people with superb taste and the knowledge to go with it and permitting everyone on his set to offer suggestions, taking them when they seemed appropriate, politely disregarding them when they did not—began in earnest in *Klute*, and the results of Pakula's approach are visible on the screen. The film is far more accomplished than *The Sterile Cuckoo*—astonishingly so, considering that it was his very next film.

Unlike his earlier projects, *Klute* did not originate with Pakula. The script, about a prostitute in danger of being murdered, written by Andy and Dave Lewis, was purchased by Warner Bros., who later—after several other directors turned it down—engaged Pakula to produce (with David Lange, Hope Lange's brother) and direct. Warners budgeted the film at a meager $2.8 million.

The script, Pakula said, eventually went through enormous changes. "It had a lateral quality; it had a tendency, I felt, to at times get 'tabloid.' But the essence of what it was about" was in the original script, and "it clearly represented the film I wanted to make."

Pakula "ran a lot of old Hitchcock pictures" when he agreed to direct *Klute*. And, he said, "I realized that I was going against one of the tenets in the Hitchcock book, which is that you don't try to do a character study in a melodrama." He decided that violating the injunction of the master of suspense was worth trying, for it was not so much the suspense element as the psychological portrait of the prostitute in the screenplay that intrigued him.

As Pakula said, "the rhythms of melodrama and the rhythms of character study are totally different. A melodrama has a kind of inevitable, relentless rhythm. A character study has a much more leisurely rhythm. It depends on certain little details and stopping to explore. And what I wanted to do was to make the melodrama and the personal drama come together, and to make them be one and the same." Combining the two genres into one seamless film constituted the greatest challenge Pakula faced. A successful combination would result in an extraordinary motion picture, but anything less would guarantee an unsatisfactory result.

Pakula also was attracted to *Klute* because of the piece's classical approach. "It's a melodrama in which the girl's tragic flaw is responsible for almost destroying her," he said. "If she didn't have this obsessive need to seduce men she would not have gotten herself into the situation; she would not be in this danger. So, to have [Bree's] voice [on the tape recorder] at the very beginning—seductive—it becomes like a siren call calling her to her own destruction." Another aspect of the script that appealed to him was that "*Klute* very much deals with power as much as sex, and the impotent and the powerful, and sex being used as power."

The core of the plot is that John Klute, a private detective from Tuscarora, Pennsylvania, comes to New York to investigate the disappearance of Tom Gruneman, who, according to the FBI, has written threatening letters to a call girl, Bree Daniels. Klute eventually discovers that Gruneman has been murdered by the same man who brutalized Bree two years before: Peter Cable, Gruneman's employer and one of the group that originally hired Klute to investigate Gruneman's disappearance. This basic plot synopsis gives no hint of the psychological depth of the characters, nor the many strands of the plot, which include:

- Bree Daniels' attempts to leave the world of prostitution
  and to become an actress or a model;
- Bree's sexual and romantic involvement with Klute, which she initiates
  in order to humiliate Klute, but discovers (to her surprise) that their
  relationship infuses her life with meaning;
- Peter Cable's neurotic dependence upon repeatedly listening to a tape
  of himself and Bree, recorded surreptitiously when she came to his office
  and exchanged money for sex;
- Cable's pathological hatred of all humanity, particularized in his
  contempt for prostitutes;
- The impact on Bree of the murder of Arlyn Page, a former prostitute
  who might have been able to lead Klute to the killer; and
- Bree's growing understanding of her motives and her character.

All of these elements transform *Klute* from a suspense thriller to a subtle psychological study—which, in turn, ratchets up the suspense at every turn.

The structure of the film is particularly complex. A close look at the first fourteen sequences in the film, most of them comprised of a single shot, hints at the structural complexity:

1. A shot of a mini-tape recorder.
2. A cheerful scene at an outdoor party with several guests, including Peter Cable, Tom Gruneman and his wife, and John Klute.
3. A somber interrogation by FBI agents of Klute, Mrs. Gruneman, and Peter Cable, several months after the previous scene. The disappearance of Tom Gruneman is discussed.
4. A policeman says that he has discovered an obscene letter from Gruneman to Bree Daniels, who claims to have received six or seven similar letters.
5. The credits, side-by-side with the mini-tape recorder. Someone—we see only a hand—inserts and plays a tape of Bree talking seductively to her "client."

6. A scene of aspiring models, including Bree, seated in a line underneath three enormous panels of models' faces, being inspected by the staff of an advertising agency. The women are treated shabbily, without regard for their feelings.

7. A scene at Gruneman's house, in which Cable says Gruneman has now been missing for six months. Also in attendance are Klute, Mrs. Gruneman, and two FBI men. The latter say that Gruneman has simply disappeared, and is unlikely to be found; Cable answers that neither he nor Mrs. Gruneman is willing to accept that idea, so they have hired Klute to investigate.

8. On the sound track, the voice of the FBI agent continues, saying that Bree has reported receiving anonymous phone calls and believes that someone is following her, as we see Bree leaving the modeling agency with her portfolio. She goes into a telephone booth and calls someone to arrange a meeting with a john.

9. The john, who is very nervous, lets Bree into his hotel room. She discusses money right away, then begins to take off her clothes as he opens the couch into a bed.

10. She fakes an orgasm while looking at her watch.

11. Bree is seen carrying flowers, walking toward a funeral home (creating the expectation that she is going to a funeral), but just before the entrance to the home, she turns right and goes into her apartment house.

12. She looks apprehensively into the dark hallway. An eerie musical theme begins. She goes upstairs, and, after another apprehensive look, enters her apartment, locks the door, and puts the flowers down.

13. In her bathrobe and holding a glass of wine, Bree sits down and smokes a marijuana cigarette.

14. Bree reads a book—*Six Signs*—in bed. A voice on the radio says that it's midnight. She turns out the light and closes her eyes, but the telephone rings. She picks it up but all she can hear is a man breathing. She hangs up in alarm. The phone rings again. The camera pulls slowly away as Bree remains awake, staring into the room. The eerie music begins again, accompanying the action.

By this time, no more than five minutes have elapsed, but the viewer has learned that Bree is a prostitute and an aspiring model; that Tom Gruneman is missing; that someone is stalking Bree; and that Peter Cable and Mrs. Gruneman have hired Klute to track down Gruneman. Beyond that, the tone of the film has been set, particularly by the cinematography—the brightness of the scene in Pennsylvania contrasts startlingly with the gray world of New York City and the ominous darkness of Bree's apartment building—and the haunting musical score, in which a female voice sings without words. The viewer sees the attitude of the advertising agency executives toward Bree and the other models, Bree's skillful plying of her trade, John Klute's stoic demeanor, Bree's frightened response to the anonymous telephone caller, and the ominous tape recorder. It is a remarkable beginning to a remarkable film.

Other important scenes involve Frank Ligourin, Bree's pimp (played by Roy Scheider, in one of his first major screen roles), and Arlyn Page, a former call girl who has dropped out of prostitution because of her drug addiction. We are also shown Bree's audition for a play at a small theatre, revealing her talent as an actress; Peter Cable's stalking of Bree, as evidenced in several scenes of eavesdropping and harassment (and one in which he violently trashes her apartment, slashing the mattress and leaving semen-stained underpants); Bree's ambivalent relationship with Klute—she is attracted to him, but is deeply disturbed that she does not feel in control of the relationship; Klute's realization that Tom Gruneman is probably dead, perhaps killed by the same man who brutalized Bree; Klute's pursuit of the killer, during which he discovers that Arlyn Page has been murdered; and Bree's relationship with an old man, Mr. Goldfarb, the owner of a garment factory who never touches her but delights in watching her undress. Finally we see the death of Peter Cable, preventing him from killing Bree.

Klute could not be called a whodunit, for the viewer learns quite early in the film that Peter Cable is the man who beat Bree two years before. Thus, when Klute discovers that Cable also killed Arlyn Page and Tom Gruneman, it comes as no surprise.

Nor could *Klute* be accurately characterized as a film in which violence is glorified. Pakula said that

> although Klute deals . . . with sadistic sexual behavior, I was very frightened of romanticizing or sentimentalizing sadism. If you think about it, you see very little violence in Klute. You hear murder. You don't see it. . . . I was not interested in showing a literal violent act. I think we're just obsessed with that today [1972]. And you can so easily glorify it, especially in this kind of film. . . . I really don't want any part of that turn-on to violence. Film is such a powerful medium. A certain naïve or deeply disturbed person, or a very young person, is my responsibility if I'm making a film that deals with sexuality and violence.

The visual design for *Klute* mattered greatly to Pakula. "I wanted to get a sense of a very claustrophobic world," he said. "I had a rather disturbing visual concept for the film. It was like the characters were subterranean . . . it was the underbelly of the world. We tried to photograph it that way." He recalled his first discussion with the cinematographer, Gordon Willis, in Pakula's New York apartment. He told Willis that he wanted "to take the Panavision screen and wipe out all the horizontals and over-the-shoulders so that [Bree] is a tiny figure, . . . always being squeezed or isolated." Further, he hoped the visual style would convey "an inhuman scale, people feeling trivial, having lost a sense of their identity, which is the essence, to me, of the psychology of prostitution." He hoped that the lighting in Bree's room would convey "a world without sunlight." Finally, he said that he "wanted a very nervous screen." How those elements could be transferred to the screen was left up to Willis, for Pakula, as he admitted, was "very vague with lenses and things like that."

As Pakula observed, the director may know the spatial relationships he wishes to achieve and how the lighting should affect the characters and the viewers, but the cinematographer knows how to transform those abstract notions into reality. He may say to the director, "Well, you want it this way, but I can get it for you *this* way." And, said Pakula, "that's when you always listen. Technically Gordon is infinitely more skilled than I will ever be as a cinematographer.[17] But the concept, that's got to come from the director."

Willis "was a huge influence on my life, artistically," Pakula said. "Gordon gave me the courage to believe in my eye." Jane Fonda uses the term "the Prince of Darkness" to describe Willis, who was able to photograph dark and potentially threatening locations more effectively than any other cinematographer.

"Alan wanted a specific look," Fonda said, "and, boy, he got it."

The production design was planned with equal care. George Jenkins originally designed three small separate rooms for Bree's apartment, basing his design on the actual apartment of a call girl. Pakula asked for a different set. "We made it into this long unfinished tunnel, this big studio room," he said. "That worked. That way I could make a visual statement with the apartment. I wanted a sense of an unfinished life, and I wanted that sense of being trapped in space, of being caught, of a compressed world, a distorted world."

In the original script Pakula received, he was concerned that the role of John Klute was so underdeveloped compared to Bree's role. Pakula told the Lewis brothers, "I am fascinated because this is a story about compulsive behavior and we must explore this kind of man." But, he said, the more they explored the character of Klute, the less complex Bree became, and that distorted the focus of the

---

[17] *Gordon Willis began his career as a cinematographer in 1970, only a year before* Klute *was filmed. He went on to photograph many of Woody Allen's finest films (among them:* Annie Hall, Manhattan, Zelig, *and* The Purple Rose of Cairo*) as well as all three parts of Francis Coppola's* Godfather *trilogy. During his three-decade career, he was perhaps the most respected cinematographer in American films.*

film. Ultimately, Klute's character remained distinctly less complex than Bree's. "There was not enough time to explore his character as fully as hers without making the structure of the film patchy and unstable," Pakula said. However, when Donald Sutherland, who played the detective, brought a complexity of his own to the role, Pakula worked with him to develop and deepen it, all the while maintaining the focus on Bree.

Still, many have wondered why the movie was entitled *Klute*, since its focal character is clearly Bree Daniels. Pakula spoke with co-author Andy Lewis about changing the title to *Bree*, but was concerned that audiences would think the film was about a hunk of cheese. Besides, Lewis did not welcome a change. In his mind, the title was *Klute*, and Pakula decided not to pursue the issue further.

A number of leading actresses hoped to be cast as Bree Daniels. Barbra Streisand said not long ago on Larry King's program that, to her regret, she had turned down the role. Indeed, Warner Bros. had sent her a copy of the script, but, Pakula noted, "I was not involved at that point. As great an admirer as I am of Streisand, still, that's not a film I would have done with anybody but Jane [Fonda]."

Pakula sent the script of *Klute* to both Fonda and Donald Sutherland, who, at the time, were living together. Sutherland was eager to participate as soon as he read the screenplay, but Fonda's decision to accept her role was an agonizing one. Pakula called to arrange a meeting with Fonda after giving her time to read the script, at which time Fonda said she was not particularly interested, but was willing to discuss it. "The script, [with its] tabloid quality, threw her off when she read it," Pakula said. "I flew to New York because I thought that she might be put off by certain things in it, and I got to New York and she said, 'I don't know what I feel about it.'"

"We talked for several hours," Pakula recalled, "and we talked about a lot of things—about women in our society and about compulsive behavior and about sexuality in our society today. It was just a wonderful freewheeling discussion, and I came out of it thinking, 'God, I'd love to work with that woman.'"

According to Fonda, the decision whether to accept the role of Bree was complicated by her emerging sensitivity to women's issues. As she described her conflict:

> I was just beginning to understand the women's movement, it was still on the surface of my skin, but I worried, Would a feminist do a movie about a prostitute? And I called a feminist friend of mine, a singer. I sent her the script and I said, "I don't know if I should do this. What do you think?" And she, who was not an actress, and had never, I don't think, had a lot of experience reading scripts, and who didn't know Alan Pakula, wasn't sure that the script would give me the room

to do what she said was necessary. She said, "It doesn't matter that the woman is a prostitute. If you can create a three-dimensional character, that's what's important, but I'm not sure the script allows you to do it." But she didn't know Alan.

Ultimately, it was Fonda's belief that Pakula was as determined as she to create a multi-faceted character that persuaded her to accept the role. "The thing that interested me the most," she told me, "is that Alan had a profound interest in and empathy for women's emotional and psychological processes. I think he was deeply rooted, himself, in therapy. He had a fascination, as I do, for why people do the things they do, and what it was that happened early on that caused them to do it. And how those things are expressed through mysterious subterranean messages that go far beyond dialogue."

Pakula's casting of Jane Fonda fit neatly into his belief that "every picture depends upon casting, and the wrong casting can destroy any story no matter how good it is." Indeed, he devoted considerable time to the film's casting, ensuring that every role would be played sensitively and intelligently.

Before the project could go further, however, Warner Bros. suddenly decided to remove both Pakula and Fonda from the film and assign it to another director and actress. But their plans did not work out. "Several people turned down Warners then," Pakula said, "and they came back to us."

Pakula scheduled a read-through with all the actors. When Jane Fonda arrived, he discovered, to his surprise, that she had become a very different person from the woman he had spoken to earlier.

At the time I had first seen her about *Klute* . . . she was not a political figure yet. And in that interim she became politicized and came to the set with this grand passion—about everything, really. She's an extraordinarily passionate woman, and I was concerned that her mind was not going to be on the film because she was very involved in so many causes. She has this extraordinary kind of concentration. She can spend all the time that somebody is lighting a film on the phone making endless telephone calls, raising money, whatever, and seem to be totally disinterested in the film, and when you say, "We're ready for you, Jane," she says, "All right, give me a few minutes," and she stands in a corner or just stands quietly for three minutes and concentrates, and she's totally and completely in the film and nothing else exists. And when the scene is right and you have it and you say you don't need her anymore, she goes right back to the phone and that world is total. It's a gift a lot of good actors have; she has it to an extraordinary degree.

Pakula refined his approach to pre-production and rehearsals while working on *Klute*. Since so much of the planning he had done for *The Sterile Cuckoo* had to be discarded, he decided that the Alfred Hitchcock method, in which everything is meticulously worked out in advance and shooting the film is simply a matter of transposing the images inside the director's head to celluloid, was not for him. Instead, Pakula said, "I try to do a lot of planning, but once the planning is done, I then throw an awful lot of it away while I work. I [do] try to keep one conception in my head, and then I try to use all the accidents that happen" on the set. "Once I start shooting a scene," he said, "I don't necessarily use what I did in rehearsal. . . . I mean, you get to a scene six weeks later when you're shooting that you rehearsed six weeks before. You're different. [The actors are] different. [Rehearsals are] a good starting point, and then you go from there." He felt "it's terribly important that I keep myself loose, to work with what is happening on the set that day in terms of my conception."

Pakula rehearsed with the *Klute* cast for three weeks. "I do a certain amount of blocking, but that's not why I rehearse," he said. "I really rehearse to get into character, to improvise, to find characters, to explore, to see what the actors' problems are and where they might go wrong. But even more importantly, what they have to give that character, because that's where the final rewrite comes—it comes out of the actors you're using. The creation of a character is an integration of the actress or the actor and the character."

As rehearsals progressed, Jane Fonda became more and more insecure, according to Pakula. Finally, she said, "Alan, I can't do it. I'm sorry. I think you should hire Faye Dunaway. I'm scared to death and I can't do it."[18] Then, Fonda said, "He *laughed!* And I guess that was the right thing to do, because had he not laughed, had he discussed it seriously, I might have [quit]. But the fact that he had unquestioning confidence in me [persuaded me to stay.]" Pakula told Fonda, "I'm not going to let you out. You'll be fine."

Pakula knew that Fonda "was genuinely scared. It wasn't affectation. Some of the most gifted people in the world are the most scared—and some of the least gifted people have all the confidence in the world. [But] I knew she was wrong."

According to Pakula, once Fonda decided to proceed, she "wanted me to tell her what to do at every second and I said, 'I'm not going to do that, you're going to have to find things, and I'll tell you when you're right or wrong, and [if I think you're wrong] I'll give you something else. But first let's reach inside yourself.' And she did."

Pakula detailed his preferred method of working with performers. "After

---

[18]*Jane Fonda's recollection is somewhat different. She remembers that her crisis of confidence occurred before rehearsals began. "The first time we sat around the big table and did a reading," she said, "I knew that I could do it, because it went really well." In any case, she confirms that she did tell Pakula at one point that she doubted her ability to play the role.*

talking with the actors, I see where their instincts take them," he said. "Sometimes [actors] will fall into what I had [imagined] in the first place. Sometimes they will do things I didn't think of that are better than I might have thought of, or just as legitimate, and in terms of their personality would be better for them to do. Sometimes, too, they will do something that is totally wrong for the scene, and then we . . . talk. But I don't say, 'You stand here. You move six inches to your left and you move a quarter of an inch to your right.' For me, the essence of getting good work out of an actor is having some strong sense of that person, and getting to know them well enough so you know what in them can contribute to the character they're playing."

Because of the fortuitous rainstorm that had occurred at the beginning of shooting *The Sterile Cuckoo*, forcing Pakula to shoot Pookie's emotional scene on the telephone, he decided to begin shooting one of the major scenes in *Klute* on the first day—the "big confrontation scene," as he called it, when Klute goes to Bree's apartment for the first time. Then, however, Pakula became aware that Fonda was still extremely insecure about playing Bree, and, "when I saw this girl absolutely terrified, there was no way I could get near that scene," Pakula said. "So I went to the production manager and I said, 'I'm throwing out the whole shooting schedule.'" Ed Fay, the production manager, had, as he was instructed, arranged for the first week of shooting in the studio, but Pakula now told him that the first week would be shot on location. As a result, Fay said, "Do you know what that means, Alan? We're [not] supposed to go on location [until] the third week. We'll have to get all new permits. It's now Thursday night and you're telling me that by Monday we're going to begin shooting in New York."

Fay and the other members of the production staff were thrown into a frantic weekend of activity, but succeeded in arranging the first scene in New York. The sequence consisted of a "totally relaxed" sequence Pakula made up for the occasion so that Fonda could "be led very gently into this." Then, as Fonda gained more confidence, "she did walk-bys and little telephone scenes," Pakula said. Not until late in the week did Pakula begin to shoot more challenging scenes requiring Fonda to fully assume her call girl persona. To prepare for those scenes, Pakula imported what he called "research people"—call girls, madams, and pimps—to advise her on the appropriate attitude and behavior.[19]

In his research, Pakula found that the attraction of being a call girl was "not sexual. Call girls pride themselves on not having real orgasms and not feeling anything for their clients sexually—but the great turn-on is that for five minutes, ten

---

[19]*A great deal of research preceded the shooting of the film. Much of it came from books. Primarily, however, the work was "the kind of research you can only do after midnight," Pakula said, "because they"—the prostitutes, pimps and johns—"don't really come out until after midnight."*

minutes, fifteen minutes, they are the center of attention of one man and his world, and they control him. For girls who have usually had terrible relationships with fathers, that's very heady stuff."

Fonda "spent a week with different prostitutes and call girls—arranged by Alan's production assistant," she said, "and on several occasions I went with him late at night into these clubs where they would go to meet up with their pimps."[20]

Fonda's next challenge was to play the scene in which she goes to a man's hotel room as a prostitute. Pakula had hired a "technical adviser," a twenty-three year old call girl who, he said, counseled Fonda, "The first thing you do is that no matter what, you get the money. You get it before, because you're not going to get as much afterwards. The second thing you do is to make sure that the man thinks he is different, that you need the money because you can't afford to take him for free, but he is different from any other john you've ever seen, that he really turns you on—because you get more money that way."

The actor in the scene played a man with little or no experience with call girls, a man who is apprehensive about his encounter with Bree. The scene's dialogue was essentially improvised. In the midst of the erotic conversation between the two, with Bree saying, "Come on, what do you like, tell me what you like," Fonda improvised a line, "Oh, I like your mind." Pakula said, "I almost destroyed the scene because I started to break up, but I stopped myself. That [improvised line] wasn't done as a gag. It came out of Jane being in character and having a simple action that was to turn on this man as much as possible, to make him think he was exciting to her. And, once given that, she was really in character, she couldn't do much that was wrong." Recognizing that she was now totally at home with her character, he offered only one further direction: to seem to remain excited by the prospect of sex and not to ask the john too obviously about the money.

One rehearsal technique Pakula did *not* employ in *Klute* was to repeat periodically the story of the film to Jane Fonda, as he had done to such good effect with Liza Minnelli in *The Sterile Cuckoo*. "I think if I'd said to Jane Fonda, 'Once upon a time there was this prostitute,' she'd have called her agent and said, 'What's happening? He's flipping out.'" Clearly, "the solutions that you've used on one picture don't help you too much on the next picture."

Fonda told Pakula, after the set for her apartment had been built but before it had been dressed, "I need to live there. Can you help me with that?" This coincided nicely with Pakula's notion, "I like the actors to live in the set." He had a toilet installed, and "she slept in the set for several nights so she could put her

---

[20] For one particular scene, Pakula described to a pimp the effect he was hoping to create. The pimp responded, "Terrific, I'm going to stage this whole spectacle for you." Pakula quickly responded, "No, you're not, thank you very much. My research does not go that far."

stamp on it, and then when she'd do her blocking"—the actor's movement from one place to another—"she knew exactly where everything was, she knew what her daily routine was." As a result, Fonda said, "It was lying in that bed every night that I was able to imagine what Bree would want to surround herself with. What books she would read. That was where the idea of the photograph of John F. Kennedy came from—particular kinds of photographs on the wall. Having a cat. What I would feed the cat. I mean, just a whole lot of specific things. I brought a lot of my own things onto the set."

Now that the production was in full swing, the amount of time given daily to the lighting of the set was enormous. Typically, the actors would work with Pakula—"we rehearsed rigorously and talked rigorously," Donald Sutherland said—between seven and nine AM, then the actors would repair to their trailers or dressing room while Willis lit the set and positioned the cameras. Not until noon or one o'clock would the actors be called again for the shooting of their scenes.

The first scene in the film, set during an outdoor party in Pennsylvania, was shot at George Jenkins's house. "It's one of the few times you really see sunlight in that film," Pakula said, "and it's the only time you see a family in the film. I wanted to start the film on a family celebration in sunlight [with] people who belong together, because you then go to an alienated world of people who don't belong anywhere, this nightmarish world, . . . and that turns to black, to darkness."

Although Bree Daniels's primary occupation is prostitution, she wishes to become an actress. In one scene in the film, she auditions for *Saint Joan*, along with many other aspiring performers. The most conventional approach to the scene would have been to show her as a talentless performer, but that was not the route either Pakula or Fonda wished to take. "Jane worked very hard on that scene," Pakula said, "and she went to a coach for the accent and the speech, and did all the things that Bree Daniels indeed would've done. It would've been easy to make her look like a bad actress, but, although she didn't bowl you over in the scene, she was perfectly competent." Still, she is given short shrift by the director of *Saint Joan*, who cuts her off in the middle of her monologue. Despite her fine reading, Pakula lamented, "it didn't necessarily mean that anybody was going to hire her. I must say that you can go to New York or to little theatres and see an awful lot of good actresses that don't get anywhere unless they persevere and persevere and persevere. But my concern in the scene was not to [have Jane Fonda] play down to it somehow, and she didn't do that."

The audition scene was important to Fonda in understanding Bree's character. "Alan and I spent many hours discussing why is it that a woman like Bree, who clearly was not lacking talent as an actress [would remain a prostitute]. We felt it was important in that scene where she was auditioning for *Saint Joan* to show that she had talent."

The attitude of the stage director to Bree's *Saint Joan* audition, which was essentially to ignore Bree as a human being, is demonstrated again and again throughout the film, particularly in the scene referred to earlier, when she is shown as an aspiring model, sitting in a line with several other young women, under three enormous posters of idealized-looking models. Advertising agency executives look at each woman in turn and comment, often insultingly, about their appearance. "I was trying to get the dehumanized feeling of these beautiful girls [seated under the posters]," Pakula said, "that they are not people; they're little dolls who have been reduced to products." (In the scene, Bree is given no more prominence than any of the other aspirants.) A later scene shows Bree in the office of a casting director who appears to be communicating with her but is in fact paying no attention to her. "What I was trying to do in all those little scenes was to show how the people she comes in contact with do not see her at all; she's just an audience for them," Pakula said.

One of Pakula's favorite shots in the film occurred "when Klute hears somebody on the roof [of Bree's apartment house] and she's seducing him [Klute] and . . . she's got her dress unzipped all the way down the back, and he walks her over to the bed because he's heard somebody on the roof that she hasn't heard . . . and you can see in the mirror that she's stroking him with her hands. You see that bare back, very erotic-looking, and he says, 'There's somebody on the roof,' and those hands just become absolutely paralyzed, and this girl who is at the height of her seductive power, on top of it all, just suddenly turns into a broken little doll, totally vulnerable, totally terrified. I love when one shot that starts out meaning something turns into something else."

Magnified sound is an important element in *Klute*. The sound of Cable's tape recorder, the ring of a telephone, the creak of footsteps on the roof—all were amplified to help in the creation of a frightening world. And the mechanics of sound reproduction play a significant role in the film. Peter Cable tapes his encounters with prostitutes; John Klute tapes Bree's telephone conversations. (A significant moment occurs when Klute returns Bree's tapes, a sign that, unlike Cable, he is not a threat to her.)

Undoubtedly the most significant sound in the film is the music. Pakula said, "The score can say things that nothing else can say. It can in some ways make you feel inside a character. On an emotional level you understand the film better because of the music." Michael Small, the composer, said that his intention was to create music that would not only "key in moments of terror," but would serve as "character music. The music—Alan called it 'the siren call'—is not only the signature of the killer, it's also the very seductive force that Bree is putting out. So it's *her* music in so many ways; it's really scoring her inner life. I also wrote a very minimalist score, in that there were certain motifs that were repeated a lot. I think the way that music works in the film began a whole style of film score I wasn't aware of at the time even existing."

Small used an ensemble of only a few instruments—as opposed to the large orchestra so common to Hollywood movies—and a female vocalist who sings wordlessly. Essential to the score, he said, was "very, very exotic percussion, weird ethnic percussion—African, Chinese, you name it. We didn't have synthesizers then, but the idea was to create a new sound."

Pakula was unable to be specific about the way in which the music was to be scored, but, said Small, "I know that Alan guided me. He kept saying, 'Don't play low notes, we already know it's scary.' He wasn't specific about the way in which it was scored, but he was very specific about what he *didn't* want. . . . He really wanted music to be a character in the film. And I think it was his idea to have the voice of the singer. Also, he was very helpful to me, because he articulated Bree's need for control, all of those things which were not in your usual movie about a prostitute."

The music was often used to let the audience know that Bree was in danger as well as to mirror Bree's inner life. "The scene where the music dovetails in function," Small said, "is when [Bree and Klute] are in her apartment alone together. She's trying to seduce Klute so he'll give her the incriminating tapes. They get very close. Suddenly his eyes look up at the skylight and he pulls away and says, 'There's someone on the roof,' at which point the 'siren call' music is played. For me at that moment, you identify that music with what she's just been doing as well as the presence of the killer. I think that she has this chilling realization that it's her own obsession with control and seduction that's haunting her, literally stalking her."

In 1971, Small was thirty-one years old and had written only one film score, for a low-budget film called *Out of It*. "It was a big risk for Alan," Small said, "to work with an unknown composer." But the risk paid off. Pakula said that Small's score "worked on a suspense level, but it also worked deeply on a character level, and it gave the film a very strong subtext, a textural richness."

As Pakula saw it, the story of *Klute* "was the story of a girl who is [almost] destroyed by her own compulsions." To some extent, this theme paralleled *The Sterile Cuckoo*, for Pookie, too, comes perilously close to being destroyed by her compulsions. Pakula admitted that he was "fascinated by compulsions, by bright, rational people who have various behaviors they cannot control." In terms of Bree Daniels, "she has a compulsion to seduce, and it's that compulsion that almost destroys her in the end."

At first, Pakula thought of his first two directorial efforts as polar opposites. He said to a friend, "One thing they can't accuse me of is doing the same thing twice. The first one was all innocence and the second one hasn't got a drop of innocence in it. They couldn't be more different." Then, however, despite the immense difference in style and tone, he realized that there was a point at which they intersected. "The major similarity," he said, "is that they both deal with kind of middle-class, controlled, repressed males. One is a boy and one is a man, falling in love with self-destructive, very alive, witty, vibrant, spontaneous, surprising women who almost destroy them."

Pakula was fascinated with exploring those qualities in John Klute, "a middle-class American, a square man who has lived his life by simple rules, almost Victorian rules, who has led a life of total decency, has controlled his baser emotions and his hostilities . . . [but] suddenly feels himself falling in love with somebody who is all the things he despises." As a result, Pakula noted, Klute learns "compassion for the human condition and some realization of his own complexities, and [becomes] a fuller and more aware and more emotionally alive human being."

Pakula felt that Donald Sutherland was "a complicated, fascinating man, mercurial and full of moods, [who] in his own way could do a male version of Bree Daniels. And," Pakula said, "there was this strangeness about him. Sometimes his eyes would stare with such intensity—and he was playing this supposedly simple character. There were a couple of times when Gordy [Willis] would say to me, 'Jesus, it's getting so I don't know who the heavy is.' The part is kind of rigid, and yet there is a complication in Donald that somehow gave it a certain kind of color."

Other actors received no less attention. "The character of Peter Cable was not that well-developed in the script," Charles Cioffi said, "so Alan would take me out to Sardi's and we would have dinner. And we would create a dossier of Peter Cable. So that by the time the camera started to roll, I was entirely into it."

At one point Fonda asked Pakula, "What made you decide that you wanted to do this film?" He answered that he had been most fascinated by the scene in which she goes to the old man's office and removes her clothes for him. Fonda said, "But you're not a voyeur. Why was it that scene?"

Pakula's response revealed the complexity of his feelings and the acuity of his psychological understanding of the characters and situation. "It's a brilliant conception, that scene, because," he said,

You have a girl who is seducing all kinds of men, obviously lots of them young, even the john you see in the hotel room is fairly young and fairly attractive, but she obviously gets no pleasure with any of them. And here she is with an old man. And the one pleasure—not erotic pleasure, but innocent pleasure—the one joyous time that she has with a john is with the old man. . . . An old man making a girl fantasize an old fashioned Schnitzlerian turn-of-the-century erotic image while she takes off her clothes. You want to say, "that's distasteful," and yet there's a relationship that works between those people, there's a joyousness about it. . . . For all its erotic qualities, it has an innocence about it. And he's admiring her for being a wonderful, romantic character and fulfilling a part of her childhood that she undoubtedly hadn't had a chance to fulfill. Well, that fascinated me. There's something heartbreaking about that scene, very moving about that scene.

Pakula used every device he could think of to communicate his feelings about the scene to the audience. He told his cinematographer, "Gordon, I want that entrance when she comes in [to the old man's office] in her boa—I want to photograph it like Josef von Sternberg photographing Dietrich. I want it felt from that man's point of view, his erotic fantasy. And I want her to walk down and come into a close-up; I want liquid lips and softness and romantic things." Moreover, he employed music by Michael Small, played on the cimbalom, that was "very middle European erotic."

The most difficult scenes to film were those involving Bree and her psychiatrist. Even before the shooting began, Fonda told Pakula that she felt uneasy about playing the scenes with the male actor who had been cast in the role. She told the director, "You know, Alan, he's a very good actor. I don't want to sound unreasonable, but I think it would be better for me if I had a woman as a psychiatrist. Bree could never reveal herself to a male psychiatrist." After thinking it over, Pakula agreed, and recast the role with Vivian Nathan. It "made all the difference in the world," he said. Fonda agreed. "Everything changed," she confirmed. Fonda asked if the scenes with the psychiatrist could be delayed until the very end of shooting, "when Bree was inside me, when I had completely internalized her," and Pakula agreed.

Pakula used an interesting technique in working with the two actresses. "I never introduced Jane to Vivian," he said. "I wanted to keep a professional relationship. So I would talk to each one separately. Jane would come out to the anteroom [of the office set] after each take. I'd talk to her in the anteroom, and I'd talk to Vivian in the office."

Pakula felt that "the only chance for the scenes [in the psychiatrist's office] to succeed was if you really felt this girl breaking down before your eyes. And the only chance I felt we actually had for that was to improvise. And we improvised all day, and I just kept feeding film into the can, and we kept going through reel after reel after reel."

After about five hours of shooting, Fonda, improvising, had "never actually said that she was a prostitute," Pakula said.

And I kept saying, "Why don't you tell her you're a prostitute?" She said, "I keep trying to tell her, and every time I try to tell her she changes the subject." And Vivian Nathan [who played the psychiatrist] said, "Every time I try to get her tell me what she really does, that she's a prostitute, she changes the subject." It got to be 4:00, and I thought, "Oh, we're running out of time," and I said to Vivian, "Okay, really give it to her. You've been very kind and very compassionate and very nice, and I would like you this time to lace into her. Be hostile, don't be so patient and kind." Because I thought that's really going to start breaking Jane down. . . . And she really laced into her. Well, the more angry she got at her, the more controlled Jane became. Relaxed, kind of happy. The exact opposite of what I'd been reaching for. We ran out of film . . . and I said, "Jane, what happened here? She was really lacing into you. Didn't that get you angry?" And she said, "Alan, for Bree Daniels that hostility is the easiest thing in the world to deal with. She's gotten an emotional reaction. When there's anger, she can be angry back if she can control it. She's made that person vulnerable. She's gotten to her."

Pakula tried again, this time instructing Vivian Nathan not to be confrontational. During the scene, Bree announces that she will not be returning for further sessions. When the psychiatrist asks why, Bree answers that she had turned to therapy so that she would not continue to lead the life of a prostitute, but that every time she passes a telephone booth she wants to pick up a trick. Nothing in her life, she believes, has changed. Then, once again, the improvisation took a direction Pakula hadn't anticipated. The psychiatrist says, "Do you feel I've failed you?" and Bree says, "No, I feel *I've* failed *you*."

Now [Pakula said], Vivian proceeded to get tears in her eyes, which I would never have told her to do. She knew what she was doing. It was a very good choice, but I would never have asked her to make that choice.

So I started to say, "Wait a minute, this is getting unprofessional. Something's wrong." And Jane said [in character as Bree], "You're crying." And Vivian said, "Well, you've been telling me through all these sessions that you don't like anybody. And you said something very nice to me, and I didn't ask you to, and I was touched. And now you're leaving me." And Jane broke into tears like a child to whom it was proven that her mother really loved her no matter what. And then Jane said, "You know what it is? I'm beginning to feel. I'm just so scared." I felt a thrill down the back of my neck. Everything we'd reached for was happening. She was really facing what her problem was, that being a prostitute was a denial of sexuality, a denial of feeling. She was coming to grips with all that, and we ran out of film. And we just said to the crew, "Quiet, just everybody be quiet and keep standing there. And we changed the camera. It was like a church. Nearly everything that's in the film with the psychiatrist was in that ten or fifteen minutes that we shot.

During the improvisation, Pakula used a single camera focused on Jane Fonda—which he came to realize was a mistake. "I should've had two cameras," he said. But, not having done so, "All I could do was to cut to Vivian smiling wisely, which is a sacrifice of Vivian as an actress."

Another scene that was "basically an improv," according to Charles Cioffi, was the long, climactic scene in the garment factory when Peter Cable attempts to kill Bree. And still another improvised scene was the dialogue on the mini-tape recorder, in which Bree hears Cable murdering Arlyn Page.

The notion of using a tape recorder as object and symbol did not occur to Pakula until a third of the way into the shooting of the film. "And then from that," he said, "came the idea of using the tape recorder at the beginning of the film. And then it became Jane's voice seducing that one man that's played back all through the picture. You hear that man listening to it and listening to it, and it's like her siren call that's leading this man on, that keeps arousing him, that keeps leading her to her own destruction." Then, finally, it is used to reveal Arlyn Page's death to Bree.

During the film, one of the methods Klute uses to try to discover if any of Bree's friends has been murdered is to take Bree to the morgue and have her look at pictures of murdered prostitutes. Although the scene was performed on a set, Fonda said, "I had actually gone down to the city morgue and gone through the real files and seen pictures of hundreds of women that had been beaten and killed. I threw up, it had such an impact on me." The impact can be clearly seen on the screen during a scene late in the film, when Peter Cable traps Bree Daniels in the garment factory with intent to kill her. He plays the tape of his encounter with Arlyn Page, culminating in Arlyn's murder.

The scene was shot without rehearsal, but, as originally planned, Bree would react to the tape with fear for her own life. However, in the only take the scene required, Fonda said, "I had a very interesting reaction to that scene, which I had not planned. I didn't act scared. I cried. And it was powerful because it was not what was expected, and the reason that happened was because when I heard him playing the tape I suddenly realized that I was listening to my girlfriend, fear was rising in her voice, and I realized that she was about to die and this was the man that had killed her. I began to cry, not out of fear but out of this feeling: there are so many of us that have gone this way. I felt such sorrow for us women who are victims of misplaced rage that men bring against us, and it was for all the faces of those women that I saw at the morgue that I cried. So in that sense it was a new kind of consciousness that was blooming in me that caused me to react that way, which caused a different kind of life to be brought to the scene."

On occasion, as when Fonda responded differently than he anticipated, actors would surprise Pakula, and those moments gave him great pleasure. "I love when things come out of the actors I don't expect," he said.

Conventionally, one might think of a suspense film in which several people lose their lives by violent means as having a rapid, staccato rhythm, but the suspenseful scenes in *Klute* are paced very deliberately, extraordinarily slowly, in order to emphasize the mysterious presence of danger—as when Cable is hiding in the garment factory and Bree walks slowly toward him (and toward the camera, eventually moving into a close-up), unaware that he is waiting to attack her—and to create a sense of fear in the viewer.

Cable menaces Bree, but he is killed when he sees Klute rushing toward him. In the original script, the scene did not take place in the garment factory. "The murderer came to [Bree's] flat and sat there and confessed everything," Pakula explained, "and then he took a gun and he shot himself. Well, guns and all that did not seem very interesting to me." Instead, Cable falls backwards through a window to his death, repeating a motif established earlier. On several occasions throughout the film Cable had been photographed behind glass, to emphasize his remoteness and isolation. "He's totally cut off from any feeling. And the violent, sadistic sexual behavior and infantile anger of being not in touch with his own emotions [caused him to become] cold and gray and dead," Pakula said.

The final scene in the film shows Klute and Bree in Bree's empty apartment, three packed suitcases on the floor. After receiving a telephone call, and turning down a "date," Klute and Bree pick up the suitcases and leave—while on the audio track Bree is heard telling her psychiatrist, "I have no idea what's going to happen. I just can't stay in the city, you know. Maybe I'll come back. You'll probably see me next week." The ending, as is so often the case in the films Pakula directed, is ambiguous. Will Klute and Bree begin a life together in Pennsylvania? Will Bree eventually return to her old life? Even the principal actors were divided in their interpretation. Donald Sutherland said, "I had the feeling that Bree and John Klute maybe had a chance of having a life together, but Alan and Jane thought that there was absolutely *no* chance that these people could have a life together."

Pakula's relationship with all his actors was creative from the beginning of the process until the end. As Charles Cioffi said, "he allowed you to invent, and if you did—that's the reason he hired you. He didn't hire somebody just to be a mouthpiece, or his puppet." Donald Sutherland characterized his experience in the film in similar fashion: "[Good acting] has to do with vigorous pursuit of truth in the character. Alan's interest in psychotherapy was just a device to getting at the most definitive explanation of a character's motives. I would sometimes ask him what he wanted out of a scene, and he was always able to tell me *exactly* what he wanted out of it, and then it was my job to go and get it."

Jane Fonda said, "He gave me the kind of help I needed, because he would always go for the psychological. He had a wonderful, and, at least for me, an unusual combination of both emotional literacy and technical interest. And he was always incredibly supportive of and attentive to my thoughts and needs."

Sutherland recalled that the joy and delight Pakula radiated when the actors were able to give him precisely what he hoped for—or possibly even more than he hoped for—"was thrilling. It didn't happen all the time, but when it did happen . . ."

Michael Small was present in the editing room during some of the post-production process. He saw a different side of Pakula than he had seen before. "Boy, he was very tough," Small said. "He had done his shoot, he had his concept, and he was very disciplined. I think he knew exactly what he wanted. If he saw something he didn't like, he would re-edit sequences. He'd also make a lot of decisions about the music, moving it around to different places."

Small's view of the film is that *Klute* was "a feminist movie in a strange way. The character [of Bree] was very round and very full. . . . So it's a genre film that transcends the genre. The thriller aspect had to work, but it was really a character-driven movie."

Klute was immediately successful with the public, but it seemed to confuse many of the critics, who wanted the film to fit into a recognizable genre. It seems remarkable, but it is true, that *Klute* was poorly received by the critics on its 1971 release, remarkable because the film quickly assumed the status of a classic, and not just with audience members. Critical opinion fairly quickly reversed direction and embraced the film. But the initial reviews were strongly negative.

Roger Greenspun in the *New York Times* seemed confused. "The actual intentions of *Klute* are not all that easy to spot," he wrote, "though I think they have more to do with its intellectual aspirations than with its thriller plot." He referred to its suspense as "contrived a terror as any I've ever seen," and said, "[D]espite the sharp edges and dramatic spaces and cinema presence [derived from] *Citizen Kane*, it all suggests a tepid, rather tasteless mush." He dismissed Fonda's performance in one sentence: "Jane Fonda, who is good at confessing, is generally successful." Greenspun's review infuriated Pakula, who felt it superficial and imperceptive. Further, he felt that Greenspun's dismissive comment about Fonda's performance showed "no understanding or comprehension of what acting is all about."

Andrew Sarris found the premise of the film improbable and "unlikely." He spoke of "the film's failure as a suspense mechanism." For *Time*'s Jay Cocks, the film was "slick" and sometimes "hoked-up," containing "an uncomfortable number of genre clichés." The scenes with the psychiatrist were "a rather clumsy dramatic device," he said, and the "balance between suspenseful diversion and romantic melodrama" was "sometimes successful, sometimes tenuous." He did have high praise for Pakula's work with Jane Fonda: "His talent with actors seems now beyond contention, and under his guidance Jane Fonda gives her best performance to date. . . . In *Klute* she is profoundly and perfectly Bree: she makes all the right choices, from the mechanics of her walk and her voice inflection to the penetration of the girl's raging psyche. It is a rare performance."

Pauline Kael also praised Fonda ("she never stands outside Bree, she gives herself over to the role, and yet she isn't *lost* in it—she's fully in control, and her means are extraordinarily economical. . . . [Bree is] one of the strongest feminine characters to reach the screen") and commended the film as "perhaps the first major attempt to transform modern clinical understanding [of the behavior of prostitutes] into human understanding and dramatic meaning." But she also called the film "far from a work of art . . . the mechanics of suspense—the lurking figures, the withheld information, the standard gimmick of getting the heroine to go off alone so she can be menaced by the big-shot sadistic sex fiend, the improbable confessions and last-minute rescues—are just claptrap . . ." She described the groundbreaking musical score as "awful" and "repetitive," and Gordon Willis's brilliant photography as "fancy excesses . . . the shadows and angles are as silly as a fright wig."

Variety found the film full of "terminal flaws . . . directed tediously and redundantly . . . a suspenser without much suspense, . . . neither a good crime drama nor a developed personal drama. . . . The only rewarding element is Miss Fonda's performance." Since *Variety*'s claim to fame was its supposed expertise in the business of show business, it predicted that "commercial prospects seem tepid."

Stanley Kauffmann in the *New Republic* was less enthusiastic about Fonda and utterly contemptuous of Pakula. Fonda, he said, was "*relying* on her talent, including her excellent voice, instead of using it. In scene after scene of *Klute*, one can see her using easy 'solutions'—easy to her anyway—instead of really freshening the moment. And since she has such ample gifts, and since her director doesn't seem to know much about *anything*, she gets away with it." He characterized the film as "one more of that new breed of rotten film that tries to be mod by taking a conventional story and telling it badly. It's basically a crime thriller, but by misproportioning it and fancying up the photography and having the call girl speak bluntly, they thought they'd sort of take a fix on the Human Condition." Pakula, he said, "is just another artistically shallow slicknik, operating in the new psychologized showbiz."

Rarely in the history of motion pictures or of the theatre has a distinguished work been so savagely attacked on its first appearance, only to be quickly re-assessed and described as a classic. Within a year of *Klute*'s release, critical opinion changed significantly. Pakula won the London Film Critics' Circle Award for Best Director. Jane Fonda won the Academy Award for Best Actress.

By and large, the public simply ignored the overwhelmingly negative reviews. The film was highly profitable on its first release and has continued to make money for Warner Bros. for years. Now firmly established as a classic, hundreds of thousands of viewers each year watch it in its videotape and DVD versions.

Pakula felt that *Klute* represented "enormous advances for me as a director. In terms of visual storytelling and use of the camera, in terms of creating a mood visually, I felt that technically it was a much more skilled film" than *The Sterile Cuckoo*, he said. So thoroughly skillful was it that it represented a breakthrough for Pakula. For the next thirty-seven years he was regarded as one of America's finest film directors. *Klute* gave Pakula the prestige to take on virtually any project he wished, and he took that opportunity to direct a dazzling array of films, many of them equally groundbreaking.

Not only was Pakula's career transformed by *Klute*, but Jane Fonda was forever after regarded as an outstanding film actress, Gordon Willis was acclaimed as a great cinematographer, and Michael Small's excellence as a composer was unchallenged. For so many of its participants, *Klute* was a watershed event.

In September 1999, Charles Cioffi attended the Gotham Awards in New York, an event celebrating independent films. All the filmmakers were asked to name the one movie that influenced their own development more than any other. The runaway winner—"across the board," Cioffi said—was *Klute*.

CHAPTER SEVEN

Love and Pain;
Love Without Pain

"[Alan and Hannah Pakula] were, almost more than any other couple I can think of, a single entity. As their life together progressed, they arrived at that idyllic place where there was no Alan without Hannah, no Hannah without Alan. His work was influenced and encouraged and enjoyed by her, as was her work by him. No one was prouder of his films, no one was prouder of her books."

—PETER STONE

P AKULA SUFFERED HIS FIRST DIRECTORIAL FAILURE with his next effort, *Love and Pain and the Whole Damn Thing*, released in 1972. Still, he enjoyed the process a great deal. For one thing, he spent the pre-production period living in an apartment off Berkeley Square in London. "Alan loved London," Michael Small said. "He loved the elegance of London. *Love and Pain and the Whole Damn Thing* was made right in the middle of the Vietnam war, and being in London provided a sense of escape."

Even better, Pakula had the pleasure of visiting with his stepchildren, Chris and Patty Murray, who spent the summer of 1971 with him. Particularly on weekends, they were able to spend a great deal of time together. Chris, who was fourteen at the time, recalls with pleasure that his stepfather would rent a car and take Patty and himself on long drives, once to Ireland.

Pakula had begun working on *Love and Pain* before Warner Bros. offered him the opportunity to produce and direct *Klute*. During the time when he was cutting *The Sterile Cuckoo* with his editors in Los Angeles, Alvin Sargent said to Pakula one day, "I have an image, an image of a boy who's eighteen or nineteen years old, and he's come back from a trip to Europe, and he wears a black armband, and he's a widower."

"How the hell did he become a widower?" Pakula asked, but at that point Sargent had no more than an image. The idea sparked Pakula's imagination, however, and the eventual result was *Love and Pain*.

Pakula "went around to every studio in town," he said, "telling the story. But since I didn't have it on paper, I got turned down by everybody. Finally, an executive producer at ABC financed the first draft after endless negotiations."

Pakula and Sargent worked out the details of the plot together. "Once I became interested in the idea, I thought of the very bold, outrageous comic strokes I could use to treat it," Pakula said. Eventually, Sargent completed the screenplay, which Pakula called "a love story of the absurd, a kind of sexual Laurel and Hardy."

Pakula returned to the executive producer at ABC who had agreed to finance the first draft. The executive said, according to Pakula, "I'd like you to take out this part and this part and this part if you're going to do it. Otherwise we won't finance it." Pakula refused to change the basic shape of the script and began making the rounds of the studios again. Finally, an executive at Cinema Center, a CBS affiliate, said, "We'll finance it if you do it with Angela Lansbury." Pakula had another actress in mind, but he found the executive's offer plausible. "Angela's a very gifted lady," he thought. "I do have certain reservations in certain areas, but it's okay, it's a very comic part, and she has a real comic sense." He went so far as to announce Lansbury's participation in the film, but, eventually, she withdrew, as did CBS. Columbia Pictures wound up financing the film, and Pakula returned to his original notion of casting Maggie Smith as Lila Fisher, a middle-aged spinster. Timothy Bottoms played Walter Elbertson, the eighteen-year-old boy who falls in love with her.

Like *Klute*, like *The Sterile Cuckoo*, the film is the story of an odd couple—and, in this case, they get married. Lila, a woman in her late thirties who suffers from a neurological disease, is touring Spain in order to escape her two elderly aunts in Bournemouth. In Pakula's words, she is "a woman of great spine and discipline, with an enormous will, but . . . is afraid of exposure to life." Walter, son of a Pulitzer Prize-winning author and brother of an accomplished maker of cellos, "has sort of withdrawn from life to a great extent," Pakula explained. "He refuses to compete. At the rather tender age of eighteen, he just seems to have given up."

Lila's disease causes her to fall down unexpectedly and at odd moments, offending her sense of dignity. But "she finds herself in this very undignified affair with this very insecure boy-man," Pakula said.

While he was making the film, Pakula said, he had "a kind of welding problem. I am attracted to welding unlikely elements together—like doing something that seems rather tragic, and then seeing the comedy in it. *Love and Pain and the Whole Damn Thing* is a romantic story that could be done rather tragically and rather somberly, but it's done with many farce elements."

Like *Klute*, *Love and Pain* (which was shown in England under the title *The Widower*) rehearsed for three weeks. Michael Small composed a score of Spanish romantic music for guitar and orchestra. Small discussed the way he and Pakula worked in post-production. "We always had a great time exploring ideas, more than any director I worked with," Small said. "We would articulate concepts and play with ideas. He really wanted music to be a character in the films. He became my mentor."

The film was shot entirely in Spain, after which Pakula and his editor, Russell Lloyd, cut the film at Shepperton Studios in England.

Pakula was particularly delighted with Maggie Smith's performance. "Absolutely remarkable," he called it, and he was not alone. Vincent Canby of the *New York Times* found Smith "magnificent (and magnificently funny)," and Timothy Bottoms "equally funny and believable." He said that the film was "such a funny and eccentric romantic comedy that, [although] it eventually goes to soap suds, [when it is revealed that Lila is dying], it can be enjoyed for two of the most intelligently comic performances of the year."

"The movie is at its quiet best, funny and affectionate, as it chronicles their unlikely courtship," wrote Jay Cocks in *Time*. He also described Maggie Smith as "a peerless comedienne." *Variety*'s reviewer typified the general critical opinion by saying that the first two-thirds of the film "is lowkeyed and totally disarming, played with enormous sensitivity by the two leads," but that the remainder of the film "goes woefully off the track and the viewer can almost feel the carefully wrought mood slip away."

Pakula readily admitted afterwards that *Love and Pain* was a failure—"roundly rejected" by most critics and by the general public, as he put it—although he remarked in the 1990s that it contained some of his best work. He said, "I have a [belief] that when you have a success people don't see the bad work and when you have a failure people don't see the good work. There's never been a film I've done where there was not something that I didn't dislike and there's never been a film I've done where there wasn't something in it that I didn't like a lot." Speaking particularly about *Love and Pain*, he confessed that "while there were charming, outrageous, farcical things in it, it didn't work at all. . . . But there is a little lonely minority out there that seems to still remember it."

Indeed, *Love and Pain* had its avid supporters, who found it a delightfully romantic and bittersweet fairy tale, but it had little appeal at the box office. Columbia Pictures, which distributed the film, lost most of its investment.

Moreover, the owner of the rights obviously doesn't believe the film would have any appeal now, as it is the only movie Pakula produced or directed that is not available on video. Still, Pakula always maintained that it "was a very bizarre little picture" for which he had "great fondness."

Michael Small said that when he worked with Pakula on *Klute*, the director's tension and intensity were apparent, but that he was far more relaxed during the shooting of *Love and Pain*, partially because "he had made a tremendous success of *Klute*, and felt that he had arrived." His personality was also undergoing a change because of the woman he had begun seeing before he came to England. Indeed, one reason that Pakula wished to direct a romantic film may have been because, at the time *Love and Pain* was being made, he himself was involved in the romance of his life.

Born in Nebraska, Hannah Cohn grew up in Los Angeles. Her parents had raised her to be "a Jewish geisha," as a friend described her, an ideal wife and mother, and an accomplished hostess. "I was Miss Perfect," Hannah said. "Quite a burden. I came from a family where you never made a mistake." Barbara Davis, who knew Hannah from the time they were both adolescents and has remained close to her ever since, said that Hannah's mother expected her to be perfect "about everything. Perfect looking, perfect grades, perfect house, perfect children, a perfect musician. . . . Her mother was a very powerful character, had a very precise view of what was right in almost every case, from manners to morals to aesthetics. I think her mother's aspirations were for Hannah to run this absolutely perfect household and to be very rich and very social."

Hannah attended Wellesley College, where she excelled academically. During her junior year she studied abroad at the Sorbonne in Paris and met Robert Boorstin, who had left an investment banking business in New York to run an oil company. Hannah and Robert were married before the year was out, then moved to Texas, where Hannah completed her education at Southern Methodist University. They soon began to raise a family of three children: Anna; then, two years later, twin boys, Bob and Louis.

Robert Boorstin was, in the words of Barbara Davis, "a man I liked very much; he had a great mind—but he was incredibly controlling, somebody who had an absolute sense of what was correct about everything. He picked out Hannah's clothes, for example. He had wonderful taste in everything—but he wasn't easy."

When Hannah and Robert were on a vacation in Greece in 1969—their first long-term holiday without the children—Boorstin died of a heart attack at the age of forty-one. Hannah, who was then thirty-five, flew home as soon as possible so that her children would not hear of their father's death from any other source. At the time, Anna was eleven and the twin boys were nine.

Hannah refused to give in to despair. "I realized I was the only person in the world who cared more about these children than anything else," she said. "So you go on. I became like a mama lion."

Later, just before *Klute* was released, a friend invited Hannah to a dinner party in New York. Another guest that night was Alan Pakula, whom she had met while she was married. As they talked, they found that they had many interests and attitudes in common, and when the evening was over, Alan said to Hannah, "I'll call you." True to his word, he called to ask her out—but not until six months later.[21] He was still bitter about Hope Lange's request for a divorce, and cautious about beginning another relationship. At last, however, in 1971, but before his divorce from Lange became final, he and Hannah began seeing one another in New York.

Pakula found the relationship awkward, at first. "To go back, after a committed relationship, to the superficialities of dating, the uncommitted quality of dating, is bizarre and unnerving," he said. "It seems as if you're going back to some adolescent conduct. The very idea of making a pass, or accepting a pass, and how far do we go and how deeply do we get involved, all of those things can be very insecure-making."

But falling in love with Hannah also caused Pakula to admit to himself that his marriage to Hope Lange was over. "If you've been married and [later] divorce, once you fall in love with someone else, commit yourself to someone else, that's the final death of the marriage," he said years afterwards, in the context of a film he made about divorce and remarriage. "That's the final killing-it-off. Divorce isn't as final as falling in love again."

Hannah returned to California, where she and her children lived. Alan was determined to continue seeing her, but continuing their relationship on the West Coast meant that Alan would have to pass muster with the children. According to Pakula's cousin, Selma Hirsh, when Alan arrived at Hannah's house in Beverly Hills, "he was confronted with these adolescent kids. Her children were taking care of their mother, supervising her activities. So they eyed him up and down, not certain whether they liked her going out with him."

Perhaps the children's initially skeptical attitude about Pakula is best summarized by Louis Boorstin's anecdote. "Alan had been dating my mother for some time when he came to visit us in Los Angeles from New York. You can't survive in L.A. without a car, and we had an extra, so my mother decided to lend it to him. I leaned out the door as Alan headed down the driveway, and yelled, 'Just remember, that's *our* car!'"

As the children came to realize that Pakula was more than "a date," that he and

---

[21] *Pakula had followed exactly the same pattern earlier with Hope Lange. He later said to Hannah, "I did that [waiting for six months to call before asking for a date] twice in my life, and I married both women."*

their mother were in love with one another, they got to know him better and grew more comfortable with his presence in the family.

Alan and Hannah went out together for two years, and their relationship ripened into love. But Alan, still smarting over the unhappy outcome of his first marriage, "was scared of getting married," according to Hannah.

In any case, marriage was impossible until Pakula's divorce was final, so they attempted to find a level of commitment somewhere between marriage and dating. Theoretically, they might have lived together, but both Alan and Hannah thought that doing so might be psychologically damaging for her children. As Bob Boorstin expressed it in 2002, neither Alan nor Hannah thought "that kids should wake up and see a man in the house. This is symbolic," he said, "of who he was, and his innate moral sense."

Soon after Pakula's divorce became final late in 1971, the pair began going out together, facing no opposition from the children. As Louis said, by that time Alan was regarded as "a member of the family." On February 17, 1973, they were married. Chris Murray, Hope Lange's son, was Pakula's best man, a remarkable example of Alan's continued closeness to his stepchildren from his first marriage and they to him.

After the wedding, Alan moved into Hannah's house because, Hannah said, "He didn't want to disrupt the kids' lives." Anna, who was fifteen when her mother remarried, was concerned only that her life might be disrupted because "we might move to New York and I wouldn't be able to ride my horse at my barn."

Anna was a straight-A student at a private girls prep school. But several weekends after the wedding, with Hannah in Texas on business, Anna was arrested for taking a pair of earrings from a local department store. Humiliated, she called Pakula, who brought her home from the police station. Because Anna's behavior seemed so out of character, Hannah and Alan were convinced that this was a form of protest about their recent wedding. Anna, who told the story as a toast at Hannah and Alan's twentieth wedding anniversary and again at Alan's memorial service, has always explained the situation differently. "I was doing what all my friends were doing and trying to fit in. I wanted to seem like everybody else. The point of the story is very simple: in a horribly humiliating situation, I called Alan. I got him off the set of *The Parallax View*, which I knew was a big deal. I did not call my grandmother. I did not call my aunt. The person I called was Alan."

Years later, Pakula made a semi-autobiographical film entitled *See You in the Morning*, in which this incident is portrayed. Anna is clearly not reluctant to discuss it, but she is adamant that the point of the story—and the reason she told it to an audience of about twelve hundred people at the memorial service—had nothing to do with any negative feelings about her mother's remarriage.

Alan yearned to return to New York City (because, he said, reflecting his concern that his abilities might be diminished by the insular Hollywood community, "I don't want to make a film about films; I want to make films about what's going on in the world"), and, after Anna's graduation from high school, broached the idea of moving east with his new family. Hannah agreed, and she and Alan moved east with the children in 1976, renting a townhouse on Manhattan's East 69th Street. Then, after buying a summer house in East Hampton, they decided they needed a larger apartment in the city because Hannah was pregnant. (Soon afterward, however, she suffered a miscarriage.) They sold Hannah's house in Beverly Hills and bought an apartment on Park Avenue in New York City.[22]

Hannah never regretted the move to New York. "I loved it," she said, "and I have never lived in California again."

Only rarely did Alan return to California afterwards, preferring to shoot his films in New York or on location. He later established an office, Pakula Productions, on West 58th Street, where he planned future projects, eventually assembling a staff of seven people.

Hannah explained Alan's love for New York: "New York was home. He was raised there and started in the theatre [on the East Coast]. He found Los Angeles rather film-centric and there were other things"—literature, politics, and friendships with others who shared his diverse interests—"that interested him."

Early in her marriage to Robert Boorstin, when she was pregnant with Anna, Hannah had written articles, book reviews, and advertising copy. Then, however, she ceased writing. Alan encouraged her to begin again, and not just the "short pieces on blue jeans and shopping bags," as she described them, that she had written in the past. "Look," he said, "You've got to do something serious." Hannah, fearful of rejection, said, "But if I fail . . . ?" Alan spoke to her as one who had experienced critical failure in the past. "I get bad reviews all the time," he said, "and when I get up in the morning I still have ten fingers and ten toes." As a consequence, when she was nearing forty Hannah began work on a biography of Queen Marie of Romania, *The Last Romantic*, which was subsequently published by Simon and Schuster. The book was greeted with accolades wherever it was published. In his review in a British journal, Graham Greene called it one of the three best books of the year, and the best biography.

Later, Hannah wrote *An Uncommon Woman*, a biography of the Empress Frederick, the daughter of Queen Victoria and mother of Kaiser Wilhelm. She

---

[22]*Ten years later, they left the Park Avenue flat because, with Anna, Bob and Louis now grown, it had become too big for the couple. Eventually they found precisely what they were looking for on East 72nd Street, and, with the help of an architect, decorated it to their satisfaction.*

was sustained by her husband's unfailing support. "Alan gives support like nobody I've ever known," she said.

He "really enabled me to write," Hannah said. He told her, "Go ahead and try it. I'll protect you if it falls flat." She described that as "an enormous gift. He gave me his protection. He honored work, successful or not." As of this writing, Hannah Pakula is working on a book about Madame Chiang Kai-shek. She also contributes occasional book reviews to the *New York Times* and articles for such magazines as *Vanity Fair*.

Bob Boorstin recalled in the eulogy he gave after Pakula's funeral how important Alan was to his mother in terms of helping her get over the trauma of her first husband's death. Not only did Alan "love her desperately," he said, "he made her whole."

* * *

Asked what sorts of things she and Alan used to talk about at dinnertime, since he was involved with his films and she with her writing, Hannah answered, "We would end up having what I call parallel conversations. I would talk about my work and he would talk about his and I think neither of us listened [very carefully] to the other."

Alan rarely spoke about his films or about the world of filmmaking when the entire family was present—or, for that matter, when he spoke individually to his friends—because, Hannah said, "I think he had a horror of producers and directors who try to be producers and directors at home. I think it was something he had probably been exposed to too often in California." Indeed, he had been consumed by ambition in earlier years, rarely speaking of anything but his interest in film. Now, however, and for the remainder of his life, that passion was balanced by his other interests, such as politics, government, art, music, and history. This is not to say that his interest in his work lessened in any way, only that it was enriched by his wish to participate in other aspects of life.

Bob Boorstin, Hannah's son, had ambitions to be a filmmaker when he was an adolescent. "There were times when I wished he *had* talked to me more about his job, because I felt I was always talking to him a lot about me and what I was doing, and I was really interested in what he did. But this was not a subject of family talk. It was not a subject outside of his working circle. And the family did not show up on the set when he was shooting. We'd show up at the premieres, and that was about it."

Hannah rarely visited the set when Alan was shooting, either, but for a very specific reason. "Alan had a theory, and I think it was a very valid one, that the director is the big daddy, and if the real family comes in, it upsets certain relationships. One night early in our marriage, when Alan was away on location, Francois Truffaut came over to dinner, and I was complaining that Alan wouldn't let me go on the set, and he said, 'Would you like him here watching you type?'"

Still, Hannah occasionally watched Alan at work "when they were shooting outdoors and I could sort of get lost in the crowd," she said.

The Pakulas hosted many parties for their friends, both in their apartment and in East Hampton. Hannah, in the words of Jan Hoffman of the *New York Times*, is "known in New York social circles as a woman of stunning, even formidable presence, accomplished in the art of the gracious dinner party." Their parties included people from all walks of life, few of them from show business, but all of them accomplished. Marilyn Berger, who, with her husband, Don Hewitt, were two of the Pakulas' closest friends, said, "They loved to have people over. Hannah is a *great* hostess." But the dinners and parties Hannah gave after she was married to Alan were not "social-climbing" in any sense. "Alan wasn't interested in 'society,'" Barbara Davis said. "He liked people that were interesting."

The list of the Pakulas' close friends is impressive for its size alone. If it seems that no one can be truly close to more than a few people, it simply didn't apply to the Pakulas. As Larry Turman observed, "Alan had a talent for friendship, which is why so many people say, 'I was so close to Alan.'" Each of the Pakulas' friends, without exception, regarded Alan and Hannah as the closest thing to an ideal couple that they had ever known. Alvin Sargent said, "Hannah was great for Alan, and they were wonderful together. They took very good care of each other, in a beautiful way."

One day, shortly before Alan was killed, he and Hannah were driving from New York to East Hampton when he looked at her and said, "You know, we don't even bother to argue anymore." As Barbara Davis said, "They were an amazing couple."

After Pakula's accidental death in 1998, Keren Saks, their close friend, said, "It was the one marriage that shouldn't have been broken; no marriage should, of course, but they were so particularly dependent and in love with each other. It seemed awfully close to perfect." Marilyn Berger added, "You can never really look into a marriage and see what it's like, but they appeared to be extremely close and very sensitive to each other's moods and feelings." Members of Pakula's family agreed. According to Selma Hirsh, "He was totally fulfilled."

Peter Stone, a close friend, summed up Alan and Hannah's relationship eloquently. "To find a woman of intelligence, talent, charm, grace, and beauty are rare achievements, but to find one and then win her love is nothing short of miraculous. And this miracle came to Alan and blessed his life for many happy and fulfilling years. They were, almost more than any other couple I can think of, a single entity."

"We were enormously happy together," Hannah said in 2002, four years after Alan's death. She added, with a catch in her voice, "It's made [living without him] very much tougher for me, I would have to say, but it was a wonderful relationship."

CHAPTER EIGHT

The Parallax View

"*The Parallax View* attempts to reveal a view of America 'as it is seen through a distorting glass which may point out more intensely certain realities.'"

—ALAN J. PAKULA

I N THE EARLY 1970S, a number of American films dealt with the notion of political conspiracy in the United States. And no wonder, for the assassinations of John F. and Robert Kennedy, Martin Luther King, and Malcolm X were fresh in the minds of audience members. The Vietnam War had caused millions of citizens to distrust its government. In addition, the depravities of the Nixon administration were being systematically exposed by Bob Woodward and Carl Bernstein of the *Washington Post*, further adding to a sense among many citizens in the United States that the country had lost its moral bearings.

Among the best of these films released in 1974 were *Chinatown* and *The Conversation*. But *The Parallax View*, more vividly perhaps than any other film, captured a sense of vague doubt about the ethical integrity of the United States, suggesting that unknown but sinister forces were somehow controlling the national destiny—or, even more alarming, that federal agencies such as the Federal Bureau of Investigation and the Central Intelligence Agency were evolving policies of their own in order to manipulate the American electorate. Elections were still being held, but democracy, the film implied, was only an illusion. *Someone*—or some group of malevolent people— was assassinating the most qualified candidates for the presidency, so that only the choice of those who controlled the Parallax Corporation (or the FBI, or the CIA, or an unidentified entity) could win election.

The Parallax View represented for Alan Pakula "a kind of despair and fear about our society," he said. "In America, most films are about good and evil. But the difference—in the American myth as compared to the European myth—is that in

America, the evil is always known. For example, in the Western, . . . evil is the guy at the other end of the street with the gun during the shoot-out. It may take you awhile to find him, but you find him, and you see him clear and sharp. He's recognizable, and he's out in the open, and you can kill him." However, by the early 1970s, America had "become a world in which heroes didn't necessarily win," Pakula said, "and not only didn't you find the heavies, not only did you not destroy the heavies, you sometimes never even found out who they were. We live in a Kafka-like world where you never find the evil. It permeates the society. . . . We live in a world of secrets, a world in which we can't even find out who is trying to destroy our society." The Parallax View, he said, "was an almost nightmare reflection of that" apprehension, "sort of an American myth based on some things that have happened, some fantasies we may have had of what might have happened, and a lot of fears a lot of us have had."

Pakula said, "The Parallax View was a whole other kind of filmmaking for me." As he said to Warren Beatty, who had agreed to play Joe Frady, the film's protagonist, "If the picture works the audience will trust the person sitting next to them a little less at the end of the film."

In reference to Love and Pain and the Whole Damn Thing, Michael Small said that Pakula wished to stretch his wings by working in all genres. In 1974, he was still stretching. Referring later to The Parallax View, he said, "I wanted to deal with action." Thus the film was conceived almost entirely in terms of an action picture—but it was considerably more than that, for he also "wanted a certain surrealism," and the style of Parallax is grounded in surreality. The surrealism was only a means to an end, however, revealing a view of America "as it is seen through a distorting glass which may point out more intensely certain realities." It was also an opportunity for Pakula "to deal with a bigger canvas, [about] man in his relation to his society." However, the archetypal nature of the characters and the surrealistic style he envisioned would not extend to the actors, for Pakula intended to employ realistic performances within a surrealistic framework that would be created by visual elements.

Warren Beatty, the leading actor, returned to the screen after a three-year absence. Beatty, who was well known for his interest in politics (he had spent much of the previous three years working on George McGovern's campaign for president), denied that the political aspect of The Parallax View had anything to do with his appearance in the film. He believed that "Every film has some politics in it, by commission or omission, whether you're aware of it or not."

Pakula searched for locations in New Mexico, but ultimately shot The Parallax View in Washington state, San Francisco, and Malibu. "I am always looking for surprises," he said. "That's one of the reasons I love to shoot on location."

Lorenzo Semple, Jr. wrote the original screenplay, taken from a novel by Loren Singer, and gave it to Gabriel Katzka, the executive producer of the film. Katzka sent the screenplay to Pakula and to Warren Beatty. Pakula admired the screenplay's "bold sketches and almost expressionist quality" and its concentration on "the mythical American hero and a lot of American myths." Later, David Giler was brought in to work on the screenplay and to further the use of "archetypal people, characters, and places," said Pakula. However, a Screenwriters Guild strike prevented the completion of the script. Pakula wished to delay shooting until he had a complete screenplay. But Warren Beatty had been signed to play the leading role, and his salary was guaranteed whether the film was shot or not. Paramount insisted that Pakula begin shooting in order to take advantage of Beatty's participation. The result was a film "made under hair-raising conditions," Pakula said. "Talk about improvisation. We had a script, and we had a beginning, middle, and end," but, other than a few scripted sequences, that was all. The situation often forced Pakula to write scenes in the morning that were used during the afternoon's shooting.

Pakula worried that he would lose the original conception of the picture in the day-to-day necessity to write and shoot a certain amount of film. He was particularly concerned that his judgment would be impaired, causing him to film whatever seemed to be entertaining, regardless of its relation to the theme. He therefore demanded of himself a strict fidelity to his original conception. This insistence did not permit the inclusion of any romantic scenes, for example, whereas such scenes are a staple of so many adventure and suspense films. Rather, *The Parallax View* never deviates from its focus.

The film begins with a shot of a totem pole, a symbol of ancient wisdom and an object of immense size. Immediately, the camera pans to Seattle's Space Needle. Pakula's notion was to "jump hundreds of years into today, and there's . . . the Space Needle, which was like an American totem to me," he said. The use of the Space Needle at the beginning of the film "made the whole beginning work for me," Pakula said, because he wanted to use classically American images. "Making those observations and throwing them away in the background while I was telling a melodrama and a chase story was a big challenge to me," he added.

Another early image in the film is of a Fourth of July parade, complete with marching bands. "I want to start with Americana," Pakula said. "And I want to start with sunlit Americana, the America we've lost."

After the audience is familiarized with the locale, the political theme is introduced. Senator Carroll, who is considering a run for the presidency, is assassinated by a waiter just as he begins to give a speech at the top of the Space Needle. Among the witnesses to the murder are the Senator's aide, Austin Tucker (William

Daniels), a local television reporter, Lee Carter (Paula Prentiss), and the film's protagonist, Joe Frady.

Joe Frady (Beatty), an intrepid journalist for a small newspaper in the west[23], determines to expose the activities of the Parallax Corporation, which, he discovers, is in the business of hiring assassins. Frady's character is a blank slate throughout. Beyond knowing that he is ambitious to further his journalistic career, the audience knows almost nothing about him. Pakula called him "the totally rootless modern man." Indeed, Frady has no home, living in one cheap motel after another.

He does, however, have a metaphorical home: the newspaper office where he works, and to which he returns several times in the course of the film. The atmosphere of the newspaper office contrasts almost startlingly with every other location. It is comfortable, cluttered, lit in warm colors, home-like; whereas every other interior is cold and forbidding, very modern but devoid of personality. Pakula said the newspaper office represented "much more simple American values, almost nineteenth-century values. It represented a family, a man [Bill Rintels, the newspaper editor, played by Hume Cronyn] who was rooted, a whole American tradition that was dying, an anachronism."

When Pakula referred to Rintels as being "rooted," he meant that in a realistic as well as a symbolic way. In the original script, one of Rintels' scenes was to take place in his house, but Pakula thought better of the idea. As a way of demonstrating that Rintels is the only truly anchored character in the film, he is shown only in his office, which is, for him, a home, whereas Joe Frady is a wanderer with no home at all.

The assassination of Senator Carroll did not occur in Semple's original screenplay. Instead, an assassination was referred to, having taken place in a motorcade in Dallas—an obvious reference to the murder of John F. Kennedy. But Pakula did not wish to mix reality with the fiction he was creating, so he chose to open his film with the assassination of a fabricated candidate. To have done otherwise, he felt, would have been exploitative and "distasteful."

The film cuts to an extreme long shot of a senatorial committee. The chairman solemnly announces that the assassination of Senator Carroll was the work of one man "acting entirely alone. . . . There is no evidence of a wider conspiracy." Throughout his remarks, the camera dollies slowly, slowly forward, finally ending with a shot of three of the senators. Underneath the dialogue is a slow and por-

---

[23]In the original script—or the section of it that was completed—Beatty was going to play a policeman, but he and co-scenarist David Giler lobbied for the character's occupation to be a newspaperman. Quite by chance, then—especially after he followed Parallax View with All the President's Men—Pakula became known as a filmmaker with a fondness for using journalists as the conscience of society, ferreting out secrets that would otherwise remain hidden.

tentous version of the anthem-like musical theme that becomes the film's signature music.

The film then flashes forward. Three years later, Frady dismisses the concerns of Lee Carter, his ex-girlfriend, when she tearfully tells him that she fears for her life, since six of the eighteen witnesses to the Carroll assassination have died in the three years since Carroll was murdered. Only after Lee dies—a suicide, according to an unseen doctor—does Frady begin to realize that a conspiracy to kill all the witnesses to the crime may be in progress.

Frady imagines that he can expose the conspiracy, giving his journalistic career a significant boost in the process. He speaks with a friend, an ex-FBI agent. In keeping with the surreal nature of the visuals, the two ride together in a miniature train in an amusement park while they concoct a new identity for Frady, one that he will not employ until much later in the film.

Searching for Austin Tucker, the former aide to Senator Carroll (who has not been heard from since the senator's assassination and is presumably in hiding), and fearful that he, too, might be assassinated, Frady goes to a small western town. The local sheriff, who has been bribed by the Parallax Corporation, pulls a gun on Frady while tons of water come pouring through an opening in a dam; Frady is thus endangered both by the possibility of being shot and the possibility of drowning. He avoids the first by pulling the sheriff into the onrushing water. We see Frady and the sheriff, dwarfed by the enormous scale of the dam, being swept downstream.

What follows offers an insight into Pakula's filmmaking technique. After an abrupt cut, we see an extreme long shot of a car driving toward the camera. The shot is held for an extraordinarily long time as the car drives ever closer. The audience is given time to wonder about the significance of the car—and why they are watching a car when their wish, surely, is to know what happened in the raging water. Gradually one can identify the automobile as a police car. Then the car pulls up at a house and Joe Frady steps out. Without a word being spoken, the questions that have been on the minds of the filmgoers have been answered. Frady obviously disarmed the sheriff, won the struggle, emerged from the water, and took the sheriff's car. Moments later, when Frady is going through the sheriff's desk drawer (where he finds a questionnaire from the Parallax Corporation), a deputy answers the telephone in another room and says, "Drowned in what? His car's right out front." Thus, another piece of the puzzle fits into place. The sheriff, we now know, is dead.

Obviously, Pakula might have shown Frady's struggle with the sheriff, his escape from the water, and his theft of the car. But by allowing those elements to remain temporarily unexplained, the sense of mystery is heightened. And the audience is made to feel that they, too, are involved in discovering the answers to the mystery, for they have pieced together the seemingly disconnected bits of information to form a coherent narrative. The technique also informs us that in this film the visual elements will tell us as much as, or perhaps more than, the dialogue. As Pakula said, "I like to try to solve certain problems in film through filmic devices rather than literary devices."

Frady drives away, the deputy in hot pursuit. The car chase—which might have been taken from any adventure movie—culminates in Frady's car crashing through a grocery store's window. Frady walks away unhurt, then, concealing himself in the back of a truck, escapes altogether.

Frady realizes that the Parallax Corporation's questionnaire is designed to identify aggressive loners, men who feel excluded from society, men with angry, possibly homicidal tendencies. He takes the test to a psychologist (Anthony Zerbe, in an uncredited performance), who helps Frady supply answers that will conform to the profile the test wishes to elicit. Again, we do not see Frady take the test. In a later scene, an agent for the Parallax Corporation congratulates Frady on his "very interesting test." We, the audience, fill in the missing details.

Frady continues his search for Austin Tucker, Senator Carroll's aide, who, he believes, will be able to tell him about the Parallax Corporation. William Daniels, as Tucker, is an enigmatic figure in the film. He says little, conveying more with body language than with speech; he also has an ambiguous relationship with his bodyguard. "One of the problems in that film that interested me," Pakula said, referring to Austin Tucker, "was sketching in characters that I had no time to explore, sketching them in one scene, and giving a sense of relationships underneath that you never explore but are there."

Tucker, terrified for his life, invites Frady on his boat so that their conversation cannot be heard. But a tremendous explosion in the aft kills Tucker and his bodyguard. We can see Frady jumping off the fore of the boat to safety.

All three men—Tucker, his bodyguard, and Joe Frady—are believed to be dead, and Bill Rintels' newspaper prints that story. Rintels is thus astonished when Frady shows up at the office. Rintels, now convinced that something sinister is occurring, vows to write a story in the next edition calling for the Carroll investigation to be reopened. Frady stops him. "It's much bigger than that," he says. "Whoever's behind this is in the business of recruiting assassins." Rintels is about to put through a telephone call to the FBI or the CIA. Again, Frady intervenes. "Don't do it," he says, suggesting (albeit hesitantly) that those agencies may have covered something up in the investigation—or, worse, that they may be somehow involved in the activities of the Parallax Corporation.

Because the Screenwriters Guild strike kept Pakula so busy writing and rewriting throughout the process of making the film (in addition to the demands normally placed on the producer-director), he was unable to devote as much attention to certain details as his co-workers had hoped. George Jenkins, for one, was concerned that he would be unable to locate a boat to blow up in time for the scene to be filmed unless he could get Pakula to focus on the problem. One early morning, ten days before the boat scene was scheduled to be shot, Jenkins came to Pakula's house and waited for Pakula to come downstairs for breakfast. As the director reached for his orange juice, Jenkins handed him photographs of boats. Although Pakula asked him to wait until he had finished his juice, Jenkins would not be put off, insisting that Pakula make a choice. Irritated at first, Pakula eventually recognized that Jenkins' request was a perfectly reasonable one. He looked at the photographs and made a choice.

Pakula used that anecdote to illustrate the need for a director to work with competent, committed artists, who become an extension of the director. Pakula did not like "yes-men," he said. Rather, he wished to collaborate with craftsmen and -women who were willing to serve the director's vision, but who were themselves artists.

In the scene following Frady's admonition to Bill Rintels not to phone the FBI or CIA, Jack Younger, the representative from Parallax, visits Frady (calling himself "Richard Paley") in his bleak motel room. Younger, a smile playing on his lips, exudes friendliness and solicitude. "If you qualify," he says with a disturbingly soothing quality, "and we think you can, we're prepared to offer you the most lucrative and rewarding work of your life." Frady is seen in silhouette throughout the scene; Younger is seen more clearly, but he, too, is often hidden by shadows.

Frady then takes another, more rigorous test, an elaborate visual psychological examination to see if he is sufficiently aggressive and antisocial to match the Parallax Corporation's definition of a potential assassin. The scene had not originally been intended for the film and was developed entirely in post-production. The original script simply indicated that Joe Frady would be given a test. But the psychological examination ultimately became the movie's centerpiece. Originally, Pakula shot a sequence in which Frady had an interview directly with a Parallax representative, but the director was not satisfied with the result. He turned to his wife's nephew, Jon Boorstin, who served as Pakula's assistant on the movie. Pakula asked Boorstin to collect photographs for him—images that might elicit emotional responses of various kinds. Eventually, the images were woven into a five-minute montage in which shots of George Washington and Abraham Lincoln were intercut with shots of lynchings, Hitler, Mao, the Ku Klux Klan, images of the Vietnam War, a pair of lovers, a comic-book hero, Jack Ruby shooting Lee Harvey Oswald, views of fathers and mothers, and a hundred other images. Pakula "worked on that for at least four months," he said. He played "endlessly" with the photographs, trying them in different order.

Ultimately, he said, the sequence "starts out with love—and that fascinated me, that you come and they test for hostility, and to find a gunman or a killer's personality, the first word is Love—and all these happy, bourgeois images, all the wonderful, ideal fathers we've been told we're supposed to have, and country, and motherhood, and everything is all as it should be. And then father becomes a Depression figure, an 'Okie' who's been hurt by society, who's worked hard and has obviously been destroyed in some way. And Mother becomes a kind of broken figure." Eventually we see a man in a prison cell, "the impotent, passive person cut off from the world. And people who are attracted to that kind of violence, that kind of assassination fantasy, very often there's a great fear of impotence, a great fear of passivity, a great fear of being destroyed by the world."

The test is intended to demonstrate that "You can be destroyed by society," Pakula said, "you can be left out, you can give in to your sense of impotence." At first, members of the audience may think that the test is logical and precise, but the images spin out of control. "Suddenly you look at swastikas, suddenly there's George Washington with a swastika at a Nazi Party rally, and there's Kennedy. And it whips you out of the unfairness of this world where everybody has everything, steak and meat and gold and fame and sex and love—and why have I been left out? But [the Parallax Corporation suggests] you can be Superman and break out and destroy and make the world well again by destroying."

In addition, "there's a whole kind of Oedipal thing," Pakula added, "where there's a picture of mother, and suddenly there's a picture of a boy who looks like he's opening his trousers. It's sort of like he's exposing himself to his mother. And using all the love images. And then suddenly the castrating father figure, . . . running after the little boy to destroy him, to punish him. And then you get the . . . confusion of fathers and authority, and authority being father, and if you kill authority, you kill father. And sexual confusion, and the confusion of sex and violence. You go from the couple making love happily—and it winds up in shooting."

Ultimately the test is designed to discover whether the candidate finds the progression of images—from fantasy to brutality and nightmare—stimulating. However, no indication is given how Joe Frady scored on the test. That omission is perhaps a flaw in the film. Pakula regretted the absence of an explanation ("I should have had it in," he said), but nevertheless believed that "Parallax depended on a certain kind of hypnosis to work. And if you stop and explain to such an extent that you break the hypnotic rhythm of the film, you [may] make it more believable on the intellectual level, [but] the thing that may pull that audience emotionally can fall apart."

Of all the scenes in the film, Pakula was proudest of the prolonged psychological examination, "designed to whip you into a kind of frenzy of rage if you are one of the people who feels left out of society, if you are one of the ones who is unwanted, one of the unsuccessful." After filming the examination sequence, Pakula slotted it into the film.

Working on a tight deadline, Michael Small then composed and recorded music for the sequence in a few days. As he recalls, "I don't think Alan even heard it. It was just one of these magical events." Only if a director has complete faith in the taste and skill of his composer is this possible. In any case, Pakula was captivated by the result. "He started out with that wonderfully simple little folk melody," Pakula said, "and then it's all very simple Americana and terribly innocent. And then it just builds into this kind of acid-rock hysteria."

Small considered his score for *Parallax View* to be his best, and not only for his contribution to the examination scene. After listening to Pakula describe the sort of film he wished to make, Small thought about various possibilities for a few days, then called and said, "Alan, I've got the idea for the score: an anthem." Pakula responded immediately, "Wow, what an idea." Small felt that the repetition of the anthem-like music worked so effectively because it was "both terrifying and very attractive. I've always been attracted by patriotic anthems—and scared by them. You not only have 'The Star-Spangled Banner,' but you have 'Deutschland Uber Alles.' The skewered patriotic anthem worked not only as underscore, but became signature for the overall point of view of the story."

Small also employs music of a different sort. As his score did so successfully for *Klute*, his music at particular, appropriate moments in *The Parallax View*—though very different in melody and instrumentation from the *Klute* music (there is no vocal line, for example)—immediately conveys a sense of mystery and danger.

Joe Frady is told to proceed to the Parallax offices. He follows a suspicious-looking man to an airport, where the man's luggage is put aboard a plane. Frady boards the plane and places a note ("There is a bomb on this plane") inside a stack of napkins on a flight attendant's cart. Agonizing moments go by—again, Pakula is unafraid to let his camera linger over a shot, thereby building tension—until, at last, the attendant sees the note, informs the pilot, and the plane returns to the airport. As Frady is seen walking toward the terminal, the airplane is heard (not seen) to explode. Whether the other passengers and the crew managed to escape is left to the imagination of the viewer.

The actions Frady has performed to this point cannot help but seem improbable, the actions of a movie superhero. In the course of the film, he has won a savage barroom brawl with a deputy sheriff without having suffered as much as a scratch on his face; he has threaded his stolen car through and around traffic, crashing the car through the window of a grocery store, and emerged unscathed, running away to safety; he has escaped a boat, blown to pieces by an enormous explosion, although the others on the boat are killed; he has saved himself, and perhaps a planeload of passengers, deplaning seconds before the airplane explodes. He seems to be John Wayne and Superman rolled into one. But the creation of this superhero is, as we shall discover, only another illusion.

In another scene played in near-darkness, Jack Younger, the man from Parallax, revisits Frady. Younger, maintaining a smile on his face, interrogates Frady about his identity as Richard Paley, which, he says, Parallax now knows to be false. Frady reverts to the identity created for him by the ex-FBI man. Throughout the scene, Walter McGinn's performance as Jack Younger is exceptional. He plays Younger almost in a seductive way, as if he were attracted to Frady and wished to protect him—a dimension that was not in the script, but that McGinn and Pakula discussed extensively.

McGinn's performance exemplified a trait Pakula tried to achieve with all his actors playing major roles: hinting at psychological qualities the script itself did not suggest the character would possess. Pakula approvingly quoted Laurence Olivier's dictum that actors should always withhold something from the audience, thus projecting a sense of mystery.

Bill Rintels, alone in his office, plays a tape of Frady's conversation with Younger—thereby informing us that Frady has surreptitiously taped the exchange. A delivery man, whom we recognize as the "waiter" who assassinated Senator Carroll at the beginning of the film, brings Rintels a cup of coffee. The editor takes a sip—and in the next shot he is leaning backwards, his eyes wide open, dead.

In a hotel's convention center another presidential candidate is assassinated. Originally, the scene was to be staged as a fundraising rally with an enormous crowd. But a series of accidents altered the nature of the scene. Gordon Willis, production designer George Jenkins, and Pakula went to the convention center location, and as Pakula tells it, "it was empty, and they were putting up all these tables, these dining room tables, which looked totally ludicrous for a banquet, an absurd place to be eating. And there was nobody in it except for these lonely waiters setting up these tables. It was terrific with nobody in it. There was something dreamlike about those tables. And [the waiters] were using these little golf carts . . . to go from table to table with their dishes and knives and forks." The scouting expedition led Pakula to revise the originally planned sequence.

In the new version, "The candidate comes in in the golf cart," he said. "It's a rehearsal. It's a story of manipulation. It becomes manipulation on top of manipulation. We'll get the kids in. We'll get card tricks going. [In the scene, a large group of teenagers manipulates flashcards of Washington and Jefferson ("the great icons of America," as Pakula called them), culminating with a collage representing George Hammond, the candidate.] We'll show them being rehearsed. We'll show how they're rehearsed to applaud [for George Hammond]. We'll show innocence being manipulated for what's supposed to be spontaneous.'"

Pakula told George Jenkins to "get red-white-and-blue tablecloths so that this man gets caught in the middle of a flag." The flag motif is tied inextricably to the theme of the film. As Pakula phrased it, as *The Parallax View* progresses, "We have the sense that the safe, open society we supposedly live in is full of dark unknowns that could be threatening us. . . and that's why at the end of it we used all those cheerful, open, American images—red-white-and-blue tablecloths and banners, all those little cheerleaders putting up their little Presidential faces—a vision we've all grown up with about America, underneath which is the mysterious unknown."

When Hammond, the candidate, is seen entering the convention center in a golf cart, he does so by driving through a rectangle of light surrounded by blackness—an extreme example of Pakula's and Willis's fondness for darkness in order to convey a sense of mystery and ominousness.

The scene in which Hammond is assassinated, followed by his golf cart plowing into tables (the momentum forcing tables into other tables) is all seen in a long shot, from a high angle. One would normally expect loud crowd noises—a large group of teenagers and adults have just witnessed a murder—but there is no noise whatever. Pakula's intention to create a surrealistic atmosphere is fully realized in this peculiar, eerie sequence.

Frady, who has been portrayed to this point as indestructible, is finally revealed to be a fragile human being. When, having realized that he is being set up by Parallax as the man who killed George Hammond—the fall guy—he attempts to run the length of the catwalk to an open door. An assassin, completely in shadow (the outline could be that of the young tuba player in the band, or perhaps Jack Younger), shoots and kills Frady before he can reach the door. Interestingly, we do not see the assassin move into place; he simply, inexplicably appears—another surrealistic touch.

Frady's death would be shocking in any event (who expects the protagonist, especially if he's played by Warren Beatty, to die before he can expose the conspiracy?), but is so particularly *because* of the many feats of derring-do we have seen him perform with such aplomb throughout the picture. Pakula said that the film "takes a lot of those American myths, all the most 'movie' versions of the indestructible hero figure, carried almost to the point of kitsch, and says 'this is what has happened to them.' The American hero character who can do anything, who can survive anything and expose the truth in the end, has been destroyed. We can't believe in him anymore."

The final sequence of the film takes place, once again, in a congressional hearing room. This time, the camera begins with a relatively tight shot and gradually pulls back farther and farther until the senators are mere specks on the screen. They have reached the conclusion, they say, that Joe Frady was a madman, "obsessed with the Carroll assassination, and in his confused and distorted mind seems to have imagined that Hammond was responsible for the senator's death." Frady, acting alone, was guilty, they conclude, of the assassination of George Hammond. The spokesman emphasizes, "There is no evidence of a conspiracy." Then, in the final surrealistic touch of the film—the senators vanish. They simply pop off the screen.[24]

Only then, as the credits begin to appear, does the final music begin. "All you hear is this John Philip Sousa-like march," Pakula said, "and we dubbed it so it didn't sound to you like it was marching across the screen. And you hear cheering crowds along with this cheerful music. But you know it's the sound of evil."

The film ends with Joe Frady dead, a victim of the very conspiracy he had hoped to expose, Bill Rintels dead, Lee Carter dead, Austin Tucker dead, the candidates dead, Congress compromised—and, it is suggested, the Parallax Corporation will continue to control the destiny of the country. One leaves the film "with the third act hanging in your hand," as Pakula said. "That was deliberate."

Pakula's first concept, he said, "was to do *Parallax* in a kind of poster style, like a series of poster images. . . . It was American baroque. That was one of my first images."[25] That explains his use of the red-white-and-blue motif at the end, and his use of the Space Needle at the beginning. As he said, "That's the old Hitchcock thing. If you're doing a picture about Switzerland, use cuckoo clocks and chocolate. In America I used golf carts and kids making faces out of cards and the Space Needle."

Some of the elements of the film—especially Joe Frady's exploits—may strike the viewer as having been borrowed from previous adventure films, but, Pakula said, "I tried to do a lot of mythic American things in that picture: barroom fights, and the whole idea of American macho." The fight sequence—and the subsequent car chase— made violence appear to be harmless, even fun. "At the end," however, as Pakula said, "violence is not fun. It's cold and it's terrifying and it's impersonal."

Much of the success of the film can be attributed to the work of Gordon Willis. The dark and brooding qualities he brought to *Klute* are taken several steps farther in *The Parallax View*. Many scenes are so ominously dark that one can barely make out the figures on the screen. Some scenes are shot entirely in silhouette. Pakula said that

---

[24]Someone at Paramount altered the ending after the film was released. In the altered version, the senators stand up and walk off the platform. Both Pakula's version and Paramount's version still exist.

[25]Pakula credited Gordon Willis with never forgetting the director's initial conception. "He never forgot that," Pakula said. "Sometimes, right in the middle of a scene, he would say that what I wanted him to do was a violation of what I wanted the [baroque, poster-ish] style of the film to be. Gordon always operates within a conception of the film."

the film's visual design was intended to reflect "a child's fear of darkness, night fears, fears in some way of being punished, that the unknown is indeed threatening, that there is something out there that you can't see that could destroy you."

Another concept of the director and the cinematographer was to "play with scale" in the film, Pakula said, "in the sense of people being manipulated, being very small figures in a large scale." Again and again—in the waters spilling through the dam, in the convention center—we see the dwarfed figures about whom Pakula spoke.

For a film without a shooting script, The Parallax View is remarkably coherent and consistent. "There were," Pakula conceded, "a few major changes along the way that I wanted to make and never had a chance." Some changes were implemented, however. The role of Lee Carter, Joe Frady's former lover, was written to be played by "a tough kind of older woman, older than Warren, wisecracking, witty, sardonic, a lady like Lauren Bacall," according to Pakula. However, when Paula Prentiss, a much younger woman, auditioned for Pakula, "looking wide-eyed and vulnerable," he reconceptualized the character as a "girl who's crashed once too often, who was in a constant panic." The results fully justified the change, he felt: "It made her death more moving."

Similarly, the role of Jack Younger, the man who recruits Frady for the Parallax Corporation, was written for "the classic ex-FBI man," Pakula said, describing him as "six foot two, easy with a gun in his jacket holster, that classic kind of man." But Pakula saw a stage production of That Championship Season, in which Walter McGinn played the role of a passive, mousy, self-hating alcoholic. Pakula began thinking about the possibility of using McGinn as Jack Younger. "You expect, when Parallax comes, to get some kind of Superman figure, and what you get is this little church mouse man with some kind of strange emotional need to pull these people out. And I changed the whole part for Walter, a little . . . man with great wide eyes," who rewarded Pakula by giving perhaps the most accomplished performance in the film. (If most filmgoers are unaware of Walter McGinn, it is because he died in 1977 at the age of forty-one.)[26]

As an example of the day-by-day changes that were made to the script, Hume Cronyn called Pakula several days before he was to begin his first scene. "It's Friday, and I work on Monday," Cronyn said. "In the script I read, I play a police chief, and you told me a couple of weeks ago when I checked in on the phone that I was going to be a newspaper editor, and I just wanted to know if you'd settled on which of them I'm going to be. I'm shooting on Monday."

---

[26]Some of the actors, Pakula confessed, were cast simply on the basis of their look. "That does the work for you. It's a small enough part, and you just want to go for an image." Such a role was that of Senator Carroll's wife, who appeared only at the beginning of the film. Pakula wanted a "wholesome" look, and used Bettie Johnson, the same actress who had played Gruneman's wife in Klute.

Pakula answered that Cronyn would be playing an editor. "Gee," Cronyn said, "it would be nice to see some pages." Pakula suggested to the actor, "You come to my house on Sunday," and they would discuss the problem of the unscripted scenes. "You know," Cronyn said, "I hope you don't think because I've had all this experience that I like to improvise or that I'm good at it. I'm terrible at things like that."

When Cronyn arrived at Pakula's house, he found Warren Beatty and the script supervisor there as well. Pakula led a discussion about the first scene between Cronyn's character, Bill Rintels, and Joe Frady. After agreeing on what Pakula called "the line of the scene"—the way in which the scene moved from point A to point B to point C—the discussion led to an improvisation. As Pakula told it, "My wife was in the kitchen and fifteen minutes or so after we talked, this rather nervous actor, Mr. Cronyn, came to the kitchen saying, 'By the way, Mrs. Pakula, do you have some Scotch Tape and some scissors and a pencil and some paper?'" Then Pakula, the actors, and the script supervisor wrote the dialogue for the scenes they had been improvising.

When the actor Jim Davis came to read for the role of Hammond, the presidential candidate who is killed at the end of the film, Pakula said, "Jim, there's nothing to read, you know? I'm making up the cockamamie speech which deliberately is full of generalities." Pakula saw something in Davis that he thought would be valuable for the role. "He had something in his character; he was the athlete. I wanted a contrast to the first man who's assassinated, who's a kind of urban liberal, a kind of John Lindsay-ish kind of figure. I wanted more of a kind of, without saying he's a conservative, but a certain kind of Texas or country figure. Well, there was Jim . . . with his white hair and a strong athlete's body. His passion is playing golf, so we [inserted] a talk [in the film] about his golf game while the tape [of his voice giving a speech] was going on. [Because] it was a rehearsal I could then use the whole bizarre thing of the tape recording of the man's voice going on, still talking these ridiculous truisms, mouthing these things as [Hammond's corpse is riding] in that golf cart and hitting those tables."

Whereas intricate work with the actors took precedence in the filming of *The Sterile Cuckoo* and lighting the sets took what seemed to the performers to be an inordinate amount of time in *Klute*, Pakula struck a balance in the filming of *The Parallax View*. "There are sequences where what is best for the actors will come before the visual effects of the film," he said. "There are other sequences where what is best for the visual effect of the film, the camera, will come before what is best for the actors. It all depends upon what values seem most important in terms of the storytelling. I don't believe in ironclad rules. I don't like to move actors around like puppets for the camera, nor do I like to come in and pretend that we're on the stage and that adjustments should not be made for visual storytelling. It all depends on the scene and the specific problems."

While shooting the film, which began in the spring of 1973, Pakula also utilized flexibility in his approach, as the following quotation testifies:

> With all the rehearsal, we come on the set and we start doing a scene. . . . I have a conception before [the rehearsal begins] about what I want. But first you see what [the actors] do, what is coming out of them. Now, one of three things happens: Either they do something you don't think is right, and you just say, "A-ha, they're making that same mistake over and over again," and . . . that makes me realize what their problem is. Or, two, they do what you wanted them to do—it was your idea [to begin with, but] they do it better, because it comes out of them. And three, they may come up with something you never would have thought of. Well, if they're well-cast, if they're in their parts, their unconscious is working like gangbusters, hopefully.

The Parallax View, in which he was working essentially without a script, carried his flexible approach to a new level. Everything was subject to last-minute changes. But, remarkably, for a film that had to be largely improvised, the picture never got behind schedule. Although the experience of working without a complete script was often harrowing, Pakula said, "It's a film I'm very glad I made and it's a film I learned a great deal from."

Soon after The Parallax View was released, the writer William Goldman met Warren Beatty and said that he would soon be working with Pakula on All the President's Men. Goldman later observed, "Novelists are always using the phrase, 'enigmatic smile.' It's a staple. In all my life, I have only seen one such enigmatic smile. It came on Beatty's face and he said this: 'Just make sure you've got it before you go on the floor.'" The meaning of Beatty's remark is as enigmatic as was his smile. Did he mean that Pakula was prone to making last-minute changes? That would hardly be surprising in a film that was being written as the shooting went along. Did he mean it as a criticism, suggesting that Pakula didn't know what he wanted from his actors? It would be satisfying to be able to offer an explanation of Beatty's remark, but, since he failed to respond to repeated requests for an interview, one can only guess at his meaning.

Editing the film took even more of Pakula's time and energy than usual. "I work very closely with the editor," he said. "I am obsessed with that, and in Parallax View more so than before." The post-production process began nearly a year before the film was distributed, suggesting that Paramount Pictures might have been nervous about the effect on the audience of the movie's explosive and disturbing political statement and surrealistic treatment.

Like Pakula's previous films, *The Parallax View* was greeted with generally condescending reviews. Vincent Canby wrote in the *New York Times* that the picture "is the sort of suspense melodrama that travels a horizontal course from beginning to end. The thrills don't mount as the film goes on. They don't even accumulate. Once they are experienced, they dissolve so thoroughly that by the end you're likely to feel as cheated as I did. The movie . . . never rewards the attention we give it with anything more substantial than a few minor shocks." Canby added, "to treat a political assassination merely as a subject for fun is frivolous." In a subsequent article, he called the film an "essentially cheap melodrama."

Much of his disdain for the film seems to be based on Warren Beatty's apparent invincibility. He points to Beatty's escape from the roaring waters coming through the spillway and comments, "Since the man is Warren Beatty . . . you know he can't be fatally clobbered." Indeed, Joe Frady survives a series of incredible threats, but, one might ask, isn't that the point? Frady seems to be a conventional action hero, almost a superhero, so that when he is gunned down at the end of the film, the attack is shocking, totally unanticipated, and provides the ultimate evidence of the Parallax Corporation's control.

Stephen Holden, in an article entitled "Movies That Reflect Our Obsession with Conspiracy and Assassination," referred to *The Parallax View* as "probably the most mindless and irresponsible of the lot." He called the plot "full of holes," but a second viewing would have shown him that, although complex, the plotting is remarkably tight. Every event, every reference can be explained by another event (sometimes seen but not heard; sometimes heard but not seen) or reference elsewhere in the film.

Holden further argued that "the interesting point is that a large public is willing to buy such a bleak paranoid vision. Today's mass audience wants to believe in omnipotent, omniscient, indestructible conspiracies." He paraphrased renowned author and historian Henry Steele Commager's contention that people were attracted to conspiracy theories because, if John and Robert Kennedy and Martin Luther King had been assassinated by deranged individuals, "life might be fundamentally senseless, chaotic, purposeless—and such a possibility was too disturbing for many Americans to contemplate."

Indeed, Alan Pakula did not accept the Warren Commission's contention that Lee Harvey Oswald acted alone when he murdered John F. Kennedy. He read a number of books suggesting a conspiracy behind the assassination, and undoubtedly Pakula's attraction to such theories accounts, at least in part, for his decision to make *The Parallax View*.

Holden contended that "*The Parallax View* is too cowardly to make direct accutions." He went on to say, "In keeping the conspirators and the candidates so shadowy, Pakula may have hoped to broaden the movie's appeal by allowing every member of the audience to nominate his own favorite demon as the evil genius behind the assassinations. If you fear the American Nazi Party or the American Communist Party, the oil industry or the C.I.A., Henry Kissinger or Ralph Nader, any or all of them might be involved in the mysterious Parallax Corporation. This film exemplifies the empty-headed, fence-straddling approach to controversial issues that has made Hollywood's political movies such a joke." Again, however, the critic misses the chilling point, which is that whoever is behind the Parallax Corporation is assassinating whomever it wishes to eliminate, regardless of the individual's ideological position. How much simpler it would be if only liberals—or only conservatives—were under attack. They could simply switch their ideological positions to escape danger. But if *everyone* is a political target, for reasons no one can understand, then the situation is far more frightening simply *because* the killings are so random and inexplicable.

In 2002, Pakula's stepdaughter Anna Boorstin lamented the often-negative reviews American critics bestowed on Pakula's work. "He was never well-reviewed in American papers," she said. "He was well-reviewed by the French, he was well-reviewed by the British. And even when American critics liked his films, the reviews tended to be more about the actors or the plot. He was never given credit for the fact that his films were extremely interesting." And, she continued, the contrast between the worldwide respect given to his films on the one hand, and the disdain of so many American critics on the other was "most disturbing" to her stepfather.[27]

However, if the initial reviews were negative, later notices were increasingly enthusiastic. As early as 1976, only two years after the film was released, Richard T. Jameson cited "the astonishing density of performance [Pakula] elicits from the merest bit-player [yielding] the kind of behavioral richness associated with the ensemble professionalism of a bygone generation of character actors," using William Daniels' performance as an example. Jameson added, "even though *The Parallax View* failed to dent the box office, every audience I saw it with was riveted to the screen," and said he found "that film to be Pakula's most exciting [and] most adventurous."

Stephen Pizzello, in an *American Cinematographer* article dealing with cinematic paranoia, said, "Few motion pictures have captured this gnawing sense of suspi-

---

[27]*Pakula himself reflected on* The Parallax View *nearly thirty years after it was made. He lamented the fact that some critics failed to understand the abstract nature of the film, and reviewed it in literal terms. "It's interesting," he said on another occasion, that a "film magazine had an article about pictures that misuse patriotic symbols and make fun of them. That's not what I was doing at all, but they mentioned* The Parallax View *in the article. It was meant to be a cautionary tale and I was saying, beware, anybody can hide behind these symbols. Symbols mean nothing; it's what they stand for."*

cion better than *The Parallax View*." In the London journal *Independent on Sunday*, David Thomson wrote that the film "does not end positively, and it lacks a likeable central character. But that's why *Parallax* gets better with the passing years. For the ambivalence of its hero is almost the most mysterious thing in the picture. . . . [T]he aloof, attractive yet withdrawn Mr. Beatty is brilliant casting, and he shows diverse moods that are very effective in this story. Notice, too, how subtly *Parallax* projects and betrays the component parts of the American dream."

Ian Johns of the *Times* of London called the film "one of the best political thrillers of the Seventies, . . . a calling card for Seventies paranoid, anti-government sentiment that was the hallmark of a generation." He added that, in contrast to later films like *Conspiracy Theory*, one should watch *The Parallax View* "to see that it's not just a heap of meaningless hokum. It can have weight, menace and far-reaching implications, and not need an insultingly tacked-on happy ending."

In its 1998 obituary of Pakula, the *London Daily Telegraph* called *The Parallax View* "perhaps his best film, [provoking] unease through image. The elliptical photography of buildings and vast hallways, and the nervous views of distant conversations convincingly suggest that the smile on the face of American democracy might be a mere seduction."

When the film was released in 1974, a series of coincidences harmed its chances for commercial success. Warren Beatty was producing and acting in *Shampoo*, and was thus unavailable to help promote *The Parallax View*. Bob Evans, the head of Paramount, had produced *Chinatown* (which was released at the same time as *Parallax View*), and, for obvious and understandable reasons, was more intent on promoting his film than Pakula's. Ultimately, however, Pakula did not blame the studio for the commercial failure of *The Parallax View*: he admitted that a film in which an American hero is killed by an unknown assassin is unlikely to attract a wide audience in the United States. But Pakula insisted that the way the film ended was not only appropriate, but that any other ending would have been a "total compromise." He felt so passionately about it that he was willing to endure the public's temporary indifference—although he felt a great deal better years later when *The Parallax View* became far more widely accepted.

The Parallax View, in common with *Klute* (and with *All the President's Men*, a film on which Pakula would soon begin working), portrays a frightening world in which ominous shadows conceal frightening possibilities. The three films have been grouped together, earning Pakula the reputation as the "master of paranoia," and, indeed, if "paranoia" is defined as Pakula intended it—as "an excessive fear of the unknown, the unseen"—the term applies to all of them. It is no wonder that they have often been referred to as "the paranoia trilogy."

CHAPTER NINE

Stepchildren

"How lucky we all were to count ourselves among Alan's students, those who were touched, not only by his art but by his humanity, those who felt firsthand his decency and his honor, those who warmed themselves by the fire of his heart. . . . For this man, who fathered no children of his own, was father to all who turned to him and to any who needed him. He had the habits and the markings of a patriarch."

—BOB BOORSTIN

FABLES OFTEN TELL OF WICKED STEPPARENTS, seldom loving and supportive ones. But Alan Pakula decisively broke with that stereotype. All of his stepchildren felt remarkably close to him. They also speak of being thoroughly nurtured and supported by Pakula.

Anna Boorstin said of her relationship with Pakula as she was growing up: "It was loving, absolutely loving. I couldn't have asked for a better stepfather. I couldn't have asked for a better father." I asked her to expand upon her response. "I would tell him things I would never tell my mom," she explained, "because she's a worrier, and Alan was not a worrier." When she was still an adolescent, she imagined that "the reason my dad died was clearly so that we could all be put back together by this wonderful man. I mean, you know, we argued, he irritated me sometimes—but he was the greatest. All my friends were jealous of my stepfather because they liked him. I know this sounds almost like sitcom material," she added, "but it's true."

When Louis Boorstin was asked if he recalled how he felt when his mother remarried, he responded, "We all sensed how happy she was being with Alan, and that made their marriage and the changes that [that] brought to our household seem natural and appropriate. Alan was a remarkably sensitive man, and he used that sensitivity to make sure that the transition went well. I can't imagine anyone handling it better. He never pushed too hard, yet he was always there if we need-ed him, and he went out of his way to make things easy for us. Alan's entry into our home brought very little conflict and lots of love, joy, humor, and stability; pretty hard to argue with that."

"From the outset," Louis went on, "Alan made it clear that he did not want to replace our father. There was no talk of adopting us, then or any time later." But Pakula quickly became a father figure for the children, listening sympathetically to their problems, providing help when he could. "What guidance he provided in those early years came mostly at the dinner table," Louis remembers, "via the 'theme of the week,' or, for longer-running matters, the 'theme of the month.' Alan chose a theme when he saw something in our behavior that needed some adjustment, ranging from silly affectations to intolerant attitudes. He would then have a go at correcting it by making us laugh at ourselves."

The children were not raised in any religion. Bob Boorstin says, "My mother and I had a very, very healthy skepticism about organized religion," as did Anna and Louis. Bob recalls that Alan, who had been bar mitzvahed when he was thir-teen, "had intensely historical feelings of being a Jew, to the point where com-ments about it, references to it, would be a regular part of his discussions about history or about current events. He didn't go around talking about being a Jew all the time. His interest in it came from what history taught us about tolerance and oppression and survival. But it was not a weekly practicing Jewish identity."

Hannah elaborated, "Alan was brought up in a traditional conservative Jewish home, loved his Jewish heritage, and identified strongly with it. He enjoyed cer-tain rituals," such as the High Holidays, "which he attended." On the other hand, Hannah was raised in a reformed Jewish home, and, although she attended Sunday school as a child, rarely went to temple as an adult. She and Alan, both of whom "regarded faith as a personal matter" (in Hannah's words), rarely spoke about their religious beliefs.

Alan's ethical system may or may not have been based upon Judaism, but his actions were those of a man who was compassionate, eager to help whenever any-one he loved needed assistance, and who possessed a strong moral compass. Bob Boorstin remembered an incident that exemplifies all those characteristics:

When I was sixteen I went to prep school, and it was not an easy experience for me. I was four feet ten when I was sixteen years old—I was four eleven when I went to college—and Alan was worried about me going off to prep school, concerned about my size and being with other guys the same age. And the first months were really tough for me. I got into a fight, I was unhappy, and so on. At one point I talked to Alan on the phone—and the next day, out of nowhere, he showed up.

He flew from Los Angeles to Hartford, Connecticut, and took me out to dinner to talk. Now, I don't know, but I've never heard of anybody with a stepparent like that. He had that unerring sense of knowing when he was needed.

Bob credits Pakula with having literally saved his life on many occasions. "The seminal event in my life," he said,

was my diagnosis with mental illness. I was diagnosed with manic depression in 1987. I had a manic episode and I was hospitalized for a month, and again in '88. And one of the things that drew Alan to me and me to Alan was his unerring support and understanding of that illness. Our relationship was made closer by my illness. He and my mother supplied the support for me. She worried about me, worried that I'd be miserable all of my life, and she had good reason to worry because I would call them at six in the morning and tell them, basically, that I was on the verge of suicide and there was nothing they could do about it. And he saved me—not physically, but mentally—many times. He had this ability to give advice and to provide perspective that I got from no one else in my life, and it's the thing I miss most. He was my stepfather and he was my best friend.

After seeing a psychiatrist who prescribed effective medication, Boorstin's illness was—and remains—under control. Later, he began to speak on behalf of the mentally ill. "The last time I saw Alan before he died," Boorstin said, "was when I gave a speech on mental illness. I was given an award by a group in New York for being a mental health advocate, and I invited Alan and my mother. It was the only time I acknowledged, to their face, my debt to them. Because I said that the most important thing that someone with mental illness can have is a supportive family, which I truly believe. I'm happy he heard that before he died, because I wouldn't be here if it wasn't for him. No question about it."

Although Pakula lived in New York after he and Hannah were married, far from Chris and Patty Murray, Hope Lange's children (who were brought up in Los Angeles), he remained as devoted to them as when they had all lived together. "Alan never stopped treating my sister and me with care and concern," Chris said. "He was a perfect parent. He was always interested in our bizarre pursuits. And a constant source of comfort and encouragement. Even when he started his new life with Hannah, he made Patricia and me feel like an integral part of his new family."

Chris now works as an actor in Los Angeles. Patricia, who acted for fifteen years, is now a photographer, designer, and horse trainer. Anna Boorstin, after graduating from Yale, moved to California, where she worked as a sound editor before becoming a full-time mother. Louis also attended Yale and, after a few years on Wall Street, went on to get an MBA from Stanford. But he has taken an unusual career path, focusing on the financing of ventures in developing countries, and he now leads a team at the World Bank Group that funds innovative environmental projects in the private sector. Bob is a Harvard graduate who worked as a reporter for the *New York Times* before going into politics and government. He went on to Washington after the 1992 Presidential campaign, working at the White House as Bill Clinton's national security speechwriter and later in the State and Treasury Departments. Today he works at a progressive think tank.

Pakula never had children of his own. After Hannah miscarried the baby she and Alan had conceived, the couple was devastated (Pakula wept when he told his friend, Lyle Kessler, about the miscarriage), but comforted by the other children in their lives: Anna, Bob, and Louis, all of whom were then in college—as well as Chris and Patricia Murray. Nevertheless, as Pakula's niece, Debby Maisel, observed, his extended family was saddened "that Alan didn't have children of his own, because he was such a very loving, giving person." Undoubtedly true, but, as Louis Boorstin said, "For a man who had no natural children of his own, Alan was father to many"—himself, his brother and sister—"all of our spouses, two stepchildren from his previous marriage, and many others of our generation whom he mentored on the job. I'd like to think that there are pieces of Alan embedded in all of us."

Pakula himself used to joke that he preferred being a stepfather to being a father, because, as Bob Boorstin explained, "it was easier that way. Because every time one of us screwed up, it wasn't his genes talking." Perhaps, however, his joke concealed the pain he felt after Hannah suffered her miscarriage.

Pakula's death in 1998 left all his stepchildren distraught. Each of them echoed Bob's sentiment: "I still feel that vacuum in my life every day."

Bob and Louis Boorstin and Chris Murray expressed another reaction in the aftermath of Pakula's death. Each of them said they felt most sorry for their own children, who would grow up without knowing the man who would have been a wise, sympathetic, loving grandfather. There can be little doubt that Pakula would have reveled in his grandchildren, for he had a special affinity for young people. As Boaty Boatwright said, "He was interested in everybody's children, and at parties, he always spent as much genuine time talking to the kids as to the adults."

In the case of Anna's children, Pakula did have the opportunity to know them before he died, and, Anna said, "He really hung out with my oldest son. He showed him movies and made him feel very special. He loved kids."

CHAPTER TEN

All the President's Men I:

Pre-Production

"I thought [Alan Pakula, as director of <u>All the President's Men</u>] and I [as producer] would balance out well together, because I think we both had a shared intelligence. My tendency, knowing about the traps in the film, was to go for the visceral and I knew he would go for the psychological, and that's exactly what happened. Our relationship was nothing but terrific."

—ROBERT REDFORD

AMERICAN FILM CRITICS MAY HAVE BEEN DIVIDED in their responses to *Klute* and *The Parallax View*, but their praise for Pakula's 1976 movie, *All the President's Men*, was nearly unanimous. And the public response was equally enthusiastic, despite many factors that appeared to militate against success. It dealt with a political theme, for example, normally not an appealing topic for a Hollywood movie. The film was based on recent historical events (the Watergate scandal that led to Richard Nixon's resignation in 1974), so everyone in the audience knew how the picture would end. It focused on investigative journalists attempting to put together a coherent story based on interviews—which threatened to turn the film into a series of marginally cinematic episodes featuring "talking heads." It attempted to dramatize the work of writers, which, historically, has proven to be notoriously difficult, both on film and on the stage. Finally, film studios, fearing that the subject matter and probable treatment would fail to draw large audiences (as well as alienate their conservative constituency), were reluctant to finance the film.

Perhaps the greatest obstacle to the making of *All the President's Men* was the public's indifference to the Watergate scandals. In 1972, a month before Richard Nixon was re-elected president, a Gallup Poll found that forty-eight percent of adult Americans had never heard of the incidents known collectively as "Watergate." And, even after Nixon's re-election and resignation, millions of Americans believed, in the face of overwhelming evidence to the contrary, that Nixon had behaved much like previous presidents, had been shabbily treated by the press, and that his fall from power was unjustified.

All the President's Men became a film because, as Pakula made clear, Robert Redford used his considerable influence to bring it to the screen. In Pakula's words, Redford said, "I know nobody wants to make political pictures because they're box-office poison, but I don't care, I'm going to get it made." And, Pakula added, "he not only made great contributions to the development of the film, but also helped create an environment in which we could all do our best work. That to me is a first-rate producer."

Redford had, for many years, harbored a dislike for Richard Nixon. At the age of thirteen, after winning a tennis tournament, he received an award from Nixon, then a senator from California. When he shook Nixon's hand, he recalled years later, he felt "absolutely nothing . . . it was just empty." And, he said, he "never believed a word [Nixon] said" during the presentation. His disdain for Nixon continued during Nixon's tenure as vice president to Dwight D. Eisenhower, and into Nixon's first term as president.

In July 1972, Redford was promoting his newest film, *The Candidate*, by traveling on a mock-campaign whistle stop train from Jacksonville, Florida, to Miami, where the Democratic convention was about to be held and George McGovern would receive the delegates' nomination for president to run against Nixon. The "campaign train" was heavily and successfully promoted: all along the way, large crowds of people would come out to cheer Redford, who was, of course, not a candidate at all, but a movie star promoting his latest film.

During this time, Redford first became aware of Bob Woodward and Carl Bernstein's articles appearing in the *Washington Post* that exposed the activities of miscreants connected to the break-in at the Democratic headquarters in the Watergate office building that had occurred just two weeks before. These articles not only identified the burglars—four Cuban-Americans and CIA employee James McCord—they suggested that the break-in had been paid for by powerful political interests. Redford wondered why the forty or so reporters onboard his train—"there was this mix of entertainment and political press, to help promote the film," Redford said—failed to show any interest in the events Woodward and Bernstein were covering. He put the question directly to several of them, and, in his words,

I said, "What the hell happened with that thing? That was all Cuban refugees?" And they all kind of raised their eyebrows and looked at each other with a shared kind of knowledge, like, "No, no, no, no." So one thing led to another and it began to filter out that there was a lot more to it than that. So I said, "What are you talking about?" There was a hint that it went all the way to the administration. I said, "You've got to be kidding." I was shocked. So I said, "What are you guys going to do about it? You're just sitting here. What are you doing on this train? This is just movies." And then they gave me a lecture about how I didn't understand how the media worked, how I didn't understand journalism and all that. They said, "Look, this guy [Nixon] is going in on a landslide and a mandate, and McGovern is going to self-destruct. Nixon's going to get in, everybody knows it, nobody wants to be on the wrong side of this guy because he's got a switchblade mentality. He's vindictive and mean. A lot of people are afraid. And the second thing is, a lot of people know this [about the Republican Party's "dirty tricks"], they're just not going to talk about it because the Democrats do it, too, it's just the standard dirty tricks thing that happens in D.C., and nobody's going to make that much out of it, people are more interested in whether Hank Aaron is going to break Babe Ruth's record."

Redford, astonished at the cynicism of the reporters, went "completely nuts," as he put it, and sneered, "So that's what journalism's turning into." The reporters responded with condescension. "Boy, are you clueless," Redford quoted them as saying. "You're so naïve about how the press works. [If you're going to dig into a story like the one Woodward and Bernstein are beginning to expose] you need an editor to support you, you need a publisher that's going to give you the money to go out and do the tracking of a story like this." Redford angrily replied, "So you guys are just going to sit here on your ass, you're not going to do anything about it but smoke your cigars and have our free booze and write a superficial story about what I'm doing and that's it?"

The reporters "just sort of laughed it off," Redford said, so the actor, disheartened, went home to Utah after the promotional campaign and began checking the newspapers each day to see if anyone was following up on the break-in at the Watergate. "And then, slowly," he said, "these little stories started coming out," alleging that the Republican Party had funded the burglary. "It started to add up to bigger and bigger stories all through the summer. And all the stories were written by the same two guys [Carl Bernstein and Bob Woodward]. And finally it broke loose. Suddenly the *New York Times* got on board with a massive headline about the Sloan jury thing [Hugh Sloan, the treasurer of the Committee to Re-elect the President, had given secret testimony concerning the activities at the Watergate to a grand jury], and Donald Segretti and the dirty tricks [Segretti, working for the Republicans, had attempted, often successfully, to plant false news stories in the press discrediting Democratic candidates], and so on." For the first time, the stories began to demonstrate the complicity of highly placed members of Nixon's administration.

However, the administration denied culpability and accused Woodward and Bernstein of scurrilous reporting. The public appeared to side with the administration. And, except for the *Washington Post*, the media tended to ignore the apparent links between the Watergate burglary and the Republican Party.

In October, Redford read a profile about Woodward and Bernstein and began to conceive the notion of making a film about the young *Washington Post* reporters (Woodward was then twenty-nine, Bernstein twenty-eight). In addition to offering a fascinating look into the murky world of political chicanery, it offered the opportunity to explore the characters of two young men who were unlike one another in every respect except their reportorial skill. Woodward, a calm, unflappable Protestant and Yale graduate, the son of a suburban Chicago judge, represented almost a polar opposite of Bernstein, a highly strung, volatile Jew whose parents had been accused of being Communist sympathizers and who had begun his journalistic career as a copyboy at the *Washington Star* when he was sixteen. That two such contrasting figures could work so well together seemed to be the stuff of which movies were made; in cinematic terms they were partners whose disparate personalities complemented one another: a latter-day Abbott and Costello, Roy Rogers and Gabby Hayes, Katharine Hepburn and Spencer Tracy. But their partnership, unlike that of their cinematic forebears, promised to produce far more than a comic contrast. Woodward and Bernstein were at the beginning of an adventure that would result in the resignation of the president of the United States.

Redford's notion was "a little black-and-white movie, very low budget, with two unknown actors, and I would produce it. It would be about what these two guys did that summer that everybody else was afraid to mess around with. It was only meant to be a small story about what they were trying to do." He attempted to contact Woodward and Bernstein, but they refused to return Redford's calls, perhaps because, as Redford later said, "they probably thought they were crank calls." Not until six weeks later, when he was filming *The Way We Were* in upstate New York, was Redford able to reach Woodward, who "was very cold on the phone, and very distant," according to Redford, who quotes Woodward as saying, "Yeah, we got your message, but we've been busy." Redford told Woodward he'd like to speak with him at greater length, but the reporter brushed him off. "Well," Woodward said, according to Redford, "we're really not interested, we're writing right now, and now's not a good time. Maybe some other time." Redford, believing that he would never be able to crack Woodward's shell of indifference, thought, "Well, okay, so much for that, and I didn't put any more thought into it."

Suddenly, however, the legal and political climate changed. In a letter from James McCord to Judge John Sirica, McCord admitted that the burglars had been hired by the Committee to Re-elect the President (known irreverently as CREEP). "All of a sudden," Redford said, Woodward and Bernstein "were vindicated. I called Woodward and I said, 'Look, I really insist that you give me just a few minutes, I just want to see you face to face; at least give me a chance.' It was April 1973. Woodward said, 'Okay, if you're here tomorrow night, in D.C., I'll meet you in a private meeting place. You don't need to do anything, just show up and I'll find you.'"

Redford, who had no idea what Woodward looked like, went to a buffet dinner in Washington, after which *The Candidate* was going to be shown. Before the film began, he was approached by a mysterious young man, who whispered, "Woodward. Meet me at the Jefferson Hotel bar in about forty-five minutes." It was, Redford said, "kind of like Deep Throat. It was very clandestine. The next thing you know I'm in the Jefferson. He admitted in our meeting that they didn't trust me, they weren't sure it was me on the phone."

Redford explained his notion of and enthusiasm for a film about the *Post* reporters. Woodward, evidently afraid of being followed, said, "Tell you what, we'll come to your apartment in New York. Don't you come near us, let us come to you."[28]

Redford told his friend, William Goldman, who had written the script for Redford's enormous success, *Butch Cassidy and the Sundance Kid*, about his meeting with Woodward. Goldman "just got wild with excitement," Redford said, and asked to be included in any meeting Redford could arrange with Woodward and Bernstein. "So," according to Redford, when the reporters visited him in February 1974, "as a friend, I invited Goldman to sit in. When they came up I introduced him. Well, the mistake was that, because I introduced him and he was Bill Goldman, they just automatically thought that he was going to be the writer. That was not the case. He was just there as my friend."

During the meeting, Goldman spoke disparagingly of the incompetence of the burglars and the cover-up. "It's almost like a comic opera," he said. Bernstein took offense at Goldman's comment, evidently feeling that the screenwriter did not understand the seriousness of the conspiracy he and Woodward had exposed. Nevertheless, the meeting continued. Before it was over the reporters said, "Look, at the end of this month, three guys are going to resign: [chief of staff H. R.] Haldeman, [assistant for domestic affairs to the president, John] Ehrlichman, and [Nixon's lawyer, John] Dean." The exposure of the Watergate scandal was

[28]*Redford said he had no doubt that Woodward and Bernstein were "under surveillance" and "under tremendous pressure." Woodward recently confirmed to me that he thought he and Bernstein were in danger at the time, but no longer believes that was the case.*

about to bring about the removal from power of two of the most powerful figures in the administration, as well as the president's attorney. Redford, astonished, said, "Oh, come on, you've got to be kidding." But the reporters said, "No, we just had information. But we don't know when this thing is going to bottom out. We're still working on the story."

Redford asked directly for the film rights to the investigation Woodward and Bernstein had conducted into the string of events that began with the burglary and was about to claim Haldeman, Ehrlichman, and Dean, but the journalists were reluctant. "Let us get back to you," they said. "We're going to be writing a book about this." Redford replied that the film he was conceiving was intended to focus only on the early stages of the investigation. "The part I'm interested in," he said, "is not the aftermath so much as what happened when no one was looking. Because that's what no one knows about. History's going to deal with the aftermath." He wanted the film to "tell the story from their point of view," he told me, "as journalists at the lowest end of the ladder, and [to be about] how two guys could affect the highest rung on the ladder—how, in a democracy, that could be possible."

Woodward and Bernstein had decided to write their book from the point of view of the burglars, but when they met with their editor, Alice Mayhew of Simon and Schuster, and Woodward said what Redford had told him, "The story of Watergate is the reporting of it," she said, "I like Redford's idea better." As a result, the book's point of view changed. Woodward later confirmed that Redford "certainly laid the seeds for the way we" wrote the book.

Alice Mayhew also suggested that the reporters give Redford the film rights. They agreed, but stipulated that work on the film could not begin until they completed the book in eight or nine months' time. Redford, therefore, had to wait, and, "in the meantime," he said, "while I'm waiting, all hell broke loose. By the time they finished it, Nixon had resigned. An amazing story unfolded while I was waiting to do this movie." Woodward and Bernstein had agreed to send their manuscript directly to Redford. However, William Goldman contacted the reporters through his agent and asked them to send the manuscript to him. The reporters, mistakenly believing that Goldman had been hired as the scenarist, did so. "And that's how Goldman ended up on the picture," Redford said.

Simon and Schuster demanded $450,000 for the movie rights—an extremely high price at the time. The original movie Redford had envisioned, costing $2 million, was no longer possible. Thus, Redford raised $4 million from Warner Bros. and contributed another $4 million from his own company, Wildwood Productions. Warners insisted that it would have to be a commercial film, and, to ensure audience appeal, Redford would have to agree to appear in it. Redford maintained that Woodward and Bernstein should be played by unknown actors "because the story was so much about unknowns," but Warners refused to budge. And if Redford was going to play Woodward, they insisted that an actor of equal renown play Bernstein. Thus, Dustin Hoffman was hired to appear, his lawyers negotiating with Walter Coblenz on behalf of Wildwood Productions. (Coblenz, who looked after money matters throughout the film, received screen credit as the film's producer, although, in every other respect, Redford performed that function.)

Once Woodward and Bernstein had agreed to the making of the picture, they allowed Redford to travel with them on their investigative routines (although Redford remained in the car when Woodward and Bernstein entered the home of the person they were going to interview).[29] Woodward also spent a great deal of time with Goldman. "I cannot overemphasize [Woodward's] importance to the screenplay," Goldman wrote. "When he was in New York he would call and we'd often meet. When I was in Washington, he gave me everything I needed in the way of knowledge and support."

Goldman wrote a draft of the script which disappointed Redford, "because Goldman writes for cleverness and he was still leaning all over *Butch Cassidy and the Sundance Kid*. He was borrowing heavily from the charm of that piece and it didn't work. It was written very quickly, and it went for comedy. It trivialized not only the event but journalism." Goldman did, however, solve the problem of how to condense the enormous amount of material in the book for a film: in his words, "Throw away the last half of the book." Although very little of Goldman's original screenplay remained when the film was finally shot, his notion of how the film should end was never altered, and was a significant contribution to the movie's success.

Redford hoped to enlist Elia Kazan as director of the film, but Kazan "was extremely turned off by Goldman's script," Redford said, "thinking that Goldman was trivializing something too important," and turned down the offer. Redford then took the script to William Friedkin, best known as the director of *The Exorcist*, because he "knew that this piece was going to have to be energized, it was going to have to have a lot of visceral and cinematic energy. It could very easily just have been a lot of typewriters and pens and talking heads and we'd be dead in the water. It needed a visceral kind of emotional energy, and Friedkin had that." Friedkin liked Goldman's script, but ultimately decided that he—Friedkin—was the wrong person to direct the film.

Meanwhile, Carl Bernstein, who said that Goldman's screenplay reminded him of a Henny Youngman joke book, had, with Nora Ephron (then his girlfriend and later his wife), written a screenplay of his own. In their version, Bernstein was

---

[29]*Bob Woodward has no recollection of Redford's presence on these occasions. "I don't think we would have taken him around and have him wait in the car," he said. "It doesn't seem quite right." But he acknowledges that it may have happened as Redford described.*

portrayed as heroic and dashing, and Woodward as a passive, rather ineffective follower. The treatment also included several scenes of Bernstein as a romantic lady-killer. Woodward, who read Bernstein's script, claims not to have been offended by it at all. He even says, "I thought it had a great deal of merit," although "it shifted the focus to Carl."

Bernstein handed his completed screenplay to Redford, who had not even been aware that Bernstein and Ephron were working on a script. Bernstein's characterization of himself made his screenplay unacceptable, but Redford was slow to come to that conclusion. Indeed, he suggested that Goldman read Bernstein's script. Goldman, offended that Redford would even consider Bernstein's rewrite, went into a prolonged sulk. Redford, realizing that he should never have permitted Bernstein to think that he could influence the screenplay, eventually told the journalist, "Carl, Errol Flynn is dead" (a remark Woodward recalls with amusement), which put an end to Bernstein and Ephron's version.

In mid-1974, Redford (with Dustin Hoffman's consent, since Hoffman asked for and received director approval when he agreed to play Bernstein) asked Alan Pakula if he wished to direct the film. Pakula's work on *Klute* had impressed Redford (who had been offered the role of John Klute, but turned it down). According to Pakula, "that is the reason Bob hired me for *All the President's Men*. He felt a tension in *Klute* that he had not felt when he read the script. And he felt that I had this strange, threatening quality in some of my work." Redford, believing that quality could be used profitably in *All the President's Men*, said, "If our project was to succeed, we'd need the same kind of tension."

Still, Redford was a bit uncomfortable about the offer he had made, not entirely certain that Pakula was the right choice. "When I thought about Alan," he said, "my initial worry was that he might be soft. I really felt this picture's got to have a very strong, visceral edge to it, to compensate for the amount of talk, and I wondered about Alan because I knew he was very cerebral, that was his main track, he was an intellectual. But when I met with him, I just felt so comfortable about our ability to communicate that I just decided to go for it."

Redford wanted Pakula not only because of his intellectual bent, but also because "he was psychologically oriented, and he was a liberal—but he was not a knee-jerk liberal. If you directed this with a knee-jerk liberal attitude you could die, because then it would have been about Nixon, which it shouldn't be. It would have been about the good guys and the bad guys instead of about investigative journalism and treating it like a detective story." Eventually, all of Redford's qualms were set aside. "Alan was so smart that I trusted him fully. And I thought that he and I would balance out well together, because I think we both had a shared intelligence. My tendency, knowing about the traps in the film, was to go for the visceral and I knew he would go for the psychological, and that's exactly what happened. Our relationship was nothing but terrific."

Pakula read Goldman's script and, like Redford, was not impressed. "*All the President's Men* is a true story about a major piece of American history," he said, "and I didn't think it should be gussied up and 'movie'd up' and souped up for 'entertainment value,' [or] that these two men should be made into conventional, wisecracking film heroes." Still, he felt, even though the prospect of filming *All the President's Men* presented "a lot of problems, I'd like to have a try at it," undoubtedly because, like *The Parallax View*, it expressed his mistrust of large and powerful institutions—a notion he would return to in subsequent films.

Pakula was at the time under contract to Universal to develop a film called *Sweeter Than Honey*, and the studio would not let him out of his contract. In December 1974, however, Universal decided to drop the project, so, when Redford called to say that Pakula was still his first choice to direct, but he needed at least an indication of Pakula's availability, Pakula was able to answer, "You called at just the right time." He tentatively accepted Redford's offer, and, although he regretted the loss of *Sweeter Than Honey* (which he said he would make at a later date, but never did), the notion of directing *All the President's Men* must have been supremely satisfying, since—as a confirmed "political junkie"—he was fascinated by Watergate.

But Goldman's script was so seriously flawed that it continued to create difficulties. Woodward, as well as Bernstein, was "*extremely* critical of the screenplay," Redford said. And the executives at the *Washington Post*, after reading Goldman's script, said, "If you make this movie, you've got us against you. This guy [Goldman] is trivializing everything, he makes it sound like it was a joke."

Pakula's adverse reaction to the script caused him to delay formal acceptance of the directorial assignment for several weeks. He then spoke candidly to Redford. "The first thing we have to do is really make sure we both have the same concept of this film before I [agree to] do it," he said. "I don't want to make *Butch Woodward and the Sundance Bernstein*: you know, Bob Redford and Dustin Hoffman loving and laughing their way through the East as they bring down the President of the United States. [A picture of that sort] may make a mint, but we would look in the mirror and not like what we saw."

Also, he said, "You can't do a whole historical overview of Watergate and all the ramifications—you're going to have the longest montage in film history and that's not what this is about. The film we're making is, 'What was it like to have been these two young men who broke through this cover-up and discovered these facts that eventually led to the destruction of some of the most powerful people on earth?'"

He was also skeptical about the two roles that had already been cast. Pakula said to Redford, "You know, Bob, . . . I'm not crazy about the casting." Redford asked if Pakula was referring to Dustin Hoffman and himself. "Yeah," said Pakula, "because to me the power of the story is that these two are unknowns. You and Dustin may be better known than Nixon." He was also concerned about Redford's playing a young, sometimes bumbling, reporter, believing that audiences would be unable to accept him in the role. He told Redford, "Bob, you know, one of the dangers of you for this film is that you seem so competent to audiences, and these guys fumble their way on to the story. You have an air of enormous confidence on the screen. Everything you do seems to come so easily and with such grace." Pakula offered a specific example: "It doesn't matter that Bob can have trouble opening a bottle of club soda in real life, like all of us. On screen, it looks like it would pop open if he just waved his thumb at it." Consequently, he feared that if Redford played Woodward, "it's going to seem too easy."

Finally, Pakula was concerned that a film documenting such a monumental period in American history ran the risk of being pompous and overblown. He wished to avoid the sort of picture in which "you could hear the drums rolling in the background," he said, "signifying that this was an important event. There is no way of writing importance and there is no way of directing importance and there is no way of acting importance. We were going to do a film that would show what it was like, and it had to be totally un-selfconscious." If he were to direct the film, he said, he would try to make everything in the picture "an immediate experience, trying to say what it was like at the time."

Pakula finally agreed to accept Redford's offer. In 2002, Redford recalled that "the moment he was on board, there was no fooling around. Once he signed on to it and got rid of some of his early questions he drove into it full-bore."

In 1975, however, Redford was more impatient, believing that Pakula was taking too long to prepare himself for the first day of shooting. Although Redford offered to give Pakula the information he needed, the director declined, needing to do his own research.

Pakula's research consisted primarily of spending time at the *Washington Post*, observing the routines of the editors and reporters, and soaking up the atmosphere. According to Ben Bradlee, Pakula spent more than a month observing, and three days at Bradlee's side, "sharing phone conversations, news conferences, [and] talks with reporters and editors."

When Pakula emerged from his sojourn at the *Post*, he insisted that Goldman's lighthearted approach to the material be eliminated. Consequently, Redford spoke to Goldman, telling him "he had to go back to work on it and really dig in. He hadn't even been down there [Washington, D.C.] to investigate it. He hadn't spent time at the *Post* or anything like that. You can't do that. You have to get down there and dig in and do some work, you've got to roll up your sleeves. But when I found out that he was also writing *Marathon Man* in the mornings, I knew that we were never going to get the kind of hard work that we needed, so I had to confront him on that and there was a falling out, because I told him I thought he was abrogating his responsibility to do this and nothing else, to do it right, and he got very huffy about it. He said, 'Why don't you do it yourself?'"

Pakula was convinced that Goldman's petulance made working with him impossible, and eventually said to Redford, "Look, I can't work with him. And I don't think he can do it." As a consequence, Redford and Pakula did just what Goldman had facetiously suggested. They checked into the Madison Hotel in Washington for a month and rewrote the screenplay themselves.

Redford recalled that he and Pakula were "holed up in the hotel, just across 15th Street from the *Washington Post*, working on the script. For almost six weeks we paced around a suite strewn with typewriters, papers, and pots of coffee. Room service must have made a fortune off us."

As a result of this string of events, Goldman alleged that Pakula's paralyzing indecisiveness had led to his dismissal. Employed to write the screenplay, Goldman said he "would meet and discuss a scene" with Pakula, "and I would ask if it was okay, and if it wasn't, how did he want it changed, what direction? For example, I might ask, did he want this shorter or longer?

"He would answer, 'Do it both ways, I want to see it all.'"

"I might ask, did he want me to rewrite a sequence and make it more or less hard-edged.

"He would answer, 'Do it both ways, I want to see it all.'"

"And now would come the answer that I always associate with Alan: 'Don't deprive me of any riches.'"

Goldman found Pakula "unable to make up his mind," and it galled him so thoroughly that, according to his account, he was unable to write productively. He further said that Redford "was disgruntled with Pakula's lack of decision," but Redford categorically denies that assertion.

Redford recently acknowledged that "Alan did appear indecisive lots of times, and I encountered that myself, but it's because his head was working, that was the kind of guy he was, he would sometimes get lost in his head, become lost in thought. And if you didn't know Alan, that could seem as if he's not paying attention or not hearing you, or not having much use for you. I *don't* think he ever had much use for Goldman, because he thought Goldman was taking a cheap road, and he just didn't have a lot of patience for it. So I think Bill picked that up, and rather than accepting it for what it was, he turned it into a problem of Alan's—and I don't think it was Alan's problem."

Redford and Pakula continued laboring to create a new script in the Madison

Hotel. Their primary job, Pakula said, was to mercilessly pare down the amount of research he and Redford had accumulated. "I spent my first months of preparation finding out everything I could about the subjects and characters, and amassing details and ideas—a constant accumulation," Pakula said. "The next step was ruthlessly boiling it down; discarding, discarding, discarding. And hoping that somewhere in the boiling process, something of the original richness was still there."

During the process of rewriting the script, Bernstein and Woodward turned over all their notes to Redford and Pakula, who used the notes as the basis for their treatment. "They were *enormously* cooperative," Redford said. "So all the stuff in the movie was really drawn from their actual diary notes of each meeting. We were literally able to take those notes and construct a kind of through-line of their investigation." Pakula interviewed Woodward and Bernstein again and again, asking them to describe the people they had interviewed in greater detail than they had provided in their book. The importance of knowing as much as possible about those to whom the reporters had spoken was imperative. Pakula explained, "In any detective story when you [are dealing with] a series of characters who last for only one or two scenes in the film, you are in danger of winding up with characters who are just lifeless puppets serving the narrative." That led to the filmmakers' eventual accomplishment: portraying the characters being interrogated in multidimensional ways.

At Pakula's urging, Redford often called Woodward while the script was being written—as frequently as three or four times a day. "What happened at this point?" Redford would ask; "What really happened?" Woodward said, "Redford was always driving toward the reality." (Similarly, Hoffman often telephoned Bernstein as he developed his characterization.)

All these activities led to a script that stayed focused on the central question of who controlled the secret campaign fund that financed the Watergate break-in and other acts of mischief. That focus led to a fascination with process: "How Woodward and Bernstein will get them [their sources] to talk, and if they will get them to talk, is the key to much of the suspense in the film," Pakula said. "If you don't have a sense of the character—why it's difficult for him to talk, what his attitude about all this is, what kind of person he is—then none of the suspense works."

In an attempt to flesh out the characters of the reporters, Alvin Sargent wrote scenes based on an idea of Pakula and Redford's, in which Woodward and Bernstein were shown with women they loved. (According to William Goldman, he wrote a scene for Bernstein and his ex-wife, after which Redford insisted on having not one but three scenes with a girlfriend of Woodward's.) Hoffman's scene was shot but had to be discarded, partly because Hoffman so overwhelmed the actress playing his wife that the scene was unacceptably imbalanced. When Pakula determined not to use the scene, he and Redford decided not to include an episode by Sargent that had been written for Woodward and his ex-wife, because, as Redford said, "we couldn't have a Woodward scene and not have a Bernstein scene."

Two years later, after the film was released, Pakula said that the omission of Hoffman's scene was "a decision Dustin is unhappy about to this day. He feels it left out the whole personalized sense of the characters. . . . But Bob and I felt we could not stop the relentless narrative drive of the film to stop parenthetically, kick off our shoes, and relax with the characters. We felt it would have made for a more leisurely film, endangering the line of tension that holds the whole experience together. Dustin felt we didn't take enough time to play the reactions of Woodward and Bernstein, particularly Bernstein."

The scene of Woodward's private life sounds as if it would have been a valuable addition to the film. As Redford noted, "it illustrated a lot about Woodward's character, since he revealed so little about himself. It's a scene where Woodward is troubled by some things and the way he's doing it; he's looking for some connection, someone to really talk to, and he has no one. Because he's become such a private, secret guy, he doesn't have many friends, he just has contacts. So it was a scene to illustrate his loneliness, and why his journalistic ego and ambitions drove him past being able to have a relationship." But the scene was never filmed.

The decision not to include sequences detailing the reporters' personal lives distressed Pakula at first. "We spent endless time—oh, God, we spent endless time [discussing] their personal lives, I can't tell you how much. I have notes up to here on it. We had scenes written. [But] reluctantly at first and then with more sureness and determination as time went on we thought, 'No, we're telling this story because of what they did, not because of their fascinating personal lives. . . . The work is what this is about. . . . If there's not a relentless rhythm to this film it's going to fall apart.' The narrative is so complicated that it depends, for comprehension, on one thing building on another thing building on another thing, and if you stop for a parenthesis and a tangent to say, 'Look at this adorable girl he's got, and look what this shows, and look how he has a difficulty with his mother,' or whatever, even if it's interesting personal stuff, it's going to stop that relentless build of that narrative."

Jon Boorstin, who served as Pakula's research assistant, as he had in *The Parallax View*, supplemented the reporters' notes by bringing in "all kinds of stuff," Redford said. "So, between his research and Woodward and Bernstein's notes, Alan and my instincts, and what information I had gathered over the year and a half to two years leading up to it, we then constructed a kind of new script.[30] And

---

[30] Bob Woodward agrees that Redford and Pakula did a great deal of significant rewriting, but believes that "Goldman had the structure [of the screenplay] basically right, and a lot of things are right out of the book. I think . . . Goldman would be able to make a pretty strong case that [the version he wrote and the script that was filmed are] basically the same, though I'm pretty sure that [Redford and Pakula could also have said] 'Well, look, it's really different.'"

then we hired Alvin Sargent, later on, to come in and do some polish work." They discarded much of what Goldman had written, but they did maintain the structure he had created for the screenplay.

Pakula and Redford labored to infuse tension and excitement into what might have seemed a tedious business: making telephone calls, riffling through call-slips at the Library of Congress, rewriting copy. They were also intent on preserving the reality of the daily routines at the *Washington Post*. They had no wish to romanticize the activities of the reporters, as so many Hollywood films set in newsrooms had done in the past. That they accomplished these intentions so thoroughly is perhaps the film's greatest triumph. *All the President's Men* does convey excitement, it maintains a level of tension throughout, but it never understates the basis of the investigative reporter's task: thorough, meticulous, repetitive work, focusing upon every detail, no matter how seemingly insignificant.

Since Pakula and Redford did not claim credit for their authorial work, William Goldman's name remains in the credits as the author of the screenplay. So thoroughly did Pakula and Redford maintain silence about their role in writing the script of *All the President's Men* that not even Alvin Sargent knew they had done so. Even when Sargent spoke to me in 2002, he continually referred to his admiration for "Goldman's script." The irony is that William Goldman received an Academy Award for "his" screenplay. "What really blew me away," Redford said, "was that he went up and received it."

Warner Bros. was becoming nervous. Each time the studio asked to look at the script, they saw that the screenplay was becoming more serious, more focused on the routines of investigative journalism, less concerned with comic byplay among the characters. "Oh God," one of the studio executives said, "this looks like it's some television documentary, some CBS white paper." Pakula assured the studio that he planned to make an entertaining film but that he was equally concerned with revealing the truth of what had happened.

Redford and Pakula initially hoped to shoot the film at the offices of the *Washington Post* and to use all of the principals in the operation of the newspaper as characters in the film. But they met immediate resistance. Katharine Graham, the *Post*'s publisher, was adamant about not wanting to be portrayed. When they met with her, Graham asked that the name of her newspaper not be used in the film. "What are we going to call it? The *Washington Bugle*?" Redford said. "This is a fact of history. I'm sorry, that we can't go along with. We're going to use it." Then Graham said, "I beg you—I *beg* you—not to use me [as a character] in the film." Redford responded that a scene had been written about her, portraying her as an admirable champion of freedom of the press, and Pakula said he hoped she would allow her persona to be represented, but she flatly refused. As she pointed out in her autobiography, *Personal History*, she was scared "witless" that the film would destroy the *Post*'s reputation.

Redford asked Graham, "Could we at least shoot the scene and then let you see it?" But she said, "No, I beg you, do not even put my name in the film." Redford and Pakula did agree, reluctantly, not to portray Graham in the film (although her name was mentioned on several occasions), despite the fact that Geraldine Page had already been cast. According to a report in *Time*, Graham "remained wary of the whole project" long after the filmmakers had won over the editorial and reportorial staffs.

Executive Editor Ben Bradlee was also involved in the attempt to keep the filmmakers from using the name of the *Post*. "We withheld that permission for a week or so," he said, "until our lawyer said we didn't have a leg to stand on, that despite our reticence we had become public figures, and they had a right to" use the newspaper's name. Bradlee was reluctant to be included in the film under his own name, as well. He told Redford and Pakula that he was concerned about being portrayed inaccurately, saying to Pakula, "You're going to go on to make other films, Bob will be riding off into the sunset in his next film, and meanwhile I'm going to be stuck for life as being to the American public whoever is playing me in" *All the President's Men*.

"I think Ben was both attracted and repelled by the presence of Hollywood," Redford said. "There's something of the star about Ben—legitimately. He's very, very charismatic, has a very powerful personality, is a real leader, and is thoroughly admired by everybody, including me. But the ambivalence that he had, as a tough, edgy kind of guy, would not allow him to completely go along with his attraction to Hollywood. The editor-in-chief in him had to put that hat on and say, 'I shouldn't be trusting this, I shouldn't be liking this.'"

For his part, Bradlee said, "Redford kept talking about trust. He kept saying, 'You've got to trust us.' We didn't understand that. We were thinking, 'Why the hell should we trust Robert Redford? Why should we turn our reputations over to him?'" But Redford's sincerity and doggedness eventually prevailed, and Bradlee ultimately agreed to be portrayed under his own name.[31]

Once Graham and Bradlee realized that Redford and Pakula were going to film *All the President's Men*, "they decided it was best to cooperate so there would be as

---

[31] *A few months later, Pakula did Bradlee what the editor called "a terrific favor," partially, no doubt, to repay Bradlee's willingness to be included in the film, and his help in persuading other principals at the Post to do the same. Bradlee said "I had promised my daughter that if she got through some high school exam that I would take her out to Hollywood so that she could watch the movie being made and I'd introduce her to Redford. Of course, I could not deliver on that, but Alan could. And so when we were out there Alan and Hannah gave a dinner to which my daughter Marina was asked and so was Bob. Then they took her to the set, and it was a thrill for her."*

much reality as possible," Pakula said. "They watched the project with hope, fear, and trepidation."

Pakula felt that the casting of Ben Bradlee's character was of paramount importance. Putting the problem in familiar movie jargon, Pakula called Bradlee "the old cowboy and [Woodward and Bernstein] were the young cowboys. He was the one they had to look up to if they were really going to look like they were in insecure, vulnerable positions. So the casting of that part became absolutely crucial for the success of their performances."

A few years before the filming of *All the President's Men*, Jason Robards, always a heavy drinker, had had too much to drink, had driven his car off a road in Malibu, and was seriously injured. His face was repaired by plastic surgery, but scars remained. After the accident, he went through rehabilitation and stopped drinking, but he found it difficult to get acting work. Redford had acted on television with Robards in *The Iceman Cometh* for educational television in New York in 1960 and had been treated with particular kindness by Robards. Now, Redford said, "I wanted to pay him back for his generosity, which meant a great deal to me." In addition, he knew that Robards possessed a "kind of rough, gruff charm, and a lot of power." He recommended the actor to Pakula.

Robards met with Pakula and said, "I look like Ben Bradlee, I sound like Ben Bradlee, and I've got to play Ben Bradlee." But Pakula needed to be convinced. He knew that Robards was "one of the great American actors," he said, "but he's noted for playing . . . the poetic failure" in such plays and films as *The Iceman Cometh*, *Moon for the Misbegotten*, and *A Thousand Clowns*. "Poetic failure is the antithesis of Ben Bradlee, who thrives on success, on being of and in the world, and on trying to be a controlling factor in the world. He loves dealing with reality. Jason and Ben are very different people. Jason's full of soul, which is one of the least-needed qualities to play Ben Bradlee. And if Jason did not have [Bradlee's] quality in the film, the whole film would go down the drain."

Pakula said to Robards, "Ben is a big star. He's just got charisma in life. He's very successful and he loves dealing with reality. And your great successes as an actor are [playing characters] who have difficulty dealing with reality, deeply sensitive, wounded, vulnerable—and that's not Ben."

However, Pakula came to believe that casting Robards might be precisely the antidote needed to keep the star personalities of Redford and Hoffman from dominating the film. "The major key to that," Pakula said, "was [that] Ben Bradlee . . . is the star personality in the newsroom. They're not. He is. And if he's not and doesn't have that power, if he can't threaten them, if he's intimidated by them, then the film's over." Redford's respect for Robards was so great that Pakula gambled it would be reflected in the Woodward-Bradlee relationship on the screen. And Redford was not alone in his admiration for Robards. "He was somebody that both Redford and Dustin looked up to," Pakula said. Moreover, Robards had the power and stature to make Redford and Hoffman "feel insecure," just as Bradlee would have made Woodward and Bernstein feel insecure.

Finally, Pakula said to Robards, "If you tell me you can do it, knowing my reservations, you've got the job." Robards said, "I can do it."

Because Robards' career was at a low ebb before *All the President's Men*, he accepted a salary of only $50,000 for his participation in the film—a remarkable bargain, considering the performance he gave. However, as Ben Bradlee said, Robards "never stopped working after that."

Another role that required careful casting was that of "Deep Throat," Woodward's mysterious informant. The character—so named because he insisted that anything he told Woodward was on "deep background" and could not be quoted or even paraphrased—demonstrated that not everyone in Washington condoned the activities of the administration. But the character also needed to communicate a sense of self-importance, a condescension to Woodward, a penchant for mystery and ambiguity, a man who signals his willingness to meet with Woodward in the most melodramatic ways—such as inserting red flags in flower pots on his balcony. Clearly, this peculiar combination of characteristics would represent a challenge for any actor. Not until after filming began did Pakula find the actor he wanted. Hal Holbrook seemed better able to embody the qualities Pakula was looking for than any other performer, so he decided to cast Holbrook, provided that Woodward would be willing to divulge one significant piece of information.

Pakula—along with virtually everyone in the world except for Woodward and Deep Throat himself—did not know the identity of Deep Throat, an identity that Woodward had promised to conceal. Pakula wondered if Deep Throat really existed or if he was a metaphorical invention of Woodward's. He was also concerned that, if such a person existed, Deep Throat might be identified before the film premiered. Consequently, he approached Woodward, saying, "I'm going to tell you who I'm casting, and if it's not right, if it's so off the mark, then tell me, because it'll be disastrous in this picture if I cast a man and it turns out, the week before the picture is released, that we find out who Deep Throat was and it turns out to be Tricia Nixon— or Golda Meir, or somebody who's so far removed from my casting that it's going to make the picture look ridiculous." When Pakula said that he intended to cast Hal Holbrook, Woodward said nothing—in effect, squelching the rumor that Martha Mitchell, the wife of the Attorney General (or any other woman), might have been Woodward's source—so Pakula went ahead with his plans. In May 2005, Deep Throat was revealed to have been W. Mark Felt, former deputy director of the FBI.

Pakula, Redford, Hoffman, Robards, cinematographer Gordon Willis, and many of the other actors and production personnel were given access to the offices of the *Post* before filming began, observing reporters at work and attending editors' meetings while an assistant director took careful notes about the behavior and habits of the employees.

Pakula said, "I made anybody with a major part in the film who was supposed to work at the *Washington Post* spend time at the *Washington Post*. . . . The most important thing was to learn how to be a good reporter [or editor]. In many ways, it's a 'how-to' picture." But this ran the risk "of doing a wax museum of a film—of getting such perfect imitations that there is no essence of reality," he said. Therefore, "After the research was done, the most important thing was to make it our own."

In other activities that he hoped would ensure accuracy, Pakula spoke to Bernard Barker, one of the Watergate burglars, to garner details that could be used in the film. He also interviewed one of the police officers who had arrested the burglars. He wished to speak to James McCord, as well, but McCord demanded too much money, and the meeting did not take place.

Pakula hoped to shoot at the offices of the *Washington Post* (again, in an effort to create as realistic a portrait as possible) in May 1975, but Katharine Graham and Ben Bradlee said that would be impossible. Indeed, Pakula and Redford soon came to the same conclusion. Whenever Redford or Hoffman were at the *Post*, female employees kept running to the restroom to apply makeup in an apparent attempt to make themselves attractive to the actors—and perhaps to be cast as extras in the film.

Photographers continually surrounded Redford and Hoffman. After ten days of preparation, the filmmakers had to give up. Pakula asked George Jenkins to build a replica of the *Post*'s newsroom on two large soundstages at Warner Bros. in Burbank, California. The wall between the two stages was removed to make one enormous space, measuring 240 feet long and 135 feet wide. The unanticipated move cost a small fortune—$450,000—and further strained the budget, forcing cutbacks that included the sacrifice of three planned scenes.

Jenkins re-created the *Post* offices down to the smallest detail. He and his assistants measured the dimensions of the newsroom and photographed it from every angle, taking careful note of the style and color of the furniture, before beginning the reconstruction. Approximately two hundred desks were ordered from the company that had provided desks to the *Post*, then were painted exactly as the desks in the *Post*'s newsroom were painted. On the desks and walls were 1972 calendars, with the appropriate date showing.

Furthermore, Pakula hired Roy Aarons, a reporter from the *Post*, to give a series of informative talks, thus ensuring that the actors would be familiar with the routine of the newspaper office.

The trash in the wastebaskets in the *Post* newsroom was collected by Jenkins and his assistants, transported to California, and placed in the prop wastebaskets of the film set. After the work was complete, Bradlee visited the set and expressed his astonishment: he felt as if he were standing in his own office, he said. "When I brought my daughter onto the set in the studio," he added, "she could walk right to my desk. She was stunned."

As in the actual offices of the *Post*, the set employed white fluorescent light, which, as Pakula said, "was rather difficult for Gordon [Willis]." But, he said, "I wanted a world without shadows; I wanted a world where nothing is hidden. The hub of this film is what . . . investigative reporters do [which is] to try to expose the truth about everything. Nothing can be left secret or hidden." Consequently, Pakula discussed his concept with Willis at length before deciding whether or not they could work together on the film. He told Willis, "I want it hard, don't soften it; I want to make the audience uncomfortable. The truth is uncomfortable, we're obsessed with the truth, so there should be harsh light."

Pakula described the color scheme of the newsroom as employing "tough poster colors—hard electric blues, hard oranges and reds, hard greens" giving one the sense "of being put in the middle of a modern poster." That, he said, became the visual conception of the film. And the lighting, which Pakula characterized as "incredibly harsh" and "ruthless," was, he said, "just marvelous, because the *Post* newsroom is in the business of communicating the truth. They do it in a place without shadows where everything is exposed . . . I wanted to show the total accessibility of everyone at the *Washington Post*—you see everything Bradlee does behind his glass wall; if he scratches, the whole office watches him—compared to the inaccessibility of the President."

The poster-like quality that Pakula wanted the photography to achieve was sufficient to persuade him that the film should be made in color. "To me," he said, "'documentary' does not necessarily mean black-and-white; it does not necessarily mean grainy; it does not necessarily mean handheld cameras. At least, 'reality' does not mean that to me."

Pakula spoke to Willis "of wanting to see lots of counterpointed action, lots of scenes with action going on in several planes deep into the background. It meant much use of wide-angle lenses. It meant a lot of the total opposite of [the sort of] photography that is being done [in the mid-1970s]. It meant going back to a crisp, hard, sharp style of cinematography."

Pakula said, "Gordy is not known for his very bright cinematography, but there's a whole concept about light in this film. . . . The world that our detective-reporters go through in *All the President's Men* is a world of sunlight. It's a world where the sun shines, it's a world where the grass is mown, houses are clean and bright

and cheerful and orderly looking. It's sunny. And in the midst of all this order-
liness and brightness and cheerfulness, Disneyland happiness, is decay and all
those crumbling things. I wanted that counterpoint."

"It was Alan who thought to tell the story of Woodward and Bernstein's heroic work uncovering Watergate as a tale of light and dark," Redford said. "The *Post*'s
newsroom, a place of truth, is brightly and fluorescently lit; when Dustin
Hoffman or I leave it, we go into shadows"—and an environment suggesting
peril—"looking for clues."

On the set, as in the *Post* newsroom, television sets were placed at several
points. This served a useful function in the film, as clips of Nixon, Vice President
Spiro Agnew, Gerald Ford (granting Nixon a pardon after he replaced Nixon as
president), and others were shown, counterpointing the activities of the *Post*
reporters. No one in the film needed to refer to Agnew's attack on the *Post*, for
example; for it was playing in the background while the employees of the newspaper went about their business.

Robert Brent Toplin, a historian who wrote extensively about the film, has
pointed out that "in scenes showing Woodward and Bernstein asking questions
over the telephone, viewers would not see the individual at the other end of the
line. By limiting the audience's information solely to the voice heard over the
phone (exactly what the reporter experienced), viewers would sense better the difficulty of trying to interpret a respondent's comments without seeing the individual's facial expressions. This format would also make audiences sensitive to the
journalists' difficulty in extracting information from a conversation before the
person at the other end chose to hang up."

On occasion, the characters on "the other end of the line" were those who,
Woodward and Bernstein felt, were threatening their safety (former Attorney
General John Mitchell, for example, shouts a very specific threat concerning a
part of Katharine Graham's anatomy). More often, they feared others who were
neither seen nor heard. Pakula said he "had a very difficult time . . . characteriz-
ing the antagonists because you don't see them on-screen. . . . So we dramatized
them in two ways. One was that you see them on television, only on television. And
the other way they're characterized is through buildings. [In the beginning of the
film] all the buildings are lovely, charming little neo-Greek temples . . . lovely and
peaceful and romantic and all on a very human scale and sunny, and as the film
goes on it gets grayer and the buildings get bigger and bigger and bigger and the
people get tinier and tinier and tinier, and at the end they're these great Fascist
stone monoliths and our reporters walking underneath are these impotent, tiny
little figures totally dwarfed by power."

Pakula said that the impact of Nixon's appearances on television, each time "at the height of his power, depends, unlike any other film I've ever dealt with before, on your knowing how the story is going to end, on your knowing more than the characters [know about] what's going to happen after the film is over."

Pakula was concerned about the amount of dialogue necessary for the audience to understand the premise of *All the President's Men*. "I don't think there's a more verbal film that's ever been made," he said, but he hoped "that audiences would sense a great deal more about the characters than was verbally revealed on the screen."

On the other hand, Pakula said that he was "bored with people who say films have to be all visual. I've often wondered what would happen if radio had started before silent film, and if films had come out of radio. I think we would have a whole different sense of what's pure and what's impure. It's absurd to say that film is only visual."

In terms of the film's content, Pakula's intention was never simply to attack the conservatives of the Republican Party, although, as he said, "a lot of people don't believe me on this, especially a few Republicans I know." He went on, "That's not what investigative reporting is about; it's exposing things about people in power, whatever side they're on. But beyond that, it's not . . . just what those men were. It says something could happen in terms of the system all the time and there is a certain kind of watchfulness and vigilance that is always going to be required. The books are never closed on those threats to our system or to ourselves."

Pakula said that the first reaction of his friends and colleagues when they heard that he was going to direct the film was, "Oh, isn't it terrific. What a noble effort," because it would expose Nixon and the members of his administration as guilty of criminal behavior. But Pakula said, "It's not my job to put these people [the conspirators portrayed in the film] in double jeopardy. They're being punished by the law and the justice system. And you're dealing with people's reputations and you do feel [the responsibility of] that."

Pakula said, "My own feeling is that this kind of corruption, this danger to the electoral system, can't be restricted to one party. I think that people who are attracted to power share similar strengths and vulnerabilities. . . . I don't think we would have refused to do a movie if it had been about a Democrat."

Pakula and Redford planned the film meticulously before shooting began. "There would be nights at three or four in the morning" Pakula said, in which he and Redford engaged in "planning, talking, exploring, examining."

At last, the script rewritten, the cast complete, the shooting began with the scene of the Watergate burglary and exteriors in the streets of Washington while the set of the *Post* was being re-created in Burbank. The cameras began to roll on May 12, 1975; shooting in Burbank began on June 26.

Alan and Felice as children with their mother Jeannette in 1934 *Collection of Debby Maisel*

Jeanette Pakula and her son Alan at the wedding of Alan's sister Felice in 1947
Collection of Debby Maisel

Alan (at right) at the wedding reception
for his sister Felice and Murray Baxter
Collection of Debby Maisel

Alan about 20 *Collection of Debby Maisel*

At the bar mitzvah of Alan's nephew Rodd in
1963. Left to right: Alan; Paul and Jeannette
(Alan's father and mother); Felice (Alan's sis-
ter); Debby Maisel (Alan's niece); Murray Baxter
(Alan's brother-in-law); and Rodd Baxter
Collection of Debby Maisel

Robert Mulligan and Alan Pakula at work

Paramount Studios

Alan with Chris and Patty Murray,
shortly after his marriage to their mother,
Hope Lange *The Estate of Hope Lange*

On the wedding day of Alan Pakula and Hope Lange *William Claxton*

Rehearsing Jane Fonda for a scene in *Klute* Corbis

Alan in 1972 *Chris Murray*

Relaxing with Robert Redford and Bob Woodward during a break in the shooting

of *All the President's Men* All the President's Men © *Warner Bros., Inc. and Wildwood*

Enterprises, Inc. All rights reserved.

Jason Robards, Robert Redford, and Alan Pakula accepting awards from the New York Film Critics Circle for their work on *All the President's Men* Corbis

Alan with Martin Starger during the filming of *Sophie's Choice* Collection of Martin Starger

Peter MacNicol, Meryl Streep, and Kevin Kline on the roof of the Pink Palace in a scene from *Sophie's Choice* *Getty Images*

William Styron, Alan Pakula, and Kevin Kline on a break during the shooting of *Sophie's Choice*
Corbis

Rehearsing Meryl Streep for a scene in *Sophie's Choice* Corbis

Clowning for the camera at a party in 1984 are Bob Boorstin, Anna Boorstin, Alan and Hannah Pakula, and Louis Boorstin *Photo by Jasmine Lindsay Forman*

With Julia Roberts during the filming of **The Pelican Brief** *Ken Regan, Camera5*

Giving the commence-
ment address at Vassar
College in 1996

Diane Pineiro Zucker; Courtesy
of Vassar College/George Laws

Alan and Hannah with Debby Maisel's son Chad on Chad's bar mitzvah in 1998

Collection of Debby Maisel

Alan J. Pakula, 1928-98 *Ken Regan, Camera5*

CHAPTER ELEVEN

All the President's Men II:
Production and Post-Production

"All the President's Men is a picture of total detail of texture, because it's
tiny little things that add up to the destruction of this man [Nixon], not one
great big giant bold stroke. So [the details create] a tiny little mosaic."
—ALAN J. PAKULA

"Alan and I were both nuts for detail. Detail has always been a big deal for
me and it was a huge deal for him. His fascination with detail went into
outer space."
—ROBERT REDFORD

FOR A LONG MOMENT AT THE BEGINNING of the film the screen
appears to be simply a vast field of white accompanied by silence. Then, suddenly, a giant typewriter key slams explosively on to the field of white—a sheet of
paper. Then another slam, followed by another, typing out the date: June 1, 1972,
sixteen days before the Watergate burglary took place. The opening sequence signals that, as Pakula said, "this is a story of the power of the word, this is a story of
the power of the typewriter, it's a story of the power of writing machines. Actually,
the opening shot of those typewriter keys set the whole use of objects in the film.
If there was ever a picture which says on the most primitive level that the pen is
mightier than the sword," Pakula said, "this is it. . . . So when the typewriter keys
come down, we had whiplashes and gunshots mixed in with that sound; not
enough so you can tell, just enough to get that CRACK!"

After we see television images of a session of Congress waiting for Richard
Nixon's arrival to give an address, a cut takes us to the Watergate office building.
Watchman Frank Wills discovers the latch to an office in the Watergate building
taped open, and calls the police.

In menacing darkness, where, for much of the scene, the audience is looking in-from-outside, we see an office being ransacked. Then the police arrive and arrest the surprisingly well-dressed burglars. Pakula said he felt that the scene, which he referred to as "the prologue," "could be better. I recut it and recut it and recut it and I went to the first preview, thinking, 'They're going to kill me in the prologue.'" But when the audience members filled out response cards after the filming, "nobody ever mentioned the prologue. It seemed fine." But still, Pakula said, he thought "I could do better" in that scene.

Steven Soderbergh, the director of such films as *Traffic* and *sex, lies and videotape*, said recently that Pakula need not have worried. "A lot of filmmakers would have gone with the obvious thing," he remarked in 2001. "We'd have a close-up here of the guy talking, or the camera would move inside the room. But it is so much creepier like this"—with virtually no dialogue and the camera being set up outside the building, then in the hallway, watching the burglary take place behind glass.

After the arrests are shown, Pakula cuts abruptly from the darkness of the crime scene to the intense white light of the *Washington Post* and the posteresque colors he was determined to achieve.

"Beyond focusing on the foreground," Redford said, "we were constantly focusing on the background [of the newsroom]. Alan and I shared a feeling about how important background detail was, because it filled in and made it a deeper piece." Redford recalled that when he and Pakula looked at the actors playing *Washington Post* reporters they would ask, "Okay, what are *these* guys doing, what is their story? Some guy, way, way in the background. *Everybody* had to have a story, everybody had to have a connection, whether it was to each other or to the group or their typewriter or a phone call, they had to be totally involved, just the way people would in a newsroom." This meant that the actors playing the editors—Robards, Jack Warden as Harry Rosenfeld, and Martin Balsam as Managing Editor Howard Simons—needed to be on the set constantly, since they were frequently visible in the background.

Passion for detail also extended to scenes outside the newsroom. "In scenes showing the break-in at the Watergate," historian Robert Brent Toplin observed, "the filmmakers used $100 bills in sequential order, just as the real burglars did, and they used the same model walkie-talkies." In addition, Frank Wills, the security guard who discovered the Watergate break-in, played himself.

During a brief scene involving two of the newspaper's editors, we see Carl Bernstein framed in the doorway just outside Harry Rosenfeld's office. Then Rosenfeld calls Bob Woodward at home to tell him to cover the arraignment of the Watergate burglars. From that point on, we remain with Woodward and Bernstein throughout the film.

Because one or both of the characters was always on-screen, the director needed to convey the essence of their characters to the audience early in the film. Pakula was continually aware of the necessity not to glamorize Woodward and Bernstein or to make them appear heroic. The story, he was convinced, was that of two ordinary, hardworking individuals proceeding—sometimes by inches, sometimes in great leaps—from one discovery to the next, eventually revealing a vast conspiracy; however, he felt it was important to show the mistakes they made along the way.

Woodward and Bernstein are shown as flawed characters, willing to ask aggressive, troubling questions (such as badgering a colleague to get information from her former fiancé, using devious means) and to deceive sources (by playing variations of "good cop-bad cop," among other ruses) in order to derive information. "I think we feel the reporters' ruthlessness in the film," Pakula said. "In dealing with an administration, part of whose tragedy was that the end seemed to justify any means . . . Woodstein [the nickname by which Woodward and Bernstein collectively became known at the *Post*] certainly did not hesitate to have *their* end justify some very questionable means. Their end was to get the story. . . . To *reveal*: that's their job, that's their hunger, and it has to be a desperate hunger for them to succeed. . . . It's a highly unsentimental line of work."

Woodward and Bernstein ask two of the women who work at the *Post* to use their relationships with men involved in the conspiracy to get information the reporters could not otherwise have gotten. "One of the people at the *Post* was disturbed by the fact that the two *Post* women were shown using their sexuality," Pakula said. But "it's not the women who come off questionably, it's the reporters who come off questionably. Because they're exploiting them."

The reporters are also shown as immensely resourceful, knowing when to refrain from taking notes if a source would be made uncomfortable by the sight of a pen and notepad, intuiting how their behavior and attitudes (even if the attitudes are feigned) might encourage a source to cooperate, and spending enormous amounts of time on information that may or may not lead to a significant discovery. Despite the flaws in their characters, Pakula clearly intended the audience to like and empathize with Woodward and Bernstein.

One way of maintaining the anti-heroic view of the reporters was in the portrayal of their characters. Woodward is shown as a mild, almost colorless character, a characteristic derived from the behavior and self-image of the actual Bob Woodward, who, as Robert Redford described him, "likes being seen as bland. He wants you to think of him that way." In fact, Redford told Pakula during early conferences, "Woodward's a boring guy. He's not the most exciting guy in the world to play, and I can't get a grip on the guy because he's so careful and hidden."

Pakula characterized Woodward as "a very controlled man [with] very controlled energy, and he's obsessed, he's obsessed with a story. Any story. Put him on a story about ratshit in restaurants [a story Woodward had actually covered for the *Post*] and he's just as obsessed about that as he is about Watergate." Woodward's bland, obsessive, controlled personality would have been difficult for any actor to portray dynamically. Pakula told Redford, "All I can give you in this film—you're not going to like me for it—is that you've got to *concentrate* and you've got to *think*, and the audience has got to be able to see you think and they've got to be able to feel your concentration. That story has to mean so much to you that it means that much to the audience. And that's tough. In half of your scenes Dustin is out interviewing people and you're playing with a telephone. But that's what it's about. That's what that kind of reporting is about."

For a time, Redford was uncomfortable in the role. As Pakula observed, "Bob felt, 'there's no part, I can't hold on to it.'" But Pakula noticed early on that Redford, frustrated in his attempts to come to grips with Woodward's character, was showing a "contained energy," as he put it. Pakula tried to capture that quality during the first few weeks of filming in Washington, as Woodward was seen hailing taxicabs and walking through the streets. "I'd say, 'Bob, get your hands out of your pockets.' There's really nothing wrong with Bob having his hands in his pockets," but Pakula was concerned about "a jaunty quality about Bob Redford," whereas with Woodward, "it's held in, it's more reserved, it's more controlled. So the hands in the pockets became a symbol. I wanted a straight, kind of linear quality." In the end, Pakula said, he was able to help mold Redford's performance through his physical characterization, even though "I lost a few on the hands in the pockets."

The key to the character, as Redford and Pakula realized before the shooting moved to Burbank, was that despite Woodward's bland exterior, he is "really a killer underneath," in Redford's words. That insight provided the actor with the key to playing the role. After he became comfortable with his approach to playing Woodward, Redford "started to get into his scenes in the newsroom," Pakula said. "He was in much better shape from the minute he did the first series of phone calls to Howard Hunt. Because suddenly there it was: he had the concentration." As the completed film demonstrates, Redford's performance caught the qualities of containment and concentration Pakula described to him as essential for the role. Pakula said, "Bob has much more range than people give him credit for. . . . I have enormous admiration for [his] work in the film."

But the director's admiration did not make the actor's job any easier. Essentially, as Pakula said, "all the telephone calls he makes are done in one set-up." Redford was concerned that the lack of variety would make his performance less interesting. After completing his first scene on the telephone, unaware that the camera position and lighting would not need adjustment, he said to Pakula, "I'll be in the trailer. When you and Gordy have the second set-up [i.e., the cameras moved to their new positions and the set lit to the director's and cinematographer's satisfaction], call me." Pakula answered, "We have the set-up for the second phone call. And we have the set-up for the third phone call and the fourth phone call and for the phone call to Howard Hunt." Redford asked, plaintively, "The same dull set-up, me and the telephone, and the camera never moves?"

Pakula nodded yes, and explained why: "Part of reporting is the agony of sitting by that phone and going from one phone call to another phone call to another phone call, and you never get off your ass, and you're trapped in there, and the tiresome quality of that work. To have done a lot of camera moves would have broken the concentration rather than intensified it. You risk boring the audience, but if I give them distractions, the picture becomes dishonest right away. [The audience has] got to know what that concentration is like, what hard work it is." Redford conveyed that agonizing hard work so well, Pakula said, that "at the end of those phone calls he's aged about five or six or ten years. He is battered by that. It's like he's been locked in there, in a sense, and that's just what I wanted."

Shooting the scenes in which Woodward and the crowd watch the television set with both in clear focus "required using a diopter lens, which is really two lenses in one—essentially bifocal glasses, in a lens sense—so you can have one field of action over here that's in focus and the plane of action closer to you on this side is [also] in focus[32]," Pakula explained. "This meant that if Redford moved his hand half an inch too far . . . his hand would go out of focus [and it would have] killed the shot. It locked him in, which actors hate. And it meant that Bob was going to have to concentrate on two things at once. I wanted to do the whole thing in one shot to keep up the intensity of going from one call to another. All the time, the camera is moving in, imperceptibly, continually for six minutes, which means that the lens focus keeps changing. It ends up, several minutes later, on a big close-up of Woodward."

During one scene, Woodward is seen alternating between calls to Kenneth Dahlberg and to Clark MacGregor, the head of CREEP, all in an attempt to learn how Dahlberg's check wound up in the bank account of one of the burglars. Redford gives a virtuoso performance as a man who is being overwhelmed by information and trying to keep the various strands clear in his mind. "It's a major

---

[32]An invisible line in the middle of the diopter lens permits the use of different focal lengths on each side. But the line must be hidden so that the audience cannot detect the use of the lens. Otherwise, the effect would seem to be merely a trick. Since the invisible line can be either vertical or horizontal, Willis and Pakula were able to conceal the line in a pillar in the newsroom or on the edge of a desk. The lens was used several times in All the President's Men.

scene," Pakula said. "One part of the screen showed Bob Redford at his desk, making calls; the other part [showed] people in the city room clustered around a television set, watching the actual news about the withdrawal of Senator Thomas F. Eagleton of Missouri as the Democratic Vice-Presidential candidate after his medical history was made a campaign issue." The inclusion of this footage (the audience hears only the audio portion of the report), which reflected badly on the Democratic Party, is perhaps the best example of Redford's contention that Pakula was not "a knee-jerk liberal."

The first time the sequence of telephone calls was filmed, the scene, including the background action, took many hours to set up, by which time Redford was tired and unable to do his best work. Pakula shot seven takes, but "in my heart I thought it could be better," he said. At the dailies the next morning, "everybody said it worked, that it was terrific. Well, the shot worked and Bob was good. He was good. He wasn't bad. In one take he was excellent here and in another take he was excellent there and in another take he was excellent here. But you could only use one take because there was no cut in it. If you cut it you just wipe out the whole hypnotic effect and the whole continuous build."

Because the viewers at the dailies had expressed such enthusiasm, Pakula kept his reservations to himself, but he was not pleased. Weeks later, Pakula ran the scene again and still found it less than satisfactory. He went to Redford and said, "Look, Bob, your work is good. It would have been even better if you'd done it earlier [in the day]. I know it's complicated to set this whole shot up again, but your concentration and intensity could be much better. I think we should take another stab at it." Redford, who, as producer, also had to take the expense of reshooting the sequence into account, was initially reluctant, but ultimately said, "If you feel that strongly about it, let's do it." The difference, after the scene was shot, Pakula said, "was day and night."

If Woodward is portrayed as a bland character, Bernstein is shown throughout the film as high-strung, nervous (he often stutters), with a tendency toward loss of control. He was, as Redford said, a perfect character for Dustin Hoffman to play: "a very flashy kind of extroverted guy, very colorful."

Pakula was continually on the lookout for moments that were ineffective because the personas of Redford and Hoffman obliterated the characters they were playing. He would interrupt scenes at such times, saying, "Oh oh oh, that's a little Redford, oh oh oh, Dustin, you're jumping all over, you're arm-waving again." Because of what Redford termed Pakula's "great taste and sensibility about overplaying and things of that sort," Pakula was able to keep the actors' own personalities in check.

This is not to say, however, that the actors' personalities were eradicated. As

Pakula said, "You use things in Bob Redford; you use things in Dustin Hoffman. The parts become an integration of the actors and the characters. It's the only way I know how to work with actors."

While shooting the film, Pakula learned that Hoffman and Redford operated very differently. "Dustin loves to talk," Pakula said. "He just loves to talk. Dustin wants to examine a scene and examine a scene and examine a scene. Bob likes to examine it and say, 'Okay, let's go. Let's do it.' He's very intuitive, he's very quick. Dusty is examining how many angels are on the head of a pin and he's only gotten to the tenth angel out of two thousand and Bob is ready to start the take, and Dustin says, 'Wait a minute. I've got nineteen hundred and ninety [more angels] to examine before we do the scene.'" Pakula's problem was, as he expressed it, "By the time Dustin is [ready] I'm going to lose Bob."

Pakula was convinced that Hoffman worked best when permitted numerous takes, and he simply ignored Redford's repeated requests to alter Hoffman's methodical work process. "There's a part of me," Pakula said, "if you start putting pressure on me I turn into a rock. It's passive resistance. Like, I'm not going to move on from this scene until I think the scene is there. I become Sitting Bull. And he [Redford] can't move me and he's so frustrated. He's producing the picture, Goddammit, and he can't move me." But, despite occasional arguments— "We had our battles," Pakula said—Redford reluctantly came to concede that Pakula's methods were not only good for Hoffman, they suited Pakula's typically thorough, methodical directorial style.

Ultimately, Redford felt that he and Hoffman "worked very well together." And, although he was ready to shoot long before Hoffman, he, too, enjoyed the process of discussing each of his character's motivation in depth before filming a scene.

Early in the film, Woodward attends the arraignment of the Watergate burglars, where he hears one of them, James McCord, identify himself as an employee of the CIA. McCord is also, as it turns out, the security coordinator of the Committee to Re-elect the President. Later, a source informs Woodward that Howard Hunt's name was found in the address books of two of the burglars, and that Hunt, like McCord, worked at the CIA. But Hunt's apparent involvement adds another dimension, for Hunt is also employed by the White House. Woodward discovers that Hunt has checked out many books about Senator Edward Kennedy, perhaps because, as a source suggests, the White House is obsessed with Kennedy, believing that he will be the most formidable candidate to run against Richard Nixon in 1972, and wants to compile a catalogue of Kennedy's personal and political weaknesses.

A search for the books Hunt has been reading (to discover if Hunt was researching Kennedy) leads Woodward and Bernstein to the Library of Congress, where a librarian presents them with thousands of call slips. This culminates with one of the most famous shots in the film, a shot conceived by Pakula. While Woodward and Bernstein are riffling through the call slips, the camera, shooting from above, with a tight view of the slips, begins rising toward the ceiling of the immense room. As seen from a greater and greater height, Woodward and Bernstein are shown as mere specks on the screen, searching through call slips that are all but invisible due to the extreme distance of the shot. The sequence was such a long and difficult one that it was telescoped with two dissolves, and cost $90,000 to film. Gordon Willis described it with understatement as "no easy trick to pull off." But, as producer-director Pieter Jan Brugge observed, the shot gave the film a "magnitude, that these guys are really looking for a needle in a haystack. Alan found visual language for the extraordinary challenge that these two guys were up against."

"Some people say [the sequence] was a tour-de-force for its own sake," Pakula said. "I don't think it was. I tried to do several things with it. Starting with those little library slips as clues, filling the screen at first, enormous in their size, and then pulling back to the top of the Library of Congress, where the reporters are so small, gave me a chance to dramatize the endless time it takes to do these things . . . It also gave me a sense of how lost they are in this thing, how tiny these figures are in terms of the enormity of the task."

From a telephone booth on the street, Woodward calls a source he has used before, a mysterious man, evidently a government official, who enjoys speaking in riddles and toying with Woodward. The man, whom we will come to know as Deep Throat, is not visible in the scene, but is heard over the telephone. Hal Holbrook conveys his apprehension at becoming involved in the story Woodward is investigating. The following day, however, Deep Throat contacts Woodward (by placing a typed note inside Woodward's copy of the *Washington Post*), informing him how to get in touch.

In the following scene, Woodward, following Deep Throat's instructions, places a red flag in a flower pot on his balcony. Then the lighting suddenly changes from bright sunlight to near-darkness. Woodward is seen taking a series of taxi-cabs to the parking garage where he will meet Deep Throat. The sequence is accompanied by slow and ominous music—the first time we have heard a musical accompaniment, and the first half-hour of the film has already elapsed.

Steven Soderbergh commented on the lighting of the scenes with Woodward and Deep Throat in the darkness of the underground parking garage. "Gordon Willis at his absolute best," he said. As a specific illustration, Soderbergh noted that "In his close-ups Holbrook's got a light right on his eyes, but it's maybe two stops down, at the very edge of perception. And there is another light off to the side that just draws a line right around him, highlighting the side of his face. He looks like a ghost." Then, when the camera cuts to Woodward, "with Redford we get skin tones, but with Holbrook it's just completely monochromatic. Deep Throat is not even human."

Pakula employs an unrealistic touch for the first and only time in Deep Throat's second scene. In the midst of the elliptical conversation between Deep Throat and Woodward (the former tells the latter not to lose sight of "the over-all"), Woodward's attention is diverted momentarily by a squealing car. When he turns around, Deep Throat has vanished. A long shot shows Woodward to be alone, although Deep Throat's utter disappearance would have been impossible in the seconds that Woodward was looking away. Again, there is a suggestion that Deep Throat is somehow not entirely real, that his mysteriousness and the apprehension it causes is somehow augmented by Woodward's imagination.

Leaving the garage, Woodward walks on the darkened street, then breaks into a run, fearful that he is being pursued. He turns to look, but no one is behind him. Again: is the danger real or only in Woodward's imagination?

Deep Throat's scenes are powerful in part because of their moral dimension. For all the character's cynicism, arrogance, and world-weariness, for all his unwillingness to do more than hint at the truth, Deep Throat and Hugh Sloan (the CREEP treasurer) are portrayed as the only figures associated with the government who appear to have had moral qualms about the Nixon regime.

Redford's scenes with Hal Holbrook as Deep Throat were characterized by Pakula as a relationship "of teacher and acolyte. [Woodward] is intimidated by Deep Throat. He's afraid of making a fool of himself. That worked well" in terms of minimizing Redford's star quality.

During Woodward's first scene with Deep Throat, Woodward says, "All we have are pieces. We can't seem to figure out what the puzzle is supposed to look like." Deep Throat's advice is both practical and cryptic: "Follow the money," he counsels. Woodward presses him, trying to get more specific information. "No," Deep Throat says, "I have to do this my way."

Deep Throat's advice leads Woodward and Bernstein to investigate the funding of the Committee to Re-elect the President. One of the people Woodward and Bernstein interview is Hugh Sloan's frightened bookkeeper (when Sloan worked for Maurice Stans, the Finance Committee Chairman of CREEP), a character played by Jane Alexander. It is also the first of several scenes giving glimpses into the private lives of those whom Woodward and Bernstein called upon: others are with Sloan, the conscience-stricken treasurer of the committee, and with Donald Segretti, who planted false stories about the Democrats with the press, but does-n't understand why his activities should be thought reprehensible.

These scenes came about largely because, in Pakula's words, "the essence of investigative reporting . . . is making people tell you things they don't want to tell you. Well, how you do that depends on who they are, so you must have a very strong sense of the characters that they interview; otherwise these characters just become devices for the narrative, which would be very boring."

As a result, Pakula said, "I spent endless time with the actors in discussions of the characters they were playing. There were things that were never verbalized in the film that nevertheless added to the suspense." The work paid off in fully developed performances. "The actor has all that going to texture his performance," Pakula noted, "and, even though his background is never discussed, the audience will feel a dimension it would not feel otherwise."

Jane Alexander's scenes are among the most effective in the film, and provided Pakula with "one of the most exciting weeks I've ever had filming anything." The first scene was shot "in a tiny little house in Maryland," so tiny that "there was almost no room for the camera." With insufficient space for the characters to move, Hoffman as Bernstein interrogates Alexander (called Judy Hoback in the film), whose uneasiness at becoming involved is palpable. Both actors are, as Pakula said, "at the top of their form" in the scene. Pakula said he "wanted this hypnotic thing where [Bernstein] felt that if he made one wrong move, if he scared her, he would lose the whole story, and the more she said the more he realized how important she was, and if he lost her he would never get it again. So [the scene] just became quieter and quieter and quieter. And in one take all I said to Jane was, 'Whisper, make it hard for him to hear you. Every take you do, lower your voice one more notch.'" In each take, Alexander spoke her lines so softly that Hoffman strained to hear. "So he's got to work, he's got to sweat," Pakula said. "He could not break into it and say 'louder' because he knew as the character she would withdraw." Interestingly, Hoffman picked up Alexander's method; as she became quieter, he lowered his voice even more. The audience must strain in order to hear them both.

The scene was shot only after Hoffman and Alexander rehearsed the script the day before, "doing a lot of re-wording, rewriting," Alexander said. Whether Pakula would have taken the same liberties with a script someone else had written is open to speculation, but since he had written a good deal of it, he had no qualms. (He did not tell Alexander that he and Redford had rewritten Goldman's screenplay.)

The scene is well-achieved for another reason, said Steven Soderbergh. "Throughout the whole scene the camera remains the same distance away from both of them. It never goes in for a close-up. It never changes its distance at all. By maintaining the same distance, it keeps the intensity building in the scene. Normally, you'd go in and out. And shooting a scene that way can be effective, too. But there is a different kind of energy that comes from maintaining the same shots. You just get a sense that these filmmakers are so secure, that they have complete confidence in their material and their performers." Not until the end of the scene does the camera pull back, a sign to the audience that the scene is over.

Regarding the lack of camera movement, Pakula said the scene portrayed two characters "caught together in time, and that's the essence of that kind of confrontation between the reporter and the person he's interviewing. You're just locked in there, and if the camera had started to move, it would have broken the whole hypnotic quality."

Jane Alexander felt that a great deal of the success of her scene with Dustin Hoffman was due to the lighting: "It's brilliant. In that scene, to have me partly in shadow. It was conducive to creating the sinister atmosphere on the part of the government." In a later scene, Woodward and Bernstein return together to interrogate "Judy Hoback." Pakula said to Gordon Willis, "I would like you to do this as if you were doing an impressionist painting. I want it lyrical, I want dappled sunlight coming through the trees."

Alexander remembered that she arrived for shooting "in a little blue dress, a summer dress that I had on. Alan said, 'That's perfect!' I said, 'Oh, Alan, that's not my costume.' He said, 'That's perfect. That's what I want you to wear. Just as you are. No makeup.'" His response gave her the feeling that he had complete confidence in her, that she was ideal for the role. Alexander recalled recently how helpful Pakula was in shaping her characterization. "It is a long time ago," she concluded, "but I remember the great directors, the great people I've worked with. It's not difficult to recall, because there are only a few of them. Certainly, for my money, Pakula ranks right up there."

Pakula's devotion to improvisation was not shared by Redford, partly because of his discipline as an actor, partly because he was perfectly satisfied with the script he and Pakula had written, and partly because of his concern that an improvised scene would require a longer time to shoot, thus extending the film's shooting time and straining the budget. As producer, Redford was also annoyed by the amount of time some sequences took before Pakula was finally satisfied. Guiding the performances of extras, lighting the set, and placing the cameras all seemed to take an eternity.

Pakula was well aware of Redford's irritation. "I know there have been times when each of us thought the other was a royal pain in the ass," he said. A rift between the producer and director was evident to Bob Woodward, who recalled, "I don't know if they parted this project friends."

If Redford was sometimes irritated by Pakula's methodical approach, he was delighted that his recommendation of Jason Robards was working out so well. At the first read-through of the script, in the cellar of the Watergate apartment house, Pakula knew that Redford had been correct in lobbying for Robards to play the role. Robards began reading—"and out came Ben Bradlee," Pakula said. "Out came this sense of, 'I'm a bigger star than you, Redford, and I'm a bigger star than you, Dustin Hoffman.' Bob and Dustin and I looked at each other. [We knew that] he had it. He came in with it. And it just stunned me."

Pakula reserved the only "star entrance" of the film for Robards. "Up until he comes on, there's almost no camera movement, very little," Pakula said. "When he comes out of his office, arbitrarily out of nowhere, we move with him down half the set; we give him a star entrance out of Belasco[33], all stops out. And you say, here comes the king." The star entrance, combined with Robards' commanding performance, worked to perfection, Pakula said, because Woodward and Bernstein "had to be cowed by him. And then, when the stories started to go bad on them, they had to be terrified of having failed him. And Jason had a glamour in that picture that I'd never seen [from him] before, and that was essential to the film."

Ben Bradlee was astonished by the accuracy of Jason Robards' portrayal—an accuracy he himself didn't recognize until it was pointed out to him. "Pakula has Robards walking out of the newsroom, in a good mood. He says, 'Go ahead and print that sucker,' or something like that. And then on the way past a desk he just swats the desk with his hand. I wasn't conscious of making that gesture, but people say I did that a lot, and Alan had obviously seen me do it."

Bradlee is the only character in the film that is in any way idealized. In Robards' interpretation, Bradlee is commanding, decisive, and wise. Still, he is not portrayed as sentimental in the least, as Pakula pointed out. "His concern is not about hurting people unnecessarily, it's, 'Is the *paper* going to be in danger?' He never says, 'Poor John Mitchell, poor so-and-so.'"

Robards found the role of Bradlee to be infuriatingly repetitive. At one point Robards said to Pakula, "My God, all the scenes are the same. [The only thing I say is] 'Where's the fucking story?' That's every scene I do." Pakula agreed that Robards had identified a problem, "the problem of orchestrating it so it wasn't all in the same key, because a lot of the writing of the scenes was on the same level."

Remarkably, although Robards played a role into which repetition was inextricably woven, he managed to give a dynamic performance in which the character seemed throughout to be changing and developing. "It was a question of orchestrating and playing different tones" for each scene, Pakula said. He helped Robards accomplish this in several ways. "The staging is different in every scene," he said, "and there is a different concept, hopefully, to each scene, and you get a different color."

---

[33]David Belasco (1859-1931), the most famous American stage director of his era, was noted for his ability to create and shape the careers of star performers.

Hugh Sloan (played by Stephen Collins), who is interviewed soon after the interview with Jane Alexander's character, is portrayed as tortured by his association with CREEP. In the first scene in which Woodward and Bernstein interview Sloan, Pakula carefully arranged the visual elements. "There's sun on the wingchair, soft light through gauzy curtains," he said. "The sun's on him . . . there he sits—a very formal portrait. We shot a medium shot and a close-up, only used the close-up for one line as the tag end of the scene, never used it for the rest of the scene because in the close-up you lost the formality, that whole sense of a modern version of the young Virginia squire—decent, aristocratic, sitting in his wingchair with a nineteenth-century convex mirror behind him, almost ready for Gilbert Stuart to come along and paint him. In the midst of this precise tableau with the shaft of sunlight, all these cheap, corrupt little facts come out—in counterpoint to what we see, and indeed in counterpoint to a simple, traditional kind of decency that we sense in the character of Sloan."

Hugh Sloan fills in another part of the puzzle for Woodward and Bernstein when he tells them, "the committee is not an independent operation. Everything's cleared with the White House." This provides the reporters with proof, for the first time, that the slush fund was controlled by the White House, and that the Watergate burglary was almost surely linked to the highest office in the United States.

As the film progresses, Woodward and Bernstein are able to link the burglars with White House consultant Charles Colson, and, by tracing the financial contributions to CREEP, implicate Maurice Stans and John Mitchell, the Attorney General.

A scene late in the movie shows Bernstein interviewing lawyer Donald Segretti (played by Robert Walden). The scene is notable—and, at first, a bit disorienting for the viewer—because Segretti is played throughout as a boyish, pleasant young lawyer, puzzled about why he should be the subject of Bernstein's investigation; but his activities—successfully sabotaging the political system (and, in particular, Edmund Muskie's candidacy for the Democratic presidential nomination) through a series of deceptions—are disreputable and shameful. Hoffman as Bernstein plays the scene differently than any other interrogation in the film. He is relaxed, friendly, seemingly sympathetic—just the right qualities to elicit Segretti's confession. At last, Segretti drops his apparent confidence and tells Bernstein that he will probably be disbarred and sent to jail.

In a later sequence, the *Post* goes to press with the story that H. R. Haldeman, the second most powerful man in the country, was one of five people to control the slush fund. However, the story is based on a faulty assumption by Bernstein, allowing press secretary Ron Ziegler, on behalf of the administration, to accuse the *Post* of making false allegations based on Bradlee's sympathy for the Democratic Party.

Ziegler's accusation is seen on the television set in the *Post*'s newsroom. The notion of using television images to project images of Nixon, Ziegler, Vice President Spiro Agnew, and others, was partly dictated by Pakula's belief that "there's something about seeing people on television or film that makes them godlike, untouchable, beyond your reach."

Originally, Pakula planned to place the television set a few feet in front of Redford, whose hands and typewriter appeared to be larger than the television screen. But Pakula was bothered by the arrangement. "So," he said, "we put a TV set way in front of Woodward so that the cheering people . . . would fill three-quarters of the screen while Woodward typing would be a tiny figure in the background, thus dramatizing the David and Goliath struggle I wanted."

Pakula builds the tension during the next several scenes. After listening to Ziegler's tirade, Ben Bradlee angrily calls "Woodstein" into his office to berate them for their inaccuracy. The tension of the film increases as it seems possible that the paper may withdraw its support of Woodward and Bernstein.

At Woodward's third and final trip to the parking garage, he insists that Deep Throat stop being coy and tell what he knows. Deep Throat confirms, "It was a Haldeman operation." And, he adds, "the cover-up had little to do with Watergate. It was mainly to protect the covert operations. It leads everywhere." He also tells Woodward, "Your lives are in danger."

Bernstein and Woodward drive to Bradlee's house late at night. Afraid that Bradlee's house is bugged, they ask him to step on to the lawn as they reveal their fear for their lives. They confess their anguish that they may have destroyed their reputations and harmed their ability to discover the truth, but Bradlee urges them to continue working on the investigation.

The film's penultimate scene occurs on the day of Nixon's inauguration to a second presidential term in 1973. A television set in the newsroom shows Nixon receiving a twenty-one-gun salute as Woodward and Bernstein are seen in the background, at their desks, reporting stories on their typewriters. "That," as Pakula said, "is really the David and Goliath image right there, and that little pecking away is going to overcome the enormous power represented in that [salute]." The scene ends, in Pakula's words, with the camera moving in "and the guns boom-boom aloud, and in the background you hear these typewriters going—of theirs, Woodward and Bernstein—and now the camera moves in, closer and closer to them, past the television screen and all the way to the back of this newsroom, and as the camera gets closer and closer to them the sound of the typewriter keys gets louder and louder, the sound of the boom of the guns softer and softer, and by the end the sound of the typewriter keys has overpowered the sound of the guns in a twenty-one-gun salute. And what is it saying? It's saying that the power of the word turned out to be stronger than the power of the President." On another occasion, Pakula said, "Thank God they had the twenty-one-gun salute, because it set up the typewriter keys as weapons."

Pakula noted, "There's never been a film I know of that has depended so much on the basic knowledge the audience has and that uses that, takes it for granted. That's deliberate." Particularly at the end of the movie, when Nixon's triumphant inauguration is being shown on the television screen in the *Post* newsroom, "the power of that shot depends upon the audience knowing what the President at the height of his power doesn't know," Pakula said, "what even the reporters typing away don't know: that in two years, what they're writing is going to force him to resign." The scene derives its power from the audience's knowledge of "how important the story was; and the suspense came from realizing how close it came to the story never getting out." Pakula added, "One of the things that makes the film work is that the audience knows how much more important this story is long before the characters on-screen do, so that little things hold them that wouldn't have held them if they didn't know."

Then—a cut to a teletype machine, printing out headlines that were written during the next two years. The headlines report the convictions of such officials as Haldeman, Ehrlichman, and Mitchell, culminating with "August 9, 1974— Nixon Resigns. Gerald Ford to Become 38th President at Noon Today." The film thus ends abruptly, in what was really the middle of the investigative process. Pakula said, "I liked the irony of ending right after their greatest defeat, the Haldeman story. They were right but their story was wrong. That was Bill Goldman's concept before I came on the film and the more I worked on the film the more I came to trust it. The two of them and Bradlee against the world; everyone saying they've obviously gone too far, while we know it goes further than that."

The teletype machine sequence was not added until after the first preview, when it became apparent that the audience needed a reminder about the impact of Woodward and Bernstein's investigative reports. The headlines on the teletype also serve to release the accumulated tension, so fully developed that *All the President's Men* seems to encompass several genres: a newspaper story, a superior detective story, a probing psychological portrayal of its central characters in the grip of fear.

At the end of the credits, rather than the customary notice that "The people and places in this film are fictitious," a notice announces that "Wildwood Enterprises [Redford's film company] assumes responsibility for the content of the motion picture, which is based on factual material from the book, *All the President's Men*." Pakula explained, "The reason for that notation at the end was that the *Washington Post* was absolutely terrified of the film being made. . . . And for good reason. [Therefore,] that was a disclaimer letting them off the hook, that the

Washington Post had no control over the material and only the film company had." Fearing that he, as the director of the film, might be sued, Pakula, through his lawyers, inserted "a clause in the contract saying that if the film I delivered [was] approved by the Warners legal department—and we were constantly checking with lawyers all along the way—that I would be indemnified from any libel suits."

Pakula was sensitive to the need to be as truthful in their portrayal of historical incidents as he and Redford could possibly be. "In terms of accusations or charges," he said, "nothing was ever said that wasn't corroborated in the book, or in [Woodward and Bernstein's] notes for their stories. That became our guideline; Woodward and Bernstein had their two-source rule, and this was our rule."

The validity of the film's conclusions are confirmed by the fact that no one accused of wrongdoing brought a lawsuit against Wildwood Enterprises. Since many of them had already been convicted of criminal behavior, any attempts on their part to file lawsuits against Redford or Pakula or Warner Bros. must have seemed pointless to the conspirators themselves.

The *New York Times* asked each of the persons involved in the Watergate scandal "to comment on whether or not the movie dealt fairly with the facts." Only three of them—two of them referred to in the film—replied. On May 23, 1976, the *Times* printed the response of Kenneth Dahlberg, the Midwestern chairman of CREEP, who called the movie "grossly inaccurate . . . a degrading, self-serving fabrication." Rather than being "nervous, scared, and apprehensive . . . somebody with something to hide," as portrayed in the scene during which he spoke to Woodward on the telephone, Dahlberg contended that he was "very straightforward and up-front." (But Pakula, who was in possession of Woodward's notes, made at the time of the phone call to Dahlberg, insisted that the film's portrayal was entirely faithful to Woodward's notes.) Charles Colson dismissed the film by saying, "I was bored." Further, he chided the filmmakers for their suggestion that Woodward and Bernstein feared "that they [were] being bugged and their lives [were] threatened. Come, come now," he wrote. "There was not a shred of evidence that anything of the sort was going on."

Critic and historian William E. Leuchtenberg also claimed that "the film particularly strains credibility when it suggests that the reporters' lives were in danger." However, as Robert Redford has pointed out, Woodward and Bernstein *believed* their lives to have been in danger because Deep Throat explicitly said so to Woodward, and the film, based upon the reporters' point of view, accurately recreates their fear. It does not show assassins chasing the reporters in the streets of Washington, nor does it allege that assassins existed.

In terms of directorial techniques employed throughout the picture, Pakula used more close-ups and medium close-ups in *All the President's Men* than he did in most of his films. This is particularly effective when the camera slowly pulls back for a long shot, for it is during those moments that the spectator can assess in his or her mind how much information the reporters have gleaned and how far they have gotten in putting together the various pieces of the puzzle. And the effectiveness of the lighting scheme cannot be minimized, for it serves as a visual metaphor for the film's theme: the attempt to extract the truth—the light—from those who wish to hide in the darkness.

The post-production work, including the editing, musical scoring, and sound mixing, was overseen by Redford as well as by Pakula. Pakula developed the idea of the typewriter keys' loud thwacking at the beginning of the film. He and Redford then decided to apply the same notion to all writing instruments. The technique is maintained throughout the film, for whenever a pencil or pen is seen writing upon a piece of paper, the sound of the writing instrument is ratcheted up slightly beyond its realistic level, so that, as Pakula said, "it was like the sound of little rats scratching their way into these huge walls of power, bringing them down in a way that all the guns in the world could not." The same technique was used when, for example, a newspaper was being unfolded.

Using sound in this way was perfectly appropriate for the film. Pakula, always known as a director who spent a great deal of time in post-production, concerned himself with sound as much as with any other aspect of his movies. "Sound is as much a part of films today as visuals," he said. "You try to orchestrate the sound track very carefully for an effect . . . That's one of the great tools you have as a director—what you do with the sound track."

Throughout the film, music is used minimally. Altogether, there is probably no more than fifteen minutes of musical accompaniment. But every note of David Shire's score adds to the film's tension—partly because it is used so sparingly.

Pakula was an advocate of the "less is more" school of art, applying that belief in many of his films, particularly as it applied to music. Michael Small, who composed music for nine different films by Pakula, said, "Alan used to use an expression whenever I would overdo a moment [with his music]: 'This film is getting too big for its own britches.'" That, as Small said, reflected "his elegance and taste." Pakula was wary of music when it was used to "push," "force," or "milk emotions." Using music in that way was a sign that the director did not "trust the actors," he said.

As the producer of All the President's Men, Redford would offer opinions during the post-production process, and, Pakula said, "Occasionally we'd disagree, but he never forgot who the director was, and it never came to a knockdown-dragout."

Pakula often said that All the President's Men was the reverse of The Parallax View, in terms of its philosophical outlook. If The Parallax View represented the destruction of the myth of the American hero (and was therefore a pessimistic film), All the President's Men represented the resurrection of the hero, and the notion that two men can right the wrongs of a vast political system (and represents hope for the future).

All the President's Men received eight Academy Award nominations, including Best Picture. Incredibly, in a field that included *Taxi Driver* and *Network*, *Rocky*—a mediocre film in contrast to its competitors—was chosen as the winner. Pakula was nominated for Best Director. Among the winners were Jason Robards for Best Supporting Actor. Robards also won the Best Supporting Actor award of the National Board of Review of Motion Pictures, and Pakula was cited as Best Director by that organization. The National Society of Film Critics cited the film as best picture. The New York Film Critics Circle voted *All the President's Men* the best film of the year, Pakula the best director, and Robards the best supporting actor. Pakula received the Director of the Year Award from the National Association of Theater Owners.

In 2003, his irritation with Pakula during the filming long forgotten, Robert Redford summed up his experience working with the director in these words:

> The reason that Alan and I got along so well was, whatever my reputation was or my image was or whatever you want to call it, it never entered our relationship. Somebody else with less than a strong ego or a sense of self would maybe have had a harder time, because it had been my project. But Alan was just terrific about that, he was very collaborative, he had respect for my position as producer and he honored that, but ego never became an issue. And as a result, his willingness to be open and accepting of ideas made the whole experience better because I could relax. We were able to work our own points of view well together, and I think that made it a better film. Also, Alan completely understood what that film was about and what it needed to be doing. And that kind of broad grip on things, I think, contributed a lot to the success of the film.

As for Pakula, he made clear his respect for Redford as a producer and also noted that his initial resistance to the casting of Redford and Hoffman had "nothing to do with their talents." After the film was released, he said, "Now I am convinced that one of the shrewdest things done in the making of the film was the casting of Bob Redford and Dustin Hoffman—and I had no part in the casting [of their roles]."

All the President's Men was scrutinized by historians, some of whom objected to the film's omission of certain developments: the work of special prosecutors, judges, and members of congressional committees, for example. However, the film did not purport to be a documentary of every aspect of the Watergate investigation; it maintained its focus tightly on the work accomplished by the reporters of the *Washington Post*. Surely, if *All the President's Men* had attempted to follow every link in the chain of events that led to the administration's downfall, it would have resulted in an enormously long, confusing, and possibly dull film.

Historian Robert Brent Toplin presented the problem concerning the dramatization of historical events:

> In presenting stories about the past, filmmakers usually focus on the exploits of one or two individuals. This approach brings history to a personal level, portraying it through the experiences of fascinating and often heroic people for whom audiences are encouraged to show sympathy. The practice of reporting on good people's struggles against adversity produces attractive drama, but it also raises some problems. Personality-oriented movies give short shrift, for example, to the effect of collective action from the masses or to the impact of long-term economic changes. Instead of recognizing subtle, complex factors that foster change, they see developments resulting almost exclusively from the actions of dynamic individuals. In this respect they borrow ideas from the "Great Man" theory of history and stretch them to an extreme. . . .

Toplin felt that *All the President's Men* had, in its focus on Woodward and Bernstein, neglected the meaningful contributions of many others. However, he gave the film high marks for its "realistic, documentary style format," saying, "The makers of *All the President's Men* . . . gave careful attention to detail, attempting to reproduce the past as it really was. This emphasis on what may be called 'cinematic realism' is evident in many films that chronicle individuals' struggles against difficult odds. . . . They portray the past in fine detail to establish the audience's belief in the legitimacy of their reports. They make their case by stressing authenticity. . . . [F]or *All the President's Men* . . . realism became a defining characteristic."

Realism and attention to detail did not go unnoticed by the film's other critics. Vincent Canby, for example, commented in his review of the picture, "The manners and methods of big-city newspapering, beautifully detailed, contribute as much to the momentum of the film as the mystery that's being uncovered." Canby called the film "riveting" and "spellbinding," and "an unequivocal smash hit." Any attempt to tarnish the film's achievement by suggesting that Woodward and Bernstein alone had brought down the Nixon administration was, in Canby's words, "to miss the point of the movie, which is to make understandable to nonprofessionals the appeal and the rewards of American journalism at its best." *All the President's Men*, was, he said, "the only narrative film I've seen that comes remotely close to dramatizing the . . . journalistic mission."

Critic Nat Hentoff said that the filmmakers "brought about a small nearmiracle in film history. This is a movie journalists can see without either cringing or hooting." Hentoff confessed, "with a certain amount of discomfiture," that Woodward and Bernstein in the film used "techniques that I and just about every reporter I know use all the time," including "shameless trickery" and "false empathy." The film "is virtually a seminar in the art and craft of interviewing," Hentoff said.

So much attention has been paid to the amount of detail in *All the President's Men* that it has perhaps been overemphasized, for that is certainly not the most important aspect of the film. More significant are the insights into how a world-class newspaper operates; how Woodward and Bernstein learn to pry information from the subjects they are investigating; the severe obstacles the reporters faced, both in deriving information and in putting one piece of information alongside another until a coherent picture emerges; how the tensions resulting from the reporters' stories build to fever pitch; and how the work of two young reporters gradually leads to the dissolution of a criminally complicit American administration. Toplin, who believes that the ultimate test of whether a film accurately reflects the history it purports to portray involves "the intelligence and seriousness of the [filmmakers'] interpretations of history," credits Pakula and Redford with precisely those qualities. "Fortunately," he says, "the makers of *All the President's Men* . . . performed well in this regard, rendering sensitive and informed perspectives on events" and presenting "an inspiring story about the value of perseverance in the face of difficult obstacles."

Despite his objections to certain aspects of the film, historian William Leuchtenberg opined in *The American Historical Review* that when it came to "providing the public policy context of Watergate," the film "succeeds brilliantly."

Ben Bradlee admitted that many links in the chain of events that brought down the administration were not shown in the movie, but, if they had been, the film "would have been two-and-a-half years long." However, he said, "The question is, does it reflect the verities of journalism and investigative reporting, and what was going on in terms of Nixon and the White House? And I thought it just did just that."

Bradlee did concede, however, that some of the tedium of the investigative reporter's process had to be eliminated in the movie. "The phone always answered when the reporters dialed numbers, and of course that doesn't happen. You always get stiffed the first time or second time or third time." Nevertheless, the methods utilized by investigative reporters were conveyed vividly to the film's audience.

An even more significant aspect of the movie's triumph is its willingness—its insistence—upon taking a decided point of view toward a political event, something Hollywood films have historically been reluctant to do. This might have been a particular problem in the case of *All the President's Men*, since the events had so recently occurred and the criminals were highly placed political figures. And, lest we forget, millions of Americans supported the Nixon administration until, and even after, the president's resignation. To make such a bold film with so clear a moral position at such close proximity to the events depicted in the picture—in a film that was designed to attract audiences in large numbers—was an act of considerable courage.

Pakula discovered that the picture was greeted differently depending upon where it was shown. At the first preview, in Denver, "We knew the audience was really with Woodward and Bernstein and really with the film," he said, but at a preview in Louisville, "the audience was more on the side of the people being questioned. The audience was thinking, 'Why don't those damn busybodies leave those poor people alone?'"

Whether audiences sympathized with the investigators or the investigated, they flocked to see the film, which grossed $7 million in its first week. The first public showing of All the President's Men was given in Washington, D.C., on April 4, 1976, followed the next day by the opening in New York City. All proceeds from premieres given in twelve cities on April 8 went to the Citizens Action Fund, an organization created to lobby on behalf of environmental and social reforms, of which Robert Redford was a board director.

When Pakula was in the process of making the film, he believed that foreign audiences would not respond to the very particular American story. But, after the British premiere, he discovered "much to our amazement we're a great success in London." The success was repeated at the Berlin Film Festival. A knowledge of specific events in the United States was evidently not necessary for the high drama of the Woodward-Bernstein investigation to resonate with audiences around the world.

Some people—William Safire of the New York Times is a prominent example—said that releasing the film during a presidential election year amounted to a vendetta against the Republican Party. But, as Pakula pointed out, "The realities are that Bob Redford wanted to make this film before that and there was no way to get it ready in time." Pakula also observed that Warner Bros., which financed and distributed the film, was also financing Richard Nixon's memoirs.

A few critics contended that the film was "too talky." In response, Pakula said, "the fact is that reporters deal with words. Theirs is a totally verbal world. The essence of this film is words, and for those in the audience who don't like to listen or don't like to read, I can only say that it's the wrong film for them."

Steven Soderbergh spoke for those who don't mind listening attentively while in a movie theatre. Soderbergh said, "This movie just has the perfect balance of all the elements. You hope for it, and you work for it, and sometimes you get it. And this is just one of those movies."

Ben Bradlee acknowledged the power of the film when he commented that young people in large numbers applied for journalistic positions after the premiere of *All the President's Men*, hoping to become the next Woodward and Bernstein. He also "thought that it was quite a wonderful genre movie about the newspaper business. If you had asked me if they could make that picture so successfully, I would have said, 'How the hell could they do that?' But they certainly did do it. There are people whose fathers weren't born who now know quite a lot about Watergate because of that movie. I think it had an amazing influence."

Robert Brent Toplin's assessment is particularly significant, as it comes from a historian who was initially skeptical that a film could deal with history in a meaningful way. "*All the President's Men* provided a valuable history lesson worth repeating to a public that suffered historical amnesia in the years following Watergate," Toplin wrote. "Too many Americans forgot what was at stake in the scandal, and consequently, they considered the crisis to be far less serious than it really was. *All the President's Men* offered them a useful reminder."

Having achieved complete success with *All the President's Men*, Pakula was in the enviable position of being able to produce and direct virtually any film he liked. He might well have chosen to concentrate on movies with political themes or films dealing with great moral questions. Instead, at least for the next several years, he chose to exercise his directorial muscles on genre films of various kinds. Some were successful, some unsuccessful, but all permitted him to explore the kinds of movies he had not previously attempted.

CHAPTER TWELVE

A Mixed Bag:

Comes a Horseman, Starting Over,
Rollover

"Directors make movies at different times for different reasons. There were
some movies that Alan signed on to do because he simply needed to make
a movie. He needed to work and he wanted to work."
—**DONALD LAVENTHALL**, Executive Vice President
of Production at Pakula Productions

ONE CANNOT PIGEONHOLE Alan Pakula as a filmmaker. Unlike
Hitchcock or Scorsese, for example, he was not particularly noted for making a
specific kind of movie. Despite the fact that three of his films—*Klute*, *The Parallax
View*, and *All the President's Men*—were dubbed "the paranoia trilogy" by many critics,
such films as *The Sterile Cuckoo* and *Love and Pain and the Whole Damn Thing* obviously don't
fit that mold. It is certainly true that he excelled with certain kinds of material and
attained only indifferent success with others, which led some to wonder why he
occasionally strayed from his apparent strengths. The answer is that Pakula considered himself a *filmmaker*, and, for him, that meant working in every possible
genre. The end result was that while he established himself as a brilliant, original
craftsman with the so-called Paranoia Trilogy—which gave him sufficient power to
produce and direct whatever he chose—he occasionally selected films to direct that
(in retrospect at least) seem baffling, as they lacked the creative elements that
would make them rise above the level of conventional genre films.

Pakula was specifically eager to make pictures that "have vast differences in
style," he said in 1974. "That's partly because I've been trying to educate myself in
different styles. I started directing late. . . . I'm doing films in different styles to
see whether I can do them or not." Although his penchant for exploring different

styles occasionally led him to direct some unsuccessful films, he rarely compromised his integrity. As Pakula's friend Marilyn Berger noted, "he made movies he could be proud of. He never pandered with his movies to popular taste. He would never have made a smash 'em, crash 'em kind of movie."

So, why did he direct sub-par films with weak screenplays such as *Comes a Horseman* and *Rollover*? Because he wished to test his skill against all of the classic forms. A model for Pakula might have been a director like Fred Zinnemann, who did superior work in genres as disparate as historical costume films (*A Man For All Seasons*), Westerns (*High Noon*), films of international intrigue (*The Day of the Jackal*), religious-psychological dramas (*The Nun's Story*), and political thrillers (*Julia*); or Howard Hawks, who was as brilliant with farce (*His Girl Friday* and *Bringing Up Baby*) as with gangster movies (*Scarface*) and mysteries (*The Big Sleep*).

But Zinnemann's and Hawks's willingness to forego specialization for versatility led them to direct some undistinguished films, and the same was true for Pakula. Two of the three films he made after *All the President's Men* and before 1982's *Sophie's Choice*—all of them quite different than anything he had attempted previously—were no better than ordinary. However, the third—*Starting Over*—was a triumph, and had Pakula decided not to direct it because he was inexperienced with comic material, his career as a whole would be less impressive to contemplate.

The first of these films, 1978's *Comes a Horseman* (originally titled *Comes a Horseman, Wild and Free*, before its title was truncated), featured an original screenplay by Dennis Lynton Clark and was a [Robert] Chartoff-[Irvin] Winkler production. Pakula agreed to accept the directorial assignment because it gave him the opportunity to try his directorial hand at a Western. It was the first and last non-urban film he ever made.

He was surrounded by artists with whom he had worked in the past, including Jane Fonda, Jason Robards, Michael Small, and Gordon Willis. But the combination of an accomplished director, fine actors, a superb cinematographer, and an expert composer could not rescue the film from mediocrity. Nor was the experience of making the film particularly pleasant.

Dissension was provided in the person of James Caan, who, as one observer put it with apparent understatement, was "not easy" to work with at this stage of his career. Nor was Caan able to conceal a condescending attitude toward his director. Jane Fonda, who said that she and Caan got along without difficulty, spoke of the amusement Caan displayed at Pakula's obvious discomfort during the filming. Pakula, whose experience of the world was largely confined to cities, "always looked a little uncomfortable and out of place, especially during the cattle drives when there was manure everywhere and it would rain, and there'd be mud, and it was dusty," Fonda said. Although Fonda regarded Pakula's predicament with affection ("That's so sweet," she thought, "that he's out here putting up with this although clearly he's not in the element he would prefer"), Caan did not share her attitude. Rather, he "viewed it pejoratively," she said, and would imitate Pakula's discomfort for the amusement of others. (Fonda does not recall Caan ever making fun of Pakula to his face.) Caan, who had spent nine years roping steers on the rodeo circuit, apparently considered Pakula an interloper in his world.

Caan liked everyone to know just how comfortable he was in rural Colorado, where the film was shot. "You'd go into his trailer and he'd be listening to country and western music, and he knew all the words. He was a rodeo rider, his pals were rodeo riders and bronc busters," Fonda said. But other sorts of activities in Caan's trailer aroused suspicion among some members of the cast and crew, who noticed that throughout the filming, Caan would enter his trailer in one mood and emerge in an entirely different frame of mind. Some believed that Caan was drinking heavily; others suspected that more potent substances were involved. Martin Manulis, an old friend of Pakula's, recalled that the director quickly came to regret casting Caan. "The idea of an actor who didn't dare to come onto the set until he had a couple of shots in the arm—he [Pakula] thought that was just disgusting. And he'd never, never talk to him again, let alone hire him."

Considering the strained relationship of leading man and director, it was perhaps impossible for the film to succeed. But if Pakula knew that the picture was destined to fail, he never said so. Indeed, he sounded enthusiastic during the shooting as he described the film as a "Dreiserian Western, [dealing] with very specific American myths" and "an attempt to deal with a classic film genre to explore character, as was *Klute*." Speaking specifically about the plot of *Comes a Horseman*, which pits two ranchers, hanging on to their livelihoods by a thread, against a wealthy cattle baron, he said he felt a "great attraction to people who fight against powerful odds for freedom and dignity, who live for values beyond the obvious material ones of today." He also discussed his wish "to explore a woman in the American West as a heroic character. In most Westerns, the woman is in a calico dress, running after the hero on the horse, saying, 'Nothing is worth dying for,' or she's a gun-toting Calamity Jane. The idea of dealing with a heroine in the West, very much a woman yet willing to fight with the same passion as men, was a great attraction."

Pakula identified the themes of *Comes a Horseman* as "the obsession with land, the obsession with freedom, the mentality of two different kinds of people who settled the West. One kind [consisted of] people who really wanted the freedom and their own piece of land and who didn't want much else . . . And, like the heroes of the classic Western genre, it is their nature to fight for survival. The other kind," embodied by the character Jason Robards portrayed, are "expansionists who have a dream of power. I see him as an outsized, giant figure caught up in a romantic, empire-building dream," Pakula said, "who is totally obsessed with what he is doing."

In the best of circumstances, such enthusiasm might have produced a Western that would be more profound than other films of the same genre, and perhaps that was Pakula's intention, but the end result is no more and no less satisfying than a hundred other films of its kind. Western movies have explored many of these themes since the dawn of American movies, and, except for its focus on a heroic female character, *Comes a Horseman* has nothing fresh to say about them.

The film was deliberately set in a time when "the kind of people who built [Western] America [were] already an anachronism, nineteenth-century people in a twentieth-century world," Pakula said. *Comes a Horseman* was made several years after the era when Western movies were a commercially viable genre, making it, too, an anachronism. Most Westerns of the 1960s and 1970s tended to parody the genre (examples include 1965's *Cat Ballou*, 1969's *True Grit*, and 1974's *Blazing Saddles*), but the solemnity of *Comes a Horseman* is unleavened by humor.

Although the action is set in Montana, the film was shot in the area near the mountain community of Westcliffe, Colorado, beginning in May 1977. Since Pakula saw the land as "a kind of central character in the film," he wanted the valley "to have a haunted look." He told Gordon Willis, "It's a *Wuthering Heights* of the West in terms of visual feeling. These people are all haunted."

Pakula was assured by the Colorado Film Commission that the weather in the valley where the picture was shot was reliably dry, but noted later that "the weather kept changing. We'd have an hour and a half of sunlight; we'd have an hour and a half of thunder clouds; we'd have an hour of rain; we'd have another hour of sunlight; we'd have some more thunder, then rain. We had a kaleidoscope of God's weather every day. For several days we even had incredible hailstorms." The variable weather, which made sticking to a schedule impossible, undoubtedly further dampened the spirits of those working on a troubled enterprise.

Comes a Horseman, set at the end of World War II, pits J. W. Ewing, a power-hungry cattle baron with a well-deserved reputation for ruthless behavior (Robards) against Ella Connors, a rancher who owns a small parcel of land (Fonda). Ewing has clearly become deranged in his obsession to secure all of the land in the valley. Years before, after sleeping with him, Ella rejected Ewing's proposal of marriage, and he has been trying to wipe out her ranch (and absorb her land into his) ever since. At the beginning of the film, Ella is portrayed as a woman who is isolated spiritually, seemingly without any need for (or ability to give) friendship or affection, apparently dead to all emotion.

Her feelings are awakened by her hired man, Frank "Buck" Atherton (Caan), with whom she has an intimate relationship (one would be hard pressed to describe it as a love affair, for Ella's character remains determinedly taciturn throughout the film), but she never manages to free herself from melancholy. Still, she is determined to counter Ewing's attempts to rob her of her property. Buck agrees to help her if she will accept him as a business partner. She agrees, and together they put up a spirited fight. At the end of the film, Ewing, now totally demented, tries to burn down the house in which Ella and Buck are trapped. But they manage (not very convincingly) to escape and to kill Ewing. A final scene conveys a sense of optimism, although nothing in the film seems to justify it.

The picture's one claim to distinction is Jane Fonda's performance, for which she gives Pakula much of the credit. She claims that she is not the sort of actor who can function well without a strong director, comparing herself to "a piece of clay, and every director that you work with molds you in a slightly different way. It's like you're a baseball player and suddenly you switch to tennis, so you get sore in different places—and that's the way it is working with different directors. Pakula managed to cause me to use different emotional muscles than I had [used] before as an actress." The mood of the film is dominated by Fonda, whose dark, brooding, unsentimental performance, capturing the essence of frontier stubbornness, strength, and self-reliance, is mirrored by the slow tempo of the film.

Whatever problems he may have given the director off-camera, James Caan's performance as Ella's laconic partner and lover is well-accomplished. But Jason Robards' portrayal is disappointingly conventional. He plays a thoroughgoing villain without originality. On the other hand, Richard Farnsworth, in his first significant speaking role as Fonda's loyal hired hand, Dodger, earned an Academy Award nomination for best supporting actor.

Michael Small, who composed the music, said that his purpose "was to write a classic Western score" for the film. That intention identifies one of the film's greatest problems. Any film in which the composer's idea—or, for that matter, any artist's idea—is at variance with the director's is a sign of trouble, for it means that unity cannot be achieved. And that is precisely what happened in the case of *Comes a Horseman*, where the tempo of the acting (particularly Jane Fonda's performance) is deliberate and brooding, the often-rousing music conveys an entirely different sense. The blame, however, properly belongs to Pakula, for he inexplicably allowed the musical score to be used, despite its inappropriateness.

Similarly, the unconventional approach taken by Fonda to her character is undercut by the observance of clichés in other performances: the demented villain without a shred of goodness; the conventional leading man; the typically crusty old sidekick (Dodger), whose death in the film is meant to represent the death of the old West.

Pakula claimed that, after completing *Comes a Horseman* and after a trip to France, he cut seven minutes out of the film. "I started playing over some of the scenes," he said, "and I thought, Oh, you hang too long there. You're saying, 'Hey, look at that,' and 'Look what Gordon Willis and I did there,' and 'How about that moment that Jane Fonda has over there?'" One of the most difficult aspects of directing is to remain objective about the work despite attempting to achieve an intense closeness with the actors and the technical collaborators. Pakula is to be applauded for his ability to recognize some of the shortcomings in *Comes a Horseman* and improve the film as a result. It is mystifying, however, that he missed so many weaknesses in the film. Had he applied the same objectivity to all aspects of the picture, he would surely have achieved a more satisfactory result.

Prior to the film's release, Pakula observed, with some prescience, "It deals with classic—or hoary—American themes. If the picture succeeds, they'll be classic, and if it fails, they'll be hoary."

Unfortunately, virtually every element in the film is predictable and conventional. Had *Comes a Horseman* been directed by a predictable and conventional director, it might be regarded as marginally successful. But coming from Alan Pakula, a man who had become renowned for his innovative, unpredictable, unconventional films, it is a distinct disappointment. It is, in the last analysis, just another movie, and a lethargic one, at that. In some respects, however, it is less than that, for the inconsistencies in the approach to the material makes the film seem pointlessly arty.

Or possibly not arty enough. As Frank Rich pointed out in his review for *Time*, "there are no emotional or intellectual mysteries to hook the audience's imagination. Every level of the movie's meaning can be found right on its surface. Since that surface is only rarely bestirred by action or drama, *Comes a Horseman* ultimately comes to nothing." Rich observed that ambiguity played a significant role in Pakula's previous movies, that it had often been "impossible to separate heroes from villains until the end." But in the case of *Comes a Horseman*, Rich said, "the cast might as well wear white and black hats."

Christopher Lehmann-Haupt said in his *New York Times* review, "As usual, though it never comes out that way in real life, the little people win. But [the film is so generic that] it might as well be the cattlemen against the sheep-herders, or the homesteaders against the ranchers, or any of a dozen rivalries that have been fought since the Western was first stamped on our collective unconscious."

Gene Siskel, writing in the *Chicago Tribune*, gave the film one of its few enthusiastic reviews. "It's a fine film," he said, "majestic at times. . . . a very special motion picture." He also wrote that, despite her appearances in *Coming Home* and *Julia*, Fonda's performance in *Comes a Horseman* was "her best . . . since *Klute*."

Jack Kroll, reviewing the film in *Newsweek*, offered a mixed review. "If the [film] doesn't quite jell, it's good to see so much sensitivity amid the sagebrush," he wrote, "and Fonda and Caan create characters who are strong and sweet without being macho or mawkish."

* * *

After Pakula served as President of the Jury at the Cannes Film Festival in 1978, he returned home to begin work on another new genre, a romantic comedy. Happily, *Starting Over* was a far more successful achievement than *Comes a Horseman*. It stands as one of Pakula's finest films, a warm, gentle, likable, whimsical comedy that is never frenetic, never obvious.

Unlike most of the films Pakula worked on in the past, he did not generate the project. Rather, James L. Brooks, writing a film script for the first time (he had already established a reputation as one of television's most accomplished writers with *Room 222*, *The Mary Tyler Moore Show*, *Rhoda*, *Taxi*, *Lou Grant*, and others), used incidents from his own life in creating his screenplay, then sought out Pakula as the director. The two of them co-produced.

The job of the producer is now, as it was in 1979, a complex enterprise, dealing with byzantine financial procedures. Consider, for example, Stanley Kubrick's 1980 response to the question of how to budget a film so that it can return money to its backers:

> Take a film that costs $10 million. Today it's not unusual to spend $8 million on USA advertising and $4 million on international advertising. On a big film, add $2 million for release prints. Say there is a 20% studio overhead on the budget: that's $2 million more. Interest on the $10 million production cost, currently at 20% a year, would add an additional $2 million a year, say, for two years—that's another $4 million. So a $10 million film already costs $30 million.
>
> Now you have to get it back. Let's say an actor takes 10% of the gross, and the distributor takes a worldwide average of a 35% distribution fee. To roughly calculate the break-even figure, you have to divide the $30 million by 55%, the percentage left after the actor's 10% and the 35% distribution fee. That comes to $54 million of the distributor's film rental. So a $10 million film may not break even, as far as the producer's share of the profits is concerned, until 5.4 times its

negative cost. Obviously the actual break-even figure for the distributor is lower since he is taking a 35% distribution fee and has charged overheads.

Pakula's background as a producer (and, before that, as a studio executive) allowed him to master such arcane information. Hannah Pakula called him a "strange combination of artist and reliable businessman. He could look at a script he was going to do and tell you what it would cost. He did not 'run over' the way that some directors do." Pakula helped Brooks raise funding for *Starting Over* from Century Associates and Paramount Pictures.

The film's major character is Phil Potter, a writer for airline magazines, who, as the movie begins, is asked for a divorce by his beautiful wife, Jessica. He is attracted to Marilyn Holmberg, a woman selected for him by his sister-in-law, Marva ("Don't hurt her, Phil. She's an extraordinarily gifted nursery school teacher," Marva tells him sternly, in a typically loony turn of phrase); but his continuing strong feelings for Jessica, his caution about becoming involved in a new relationship, and his shy nature, combined with Marilyn's fear of commitment, prevent Phil and Marilyn from getting together until they can resolve their problems.

Later, Phil's difficulty in coming to a decision about his relationship with Marilyn is painfully shown (but comically portrayed) when they decide to move in together. They go to Bloomingdale's to select a couch. Phil, after suffering a bout of hyperventilation, collapses on a display mattress and is unable to move until his brother, Mickey, a former psychiatrist, arrives to give him a Valium and a paper bag to breathe into—to the applause of an appreciative crowd of onlookers. After an unsuccessful attempt to reunite with Jessica, Phil, determined to win Marilyn despite all obstacles, asks a friend to drive him to Bloomingdale's, where he buys the couch that has become symbolic of his inability to commit to Marilyn. With his typically sly sense of humor, he wins her over. In the film's final shot, we see an overhead view of Phil's friend's van parked on the street and hear Marilyn's voice, exclaiming happily, "You got the couch."

The essence of the film's appeal is that its treatment of the characters is humorous throughout, but they and their underlying problems are not belittled. All the characters are recognizable as appealing people in whom we can recognize ourselves. Even Jessica is not caricatured (except for her woefully unmusical singing). One senses that the filmmakers have real affection for their characters, for the movie never condescends to them, as so many comedies do; never does its comedy depend on the spectator's feeling superior to the characters. *Starting Over* elicits smiles from its audience rather than laughs—in the mode of such films as *Roman Holiday*.

Pakula's direction was influenced by that of George Stevens, whom he had known and admired when he worked at Paramount in his twenties. Stevens's *Woman of the Year*, the first of the Katharine Hepburn-Spencer Tracy films, is one of the funniest American films, but, unlike most comedies, it is paced deliberately, rather than frenetically. Pakula was particularly impressed by a sequence near the end of Stevens's film, when Katharine Hepburn's character, a career woman who has never cooked a meal in her life, attempts to prove to Tracy's character that she can make him a good breakfast. During the scene, the coffeepot boils over, burnt toast pops out of the toaster and onto the floor, waffle mix overflows the waffle-maker, and Hepburn is gradually reduced to tears. Pakula felt the sequence was all the funnier because "George gradually, slowly, taking his time, builds each prop in the kitchen, and the more frenetic Katharine Hepburn gets in trying to show she can be a good housewife and cook a breakfast for Spencer Tracy, the calmer the camera remains, just sitting there calmly, observing all of these things, rather stoically. . . . It takes a lot of daring and courage to take your time with comedy." Pakula demonstrated precisely the same courage in his deliberately paced direction of *Starting Over*. To do otherwise, he said, to succumb to the temptation to speed everything up, as most directors do with comic material, is to confuse comedy with cartoons.

Starting Over is a film for and about grownups. Unlike nearly every romantic comedy made since the heyday of Hepburn and Tracy, the characters are mature (Marilyn is in her mid-thirties, Phil probably in his early forties) and do not behave like lunatics. The dialogue is gently, rather than hilariously, funny. (Two examples: after Phil first visits Mickey and Marva, clearly upset by his separation from Jessica, Marva says, "Call if you get sad." He asks, wistfully, "Can I call if I get happy?" Later, after Marilyn and Phil have sex for the first time, Marilyn emphatically defends her behavior. "I'm no one-nighter," she says, angrily. "I'm a teacher going for my master's.")

The situations, too, are amusing rather than hilarious. At one point, Phil takes a job teaching writing at a junior college. He prepares a handful of elaborate notes for his first lecture. Nervously he enters the classroom and delivers the "lecture," which lasts for all of four minutes. A student in the class points at the clock and reminds Phil that he has fifty-six minutes to go. Phil sheepishly announces that he is prepared to answer questions for the remainder of the class. Any beginning teacher will be able to relate to Phil's predicament. Similarly, all the comic events in the film evoke a smile of recognition.

Alan Pakula, whose divorce and remarriage were such significant events in his life, had no difficulty empathizing with his characters even as he poked gentle fun at their behavior. "A man and a woman committing themselves to a life together is one of the most heroic acts in the world," he said while the film was being shot.

Although Brooks's screenplay was written without Pakula in mind, the writer spoke to Pakula "a lot about Alan's experience with divorce during the revisions I did." Eventually, the director made the material so thoroughly his own that when his cousin Selma Hirsh saw the film for the first time on television, she thought—without knowing that Pakula was the director, having tuned in after the credits—"that's Alan. Just like the main character, he had difficulty separating from his first wife, and both Alan and the character had a delightful sense of humor." Brooks agrees that Pakula was far more than a "hired gun" executing the writer's ideas. "It became his film," he said.

Don Laventhall, who was working on a Pakula film for the first time (as a production assistant) during *Starting Over*, observed an "amazing synergy" in the relationship between Pakula and Brooks. The screenwriter also spoke of that synergistic quality when he observed that Pakula's inventive staging caused some of the scenes he wrote to be a good deal more amusing than Brooks had intended. One example: it was Pakula's idea to have the Divorced Men's Workshop angrily confront the members of the Divorced Women's Workshop in the basement of a church while Christmas carols are heard upstairs; during their scene, one of the film's most charming, hostility turns to warmth at the first pleasant word. "Alan thought of that Christmas finish," Brooks said, crediting Pakula with the success of the scene.

Casting Phil Potter would be critical, Pakula realized. As he said, the role "was of a rather ordinary man being rejected by his first wife, and going on to have to lick his wounds and try to make a new life for himself. It's hardly the great leading man part."

He had a hunch that Burt Reynolds, known for his action movies, would give a convincing performance as the wry, soft-spoken Phil Potter. The role would require a subtle and skillful comic actor, and Pakula, who found Reynolds "an extraordinarily endearing man," believed that the actor could jettison his acting persona and convey an aspect of himself with which audiences were unfamiliar: "a kind of genuine sweetness . . . very caring, vulnerable," in Pakula's words.

However, Reynolds had to demonstrate to the producers and to associate producer Douglas Wick that he could convey those qualities on-screen. He was, after all, perhaps the last actor one would think of in connection with Phil Potter's character. Reynolds had no doubt that he could play the role satisfactorily. "It was," he said, "the first part I read that was *me*. Ironically, people say—and in all the reviews they talk about—what a stretch it was for me to play this part, when I knew that it was closer to me than anything." Reynolds, who was then the number one box-office film attraction in the world, not only agreed to test for the role (an unusual concession for such a successful actor), but tested eleven times before the filmmakers were convinced that he was an ideal choice.

Resisting any temptation to perform as he had so often in the past, Reynolds gives a quietly understated comic portrayal. An article in *Newsweek* confirmed the wisdom of Pakula's selection. "Under Pakula's handling, Reynolds is gently, rue-fully funny," the reviewer observed. Other critics concurred.

Reynolds's performance effectively contradicted the belief that Pakula was a more effective director with women than with men. Nor did Charles Durning, who played Reynolds's brother, Mickey, feel that his gender was a barrier to receiving expert direction from Pakula. "He's just a terrific director," Durning said, "and a man who has an eye for the camera and an eye for story and knows what's good and what's bad, and is so gentle in his approach to you that you don't think he's directing."

Both Jill Clayburgh and Candice Bergen received Academy Award nomina-tions for their work, and one could argue that Reynolds deserved that recognition as well. Reynolds certainly thought so. He could barely conceal his anger when the nominations were announced. "Jill was nominated, Candice was nominated, Jim Brooks was nominated, the movie was nominated, Alan Pakula was nominated [actually, neither Brooks, the film, nor Pakula received nominations]. Guess who wasn't nominated?" he said bitterly.

During the filming, Reynolds, whose aversion to doing more than a few takes of a given scene is well known, clashed repeatedly with Pakula, who always preferred to choose from among many takes when he was assembling the film. "Burt was tough," James Brooks said. "Once Burt got past three takes, which is really noth-ing, he would start to get nervous, and he would act out, and he would say, 'What else do you want after three takes?' The greatest actors in the world do forty."

Reynolds turned the disagreement into an amusing anecdote—but, in fact, the conflict in his and the director's styles was never fully reconciled. Reynolds said that during one scene, "we go up to about take fourteen, and I keep saying [to Pakula], 'What can I do to please you? I mean, what can I change?' And he'd say, 'Just do another one.' So I did another one and he said, 'Perfect!'" Reynolds, eager to get off the set as quickly as possible, ran to his trailer, only to have Pakula knock at the door a few moments later. "Burt," he called, "it's Alan. Why are you here?" Reynolds, frustrated, answered, "You said, 'Perfect.' I've never been better than perfect. I can't do another one. I mean, what do you want?" Pakula laughed, rec-ognizing that Reynolds' logic was unassailable, but he still insisted on another take.

According to Reynolds, from that time on, "every time we'd do a take, [Pakula would say] 'Per—no, not perfect, Burt. Good. But not perfect.'"

One reason why Pakula insisted on far more takes than Reynolds wanted was because he wanted to leave "room for spontaneous gestures and ideas," Candice Bergen said. As in all his films, he encouraged improvisation, and a good deal of the comic business that supplemented the film's dialogue occurred as a consequence of that method. Jill Clayburgh said that Pakula's ability to select improvised business that supported the humor while gently rejecting what did not was the key to his success as a director of comedy. "It's not that lots of wonderful ideas aren't always on the table," she said, "it's the intuitive sense [on the director's part] to grab onto an idea that is special." She also credits Pakula with never cutting an actor's creativity short. "He wouldn't say, 'Oh, that's too much,' or, 'That's too silly.' He didn't censor what you were doing."

Just as Pakula took a chance with Burt Reynolds based on a hunch that the actor could give a subdued comic performance, he was determined to cast Candice Bergen as Jessica, although Bergen herself doubted that she could play the role. Initially, she wished to play Marilyn, but soon came to realize that, in her words, "I didn't have any of the experience or background to do Jill's role."

Pakula took Bergen to lunch at the Café des Artistes in New York and, by the time the meal was over, had persuaded her to play Jessica. As Jim Brooks said, "Alan came back with her cast. I think the wine flowed and Candy got the part."

Bergen had never played comedy before, but, as she said, "Alan was shrewd enough and smart enough to use me very effectively. And the fact that he was able to make me feel safe enough that I could behave so foolishly" gave her confidence in her comic ability.

Bergen, as Jessica, plays a woman who, despite all evidence to the contrary, believes she is a talented singer and songwriter. The screenplay called for her to sing several songs written by her character—but the comedy lies in the fact that the hackneyed songs (written by Marvin Hamlisch and Carole Bayer Sager) are performed dreadfully. No performer wishes to give a dreadful performance, so Bergen, despite knowing full well that her character was not supposed to be a gifted singer, worked with a vocal coach and sang the songs with some skill when Pakula first heard her. Later, he recalled his feelings: "It's not wonderful singing, but it's not bad. It's just neither here nor there. What is . . . funny about this character is her outrageous belief that she's a wonderful singer when reality does not back that up."

Pakula was uncertain how to break the news to Bergen that her singing needed to be worse. "One of the most difficult directions I've ever had to give was to

Candy Bergen in that film," he said. When she asked, "Well, what do you think?" Pakula, knowing that "we all want to do something the best we can do it," nevertheless summoned up the courage to say, "But it's not bad enough." Bergen said, "You mean you want me to make a complete fool of myself?" Pakula answered, "Yes, that's exactly what I want you to do."

Bergen still vividly remembers the first scene in the film, when she breaks into song. "The crew were holding pillows over their ears," she said. "Doing the song, which I think was on the first day, was, for me, a considerable act of courage—to get up the nerve to sing that badly, that loudly, and to really commit to that rather than stand back and wink while I was doing it." But the result, she found, was "incredibly liberating." Pakula was delighted when Bergen, "sport that she was, . . . went out there and sang her lungs out."

Bergen was daunted by Pakula's expectations, but comforted by his solicitude. "I would never have taken the chances I took on *Starting Over* with anyone else," she said. "The set was just the safest and most secure of havens, where you could take real chances and know that you would not be made to feel ridiculous."

She felt that her lack of training put her at a disadvantage, particularly because the role called for "someone who was very confident and quite sure of herself, and had an obliviousness to a lack of talent." Pakula told Bergen, "You as Candy try to get from one end of a room to the other as quickly and unobtrusively as possible, but [as Jessica] you have to be very confident about the way you move and be confident about yourself." He worked with her until she found a manner of walking that was appropriate for Jessica, then addressed other aspects of her character.

"Alan really extended himself," Bergen said, "and loved the process, as well. You see that in his films. You see that in his casts, and you see that in the performances. We felt that he was so responsive, and he would never undermine his actors. It was really an experience that is, unfortunately, not so common." She credits the performance Pakula helped her give in *Starting Over* with "starting my work in comedy." Eventually, she played the title role in the successful television comedy *Murphy Brown*, amply demonstrating her rich comic gifts.

Jill Clayburgh, then at the height of her career, was everyone's choice to play Marilyn from the outset, and her performance fully justified their confidence. She thoroughly enjoyed both her role ("Playing Marilyn in *Starting Over* was like exploring the most vulnerable part of myself," she said) and the filming process. She credited Pakula with bringing a "devilish glee" to the set each morning, thereby helping to establish the comic tone of the picture.

However, after the film was edited, Pakula was dissatisfied with the results. Clayburgh asked if he could identify the problem. He said, "I have to go back. I used too many close-ups on Burt and you in the first assemblage, and it's not as funny as it ought to be. I need to go back and find wider shots." As it turned out, Pakula's re-editing was precisely what the film needed, giving it the droll flavor it lacked in the initial cut.

Although not all Pakula's films were re-edited to such an extent, he confessed "that I just love being in the editing room, and so it's very hard to get me out," because it gave him the opportunity to refine the work he had done on the set. "You have to keep looking at [your work] and saying, 'What's wrong?' Because as long as you're involved in the cutting process and the post-production process, you can do something to help [the film] if you face its problems. [The film] is alive to me. It has a life I am nurturing and trying to bring to maturity in some successful form. And while I'm doing that, it's fascinating."

The ability to view his work objectively and modify it when necessary was a characteristic that set Pakula apart from other directors. Clayburgh said, "one of the things about Alan that really made him a cut above was his ability to question himself. I think a lot of directors get in a position of power and they surround themselves with people who say everything they do is brilliant, and they don't ask themselves the really hard questions." Pakula asked the hard questions. And if he didn't like the answers, he would re-enter the editing room and begin again.

Clayburgh also appreciated Pakula's patience during rehearsals. "He never rushed me," she said. "He accepted the process [of making a film] for the lumbersome, difficult thing that it is, whereas a lot of directors get antsy with it."

Many actors who worked with Pakula have commented on his propensity to get as comfortable as possible during the shooting of a film. He would invariably take off his shoes, shed his wallet, his keys, and his watch, and, as Hannah Pakula described it, "He'd dance around like a kid. He just loved it."

Candice Bergen said, "When he takes off his shoes he seems to become weightless. And when he was pleased with a scene, he would *hop* behind the camera. If things were going especially well, he would hop a couple of times. We came to see it as a rating. It became like a one-hop or a two-hop scene. If, by chance, you got a three-hopper, you really went home happy."

Jill Clayburgh spoke warmly about his "boyish, mischievous giggle," and recalled how "he dressed so elegantly and then always took his shoes off." Pakula said that this seeming eccentricity had a specific purpose. "I take off my shoes when I'm directing, and I take out my watch, I take out my wallet, I give it to the assistant director. I don't want reality around me." He didn't need a watch because "the clock is ticking in my mind," he said. "I know what's going on. [Shooting a film is] pretend, it's after school, it's fun, and if the actors see this and they get loose, wonderful things can happen. If they get tight . . . you're in trouble." In order to further relax his actors—or perhaps simply because his boyish nature overcame him— Pakula "bounced up and down," Meryl Streep said, "when something we did [in *Sophie's Choice*] delighted him. He would clap his hands and he cried."

In Pakula's work with actors, Jill Clayburgh said, he was not the sort of director who tells the actor precisely what to do. Rather, "he was more of a responder to what *you* did. He would say, 'What would *you* like to do?'" and, as long as it fit within Pakula's general conception of character, he would encourage the actor to try various approaches to a scene. He would often film several of those approaches, allowing himself time to think about which one he preferred before cutting the film.

Bergen confirmed Clayburgh's view. Pakula "was somebody who very much wanted to see what an actor brought to the table," she said. "He did not impose himself on an actor. He would rehearse and rehearse and rehearse, and wait to see what was going to evolve out of that process."

Although Pakula encouraged the actors to improvise physical business during rehearsals, he did not permit the actors to tamper with the dialogue because Brooks's script was so meticulously crafted. Even if he had been tempted to permit improvised dialogue, he would have been dissuaded by the presence of Brooks, who, as co-producer, was on the set for the first few weeks of rehearsal. Shortly thereafter, however, Pakula had to tell Brooks that he was making the actors nervous "because," Brooks said, "I was making faces and I was doing all these acting-out things that writers do when they're passionately involved. Nobody ever barred a writer from a set more gently and diplomatically than when he barred me from the set."

Starting Over was shot in New York and Boston. For the next nineteen years, until the end of his life, Pakula continued to shoot in New York or on location whenever possible.

Soon after *Starting Over*, Brooks embarked on a directorial career, thanks to Pakula. When Jennifer Jones sent Pakula a copy of *Terms of Endearment*, she asked, "Would you be interested in doing this?" Pakula was involved in preparing *Sophie's Choice* and decided to pass, but he told Jones, "I know somebody who never directed before but he'd be wonderful for this material, for the eccentricity of the material, and that's Jim Brooks," who directed the film to critical acclaim.

Brooks, who carefully observed Pakula's work with the actors and in post-production of *Starting Over*, told me, "any initial thoughts I had about directing came from studying him." Brooks has since gone on to become one of the most successful directors in film.

Starting Over is such a skillful picture that Pakula's ability as a director of comedy is unquestionable. Had he worked more frequently with the form, he would surely have become recognized as a master of the genre. Janet Maslin wrote in the *New York Times* that *Starting Over* "manages to be fast and funny while it breaks new ground. There's a kernel of truth here. There are a lot of good laughs, too." Jack Kroll said, "Pakula gives this fable a light, sensitive touch, letting the laughs come naturally from a realistic texture. . . . You laugh all the harder because the movie never winds up to hit you with a boffola." *Time* found *Starting Over* "a perfectly charming movie" and *Variety* called the film "a delight. . . . Audiences may wince at Bergen's autobiographical ditties, or shudder at Reynolds misguided love affairs, but the essential link between comedy and reality is never absent."

* * *

Pakula's next film, *Rollover*, is clearly the worst film he ever directed. Perhaps its inadequacy was partly due to a family crisis that commanded much of his attention for several years.

In 1979, the extended Pakula family celebrated the birthday of Murray Baxter, Alan's brother-in-law, at Alan and Hannah's house in East Hampton. Murray's daughter, Debby Maisel, noticed a protrusion on the neck of her mother—Alan's sister—Felice. Debby asked her mother what had caused the injury, and Felice responded that she had hit herself with a hair dryer. Debby alerted her father to her fear that the protrusion might be cancerous, but Felice, desperately afraid, told her husband, "If you make me go to a doctor, I'll divorce you." Despite the entreaties of everyone in the family, she refused to seek medical attention.

Alan and Hannah, recognizing that arguing with Felice was futile, agreed not to say anything to Alan and Felice's parents, since it appeared likely that they might die before Felice did, and, in Debby Maisel's words, "they'd never have to know."

For the next five years, Felice lived on (as did her parents), during which Alan became closer than ever to her and "very, very attentive." Finally, in May 1984, Felice became so ill that the family called Alan in Europe, where he was making *Dream Lover*. Pakula flew home on the Concorde, knowing that he would have to tell his parents that Felice had only a brief time to live. Paul and Jeannette, now in their mid-nineties, had no inkling until then that their daughter was ill.

Felice died on Christmas Eve, 1984. Paul survived until late 1990, Jeannette outliving him by five months. Both of them were ninety-six years old at the time of their deaths.

Rollover, a story of skullduggery in the world of high finance, was set in California but shot in New York. Perhaps Pakula agreed to direct *Rollover* as another expression of his mistrust of large and powerful institutions. In an interview, he said, "Little is known about modern banking. I wanted to show bankers as people who, in the present set-up, are entrusted with huge sums of money and forced to gamble it."

Jane Fonda's company, IPC Productions, financed the film, commissioned the screenplay, and hired Pakula to direct. Presumably, Fonda hoped that the film would make an important social statement, for all of the films she and her partner, Bruce Gilbert, produced (such as *Coming Home*, *9 to 5*, and *The China Syndrome*), were calculated to alter people's attitudes about significant issues. A less charitable characterization would be to call them illustrated lectures.

In the abstract, it is praiseworthy that a film should attempt to explain to a general audience the international monetary system and how it can be subverted. But *Rollover* is so confusing, so obscure, that one learns nothing—except, perhaps, that bankers are scheming evildoers, which does not seem to be the point anyone wished to make.

Or perhaps Pakula's main motivation in agreeing to direct the film was because he wished to work with Jane Fonda once again. But the results are so indifferent that one suspects his ill-advised decision to make *Rollover* was based simply on Pakula's wish never to be without a project.

Fonda plays Lee Winters, a former film actress who runs a multinational petrochemical company after her husband is murdered. Hub Smith (played by a miscast Kris Kristofferson), a wheeler-dealer whose specialty is salvaging troubled companies, persuades Lee to assume control of her dead husband's corporation, and spends much of his time helping her consolidate her power. However, the agents of high finance are shown to be sinister and conspiratorial. Thanks to a string of absurd coincidences (among them: Lee happens, by pure accident, to empty the contents of a cigar box into a wastebasket and find an incriminating tape that leads to the discovery of a scheme to control the monetary systems in devious ways; Hub just happens to find the villain's diary, containing the computer codes that will allow Hub to reveal the nefarious scheme in detail; the villain returns to his office just a fraction of a second too late to catch Hub running off copies of the incriminating material. Still more examples of the plot turning on improbable happenstance could be offered, but perhaps no more are necessary), Lee and Hub are able to expose the conspiracy, tracing it to the villainous Maxwell Emery (Hume Cronyn). Still, a worldwide depression is created when (for reasons that elude understanding) the Arabs withdraw their funds from all United States banks. Lee and Hub are among the victims, but at the end of the movie pluckily suggest that they're going to start over—together.

Nearly every scene in the film misfires. The love affair is difficult to accept because of the lack of chemistry between Fonda and Kristofferson. The element of suspense often falls flat, as when an attempt is made to kidnap Lee. But the attempt does not succeed and the plot device leads nowhere, so its point is utterly lost. Even the murder that begins the film is simply a set-up for the story to come, not a meaningful strand of the plot.

The film is dominated by endless talk about arcane financial matters. David Shaber's screenplay is so full of technical jargon that even those who are familiar with the world of finance found it incomprehensible. According to Marilyn Berger's husband, Don Hewitt, "We went to the premiere, and in the middle of the movie, Marilyn turned to me and said, 'I know more about this subject than anybody in this theatre, and *I* don't understand this movie."

Why Fonda, Gilbert, and Pakula chose to cast Kris Kristofferson is a mystery. Kristofferson performed effectively in many films, but he is at sea in the role of a financial mastermind. Pakula was frustrated by his inability to deliver a convincing performance, but, unlike his disapproving attitude toward James Caan, he felt no antipathy for Kristofferson. If anything, the problem derived from the director's poorly conceived casting. The only justification is that other actors who were considered for the role did not accept it[34] and Kristofferson was cast at the last minute. As Pieter Jan Brugge said, "You can't always get who you want." Celia Costas, who was the film's location manager, recalls that "everyone in the production office was thinking of who would be good as the male lead in the movie" and passing on their suggestions to Pakula. "Basically," she said, "people had run out of ideas and the engine on the movie had already started, so you had to hire somebody or you were going to delay, and in those days, once a movie started up and started going forward, you didn't decide that you were going to wait nine months for so-and-so to become available, you just went with whoever you could hire in the time frame you had."

Jane Fonda felt that Kristofferson was insecure throughout the picture—in much the same way that she was insecure during the rehearsals of *Klute*. However, as she points out, Kristofferson's intelligence was not an issue: "He's a Rhodes Scholar," she said, "he's brilliant. But it was difficult for him to get inside the skin of a Wall Street person."

Actors do not perform in a vacuum. They are inevitably affected by those with whom they share the screen. Perhaps as a result, Jane Fonda's performance is far below her usual standard. She fails to infuse her character with any warmth, leading the viewer unmoved by the various plights in which she finds herself. The supporting cast fares no better, although Hume Cronyn may be singled out as giving the most compelling performance.

---

[34]*Don Laventhall, a production assistant on this film as well, recalls taking a copy of the script to Robert Redford's apartment in New York.*

Pakula persuaded businessmen to play businessmen in the film. "Some actors get pompous when they act businessmen," he said. And he prevailed upon Marilyn Berger, who was a television interviewer at the time, to play just such a role in *Rollover*. She improvised an interview with Cronyn (whose answers were scripted). To prepare for the "interview," Berger studied international banking.

Berger was not the only friend cast in *Rollover*. Several of Pakula's friends participated as extras. One was Michael Small; another was the director's wife, Hannah. It is almost as if, knowing the film had no chance to be successful, Pakula was determined to make the process as enjoyable as possible.

Looking back at *Rollover*, Jane Fonda says that her dominant impression is not of a hapless director or a miscast co-star, but "that we couldn't get the script right. I loved what we were trying to do, it was important," she said, "but I just don't think that the story worked."

For all its immersion within the financial milieu, *Rollover* is a highly conventional melodrama, featuring clearly delineated "good guys" (Hub and Lee) and "bad guys" (nearly everybody else). The cinematic style contributes to the film's melodramatic emphasis, repeatedly offering sinister close-ups of the villainous characters. Whether the film is judged as a serious study of international banking or as an entertaining thriller, it fails on both counts. Unsurprisingly, it was not commercially successful.

Perhaps one can understand the superficiality of *Rollover* when one realizes that Pakula had already read and begun to prepare the screenplay for *Sophie's Choice*, a project of immense importance to him—and that he may simply have lost interest in *Rollover*. Still, although he had indeed started thinking about writing and casting *Sophie's Choice*, it is impossible to envision so professional a craftsman simply giving up on the film he was making. After considering all possible reasons for *Rollover*'s incompetence, one remains bewildered. It seems impossible to reconcile the fact that the director of this film was the same man who directed such masterworks as *Klute*, *The Parallax View*, *All the President's Men*, and *Starting Over*.

Variety called the film "fundamentally disappointing," although it noted, "Pakula's previously displayed expertise at conveying pervasive paranoia triggered by massive conspiracies at high levels is perfectly in tune with the story's aims." *Newsweek* praised Pakula's portrayal of the world of high finance ("the frenzied cacophony of the trading rooms, where millions of dollars are exchanged in screaming telephone calls; the chilly glamour of boardroom offices and joyless corporate parties"), but little else. And Richard Schickel, writing in *Time*, noted that Pakula "is a true stylist, a man who sees the world through a slow-panning lens darkly" and for whom "the corridors of power are menacingly dim and hushed," but concluded, "in the end [*Rollover*] just does not wash. One is left with a succession of classy, spooky images, a titillated but unsatisfied imagination, and the feeling that there is both less and more here than met Pakula's excellent eye."

In her review in the *New York Times*, Janet Maslin said, "The cleverness and proficiency of Mr. Pakula's other work are astonishingly absent here, as are the shrewdness of Miss Fonda's better performances and the easygoing charm of Mr. Kristofferson's." Maslin also commented upon Michael Small's "uncommonly loud and vacant score." Indeed, it is virtually impossible to find anything to praise in this confused and confusing movie.

Nevertheless, in terms of the arc of his career, Pakula's trajectory was still ascending, interrupted only briefly by the failure of *Rollover*. Indeed, the film he had begun to prepare before *Rollover* was completed can arguably be described as his greatest achievement.

CHAPTER THIRTEEN

Off the Set

[Alan Pakula was] "an interesting combination of a very public and a very private man. He was also a powerfully involved family man. Alan was a very complicated human being—very sensitive, very connected to his roots. He was one of the most unspoiled people in the movie business. He would rarely speak about Hollywood. I think he was much more interested in life."

—PETER JENNINGS

REGARDLESS OF THE SUCCESS OR FAILURE of Pakula's individual films, one element in his life remained constant: his fulfilling personal life, which was marked not only by extraordinary relationships with his wife and stepchildren but by a remarkable number of deep friendships.

In the process of discussing Alan Pakula with co-workers, friends, and relatives for this book, a pattern emerged: with near-unanimity, they found him to be compassionate, sympathetic, unfailingly pleasant, and extremely bright. Some people—but an amazingly small number—found flaws in his personality, but even they regarded the flaws as minor, often as endearing. Of the hundreds of people I interviewed or who were quoted in other sources, no more than two or three had anything resembling a negative opinion of any aspect of Pakula's character. The sum total of each individual's testimony about his good nature, good character, and good intentions is simply overwhelming.

Pakula's friend Polly Kraft described him as "funny, witty, enormously perceptive." Lauren Bacall called Pakula "a loyal friend, a very, very good human being, a man of charm and wit, an immense talent." When Jason Robards heard about Pakula's death in 1998, he said, "I can't believe it. I not only worked for him, I loved him very much." Jane Alexander echoed Robards' words: "I loved him," she said; "I just thought he was a very special person." These are not carefully selected utterances to portray the man in a rosy light; they are typical. Even William Goldman, one of the few people with whom Pakula did not get along, called him "one of the last gentlemen in the movie business. We had mutual acquaintances in the business and they said nothing but good things about him as a human being. Neither can I."

If one word emerged more than any other in people's descriptions of Pakula, it was "gentleman." Harrison Ford said, "That's the first thing that comes to mind. A gentleman." Charles Cioffi also used the "g" word: "Alan Pakula was a step above and beyond all of them, as far as being a gent; educated, articulate, his kindness was unmatched. He was, without question, the nicest and the classiest man I have ever known in show business."

Another who categorized Pakula as a gentleman was Peter Stone, "because he was the true definition of that word: he was a gentle man. Anyone who ever came in contact with him, including the fools that even he found so difficult to suffer, were treated with a gentlemanly civility that few in his profession . . . or in any profession, are able to maintain."

These encomiums came not only from Pakula's friends or from those in the film business who hoped he would hire them. Gretchen Babarovic, Peter Jennings' assistant, told me, "Alan Pakula is the one man who, whether he was speaking to Peter Jennings or to me or to the parking lot attendant, made you feel as if you were the most important person in the world. I've never met anyone like him. He was a very special human being."

Pakula was as generous with strangers as with friends. "You could walk down the street with him and he would never pass someone who had their hand out without putting money in their hand," Don Laventhall said.

Pakula's relatives, as might be expected, have only the highest praise for him. In an earlier chapter, his stepchildren's love and respect have been amply documented. Louis Boorstin's comment is appropriate here, however: "He was an extraordinary man. I'd like to be able to give you something more controversial—biographers always like controversy because that makes it more interesting—but there wasn't. We had a wonderful relationship. He was an extraordinary man."

Other relatives praised Pakula in similar terms. His niece, Debby Maisel, called him "an unbelievable person. He was so kind and thoughtful and he really cared about you. When he spoke to you, you felt you were the only person in the world."

I asked Selma Hirsh, Alan's cousin, how Pakula changed as he got older and became a successful film director. "He grew more compassionate than ever," she said. "He was affectionate with his family, always affectionate, always devoted to his family."

Don Laventhall, who worked closely with Pakula on a daily basis for years, first as his assistant, later as Executive Vice President of Pakula Productions, and finally as associate producer of two of Pakula's films, characterized him as "a great lover of people. When he got on a plane, and people would ask him, 'What do you do?' he wouldn't tell them he was a movie director because he didn't want to talk about himself. He'd say, 'I'm a psychiatrist,' so that he could get people to talk about themselves. He was very interested in other people."

Hannah Pakula also spoke of her husband's fascination for learning about other people's lives, and said that Alan "had the ability to draw people out." She recalled that when they attended parties together, she would often be stopped after dinner by whomever had been seated next to Alan at the table, and told, "Oh, Alan is so wonderful. I told him my whole life story." Selma Hirsh used virtually the same words, saying that when she would bring a friend to the Pakulas' apartment, "he would chat with her until he had gotten her whole life story out of her."

Ben Bradlee observed, "I thought he was Freud reincarnated. I never saw a guy who sort of intuitively could get to understand people, and who was so open-minded about people. We got along like smoke from day one, we really did. I was so impressed with him. You know, the Freud analogy is not crazy. He knew about my brother, and mother, and father—God, he knew my family. He knew them so well, and he was so caring. Some part of his brain was filled with sympathy for people. He understood people's difficulties and people's frailties, and made adjustments for them."

In Bradlee's autobiography, he pursued the analogy to Freud further. Pakula, he said, "even looks like Freud, gently listening, analyzing the passing scene, quietly absorbing information and impressions from all around him with a glint in his eyes, and a trace of a quizzical smile on his lips."

Marilyn Berger was also taken by Pakula's interest in others. "Alan was a person who, unlike many people in the movies, was interested in what *you* were doing," she said. "He would like to know about a story Don [Hewitt, her husband, the producer of *60 Minutes*] was working on, for example."

Hannah's view of her husband is obviously influenced by her love for him, but her opinion is no less valid for that reason. "He was a delicious human being to live with because of his wonderful sense of humor," she said. "It was a blessing. He had the ability to make you feel good."

Pakula maintained his sense of humor and his interest in other people even when he was deeply involved with work on a film. He refused to allow his work, however stressful, to negatively impact his life away from the set. He "was living proof that working and being successful in the film industry does not mean that you can't have a loving, happy, rich, and fulfilling personal life," said Pieter Jan Brugge, the husband of Pakula's stepdaughter, Anna, and a co-worker on several of Pakula's films.

The actors who worked with Pakula were effusive in their praise of his qualities as a human being. Hume Cronyn said, "Alan was a *very* good friend. When I think of him it's always with great affection. He was a generous man." Charles Durning called Pakula "just a gentle, warm, lovely human being." Gregory Peck said, "Alan Pakula was one of the most honorable men I have ever met." Kevin Kline could not sum Pakula up briefly, he said, because "he was complicated. The elements mixed in him in paradoxical ways. He combined, uniquely, passion and intelligence, humor and gravity, madness and rationality, earthiness and refinement. Always generous, always kind."

And at least equally as kind and generous to women as to men. "He liked women a lot," Celia Costas said. "He liked talking to them, he liked talking about them, he felt very comfortable expressing his ideas to women." Catherine Solt, Pakula's personal assistant, agreed: "He was wonderful with women; he just was. He was charming with women. He made them feel very special."

Jill Clayburgh was more specific. "He was flirtatious and gentle, but never in a way that was off-putting. It was just a sort of intimate, charming manner. Not to say that he didn't like men, but he was very comfortable around women."

Charles Cioffi felt that Pakula "was just a guy who liked women. He liked to be carried away by their flirtations—and all actresses are flirtatious. I think he was very attracted to pretty women."

Jane Fonda said, "He had a profound empathy for women's emotional and psychological processes. Really, he was a woman-friendly man. I don't know why that is, because he was certainly a man, it's not that he identified with women. I'm not sure whether it was that he tended to be more interested in women, or that the parts [in his films] were better-conceived for women—or maybe they went together."

Pakula was, in some respects, a curious mixture of liberal and conservative. Liberal in his politics—"I think he was essentially liberal, but not in a doctrinaire way," Ben Bradlee said; "I think he was interested in truth, in the pursuit of truth." Adventurous in his filmmaking—"the breadth of his imagination is startling," Meryl Streep said, "and it's unusual"—he was conservative in other respects, particularly in his dress. He normally wore a tie and a tweedy jacket, khaki pants, and a button-down shirt, although he took off his shoes nearly everywhere—at home, on the set, in the office. "He liked to nest, you know, and get really comfortable," Catherine Solt said. "And yet he was very formal at the same time; he almost always wore a suit to the office, even on days he didn't have to—he just *did*."

Chris Murray remembers when, in 1969, Pakula took him and a group of his teenaged friends to a rock concert. Chris and his friends were all in hippie garb, but Alan wore his customary suit and tie. He also took a movie camera and hung on "to the light tower, trying to get some footage out of this incredible spectacle," shooting through "a haze of reefer smoke."

Despite the care he took with his wardrobe, Pakula always seemed to have a rumpled look. "He was natty," Michael Small said, "but he looked like the Yale professor, the morning after being natty." Debby Maisel observed that Pakula "always looked nice, but in a professorial way, not in a stylish way."

In many respects, he resembled the stereotype of the absent-minded professor. Maisel remembers that when Alan and Hannah came to visit her and her family in New Jersey, "Hannah would do the driving because Alan would invariably get lost.[35] He was very smart, but there was a piece of him that was absent-minded."

This quality was carried to extremes when he was concentrating on a film he was making. One day, during the shooting of *Starting Over*, he remarked to the makeup artist, "That's an awfully attractive woman over there." The makeup man looked at him with astonishment. "Oh, for God's sake, Alan," he said, "that's your wife!"

If Pakula was a man without substantial character flaws, he was certainly a man of many quirks. Anna Boorstin attributed several of her stepfather's eccentricities to the fact that he was left-handed, but when he attended grammar school, he was forced to learn to write with his right hand. "He had all these bizarre brain disconnections," she said, "so he would literally walk around the house with a newspaper in one hand, saying, 'Where's my newspaper?'" She became "Little Miss Helpful," as she characterized herself, asking Pakula questions such as "Did you remember to take your keys out of the car?"

"One of my favorite Alan moments was when he took me to see *Kind Hearts and Coronets*" while she was in high school, Anna said. "We were driving down Santa Monica Boulevard and he was proving to me how screwed up his brain was while we were driving. He took two pens and one or two pieces of paper, and while he was driving he wrote his name in mirror writing on one side and the right way on the other side. I mean, this was the ultimate in cool. And goofy, too."

Also just a bit on the goofy (or, perhaps, compulsive) side was Pakula's daily nap ritual. Rather than simply lie down on the sofa in his office, he would remove his trousers, put them on a hanger, and hang them on the back of his office door.

Another of Pakula's quirks was to keep a king-size mug of coffee in his hand or nearby, particularly when he was working on a film. Jack Hirshberg, who observed Pakula filming *All the President's Men*, told of the director's dependence on his coffee mug: "It wasn't that he drank so much coffee; sometimes a single cup lasted hours. It was the cup he needed . . . Frequently it was almost empty, but

---

[35]But Anna Boorstin's recollection was somewhat different. Although she acknowledges that Pakula "was absent-minded; it's easy to imagine him missing an exit or a turn completely because his mind was elsewhere," she adds "he did have a good sense of direction. My whole family (especially Mom, me, and Robert) are clueless when it comes to senses of direction. We joke that my mom can get lost going around the block. So, Mom would drive and Alan would steer. She would keep him focused by asking where the heck she was going, and he would know—as long as there was someone to tell him he needed to pay attention."

occasionally he would raise it to his lips to take a swig without ascertaining if there was any coffee left. After a while, the crew began to drop cigarette butts and ashes in the mug when Pakula wasn't looking. Perhaps a half-hour later he would lift the cup to take another swallow—but never once did he gag, spit it out, or so much as indicate by a twitch of his face that he had even noticed. Nor did he once complain of stomach discomfort. It was a remarkable performance, rivaling the old time vaudevillians who used to chew razor blades."

Anna Boorstin bemoaned (with amusement) Alan's, and Hannah's, chronic lateness. "Each of them was later than the other," she said. "If they asked my brothers and me to make a dinner reservation, we'd call and make them half an hour later so we wouldn't be embarrassed." For Robert Mulligan, Pakula's habitual lateness was less amusing. "He was often late for all kinds of things," Mulligan said, "or, at best, he'd arrive at the last minute, out of breath and full of apologies. I don't recall that he ever missed the start of an important meeting, but everything else was at risk: airline schedules, social affairs, lunches, dinners, and assorted travel arrangements and appointments of all kinds." Mulligan, both by nature and because of the discipline imposed on him by his vocation as a television director, was always punctual, often early. But "Alan was going to be late. The only question was—by how much? Early on it drove me to distraction." Eventually, even Mulligan ceased to become annoyed, partially because Alan "was always so apologetic—and breathing so hard—you just had to forgive and forget. And laugh. It was just—Alan."

Michael Small felt that Pakula's absent-mindedness wasn't entirely unintentional. When Pakula was deep in the throes of making a film, Small said, "he was very tunneled. He didn't always want to talk to you, because he was preoccupied. Sometimes he'd almost hide so he didn't have to see me. He didn't like to make small talk. He'd become so obsessed with what he was doing."

Alvin Sargent, whose relationship with Pakula dated from the 1940s, thought that Pakula wished to exert subtle control in his relationships. "Alan and I would talk on the phone often," Sargent said, "and he would finally say, 'I gotta go.' So he would go. And one day we were talking and something came up and I said, 'I have to go.' And I realized that he wouldn't let me go. Not because he loved me, but because he didn't want *me* to be the one to go." Sargent also observed a side of Pakula that few others saw: "He could be snarly when he didn't get his way. You could see it. He couldn't hide it. If he believed that his way was the right way, he wasn't going to back down."

Keren Saks, too, was aware of Pakula's thorny side. Although she stressed that her dominant impression of Pakula was of a kind, compassionate, articulate, and intelligent man, she also perceived him as a man "who could get angry. He had a look, when there'd be a topic of conversation, when somebody took a point of view about [something] which he felt very strongly, and took the opposite side. He'd get kind of 'big,' and he'd sit up straight. But he never yelled. He could make his points without shouting."

One reason Pakula did not resort to shouting was because of his imposing physical presence. At six feet two, he was considerably taller than many of his friends. ("It's better to be a short director," he once said. "You don't get into the shot so much.") He sported a beard (first red, then brown; then, in his sixties, gray), had green eyes and brown hair. He remained slim by maintaining an odd diet—"chicken salad in the mornings," Chris Murray recalls.

Physically, he was "sort of held in," Meryl Streep said. Donald Sutherland spoke of Pakula's "stiff neck," and he wasn't speaking metaphorically. Jane Fonda recalled Pakula's odd appearance during the shooting of *Comes a Horseman* in rural Colorado. "Alan was a very urban man," she said. "He always had spit-shined loafers and well-dressed khaki pants"—clothing that was inappropriate for the setting and clashed jarringly with the blue jeans and boots worn by everyone else.

Pakula was out of place in any environment that might be termed athletic. Colleen Creedon said about him, "I saw him in the pool [at the house he owned with Hope Lange], but I don't think I ever saw him swimming in it." "He liked to ride a bicycle," Hannah Pakula said. But, she added, "he wasn't very good at it." His nephew, Rodd Baxter, said, "You never heard of Alan doing anything athletic. Never heard of him playing tennis or golf."

Although he had no formal musical training, Pakula had a remarkable affinity for the piano. "If you could sing a song, he could pick it out in no time," a relative said. "He was incredible. He had a great, great ear." Hannah added that Alan had perfect pitch. He often sat at the piano and improvised melodies—but they were never written down, and were not heard again. Hannah "threatened to put a tape recorder in the piano," she said, "but I never did." Pakula played the trumpet when he was in college, and gave his trumpet to stepson Chris Murray as a gift from the tooth fairy when Chris was five years old.

All his friends and family members refer fondly to Pakula's sense of humor. One example: the Pakulas invited the Israeli Uri Geller to dinner one evening. Geller was famous for his supposed ability to bend spoons and keys by concentrated attention alone. Consequently, before Geller arrived, according to Michael Small, "Alan was running around telling Hannah, 'Hannah, hide the silverware, hide the silverware!'"

Pakula loved to laugh. Chris Murray remembered "when he took me to a Woody Allen film and I was literally embarrassed because Alan was laughing so loud—a wonderful laugh that sounded like a freight train gathering momentum, and then blasting out."

But if Pakula could laugh easily, he also "understood the dark side of human nature and human behavior," as Bob Woodward said. Pakula told Woodward about the years he had spent in psychoanalysis, and, Woodward concluded, "I don't think somebody would do that for so many years who wasn't trying to work out some agonies and uncertainties. Some people radiate a sense of, I've glimpsed the abyss. Maybe indirectly, maybe directly, but I've glimpsed it, I've seen it, I know it." However, if Pakula was plagued by such knowledge, he shared it only with his psychiatrist—and through his films. One might say that directing films had a therapeutic effect on him, allowing him to work through problems that in the past had driven him to the analyst's couch. As he once remarked, "I think when you do a film, there's a part of you in each character, or vice-versa."

Ben Bradlee was also impressed by Pakula's enthusiasm: "I kept up with him very closely afterwards—I saw him until he died, and he was such fun to talk to because he wanted to talk about what people were like. It's very seldom that you find people who do that. Usually they want to talk about themselves or their own efforts, but Alan was always saying, 'Well, what was Katharine Graham like?' or 'What are Woodward and Bernstein *really* like?'" Bradlee and his wife, who, like the Pakulas, have a house in East Hampton, became friendly with Hannah as well as with Alan. "They're so straight and caring and they've both got good senses of humor. Alan, especially, had a *great* sense of humor," Bradlee said. "He laughed a lot. And he listened well. Jesus, he listened well. And I think he heard, when he brought his mind to bear on it, he *heard* what people were saying."

An enthusiasm that could reasonably be described as boyish characterized Pakula until the end of his life. "When you're working with wonderful collaborators, there is this exhilaration that's like, 'Hey, I'm Tom Sawyer and he's Huck Finn and we're making a movie together, and, hey, what if we did this?'" he said shortly before he was killed. Debby Maisel recalls another of Pakula's boyish qualities. When he was an adult, "Alan would skip as he walked down the street," she said.

Writer Dennis Brown speaks of Pakula's "Candide-like innocence and enthusiasm about filmmaking." But Pakula's enthusiasm was not reserved for filmmaking; it extended to all walks of life. "He was young in thinking," Debby Maisel said, "and that's why young people would gravitate to him."

Keren Saks, who, with her actor-director husband Gene, often socialized with the Pakulas, said, "I miss him so terribly. When he died, I felt that something substantial and very supportive in my life was suddenly gone." At one point in her life, when she was thinking of changing careers, Pakula "would sit and talk to me," she said, "and he'd look me in the eye and he'd put his extraordinarily intelligent and creative brain to work. He came up with ideas that I didn't have, and he'd suggest how to do them. At one point he said I should do a cooking show and he'd direct it! He had ideas about all the particulars. I mean, what kind of friend! And, you know, he didn't just talk about it. He really would have directed it. He was dead serious."

Barbara Davis recalled a similar occasion. When she began writing full-time she was feeling insecure about it, having "done not very much except journalism during the sixteen years of my first marriage." As a result, she was reluctant to send her work to agents and publishers. Pakula took her out to dinner and told her, "You really have to decide whether to risk writing what you want to write and trying to publish and sending it out—and run the risk that you're really not very good. Otherwise, people might say, 'Oh, she had such a gift, but it was never used.'" Davis called Pakula "a wonderful friend. I think he was a very good man—an amazingly good man. I think he was incapable of doing anything dishonest or dishonorable. He was faithful to old friends. I think that was an important part of who he was and who he wanted to be."

Marilyn Berger said that "Alan as a friend had a tremendous capacity for intimacy and gentleness, and he genuinely cared about his friends. He was there when there was a problem. There was a great sense of caring about him. I just think he was a genuinely gentle soul." Horton Foote said, "I always knew if I needed anything—advice, kindness, reassurance—where it was to be found."

Peter Jennings, too, found Pakula to be a person with whom he could discuss personal problems. "If there was something happening in my life, he had a sound opinion about it," Jennings said. "He was a person in whom I truly believed I could confide." Jennings summed up Pakula as "such a special person. At least with me, he had no airs. He was very quick and very thoughtful. He cared passionately about human rights, about cinema, about teaching, about other people."

Gene Saks's initial impression of Pakula was that he was "very formal and, therefore, rather cold," but he soon "found [Pakula] not only warm and friendly, but somebody who took a particular interest in me in such a way that it was really very comforting and flattering. I mean, he genuinely wanted to know me and to know my feelings, my thoughts, and what was going on inside me. Which is very touching. You know, it happens so seldom that somebody takes a very personal interest in you and wants to learn something about you."

Catherine Solt said, "Once you had his trust, he was extremely kind and very generous. If Alan liked you, then you became sort of like family. When he took you into his immediate circle, he was very interested in people's lives. He'd ask a lot of questions. 'How do you feel about *this* and about *this*?'" She found "something professorial about him," and as the daughter of two professors, she would know.

Solt witnessed Pakula's generosity on several occasions. "He was very compassionate. With the people he loved who were having trouble, he'd always talk about it and worry about it. He would help financially, he'd call people to find out what to do. For instance, if somebody was having a medical problem he'd call up people he knew to find out who the best doctor was. And that made all of us [working at Pakula Productions] feel very safe. We always had the best. Alan would say, 'We need health insurance, so what's the best we can get?' He was always like that."

Her dominant impression of her boss was overwhelmingly favorable. "He had an amazing life, and it was very broad," she said. "And because he was so smart and so interested in so many things and knew so many people, and made sure that that was a big part of his life, I think that that really influenced his selections [of what films to make], and his films in general, and what he brought to his films. He surrounded himself with amazing people all the time. And he loved ideas, he read a lot. There was nothing you could talk to him about that he didn't have an opinion on, that he didn't know something about, and you couldn't figure out how he could have so much time in the day to know all that stuff."

But Solt was aware of a flaw in his personality—or, rather, a worthy attribute carried to extremes. She felt that in many cases Pakula "was almost too nice. He wanted very much to be a nice guy and not to offend people. He cared very deeply if he felt he had hurt someone. He was apologetic."

Boaty Boatwright felt that Pakula "worried too much about offending or hurting people or what people might think of him. Alan always wanted people to like him." But Larry Turman, Pakula's agent in the 1950s, had another take on this aspect of Alan's personality. He felt that Pakula was so determined not to offend others partly because it worked to his professional advantage. "Alan had a quality, the ability to be totally indifferent to somebody as a professional and perhaps even as a person and yet convey warmth, intimacy, and total connectedness. It was a skill. I've been in meetings with him with various people. He could be wonderfully disarming. He could reveal something seemingly very intimate about himself, which would engender a response in which the other person would open up everything. That was a quality he had. The best directors, and also producers, are also seducers, and Alan was fabulous. Put him in a room with anybody and they'd say, 'Yes, I want to work with this guy.'"

Pakula was inherently modest, never seeking publicity for himself. Hannah sometimes became indignant on his behalf. On one occasion, she saw and was irritated by an advertisement for one of Pakula's films that did not feature his name prominently. Her husband quietly assured her, "Don't worry. The people who need to know, know I directed it." Hannah characterized her husband as a "most singularly modest human being."

Don Hewitt's view of Pakula was also informed by his friend's modesty. He thought of Pakula as "a guy that I would trust with anything. Alan was as trustworthy as anyone I ever met in my life, and had a marvelous sense of humor about the Hollywood scene. He never got seduced by Hollywood, because he had a wonderful sense of perspective and he knew where movies fit in the overall scheme of life. There are so many guys out there who take themselves so seriously. It's like they would have you believe that Hollywood is the be-all and end-all of America. I don't think Alan ever thought that."

Pakula's modesty sprang from his strong sense of his identity as an artist, and an objectivity in assessing the quality of his own work. "A lot of it has to do with who you are, who you think you are," he said, "because when you do public work, when you make films, everybody tells you what they think and they tell you in print and they tell you on television, and you will get as many different reviews as there are reviewers, and somewhere you have to go through all of that and come out of that saying, 'Yes, but this is what I tried to do and this is what *I* think I did and this is what I don't think I did.'"

Hewitt (who like Pakula, the Bradlees, and Peter Jennings owned a house in East Hampton) said of Alan, "I never knew a better man. . . . He came as close to being a brother as a friend could be."

Pakula was an avid follower of current events. "He was as perceptive about the world around him as he was in his personal life," Hewitt said. Pakula, reflecting upon his interests, said, "I am very interested in political society; I am very interested in society as a whole." Hannah Pakula confirmed that "he was kind of a political junkie." Peter Jennings added, "If something happened in the world, he always had an opinion on it. Always, he was very interested in politics, *deeply* interested in politics. A very, very committed liberal, very committed about civil liberties, very opinionated." Furthermore, Pakula told Jennings that he watched ABC News regularly. And, said Jennings, "he had very strong opinions about what we [at ABC] did or did not do." Those strong opinions often manifested themselves when he "watched the talk shows on television and yelled back at them," Hannah said.

Pakula had strong opinions about everything, for that matter. Peter Stone said, "His powers of concentration were formidable. It was impossible to interrupt him when he was in the throes of expounding, describing, or analyzing. Not that he refused to allow any interference; it was simply because he wasn't aware of it. And after several frustrated attempts to break into the conversation, the only thing left to do was to shut up, wait, and finally, to laugh. One day I remember telling him that he was even more concentrated than frozen orange juice—but, typically, he didn't hear it. Or, because he was a gentleman, he pretended not to hear it."

One subject on which Pakula had strong convictions was human rights, especially insofar as it applied to creative artists. He helped Hannah found Human

Rights Watch/Film Watch, which "was created to monitor and protect the human rights of filmmakers and film programmers who are threatened or censored or otherwise abused for their expression through film." Members of the organization encouraged American filmmakers to write to heads of state in which foreign directors were unable to function freely. Hannah Pakula became co-chair of the Freedom to Write committee of the PEN American Center, and is a member of the Council on Foreign Relations.

Alan Pakula, moved to activism by his experience with his stepson Bob, actively supported and raised funds for the National Alliance for the Mentally Ill. He was also a member of the American Civil Liberties Union.

As a renowned film director, Pakula was often asked to make speeches, for many of which he had virtually no time to prepare. However, as Hannah explained, "Alan was very good on his feet and he spoke extremely well and without notes. He would have to give a speech somewhere and we'd be on our way down in the car, and he'd say, 'Just be quiet for a few minutes; I want to think about this.' Later he'd get up to speak, and I'd sit there with my mouth open, he had such an ease and a gift for doing this." She recalled an event at Trinity College in Dublin at which Arthur Schlesinger and George Mitchell—whom Hannah called "professional speakers"—were among a group of lecturers, one of whom was Pakula. During lunch, Pakula excused himself "and went over to the side and made a few notes." The other speakers "had these beautifully, carefully written and typed-out speeches. When Alan spoke, none of the professionals could believe" how concise and fluent his presentation was.

To Catherine Solt, Pakula seemed remarkably lucky. "He'd always be late for things because he was so busy—but then it would always work out. Or he would lose things—but they'd always be returned. He was sloppy in some ways. He would walk out of the office with his wallet half-hanging out of his pocket."

Then, recalling the accident that took Pakula's life, Solt said, pensively, "I *never* thought it would end that way. Before he died he seemed to have a charmed life. I thought he would live to be a very old man, and he would have this nice, privileged life."

I asked Don Laventhall if he was aware of any unresolved crisis in Pakula's life, a life that seems to have been so fulfilling and so nearly free from conflict. Laventhall reflected for a moment, then observed, "I think Alan had a real sense of his mortality and the physical frailty of life, so he was careful, physically—which is ironic, of course, considering what ended up happening."

CHAPTER FOURTEEN

Sophie's Choice I:
Pre-Production

"Sophie's Choice was as much a labor of love for me as any film
I've ever done."

–ALAN J. PAKULA

"Nobody loves an adaptation. Not literary enough in that it proceeds
through pictures, not cinematic enough in that it has its origin in words,
it finds itself in a no-man's land, caught somewhere between a series
of conflicting aesthetic claims and rivalries. For if film threatens literature,
literature also threatens film, and nowhere so powerfully, in either
instance, as in the form of adaptation."

–JOY GOULD BOYUM, *Double Exposure: Fiction into Film*

T HE NARRATOR OF *Sophie's Choice*, both in the novel and the film, is
Stingo, a sensitive, aspiring young novelist who moves from a small town in the
South to New York City, but the main characters are Stingo's upstairs neighbors
in Yetta Zimmerman's boarding house: Polish-born concentration camp survivor
Sophie Zawitowska and her lover, the brilliant but unstable Nathan Landau.
Stingo's life becomes interwoven with the lives of Sophie (with whom he becomes
deeply infatuated) and Nathan (whom he believes to be a research chemist at Pfizer
and whom he admires more than anyone he has ever known). Nathan is fatally
attractive, both to Sophie and to Stingo: a gifted musician, an apparently skilled
scientist, a widely read intellectual with remarkable verbal gifts. He is not only
Sophie's lover; he is also her tormentor, brutally questioning why she survived
Auschwitz when so many thousands of Jews died there. He is not only Stingo's
friend and supporter, but a malignant force who accuses Stingo of coveting

Sophie. A paranoid schizophrenic (as described by his brother) who is also sub-ject to manic-depressive episodes, Nathan alternates between tender concern for Sophie and mad outbursts in which he accuses her of infidelity and threatens her life. His instability is increased by his misuse of drugs.

In his novel, William Styron created a brilliant, haunting narrative, inter-rupted frequently by lengthy philosophical discourses (which, depending on one's inclination, are either the novel's best feature or an irritation to be endured). In his film adaptation, Pakula dispensed with the discourses and focused on the action, which is so profound and evocative that a philosophical point of view emerges strongly.

It is unusual for a drama of the Holocaust to focus on a persecuted Nazi vic-tim who is not a Jew, but a Catholic. Some reviewers criticized Styron, saying that his focus on Sophie's tragedy diminished the experience of six million Jews.[36] But Alan Pakula, a Jew, did not agree. An estimated five million non-Jews were also murdered in the Holocaust; brutality against a member of the human race is a crime against all members of humanity and the focus on Sophie hardly altered the historic fact that most of the inmates in concentration camps and most of those put to death were Jewish—as Nathan reminds the reader of the novel and the view-er of the film again and again, for Nathan is obsessed with Nazi barbarity and Jewish victimization.

As Sophie's Choice unfolds, both Stingo and the reader wonder how Sophie came to be a victim of the Nazis, and what the nature of the "choice" was that she faced. Sophie fends off Stingo's questions with bits of information, some of which turn out to be truth, some lies—or, perhaps more accurately, childhood fantasies. But the truth is ultimately revealed in a series of flashbacks, spiraling backwards from

---

[36]Elie Wiesel, writing in the New York Times, agreed that "not all victims [of the Holocaust] were Jewish," but argued that "all Jews were victims." To suggest that others suffered on the same scale as Jews was a mistaken notion, he maintained: "If every-body was a victim, then no one was. If everybody endured as much as the Jews, then it means that the Jews' suffering had no spe-cial significance." Wiesel further suggested that only survivors of the death camps could legitimately use the Holocaust as a subject for memoir or fiction, for "those who never lived that time of death will never be able to grasp the magnitude of horror. Only sur-vivors of Auschwitz know what it meant to be in Auschwitz." William Styron countered, "I don't think for an instant that anyone can object to the fact that Jews, quite properly, say they were the chief victims. Indeed they were; there is simply no doubt about it. In fact, I think it can be argued that the phrase 'the war against the Jews' describes what the Nazis were doing to a great extent. . . . But I am troubled nonetheless by a certain ungenerosity that does not allow the understanding that there were, indeed, not just thousands, not hundreds of thousands, but millions of non-Jews who died just as horribly as the Jews, although perhaps not as methodically. It has to be remembered that the population of Auschwitz at any single time was largely Gentile, not Jewish. The Jewish victims were being exterminated, to be sure, and the non-Jews were dying in their own particular way, which is to say that they were slaves who were being starved to death, and they died just as verifiably as those who went to the gas chamber. . . . To be sure, they did not suffer the direct extermination process, but they died horribly of disease, torture, starvation, medical exper-iments, and so on." Styron quotes Simon Wiesenthal as saying, "I always insist that we talk about not the six million Jews, but the ten million, or the eleven million or whatever number of people, Jews and non-Jews, who were direct victims of the Nazi terror."

the "present day" of the novel and film (the late 1940s) to the mid-1930s. In that reverse chronology, we see or are told about Sophie's father, whom she claims to have been a brave defender of human values, but who is revealed to have been an anti-Semite and an advocate of Hitler's "final solution"; Sophie's arrest for stealing a ham to feed herself, her husband, and her two small children; Sophie's existence at Auschwitz, where she was imprisoned by the Nazis; Sophie's attempt to win freedom for her son by appealing to the Nazi Commandant Rudolf Hoess; and, finally, of the dreadful choice presented to her by an S. S. physician when she arrives with her children at Auschwitz: to select one of her children for extermination, in exchange for which the physician will spare the other.

Styron's novel was praised in some circles as an "American masterpiece" (Paul Fussell, *Washington Post Book World*) and strongly criticized in others. In the words of critic Barbara Tepa Lupack, "Some readers and critics, male and female alike, saw in Sophie's victimization a portrait of what they alleged was Styron's own misogyny and in the narrative voice of Stingo . . . Styron's narcissistic appropriation of Sophie's tragedy." Other criticisms of *Sophie's Choice* were leveled by several Holocaust scholars, who took umbrage at Styron's very use of the Holocaust as the stuff of popular fiction.

William Styron was not unfamiliar with controversy. His earlier novel, *The Confessions of Nat Turner*, had drawn similarly passionate responses, both in its favor and in opposition. In the case of *Sophie's Choice*, he said, "I don't know of a woman in modern literature who has suffered so much at the hands of men as Sophie has." To suggest that he used the character to vent his own misogyny appears absurd on its face, for Sophie is portrayed as the victim of cruelty (most of it committed by men) of all kinds: political, religious, sexual, et cetera.

Having seen a pre-publication announcement for Styron's book in *Publishers Weekly*, Pakula asked for and received a set of the galley proofs of *Sophie's Choice* before the novel was published in 1979. He began reading the book one Friday evening, stayed up all night, and had finished the novel by morning (a monumental feat in itself, since Styron's novel is long and complex). When his wife Hannah woke up, Pakula said, "I want to make this into a movie. Please read it." She did, completing the book on Sunday night, and told Pakula that she shared his enthusiasm.

Later, in an interview, he elaborated. "When I read the galleys of *Sophie*, I knew I had to make it. What was fascinating to me was that it's the story of a man coming in and saving a woman—at the same time he destroys her. And it's told from the view of a young boy . . . who is pulled into their vortex, but who really would like to save them both—and fails." Echoes of earlier Pakula films—*The Sterile Cuckoo*, *Love and Pain and the Whole Damn Thing*, and *Klute*, for example—are apparent.

He was able to see some of himself in Stingo, who, "when those Jews were going to their deaths . . . was worrying about an adolescent dance. . . . Similarly, on D-day, I had my Latin final exam at the Bronx High School of Science, and that was what I was worrying about when men were dying in Normandy. . . . Maybe that's part of the attraction of *Sophie's Choice*, that it's told from the point of view of Stingo, who feels about that era as I do in many ways—that he was so obsessed with his own growing pains that the rest of the world was not as real as it should have been." Furthermore, Stingo's story encapsulated "the American loss of innocence," Pakula said, "and the adolescent dream I had of trying to save somebody I loved." At another time, he admitted, "I seem to have an obsession with loss of innocence," a theme that is apparent throughout Pakula's work.

Other aspects of the novel were equally compelling to him. He was fascinated by the moral and political question at the novel's core, which he defined thus: "The final evil that Styron dealt with was that the victim is made to feel responsible for being a victim. The victim is left with the guilt. The final monstrosity: to have your loved one destroyed, and you are left feeling that you are the guilty one."

Pakula encountered Styron at a party in New York and introduced himself to the novelist. He must have known that Styron would be there, for he carried the galleys of *Sophie's Choice* to the party with him. He told Styron, "I'm so eager to make this. I've read your book. I hope I can do it." Styron, for his part, said he "immediately warmed to [Pakula]. I liked him enormously."

Pakula's agent, Stan Kamen of the William Morris Agency, had acquired the galleys for Pakula, who paid $750,000 for the film rights. Another Kamen client, Keith Barish, a real-estate developer, was looking for an opportunity to break into films as a producer. Consequently, Kamen suggested that Barish buy the rights to the book from Pakula. Barish did so in May 1979, after which he and Pakula took the idea for making a film from one major studio to another. One by one, their overtures were rejected. Many of the reasons must have sounded familiar to Pakula, for he had encountered the same sort of resistance on earlier films: the story was not commercial, it did not have a happy ending (as Pakula said, "double suicides are not necessarily the easiest thing to get financed"), and he was determined to cast it with little-known performers.

However, the search for a production company ended when Martin Starger, president of Lord Lew Grade's production company, Marble Arch, responded positively to the notion of turning *Sophie's Choice* into a film. But Pakula was wary of the reactions he had received from the executives he had previously spoken to about the project. Over lunch, Pakula warned Starger, "If you think I'll change the ending or make it a romance between a young boy and a Polish woman, don't bother to talk any further." Starger responded that he had no wish to alter the ending or to do violence of any sort to Styron's novel. "It won't be an easy motion picture with mass appeal," he conceded, "but it might be an important one."

Starger's attitude impressed Pakula, who said, "I suppose I decided to do the picture with Marty because we talked about 'the book.' We didn't talk about 'the property.' . . . I have one rule. I'd rather go with someone who has a passion for the book because he'll sell it better. At the last minute, others will try to sell it as something it isn't or get scared and not sell it at all. And this picture will take selling."

Starger called his boss, Lew Grade, who had suffered anti-Semitic persecution before leaving Russia for England. Grade said, "Tell me about it." Starger presented him with an outline of the novel. "Do it," Grade replied, and the process of bringing *Sophie's Choice* to the screen began.

Negotiations between Marble Arch and Pakula lasted for three days. The contract the parties signed in July called for Marble Arch to pay Pakula a fee of one million dollars to direct the film, for Starger to serve as executive producer, and for Barish to be billed as producer. The company would have worldwide distribution rights.

Starger established a $12 million budget, and authorized Pakula to hire a screenwriter. But for this project Pakula felt such a special affinity that he wished to write the screenplay himself. Pakula told the press, "I have rarely felt this kind of passion for anything in my life," but compared it to the sustained excitement he felt when he was producing *To Kill a Mockingbird*. Indeed, *Sophie's Choice* "was as much a labor of love for me as any film I've ever done," he later said.

Styron elected not to play an active role in the adaptation. ("I think he might have wanted me to work with him," Styron said, "but I didn't particularly want to, so I stayed away.") He told questioners, "I have a great deal of confidence in Alan Pakula, who's directing and writing the script, and who has a marvelous sensibility."

Pakula found the screenplay extraordinarily difficult to write, both because of the necessity to balance the scenes set in 1947 with the flashbacks, and because massive amounts of material had to be excised. But he was determined to preserve the core of the novel in his screenplay. "It's [to be] a mystery film," Pakula said, "it's a film about ghosts. And gradually [the audience discovers] what the ghosts are, what the mystery is, but only very gradually. [The screenwriter must tease] the audience to want to know more and more about what really happened. . . . In order to create suspense, you must build an audience's interest, you must give them enough information to want more [about] Sophie. . . . [it is] very difficult to have a film taking place in both times, past and present, in that way, and keep the suspense in both time periods strong."

Pakula and Styron conferred often during the process of creating the screenplay, and Styron appreciated Pakula's wish to solicit his opinion. "We had several long lunches," Styron recalled, "in which he described his general outline. But then he went ahead and did it by himself." Styron recalled that even as Pakula "was describing the project before he began writing, I was aware that he had an entirely different take on the film, in the sense that his view of what the film would be would not have been my projection. But I understood even as he spoke that his own vision of the film was valid. It wouldn't have been my way, but it was his way, and I realized that, different as it was, he was doing no violation to the general spirit of the book."

Pakula worried whether his middle-class background, growing up in New York, might make him less than an ideal choice to write a screenplay and direct a film about the Holocaust. He was concerned that any film might trivialize the event, which he was determined to avoid. Moreover, he wondered if an American could create an authentic portrayal of the time and place. However, he vividly recalled his fear of the Nazi threat when he was a child. "I can remember hearing Hitler on the radio," he recalled, "his harangues, that distorted voice, and realizing that if he ever got to America, I'd be in trouble," although neither he (nor anyone else in the United States) was aware of the death camps at that time. But, as he said, "If my grandparents had not come to this country . . . and my sister and I had been born in Poland, without question we would have wound up in the ovens . . . in Auschwitz or in some comparable place."

He was also motivated to direct the film because, as he said, "There's a lot of thematic material here that's . . . interested me for a long time. . . . There's the complexity of the relationship between Nathan and Sophie, as seen through [Stingo's] eyes. There's the strange mixture of life-giving and death-giving in the relationship, the ambivalence of love carried to its most intense extreme." Finally, Pakula said, "there's something else I strongly relate to. Maybe many men do, I don't know. The whole idea of being in love and thinking you can save somebody. For me the tragedy is when you can't and you have to realize the limits of your power."

In terms of a novel's suitability for film adaptation, there are two kinds of books, Pakula maintained: one "that has an interesting idea, but you feel the book itself is not a film, so you change it until it becomes one. The other is a book that must in some way be translated. If you translate successfully, the movie will have the life and soul of the book, and the core of the same emotional experience. People will think they're seeing the book on the screen." *Sophie's Choice* was in the latter category, Pakula believed, although the book required a great deal of pruning and rearranging. In many respects, he borrowed metaphors from the novel and translated them into visual terms for the film. One example is the significance of photographs, and their impact on Sophie and Nathan, which are used evocatively and symbolically both in the novel and in the screenplay; the importance of music in both is another example. And the use of the Brooklyn Bridge as a metaphor for Stingo's passage into manhood—an element that Styron did not envision—gives the film a richness of its own.

The Brooklyn Bridge, Pakula said, "represents the noble spirit of man, the great achievement of man." Further, he said, "the bridge is like a modern cathedral, and the Brooklyn Bridge looks like one." Indeed, the bridge's vaulted supports gave the impression of "arches with great gothic windows." In the scene in which Nathan somberly, with a sense of formality, pays tribute to Stingo's literary ability, Pakula used the bridge to show "almost a medieval ceremony of recognizing [Stingo] as an artist." In that way, "the Brooklyn Bridge became a core image to me in the film," Pakula said. The director also related the poignancy of Nathan's gesture to his own life. It was, he said, "something I longed for at Stingo's age from an older man: recognition of my talent, recognition that I was worthy."

Of course, no film could possibly include every incident or allusion contained in a five hundred page, richly detailed novel, and Pakula does not attempt the impossible.[37]

On the other hand, a film image conveys in an instant what a writer may require several pages to communicate. It would be pointless to catalogue every incident in the novel to see if each incident is contained in the film (as some have attempted to do; one is Barbara Tepa Lupack in *Take Two: Adapting the Contemporary American Novel to Film*—although her catalogue is perceptive and thought-provoking), for the obvious reason that fiction and film are different media. A novel and a film may resemble one another in some respects, but the test of whether a film is successful is not whether it conforms closely to the book from which it is adapted. The film must be judged on its own merits.

Some of the elements of the novel that Pakula excised, are, in fact, present *non-verbally* in the film, as some admirers of the novel are unable to (or refuse to) see. An actor's shrug can convey a world of feeling, but not if the spectator is mentally compiling a catalogue of the things the character does not say or do that he said or did in the novel. A camera angle can offer an interpretation; a cut can say one thing while a dissolve says another. Film, like prose, possesses grammar and elegance; confusion arises when one is only willing to settle for the comprehensiveness of prose in a more selective form of artistic expression.

An example: when Stingo checks into a hotel with Sophie late in the film, the bellhop says, "Thank you, Reverend." The screenplay offers no reason for this seemingly peculiar form of address, whereas, in the novel, Stingo elaborately cre-

---

[37]*Early drafts of Pakula's screenplay endeavored to preserve a great deal of material that would have given the film more than a four-hour running time (with intermission). Eventually, however, Pakula eliminated nearly all incidents that did not contribute directly to the story of Sophie and Nathan. The length of the final film is two hours, thirty minutes.*

ates an alias, Reverend Entwistle. Those who are critical of Pakula's screenplay suggest that, without elaboration, the "Reverend" reference is pointless and may as well have been omitted. But doesn't the use of the honorific at least *suggest* that Stingo, embarrassed to be registering at a hotel with a beautiful young woman, has given a false name to the management? If so, Pakula has indeed added texture without elaboration.

Pakula's use of mirrored images constitute a poetic form of screen expression, as does the play of light and darkness in the film, the amount of space between the characters, the way in which rooms are decorated, the musical accompaniment of various scenes, the heightened (or diminished) use of sound. The many ways in which photographs, windows, and circles are used in the film were noted admiringly by critic Barbara Tepa Lupack.

In his final screenplay, Pakula condensed several chapters in which Sophie comes to learn that the father she so idolized is, in fact, a vicious bigot, into a moment or two of screen time. The only glimpse of Sophie's father in the film is in an old photograph. Still, as the film progresses, Sophie gradually reveals more and more to Stingo about her attitude toward her father. "The structure of the film," Pakula said, consists of "peeling away the lies, the denial, as she gradually reveals the truth, gradually faces herself."

Few screenplays have been subjected to more intense scrutiny than Pakula's. Several scholarly articles have compared the screenplay to the novel, generally in order to demonstrate the values that have been lost by condensing Styron's work. Some of the comparisons are so finicky as to be absurd. One, for example (Benjamin Dunlap's "Pakula's Choice"), takes Pakula to task because he changed Stingo's narration in the novel ("Even back then, cheap apartments were hard to find in Manhattan") to the line in the screenplay ("In those days cheap apartments were almost impossible to find in Manhattan"), and attributes the change to philistinism. Dunlap also criticizes Pakula for having Stingo bring home a case of Spam rather than (as in the novel) corned beef.

Some observers criticized Pakula for omitting a significant portion of the novel that follows Sophie and Nathan on a trip to Connecticut, during which they make frenzied love and Nathan attempts to pull Sophie toward his goal of mutual suicide. The sequence appeared in Pakula's early drafts of the screenplay, but, ultimately, he felt it had to be dropped (over the objections of his Sophie and Nathan, Meryl Streep and Kevin Kline) because it did not include Stingo. He was concerned that "the balancing act of keeping the audience focused on the story" of all three characters would "fall apart."

If Pakula's screenplay deserves criticism, one may as well focus on what he *did* preserve from the book as on what he omitted. For example, the scene in which

Stingo attempts to seduce the apparently eager Leslie Lapidus (only to find out that Leslie could "say fuck but could not do it") is, although well played, too remote from the theme and the mood of the rest of the film to be effective, regardless of how apt the episode may have been in the novel. Thus, the process of transferring the novel to the screen was, to a great extent, one of condensation, of winnowing the incidents in the novel down to those essential for a vivid shooting script.

In many cases, the problem was how to condense novelistic material without muddying the viewer's understanding of what was transpiring in the film. As one illustration of how the substitution of an element in the novel served to propel the film forward, the book on which Stingo is at work in the film is an account of his mother, which leads ultimately to Sophie's revelations about her father, thus condensing a considerable amount of the novel. Another is the scene in which Nathan, Sophie, and Stingo all collaborate on a piece played on Sophie's piano, economically demonstrating the progress of their friendship. Still another is the final scene, when Stingo recites Emily Dickinson's "Ample Make My Bed" over the dead bodies of Sophie and Nathan, echoing Nathan's earlier reading of the poem to Sophie after he rescues her from near death and nurses her back to health. (Stingo thinks but does not speak these lines in Styron's novel.)

Another echo of nineteenth-century American literature occurs very early in the film (and the novel), when the narrator says, "Call me Stingo," a conscious evocation of the opening line of *Moby Dick*. Pakula said he included the line because *Sophie's Choice* "is written in a perfectly classic narrative style, like a nineteenth-century novel," and because, like *Moby Dick*, *Sophie's Choice* deals with "a young man encountering good and evil, love and death."

After each rewrite of the script, Pakula contacted Styron, discussing the changes he had made; then another rewrite would follow. In all, Pakula's work on the screenplay alone consumed two years. Styron, who did not see the script until the final draft, restricted himself to no more than an occasional criticism or suggestion. But Pakula made clear that he was vitally interest in Styron's response. Styron recalled that one scene Pakula had written did not seem to the novelist to be appropriate. "I remember there was one scene in which, perhaps to illustrate the volatile nature of Nathan, he had him breaking into a stable somewhere in the park, presumably in Prospect Park in Brooklyn, and getting on a horse and riding around in sort of an antic way, and I felt that that really did verge on violating the spirit of my book. And I told him so. I said I understood what he was after, but I felt it was not consonant with the way the book was ordered, to have Nathan, this urban, Jewish type, riding on a horse. So he cut it out."

Other scenes caused Styron a momentary hesitation, but, believing that they did not violate the novel's spirit, he did not request that they be changed. "An example," Styron said, "would be when the three main characters go out on the Brooklyn Bridge to celebrate and they crack open a bottle of champagne in a helicopter shot. Well, I didn't have any such scene in the book, and I never mentioned the Brooklyn Bridge. But I realized in that case that this was Alan's vision, and since it did no betrayal of the book, since it was perfectly in spirit with the book, I figured, well, that's Alan's prerogative, let him do it. And it was a very effective scene, although it resembled nothing in the book."

Originally, Marble Arch Productions hoped that the screenplay would be written in less than a year, allowing the film to open in the fall of 1981, but Pakula refused to be rushed. One draft methodically followed another. "It was a slow process," Martin Starger said, "but the results were worth it." Release of the film was delayed by more than a year beyond the original projection.

While Pakula was working on his adaptation, Styron's novel swiftly moved to the top of the bestseller list, fulfilling Pakula's hope for the novel's success. "That always gives a book the aura of being commercial," he said; "it allays the anxieties and concerns" of producers and film executives.

Keith Barish, the producer, was also pleased that the novel did so well, for its success disproved the judgment of those who had told him he was crazy to pay $750,000 for what they considered to be a non-commercial property. It also confirmed Barish's belief that "there's an audience for this kind of movie, a movie that has something to say." Barish found it ironic that, in earlier years, "the studios were making important pictures and the independents were making the horror movies, the B-minus movies," whereas, in 1982, he said, "it's reversed. Studios are doing *Star Wars*, *Porky's*, kids' comedies. And the independents are doing *Sophie's Choice*, *Chariots of Fire*, and *On Golden Pond*."

Meryl Streep first heard about the role of Sophie when she was a student at the Yale Drama School. Robert Brustein, dean of the school, had read *Sophie's Choice* in galleys; he told William Styron, who, like Brustein, summered at Martha's Vineyard, that a student of his at Yale should play Sophie. Styron indulged Brustein, but didn't take the suggestion seriously.[38]

Long before he completed the screenplay, Pakula spoke to Streep about playing the role. "I had just started the screenplay and I had no idea what she would do with the part," he said. "I couldn't imagine her in it, yet I knew she was a great actress because I had seen most of her work. I said, . . . Meryl, if you want to run the risk of committing yourself to do this film before I finish the screenplay, I'll run the risk of committing to you without knowing what you'd be like with a

---

[38]*A few years later, when Pakula was seriously considering casting Streep, he mentioned talking to her about the possibility of playing Sophie to Styron. "Oh yeah, it's that kid," Styron said, recalling his discussion with Brustein. "Well," Pakula answered, a bit defensively, "she's grown up."*

Polish accent.' She said she would like to wait until she saw a screenplay. I said, 'Fine, but you have to know that since I can't be sure you're going to do it, I have to go look elsewhere.'"

Pakula knew that the film would succeed or fail on the basis of the performance of Sophie. As the screenplay progressed, he came to believe that a European actress should play the role, and most strongly considered Liv Ullmann, who, although "ten years older than Sophie, could play the harsh realities and the ambivalences" of the character, Pakula said. Of equal importance, "she was a woman with whom a young boy would fall in love." Ullmann was interested, but it took so long for the screenplay to be completed that she had other commitments by the time it was finished.

Pakula considered other possibilities, such as prominent European actresses Marthe Keller and Hanna Schygulla.[39] Even more desirable, he believed, would be to use a foreign actress who was completely unknown to American audiences. On a casting trip in Europe for Pakula, Douglas Wick (who had been an assistant producer of *Starting Over*) came upon Magda Vasaryova, a Czechoslovakian actress, who, although experienced in the films of her native country, was unfamiliar in the United States.

When Wick communicated his discovery, Pakula invited Vasaryova to New York, where she auditioned for him at his office. He made a long, improvised test (comprising six videotapes) with Vasaryova, in parts of which she assumed the character of Sophie while Pakula asked her questions about her background and her attitudes. Don Laventhall, who was Pakula's research assistant on the script of *Sophie's Choice*, described the tapes: "He asked her questions about what it was like growing up, what it was like being in the concentration camp, questions about her family. And describing the moment of losing her child. And the *tears* streaming down Magda's face. It was amazing. It's been twenty years since I saw it, but I haven't forgotten it." Hannah Pakula recalls the test as "fascinating . . . quite a performance." Alan Pakula was equally impressed, so much so that he became convinced that no one else could play the role. Vasaryova was, he said, "a lovely Czech actress who for me *was* Sophie."

But Martin Starger was unenthusiastic—and, as the representative of Marble Arch Productions, he had the right of casting approval. Although, as he said, "there might be someone out there who no one ever heard of or who no one had ever seen, who could bring Sophie to the screen without anyone's memories of other roles," he was unimpressed by Vasaryova's test. "It was very clear that she had

---

[39]*Barbra Streisand, who, years before, had expressed interest in playing Bree Daniels in Klute, now told Pakula that she was willing to forego a salary in order to play Sophie, although she wanted to receive a percentage of the gross profits. Goldie Hawn, too, made every attempt to win the role.*

a great deal of difficulty with English," Starger said. "I remember a conversation with Alan when I said, 'You know, Alan, this is a very difficult picture on very difficult subject matter, and you're making it more difficult. You want to use an unknown—which is fine, you could be right about her, your instincts have been good about actresses—but she doesn't speak the language. It's too difficult." Instead, he recommended that Pakula reconsider Meryl Streep, who had recently won an Academy Award for *Kramer vs. Kramer* "and was a very important actress, getting role after role, and she seemed to be a perfect possibility for Sophie."

Streep's interest in the role had gradually increased, as a result of having read Styron's novel. The book triggered vivid childhood memories. She recalled "when I was ten, and my mother dropped me off at the library, and I opened a book and there were photographs of the Lebensborn program, where children were taken in transports, supposedly to be adopted, and one of those transports just ran out of gas, and the drivers walked away and left those children, and they starved and died. And then the allies came and saw the piled-up bodies in the back of the truck—and I will never, ever forget that image. It formed the basis of my emotional understanding of unimaginable horror."

Despite Starger's suggestion and Streep's growing interest, Pakula insisted that Magda Vasaryova could capture Sophie's qualities better than any other actress. Starger maintained that the film—not likely to have significant commercial appeal unless a recognizable name were cast in the title role—needed an American star. "That's the age-old debate," he said. "You could make an argument for [casting unknowns in all films], but that way there would be no such thing as movie stars, because you'd have a new actor playing every role."

Starger told Pakula's agent, Stan Kamen, about his concerns. Kamen responded, "What can you do? That's what Alan wants." Starger said, "Look, I don't want to force anyone to do what he doesn't want to do, but this is just the wrong move for this picture." Starger said that Marble Arch would have to pull out of the deal if Pakula insisted on using Vasaryova. He suggested that Pakula and Barish be given time to see if they could find another company that would be willing to finance Magda Vasaryova in *Sophie's Choice*. Starger told Kamen, "I believe in the subject matter very, very much. If somebody's willing to make this film with her, I'm not going to stand in the way, as much as we want to make it." Starger gave Pakula and Barish three months to try to make a deal elsewhere.

During that period, while Pakula tried without success to persuade other production companies to finance the film with Magda Vasaryova, Meryl Streep asked her agent, Sam Cohn, to find out if she could speak to Pakula. "Just see if you can get me in to talk to him," she said. Cohn contacted Pakula, and said, "Meryl is embarrassed to call you because you didn't send her a script. She knows you're not interested in her any more, but she sneaked a [still-unfinished copy of your] script and she would like to play it. She loves the book, she's fascinated with the character. She has fifty pictures she could be doing but she would like to do this. Would you talk to her?"

Pakula considered his response only briefly. It had already become evident that casting Magda Vasaryova might be an impossibility. "Well," he said, "who am I not to talk to one of the great actresses in the world?" In the late summer of 1981, Streep visited Pakula at his office and offered to audition for him—a most unusual procedure for an actress who had just won an Academy Award for her appearance in *Kramer vs. Kramer*. But, believing that the script was "the best thing I'd ever read," she was determined to make every effort to win the role.

She "took a great deal of care with what I would wear" to the audition, she remembered, selecting an outfit that would suggest the sort of dress Sophie might wear. "There was a store up near where we lived in the country, and they had little sundresses there, I remember it was twenty-five dollars. And it was very cute and sort of very feminine, not stylish for then. It was a cheap little sundress—but in the movie, I wore something very similar to it that Albert Wolsky designed, so I must have been on the right track." Indeed, Pakula's impression was that Streep had worn a Polish peasant dress to the meeting.

At Pakula's office, the walls were covered with photographs of Magda Vasaryova. Streep said to herself, "You haven't got a prayer, Cookie." She could see at a glance that Vasaryova was—visually, at least—an ideal choice for Sophie. "She was younger than me, and beautiful, and authentically Eastern European," Streep said. Still, the role was so enticing that she determined to persuade Pakula of the intensity of her interest. "Has there been a character that interesting in the movies in a long time?" she later said. "There are so many choices throughout the film—whether she should live with Stingo or die with Nathan, whether she should kill herself in church or live with the guilt of refugees. But what is great about her is that she does make the choices, but then, if she has made the wrong one, she doesn't quit. She goes on." Streep was unwilling to give up a role of such dimension without a struggle.

As she recalls, Pakula began the meeting by saying, "You're a very nice actress and everything, but I'm quite sure that I want the authenticity [of a European performer], it's very important to me to have that with this character. And you are strong, admirably strong. This is the story of a girl who has no heroism in her. This is the story of a girl who has no courage, it's her terrible problem, and you're just the opposite of that. And there is an open sensuality about this woman in her relationship with Nathan, and you are a very dignified woman."

Streep recognized that she probably had little chance to change Pakula's mind about casting a European actress, but told him, "I just want you to know how passionately I feel about it and how much I want to do this and how deeply I relate to this character."

Pakula was impressed by her enthusiasm for the project, by her confidence, and by the reputation she had already established. "Meryl Streep seemed a woman of great strength, great intelligence, great craft," Pakula said. "I had no idea what she was going to do with the part and I couldn't imagine her doing it. Yet I knew that she was a great actress." Coincidentally, director Andrzej Wajda, who had directed Streep in a production at the Yale Repertory Theatre, told Pakula that he thought Streep would be an ideal choice to play Sophie—a recommendation that must have been significant, coming, as it did, from an eminent Polish artist.

The discussion with Streep—there was no formal audition—did not quite convince Pakula to cast her rather than Vasaryova, but it made him doubt his certainty. "Eventually," he said, "there were only two people in the world I could see in the part: Magda and Meryl."

Before she left Pakula's office, Streep asked if he had anyone in mind to play Nathan. Pakula immediately responded that he had already offered the role to Kevin Kline. "Oh, he's amazing," Streep said. "He'd be a perfect Nathan."

The following day, Pakula called Kline and told him, "Meryl Streep came in yesterday and knocked me out. She was so passionate in the way she talked about it, and wanted to do it so much that I'm going to throw out all my original ideas of what I thought this character should be." Pakula then called Martin Starger and said, "Marty, I've been thinking. Why don't we go with Meryl Streep?" One influence in changing his mind, he observed later, was his recollection of his initial reluctance to cast Jason Robards in *All the President's Men*. He remembered how close he had come to not casting an actor who had proven to be brilliant, and he did not want to risk repeating that near-mistake.

Still, however, Streep wished to see a completed screenplay before committing herself to *Sophie's Choice*, and Pakula was not ready to show it. So he agreed to direct *Rollover* while Streep made *The French Lieutenant's Woman*. Later, Streep managed to obtain a copy of Pakula's completed script and let him know, through her agent, that she was ready to accept the role if Pakula still wanted her. He told her that he would give her a definite answer within ten days. In his words, he "went home, slept on it, woke up, and thought: she has the kind of passion I had when I read the book." Still, he continued to deliberate for a few more days, during which he wrestled with his fears that her personality might prevent her from portraying all of Sophie's essential qualities.

Pakula later said that he remained concerned that the strong-willed Streep might bring too much inner strength to the role, that she might turn Sophie into a character with the force and vigor of Joan of Arc. He continued, "The tragedy of Sophie is her vulnerability, and the fact that she feels totally lacking in heroic qualities in this time that seems to demand an almost impossible heroism—a time which beyond forcing monstrosities on the victim, forces guilt as well."

As Pakula had told Streep in his earlier conversation with her, a quality Sophie had to possess was a sexual voraciousness, a hunger for physical contact to lessen her despair over the deaths of Sophie's daughter, her husband, her father, and the inevitable loss of Nathan. Sophie's need for sex is desperate, unending. In William Styron's words, "Sophie and Nathan were possessed by some sort of demons that caused them to devour each other, and that involved a great deal of erotic lunacy." He further explained Sophie's need "to drive away the memory of the horror of Auschwitz through erotic realization with Nathan. . . . My character of Sophie came from a profoundly repressed background," Styron said. "A Polish Catholic girl with all the repressions of Catholicism of that period, of the thirties. She was coming from death into life, and sex at the hands of Nathan was a life force in itself."

Streep as Sophie would also have to suggest that much of the story she tells Stingo is a lie, told to protect her self-image and, perhaps, to preserve her sanity—but the lies must be so convincingly told that Stingo cannot be aware that he is being deceived. The audience, too, must not be able to discern that Sophie is not telling the truth—and when they discover that she is lying, they cannot lose interest in or sympathy for the character. They must wonder, however, what layers of truth she is withholding, and why she is doing so.[40]

Ultimately, Pakula's instinct that Streep would be able to portray the Sophie he envisioned prevailed. More than any other quality, he maintained, he had been persuaded by Streep's passion for the project. "I'll always go with passion," he said.

Pakula's casting of Kevin Kline as Nathan occurred after seeing him on Broadway in *The Pirates of Penzance*. "He thought the guy was just amazing," according to Don Laventhall. The ability to play the broad, comic role of the Pirate King would not necessarily seem applicable to playing the charismatic, brilliant, tormented, tragic Nathan, capable of frenzied rage and irresistible charm, often swinging almost instantaneously from one to the other—but Pakula saw an energy that he thought was precisely right for Nathan. "I was dazzled," Pakula said. "He had a certain capacity for joy, the life force, the humor so essential for Nathan. Nathan's supposed to have a fatal glamour, which he had."

After considering Al Pacino (who, Pakula said, did not have quite the right

---

[40] Styron said that when he was writing the novel, "one of the stunning moments of realization that came to me as a writer was the understanding that [Sophie] was lying. This was the key to the book: that she was telling both the author, me, and Stingo, my alter ego, a lie about her father."

touch of "bourgeois Jewishness"), Dustin Hoffman (who lacked "Nathan's sado-masochistic romantic quality that makes people of both sexes fall in love with him"), and Robert DeNiro (who possessed "the charismatic quality but not the humor"), Pakula decided to follow his instincts and cast Kline, whose only previous film experience had been the movie version of *Pirates of Penzance*, which did not open until after *Sophie's Choice* was released. (In effect, then, *Sophie's Choice* was Kline's film debut.)[41]

Kline characterized his portrayal of the Pirate King in *The Pirates of Penzance* as "insanely athletic and idiotically physical. The whole concept of the character was that he was hyperactive—and it was fun, it was silly. Alan said [in reference to Nathan in *Sophie's Choice*], 'That's more important than a brooding, internalized, tortured [characterization]; what's tragic about him [Nathan] is that he *could* be this extraordinary person if he weren't afflicted.'" Those qualities, essential for Nathan, would also reveal the capacity for joy in the actors playing Sophie and Stingo, Pakula believed. "The most difficult thing in the picture," he said, "is not the tragedy that has occurred so far, but always making sure you get a sense of the characters' capacity for life. That's what makes them tragic and fascinating, not just pathetic."

A two-time Tony Award winner (for his stage performances in *On the Twentieth Century* and *The Pirates of Penzance*), Kline first became aware of the role of Nathan when a friend of his read Styron's novel and said, "There's a part in here that you would be perfect for, but some movie star will play it. You'll never get it." As a result, Kline did not read the book until Pakula offered him the role. Pakula told Kline, after seeing him in *Pirates of Penzance*, "I'm not going to screen-test you. I don't need a screen test." Kline was even more surprised when Pakula told him that he didn't even need to read for the director. But Kline insisted, saying, "No, let me read for it. I don't want to show up on the first day," only to discover that he could not meet Pakula's expectations. But Pakula demurred. "I don't need you to audition," he said. "Your passion is more important."

If playing Sophie convincingly was crucial to the film's success, playing Nathan was equally important. Kline had to believably portray Nathan's endearing generosity and his vicious cruelty, his irresistible charm, and his tortured mind. Kline found the character fascinating. "His passion, his heroic qualities—he was born in the wrong century," Kline said. "He was trying to live a heroic life in an unheroic age. He was completely deluded, of course. But I adored his sense of humor; as vicious and as harmful as it was, it was also joyous. This man was

---

[41] Pakula had some previous knowledge of Kline, who had auditioned for a role in Starting Over. (Kline still recalls that Pakula "was such a gentleman. You never felt like cattle being herded in and out, everyone was treated with great courtesy.") Pakula had also seen Kline perform some years earlier in Loose Ends, a play by Michael Weller.

capable of a tremendous appreciation of life. He could listen to Beethoven and be absolutely filled with his love for the music, and yet he toys with death, flirts with death, even as he is living much more intensely than we are. He had a wonderful sense of ritual, a sense of event. And his sense of truth:. he's living a lie, and yet he sees truth as only a mad person can. He lived with the horror of life; the rest of us are protected by our so-called sanity."

Not until late September, several months afterward, did Pakula find Peter MacNicol, then twenty-four years old, and offer him the role of Stingo. Or, more accurately, MacNicol found Pakula. He had been roaming around Europe and the United States in an attempt to resolve his doubts about becoming an actor. His first film appearance, in *Dragonslayer*, had left him depressed and uncertain that acting was an appropriate career choice for him. During his travels, he was completely inaccessible, even to his colleagues in the theatre, with whom he had not been in touch in months. Suddenly, however, while in Minnesota, an inner voice told MacNicol that he should immediately call his agent in New York. "It was the most compelling kind of voice," he said, "the kind that says, 'Hurry home, you left the oven on.'"

His agent said to return right away, for Pakula was scheduled to audition actors for Stingo for just one more day, and Alixe Gordon, the casting director, had recommended that MacNicol be given an opportunity to read. MacNicol showed up just in time. Following his audition, Pakula told Kevin Kline that only a few days before he was prepared to cast another actor as Stingo, but "Peter MacNicol came in yesterday and knocked me out."

Pakula, who had auditioned fifty actors for Stingo, decided, in a rare hasty decision, to cast the young actor who had just appeared. Thus, although Pakula's notion of casting three unknown performers in the film was not practicable, both male leads were played by actors virtually unknown to film audiences.

The role of Stingo is a difficult one to portray; the character primarily reacts to the stimuli provided by others rather than initiating action. But, despite a certain passivity, Stingo is as pivotal a character as either Sophie or Nathan. Pakula saw the film not only as the story of Sophie, but as "a story of the journey of this boy . . . it is the journey . . . from boyhood into manhood, and from an ambitious, dreaming young man to a full-fledged artist."

Meryl Streep prepared with near fanaticism to play the role of Sophie. She learned Polish in three months from a coach Pakula recommended. Streep and Pakula both felt that she should learn the language rather than attempt to speak English with a Polish accent. "The lady came every day to my house," Streep said, "and gave me two hours of lessons. I didn't want to do some generic Eastern-European [accent], and I thought it would give me an idea of how [Sophie's] jaw would move when she spoke . . . and to understand Polish from the inside out." The language offered particular difficulties with pronunciation, but near the end of her work with the coach, she told Pakula, "I was making sounds with my voice today, Polish sounds, and I began to feel something happening." To maintain her skills, she spoke English with a Polish accent both at home and on the set. So convincing was her accent that on one occasion her little daughter did not recognize the sound of her mother's voice.

Kline, the son of a Jewish father and Catholic mother, prepared to play Nathan by researching those ethnicities, and by reading the works of R. D. Laing as well as books about the Holocaust. Since his father had not been religious, Kline knew little about Judaism. So, he said, "I had some informational, emotional, and psychological work to do. It had a pretty strong impact on me, in terms of understanding what it meant to be a Jew in 1947 when people were finding out about 'the Final Solution.'" In addition, Kline thought deeply about "Nathan's guilt about not even being part of [the resistance to Nazism], about being safe and sound in Brooklyn while his people were being annihilated." Nathan's guilt assumes such proportions that, "in his madness, [he] intensifies it so that he and Sophie are just made for each other," Kline said, "these two tragic characters who were destroyed by their guilt, [their] sense of survivors' guilt."

Peter MacNicol's job was a particularly difficult one, for, as he said, "Stingo lives in [Nathan and Sophie's] pauses, and only in their pauses," reacting to the stimuli they provide and reflecting their moods. In addition, MacNicol was physically wrong for the role, short and slight whereas the Stingo of Styron's novel was well over six feet tall. More importantly, the role called upon him to investigate a side of himself he had not hitherto examined. "Finding the common ground between Stingo and myself was to go into the loneliest country in my own life," he said, citing Stingo's "complete awkwardness, his bashfulness, his uncertainty about himself."

A three-week period of rehearsals was held in New York with Streep, Kline, and MacNicol. Pakula began by saying, "Look, this movie is all about you three. It's all got to come from you. This is not about fancy camerawork or tricky editing. It all starts with you." Pakula said that his main responsibility during the rehearsals was "to make sure we understand [the interplay of the characters' relationships] in each scene."

Rehearsals were complicated by the fact that Kevin Kline had only the night before returned from England where he had completed shooting *The Pirates of Penzance*. But after "the usual five cups of coffee," Pakula felt that the mood was right for rehearsals to commence. He began with a brief speech: "You have the parts, there's no reason to be nervous, I'm not expecting performances, just relax, we're just going to explore . . . and don't bother about acting." Pakula read aloud the descriptions of the set, then listened to Kline and MacNicol begin to read in the relaxed way he had asked for. Then, he said, "Suddenly Meryl opened her mouth. Now, we had been sitting around chatting over coffee for over an hour and she [had] sounded like Meryl Streep, and this voice came out and this accent, and I said, 'Where's Meryl Streep?' because it was so different from the woman I had been speaking to five or ten minutes before.' I couldn't believe it was coming out of her. It was such a shock to me that it took me a while to get used to it. Kevin's mouth fell open. He could barely speak for the rest of the reading, he was absolutely stunned. I've never worked with an actress where I thought I was working with two separate people. One was Meryl Streep and one was Sophie Zawitowska."

Not only did Streep sound different when she first read the role of Sophie; Pakula said "she *looked* different. When she was Sophie she was one person, and [when] I'd talk to her when she was Meryl Streep, I felt [as if] I was talking to somebody else." But by the end of the read-through all of Pakula's reservations about Streep's transformation had dropped away. Streep, who felt that she had only been tentatively cast until that point, could sense that "everything in Alan relaxed," and that it was at that first reading that she actually won his confidence.

In the days leading up to the first rehearsal, Kline, busy with another film, had barely had time to think about *Sophie's Choice*, but he was now confronted with an actress who had spent months learning a Polish accent and preparing her role. "He hadn't had a chance to even look at the part," Pakula said. "At the first reading he was still a pirate, and trying to relax and have his coffee, and then suddenly Meryl came out with this accent and Kevin was practically paralyzed. It was this exquisite performance already coming out of her and he was still half in Gilbert and Sullivan—still a pirate in his own mind," Pakula said. "He turned out to be remarkable—but he had to play catch-up, because Meryl had been doing nothing for months but working on this role."

Further complicating matters was that Streep and Kline preferred diametrically opposed methods of rehearsing. Streep, Pakula said, "was totally content to sit around the table for three weeks and basically read, ask questions, ask one question after another question after another question." On the other hand, Pakula said, "Kevin works through his body and his nerve endings and sometimes his body leads him to things. He starts to feel the character when he moves." Thus, Kline hoped that Pakula would give the actors their blocking so that they could develop their characters while walking, standing, and sitting as the characters would walk, stand, and sit, whereas Streep did not wish to budge from the rehearsal chair.

Later, she explained why. "I find it sort of putting the cart before the horse to decide on certain blocking and where you're actually going to stand before you walk into the room that hasn't yet been furnished," Streep said recently. "You don't know where the cushion will be, what will catch your eye, you don't know your favorite corner and where you would go. How can you do that in the absence of these things? You can't. They all happen—acting only happens in the moment in which it happens. So you can get ready, and you know how your character feels about things, and you can write reams about that, but as to how she'll feel when she walks in her own bedroom, you have to wait until you get to the bedroom to know that."

Eventually, Kline came to feel comfortable with Streep's approach, although, he said, "it took me about halfway through the film before I learned to *love* the method, where you know the words but you go in and follow an impulse, you capitalize on any felicitous accident that occurs. You're open to react to whatever's in the air or whatever you're feeling."

Streep is certain that Pakula was entirely comfortable with the approach she preferred. "Alan *loved* the discussion," she said. "I've never seen any director that loved the discussion so much. Most of them will [discuss the characters] dutifully and with a smile on their faces, but they just want to get on with it, just shoot the damn scene. Alan was really more interested in the exegesis of the text than in the actual getting up there. He just loved exploring the possibilities and the motivations within a specific moment." The "first read-through" actually took three weeks, because Pakula and the actors discussed each moment, each motivation, each relationship, and each implication as they read.

And it was not only the process that Streep enjoyed, Pakula's sensibility was entirely in tune with hers. "I always thought of him as a novelist with a director's hat on," she said, "because he thought about film in a literary way. He thought about layers of things and textures of meaning that a lot of people don't think about. It felt as if he sat back and let this story, as portrayed by the three of us, unfold, that he was letting it happen, letting us do what we wanted, but I think that's because he had constructed the structure himself, he had made the architecture of the scene himself; he had conceived it."

Kline recalled Pakula saying "'it was that time spent together [in the rehearsal room], getting to know each other and feeling comfortable with each other, which will pay off" in the eventual filming. And, all the actors agreed, the time spent seated around the table, discussing every aspect of *Sophie's Choice*, did indeed draw them together, mold them into an ensemble, and make their interaction in the film quite extraordinary.

The complete set of the interior of the Pink Palace (the house in Brooklyn in which all the central characters live), containing all the rooms used in the film—Stingo's room, Sophie and Nathan's room, the stairway, the hallway with the telephone—had already been built on a soundstage at the time of the rehearsal period, and, although Pakula did not use it for staging at that point, he felt it was useful for the actors to become used to the environment. On one occasion, he and the actors ate lunch together in Sophie's room. "I like the actors to live in the set," he said, "I like them even to sleep over in the set, which they did in that picture several times." Sleeping in the set released Kline's imagination—and his energy. The day after being confined all night long in Nathan and Sophie's room, according to Pakula, Kline was virtually exploding with energy "because he [had done] all these [physical] things to entertain himself. He [Kline] said, 'I want to know what it's like to be locked in that place and have to create a life of the imagination, because I have no world outside.'" Pakula concluded that the experiment "was actually very helpful to the picture."

At last, he staged one scene in Sophie's bedroom. By that time, all of the actors had worked their way under the skins of the characters they were playing. "And," Pakula said, "the blocking practically fell into place. It ended with the wonderful moment at the piano [when Nathan begins to play and everyone joins in].[42] . . . That's when this film started to come to life for me."

Kevin Kline elaborated, "One day, we all got around the piano, because it was a scene where Sophie was going to sing various Gershwin songs in a thick Polish accent. And then we tried various things with her playing. But she didn't play and I did, so Alan had me play and then he kind of evolved this thing where she's sitting at the piano but can't play anymore, so he said, 'You play it for her.' So I went and just put my arms around her and I played this piece which he chose for me. So that kind of evolved just from a very relaxed kind of rehearsal situation, without us getting up and blocking anything."

Pakula allowed—even encouraged—his actors to depart from the script whenever they were inspired to improvise a meaningful line. Although he had labored carefully on the screenplay for two years, he had no compunctions about allowing the actors the freedom to depart from it. "I felt nothing but liberty," Meryl Streep said. "I felt completely free."

Kline's understanding of the film Pakula and the actors were about to make was clarified by the extensive discussion period. It would have been a terrible diminution to film Styron's book as a "lots-of-Kleenex emotional experience," he said, for "it raises some important questions, dangerous questions about the nature of evil, the banality of evil, about guilt, about love." Indeed, that was the challenge when shooting began.

---

[42]*Kevin Kline's musical background—his father had played piano, and Kline was a music major at Indiana University—served him well in this scene, in which he played all but the last few notes of the piece. After the filming of* Sophie's Choice, *he used the money he made to purchase a grand piano.*

The three principal actors felt that they were sharing an unforgettable experience, one that no one else could possibly share in or fully understand. Pakula said, "What I loved about the rehearsals, if they had done nothing else, it made those three people comrades and they [loved] each other. Meryl was spectacular in bringing people together. But they all did. So there was this sense of warmth and sharing by the time we got to shooting the film."

But Pakula was concerned about telling Streep and MacNicol of decisions he had reached at the end of rehearsals, fearful that it would upset them. In MacNicol's case, the decision was to further cut the screenplay, eliminating MacNicol's most poignant scene. The actor was "devastated," according to casting director Alixe Gordon.

The new information Pakula had for Streep also had the potential to cause discontent. Until just before the film began shooting, Pakula intended to film the concentration camp scenes in the English language. But at virtually the last moment, he changed his mind. "I decided that they should all be done with subtitles, in different languages. Now, poor Meryl had just been sweating out the Polish accent, and I thought, 'Oh God, she's going to kill me. Now she has to speak in German, how's she going to do that?' I remember going to her with fear and trepidation [and said], 'I decided we have to separate this from the American part because it is another world and we really should feel the other languages—otherwise the world is just not going to work. I should have told you this six months ago.' And she was very calm. . . . She said, 'Get me a German teacher.' We [planned to shoot] all the European sequences last . . . and she said, 'I have all that time, we're shooting the American part, I'll learn it.' And I said, 'When will you have time to learn it?' And she said, 'Just get me a German teacher.'" By the time the scenes were shot, Streep's German was flawless.

CHAPTER FIFTEEN

Sophie's Choice II:
Production and Post-Production

"The number of questions that have to do with money in filmmaking classes frightens me to death. . . . And it does frighten me how many of you are obsessed by how much money is spent in advertising a film, how much money people have made on a film, how much they're going to make on the next film. It's something fundamentally rather unhealthy.

I think you have to question your assessment of what is a successful picture and what isn't a successful picture. You must question the thinking in the industry that a successful film is a big-grossing picture. There are dozens of ways of making a successful film."

–DAVID PUTTNAM, producer of <u>Chariots of Fire</u>,
<u>Midnight Express</u>, <u>The Killing Fields</u>, et cetera, speaking
to students at the American Film Institute

"Some directors take jobs and they think, will this be a commercial hit? Or they work to answer and confound their critics. But Alan did work that fed his soul, and sought to answer all the endless questions of life."

–MERYL STREEP

ON THE FIRST DAY OF SHOOTING, March 1, 1982, filming began at the Gould Memorial Library of Bronx Community College in New York. Pakula knew something of which the actors were unaware. The night before, he had learned that Lord Grade's organization, Associated Communications Group (the parent company of Marble Arch Productions), was in financial difficulty and might be taken over by Australian Robert Holmes a Court. Pakula worried that he might have to stop shooting at any time. He chose not to tell the actors in order not to demoralize them, but he was deeply afraid that the effort put into the writing of the screenplay, the pre-production planning, and the long read-through would be for naught.

Streep, Kline, and MacNicol surprised Pakula by hiring a string trio to play during the lunch break to celebrate the first day of shooting. It "broke my heart," Pakula said, touched by the gesture. "There was a camaraderie on this film that was very special," he said. "It was a passion for the work we all shared."

Moved by the actors' gesture, he was in such emotional turmoil that he felt compelled to tell at least one of them about what he believed to be the film's precarious financial state. He continued to withhold the news from Kline and MacNicol, but pulled Streep aside and said, "You've got to know this picture may never be finished. It may be done by tonight or tomorrow." He further confided to her that he had mortgaged his home in an attempt to secure the film. "I think it was something he confessed to me because he knew how much I loved the project and was devoted to it," Streep said, "and he thought I'd understand his anguish." She added, "I was very moved that he shared this with me."

The scene they shot on the first day was a sequence in the library in which Sophie, desperately ill and looking like a specter of the Sophie that will be seen in the Pink Palace, faints while trying to check out the work of "Emile Dickens" and is rescued by Nathan. Shooting this scene, showing the first meeting of Sophie and Nathan, before shooting the scenes after they became lovers (but which would precede the library scene in the film) was, for Kevin Kline, "a perfect way of working. We got to know one another on-screen in the natural order. That enabled us to grow on camera." Insofar as was possible, Pakula hoped to shoot the film in logical sequence (though not chronological sequence, since the film jumps backwards and forwards in time).

Sophie's appearance in the library is a shock when the viewer sees it in the film. Pakula said, "the contrast of seeing her at her most beautiful and most romantic and happiest [in the Pink Palace], to the tragic, half-dead person who came to this country" is like being punched in the solar plexus. "And one of the things that helps you pull that off," Pakula said, "is having an actress like Meryl, and what she did in going from a sensuous, totally alive-looking woman to somebody hanging on to life by the thinnest of threads. She makes it look simple, but don't believe that for a second."

One shot in the scene in the library is reminiscent of a shot in *All the President's Men*, a high angle shot looking down at Sophie and the library's patrons. Pakula said, "It's an 'eye of God' shot, and I do a lot of eye of God shots. The impersonal presence making us all such fragile, tiny creatures. We think we have control, but we're really just tiny beings in this world. It's one of the things I feel about life."

Things went so smoothly and so thrillingly during the first days of shooting that every element of the film seemed to be coming together in ideal fashion. "I knew after this I would *kill* to keep this picture going," Pakula said. Fortunately, the takeover by Holmes a Court did not interfere with the filming—"It was already too far along in the process," Martin Starger said—and Pakula was able to continue. The budget was adjusted, from $12 million to $13.5 million.

Kevin Kline still recalls Pakula's thoughtfulness in sparing himself and MacNicol the knowledge that the film might have been shut down. "In fact," he said, "Alan constantly took great pains to create a kind of bubble around each of us, to protect us." Kline gave the following example: "Alan helped me choose a make-up artist, because, he said, 'The makeup artist is the person you spend the first forty-five minutes of the day with, and it's got to be the right person.' That's what I mean about creating this protective bubble—to care about who will be doing the makeup, that it will be someone who respects your need for quiet or concentration, not some putz who's going to gossip and play the radio while he's making you up."

As he had done for other performers in previous films, Pakula created what Meryl Streep called "a safe haven for emotions to show themselves. Alan did that almost better than anybody I've ever worked with," she said. "He so completely and invisibly created this world where everything was allowed. . . . We trusted him. I've thought a lot about it since we shot the film, and I've tried to figure out what it was that he did, specifically, but it was really something intangible . . . like an embrace. He embraced his actors and said, 'You're safe here. You can go as far as you want.'"

Although shooting was now in progress, the rehearsal process continued each morning. For several hours Pakula and the actors would rehearse the scenes they were about to film. As Streep described the process, "When we came in in the morning, we'd get into makeup and we'd report to the set, and then he'd send the entire crew away to what he called the tent, which was the catering facility. They would all have a three- or four-hour coffee break while we rehearsed and blocked, changed our minds, and did it over and over again until it felt like something lived. And then he'd bring Nestor [Almendros, the cinematographer] in. Nestor would look at it and decide how to light it. We'd go away, Nestor would light it while we had lunch, then we'd come back and shoot all afternoon. We'd shoot three, four, five, maybe more pages a day, which in movies is very ambitious. In those days I was still shopping for and cooking dinner, and I was able to do that every night. We were always off by six-thirty. It's extraordinary. I've never seen any other director be able to do that. It was the director's level of preparation and deep understanding [that permitted the unvarying schedule], and the confidence to allow that kind of exploration in the mornings."

Pakula described his method of daily work while shooting: "I just want the actors not to be afraid to expose themselves, to try ridiculous things, to make fools of themselves."[43]

During the morning rehearsal sessions, Pakula's attention was so powerfully concentrated on the interaction with and among the performers that he was able to hear irritating sounds that no one else was aware of. "He would hear an electric saw in the next soundstage," Kevin Kline said. "We'd be rehearsing and he'd say, 'Wait, wait, stop!' And he'd go and tell them to stop that sawing. I couldn't hear it. No one could hear it but Alan."

Although Pakula did not work the same way on every film, his technique on *Sophie's Choice* was to allow everything to flow from the actor's impulses. For example, when shooting most pictures, the director will inform the actors where the cameras will be located before they begin rehearsing a scene; but, in the case of this film, the results of the mornings spent with the actors determined many different elements, including camera placement. "Sometimes," according to Kevin Kline, "someone [on the crew] would say, 'Well, maybe if you'd just bring [the actors] a little more over to this side of the room, it would be a better shot.' But they had to fit their art around what the actors had created. That's never happened to me on a film set since then."

Pakula also surprised Kline by inviting the principal actors to watch the dailies. Earlier in his career, Pakula had preferred that actors not watch dailies, but he encouraged them to do so during the filming of *Sophie's Choice*. "At the end of each day's dailies," Kevin Kline said, Pakula would discuss with the actors which takes he preferred. Then he would solicit their opinions. Kline would say (for example), "'I like the first part of Take Three and then the last part of Take One, don't you agree?' And," he stressed, "we agreed almost every time." As Kline saw it, the process of selecting which takes would be used in the film "was a collaboration" among Pakula and the actors.

The discipline of film acting, new to Kline, represented a difficult adjustment. He had grown accustomed to honing a performance through weeks of rehearsals and months of performances before live audiences. But "doing a film is like a combination of a first read-through, opening night, and closing night every single day," he said. "You're confronting the material for the first time, talking about it and doing it for the first—as well as the last—time, and for a stage actor that takes some getting used to."

---

[43]Meryl Streep was acutely aware of the security Pakula provided for her and her fellow performers. "Alan knew the secret of directing actors," she said. "He'd make a home for you. He'd make a place, respectful and safe, and there we'll be daring and vulnerable and funny and free. He trod very gently through the actor's world of feelings." Kline echoed her assessment when he said, "An atmosphere was created in which you could take as many risks as possible. Alan encouraged you to go all the way out on a limb and to trust him to catch you if you fell."

Kline was concerned about playing Nathan's inherent theatricality—which might seem to the audience to be overplaying. "I can see the reviews now," he said. "Kevin Kline obviously didn't learn the lesson of how screen acting is different from stage acting, and he's given a theatrical performance here." The necessity of reducing the size of a performance that might be acceptable in a two-thousand seat theatre to a medium in which his face might be forty feet tall was formidable. "The sound guy on *Sophie's Choice* kept saying, 'Could you just scream *softer*?'" Kline remembered. Indeed, the performance Kline gave in the film *is* highly theatrical (anything less would have been a betrayal of Nathan's character), but perfectly controlled.

One of the most striking scenes in *Sophie's Choice* shows Nathan in his apartment, vigorously "conducting" a recording of Beethoven's Ninth Symphony. Nathan, in a frenzy that reveals his love of music and at the same time hints at his lunacy, is reflected in six windows in an alcove—further giving the impression of a fractured personality. The idea for shooting the scene in that way occurred when Kline, who asked to sleep on the set one night (Peter MacNicol spent the same night sleeping in Stingo's room downstairs), noticed his reflection in the six windows, and recommended the shot to Pakula. Nestor Almendros lit the set and positioned the camera so that the shot could capture all of Nathan's reflections. Kline was elated that his suggestion was taken. "To be allowed to make suggestions that are in fact, cinematographic, that was typical of the kind of atmosphere that Alan created," he said.

That scene solved another problem that Pakula had been grappling with: showing Nathan's appreciation for high art, a characteristic that Styron had portrayed in the novel by discussing Nathan's appreciation of literature. Pakula was intent on finding a cinematic equivalent, and Nathan's frenzied conducting offered the solution, simultaneously demonstrating his passion for music and what Pakula called "the manic, manic quality of this man."

After shooting four or five takes of a scene, Pakula would say, according to Kevin Kline, "I'm happy. I've got what I need. Are you happy?" Kline was astounded. As "the new kid" (as he described himself) he did not expect to be consulted. But, realizing that he had a choice, he would say, "Well, I'd like to do one more, try something else." Pakula would say, "Fine," and they would begin shooting another take. Kline's enthusiasm for retakes was insatiable. After a while, Pakula would ask him, "Aren't you exhausted? We've covered it every which way." Speaking in 2003, Kline said, "I've rarely seen that kind of indulgence on any of the subsequent films I've made. He really did spoil me."

Pakula's method of working with the actors, as described by Kline, is particularly worthy of note. "From day one, he indulged our every impulse," Kline said. "I remember, he would let me put up whatever [object] I wanted off-screen.

There was a scene in Nathan's room when Nathan goes on a rampage about tracking down various Nazi generals and bringing them to justice. I had to look at something and to react I put up pictures of various war atrocities, anything that would generate the appropriate emotional response."

Pakula told Kline when filming began, "Whatever we've talked about earlier, when the camera's rolling, if you get another impulse, fuck what I said. Follow that impulse. This character has to be unpredictable, he has to be impulsive. I want you to find your own madness. Don't try to replicate the description of madness in the book. It has to be so personal, you have to find your own particular madness."

When scenes were filmed, Pakula would occasionally take an actor aside and, in Kline's words, "whisper things in between takes and tell him or her to do something that would keep the other actor fresh. It might be an off-screen line, if it's their close-up. After two or three takes, giving the line as written, we'd then say other things to make it fresh for the actor."

Pakula confirmed that he used that technique often. "When actually shooting," he said, "I will very often change one actor's performance by talking to the other actor [privately], asking for a change. Because if you're working with a good actor, [he or she] will respond to the change."

Often, when actors appear in close-up, reacting to an off-stage character, directors use a stand-in to give the off-stage lines. For Pakula, however, that convenience threatened to mar the reality of the on-screen actor's performance. Therefore he insisted "on having the actual actors read off-screen cues during close-ups, so that the actress is reacting to other characters, not some prompter."

Pakula also maintained a sense of reality by varying one actor's blocking without informing the other actors that he was going to do so. Kline recalled "a scene where Nathan and Sophie were sitting up on the roof and Peter was supposed to come out through the window. After three or four takes we're expecting him to come out of the window as usual, but Peter starts climbing up the front of the roof. It was a complete surprise. Alan wanted to capture the actors off-balanced, surprised. And that's what *we* all wanted. We all tried to surprise each other and make it fresh."

Pakula also wanted a sense of spontaneity, even if the lines in the screenplay were not spoken precisely as he had written them. In one of the first scenes in the film, for example, Nathan tells Stingo where he is employed. But, as Kline said, he kept stumbling over his lines, so Streep (as Sophie and in Sophie's dialect) filled in the words for him, finishing his sentences. Pakula used that take because, despite Kline's stumbles, it had an authenticity and a spontaneity that other takes lacked.

Anything that might disturb the reality of the actors' performances had to be eliminated. On one occasion, for example, Kline visited the set on a day when he wasn't called. As he tells the story, "It was a scene when Nathan runs off, he disappears, and Sophie and Stingo are in Sophie's room worried about him and wondering what's happened, and Stingo tells the story of his mother. I came in around lunchtime and Alan saw me before Meryl or Peter did. He whispered to me, 'You can't be here.' I said, 'Why not?' And he said, 'Because I want them to miss you.'"

Perhaps because everyone felt a special responsibility to bring the heartbreaking story of *Sophie's Choice* alive, the actors and Pakula reveled in the process of rehearsing and filming from beginning to end. "I was happy," Meryl Streep said. "I was happy from the first day we started shooting until the last day."

Pakula realized quickly that Streep's approach to the role paralleled his, but her portrayal of the character was even more detailed than the performance he had envisioned. Consequently, he refrained from offering specific suggestions, except when asked. "I would never push Meryl in any direction of my own until I saw the direction she chose to take," he said. "Often, it was not what mine would have been; but it had more authenticity, more originality." For Streep's part, if she had any specific problems with which she needed help from the director, she would unhesitatingly ask Pakula. "He knew everything," she said. "He was like a rabbi. He's the person you went to with everything." Pakula returned the compliment, saying about Streep, "I've never worked with an actor who seemed . . . more different from the character she's playing—and who seems absolutely to become somebody else."

Streep recalled that she came home from rehearsal late one afternoon and, with a sense of wonder, said to her husband, "I can't do anything wrong with this. I can't make a wrong move." Normally, Streep told me, "I'm full of missteps and second thoughts, but some things are just kind of blessed, and [with Pakula] you feel that every instinct to move or to act is justified somewhere deep in the character's backstory. I think it was an extraordinary shoot."

Throughout the film, Nestor Almendros's camera often lingered on Meryl Streep's uncannily expressive face, which registered extremes of emotion with extraordinary virtuosity. Whether Sophie was joyful at seeing Nathan, in despair at Nathan's unjustified accusations, painfully recollecting her history in Poland and Germany, or trying to comfort Stingo after an outburst by Nathan, Streep's every response seemed genuine, unforced, and often moving. She projected a sensuousness, an open sexuality, appropriate to Sophie. Her voice, too, vividly expressed the character. Those who had seen her in *Kramer vs. Kramer* and *The French Lieutenant's Woman* could barely recognize the actress' vocal quality. This was not simply a matter of speaking with an accent, but of placing and using her voice differently.

Shortly after shooting began, Peter MacNicol, who had told Pakula how thrilled he was to be working with Meryl Streep during rehearsals, came to the director in despair. "Alan," he said, "she's so different, she just ignores me, she's obsessed with Kevin Kline and she doesn't pay much attention to me. It destroys my morale." Pakula reported MacNicol's complaint to Streep, who said, "Alan, at this point I [as Sophie] am in love with [Nathan, to the exclusion of everything else]; he [MacNicol] means very little to me, he's a stranger. His time will come." And, Pakula noted, when the proper moment came, "it did."

Pakula worked patiently with MacNicol to achieve the sort of character he wished MacNicol to portray. He told the young actor his ideas about Stingo, and, according to MacNicol, "we settled on Stingo [as] the sensitive observer of things, and that was to be the keynote of the performance."

Pakula employed a time-honored device in *Sophie's Choice*, but one that had long since gone out of fashion: the narrative voice-over by a main character, looking back on the events years after they took place. In this case, Stingo, the narrator of the novel, also narrates a portion of the film. MacNicol was originally scheduled to read the narration of the older Stingo. But he was unable to develop a convincing older voice. "I tried to wreck my voice by drinking cognac and smoking Camels," MacNicol said, but it didn't work. Finally, Josef Sommer was enlisted to read the narration.

Pakula was deeply touched by the closeness he achieved with his actors and the sensitive way in which they took his direction. "It seems strange to say of this tragic film," he observed, "but it was one of the happiest filmmaking experiences of my life, from the time of reading the book through working on the screenplay and certainly to the shooting of the film, to the very end of it. There are some filmmaking experiences where you feel the wind's in front of you and you fight just to raise your hand and take a step forward, and other times when the wind's in back of you and you feel freed."

Most of the picture was shot in Brooklyn (Prospect Park, where Sophie and Stingo had shared a picnic lunch in Styron's novel, was used as the film location as well). During the Prospect Park scene and in a scene at an amusement park, cinematographer Nestor Almendros attempted to reproduce the look of "a cover of *Life* magazine in the 1940s."

Many of the interiors were filmed in the Camera Mart studios in Manhattan. A house at 101 Rugby Road in Brooklyn, after being painted, served as Yetta Zimmerman's "Pink Palace." (The crew repainted the house its original color after the filming there was completed.) The audience's first view of the Pink Palace—only a few moments into the picture—suggests an absurd quality, a suggestion that the film may be a comedy. Then the landlady, Yetta, is introduced, and, in her plumpness, her coy flirtatiousness, her Yiddish accent, she reinforces the comic quality. ("The Yiddish Art Theatre's not dead," Pakula said of Rita Karin's nearly overblown performance of Yetta. "With some actors you have to bring them up, and with some you have to say, 'Less, less, less.' Yetta was of the latter variety," he said, adding, "but dear, dear.")

Stingo rents one of the rooms at the Pink Palace. After Stingo enters, he hears the sounds of a couple making love upstairs—with such force that the chandelier on the ceiling shakes. Again, the effect seems comic; there is as yet no hint that the audience is about to see a searing tragedy unfold. The lighting of the film to this point is suffused with sunlight and brightness. Pakula told Nestor Almendros when they first discussed the cinematography, "I want the present tense to be so alive, I want it to be Rubenesque in colors, the sensuality. That's what these people [Sophie and Nathan] represent: life to this boy [Stingo]." But as the sounds from above become less amorous—an argument has broken out between Sophie and Nathan—the lighting begins to reflect a more mysterious and sinister quality. The same people who have represented life to Stingo "will also represent death," as Pakula observed, and the argument is the first sign that the tone of the film will eventually shift.

Later, Stingo watches, astonished, as Nathan, shouting vicious epithets at Sophie, runs down the stairway and out of the house. Stingo tries to calm the inconsolable Sophie. Even in her tearful state, one can sense that Stingo is attracted by Sophie's beauty and her vulnerability.

Still later, Sophie tells Stingo how she and Nathan met—at the library, in the scene that was shot on the first day of filming. After Sophie faints during that scene, Nathan takes her to his room at the Pink Palace. The only light is apparently provided by candles, giving the scene a warm, romantic glow—as befits a scene in which Nathan (who, in this flashback, as told by Sophie to Stingo, shows no sign of madness, only solicitude) treats Sophie with infinite tenderness and begins the process of nursing her back to health.

After this sequence, the adult Stingo's voice describes his interpretation of the events. One of the most intriguing structural elements of the film is that we see or hear Sophie's point of view, then Stingo's point of view (or vice-versa), and it becomes clear that they view reality differently. The audience is left to make up its own mind whose view of reality is, in fact, closer to the truth—if, indeed, there is an objective "truth."

Pakula, who said he liked to give sequences titles in order to remind himself of the most important element in the sequence that must be emphasized, called this sequence "the saving of Sophie by Nathan, and their falling in love." (The first sequence in the film, he said, was "Stingo falling in love with them and the three of them becoming comrades together.") A later sequence was titled, "Nathan's recognition of Stingo's gifts." Had he not used the titling device—or a similar device that would have achieved the same purpose—Pakula believed he would have wound up "with wonderful scenes that just don't tell the story, or damage the story by confusing the audience's concentration."

As Sophie's health returns, she and Nathan begin a passionate affair. Streep said, "I think that people who go through a certain kind of horror become numb and have no feelings sometimes. And I think Nathan made her feel alive, even in the most horrific moments of their relationship." That relationship, Pakula said, represented "the most glorious part of erotic love, which is erotic love as a savior; he literally saves her life—and at the same time it was dealing with erotic love on its darkest, most compulsive, most obsessive side; erotic love as a destroyer."

After the film was completed, William Styron said that he felt the movie slighted the sadomasochistic eroticism of the book (and surely that quality does not occupy the space or the significance it receives in the novel), but Sophie's sexual ferocity is a significant aspect of Streep's performance and Pakula's screenplay, although admittedly many degrees less ferocious than the Sophie of Styron's novel. One reason for the alteration was caused by the contrast between Streep and Peter MacNicol, who, as Sophie and Stingo, make love near the end of the film. Pakula wished to invest Stingo's and Sophie's scene of lovemaking with greater eroticism—"There's no question that Styron's Stingo was lustier," he said— but felt he had to emphasize the tenderness instead because the combination of MacNicol's innocence and Streep's sensuality "looked like a boy and his mother, so you have to go with what you have."

Early in the film, Stingo, an aspiring novelist, is writing a memoir about his adolescence in the South. Afraid that the quality of his work will be derided, he shows it to no one, but Nathan manages to pilfer a copy. After reading it, Nathan ceremoniously takes Stingo and Sophie to the Brooklyn Bridge, where he proposes—in the grandest manner imaginable, climbing one of the supports of the bridge and pouring champagne into three glasses—a toast to Stingo as the next great American writer.

Because of the wind and traffic noises on the bridge when the shot was filmed, the microphone was unable to pick up Kline's words, so the audio portion of the scene had to be dubbed in the studio. "Kevin did a wonderful job," Pakula said. "We never could have gotten this kind of intimacy" in the scene unless the words had been dubbed in post-production. At the end of Nathan's salute to Stingo, he flings his glass of champagne in the water below. "This is my way of trying to show that Nathan was 'utterly, fatally glamorous,'" Pakula said—"One of my favorite expressions from Styron['s book]."

Pakula admitted that he gave considerable thought to cutting the scene with Stingo and Leslie Lapidus. "It seems curiously different in style to me from the rest of the film," he ultimately said. However, the contrast of Stingo and Leslie's "adolescent groping compared to the genuine, romantic passion of Sophie and Nathan" was too great for him to resist. He found Greta Turken's performance endearing, and loved "all the endless underwear" that Leslie wears and Stingo tries—ultimately without success—to remove. "I took my own teenage lust for garters and stockings and all those things, at that time . . . in my life," Pakula said.

Later, Sophie tells Stingo of her ordeal in Europe. Stingo listens sympathetically and appears to be clearly moved. "Peter's wonderful in this scene," Pakula said, "but it could have another layer, where he just feels this swelling of passion, wanting to take her in his arms in such a powerful way. That's the beginning of his rise into real manhood." Pakula regretted that he had not been able to bring out that quality. "The caring is here, the sweetness, but that kind of tension is not here at this point: he's now in love with her, and as a man [he should] just want . . . to take her in his arms and protect her forever."

Pakula also wished that MacNicol had had another quality in the scene in which Nathan returns to the house and—to everyone's complete surprise—accuses Stingo of having slept with Sophie. "That should have appealed to some of the boy's guilts," Pakula said, "because he did lust after her in many ways." (Of course, since the lustful quality of the previous scene was missing, there could be no possible guilt in this scene.) "There's a kind of Oedipal triangle in this," with Nathan as a sort of father figure to Stingo, Pakula continued; "and they're both fighting over the same woman. Stingo finds himself, in his secret heart, longing to take her away from [Nathan]. . . . But as played by Peter, and, obviously, as directed by me, the boy . . . comes out much more as an innocent, without that kind of subtext."

Pakula was not entirely happy with one other scene of MacNicol's. When Stingo confronts Sophie after having learned the truth about her background, he feels deceived and confused. "What I see in there is hurt, and passive-aggressive punishment," Pakula said, "and it's okay, it's good, but the director and the actor could do better. Now, I like the scene, I think it's a good scene, it's well played, but . . ." He wished that he could have invested the scene with more complexity. "Give me two weeks of reshooting, or even six days," he said, and he would have been able to layer the scene with greater texture.

On the other hand, Pakula thought that MacNicol was "wonderful" in most of the film, particularly in his reactions—to Nathan, to Sophie, to Nathan's brother (who tells Stingo that Nathan is a paranoid schizophrenic), and to the letter telling him that Sophie and Nathan are dead. MacNicol brought a fragility to Stingo's character that is not present in the novel; that quality gave MacNicol's performance a significant resonance, although it did not permit him to explore Stingo's more aggressive instincts.

Sophie and Stingo, waiting for Nathan to join them, enjoy a picnic lunch in Prospect Park. Nathan arrives, wildly excited, claiming to have made a remarkable chemical discovery, one that might lead to the Nobel Prize. He is manic, almost out of control. The scene, Pakula believed, was "where Kevin started to really get [a sense of madness] in the shrillness of his laugh. This is very difficult to do for an actor, because he's telling total lies, because he's created this idea of himself as a scientist, and he's celebrating this great discovery, and it's all made up in his mind, and yet he must believe it. If he does it as if he's telling a lie, it doesn't work." Later, when Nathan's madness is even more clearly revealed—when he accuses Sophie of sleeping both with Stingo and with her boss, Mr. Katz—"we did many, many takes," Pakula said. "There [were] so many ways to play this scene, and Kevin [was] very imaginative and inventive, and tried twenty or thirty of them" before they arrived at the approach they deemed best. Kline's ability to find so many ways of playing a given scene offered Pakula a plethora of choices through-out the film.

As shooting progressed, the actors continued to be deeply moved by the story they were telling and the camaraderie they had developed. Mistakenly, they thought that Pakula was less affected by the experience than they. Meryl Streep explained, "A director is somebody who has to sort of sit beside the action of the movie and affect it, but not be in it. So as a director Alan sat back and resisted showing us how he felt about everything." As a result, neither she, Kline, nor MacNicol realized the degree to which Pakula had been moved. One day, as the actors were facing their mirrors and making up, the director entered the dressing room. "We were all lined up in front of the mirror and could see him in the door-way behind us," Streep said. "And he had tears in his eyes. He was ashen. So we all whirled around, and we said, 'What's happened? What's wrong?' He said, 'We're halfway done. We're halfway through the movie, and it's going to be over.' It was the first time that I'd really understood that it wasn't just the three of us, that Alan was in our story. Alan was in it with us, and he revealed his feelings that day. It was the first time I saw what he had been holding back: his love for this project and for us."

Most of the second half of the movie, which consists primarily of flashbacks, takes place in Europe. Pakula planned to shoot those scenes in Poland, but polit-ical problems in that country prevented him from doing so. When the company was denied permission to film in Poland, it began to create a facsimile of Auschwitz in Yugoslavia. In a budget meeting, Martin Starger objected to one expense, and Pakula misinterpreted Starger's concern to mean that Marble Arch

Productions might not shoot the Auschwitz scenes in Europe. Pakula told Meryl Streep about his fear. Streep, in turn, worried that the proposed change would severely affect the film. It seemed likely, she said, "that they weren't going to shoot that part in Europe at all—that they'd just let Sophie *tell* the story," which would have severely diminished the impact of the tragic events at Auschwitz. She called Pakula after rehearsal, telling him how negatively she believed the film would be affected by foregoing the European location. By this time, he had received assurances from Starger that plans to shoot in Europe were unchanged, so he informed Streep that the company would soon move to Yugoslavia, where all the European sequences would be shot.

But another crisis occurred, this time concerning the Polish actors. Pakula received a call from his friend Andrzej Wajda, who told him that Film Polski, the official Polish film agency, had instructed all Polish actors to have nothing to do with *Sophie's Choice*. The actors who had been cast were officially told that they would not be permitted to return to Poland if they performed in the movie. "The Polish government's objection to the film as well as the book," Pakula said, sarcastically, "is that it defamed Poland by implying there'd been a history of anti-Semitism" in that country. Pakula told the Polish actors who had been cast in the film that he would release them from their contracts if they wished. "I did not want to destroy their lives," he said. "However, all but one of them said . . . they would risk it, and indeed they did play in the film."

Even when the company moved to Yugoslavia, Pakula continued to rehearse his actors in the morning, but, because most scenes included many actors, there was less opportunity to explore each scene in depth.

The first scene in Poland (shot in Zagreb, Yugoslavia) portrayed a period approximately a decade before the scenes in the Pink Palace. Consequently, the audience sees a much younger Sophie—and the change in Meryl Streep's demeanor as well as her appearance is startling. Pakula admitted that a small part of the difference was created by makeup, but "it's inside that the difference comes; it's acting," he said. "There's no makeup to make her feel younger. [In this scene] there's a kind of insecurity, her womanliness is gone. In the present, she's a full-blown sensuous woman, and here [she] is a kind of fragile, not-totally-formed young woman."

Pakula did not want to film the flashbacks in black-and-white, but he did want a different look, so, in contrast to what he called the "almost overripe colors" used for the scenes in New York, he opted for a desaturated process. Nestor Almendros also photographed Sophie through a screen at times, lingering on her face when she is lost in memory. Sometimes, when a character is in the midst of a monologue revealing her recollections, directors will use "the camera running around the back of her head because [they] think the audience is going to be bored," Pakula said. But "everything is the inner life of this character and to try to juice it up with camera movement would only confuse [the audience's] concentration . . . So you hold and stay and be inside of her. If that doesn't work, it's not working anyway, so juicing it up with a lot of camera work is not going to help you."

In order to create a striking contrast between the well-fed Sophie under Nathan's care and the emaciated Sophie in Auschwitz, Streep ate, in her words, "like a pig during the whole first part of the filming," gaining ten pounds. Then, she said, during the scenes filmed in the concentration camp, "I didn't eat for about a month. And when I say I didn't eat I mean I didn't eat *anything*." She lost twenty-five pounds.

The Auschwitz concentration camp, built from the original German plans (which had been captured by the United States Army, who made them available to the filmmakers), was re-created in Zagreb by Yugoslavian workers under the supervision of the production designer, George Jenkins. Crematories were built in the background.

Pakula, a fanatic for detail in any case, was even more devoted to accuracy in the scenes set at Auschwitz in *Sophie's Choice* than on other occasions. He hired a survivor of Auschwitz, Kitty Hart, the author of *Return to Auschwitz* and the narrator of a PBS documentary of the same title, to work with him and the actors in the Auschwitz scenes. Pakula said, "I would never do Auschwitz without having somebody by my side to say, 'This is the way it was; this is not the way it was.'"

When he asked for her help, Hart said, "Mr. Pakula, I had *my* experience at Auschwitz. There are six million different [Jewish] experiences in the Holocaust, mine was one. I am not a historian. I can only tell you what it was like for me, what I saw, what I observed." Her honesty and humility impressed Pakula. When the *Sophie's Choice* company went to Yugoslavia to film the Auschwitz scenes, Kitty Hart "stayed by my side at all times," Pakula said.

Kitty Hart said that her job with Meryl Streep was "merely"—merely!—"to help her to learn how to behave and walk and dress." Walking at Auschwitz was no easy task, Hart emphasized, for "you got stuck in the mud," requiring a painful shuffle rather than a stride.

During Sophie's trudge through the mud from the concentration camp building at Auschwitz to the Commandant's headquarters, hundreds of hands are extended to her—the hands of inmates, desperately pleading for help, a vivid image of the prisoners' loss of individuality, for we see no faces and hear only the word for "water" spoken in thirty different languages. When Sophie reaches her destination, the camera rises so that the spectators can see over the wall. They are confronted with an amazing sight: a pleasant garden representing the front yard of Nazi Commandant Rudolf Hoess' house, filled with children playing happily—a painful contrast to the bleakness of the concentration camp.

The scene, Pakula felt, was one of the best in the film. "The camera just goes over the garden fence, it just goes right over the filth and the mud and the horror and the stench—right over the fence and the barbed wire to this fantasy garden of this middle-class existence, Eden for . . . this bourgeois German family. . . [who represents] the banality of evil, the evil of the people who created the Holocaust. . . . Just that simple little lift of the camera right over into the garden, and the contrast of the pretty bourgeois garden, and the horror, to me said almost everything about the inhumanity of man to man: How man can cut off the horror of what he's doing, how other people can become an abstraction, how destroying [others] can become meaningless because you're only worrying about your own problems."

An alternative way of shooting the scene would have been to emphasize the evil by showing the garden "as if in some total nightmare, using all those distorted expressionist techniques," as Pakula phrased it. But he preferred to emphasize the mundane. "I felt that the power of the material was so great that it would be hideous to overdramatize it, to get in the way of it," he said.

The Hoess family is portrayed not as monstrous conspirators in a crime of historic proportions, but as banal, bourgeois careerists. Hoess' wife almost ludicrously nags her husband with her fear that they will be posted to a less desirable concentration camp; she gaily prepares a birthday cake for Heinrich Himmler, hoping that it will advance her husband's career; and her nine-year-old daughter says at one point that Dachau was so much more fun than Auschwitz. As Pakula said, Hoess and his family were not portrayed "like Hollywood Nazis at all. They're concerned with decent, middle-class family life, bringing up their children, the woman worried about her husband losing his job at Auschwitz because it's such a good job."

Later, he amplified on his approach: "To see this 'wholesome'—in quotation marks—German family, with a tortured man, tortured [because he might be] kicked out for not doing a good enough job of killing enough people at Auschwitz, and because he wants to protect his family with his good job so that they'll eat well; a wife who's worried about her family and giving [her husband] a bit of a henpecking . . . the ordinariness of them is the key to the horror."

Pakula hoped that the triviality of the Hoesses's concerns in comparison to the devastation for which Hoess was responsible would cause the audience to look inward. The characters on the screen "are people like ourselves," he said; and it was in ourselves that "I wanted people to feel there could be this kind of evil. It's not somebody else. In all of us there's the potential of caring so little about others and worrying so much about ourselves [that we] can become instruments of evil as well.

. . . I don't like letting the audience off the hook, and saying, 'Oh, well, that makes us feel good because we never would have done something like that.'"

A German child (Melanie Pianka) played Hoess' daughter, Emmi, who is tempted to turn Sophie in for stealing a radio, but refrains from doing so. Instead, she interrogates a terrified Sophie in her bedroom, decorated with lace curtains on which swastikas are sewn. Melanie spoke no English, so Pakula directed her through a translator. For a while, she seemed oddly unresponsive to his direction. Then Meryl Streep told him, "Alan, I don't know that much German, but I know enough to hear that [the translator is] not giving your directions, she's giving the opposite." What happened, Pakula later discovered, was that the translator felt that the girl "was not [doing] enough acting, that she should act more for her money," so the translator was, in essence, ignoring Pakula's direction and "telling her how to act." Pakula was forced to replace the translator—after which Melanie Pianka gave him precisely what he wanted. "The girl's a brilliant actress," he said; "she never commented, she never thought of herself as evil. . . . She just plays . . . the reality of the scene."

Sophie manages to gain employment as Hoess' secretary, desperately hoping for an opportunity to plead with him for the life of her son. Despite Hoess' attempts to seduce her and despite his crippling migraine headaches, she manages to plead her case, but to no avail.

Gunther Maria Halmer, who played Hoess, "was very concerned," Pakula said, "that all of us would think he was an evil man because he was playing this evil part, and we had to keep reassuring him that we didn't dislike him and that we didn't confuse him with the character."[44]

A four-year-old American child named Jennifer Lawn was cast to play Sophie's daughter. A Polish speaker, the child had only accompanied her older sister to an audition, but she was the one the casting director, Alixe Gordon, had settled upon and recommended to Pakula. Meryl Streep helped audition the girl. "Well, Jennifer," she said, "I hear you can speak Polish. Would you speak Polish to me?" Jennifer sang "Happy Birthday" in Polish, and, as a result, was given the role. Streep then spent weeks bonding with the child, trying to create a mother-daughter relationship that could be believably transferred to the screen.

As the train in which Sophie and her children are riding comes closer to Auschwitz (in a flashback showing an earlier time: the first arrival at the concentration camp), we see for the first time the source of the haunting flute music that has played repeatedly on the audio track. It is a melody—we realize for the first time how simple and childlike the melody is—played by Sophie's daughter on her

---

[44]*Halmer, who spoke in German in* Sophie's Choice, *played the same role in* War and Remembrance *in 1989, speaking English with a German accent.*

recorder. Pakula said the woodwind solo represented "innocence—innocence that we will see destroyed later on."

When the train arrived at Auschwitz, Pakula chose not to show scenes of cruelty taking place around and behind Sophie and her children. "There's a certain kind of pornography of horror," Pakula said, "and bathing [the screen] with every horrible moment, that can wipe out the humanity and it just becomes like a museum of horrors." Thus, when Sophie is forced to confront the choice imposed on her by an S. S. doctor—to select which of her children she will send to the crematorium, so that the other may live—her terrible dilemma becomes all the more vivid.

When Streep was first given the scene, "I read it once . . . and never read it again," she said, "because I couldn't stand it. And I think I didn't [re-read the scene] because I was Sophie, I was in denial. I knew it was coming . . . and it was something I never wanted to look at."

Moments before the scene was shot, Pakula told his assistant he wished to speak to Karlheinz Hackl, the actor playing the S. S. doctor. "We have him in there sitting in a [room] with the little girl," the assistant responded. Pakula exploded in one of his rare moments of anger. "What?" he shouted. "She's a little girl, she reacts to this being her reality. [If] you are getting them to be friendly, she'll feel safe with him. Are you out of your mind? She's got to be afraid of him. You get him out of there . . . and I don't want him to see her until he's on the screen and he scares the hell out of her by his presence." Pakula, knowing that four-year-old Jennifer Lawn could not possibly be expected to give a convincing portrayal of fear, would have to be truly frightened. He said to himself, "There goes the scene. The little girl will never get it again. There goes the picture. If this scene doesn't work, there is no picture. I almost had a stroke." Pakula noted that Hackl "didn't do anything cruel with her. I don't believe in doing that to a child." But the fear on Jennifer Lawn's face in the scene was obviously genuine; no child of her age could have acted so convincingly.

When Sophie, having been forced to make the dreadful choice imposed on her, sees her daughter carried away, Meryl Streep said, "I had no idea how I was going to play the scene." She thought she "would be crying buckets, and when it came, what happened was this silent scream." Her mouth opens wide, but no sound emerges. Streep thought she was screaming, she said. "I thought I was screaming as loud as I could. It was like being in a dream." Pakula, who, like Streep, expected a flood of tears, was also surprised, but found the moment "more real" than he had anticipated, perhaps because it was "less conventional." It is no exaggeration to call the sequence—from the train's arrival at Auschwitz, through the doctor's insistence on Sophie's choosing which of her children shall live and who will die, to the silent scream—one of the most disturbing and powerful ever recorded on film.

On the final day of shooting in Zagreb the cameras began to roll at nine AM. Pakula, concerned about losing the actors' intensity, kept working throughout the day and night, determined to complete the scheduled scenes, not finishing until 4:15 in the morning. "It was," he said, "one of the more barbaric decisions ever made by a film director."

Then Pakula took everyone to the roof of the hotel where they were staying for a celebratory breakfast. "It was one of the most unforgettable nights of my life, and certainly one of the longest," he said.

After Sophie has told Stingo the story of her ordeal at Auschwitz, a scene at the Pink Palace shows Nathan calling from an unknown location. He has descended into utter madness, threatening to kill Sophie and Stingo; for emphasis he fires his gun so that it can be heard clearly over the telephone.

Stingo determines to escape New York with Sophie. He plans to take her to his home in the South, where he intends to marry her. On the way, they stop at a hotel, where, at last, Stingo consummates his desire for Sophie. The scene is gentle, "kind of lyrical, almost, and beautiful, instead of being animal-like as it is in the book," as Peter MacNicol said.

When Stingo awakens, he finds a note from Sophie. She has returned to New York, the note tells him, because she must be with Nathan. Generously, she calls Stingo "a great lover."

The flute music is heard for the last time when Stingo returns to Brooklyn to discover that Nathan and Sophie are dead. As Annette Insdorf points out, the music "not only serves as a counterpoint to the dramatic tension of the couple's joint suicide, but links these deaths to that of [Sophie's] daughter."

The suicide was instigated as much by Sophie as by Nathan, William Styron said. "They were both joined in this mutual need to die." Long before Sophie's death, the audience learns that she had attempted suicide earlier, when Nathan sees the scars on her wrists soon after he rescues her at the library.

Pakula hoped that the penultimate image, of Sophie and Nathan lying on the bed as Stingo recites Emily Dickinson's poem, would convey to the audience that "in some way in death [their] love survived. . . . [The film ends] with rebirth to me, not just with death." Peter MacNicol, too, thought that the ending contained an element of rebirth. When Stingo is seen crossing the Brooklyn Bridge at the end of the film, he felt that the audience "is left feeling kind of ennobled, in some strange way."

The very last image the audience is left with is that of Sophie's face. The image is somewhat faded; the face seems to be burned on to the screen as it is seared into Stingo's memory.

Pakula, with his considerable experience as a producer, "was a very good man when it came to understanding and adhering to a budget," Martin Starger said. "He was a very knowledgeable production-oriented director. He knew budgets extremely well, having made and adhered to them. And he was very professional. Absolutely a film professional." Pakula was, however, "with all fondness and respect for his talent, not the fastest person in the area of filmmaking," in Starger's opinion. "He was very slow in thinking through things, directions often did not come quickly. A good part of that [was because] he didn't shoot from the hip. He thought things out very, very carefully, all sides, and didn't jump to decisions." The result of Pakula's methodical process was that he wound up making a magnificent film, but sometimes at the expense of frustrating his co-workers. As Starger said, refusing to make hasty decisions "is often very good, and often not so good, because things are moving around you and you gotta make decisions."

Pakula's methodical approach was just the right way to deal with a crisis, however. Starger remembered, "On the first day of shooting what was the Auschwitz camp in Yugoslavia, there were all kinds of problems." Special effects technicians, hidden behind the chimneys, began to feed fire into the chimneys in order to make smoke appear at the right moment, but the chimneys, built to less-than-ideal standards, caught fire and burned down. Starger said, "This is a nightmare, as you can imagine. We're in the middle of nowhere. The fire truck consisted of a horse-drawn wagon with little pails of water. But Alan, there he was, totally in command. He calmly assessed it. 'Everybody take off,' he said, 'we'll get it right.' He was a very in-control director."

Starger had no doubt that, despite Pakula's occasional indecision, he was the ideal director for *Sophie's Choice*. "He felt and loved that story," Starger said, "and I think that passion that he felt—and he was not a passionate man ordinarily, he was almost talmudic at times, in conversations—is what is felt on the screen."

Meryl Streep said that the stories of Pakula's indecisiveness "might have been in the areas in which he wasn't really interested, like the location of the lunch van. This is the kind of question that comes to a director, believe it or not. Those kinds of question were, I think, of secondary interest. If he wasn't interested in them he probably wouldn't have responded to them in a timely fashion. The questions in which he *was* interested, which had to do with my part of the moviemaking, the actor's part—the story, the motivations, the characterizations—those he was always willing and eager to dive into, any exploration of those problems."

It is not only Pakula's passion but his artistry that is evident in *Sophie's Choice*. He employs admirable restraint throughout. He never sensationalizes, never provides the viewer with gratuitous images of beatings, killings, or other horrific acts, concentrating instead on the horrors specific to Sophie's story. Some directors would have exploited the Holocaust gratuitously (many directors have done so), but would thereby have run the risk of trivializing this most despicable period in modern human history.

Pakula told his composer, Marvin Hamlisch, "The film is so emotional, the film is about such horror, that it runs the great danger of becoming emotional pornography. I would like something that gives a kind of dignity." Hamlisch's music, including the solo woodwind music that we eventually learn is played by Sophie's daughter, is superbly written, projecting all of the heartbreak and anguish of the film's characters. Pakula hoped that the central musical theme would "ennoble" the characters, with "a gentle lovingness and [lyricism]." He felt that the music did just that, seeming "to surround and protect" the characters.

Music and its importance to Sophie was a central theme of the novel, so much so that Styron said that "people who fail to understand that may well fail to grasp the book on one of its most important levels." Barbara Tepa Lupack, pointing out that "classical music was Sophie's attempt at preserving her own precarious sense of self and her link with those whom she loved," commends the way in which music was employed in the film. "Though somewhat downplayed, the motif of music remains pervasive," she writes. "Pakula makes clear to the viewer that music is one of Nathan's greatest gifts to Sophie: classical works as well as more popular songs emanate from their phonograph, and even while picnicking at Prospect Park they dance to the radio's waltzing sounds. Moreover, for her birthday, Nathan surprises Sophie with a piano."

Marvin Hamlisch found the process of working with Pakula "astounding," because the director "was really like a musician. He could talk to you in musical terms, as opposed to just saying, 'I want it to sound angelic.' He could really be very specific about the kinds of sounds and the kinds of feelings he wanted—and particularly the kinds of subtleties like where the irony should be pointed up." Pakula knew with a precision that Hamlisch found remarkable exactly what the score needed. "He was very quick to let you know if something wasn't working," Hamlisch said. "When I was at home in my apartment I used to play music for him with the film playing, and he might say, 'Why don't you start this two seconds later?' He had a great sensibility for that. And I think that sensitivity and that ability and that kind of allowing your emotions to really work—I think that embodied his whole work and probably his whole life. And I loved that, loved working with someone like that, because I'm a very emotional person."

The filming was such a thrilling experience for the actors that, despite the horrific action portrayed in the film, they hated to see the shooting end. "The only really tough thing about the part was saying goodbye to it," Meryl Streep said. "I could have played it forever. It was wonderful, the best thing I've ever experienced." And, she said in 1998, Pakula's decision to cast her as Sophie was "the greatest gift of my career. . . . He was," she said, "our benevolent god, overseeing our destiny . . . He was organized and civilized and passionate, but unhurried, and he was demanding only of the truth."

Streep's desire to continue her association with *Sophie's Choice* was so great that she asked Pakula to allow her to dub her own lines in the French version. Pakula was doubtful, since speaking French with a Polish accent presented an entirely new problem. Then he remembered that Cecile Insdorf, an Auschwitz survivor of his acquaintance, spoke fluent French with a Polish accent. He asked her to coach Streep, but Insdorf was too busy teaching and advising French students at Hunter College. As a compromise, she agreed to speak all of Sophie's lines into a tape recorder, and Streep used the tape to perfect her French-Polish accent. Streep and Insdorf did not meet at the time—but many years later, at a National Board of Review Gala in New York, Cecile's daughter, Annette, introduced herself to Streep and suggested she might wish to meet her mother. When Streep gave her a puzzled look, Annette told her that Cecile was the person who had made the French tape. Streep then greeted Cecile warmly. The two have remained friends ever since.

Kevin Kline said that his experience in *Sophie's Choice* "was the most wonderful film or acting experience I have ever had, and am likely to ever have." Pakula "spoiled me for all directors after him because he was an ideal director, I thought. He had a kind of intellectual acumen that was tempered with a humanism," Kline said. "I always thought of him as a kind of *mensch* with great intellectual powers."

Sophie's Choice premiered in New York on December 5, 1982. Hannah Pakula recalled the first showing of the film. "The audience just sat there when it was over. Not a sound. Nobody got up." That response was reproduced everywhere the film was shown. Spectators, often in tears, devastated by Sophie's progression— from victim of her father's intolerance to the horror of the concentration camp to Nathan's brutal treatment to the film's tragic conclusion—remained in their seats long after the final scene had ended.

Those studios that had called *Sophie's Choice* non-commercial were fundamentally correct. Although the box-office receipts exceeded $30 million, the film's initial budget, promotional costs, and miscellaneous expenses prevented it from being more than a modest financial success. But box-office income can hardly be used to measure the magnificence of the filmmakers' accomplishment.

William Styron's reaction to the film was not uncritical, although his general response was enthusiastic. "I think the great virtue of the film is that it extracted the essence of the book, the central story," he said. "I thought it did an awfully good job of capturing the basic outline." Further, he said, "I think I was as well served as anyone who's written a complicated novel." He was particularly impressed by Meryl Streep's performance. "I think that seeing where she does make that ultimate choice is done with absolute, perfect precision and horror," he said. "It couldn't have been improved upon." On the other hand, he was disappointed with Peter MacNicol as Stingo. "I felt that Peter MacNicol was miscast," Styron said. "I never felt he was the right person for Stingo; he was too callow, too boyish, with not enough real stature or intellect." The fact that Stingo was intended to be a portrait of Styron in his youth may have prevented him from envisioning a Stingo that was, in many ways, unlike himself, however.

Meryl Streep's performance is one of the great examples of the actor's art. It is a cliché and a misnomer to say that an actor has *become* the character he or she is portraying (such a mystical transference of personality never occurs), but Streep *seems* to be Sophie in every fiber of her being. Her performance may be numbered among the most astonishing in film history, one that may legitimately be placed alongside Liv Ullmann's in *Face to Face*, Giulietta Masina's in *La Strada*, and Maria Falconetti's in *The Passion of Joan of Arc*. Streep received many awards for her portrayal[45], but awards pale in significance compared to the performance itself.

Among the most remarkable aspects of this remarkable film, however, is that Streep does not dominate the landscape. Kevin Kline is equally brilliant. Although the Nathan of the film does not commit some of the more barbaric acts of the novel, Kline vividly suggests the character's barbarity in subtextual ways. Peter MacNicol's role is less flamboyant than Sophie's or Nathan's (and, unlike the novel, Stingo's role in the action is reduced), but his performance is well-crafted and sensitive; given the job of responding to the action of others, he does so with delicacy and finesse. The supporting actors, too, are superbly integrated into the film. Even very small roles—such as the librarian who humiliates Sophie (Meryl Streep's former fellow student at the Yale Drama School, John Rothman) and the S. S. doctor who forces her to make her horrifying choice (Karlheinz Hackl)—are excellently played.

Pakula was more moved by Meryl Streep's performance than by that of any other actor he worked with. "I've worked with some of the most gifted actors in

---

[45] *Among the nominations and awards for* Sophie's Choice *were the following: The New York Film Critics Circle cited Meryl Streep as best actress and Nestor Almendros best cinematographer; Streep was also recognized by the National Society of Film Critics. Streep won the Academy Award, while Pakula was nominated for his direction and his screenplay, Nestor Almendros for his cinematography, Albert Wolsky for his costume design, and Marvin Hamlisch for his score. British Academy Film and Television Awards were given to Streep as Best Actress and Kline as Best Newcomer; Streep won a Golden Globe, while the film was nominated as Best Motion Picture and Kline as New Star of the Year. The Robert Festival from Denmark called* Sophie's Choice *the best foreign film.*

films," he said. "The word 'genius' is thrown around a lot. But I think Meryl has it. Critics resent it and patronize it, but she's not just an actress acting." Her performance in *Sophie's Choice*, in a way that may be impossible to define, transcends "acting" and enters another realm.

Still, Pakula continued to think wistfully of the film he might have made if Magda Vasaryova, who, he felt, also possessed the ability to achieve greatness, had played Sophie. "If I had done that film with [Vasaryova] it would have been quite a different film," he said. "Maybe not better and maybe not worse, but different."[46]

Pakula's well-deserved reputation as a "woman's director" was enhanced by Streep's portrayal of Sophie. "Alan was excellent with Meryl. She gave a wonderful performance, and there are reasons for it," Martin Starger said, giving Pakula more credit for the performance than the director himself was willing to take. Streep's fine performance does not mean that Pakula paid her more attention than he did to Kline, MacNicol, or any of the other men. Starger noted, "I was not aware of any frustration from any males in the cast at all. If there had been a real problem I would have known about it, because they would have talked to me."

One critical response to *Sophie's Choice* varied so greatly from another that one cannot speak of a critical "consensus." On the negative side, Pauline Kael thought the film faithful to the book but "an infuriatingly bad movie." Kael disliked Meryl Streep's performance, as well. Stanley Kauffmann preferred the film to the "gummy rhetoric" of the book but liked neither. John Simon said that he liked neither the movie nor the book (but admitted he had not read the novel carefully).

On the other hand, Janet Maslin in the *New York Times* was deeply impressed by the film's unity and emotional truth, "its inexorable momentum," turning a "suspenseful, troubling novel [into] a movie that is even more so." Maslin was most taken by Meryl Streep, who "offers a performance of such measured intensity that the results are by turns exhilarating and heartbreaking." Vincent Canby, in a subsequent article for the *Times*, wrote that Streep portrayed "a complete woman . . . a woman of the sort of passionate humor and sorrow and sexuality seldom seen in movies. Her performance is a ravishing combination of technical skill and mysterious artistry, and how such a fusion is achieved, I've no idea. All one can do is appreciate it." Still, Canby found the film "just a little too studied and self-conscious . . . for it to be completely satisfactory."

Other critics, however, admired the film without qualification. Kathleen Carroll in the *New York Daily News*, for example, called *Sophie's Choice* "a film that casts a powerful uninterrupted spell. . . . Miss Streep accomplishes the near impossible, presenting Sophie in believably human terms without losing the scale of Mr.

---

[46]*Magda Vasaryova's disappointment about losing the role of Sophie was perhaps assuaged to some degree when she became the Czech ambassador to Austria in 1990.*

Styron's invention." *Newsweek*'s Jack Kroll said of Meryl Streep, "the accent and the expressive Polish and German she speaks in the European sequences are not virtuoso stunts; they are thrilling expressions of character, like the feats of a great musician or dancer that ravish the senses while they enlighten the heart." About the movie as a whole, he wrote, "*Sophie's Choice* is a film drenched in sorrow, a choral lament for the monstrous pain and cruelty of the 20th century. It must be one of the saddest movies ever made . . . courageous and intelligent . . . a gripping and oddly liberating film . . . remarkable."

CHAPTER SIXTEEN

On the Set

"The whole world was the canvas of discussion in the course of the day [while filming a picture]. We generally, all of us [Pakula and the members of his inner circle, those who worked with him often] would discuss current events, we would discuss politics, we would discuss literature, we would discuss the movie a little bit. Alan was interested in the larger context of life."

—CELIA COSTAS

CELIA COSTAS, who recently produced HBO's *Angels in America*, had this to say about working with Pakula—as she did on many films: "I just loved him so much as a human being, as a man, as an intellectual, as an artist. There was no part of him that I didn't like." Costas recalled warmly the times she served as Pakula's location manager. Both on the set and during breaks, the atmosphere was always stimulating, electric.

Everything that happened in the course of the day, whether it be politically or on the movie, had a context, and that was what was so unique about him, because there are so few people in the film business who function that way. And that had a lot to do with his being a New Yorker. Every single waking moment was not spent concerned with the movies we're working on, or the movies we will work on, or the movies we're trying to get to work on. Alan just took the experience of making a film and put it in the context of living his life. And he did it for all of us [who worked with him]. And thus, we all did it. The personality and the qualities embodied by a director on a movie permeate the entire experience for everybody. And because he was smart, intellectual, rooted in the accomplishments of the past, a student of the films of everyone who had gone before him, it made every experience that he was part of a good one. Some more difficult than others, some more successful, obviously—but they were always challenging, terrific, stimulating.

A few of Pakula's collaborators mixed some criticisms of him in with their praise. Gordon Willis, who served as cinematographer for nine films directed by Pakula, and whose feistiness is legendary, seemed to admire Pakula and to be critical of him in about equal measure. "We had a really good relationship," he said. "We had a lot of respect for each other. He was one of the most intelligent people I ever worked with. But he had a way of having these attacks of self-righteous indignation, he'd feel put upon at times—not by me, although I would do it every now and then—but [there were times when] if he didn't get his way, he'd be kind of like a little boy."

Willis was also occasionally frustrated by the director's inability to match his level of expertise as a cinematographer. "One of his problems, and he's not the only one," Willis said, "he was not able to transpose what he was looking at when we were shooting it, on to a screen image. He'd be shooting certain actors in a certain way, and then when he'd see it on the screen later, in dailies," he would be dissatisfied with the results.

William Goldman's complaint that Pakula was unable to make up his mind ("Don't deprive me of any riches") resonated with Willis. He called the director "very indecisive. He would have problems with, 'Well, we could shoot it *this* way, we could shoot it *that* way.' He always wanted to know, 'What are my options here?' Well, if you're going to define an idea you don't want too many options. Sometimes if you permitted him to have that many options while we were shooting, he forgot what he was doing. You have so many options that you lose the basis of an idea. He really didn't want to put both feet down and say, 'This is it.' Mostly he wanted to think a lot." In general, Willis said, "I'm kind of a carnivore when I'm getting things done. I want to get it done, and anything that gets in the way gets pushed aside until I get it done. He had a tendency to sort of think too much at times. So every now and then we'd have this push and pull—mostly me pushing— to get it done."

Chris Murray remembered his irritation with Pakula's inability to reach a decision when Murray was fourteen years old. He, his sister Patty, and Pakula were all traveling in England in a rented car. "You know, he wasn't the most confident driver in the world," Chris said, "and put him on the wrong side of the road with his stepchildren in the back, it's not the easiest circumstance. But we're looking for a little parking structure and he just couldn't decide whether or not to go down this one street, and the traffic is backing up behind him and honking, and I yelled, 'Do *something*, for God's sake!' Sometimes it got annoying."

Anna Boorstin, Pakula's stepdaughter, felt that "indecisive is probably the wrong word. It was also one of his best qualities, because he listened to all sides of a story. He was very open." An anecdote she told may be interpreted as revealing

Pakula's indecision, or, perhaps, his wish to function as a director even in his private life. She recalled that "when we [the family] went to restaurants he would have to arrange us. We couldn't all just sit down, and if we did just sit down he would move us around afterwards."

Pakula himself would not have contested the notion that he was unwilling to reach decisions too quickly, especially in the realm of film direction. He said, "I can see twenty-five different points of view and vacillate among them, and have another fifteen ideas in mind. I can change my mind, then change it again and again. I want to keep it open and explore until it becomes evident time has definitely run out and the scene has got to be shot. And even then, I'll reshoot it—and again—and again."

Several actors, however, characterized Pakula as thorough rather than indecisive. One is Jane Alexander, who played a small but significant role in *All the President's Men*. She said, "I don't feel that [he was indecisive] at all. I think [suggesting that he was indecisive is] a natural response of people" like writers and cinematographers, who "don't understand fully how a director does his work."

When asked whether he found Pakula indecisive as a director, Hume Cronyn—who appeared in four of Pakula's movies—offered a one-word answer: "No." Jill Clayburgh also felt comfortable with the pace of Pakula's decision-making. "He really wanted actors to be free and discover things," she said. "I guess you could call not being definitive being indecisive. I *don't*."

Dianne Dreyer, Pakula's script supervisor[47] on *The Pelican Brief*, said, "I would never have called Alan indecisive," she said. "What I would say is that he would never make a decision that was uninformed."

Pakula said that the chaotic nature of any film set and the constant demands on the director could be so daunting that it might force any director into indecision. "The worst thing to me about making a film is that there are just so damn many people. The essential lack of privacy. You're like this comet with a huge tail. Every time you move—whoosh!—in back of you, they're all there. And all of them with questions, waiting for you to give an answer. That's why when you get in the editing room it's all so wonderful. Suddenly there is this kind of medieval cell, this monastery, where . . . you can work in peace on your film. It is the most difficult thing, working without that privacy."

Pieter Jan Brugge, who has made films with directors such as Michael Mann

---

[47]Pakula noted the importance of an efficient and personable script supervisor—often the only person attending rehearsals with the director and the actors, making detailed notes about any changes to the script, the blocking of the actors, and any comments made by the director. "It's very important, I find, to get a script supervisor who's compatible with me and the actors," he said. "It's amazing how close you get with her [script supervisors, once commonly referred to as "script girls," are almost invariably women], and if the actors feel uptight in front of her, it can affect the whole work."

and Warren Beatty, and who himself directed *The Clearing* in 2004, found Pakula neither more nor less decisive than other directors. He observed that, as a director, "you don't want to make decisions too quickly, because the creative process is ever-evolving. Alan understood that once you make a decision and lock in a choice, it's very difficult to change it. Obviously, you can change your mind but you pay a price, whatever that may be from a logistical, financial, or creative point of view. But Alan was a man who was particularly interested in exploring, digging under the surface—and once you start, there is no stopping."

Brugge also noted, "Procrastination at times is a very useful element in the creative process, because when you're racing up against a deadline and an important decision has to be made, and you're either going to sink or swim, the adrenaline starts to flow and exciting things start to happen in your mind. There are people who perceive this as being indecisive. I don't. It's an essential part of the creative process."

Don Laventhall, Executive Vice President of Pakula Productions and an associate producer of *The Pelican Brief*, responded to the notion that Pakula was indecisive by explaining, "One thing about Alan is he never liked to be nailed down, because he liked a living process that was never done until the last shot was in the can and the last frame was edited. If you tried to pin him down, that would stop the process for him." Laventhall elaborated:

He always had the whole picture in his head, but he didn't always know how he was going to get from point A to point B to point C. But he knew he had the craft to get there. And he very much relied upon and trusted other people's creative processes to solve a lot of those problems along the way. So the process of making a film, as chaotic as it may have seemed, [encompassed] a vision underneath the surface that was in Alan's head, and as a filmmaker and a producer he knew where he was going. Not everyone knew everything that was in Alan's head. And some personalities can handle that and some can't, and the people who kept working with Alan over and over again are the people who thrived on that process of discovery.

Moreover, Laventhall said, Pakula's process was sometimes a slow one because he "wanted to have a good time when he was making a movie." When asked for an example, he explained, "Well, Alan would like to dress a set. Let's say the townhouse in *The Devil's Own*, where the judge lived. I think they must have dressed half the townhouse because Alan wouldn't say for sure where he was going to shoot a specific scene, or a shot. That could be frustrating to a set decorator or a designer or the studio that's paying for the time, but it represented the creative process for him."

When Laventhall first began working at Pakula Productions, he witnessed the only display of temper he ever saw from Pakula. "I said to him, thinking this was the right thing to say—we were preparing to go to Los Angeles to meet with the studio executives that we were working with—I said, 'Why don't I go out there and see what they're interested in doing?' And he just *exploded*. He said, 'I don't give a *fuck* what the studio executives are interested in. It's what *I'm* interested in that matters.'"

The story might suggest that Pakula was obsessive in wanting exclusive control over his work, but Laventhall did not see it that way. "I don't think it was control," he said. "I think it was the artistic process. . . . It was, 'What is the point of making this movie if it's not something I want to be doing?'"

Moreover, Laventhall found Pakula's outburst liberating. "That was the defining moment for me, working with Alan," he said. "It was fantastic. I realized that I don't have to care what those executives want. All I have to do is pay attention to what Alan wanted. That's what I did after that. And it made my job much easier."

On the basis of the fine performances given by Liza Minnelli in *The Sterile Cuckoo*; Jane Fonda in *Klute* and *Comes a Horseman*; Maggie Smith in *Love and Pain and the Whole Damn Thing*; Jill Clayburgh and Candice Bergen in *Starting Over*; and Meryl Streep in *Sophie's Choice*, Pakula gained a reputation as a "Woman's Director," one who was particularly adept at evoking outstanding performances from women. "I think he was far more successful with women than with men," Michael Small said. "He was interested in the way a woman thinks."

Pakula was asked on one occasion if he had a specific method he used when directing actresses. Women are "all different," he replied. "It seems to me we should have learned in this post-feminist time that not only are women different from men but each is different from the other, and you don't treat them [all] the same way because they're women. . . . There is no way that I sit down with a woman like Meryl Streep or Jane Fonda or Liza [Minnelli] or Candy [Bergen] or Jill Clayburgh or whoever and say, 'All right, this is the part, this is what it's like, and I don't want any questions.' First of all, I may think I know a lot about women. But they're the real article, and if somewhere inside their unconscious they haven't got something to give that character that I don't know about, then I've miscast those people. Each one is different, each one needs different things."

On every project, his understanding of motivations and behavior was apparent to everyone with whom he worked. "If I had to summarize Alan," Robert Redford said, "it's to say that he was psychologically oriented in his work, he was a guy that was deeply aware of psychology, and he liked to play the therapist. When you'd have conversations with him, he would quickly hook into you on the psychological level: 'Oh, that's interesting. You know why you're doing that? That's because your mother did . . .' I can't tell you how much fun it was, because you'd take every character apart from a psychological perspective, and I think that was his main forte. It showed in his work, and it made his work very exciting to be involved with. We used to have such a great time [on *All the President's Men*] psychoanalyzing all the characters."

Working with actors "fascinates me," Pakula said, "because it is an exploration of character—the kind of thing that interested me in being an analyst, except you're not doing it for therapeutic reasons, you're doing it to find out what there is in that person that'll be right for that character."

Another interest of Pakula's—studying the work of other directors—was put to good use in his career. He admitted that he was influenced by a number of foreign and domestic filmmakers. Jean Renoir, he said, "is the one I would say I feel closest to," also mentioning his admiration for the works of Ingmar Bergman and Federico Fellini (particularly *8½*, which he saw many times). Among American directors, he observed that "there is no way to have made a sound film after 1940 without being influenced by [Orson Welles's] *Citizen Kane*." He also praised the films of George Stevens, Alfred Hitchcock, and Billy Wilder, all of whom were active when Pakula worked at Paramount in his twenties. He enjoyed many movies with political themes, particularly *Dr. Strangelove* and *The Manchurian Candidate*, both of which he recommended to his stepson, Bob Boorstin. Most influential were "all those films I saw when I was eleven, twelve, thirteen, fourteen years old," he said, "sitting in a movie theatre on a Saturday afternoon, when the life on the screen seemed more real than my own life outside. I would say my films are a product of my childhood in that I'm attracted to a certain old-fashioned, thirties and forties type of storytelling."

However, he did not emulate any individual when he evolved his own directorial style. "You can suck up certain techniques," he said, but "you can't imitate anybody else." He maintained that the challenge for any director was to look within, to examine one's own attitudes and beliefs, and to discover *unique* ways to transfer those ideas to the screen.

He did admit to employing—but not imitating—some of George Stevens's techniques, such as improvising the blocking and business within a scene just before shooting it, and shooting many takes from varied angles, so that he would have many options when the time came to work with his editor.

But Pakula felt that Stevens had succumbed to pretentiousness in his last films, a fault he was determined to avoid. He said,

> You've got to respect your material, respect it enough to want to sacrifice your reputation to make it work, but you've also got to be able to . . . have fun with it and not look at what you're doing as if this is God's work and now I'm creating

"Art." That's the way to become a pseudo-artist, and pretentious, and I think, tragically, some major Hollywood careers ended with great directors making bigger and bigger films—in quotation marks, more and more "important" films. And talent dried up. I can think of one example in particular. One of my favorite directors is George Stevens. I [recently watched] a film he had done called *The More the Merrier* with Jean Arthur, a delicious little comedy . . . done in the forties, on the housing crisis in Washington, and the next night I went to see the opening of [Stevens's 1965 production of] *The Greatest Story Ever Told,* and at the intermission—this shows how insensitive I can be—I went up to George and said, "My wife and I stayed up until two in the morning watching *The More the Merrier* on television and it's just great." I think if he could have hit me, he would have at that point. But, you know, maybe if the title had been *The Second Greatest Story Ever Told,* he might have had a chance with it.

* * *

Catherine Solt, who worked for Pakula at Pakula Productions and on several of his films, saw a side of him that his friends never witnessed. "He could be a little fussy sometimes, even a little bit spoiled," she said. "There was always a sense that he was a special person. And he liked to be treated that way. You made sure that there was a certain deference. You made sure that things happened the way they were supposed to happen—that you got him into the right restaurant, for instance. He liked that. He liked things a certain way. He was a strange combination of being easygoing and kind of a *prima donna* at the same time, in the sense that if he didn't want to be disturbed, you didn't disturb him. At first it was a little intimidating."

As an example, she said, "I went on movie shoots with him. On location, I set up his camper, I picked out what he ate, I chose the kind of blanket he had. And those were all things that were really important to him. I remember when we were doing *The Devil's Own*, and I was preparing his New York trailer. I did the best I could, but I didn't check with him before I made some decisions. And I remember there were mirrors on the kitchen cabinet—and he hated it. I remember having to spend an entire weekend redoing the whole thing. The colors weren't right, the mirrors had to be taken away. He'd be fussy about things like that. He'd say, 'No way. I just don't like this. This doesn't work, and do something about it.'"

Celia Costas, despite the high regard in which she held Pakula, admitted that "he could be extremely difficult. You didn't want to be at an airport with him when he or the airline lost his luggage. Sometimes he got very grand and very cross." When Pakula was shooting on location, before Catherine Solt took over the task of catering to his whims, it often fell to Costas to "go into a hotel room before Alan arrived and move around the furniture. And if I didn't keep track of all the little details, he would turn to me and say, 'Celia, you know I *hate*' whatever it might be, or 'You know I don't like to sit in front of a mirror.' At restaurants he never liked facing any kind of mirrored image of himself. I knew over the years exactly what table he would like, what seat he would like, what situation he would like, where he would feel comfortable."

Clearly, then, Pakula occasionally showed his temperamental side to his coworkers. Catherine Solt stressed, however, that Pakula was no more demanding or temperamental "than anyone else I've worked for who has that kind of prestige or responsibility. In fact, he was far more warmhearted and more generous and more kind than most."

CHAPTER SEVENTEEN

Where is the Audience?

Dream Lover, Orphans,
See You in the Morning

"Alan had a way of dusting himself off after failures. I'm sure that Alan
knew he would work again, because his dance card was always filled
up—because actors loved to work with him. . . . People were always courting him. In so many ways during his life, he was one of the lucky ones."

—**HARRY CLEIN**, Alan Pakula's publicist

THE CHRONOLOGY OF PAKULA'S MOVIES shows that four years
intervened between *Sophie's Choice* and his next film, *Dream Lover*. That apparent fal-
low period did not come about because *Sophie's Choice* was so immensely fulfilling (or
taxing) for Pakula, however. Rather, the seeming hiatus for a man who had brought
a film to the screen at least every other year since 1962 was only an illusion. Pakula
almost immediately followed *Sophie's Choice* by working on an adaptation of Bette Bao
Lord's novel, *Spring Moon*, which he intended to film in China as soon as he could
find suitable performers. By the time he found them, however, his parents were in
fragile health and in their nineties, and he did not want to be in China in case a
family emergency arose, so *Spring Moon* was temporarily shelved. Later, when the
project again became possible, the brutal suppression of dissidents in Tiananmen
Square occurred, and Bette Bao Lord expressed her preference that *Spring Moon* not
be made, which put an end to the proposed film once and for all.

Dream Lover was filmed in early 1984 and ready for the public by the end of that
year. However, MGM/United Artists, obviously dissatisfied with the result, did
not distribute it until 1986. The delay marked the beginning of a difficult period
during which Pakula's next three films were all commercial failures—"disasters"
might be a more appropriate word.

Dream Lover, with a script written by Jon Boorstin, Hannah's nephew and Pakula's trusted assistant (on *The Parallax View* and *All the President's Men*), attracted so few people to the theatre that it grossed less than $800,000, far less than it cost to make. Of course, no work of art should be judged by its commercial appeal alone; in the case of *Dream Lover*, however, the film proved to be problematical on all fronts: artistically uneven, commercially unsuccessful, and a source of personal anguish.

Pakula and Boaty Boatwright, then MGM's East Coast executive on *Dream Lover*, differed about Pakula's wish to direct the film. She made clear her belief that the film wasn't "worthy of his talents" (Alixe Gordon, the casting director, also "really hated that script") and that his desire to cast Kristy McNichol—when scores of talented actresses "were dying to do it"—was misconceived. Boatwright felt that Pakula enjoyed going "against the grain" in his casting, and believed his impulse sometimes led him astray.

However, Pakula was determined to add Kristy McNichol to the list of actresses whose careers had been given a boost by appearing in Alan J. Pakula films, despite her reputation as a difficult and temperamental performer. Gordon strongly recommended McNichol, and, since she and Pakula "had the same taste in actors," according to Gordon, Pakula was eager to cast her.

Casting was always a matter of paramount importance to Pakula. "If you are working with people you don't have a rapport with—who don't relate to you—you're already in trouble," he said. When casting, he looked "for something in the actor, something hopefully in his unconscious. Because actors can't bring you something that's not inside them, no matter how much they may transform it to be used for a character. Finally, they must use some things from within their own emotional equipment." If Pakula believed that an actor was incapable of offering exciting and unexpected twists on the character he was auditioning for, he wanted no part of him. Kristy McNichol, he felt, was capable of offering something extraordinary.

Nothing in McNichol's previous work as a teenage performer on television offered a hint that she was capable of playing such a demanding role, but Pakula was certain she would do it justice. When Pakula and McNichol met for the first time, he asked her "if [she] was emotionally ready to do a film like *Dream Lover*." She assured him that she was. "I'd been through a lot of things and I'd come out of them," she said, adding, "I felt like I could handle it."

Pakula told McNichol that the movie would be her "showcase," and she was equally pleased to be working with Pakula. "We just clicked," she said, adding that she had been typecast for years in films and on television and that Pakula had offered her a way to free herself from the continual "good girl roles" (as she called them) that she had been playing.

Pakula described the main character as "a young girl who has spent much of her life denying and repressing a great deal and, because of certain things that happen in the story, all that she represses comes back to haunt her." He was intrigued by the fact that the first film he produced, *Fear Strikes Out*, had dealt with a young person oppressed by his father, who needed to break away in order to lead a fulfilling life—and now, nearly thirty years later, *Dream Lover* dealt with the same subject.

He spoke of the film as "another attempt," like *Klute*, "to combine melodrama with character study." It was also another opportunity to work on a project that intermingled dreams and reality, precisely the sort of story he enjoyed telling. However, the script needed a great deal of work, and Pakula tried to help Boorstin shape it before filming began.

Dream Lover portrays Kathy Gardner, whose waking life is professionally successful and romantically promising, but whose dream life is filled with terror. She suffers from recurring nightmares so frightening that they threaten to obliterate her waking life. Kathy's father, Ben (played by Paul Shenar), is an emotionally abusive father who is unwilling to allow his daughter the freedom to live her own life. The film hints at a sexual relationship between Ben and Kathy, but the suggestions are evidently only illusions. At one point, for example, Ben and Kathy appear to be in bed together, but it then becomes apparent that Ben is under the covers and Kathy is seated on top of the bedspread. When, in an early scene, before the audience knows who the characters are, Kathy is seated next to her father in a box at the opera and he puts his hand over hers, one assumes that Ben is Kathy's husband. Later, Ben and Kathy kiss one another on the lips.

The filmmakers obliquely suggest a sexual relationship at every turn, only to expose it as an apparent illusion. Still, an Electra complex, in which the daughter unknowingly returns the feelings of her father, who covets her sexually, is clearly implied. Kathy is also conflicted by the relationship she had with her now-dead mother, who—at least in Kathy's dreams—is cold and remote. The relationship with her parents prevents Kathy from attaining a healthy maturity.

In the course of the movie, Kathy becomes the victim of an attempted assault in the kitchen of her apartment. She defends herself by blinding the intruder with a pot of boiling milk, grabbing a knife and stabbing him. Afterwards, she dreams repeatedly about the incident, reliving the terror she experienced when the event occurred. This nightmare becomes interwoven with her dream of childhood, in which she walks—terrified—down a hall into a bedroom, the window of which leads to a picnic occurring in the nineteenth century—except that her father and others she knows are among the picnickers. In her dream state, Kathy is able to fly through the window and join the picnic.

Until this point, the film is compelling and well-achieved. It begins to descend into conventional melodrama, however, when Kathy, desperate for help, goes to a sleep clinic, where a research assistant, Michael Hansen (played by Ben Masters), attempts to help her through the use of medical experiments. The dialogue, too, descends into cliché. When Kathy volunteers to take an injection, for example, Michael tells her, "This is totally new ground. We have no idea what the risks are. The experiment is not approved for human beings."

On a flight to London, Kathy stabs her boyfriend Kevin with a plastic knife. But is she awake or is this a dream? Does she know it's Kevin that she's stabbing, or is she dreaming of the intruder? Or of Michael? Or of her father? At this point, "dreams" and "reality" have become utterly confused, both for Kathy and for the viewer—an effect the filmmakers were undoubtedly attempting to create.

In Ben's London hotel room, the following events occur (or do not occur, for reality has become so tenuous that it is impossible to separate it from illusion): the hotel becomes a medieval castle; Ben and the intruder morph into one; Kathy stabs Ben in the shoulder; Kathy jumps from the high balcony of Ben's apartment; Michael does or does not catch her. The final shot is a close-up of Kathy, who is either alive, dead, sane, insane, dreaming, awake, free of her nightmares, trapped within a nightmare—the alternate realities are so plentiful that one has no idea what has happened, is happening, or will happen. The suggestion is that "reality" has been obliterated altogether. Viewers can select which ending they prefer—an arresting idea, but, ultimately, an unsatisfying one, for the ending goes beyond ambiguity to complete obscurity.

In its attempt to create a psychoanalytical world so complete that it virtually annihilates reality, the film is only occasionally successful. The story is believable in the movie's first half, but often ludicrous thereafter. The performers are generally good, but McNichol often seems passive to the point of immobility. Some scenes are penetrating, but they stand side-by-side with others that are utterly unconvincing.

For the second time, Pakula collaborated with cinematographer Sven Nykvist. They had worked together on *Starting Over*, but that comedy was an unusual departure for Nykvist, who is best known for his cinematography for the introspective, philosophical, intensely dramatic films of Ingmar Bergman. In many respects, *Dream Lover* seems to be more of a Nykvist film than a Pakula film, for it utilizes so many of the characteristics of Bergman's pictures: close-ups and extreme close-ups, held for long periods of time, highly restricted camera movement, a dark palette. One wonders if Pakula wanted Nykvist to photograph *Dream Lover* because he thought of it as a Bergmanesque film, or if Nykvist, employing his customary style, turned the film into a picture suggestive of Bergman's influence.

The visual style is not the only aspect of the film that resembles Bergman's techniques. A loudly ticking clock, the ambiguous relationships between parents and children, a surreal world, the confusion of dreams and reality, the inability of the leading character to find fulfillment—these are all themes familiar from such Bergman masterpieces as *Wild Strawberries*, *Cries and Whispers*, *Through a Glass Darkly*, and others. All too often, *Dream Lover* seems like a pale imitation of a Bergman film.

After working with Kristy McNichol, Pakula said, "I think she's one of the most gifted actresses I've ever worked with. [She was] absolutely remarkable in it. . . . She had a sense of that character." One can accept Pakula's praise without embracing his enthusiasm, however, for McNichol, despite her understanding of the role, was not fully able to communicate the character's complexity to the viewer.

Most of the film was shot in England, although several weeks of filming took place in New York. As he had so often in the past, Michael Small composed the musical score for a Pakula film. Since Kathy played the flute, Small wrote music for her as well as background music. Small admitted that the film was "kind of a disaster in some ways, but," he said, "at least it was trying for something very, very unusual."

In an interview in the 1990s, Pakula said, "There are a few visual sequences in that film that I find some of my most interesting work." He immediately went on to confess, "Other things about the film did not work, unfortunately." Evidently, that realization was not present in 1984, however, for, when Pakula screened the film for some friends and co-workers before its release, his publicist and long-time friend, Harry Clein, told him that the film "wasn't up to the level of [his] other work." Others, said Clein, were telling the director "that this was some of his best work," and Pakula was so angered by Clein's response that they had a falling out.[48] As a result, they did not work together again for several years, although, when they did, according to Clein, "our friendship was actually deeper" than before.

One of the few reviews of *Dream Lover* appeared in the *Los Angeles Times*. Patrick Goldstein's notice was overwhelmingly negative. He began, "*Dream Lover* is the worst kind of sleeper, a sloggy zonker that has all the energy of a sleepy St. Bernard and the clarity of your Aunt Emma after she's popped a few Valium." No element of the film relieved his boredom. Calling the character of Kathy "a listless door-mat," Goldstein said, "the filmmakers have her wander around in such a passive, shell-shocked fog that it's almost impossible to develop any real interest in her struggle to retain her sanity." The critic seemed puzzled in his assessment of

---

[48]*Pakula's response would not have surprised Lauren Bacall, a friend who felt that the director "was very protective about his own work, and if you questioned that, he would almost physically blanch. He didn't want to hear from anybody else [about his films] unless it was good news. I always got along wonderfully with him and was very fond of him," she was quick to add, "but I noticed the edge that he had."*

Pakula's work: "Even crack director Alan Pakula . . . who's normally at his best with vivid thrillers, can't add much electricity to this dreary psycho-thriller."

The film ran briefly in Los Angeles, played for a week in Boston and San Francisco, then was withdrawn from American theatres. It did win recognition, however, from the Avoriaz Film Festival in France, which awarded *Dream Lover* its Grand Prize.

Jon Boorstin, the movie's screenwriter, wrote an article for the *New York Times* about his despair over the film's critical failure and its inability to attract audiences. The article is one of the most remarkable examples of self-abasement ever written, as Boorstin excoriates his wife, "career woman that she is, [who] felt my success was her future," speaks of his despair "In my blackest moods, when I think of giving up, I realize I can't afford to. . . . [L]ike other dispossessed workers, I feel too old and too set in my ways to start over," and blames himself for "hiding behind my artistic pretensions." Particularly hurtful to Pakula was Boorstin's statement that Alan (whom he only refers to as "the director") was indifferent to the movie's fate. "The director," he wrote, "with some 20 films under his belt, went right on to another project. Our movie was a blip on his career." Boorstin went on to say that he and "the director . . . avoided each other for a year after the movie didn't open [in wide release]."

The defeatist tone of the article must have depressed Pakula, who was himself, in the words of his stepdaughter Anna, "nervous about his career" because of the failure of *Dream Lover*, but the allegation that he blithely went on to other projects without a second thought for Jon Boorstin infuriated him. He had directed Boorstin's screenplay when no one else in the film industry was willing to do so, and the result was Boorstin's public attack. He felt deeply betrayed and angry—all the more so because Boorstin's article appeared just as Pakula's next film, *Orphans*, was about to be released. This was the worst possible time for an article to appear in a prominent newspaper alleging that the director had behaved cavalierly to his nephew.

Pakula was extremely upset both by Boorstin's charges, which he considered unfair, and by the timing of the article. Neither ever worked with the other again, and, as a family member said years later, "I think they each remained prickly and distrustful of each other, but Alan was a complete gentleman about dealing with Jon, no matter how upset he may have been."

Harry Clein suggested that there was a kernel of truth in Boorstin's attitude, that Pakula's response to the film's failure undoubtedly was not as acute as his nephew's. "Alan had a way of dusting himself off after failures," Clein said. "I'm sure that Alan knew he would work again, because his dance card was always filled up—because actors loved to work with him." Indeed, Kristy McNichol said, "I'd love to work with Alan again. I'm so spoiled now. I don't want to work with anyone but the Alans of the world." But McNichol's comments were offered shortly before the film was released. They seem ironic in the light of the disastrous critical and commercial responses to *Dream Lover*.

* * *

Pakula referred to his next film, *Orphans*, as his "plovie"—half-play, half-movie. Eleven years before he began work on *Orphans*, he described the theme of a film he hoped to undertake one day: "a child's fear of darkness, night fears, fears in some way of being punished, that the unknown is threatening, that there is something out there that you can't see that could destroy you. Not a realistic fear of the unknown, but one that comes out of internal fears for oneself—one's personal anxieties being directed onto something outside of oneself." The theme would find expression in *Orphans*.

Orphans had begun as a play by Lyle Kessler about two feckless brothers living in a ramshackle, rundown, filthy house in north Philadelphia, the paint peeling off the walls, the furniture in disrepair, empty cans of tuna fish scattered everywhere. Phillip, a man in his early twenties who behaves as if he is nine years old, apparently both illiterate and retarded, dresses sloppily, his hair long and shaggy, his shoes perpetually unlaced (because he never learned how to tie them). Treat, his older brother, a small-time thief who frightens and intimidates Phillip, does not allow his brother to leave the house, claiming that the air would kill him. Phillip, then, is a virtual prisoner.

Treat brings Harold, who claims to be a businessman from Chicago, but is clearly a mobster, to the decrepit house, in order to rob him of his briefcase. Harold, recalling the movies of the 1930s, refers to Treat as a "dead-end kid," but Treat, not understanding the reference, continually and emphatically denies that he is a dead-end kid. Treat, having decided to hold his visitor for ransom, ties the drunken Harold to a chair. The next morning, however, Harold frees himself and roams the house, making himself at ease. Treat anxiously tells Phillip, "This guy's takin' over!" Although Treat brandishes a knife, Harold, blasé and unaffected, relaxes on the sofa with a cup of coffee. When Harold offers Treat $1,000 per week to be his bodyguard "and all-around man," the agitated Treat says, confusedly, "*I* kidnapped *you*. Who's in control here?" Harold pulls a gun on Treat, but, even without the gun, it's abundantly clear that he has taken over.

After the passage of an unspecified amount of time, Harold has taken on the role of the boys' father and, through the use of parables and object lessons, has transformed their lives. The transformation is evident in their appearance. Phillip, his hair cut neatly, wears a handsome sweater, Treat a smart, tailored suit.

Harold cheerfully supervises Phillip in painting the house and putting it in good repair. In a short time, the house is a model of cleanliness and stylishness. Just as Harold imposes order on his physical surroundings, he does the same with Phillip, transforming his life. Harold builds Phillip's confidence, encourages him to go outside the house, even provides him with a map of the area should he get lost. Afraid of what might he might encounter, but encouraged by Harold's support, Phillip overcomes his fears and goes outside, liberated from the role he has always assumed as Treat's simple-minded foil.

Resentful of Harold's assumption of power within the household and his bonding with Phillip, Treat can barely contain his rage and frustration. Recognizing that he has lost all control over Phillip, Treat rips up the map and tries to strangle him, nearly killing him. "I guess you don't need me anymore, huh, Phillip?" Treat says, pathetically. "I guess you can get along without me." Harold, returning from downtown Philadelphia, enters, a gaping wound in his stomach, presumably shot by a mobster. As he is dying, he drops on to the couch and tells the distraught Phillip not to worry: "You'll never be lost again," he says. Treat collapses, both physically and emotionally. He crawls over to the lifeless Harold, then, feeling a terrible pain, screams and cries out, "No, no. Don't leave me, Harold." Phillip tries to comfort him, but Treat, inconsolable, can only confess through his tears, "I *am* a dead-end kid, Harold! I *am* a fucking dead-end kid."

Harold's freeing Phillip from his confinement, and, by becoming his surrogate father, freeing him from his orphan state, are obvious themes of the film. Another is Treat's journey from violence and consciencelessness to emotional vulnerability. Some aspects of the plot and the characters, on the other hand, are never clearly defined: who Harold is, precisely what he does, precisely what he hires Treat to do, who shot him before the final scene. Thus the play/film is both clear and obscure, but the obscurity of the plot is not a deterrent to the audience's interest in and empathetic response to the characters. It is, in fact, one of the "plovie's" strongest and most intriguing characteristics.

Orphans is a fascinating piece, which resonates on several levels: symbolic, realistic, psychological, and theological.[49] Its power is no less deeply felt on the screen than it was on the stage.

Pakula said that, in the past, he had "always avoided [using] plays [as source material for films] because they were so claustrophobic"—generally confined to

---

[49]*Donald L. Carveth offers an intriguing psychological and theological analysis of the play in an article in* PsyArt. *He examines* Orphans *from Freudian and Lacanian perspectives, among others. The ending of the play, in Carveth's interpretation, shows Harold as a crucified figure, "but, witnessing and in a sense identifying with this crucifixion, Treat himself undergoes the painful but liberating disintegration of his false self and the tentative emergence of his true self—a death and resurrection through which he is finally able to recognize and acknowledge his identity as one of the community of 'dead end kids.'"*

one or two sets—"and then I took one of the most claustrophobic plays I'd ever seen to make a film." Indeed, claustrophobia is a vital element in the piece. The play derives its meaning from Phillip's confinement to the house and—near the end—his release.

Pakula saw the play in its off-Broadway production, and "was touched and amused by it"; but, as he watched, he believed it had no potential as a film. "Then," he said, "when the boy went outside in the play, the first time he breathes fresh air and sees the sky since he was a small child, I said to myself, 'There's a movie!'" He felt that, if he could maintain the audience's interest until Phillip's liberation, showing "the release of that young boy, that child-man, [a film] could be extraordinary. But for that to work, he's going to have to be locked in that house all the time."

Beyond Phillip's liberation (from his brother's dominance as well as from the house), other themes are present in the play. "First of all," Pakula said, "it is a story about parenting, it is a classic wild-child myth, and it is a story of children who've never had a father and who find a father in this outrageous way. . . . And there's a man [Harold] whose life is coming to an end and in parenting these two boys he has a chance for a last redemption." Pakula said that he only realized after shooting had begun why he was so attracted to the material. Perhaps, he thought, it was because he had five stepchildren but no children of his own that Kessler's play was particularly moving to him.

The director also found other elements appealing. He was fascinated by Harold, who, on one hand, is "the gangster on the lam," but is also the source of Phillip's liberation and a surrogate father to both boys. He also found Treat, "who's turned all of his emotion into aggression because he's terrified to feel because he's been so deeply hurt," a fascinating character.

Pakula also felt that Lyle Kessler's play did not end as pathetically as it might have seemed. Treat's cry of rage at the end of the film, Pakula believed, represented a breakthrough into a different, more humane sort of life. "I think there may be a beginning for him," Pakula said, "and in that way I don't see the ending as tragic."

Deeply moved by the play, Pakula got in touch with Lyle Kessler and conveyed his enthusiasm for the play and his passion for filming it. He would, he said, shelve his other projects and turn his attention immediately to *Orphans*. Furthermore, he made it clear that he wanted Kessler to write the screenplay. Kessler had been contacted by other producers and directors, but Pakula's passion for the play and his "deeply respectful" attitude persuaded Kessler that Pakula was the appropriate director for the film.

Turning the play into a film offered many problems, the first of which was whether or not to maintain the claustrophobia of the single set. Pakula remembered hearing Alfred Hitchcock say that the difficulty with films based on plays is that the director feels the need to "open them up"—and, as a result, "they let the air in and all the tension out." Pakula decided to keep the tension in. The vast majority of the action occurs inside the house, but Lyle Kessler wrote a prologue that would be played in a public park, to "give a sense of the world outside, so that when you got inside that house you knew what it meant to be locked in." In that outdoor scene, Treat robs a stranger on a park bench of his money, turning violent when he discovers that the man has abandoned his family (as Treat and Phillip, the orphans of the title, have been abandoned by their father).

The film makes no effort to conceal the fact that it began life as a play, for it retains the basic structure: two acts in several scenes, confined primarily within a single set on the edge of a northeastern city.

Pakula saw *Orphans* on stage in London[50] as well as New York. He was so taken with the performances he saw Kevin Anderson (as Phillip) and Albert Finney (as Harold) give in London that he cast them in the movie.

The role of Phillip, Pakula said, "demands a very particular kind of talent. Phillip is a boy who is semi-civilized, totally unschooled, but who has amazing powers of observation" and is able to imitate everyone he sees, including game show announcers on television. "The character lives most of his life in his own fantasy world because the only person he sees is his brother, and he's confined to this house. I felt that the part required enormous invention and something that had to come from inside. Kevin had that on the stage, and," he said, after the film was completed, "I think he has it on the screen."

Taking into account not only the film but the three stage productions of *Orphans* in which he appeared, Kevin Anderson spent two years playing Phillip. His long acquaintance with the character meant that "if Alan asked me to do a scene a specific way, I had probably done it that way for at least a week somewhere. I had so many options, because night to night things always changed in the theatre. It was exciting to be able to lay out all my ideas on the table and see what Alan liked and didn't like."

Pakula was concerned that Anderson might not be able to divorce himself from the performance he had given onstage, that "he would be so locked into the role that he might not have the freshness the film needed." Anderson "knew where all the laughs were," Pakula said, "which is fine up to a point, but the camera recognizes this and sees it for dishonesty. . . . And so, with Kevin, it was a question of trying to keep it fresh and to start as if it was happening for the first time for him."

Indeed, Anderson said that he had "difficulty attaining the same hyped-up

[50] *First performed at the Steppenwolf Theatre in Chicago, the play next played off-Broadway in New York, then was produced in London.*

feeling I had during the play. Particularly in [the off-Broadway production in] New York, where the air-conditioning wasn't always working, I was used to being soaking wet for most of the scenes from doing all that physical stuff and dancing around on stage. Whenever I stopped, my heart was always beating fast. When I did the film, I found not having that [perspiration] affected my performance. That high had always been there for me on the stage, I never had to think about it. So on the movie set, I had to work up a real sweat before some major scenes."

In the end, Pakula felt that Anderson had found the way to play Phillip appropriately for the camera. "He just started from scratch; it became a new adventure for him," Pakula said.

Albert Finney saw *Orphans* on stage in New York and brought it to London, where he played Harold. Pakula saw Finney's performance, and, although he auditioned many major American actors for the role, he could not get Finney's performance out of his mind. The role "needed an outsize quality," Pakula said, and, "Like many English actors, [Finney] can play something that is beyond life size."

Pakula went outside the cast of the stage production to find an actor to play Treat. When he sent the script to Matthew Modine, who had just completed filming Stanley Kubrick's *Full Metal Jacket*, the actor thought he was being considered for the role of Phillip. Modine's head was shaved (for his role in *Full Metal Jacket*) and, with his considerable height, "looked intimidating," Pakula said—one of the qualities he was looking for in the actor who would play Treat. Pakula was surprised by Modine's humor. During their conversation, "he made me laugh a lot," the director said. "I saw colors that were not [evident] in the roles he'd done."

Pakula interviewed other actors, but, he said, he "kept being haunted by Matthew. He was a risky choice. I don't think I've ever cast anyone before and had less idea of what he was going to do with the role," but his instinct told him that Modine had the capacity to bring Treat to vivid life on the screen.

Early rehearsals were disconcerting, for Modine seemed unable to find his way into the role. "None of the jokes were working," the actor said. "We started to wonder if it was all a mistake." Wonder turned to concern as the various approaches Modine tried brought him no closer to the character. Two devices the director employed eventually solved the problem. The first capitalized on the fact that Anderson had played in *Orphans* in New York and in Chicago, while Finney joined him on stage in London. For Modine, however, the encounter with the text did not occur until he began rehearsing for the film. "Kevin and Albert were very good friends in London and continued their friendship," Modine said. "They had a really good repertoire of shtick they would do, which alienated me because I wasn't in on the joke." Modine's resentment of his fellow actors precisely reflected his situation in the play, when Harold bonds with Phillip. "Treat has the same

alienation," Modine said. "It was in Alan's interest to encourage that kind of separation, and it worked. I'd never been subjected to that kind of psychological
preparation in acting before."

After Finney and Anderson helped Modine feel the sense of alienation Pakula
wanted, Finney helped to create the world of the film by adopting a paternal role
with both of the younger actors. "He worked with them," Pakula said, "he hung out
with them, he was paternal with them, he was generous, he was loving—and he created that relationship with them. Actors can help each other sometimes more than
a director can, and if they can build the relationships between them—and you [as a
director] can encourage that—you're going to get those relationships in the film."

Still, Modine felt uncomfortable playing Treat. Then Pakula hired a speech
teacher to work with the actor, attempting to formulate what Modine called a
"white trash, urban guerilla" accent. "Matthew," Pakula told Modine, "if you get
the speech you will get the character, because that speech comes out of an attitude,
it comes out of a macho thing that says, 'I am a man and I am tough,' [even
though] inside you are scared shitless and you don't know who you are. So if you
can find the speech you're going to find the part." When, after a period of study,
Modine mastered the accent, "suddenly," he said, "everything fell into place."

Pakula's greatest concern was that Modine would create the impression of a
middle-class character, whereas "this is a street boy. Without the toughness," the
character—and the movie—would not have worked, Pakula said.

Treat's toughness was mixed with fear of losing control. When, early in the
film, Treat comes home and is unable to find Phillip, "you see the fear on
[Modine's] face," Pakula said. "Tough as he is," the relationship with his brother
is the only one he "has in life to hold on to."

Lyle Kessler was pleased with Pakula's direction and with the performances of
Modine, Finney, and Anderson. However, he felt that Pakula distorted Treat's
character in that Kessler intended Treat to be a totally violent man "who had no
impulse control." Only at the end, when Treat breaks down, should the audience
become aware of his vulnerability, Kessler felt. But Pakula recalled his days at
Warner Bros., when he worked on Bugs Bunny cartoons. He explained to Kessler
that Bugs was never randomly violent; although Bugs poked his finger in someone's eye or hit someone over the head with a stick, the writers took pains to portray the victim as someone who deserved to be poked or hit.

In the film of *Orphans*, this idea can be seen in the first scene, when Treat does
not turn violent until he learns that the man on the bench has abandoned his family. "But," Kessler said, "in essence, it was the opposite of the character of Treat
in my play. Treat was totally violent. He didn't care. He didn't assess who he was
robbing or who he was cutting. Not until the end of the play do you discover where

all that rage was coming from. To me it was important to go as far as you can with that violence, so that by the end of the movie it would have had the power that I think the stage production had." But this was Kessler's only fundamental criticism of the direction. Otherwise, he regarded Pakula as a brilliant director who "had great, great character and was wonderful and respectful to me. He embraced my participation. I appreciate what he did with the film."

Pakula showed special consideration in his dealings with Kessler. As one example, he wanted to change the location of the play from north Philadelphia to New Jersey. Kessler said, "He invited me to his apartment. He was worried that I was going to get very upset about that and he wanted to be alone with me when he told me about it." Kessler wasn't the least bit upset ("That wasn't a crucial issue," he said), but he was deeply impressed that Pakula should value his opinion so highly. "You know, another director wouldn't give a damn what the writer thought," Kessler said; "he would just change it and do whatever he wanted."

More substantive was the occasion on which Pakula sent Kessler a videocassette with the first edit of the film, and asked Kessler to offer his opinion. "I looked at it," Kessler said,

> and there were about eight or nine pieces there where I thought the editing wasn't working, and I could see, from a fresh point of view, what they could do to fix that. So I came in [to Pakula's office] and we all sat down. Alan was there with the co-producer and the editor and some other people, and he asked my opinion. I began to give him my reactions, and the atmosphere in the room was like I had just told God he didn't know what he was doing. It was almost ludicrous in the way all these people jumped in and started to cut me off.
>
> But Alan said to them, 'Wait a minute, wait a minute, why can't he say what he wants to say?" So he stopped them cold in their tracks. And, in fact, he put all my suggestions in the movie. Now, with some directors maybe you're not allowed to make suggestions or it's considered irreverent to criticize the editing, but Alan was wonderful that way. His ego was not involved. That was the great strength of the character of the man.

In the film, the isolated house in which the action take place was an existing structure, one of the last houses left standing in the massive redevelopment effort in Rockaway Beach, Queens (although the film's locale was Newark, New Jersey). The interior was built in the Kaufman-Astoria Studios in New York. Thus, all rehearsals could be held within the set. As he had done with Kevin Kline and Peter MacNicol on *Sophie's Choice*, Pakula suggested that Anderson spend a night on the set, since the "house is Phillip's whole world" and "there's no way that Kevin could [know every room of the house intimately] just by sauntering on the set the first day of shooting." Anderson stayed on the set not for a single night but for more than a week. "One morning," Pakula said, "I told him, 'We're going to start charging you rent.'"

Anderson's familiarity with his surroundings did more than make him comfortable as an actor; it dictated the way a scene was staged. On one occasion, when Treat can't find his brother in the house, Pakula said, he instructed Anderson to hide somewhere on the set. "Well," Pakula continued, "Matthew looked all over—he tore things apart, he threw things around—and no Kevin. . . . So Matthew continued looking and finally saw Kevin under the springs of a mattress. And that's how that scene got staged."

Given the abstract and elliptical nature of *Orphans*, Pakula took care not to burden the actors with too much information, feeling that it would simply be too much to absorb. "I don't necessarily tell them the conception of the visual style of the film," for example. "It's important that the cinematographer knows it. It's important that your editor knows it, and your art director, and all those other people. But what actors have to know has to do specifically with their characters and their interaction with other characters. Those are the things they can act, whereas abstract concepts would only confuse them. If you say, 'I'm reaching for kind of an absurd romantic quality,' the actor says, 'I'm supposed to play an absurd romantic? How am I supposed to do that? I'm supposed to play American baroque? What the hell is that?' Well," Pakula said, "that helps *me*. It may help the art director," but, although the director "must communicate [his basic] concept" to the actors, "you communicate [only enough information] about a film that will help the people you're working with."

One of the memorable moments in *Orphans* occurs when Harold puts his arms about one or both of the boys and says, "Let me give you some encouragement." Pakula adopted the line for himself. For years afterwards, whenever he saw a member of his cast or crew looking downcast, he would put his arm around him or her and say, with Albert Finney's inflection, "Let me give you some encouragement."

The film was made with remarkable swiftness: nine weeks, including the three-week rehearsal period. Shooting was completed in November 1986. For Modine, the entire process "was like going into this pressure cooker," he said, "with steam and the whistle going."

Pakula and his cinematographer, Donald McAlpine, and the production designer, George Jenkins, back-lit the windows of the house, so that when Phillip looked outside, the audience could see nothing—thus emphasizing Phillip's hermetically sealed world. "Some people criticized that," Lyle Kessler said, whereas "other people liked it."

Worried about the possibility that *Orphans* might appear to be sentimental, Pakula asked Michael Small to use music sparingly, to allow silence to serve as the background for most scenes—as it had so effectively in *All the President's Men*.

Orphans is a successful film on almost every level. Although it is clearly rooted in a play with a single set—a valid metaphor for a drama about the inability to break free from confinement—and only three characters, Pakula's and Kessler's addition of a few brief scenes are sufficient to infuse the film with cinematic vitality. The result is a movie that—at least until the final scene—does not feel stage-bound. As to the performances, Anderson's frenetic, highly physical, near-acrobatic performance is impressive, and Finney, who has often created caricatures in his films, delineates a believable human being in *Orphans*. Moreover, Finney's portrayal infuses Harold with a mythic dimension, and the character would not succeed without it, for Harold must be seen on both a symbolic and realistic level. Modine is equally successful as the conflicted, superficially confident but deeply insecure Treat. The action portrayed in the film is fascinating, partly because of Kessler's technique of withholding certain facts from the audience, which adds to the film's mystery.

Like the reviews for *Sophie's Choice*, the notices for *Orphans* were either enthusiastic or scathing. When the film was released in September 1987, Vincent Canby of the *New York Times* said, "The unusual accomplishment of Mr. Pakula and Mr. Kessler . . . is that they've actually enriched the possibilities of the original comedy-drama, [and the picture is] a very successful example of the stage-to-film transfer of a play that seemed to be the sort that demanded its original, claustrophobic setting. . . . Mr. Pakula's achievement is in making a film that's simultaneously theatrical *and* cinematic. *Orphans* honors both worlds."

The anonymous reviewer for *TV Guide's Movie Guide* agreed. *Orphans* marked the return of Pakula to "top form," the critic said, adding that "It's not often that a play can survive the transition from stage to screen without suffering some loss. *Orphans*, however, [succeeds in doing so]. . . . Part fairy tale and part heightened reality, *Orphans* manages to strike an emotional chord with almost everyone who sees it."

Expressing the opposing point of view was Roger Ebert in the *Chicago Sun-Times*. Plays are intended to be performed on the stage, he contended, whereas "movies work best when they break out of the box, when they spring free from the physical constraints of space and time." Ebert's negative review was "not intended as a criticism of the filmmakers," he wrote, "but simply . . . an observation about the nature of the material."

Two reviews appeared in the *Washington Post*, and both were clearly disdainful of *Orphans*. Desson Howe, who called Kessler's play "nothing but amateurish gallery-playing" and the film "much ado about nothing," apparently missed the parable-like, mythic dimensions of *Orphans*, while Rita Kempley said that Modine and Anderson "scramble and grapple like demented gerbils in performances that may have worked for the [theatre] playing to the balcony but that overwhelm on screen." Similarly, she characterized Pakula's direction as "clearly overwrought."

Filmgoers had little opportunity to decide for themselves, for Lorimar released the film only to twenty-five theatres. Even in those limited venues, few people attended, partially because of a misleading advertising campaign, for which Pakula accepted some blame. He approved a poster showing Harold bound and gagged in a chair with Treat and Phillip standing mysteriously over him. The poster suggested that the film would be "a farce," Pakula admitted, "and obviously it's not a farce, and I think it was misleading and I don't think it helped." He could not say whether a more accurate pictorial image would have saved the film commercially, "but at least we would have gone down honestly. That's always the best way to go down."

Regardless of the cause, the film certainly went down: it took in only $400,000 at the box office, half of that in the United States. Even though *Orphans* was a low-budget film, it did not begin to recover the costs Lorimar Productions had provided. Still, Pakula could draw solace from the quality of the film. The screenplay, the performances, and the direction all mark it as one of Pakula's best efforts.

If Pakula was upset by the film's failure to attract audiences, he spent little time dwelling on it. He and Hannah spent two or three weeks in Italy, where, as he said, "we *drowned* in art." It was the first time they traveled to a foreign country purely for pleasure. On his return, he concluded that the break had been good for him and could be successfully applied to other filmmakers. "You have to keep a life for yourself outside of film," he said. "We should all be required to take a year off and do something else."

* * *

Regardless of the mixed reviews so many of Pakula's films received, most of them proved popular with audiences and made money for their backers. Now, however, after consecutive box-office failures, one might have thought that the director would have a difficult time arranging the financing for his next film. But the next film he had in mind was, as Celia Costas said, "something he wanted to do, and he was going to keep chipping away at it until he figured out the financing. He had a very good relationship with Lorimar. They knew he was a very fiscally minded director, never profligate in any way." In addition, "a film by Alan J. Pakula" was still a credit valued by motion picture studios, so Lorimar provided the funding for *See You in the Morning* in 1987.[51]

The film is a thinly disguised account of Pakula's divorce from Hope Lange and subsequent marriage to Hannah Boorstin. Although he insisted that the events in his life only offered the outline of the film, which was basically fictional, not intended as "true confessions," he admitted, "on the other hand, I couldn't have written it at all if I hadn't had comparable experiences."

Pakula disregarded the advice of Boaty Boatwright, by this time his agent, not to make the film. He was determined to make a picture based on his own life that was so personal, she felt, it was a risky choice, at best, to appeal to a wide public. "I guess because I knew about his past [that] I felt it was opening too much of his life, his pain," she said. But Pakula had long harbored a desire to turn the events of his life into a movie, combining them with fictional incidents, but he told no one but his wife Hannah that he was working on a screenplay about their courtship and marriage. "If I do this film," he told her, "everybody's going to think it's us. They're all going to think they're looking inside our bedroom." Hannah responded, "If you worry about that, you're not going to write anything." Armed with his wife's approval, he completed the screenplay.

See You in the Morning was an attempt, among other things, for Pakula to show how he had both resolved and further complicated the problems in his own life by marrying Hannah and becoming stepfather to her three children. Although largely biographical, it would fictionalize certain elements of their relationship and, in that way, become universal. Pakula said that he "wanted the film to be some kind of celebration of the power of human beings to start over again, to love and commit again. And not just adults, but kids."

The movie, Pakula said, is "about people who've had other lives and now are falling in love . . . again. It reflects my feelings about love—romantic love—and the family . . . It also reflects my optimism."

So thoroughly did the film's main character parallel his own attitudes and experiences, that, when describing the character in an interview, he often shifted pronouns so that it is never quite clear whether he is speaking about himself or the character in *See You in the Morning*. "Coming out of a bad experience, a relationship that failed, there's a part of you that matures underneath that," he said. "But there's a part of you that goes back to younger kinds of insecurities and vulnerabilities. Rejection can do that to you." Thinking of Chris and Patty Murray, but describing

---

[51]*By the time the film opened, Lorimar Pictures had been taken over by Warner Bros., which proceeded to distribute* See You in the Morning.

the character in the film, he continued, "It means closing the door on ever living with his [first set of] children on an ordinary daily basis as a father. And being there is finally a major, major definition of parenting." Pakula's rambling discussion clearly demonstrated how close his fictional persona was to himself—a factor that may have made it difficult or impossible for him to view the film objectively.

In the movie, Larry Livingstone, a successful New York psychiatrist, divorces his first wife (a television model) and falls in love with a widow, Beth Goodwin. They, their friends, their apartments, and their clothes all tell us that they are upscale members of Manhattan society. The film's focus, it soon becomes clear, is on the relationship between Larry and Beth, both of them sensitive and perceptive, but incomplete without a romantic partner.

Although *See You in the Morning* is not a precise duplicate of his own story—in the film, for example, Beth has two children whereas Hannah had three; Hannah's first husband, unlike Beth's, did not commit suicide; and Alan and Hannah's courtship took place in California, not in New York—many of the incidents are taken directly from his life. For example, an incident in the film showing Larry's stepdaughter, Cathy, caught shoplifting in a department store was taken directly from the incident in Anna Boorstin's life shortly after Hannah and Alan were married. Another scene, in which Larry spends the entire night in a sleeping bag on the floor of his stepson's room when the boy is ill is precisely what happened with Pakula when Bob Boorstin was fourteen. And, of course, the emotional turmoil the characters go through before and after deciding to irrevocably commit to one another mirror Alan and Hannah's feelings years before.

The first sequence shows Larry's apparently idyllic marriage to his first wife, Jo, come to an end when she abruptly asks him for a separation. Shortly afterwards, Beth's first husband, a concert pianist whose career has ended because of a paralyzing injury to his left hand, commits suicide—tastefully, off-screen. Later, Beth and Larry are introduced by a mutual friend at a party, fall in love, and begin to deal with the many problems their love creates: How will Larry cope with marrying a woman with two children? How will Beth deal with her guilt over her husband's death? How will Beth's children take to Larry? Will Larry be able to resist the attraction he still feels for Jo? If Larry marries Beth, will his relationship with Robin and Billy, his two children by Jo, be adversely affected?

Beth is portrayed as a woman who has given so much to others that she is afraid to seek her own happiness. Her children, feeling guilty about their father's suicide, are conflicted about accepting Larry as a stepfather. Robin and Billy are fearful of losing Larry's love. Larry's function in the film is to solve all of their problems even as he resolves his own loneliness and adapts to his new circumstances.

After three years of courtship, Beth and Larry are married, but she remains plagued by guilt over her husband's suicide, tormented by thoughts that her remarriage may have been the worst possible choice for her children, and certain that any talent she once possessed as a photographer has been dissipated by a lifetime of sacrificing herself for her family.

To rebuild Beth's confidence in herself, Larry encourages her to go to Russia on a photographic assignment she's been offered (as, in life, Alan encouraged Hannah to undertake the writing of a biography). In Beth's absence, her children Petey and Cathy come to love Larry, thanks in large measure to Larry's acceptance of their acts of rebelliousness. Larry assures Robin and Billy that they will forever remain his children and that he will always include them in his life. Larry and Beth, despite going through a series of crises, commit more deeply to one another.

But if Larry's wisdom and maturity are responsible for bringing happiness to the lives of everyone he encounters, they seem to the viewer to be somewhat irritating traits. Has any man, even a seasoned psychiatrist, ever been quite as wise and mature as the Pakula-surrogate portrayed by Jeff Bridges? Larry would be a more believable (and, perhaps, more likable) character if he had more than a few minuscule faults.

The film rather uneasily intermixes romantic comedy with the anxieties of children and the angst of middle-aged characters trying to decide if they should commit to new relationships. One such comic episode occurs when Larry, distressed that he may be about to lose Beth because he has not shown her how much he loves her, strips down to an oversized diaper, holds a bow and arrow, mounts a pedestal, and poses as Cupid. Taking her by surprise as she enters the apartment, he then proposes to her. Unfortunately, the incident is neither funny nor believable.[52]

The structure of See You in the Morning calls for numerous flashbacks, each of which illustrates an incident from the past. One critic described the structure as "glibly elliptical," explaining, "At the slightest provocation, one of the characters will stare off into space pensively, prompting yet another poignant flashback."

In some respects, See You in the Morning seems to be a retelling of Starting Over, but from a non-comic point of view. The basic plot—a divorced man falling in love with and deciding to marry another woman—is the same in both films, and some of the scenes are similar. For example, both movies include scenes of a group therapy session. However, the expertness which characterized Starting Over is rarely evident in See You in the Morning.

When Pakula looked for actors, he was at least equally concerned with finding

---

[52]The Cupid image was intended only as a joke by Jeff Bridges, who donned the diaper as a prank during a rehearsal. Although no such scene existed in the script, Pakula insisted on using it in the film. At early showings, he said, the audience reacted "with a huge roar, a roar of delight," confirming his belief that the sequence was irresistibly funny. One wonders if Pakula was gauging audience reaction objectively, for the scene is, at best, awkward. One critic later termed it "terribly twee."

congenial personalities as with casting the most talented performers. No longer content to work with anyone who might bring temperament to the process, he said, "At this point in my life it's not just a matter of working with wonderfully talented actors but working with them without tension, in a certain area of trust and relaxation where we get the best from each other." At sixty-one, the days when he was willing to work with an actor like James Caan were over. He stipulated that he did not wish to forego creative tension, for that can be productive. "You can have interesting critical disagreements that come out of respect, not contempt," he said.

Pakula's cast included Jeff Bridges, Alice Krige, Farrah Fawcett, Linda Lavin (as the mutual friend who introduces Beth to Larry, and dispenses wise counsel to both characters throughout the film), and Drew Barrymore and Lukas Haas (as Beth's children, Cathy and Petey). Alice Krige, the least known of the principal actors, had played successfully in *Chariots of Fire* and six other films. Pakula had spoken to Meryl Streep about playing the role, but, as Streep said, "it just didn't happen—although I wanted to work with him again."

After casting the film, Pakula spent the first week of the four-week rehearsal period attempting to create a family atmosphere, on the theory that "You can't imbue an actor with passion and caring about family and children if it's not there to begin with." He believed the process was successful. "Any film develops a sense of family before it's done," he admitted, "but it was even more so on" *See You in the Morning*.

As he did for *All the President's Men* and other films, Pakula shared information about the characters with the actors and his other co-workers that was not in the screenplay. Michael Small, who composed the music for the film, observed, "It was a brilliant way of working because he never told the actors how to act, but he gave them some more information to respond to that was not in the script. He gave them a past. He told them the background of why Larry and Jo were divorcing, but you never saw it." When Pakula was responding to musical themes Small composed, "he'd say, 'No, this character wouldn't have this kind of music.' He'd tell me something that was more the essence of the character than something in the script would reveal."

Pakula's technique worked perfectly for Alice Krige, who—in a comment reminiscent of remarks by Jane Fonda, Meryl Streep, and others about Pakula's ability to bring the members of a company together—praised the director for creating "a wonderful community for people to work in."

Although Pakula wrote the screenplay for *See You in the Morning*, he was not proprietary about the material he had written, allowing the actors to improvise scenes when he felt that they could achieve better results through improvisation than through following the scripted words or the blocking indicated in the screenplay. One semi-improvised scene, when Larry returns home after visiting his ex-wife, Jo, took the place of an episode in which Beth was to angrily confront her husband when she found lipstick on his pajamas. Instead, the filmed scene substituted Beth sitting quietly on a sofa, leaning against Larry, while he confesses that he was tempted to sleep with Jo. Undoubtedly, the change eliminated a melodramatic confrontation, which would ordinarily be a wise choice—but in a film that is so placid, so devoid of significant conflict, a scene of angry confrontation might have provided an effective contrast.

Pakula's stepchildren, Patty and Chris Murray, both played patients in a brief scene showing Larry observing patients in a therapy session. It is the only occasion on which we see Larry at work. The scene, Chris Murray said, "was all improvised. Alan set us all down individually in front of Jeff Bridges, and we talked about why we were in group therapy. Then he put us all together and rolled the camera. You get about twenty seconds [actually, closer to a minute] of it in the film, but it took an entire day to shoot."

During the filming, Pakula would clear the set every day at five o'clock, then discuss the day's progress with the actors and selected members of the crew, who were asked to offer their opinions about the scenes they had filmed. As a result, some scenes were radically altered, others removed from the film entirely. "It takes a special kind of courage and imagination to throw everything away and start again," Alice Krige said.

As Pakula hoped, the actors in *See You in the Morning* seem to genuinely care for one another, and their performances are uniformly good—so good that they are often able to conceal the clichés and sentimentality of the dialogue. (For example, when Beth's daughter says that the house into which the family has recently moved is probably inhabited by ghosts, Beth responds, "They're cozy, friendly ghosts who'll watch over us . . . because we love their house." In another scene, Sidney says to Larry, "Beth is a terrific photographer who'd be a household word by now if she hadn't devoted her entire life to her family. She's also a wonderful woman.")

Much of the dialogue is also characterized by a kind of psychobabble. Beth says about her son, "I practically had to force Petey to stop practicing [his cello] last night. I think he's trying to make up for all the practicing he didn't do when his daddy was alive." A psychiatrist tells Beth, "I wish you could be more forgiving of yourself. Might set a good example for the kids." Larry tells Beth, "You can't spend your life in bondage to your guilt." He tells Beth's daughter, "You've been under a lot of pressure lately. Just when you think you're an adult you're expected to turn back into a child."

The warm atmosphere that Pakula created suggests that the ambiance that surrounded the filming of *See You in the Morning* was as pleasant as any film he ever made. If directorial achievement could be measured by that standard alone, *See You in the Morning* would have been a thoroughgoing triumph. However, the mood established by the director is only a means to an end, and that end—a vivid, satisfying film—simply was not achieved in *See You in the Morning*.

Perhaps Pakula's personal involvement in the situations portrayed in the film interfered with his ability to create an exciting movie. But Celia Costas, who worked as assistant unit production manager on the film, does not think so. She says that the director's behavior on the set of *See You in the Morning* was no different from his behavior on any other film, "because his goal was to entertain people," not simply to tell the story of his relationship with Hannah and her children.

Most enterprises contain a built-in objectivity. If the director is overly enamored of his work, the producer can point out the flaws; if the screenwriter is overly protective of his or her dialogue, the director can indicate why other dialogue might be more appropriate. In this case, however, Pakula served all three functions, with the result that there was no objective voice to check the film's sentimentality and facile approach. That objective voice might have made all the difference, but, sadly, it was absent, and the film suffered as a result. The Alan Pakula who had so tastefully scissored extraneous material from *All the President's Men* and *Sophie's Choice* seemed to lose his objectivity in this occasionally awkward, often maudlin film.

One can imagine that the film would be both funny and moving to Alan, Hannah, and Alan's stepchildren (indeed, Hannah says, "It was a very special film to me"), but anyone who was not directly involved in the events depicted in the movie is likely to be unmoved, despite the fact that the film is a reasonably pleasant depiction of the difficulties of multiple interpersonal relationships. There are times when it even verges on the affecting, but it never manages to takes wing. It lacks the warmth of *Starting Over* and the tension of so many Pakula films. Ultimately, one feels smothered by good taste and sentimentality, and longs for a good, cathartic moment, rather than the endless series of intelligent, insightful analyses of behavior that make up so much of this film.

Vincent Canby's review skewered the film for several of its defects:

See You in the Morning works in the manner of an advertising layout. It keeps telling its characters that they "deserve" this or that new product, which, in the film's terms, is "happiness," something to be acquired by trading in the old, out-of-date guilts stored in the attic.

It's possibly the ultimate consumerist movie, not only for the prettiness of the physical environment it offers, but also for the way it manages to keep all of the truly serious emotional ugliness off the screen.

Mr. Pakula can say he wasn't interested in making a movie about emotional ugliness. However, the manner in which he avoids dealing with one suicide [and] one divorce [Jo's] motivated by ferocious ambition . . . suggests less that his characters are mature than that they are incredibly stupid and incurably self-absorbed. . . .

Though they are supposed to be intelligent, Mr. Pakula gives his characters dialogue that persuades us that everything they know about life comes from reading self-help books not of the first rank.

See You in the Morning, Pakula's nineteenth film, opened in New York on April 21, 1989. Canby, in his notice, found the picture "fairly ghastly," despite the screenplay's "occasionally decent moments." Canby enjoyed the actors' performances, except, he made stingingly clear, for the scene in which Bridges dresses as Cupid. Hal Hinson, in the *Washington Post*, called *See You in the Morning* "a droning bore" and an example of "unprocessed psycho-drivel."

Roger Ebert concluded his review with gentle mockery—or perhaps savage mockery, masked by the illusion of gentle humor: "I liked the people in *See You in the Morning*. I just wish they felt free to like themselves more. Actually, I don't really know if that's true. It's just that after listening to them for almost two hours, I find myself thinking in phrases like that. Phrases about liking themselves more. Maybe I'm only saying that. Possibly I have a resentment against them. It's hard to be sure. I'll see you in the morning."

When Pakula asked Boaty Boatwright for her honest opinion of the finished product, she confessed that she didn't like the film. "I think he was very, very hurt, and very, very cross with me," she said. "He worked long and hard on that, it was something very special to him, and he wanted very much to make that movie." Like its two immediate predecessors, *See You in the Morning* failed to attract sizable audiences, grossing less than $5 million, a disastrous showing for anything but a small-budget production—and the film was a reasonably expensive one to make.

Pakula's insistence on making personal films occurred at the very time the movie business was changing significantly. When *Jaws* was released in 1975, it broke all box-office records and altered the way movies were marketed. Film studios realized that the surest way to make a great deal of money was to open a picture simultaneously in hundreds of locations in the hope that the opening weekend's grosses would be so spectacular that the film would immediately show a profit. The only way to make this strategy viable was to turn out films that were likely to appeal to great numbers of people. The strategy worked, especially in such cases as *Rocky* (1976), *Star Wars* (1977), and *Raiders of the Lost Ark* (1981)—and the many sequels to which each film gave rise. Movie studios were so pleased about these events that they rarely approved the making of pictures that did not fit into the pattern, which effectively precluded the financing of "personal" films. Thus, Pakula's insistence on maintaining a personal vision was an act of defiance as well as integrity.

Somehow, despite the commercial failures of *Dream Lover*, *Orphans*, and *See You in the Morning*, Pakula managed to remain, in Harry Clein's words, "at the top of lists. People were always courting him. He was lucky, one of the lucky ones in life." Thus, even with three consecutive box-office fiascos, and with the director now in his sixties—in a culture and a profession that, then as now, tends to worship youth—Pakula remained in demand. Still, even with his willingness to continue making films that might result in box-office and critical failure,[53] he must have realized that he needed to follow *See You in the Morning* with a commercially success-ful enterprise in order to remain one of the most sought-after directors in the film world.

---

[53] Harry Clein said that Pakula's indifference to the opinions of critics and even to the response of the public was genuine. Once a film was completed, Clein said, Pakula "never looked back."

CHAPTER EIGHTEEN

Finding the Audience:
Presumed Innocent, Consenting Adults, The Pelican Brief

"When Alan and I worked together, [he allowed] me to delve into things
that I hadn't done on-screen before. What I remember from him was just
an incredibly comfortable, positive atmosphere that was very encouraging,
very broadly accepting. And I remember Alan as being emotionally
engaged by what the actors were doing. I felt really comfortable with him."
—HARRISON FORD

Pakula found his way back to public and critical favor with his
dazzling adaptation of Scott Turow's legal thriller, *Presumed Innocent*, in 1990. The
book is a splendidly written exploration of the mind of its leading character, Rusty
Sabich, who narrates a story of political, social, and sexual tension. The film maintains the complexity of the novel, perhaps even deepening it with its sensitive direction, finely acted portrayals, and effective musical score. It is one of Pakula's finest
achievements, ranking among the four or five most effective films he directed.

Turow's novel revolves around Rusty Sabich, a prosecutor in Kindle
County—a fictional location, but clearly recognizable as Cook County in
Illinois—who is assigned to investigate the rape-murder of a co-worker, Carolyn
Polhemus, with whom he has been having an affair. All the evidence points to
him as the prime suspect.

Rusty hires a respected attorney, Sandy Stern, who smoothly demolishes the
prosecution's assertions of Rusty's guilt at the trial, and, as a result, the judge dismisses the case. But the real reason for the dismissal is Stern's implication that he
knows the judge took bribes years ago. So Rusty is freed, but it seems to the reader that he must be guilty. Later, however, while working in his yard, Rusty discov-

ers blood on a garden tool. His wife sees Rusty holding the weapon, and, to his utter surprise, she admits that she murdered Carolyn and, having injected Carolyn's corpse with Rusty's semen, made it seem like a rape. (Her purpose was to leave gynecological evidence that the crime was committed by a man; and a specific man: her husband.) Rusty does not turn her in. As he says, he cannot deprive his son of his mother. But, as he also says, every crime has its price—a price that Rusty will pay for the rest of his life, knowing that his wife is a murderer and that the system of justice to which he has devoted his life is basically corrupt.

Making a film of Turow's novel was not Pakula's idea. Initially, Sydney Pollack and Mark Rosenberg, who had formed Mirage Productions, intended to produce with Pollack as director and Frank Pierson as screenwriter. When Pollack and Pierson met together to discuss the script, Pollack said that, rather than setting forth a specific approach he wished Pierson to take in the adaptation, he preferred that Pierson write without preconception. Pierson agreed, but pointed out, "There are so many ways this could be done." Trying to settle upon a particular approach with which the director would be comfortable, he asked Pollack to free-associate. "What is this movie about to you?" he asked. Pollack thought for a moment, then answered, "Sex and blood."

"So," Pierson said, "I went away and wrote for several weeks and I brought him back a first draft in which the first scene was a staging of the murder scene itself, which is entirely ambiguous about who is there and what is happening, but it's all about sex and blood. And then we find in the room a man, Rusty, who is in charge, and the police are examining the evidence on the body, and then, as it begins to develop, we discover who he is and what the relationship is, and the story unfolds from there. But the emphasis is still on the sex and the blood. I liked it a lot, Sydney liked it a lot," and they began the process of revising the script together.

But the collaboration was short lived. Pollack, who was producing *Rain Man*, received a call from that film's leading actor, Dustin Hoffman, asking him to take over the direction of the film. Since doing so would make it impossible for him to continue with his plans to direct *Presumed Innocent*, Pollack asked Warner Bros. to release him from his commitment to that film. Warners agreed to release Pollack "on one condition," Frank Pierson said, "and that was that he remain as producer and that he find a director of equal stature to himself to take the project over—and that was Alan Pakula." (Eventually, Pollack decided to turn the direction of *Rain Man* over to Barry Levinson.)

Pollack and his co-producer, Rosenberg, sent Pierson's adaptation to Pakula in the spring of 1988. Pakula read Pierson's sex-and-blood screenplay and conditionally agreed to direct the film. However, his response to the screenplay was not informed by knowledge of the book, for, at that time, he had not read Turow's novel. In addition, he was still working on *See You in the Morning*, and unable to take on a new project for several weeks. He suggested that he and Pierson meet in New York after his work on *See You in the Morning* was completed. Three weeks later, they met in Pakula's office, by which time Pakula, who had originally responded favorably to Pierson's "sex and blood screenplay" but had now read Turow's novel, had undergone a change of attitude.

He no longer regarded the first draft of the screenplay favorably. It was "all juiced up," he later told an interviewer; "it opened with a couple making love and you couldn't see who they were in the dark, and they're going at it and making the animal with two backs, and suddenly you cut and there's a body on the floor—and you didn't know who those people were, you didn't know anything—and I thought, No, let's start in a quiet way, let's involve [the audience] and say, 'This [Rusty] is Everyman, this could be you, this quiet man could be you'—and then get them to this dark world and then go into feelings that make them very uncomfortable. . . . The tension in the book came for me out of it being about such dark, passionate, violent, almost lurid acts and feelings, but told by this man in the first person in this lawyerly, controlled fashion." If Pakula were to direct the film, a new approach to the screenplay would be required.

He told Pierson, "You know, I love the book. I love the screenplay [you wrote], but, to me, this is not the movie I would make of the book." Pierson asked Pakula, "Okay, free-association. What is the book about to you? What is the movie you want to make out of it?" Pakula's response was considerably more detailed than Pollack's had been.

"It's about law and it's about order," he said, "and it's about the fact that the universe has a meaning and that the meaning is expressed on the human scale in terms of the legal system of justice which must be made to work, because if it does not, nobody has any guarantee of justice in this world. And that's what Rusty relies on, and when he gets in court and discovers that he's accused of a murder that he knows he did not commit, his faith [in the legal system], the very thing that supports him and enables him to live his life, is completely undermined—that's what the story is about to me."

Pierson, not at all upset that Pakula wished to discard the "sex and blood" approach, agreed that Pakula's interpretation of the book was perfectly valid. But, he said, "It's a completely, absolutely different screenplay than the one I have written, and I don't know whether I can switch gears. I've never been through anything like this. I'd love to work on it, but let me think about it."

During the next two weeks, Pierson realized he would have to throw out everything he had written, go back to Turow's novel, and begin again. He agreed to do so, and from that point on, Pakula and Pierson worked together closely, Pakula outlining the scenes he would like to see dramatized and Pierson, on his own, shaping the scenes into screenplay form.

Pierson described the change in the opening scene. "Far from being [the] impressionistic and somewhat melodramatic depiction of a rape-murder-sex scene with a kind of ambiguity built into it that I began for Sydney Pollack, [the new version] started with something that is essentially taken from the book itself, with the empty courtroom and with Rusty's voice talking about the necessity of a jury coming to some sort of conclusion in the face of all the ambiguities" of any judicial proceeding.

Pakula had by now become vitally interested in the project, for a number of reasons. Primarily, he felt himself drawn to the plot of the novel (which he summarized as that of "a repressed man, controlled man, who falls in love with a self-destructive woman," or, as he put it on another occasion, "a story of a rational, decent, responsible man, the embodiment of morality, whose life may be destroyed by an uncontrollable sexual obsession for one woman"), which echoed the plots of so many of his earlier films (e.g., *The Sterile Cuckoo*, *Klute*).

Secondarily, he admired Turow's book greatly. It was, he said, "a wonderful exploration of our system of justice. Scott Turow is a passionate attorney and writes with a real insider's viewpoint. On one level, I thought it was a chance for me to explore [the system of justice] the way I did with journalism in *All the President's Men*." Thirdly, he wished to direct a suspense film, which "gives me a chance to use all the film craft in a more intense way than in any other kind of genre. It gives you an opportunity to be much more specific in design and intention, because every detail becomes heavy with possibilities."

Pakula signed to direct *Presumed Innocent* in January 1989—a rare occasion on which he directed a film he did not produce—and shortly afterwards offered Harrison Ford the role of Rusty Sabich. Pakula considered a number of well-known actors to play Rusty, but offered the role only to Ford. "Indiana Jones may be his primary image," Pakula said, "but Harrison comes across as Everyman. There is an extraordinary sense of decency that comes through about Harrison on the screen." He also said, "For all his success and great popularity, Harrison has a depth to his talent that people are not altogether aware of yet. He has an enormous range with a first-rate intellect."

When Ford, with his great appeal to filmgoers, agreed to appear in *Presumed Innocent*, Pakula saw the possibility of a first-rate film with considerable commercial appeal—the sort of film he had not directed for more than a decade. Moreover, the budget for the movie, a modest $20 million, would enhance its possibilities of commercial success.

But, as Pakula knew, the film faced several obstacles. "It's one thing to be fascinated by the book and another thing to think you know how to make a film of it," he said. Beyond that, there was the fact that the novel had sold more than five million copies, and had resided on bestseller lists for more than a year. Thus, a vast number of potential viewers already knew the identity of the murderer. "Why bother to make the movie?" a reporter for the *New York Times* asked Pakula, who answered, logically enough, "What about *All the President's Men*? I think people who went to that movie of mine knew beforehand how Watergate turned out."[54] Besides, Pakula argued, "seeing the movie and reading the novel are separate experiences. One is no substitute for the other."

Even if those who already knew the ending could be persuaded to see the film, there was the problem of holding the attention of those who were unfamiliar with the novel. As Pakula said, "One of the core problems for an audience at *Presumed Innocent* is that you are expected to spend most of your screen time with a man whose guilt or innocence you do not know—and at the same time you must care about this man because he's the one who's going to take you through the story. If [the audience does not] care about him, it's a very cold experience."

Harrison Ford met with Pakula and Pierson while the screenplay was being written, and read the script aloud, helping Pierson tailor his script to the leading actor. "It was," Pierson said, "a very collaborative and alive" method of working. Ford's contribution to the screenplay was not insignificant, for, as Pierson said, "Harrison Ford was always looking to find ways to do things with less dialogue— which is fine by me. So a lot of what we were doing when we talked together was a matter of paring it down."

Later, Pierson worked on the script in California while Pakula remained in New York. Pakula's goal was to retain the novel's approach, to relate "a story about the most unreasonable, most irrational emotional act, told by a character who tells it in a voice of reason," he said, stressing that he "wanted the audience to relate to this man and say, what is it like to be accused of this kind of a murder and to have done something that's so outside your character? [The accusation] turns out not to be true, but you have to go through this horrifying experience with this man."

Pakula at the time was computer-illiterate, but Pierson recommended that he buy a computer and word-processing software, enabling them to communicate regularly by e-mail. Thus, they began a long-distance collaboration. After Pierson submitted a draft, Pakula would respond with notes, or rewrite scenes to his satis- faction, then send the revised version to the screenwriter. Pierson "would rework it with my computer, sometimes rejecting it, sometimes accepting it, sometimes just rewording it," he said. "It really became a kind of wonderful give-and-take, equivalent to what happens between actors and directors in early rehearsals, where you just create ideas back and forth."

---

[54]*Harrison Ford's responded to the reporter's question with a question of his own: "You mean like the screen version of the Bible?"*

Pierson thoroughly enjoyed the process, but "toward the end of it we began to diverge. The main problem was that Alan loved the book, so he wanted to put everything in. And it became a kind of interesting relationship in that sense. It's the opposite of what usually happens between directors and writers, where the director is always saying, 'Oh God, we've got to cut this, that doesn't work, we've got to take that out,' and the writer is saying, 'Oh Jesus, no, the story doesn't work without that.' It was the other way around. *I* was the one who was saying, 'Listen, Alan, we have to cut this.' At one point I said, 'Let's cut the whole first third of the screenplay.'" Rather than cutting, however, the more Pakula worked on the script, the longer it became. Pierson feared that the problem of excessive length would not become evident to Pakula until he entered the editing room, and then he would be forced to make radical cuts, with the result that "all the little character touches" would be removed from the movie.

Ultimately, Pierson says, the script that was filmed was one that he and Pakula arrived at jointly. However, he maintains that his fears that too much material would be excised during the editing process proved correct. "When I see the movie I don't understand how people can really, truly understand what's going on," he said, "because so much has been cut out in the editing room."

Pierson's first viewing of the completed film disturbed him. Pakula had restored some scenes that they had previously agreed to cut and excised some sequences they had not discussed.[55] "There were things in it that I felt did not represent the best of me as a screenwriter," he said, "and I did not want my name on it solely. So I called him and I said, 'Alan, we worked on this together, and there are some things you've done which I'm not happy with, as you well know, because we've discussed them in great detail. So I want your name on the screenplay.'" Thus, for the first and only time in his career, Pakula was credited as a co-screenwriter.

Pakula wanted Gordon Willis, with whom he had worked so often in the past, to serve as cinematographer of *Presumed Innocent*, but he felt compelled to tell Willis, "Gordy, if you want to do this film you're going to be stuck with [my conception] because I don't see much [camera] movement. I want a lawyerly style for this film." Later, Pakula elaborated on the approach he preferred: "I [didn't] want a lot of camera movement in this [because] I just want[ed] to present it. Here it is. I want the camera to be very controlled. And then maybe in some way we get a sense of the controlled, rational quality of the book. I chose to do it in an understated way because I felt the events themselves were so flamboyant that I wanted the camera to

---

[55]And, Pierson said, "interestingly enough, Alan cut some things which were his ideas, which were absolutely terrific, and I said, 'Alan, why are you doing that? That was a great idea.'" Pakula would answer, according to Pierson, "Well, it wasn't in the book." Pierson came to feel that Pakula was too faithful to Turow's novel, that the completed screenplay followed the book more closely than necessary. Indeed, Pakula said, "I believe we've been true to Turow, told the story in the same cool, controlled lawyerly style."

be a counterpoint to that and just be there as an objective reporter." Willis agreed, in Pakula's words, "to use the camera in that way, as an observer."

Willis and Pakula, in their many previous collaborations, had used close-ups in moderation. In this case, however, close-ups were employed frequently, because, Pakula said, "I found that [the audience] would concentrate much more in [the scenes of] exposition if [the actors] were in close-ups."

The film also reunited Pakula with many other artists he had worked with in the past, including production designer George Jenkins, costume designer John Boxer (who had served the same function in *Starting Over*, *Orphans*, and *See You in the Morning*), and editor Evan Lottman (*Sophie's Choice*, *Rollover*, *Orphans*, *See You in the Morning*).

Before shooting began, Ford and Pakula observed a murder trial in Detroit for a week; the chief assistant prosecutor became Ford's guide and technical adviser. During shooting, William Fordes, once an assistant district attorney, was present on the set as technical adviser, and Scott Turow was consulted when the filmmakers had questions.

The picture was filmed at the Kaufman-Astoria Studios in Queens (where a replica of a courtroom in Cleveland, Ohio, complete with a reproduction of an enormous mural, and the offices of the prosecuting attorney were built), with additional scenes shot in Detroit, New Jersey, and Windsor, Ontario.

Shooting began in the late spring of 1989. Wary of Pakula's record of losing money on his last three films, Warners "was not particularly generous" in allocating money "at the beginning," Celia Costas, the film's location manager, said. "They kept us on a very, very tight leash, because his stock as a director [had fallen]. True, it was a bestselling book and a [very popular] lead actor, but in an uncharacteristic role. So the studio approached it in a very measured way."

At the first reading of the script, Brian Dennehy, who played Raymond Horgan, said, "It was fascinating to sit around the table . . . and hear the script read . . . That day was one of those special days that happens every once in a while in this business when you hear a script that's been carefully prepared from a great book . . . read skillfully by fifteen or twenty really terrific actors—all of that, of course, due to Alan's preparation and thinking about the project."

Harrison Ford was called upon to give the most subtle performance of his career. Friends warned him, he said, that "this was a tough role because Rusty is such a passive, interior character. Though Rusty's in every scene, all the action takes place around him. Things happen *to* him." As he observed, "the biggest activity the character participates in is off-screen and over before the film begins. So this was a character that really depended on the representation of his interior life and his relationship with the people around him. But he didn't have a hell of a lot to do. The relationship with Carolyn Polhemus was in flashback . . . So that was the difficulty of the character for me, keeping him active, keeping him interesting—and without very much to do."

In the lengthy trial scene, Pakula said that "Harrison must sit silently . . . as other, more colorful characters like the judge occupy the stage. He can't ask, 'Where's *my* aria?' That's tough to do, and it takes courage." Ford accepted the limitation as a challenge. "Those courtroom scenes forced me to do different things as an actor," he said, "especially in close-ups. Getting across my reactions without speaking is key at that point in the film. My eyes and face must tell the story." Pakula said, "Harrison was [playing] a man who would never talk about what's going on inside him, and I was trying to give the audience a look inside," an insight that the other characters in the film are unable to obtain because of Rusty's reserved and repressed nature.

Ford's confidence in Pakula was buttressed when, during filming, the director, as was his wont, spent a great deal of time in discussion with the actors "before we got to the stage, which is the way I like it to be," Ford said, adding, "For me, the acting part is the easy part. The hard part is deciding what to do, what helps best serve the story. I'm not one for learning to act on the set. Either you know how to get somewhere or you don't."

Pakula, who always enjoyed rehearsing, was challenged by Ford to find an alternate approach, because Ford admits that he is "not much of a fan of rehearsal." His preferred method, he says, is "just to get there [i.e., the set] and go for it, and depend on what I get from other actors and what I get from the environment." However, although Pakula discovered that "Harrison was very unenthusiastic about the idea of three weeks of rehearsal before *Presumed Innocent*," he said that Ford was eventually "very grateful for it, because I don't use it in exactly the way I would if I was doing a play. I try to . . . find out what is right in [the actor] for the part, so we explore what can happen. We worked some things out, but we'd mainly explore. And then when the day of shooting comes, which may be five or six or seven or eight weeks later, I may do something entirely different, but meanwhile they've had a chance to explore the part."

Ford found Pakula to be the ideal director for the material, and Pakula reciprocated in his admiration for Ford's performance. Their friendship would endure, as Ford later chose Pakula to direct a subsequent film. He said of his work with Pakula on *Presumed Innocent*: "When Alan and I worked together, we were well-matched. [Rusty] was an unusual character in the string of things I had done up to that point, and that was exciting for me, to have the opportunity to play a different kind of character. And Alan was interested in allowing me to delve into things that I hadn't done on-screen before." Ford called Pakula "a natural guide to inner realms."

Ford used the information provided by the novel to promote and deepen his understanding of Rusty's character. Somehow all of his ideas about Rusty coalesced when it occurred to him that Rusty's hair should be cut short. "To me, the haircut represented a guy who did not have an ego investment in this relationship with Carolyn," Ford said. "He wasn't a guy that was pursuing an affair for purposes of ego. He was caught up in an obsession with this woman." The belief that all of this could be communicated by a haircut might seem unlikely, but if the haircut persuaded Ford that it was the appropriate physicalization to communicate his character's most essential traits, it gave him an added degree of confidence and therefore served its purpose. "If it helped him give that performance," Pakula said, "then it was necessary." And Ford, who has said, "I see physicalization of character as being critical," is always vitally concerned with the appearance of the character. In the final analysis, however, it is Ford's wariness, his contained energy, and his fear of exposure that most eloquently conveyed Rusty's character.

Bonnie Bedelia played Barbara, Rusty's wife, seeming throughout to be sympathetic with her husband's legal problems, supportive and helpful, despite her own sense of betrayal at Rusty's infidelity. She is no less convincing at the end of the film when she reveals that she murdered Carolyn. "There [was] a problem," Pakula said, "where Bonnie Bedelia had this huge soliloquy in which, at the end, she tells what happened. It takes a certain suspension of disbelief to believe that this bourgeois woman had been so desperate that she could have committed this crime in this incredibly inventive, extraordinary way, although Scott Turow is very clever in the way he sets it up. But it is a shock. This takes place in a very long speech. Now you're really in the hands of your actor there, because she had to make all of this exposition work and bring [to] it some personal emotional quality that makes you believe her and even feel compassion for this woman. I thought she accomplished this remarkably—but you come to realize that the whole picture's in the hands of this actress, and if she can't make this work, the whole picture could just fall apart at the seams. It's one of those terrifying moments when you realize how fortunate you are to have a consummate actress like Bonnie."

Pakula was asked why he had Barbara *tell* about her crime at such great length rather than showing it. "To suddenly cut into a flashback of what she did, I thought, . . . [and] to show some of [her elaborate methods] would be absolutely ridiculous. But beyond that, I wanted to stress a personal humanity, that this woman did it out of her own pain, and, yes, madness," he said.

The fact that the film ended with Barbara's long confession occurred only because of Bonnie Bedelia's tenacity. Pierson and Pakula "went through hell," in Pierson's words, "working out how to end the movie." Pierson's notion was to use Barbara's confession at the *beginning* of the trial. If used at that point, Pierson said, "Rusty and Barbara would then have to go through the ordeal of the trial pretending that all was perfectly fine between them, with the suspense for the audience being the issue of what the characters would do at the end of the trial—depending on whether he was acquitted or convicted." Pakula rejected the idea, however, largely because he felt it violated Scott Turow's structure in the novel. So, before the actors were cast, Barbara's speech was eliminated from the script.

But Bonnie Bedelia, having read the book, guessed that such a scene must have existed at one time and "snooped around to find any earlier drafts [of the screenplay] she could persuade anyone in the office to let her have," Pierson said. Someone found a copy and gave it to her. After learning the speech, she asked Pakula why it had been eliminated. "I cut it because I don't think it's playable," he told her, adding, "I don't think anyone will ever believe it." Bedelia then played the scene for him, and, as Pakula later told Pierson, "She just knocked me for a loop. It's wonderful." As a result, Barbara's confession was restored, but shifted to the end of the trial.

Bedelia appreciated the trust Pakula placed in her ability to play her role without the aid of heavy-handed direction. "There are directors who feel they have to direct even when no direction is needed," she said. "You get the feeling that they don't feel like they're doing their job unless they're busy telling you what to do or suggesting things, and Alan has the experience and wisdom as a director to leave you alone when it's going well. He also made me, at least, feel loved and appreciated, which is a very liberating feeling. It makes you feel you can go out there and possibly make a fool of yourself . . . and it's okay. I liked very much working with him."

Brian Dennehy praised Pakula's direction of him in *Presumed Innocent*, but, beyond that, he commended him as "an artist—in a community where that word is abused constantly. He's an artist in the sense that he has a vision of popular film as a way of expressing ideas and emotions that we can all respond to."

Paul Winfield played the crucial role of the corrupt judge, Larren Lyttle. In rehearsal and in the early days of shooting, Winfield's approach gave Pakula reason for concern. "He was pushing like mad," said the director, "and I finally went and I said, 'What is it, Paul? What's going on?' And he said, 'Well, all my friends who've read the book say, 'This is the part of a lifetime for a black actor. I'll never get a part like this again.'" Pakula realized that Winfield, feeling, "Oh God, there's so much at stake, there's so much at stake," was inflating the role with an importance out of proportion to the character's function in the script, treating it, in his words, as if it were "the Bible or something." He said to Winfield, "Paul, the hell with your friends. It's after school, so just pretend that . . . we're just having fun. What the hell, it's just *Presumed Innocent*." Freed from the burden of having to make what he had thought of as a monumental contribution, Winfield relaxed, and gave an admirable performance as Larren Lyttle.

"You've got to feel that way," Pakula insisted. "You've got to respect your material, respect it enough to want to sacrifice your reputation to make it work, but you've also got to be able to . . . have fun with it and not look at what you're doing as if this is God's work and I'm now creating Art."

In all circumstances and with all of his collaborators, Pakula attempted to eliminate—or, at the very least, reduce—tension on his sets. He said, "There's a certain amount of tension that [inevitably] happens in films," he said. "Some directors work very well under tension, and they get actors who work very well under tension. Well, I like to work as if it's really 3:30 in the afternoon, and we're all in high school, and we're all doing what we do just because it's what we want to do. . . . I just find that if it seems like play therapy, the best work gets done."

When, as occasionally happened (as in the case of Paul Winfield), an actor went off-track, Pakula would subtly guide the actor in the appropriate direction. "Guide" is the operative word, because Pakula thought that *showing* or *telling* the actor what to do was ineffective, causing him or her to perform without spontaneity or creativity.

Actors, Pakula said, "can do something that they think is wonderful, which *is* wonderful, but it's just wrong for the story, it's wrong for the narrative." In such a case, Pakula said, it was his job to "keep an overall sense of what's going on" and to help the actor rethink his or her approach.

One of the highlights of *Presumed Innocent* is Raul Julia's suave, elegant, highly controlled performance as Rusty's lawyer. Julia gave many fine performances in his career, but his portrayal of Sandy Stern is perhaps his best. Another outstanding characterization was that of John Spencer as Rusty's friend, Detective Lipranzer. But every actor in the film is shown to advantage, with each performance excellently achieved. Because of the subtle performance—as well as the screenplay, the direction, and John Williams's excellent score, perfectly attuned to the mood and tone of the film—Turow's complex novel of legal and moral issues is even more successful in the movie version. It is, as all mysteries should be, taut and suspenseful. Beyond that, the characters and plot are so complex, demanding every bit of the viewer's attention, that the film richly rewards a second viewing.

Although Pakula intended the film to be a popular success, he succeeded in his intention not to slight the moral, psychological, and legal aspects of the novel. "We tried to show how the system works, for good and for bad—that the pursuit of truth and the system of justice may not be the same thing," he said.

When *Presumed Innocent* was about to be released, the distributors became concerned that moviegoers might choose not to attend the film if the ending was known in advance. "Warner Bros. and the filmmakers would greatly appreciate the press' cooperation on two matters," the studio noted in a press release sent to critics. "(1) Please don't reveal the ending. (2) Please don't reveal if Rusty Sabich is guilty or innocent. We thank you for helping us keep this exciting suspense thriller a real mystery."

Janet Maslin, in her review in the *New York Times*, did not divulge the identity of the killer. Instead, she praised Turow's "spellbinding courtroom novel" and discussed the difficulty of turning the book into a satisfying film. (The novel "involves the analysis of a murder case that has many strands, much forensic evidence of a highly clinical kind, and a lot of interrelated minor characters. The plot is too potent to be readily abbreviated, and almost too intricate to be set forth in only two hours' time.") Nevertheless, she commended Pakula for directing "an intense, enveloping, gratifyingly thorough screen adaptation of Mr. Turow's story." The film, she noted, "is notably more subdued" than Turow's novel, "but this director's best work . . . can make restraint a great virtue, turning it into a slow-burning fuse."

Roger Ebert, saying that *Presumed Innocent* has at its core one of the most fundamental fears of civilized man: the fear of being found guilty of a crime one did not commit," commented that the film is compelling for audiences precisely because "everybody knows that fear." He found Harrison Ford's "taciturn and undemonstrative acting style" appropriate for a character who "at every point must seem plausible both as a killer and as an innocent man." Ebert praised all the performances as "clever," the screenplay as "subtle," and the film as "quiet, brooding, and secretive." The audience Ebert watched the film with, he noted, "watched it with a hush."

Rita Kempley, in the *Washington Post*, called *Presumed Innocent* "a solid whodunit, driven by subtext and the intensity of Ford, Greta Scacchi as the predatory other woman, and Bonnie Bedelia as the wronged wife." The film "inquires into the nature of justice itself," she noted, but lamented that "the movie, for all its striving, lacks the passion it so assiduously courts."

As everyone hoped, *Presumed Innocent* was not only a superb film but a box-office success, grossing more than $86 million domestically and $145 million worldwide. For Pakula, the film repaired any damage that might have been caused by his three previous films, all of which had failed so conspicuously to win commercial approval. As Pieter Jan Brugge said, "Every filmmaker is interested in commercial success. He wants the film to be seen by as large an audience as he can reach. It offers you the opportunity to continue to make films, and most importantly it brings you greater creative freedom." For Pakula, those were precisely the issues. As a result of *Presumed Innocent*, he was, once again, highly respected as a director; and, he soon found, his skills as a producer were no less in demand.

Perhaps because of the success Pakula enjoyed with a suspense film, his next two pictures were also thrillers, although lacking in the psychological complexity of *Presumed Innocent*. He was asked by Buena Vista Studios to produce and direct *Consenting Adults*, a *film noir* thriller in the Alfred Hitchcock mold. The script was undistinguished and obviously needed a great deal of work, but, as Celia Costas said, "Alan was always intrigued by that which he had never done before" and "wanted to try his hand" at a "simple little thriller." Don Laventhall added, "There wasn't something that was lined up and ready to go at that time, so this gave him an opportunity to make this film and do what he loved doing, which was working with actors."

Years earlier, Pakula had told an interviewer, "The more I direct, the more I am fascinated by film, the more I try to extend myself to see what I am capable of, and the more different kinds of cinematic vocabulary I would like to master. The best way to do that is to work in different styles. Fortunately, studios pay me very well to do different kinds of films, so I've been taking advantage of it. As long as my successes outnumber my failures, they will pay me well to learn."

Pieter Jan Brugge, who served as executive producer of *Consenting Adults*, felt that the script he read seemed an unlikely candidate for an Alan Pakula production; consequently he asked Pakula, "Why do you want to make this film?" The answer he received was, "This movie offers me the opportunity to continue to exercise my craft."

Pakula read several books about Hitchcock in preparation for the filming, and, when he cast Rebecca Miller (Arthur Miller's daughter, playing her first sizable film role as the *femme fatale*) and made her bleach her hair, it was intended as a sort of homage to Hitchcock. Unfortunately, the film is, at best, a pale imitation of Hitchcock's work. Moreover, Pakula's method of directing disconcerted his actors, and the public showed little interest in seeing it.

Consenting Adults' only claim to fame is that it provided Kevin Spacey with his first leading role—and Spacey took advantage of the opportunity by giving a dynamic performance as the psychotic Eddy Otis, with just the right touch of eccentricity and sly humor. In the course of the film, Eddy commits one murder and attempts another before being stopped by Kevin Kline as the man Spacey has managed to frame for the murder he committed.

The setting is Atlanta. Kline portrays Richard Parker, a composer and conductor of advertising jingles who is obviously bored and frustrated by his occupation—and, perhaps, by everything else in his life, including his wife, Priscilla (Mary Elizabeth Mastrantonio), who is equally bored by him. Eddy, a financial adviser, and his voluptuous wife, Kay (Rebecca Miller), move next door to Richard and Priscilla. Eddy taunts Richard about his refusal to take chances, his unadventurousness. Eddy's charges parallel Priscilla's; during an argument, she says to Richard, "When was the last time you took a risk?"

Richard finds himself becoming attracted to the seductive Kay. Eddy says to Richard, "You want to fuck my wife, don't you?" Despite Richard's negative response ("You are insane, Eddy"), it is clear that Eddy has read Richard's mind accurately. Moreover, Eddy's glances in Priscilla's direction tell us that he is as attracted to her as Richard is to Kay.

Until this point, the film is reasonably engrossing, and the characters appear capable of sustaining a story of intrigue. After that, the film deteriorates rapidly. Ultimately, it seems more like a parody than a suspenseful thriller.

Eddy suggests that he and Richard swap wives. He encourages Richard to enter Eddy's house late at night and crawl into bed with Kay, who, he suggests, will not be aware that the man making love to her is not her husband. When Richard does so, the film becomes almost laughably implausible. The plot becomes so intricate and elaborate that it need not be summarized in detail. Suffice it to say that each scene is a bit more bizarre and less believable than the one that preceded it.

One looks in vain for the sort of social or personal relevance Pakula's films were noted for. He told Kevin Kline on several occasions that he intended the film as a social satire, although the point of the satire is obscure. If a satirical point of view in the first section of the film (of suburban middle-class life, presumably) is offered, it is completely overwhelmed by subsequent, improbable events.

Boaty Boatwright said that Pakula "worked very hard on the scripts of his films, and I think he always improved them—except once, and that was *Consenting Adults*. It never was a good script, and it didn't become a better one."

Pakula rewrote the second half of Matthew Chapman's screenplay, and did not show the revised version to the actors until a week before shooting began. For whatever reason, the story and characters are so full of inconsistencies that the film is impossible to take seriously. One may acknowledge that the conventions of the thriller genre permit occasional lapses of logic and consistency, but *Consenting Adults* strains credibility beyond permissible limits.

Mary Elizabeth Mastrantonio, who signed to play Priscilla on the basis of the original script, arrived from her home in England to find a very different screenplay. Pakula told her, "You're going to be the victim, not the villain." Explaining the change to Kevin Kline (who preferred the original ending, in which Priscilla was the mastermind of the plot against Richard), Pakula said, "I can't believe you could be married to the same woman for fourteen years and not know about her murderous side."

Kline looked forward to working with Pakula for the first time since *Sophie's Choice*. He told Mastrantonio, with whom he had previously worked on stage, "You're going to love working with Alan, there's no director you have worked with or will work with again who makes it more about the actor. It's all about coming off your impulse, and you'll see, there won't be a cinematographer or a crew [present], we'll work it all out, and it will be all about the acting." But Kline's expectations were immediately dashed, for, "from the first day, it was all about the camera." Confused, Kline said to Pakula, "This is so different from *Sophie's Choice*." Pakula, maintaining that the shooting style should correspond to the material, responded, "This is totally different. This is all about suspense and having a field day with the camera."

Kline was shocked. He recalls Pakula "talking at great length about the color of the wall, and rethinking a whole scene so that they could get the crane into the room and do a shot." The director, in Kline's recollection, spent most of his time "working it out with the cinematographer," paying relatively little attention to the actors.

I asked Kline if he eventually became comfortable with Pakula's method. "No, frankly, I preferred the old way," he answered. "Alan explained to me how the style of this movie had very much to do with the visual style, with the camera. I didn't appreciate it until I saw it, and I thought, 'Oh my God, he uses these long lenses and uses these wonderful effects with the camera.' He really knew his shots and his lenses, and what the camera can do, and color, and everything else. That's what interested him about that material, not, 'Can I get really great performances out of my four lead actors?'" Mastrantonio, less appreciative of Pakula's concerns, was reported to be disconcerted and unhappy throughout the filming.

Because of the constant script changes, shooting continued for a considerably longer time than anticipated. Kevin Kline recalls shooting "a scene in a car with Mary Elizabeth, and as we're driving along I look out and see a poster for the movie. It was that close to the release date."

Michael Small felt "that with that film Alan was struggling, perhaps unsuccessfully, with making a 'studio movie.' I don't know if Alan would ever have admitted it, but I think there was an attempt to please the studio executives. I think that because [the dailies weren't] coming across in performance there was an attempt on Alan's part to hype things up, to make them more than they were, which is not typical Alan. Usually he would like to make less of it."

Pieter Jan Brugge, the film's executive producer, concedes that Buena Vista was disappointed with the film. "Disney hoped for a different commercial outcome," he said.

Still, Brugge contends that despite Pakula's statements to Kevin Kline about the camera's pre-eminence in *Consenting Adults*, the director tried "to bring a level of psychological reality to the characters. Additionally, he tried to emphasize the moral ambiguities inherent in the premise of the film. An adulterous set-up can be very threatening to an audience; there are real human consequences to these actions. In the end, the material couldn't handle this approach and the final product wasn't particularly successful. Also, I don't think that at the time Disney asked Alan to direct the film they fully considered or understood the potential consequences of how his style as a director would influence the movie. So there was an element of disappointment about that."

If, however, Pakula's interest was to investigate the psychological scars left by an adulterous affair, one might expect less emphasis on suspense, murder, and the bizarre psychoses so inventively portrayed by Kevin Spacey. One might also expect fewer preposterous details, of which Eddy's machine gun (with which he tries to kill Richard) is representative. Kevin Kline recalls saying to Pakula, "He can't have that kind of machine gun, that's for drug lords. He's a con man."

Pakula, uncertain until the end of filming how the movie should conclude, shot two endings. According to Brugge, the final preview of the film took place in a multiplex in New Jersey, in two side-by-side theatres, each showing a different ending. The so-called "happy ending" tested better. "The audience," Brugge said, "wanted the comfort of knowing that the couple had survived the ordeal, that Richard and Kay and their daughter were back together again, that the family unit had been restored." The studio pressed Pakula to accept the "happy ending" and Pakula complied, thereby destroying any possibility that the film could be interpreted as anything but a thoroughly implausible melodrama.

Brugge, it should be pointed out, does not concur that the film is unsuccessful as a thriller. "In terms of his reasons as to why he wanted to do the film, to exercise his craft, he did succeed," he maintains. "The film has some wonderful stylistic elements and shows great control of Hitchcockian-like suspense. I do believe that he did some very good and interesting work in this film." Moviegoers and most critics disagreed, however.

Janet Maslin's *New York Times* review called the film's characters "even more far-fetched than most . . . of the demon nannies or spouses or school friends who have lately become movie fixtures," the production design "annoyingly bland," and the story "skin-deep." Still, "watching the plot unfold remains fun," she said, and the character of Eddy, though a "ludicrous caricature . . . helps to keep matters interesting." Kevin McManus in the *Washington Post* gave the film surprisingly high marks: "a great little thriller and a home run [later in the review McManus revised his evaluation to a triple] from director Alan J. Pakula." On the other hand, Hal Hinson, also writing in the *Post*, called the film "boneheaded," and the second half of the film "as mindless and sloppy as the first half is sharp"—although he said it was "tremendous fun watching the subtle ways in which the characters express desires that are not entirely conscious, even to themselves."

Hinson's effusive praise for one aspect of the film combined with his utter disdain for *Consenting Adults* as a whole is understandable. One expects an Alan J. Pakula film to be intelligent, psychologically acute, and socially relevant. Insofar as the film reflects those qualities, it is praiseworthy; insofar as it settles for nothing more ambitious than melodramatic nonsense, it is severely disappointing. All things considered, in the context of Pakula's directorial career, *Consenting Adults* can only be seen as a failure. Only *Rollover* is a less satisfactory film, and fractionally less satisfactory, at that. Any of a hundred others could have directed and produced *Consenting Adults*, which entirely lacks the integrity of Pakula's better works.

The box-office returns reflected the film's lack of distinction. *Consenting Adults* took in only $28.6 million worldwide, $21.6 million of that domestically. It represented a severe drop-off from the figures for *Presumed Innocent*; and, had Pakula's next film not proven that he still possessed the ability to appeal to a wide audience, it would likely have jeopardized his ability to get another film made.

*　*　*

But Pakula's next project turned out to be his greatest commercial success. *The Pelican Brief*, released in 1993, once again demonstrated that any notion Pakula's career was on a downhill slide was premature—although, to be sure, his ability to create a film that would express the ideas and values most important to him was limited by the source material, the influence of Warner Bros., and the casting of Julia Roberts.

The Pelican Brief is a workmanlike novel of intrigue by John Grisham. Its strength is in its plotting, its weakness in the characterizations. Pakula turned it into a better, more suspenseful film, and gave the characters a bit more dimension than they possess in the novel.

Don Laventhall, then vice president of Pakula Productions, became aware of *The Pelican Brief* when John Grisham's agent sent Laventhall a copy of the synopsis that was being submitted to publishers. On the basis of the synopsis (eighteen pages long, as Laventhall recalls), Pakula bought the rights to the property and began to make plans for a film. Later, he read Grisham's novel, and enthused, "he just tells a wonderful yarn, he's a wonderful, old-fashioned storyteller . . . in the happiest sense of the word."

Briefly, the plot involves law student Darby Shaw, who writes a brief on why two Supreme Court justices were assassinated. When she finds her life in danger, she realizes that her theory may be correct. She contacts a newspaperman, Gray

Grantham, who was the last reporter to interview one of the assassinated justices. Grantham joins Darby in trying to discover who is behind the assassinations. Thanks to their investigation and the ensuing revelations, the United States is rescued from a massive conspiracy.

The Pelican Brief represented a return to themes Pakula had explored in *The Parallax View*, *All the President's Men*, and *Rollover*: "the relationship between the individual and power," as he put it. Once again, as in those earlier films, we follow protagonists who represent integrity, endangered by large, impersonal, powerful institutions. *The Pelican Brief* may have been a less profound exploration of the idea than Pakula might have hoped, but the opportunity to comment on the state of American society—not just the wish to direct a commercially successful movie—certainly influenced Pakula when he decided to make the film.

Pakula, the owner of the film rights, took the project to Warner Bros., which needed little convincing to finance what they fully expected would be a fiscally successful enterprise. Pakula, too, believed that the combination of Grisham's material and a major star (in this case, Julia Roberts) would all but guarantee commercial success. Indeed, he chose the project in large measure for that reason, believing that such an outcome would help him raise money for his next project, which he envisioned as a much more personal film.

Laventhall, who also served as associate producer of *The Pelican Brief*, observed Pakula's unique method of adapting Grisham's book into a screenplay. "What he did," Laventhall said, "was to take the book and transcribe it page by page into script terms: all the visuals, all the dialogue, so that when he was done the first draft was about 350 pages, about three times as long as [a screenplay would ordinarily be]. And then, he'd go back and start revisiting and revisualizing the material, and cut down from there." Pakula's rewrite took advantage of his understanding of film technique, for he knew how to condense paragraphs (sometimes pages) of material into a single visual image, and recognized what could be cut entirely and what needed to be expanded or added for an effective screenplay. In addition, since he would also produce the film, he was concerned with the cost, and found ways to sacrifice some scenes and expensive locations from the book without damaging the structure of the narrative.

Pakula's freedom in adapting the novel to the screen was severely limited because, he knew, Grisham's book was certain to become a bestseller. (The shooting began before the book was published, although Grisham's manuscript was complete by that time.) Even more than *Presumed Innocent*, people would buy tickets to the film expecting to see characters with whom they were already familiar and anticipating a plot that would remain faithful to the story told in the novel. As Don Laventhall points out, "there were certain things that *had* to be followed in terms of the story. Alan didn't have much freedom to change it. So the story was the story, and he worked within that. But I think that Alan really felt that it was a relationship story rather than anything else"—i.e., a film in which human behavior takes precedence over violent action—"and that while you had to keep the engine going and keep the story moving, it really came down to a story about two people who cared about each other."

Grisham's novel did not permit profundity, for its very premise is too improbable to be credible—except as an exciting yarn. In the novel, the only obstacle to the success of a scheme to sabotage the Constitution is the deductive power of Darby Shaw. Since logic and credulity are strained by the notion that a law student, working with a newspaper reporter, could uncover a conspiracy of such massive proportions, the film Pakula made is far less convincing a portrayal of the seamy side of American society than *All the President's Men* and *The Parallax View*. Still, as long as one is willing to suspend disbelief, the book and the film both spin an effective tale of suspense and intrigue.

If Grisham's suspense novel is a less than outstanding but perfectly acceptable example of the genre, the same may be said of the film. But, in scene after scene, Pakula's screenplay sharpens and gives dimension to a book that is little more than an adventure tale. For example, Darby is described by Grantham in the book as a "smartass"—and she fits the description. Her wisecracks stand in jarring contrast to her frequently expressed fear of assassination. But in the movie she is traumatized throughout by the various attempts to kill her and a successful attempt to murder her lover. With one exception—at the very end of the film—she is entirely, almost painfully serious. In Grisham's book, Darby's lover, Thomas, is murdered despite his lack of any personal relationship with either of the assassinated justices; whereas in Pakula's screenplay, Thomas was Justice Rosenberg's former law clerk and considered Rosenberg his mentor, thus giving Thomas a personal stake in finding Rosenberg's killer. More importantly, the film shows a growing warmth and friendship between Darby and Grantham, whereas in the novel Grantham's feelings for Darby are primarily sexual.

Although the language of Pakula's screenplay is closely modeled on Grisham's dialogue, scenes in the film are often sharper than those in the novel. Pakula frequently reduces many of the words Grisham supplies for his characters, allowing the actors to convey meaning with a look, a shrug, a well-timed pause. The actors use such techniques to add resonance to the dialogue, thereby expressing emotions that Grisham does not even hint at, giving further depth to their characters. Denzel Washington is particularly skillful in this regard.

The essence of drama is character change. All first-rate plays and films show their main characters in the process of development. On the other hand, character change is rarely present in melodrama, where the plot takes precedence to such a degree that it reduces character development to insignificance. Pakula discussed a moment in the film in which both Grantham and Darby undergo significant change: "One of my personal favorite scenes in that picture is a very simple scene in which she suddenly felt terrified after she's been to see the law offices of these people who are the conspirators and the people who are after her. And she comes out, she's terrified, and she's lying on this bed and Denzel's character is there and he's seen the pain she's going through, and he, who had insisted that she keep on this case, and that she not go, not leave, not run away—now all he says when he sees her terror, is, 'I think it's time for you to leave.' And all she says is, 'I'm going with you.' And he is changed in that he now cares enough about her that he wants to protect her, she's more important than the story. She's changed in that he and the story have become more important to her."

The character change to which Pakula refers is present only in the film. In the book, the characters of Darby and Grantham do not change in any significant way. The novel, then, can be characterized as a melodrama about a criminal conspiracy. The film, on the other hand, is primarily about the development of a relationship between Darby and Grantham, set against the background of a criminal conspiracy and its suspenseful ramifications.

Not every alteration that Pakula made to the novel was wise. In Grisham's book, Darby is said to be buying and discarding clothes in every city, in order to make her more difficult to identify. Pakula's screenplay eliminates this detail, with the result that Darby seems inexplicably to have an inexhaustible supply of clothes—or that Julia Roberts, in an old-fashioned movie-star convention, owns an inexhaustible supply of costumes.

The nature of the villain's involvement with the assassinations is byzantine and difficult to grasp in the novel—but almost incomprehensible in the film, since Pakula does not spend the time that would be necessary to explain it fully. Alfred Hitchcock spoke of using a "MacGuffin" in his films, which he explained as the reason for a mystery's existence, although the audience really doesn't care to know any more about it. In just such a manner, the villain (who never makes an appearance, either in the book or in the film) is the MacGuffin in *The Pelican Brief*.

As Pakula prepared to shoot the film, he asked Cathy Solt, his assistant, to supply him with research about the presidency, the Supreme Court, legal procedure, and other details. "I gave him tons of material," she said, "because he couldn't get enough. He loved information."

Pakula immediately visualized Julia Roberts as Darby Shaw—not surprisingly, since Grisham had her in mind as he wrote his book. Pakula faxed the screenplay to Roberts, who was in Ireland. Halfway through the fax, her machine broke down, but, based on the sixty-five pages she read, she called Pakula to say that she would be eager to perform in the film. Roberts was expensive (she received $8 million to appear in *The Pelican Brief*), but her presence would no doubt draw many people into the theatres. By 1993, she had become known as one of the few performers who could "open a movie"—that is, attract enough people to its opening weekend to guarantee its financial success.

Roberts recommended Denzel Washington to Pakula. After pondering other actors to play Gray Grantham and discussing the idea with colleagues, Pakula agreed that Washington would be an ideal choice. Since Grantham in the book was specifically referred to as Caucasian, it was both unusual and courageous for Pakula to cast a black actor opposite Julia Roberts in a large-budget Hollywood film.

Some critics suggested that Pakula was too timid to show Darby and Grantham in a romantic relationship, attributing his reluctance to the fact that the characters were of different races. But, whether Grantham had been cast with a white or black actor, Pakula's intention was to show the growing emotional closeness of the characters and to hint at, rather than show, romantic involvement. In the scene in which Grantham tells Darby that she should leave, for example, "No one ever says, 'I love you,'" Pakula explained, "but for me, if you look at those two people, it's a total love scene. And that, to me, is a much more interesting love scene than the usual clinch and the usual, 'I love you, I love you, I love you.' When people say 'I love you' too much on screen, I begin to question it. It's always more interesting if the emotion is so deep that it can't be said that easily or if the audience feels that they're saying it for them."

A strong set of supporting actors (including Hume Cronyn as Justice Rosenberg, Sam Shepard as Thomas Callahan, John Heard as Thomas's FBI friend, James Sikking as the head of the FBI, et al) was assembled to fill out the cast. The film was shot in Washington, D.C., New Orleans, and New York City.

The Pelican Brief was the fourth Pakula film in which Hume Cronyn appeared. Shortly before his death in 2003, he described the director as "something of a rarity: he was a director who knew how to direct. There are some brilliant directors who are really not very good with actors. They're brilliant with the camera or various forms of execution, but they can't tell an actor how he can achieve a certain effect which may be wanted. Alan was somebody who you were lucky to get as a director. He had the gift of communicating with actors, and could certainly make clear what he wanted. And he had the patience to wait until the actor could give it to him—or else, change the approach to whatever the particular problem was."

Pakula's stepson Chris Murray, who played a CIA operative in the film, felt that Pakula was subject to studio pressures from which he had previously been immune. "I think that at that point he was struggling with the idea of not being an equal player in terms of the stars, the director, the studio," Murray said. "In all the other films, his clout, and, therefore, his confidence, was enough to carry him through difficult decisions, because he had the final word. But *The Pelican Brief* was very much a Julia Roberts film, even though it was an Alan J. Pakula production. And I think that was the first time that he ran up against the concept of being a graybeard in this business, in spite of his track record."

But, as Don Laventhall pointed out, Pakula had final cut. "He would never have signed on to a film if he didn't," Laventhall said, "so that alone excluded any unwanted feedback from the studio. He did appreciate what the studio executives had to say, and he certainly took it under consideration, but if he didn't agree he didn't do it."

Pakula and Roberts thoroughly enjoyed working with one another throughout the making of the film. Hannah Pakula said to her husband, "I can always tell when you met with Julia because you always have a smile." Roberts said that Pakula allowed her the "time and the freedom to find things in the material. He knew when to give me my space or when to squeeze my hand."

Pakula especially admired Roberts's performance in a scene in a hotel room. "She had this containment when she told the story of what she'd been through to this reporter, and how she was in fear for her life and how attempts had been made upon her life because she had survived this assassination and because she had come up with this theory about the assassination of the Supreme Court justices—and there was this kind of mystery, you felt that beyond the facts there was something so haunted in that woman, in that character." About her performance as a whole, he said, "She was really, really strong in the role. Julia went from being this delicious girl to being this mysterious, remarkable woman with a . . . maturity that happened right there in that film."

Roberts was equally enthusiastic about her relationship with Pakula. "I'm telling you, this was a dream," she said, referring not only to working with Pakula, but with Denzel Washington and Sam Shepard, as well.

Pakula said, "I was blessed with Denzel Washington, a spectacular actor who is at the top of his form." Washington admired authentic detail nearly as much as Pakula. In an attempt to understand as much as possible about the routine of a reporter for a large metropolitan newspaper, he spent time observing and consulting reporters from the *Washington Post* (although, in the film, the name of the newspaper for which Grantham works is the *Washington Herald*, rather than the *Post*, as it was in Grisham's novel).

All of the actors in the film are well cast and deliver solid performances. Denzel Washington portrays Grantham so well that it is difficult to envision another actor in the role. Roberts is limited by her character, as she and the director chose to approach it. Rather than having her play the wisecracking heroine, Pakula's direction emphasizes her terror of being murdered by the assassins who are pursuing her; thus she is given little opportunity to develop any other dimension.[56] Robert Culp, as the slightly oafish president who spends most of his time playing with his dog in the Oval Office[57]; Tony Goldwyn as his chief of staff, the man who truly runs the country; and Stanley Tucci as the sinister (but unquestionably gifted) assassin, Khamel, stand out among the supporting cast.

An uncredited actor in the film is Alan J. Pakula, whose voice is heard narrating a *Frontline* documentary about the unexplained death of a lawyer who had been involved in a case against the film's villain, Victor Mattiece. Since Pakula also was heard in *The Parallax View* and *Rollover*, one wonders if his off-screen appearances were manifestations of vanity; or, as one observer suggested, "Alan's voice was always the voice of reason" (although that hardly explains his narration of the malignant personality test in *The Parallax View*); or, as his stepdaughter Anna guessed, Pakula may have used his own voice on a temporary recording (known as a "scratch track"), with the initial intention that an actor would eventually be hired—but, in the end, decided he might as well retain his own narration.

Pakula's willingness to allow the members of his crew to contribute opinions during filming paid dividends in *The Pelican Brief*. During the making of the picture, "we were doing a shot with a crane," Dianne Dreyer, the script supervisor, said.

Dick Mingalone, the camera operator, was seventy-five feet up in the air photographing a guy looking over the edge of a rooftop down on to a parking lot. He was reacting to the fact that the car he had rigged had just successfully exploded. We did a few takes. Alan was watching a monitor on the ground below and I was next to him, along with the cinematographer. The image was dark but Alan liked the shot and called for the assistant to check the gate.[58] Immediately, Dick hollered down from his position in the air, "ALAN!!!" Alan stood up, adjusted his windbreaker and said, "Yes, Dick?" Dick hollered something like, "I dunno what it is, but to me, to my eye, the guy doesn't look like a perpetrator." Several of us suppressed laughter but Alan brought down the crane, talked to Dick, and then spoke to the actor. It turned out that the actor was afraid of heights, and Dick could see it in his eyes.

---

[56] "One thing that Alan was adamant about getting," Don Laventhall said, "was Julia Roberts smiling, which explains that final moment, with her smiling [broadly] for the first and only time in the entire film. That was added much later," after the rest of the film had been completed.

[57] The sets for all scenes inside the White House were originally created for another Warner Bros. film of 1993, Dave.

[58] The "gate" is the apparatus through which film passes as it is exposed to light, the aperture unit of the camera. Therefore, checking the gate ensures that the scene is sufficiently lit to insure visibility.

Pakula discussed the problem with the actor, then reshot the scene until it had precisely the quality he wanted. But the original take, marred by the actor's inability to conceal his fear, might have appeared in the film had it not been for the observation and suggestion of the camera operator. And the camera operator would not have felt free to express his observation in an environment other than that established by Pakula, in which the ideas of all members of the crew were heeded and respected.

Because Pakula saw filmmaking as a collaborative endeavor, rather than one in which the director is the sole creative artist, he selected co-workers who agreed with his point of view—co-workers who were, in the words of Pieter Jan Brugge, the film's co-producer, willing to "enter into that dialogue. There are people in the business who are not interested in that dialogue. They would like to do their own thing and that's it. But that's not what Alan was about."

Brugge went on to say that Pakula "genuinely loved collaboration and the interaction with both the cast and the crew. He wasn't a director who concerned himself only with the cast; he also dealt, very extensively, with the crew." Indeed, Pakula said, "The importance of casting holds not just for the actors but for all the key people—your cinematographer, your production designer, your costume designer. In the end, if the film is successful, it is a synthesis of so many people that it is impossible to remember who did what and when. I don't want to work with anybody who I don't feel has something to give, has some idea I might not have thought of without them. In whatever department. . . . I'm not making one-man pictures. . . . You might as well use those collective talents and some way make your work a synthesis of all those minds." Therefore, he would let all the people with whom he was working—"the visual people and the sound people," as he put it, "know that their ideas are welcome."

He realized that such openness to other people's contributions ran the risk of making "a totally bastardized picture full of everybody's 'good ideas,'" but suggested that that would not occur as long as the director retained his "very specific conception" of the film.

Patricia Anne Doherty, *The Pelican Brief*'s assistant unit production manager, fully appreciated Pakula's concern for the opinions and sensitivities of the crew. "He interfaced differently with all of us," she said, "but in a very caring and loving way. He appreciated what everybody's job was, he knew everybody's name, and he had very specific individual relationships with everyone."

Dianne Dreyer spoke about an instruction Pakula gave her after hiring her to be script supervisor on *The Pelican Brief*. It proved to be "tremendously significant in my career," she said.

He told me to keep his . . . thoughts, reactions, ideas, possible camera angles, alternatives to text, the comments and inspirations of actors, all that I could glean by being present at his side during location scouts as well as rehearsals—in a box, and to open the box and remind him of them at the appropriate moment. Although I had just met him, he sensed something in me that he immediately reacted to, capitalized on. He demanded that I pay attention to things far beyond the technical responsibilities of a script supervisor. He wanted me to think about the story he was telling, to choose what to resurrect from the box that had been filled during the long period of time that spans an initial meeting and the day you actually shoot a scene. No task could have been more personally inspiring and challenging to me.

In Grisham's novel, Darby wears wigs and disguises to throw the assassins off the track. In the film, a different technique is used. "We found a way to make her as invisible as possible," Albert Wolsky, the costume designer, said. He used "no color in her clothes, only beiges and taupes," so that she would blend into her surroundings. Similarly, "Alan wanted all of the hotel rooms to be very drab and anonymous," according to Philip Rosenberg, the production designer; "so we created a palette of wallpapers, drained of colors, mostly mauves, none of them memorable."

The Pelican Brief is one of the few Pakula's films not shot by Gordon Willis, and perhaps the film would have benefited from his unique style of photography. Stephen Goldblatt's work is entirely professional, but the film has a glossy look that combines with the slickness of the material to produce precisely what might have been expected: a slick and glossy film.

The Pelican Brief took in more than $100 million at the box office in the United States (the only film of Pakula's to reach that figure on its initial release), and nearly as much worldwide. If Consenting Adults had led some to question Pakula's commercial instincts, The Pelican Brief dispelled all doubt. "Based on financial success, and what the studio would consider success, it was certainly his most successful film," Don Laventhall said.

Among the reviewers, Janet Maslin of the New York Times best summed up the popular critical opinion. Grisham's book, she said, was written as "instant movie material," and Pakula turned it into a film "with all the glossy professionalism he can muster." She described the film as "the closest thing to an exact transcription of Mr. Grisham's novel as might have been imagined," although, in fact, Pakula's screenplay does not follow the novel slavishly, adding layers of characterization here, eliminating characters and incidents there, in almost every case sharpening and improving the original material.

Many critics were unable to muster any enthusiasm whatsoever for The Pelican

Brief. Desson Howe, writing in the *Washington Post*, for example, was scornful. "Visiting aliens wishing to experience America's movie culture at its cutting-edge worst should" see *The Pelican Brief*, he wrote. Pakula, he noted, "replays his own suspense clichés in the film. In his scheme, Roberts functions primarily as a vulnerable bird (with glamorous plummage [*sic*]), stalked by would-be killers in crowded Mardi Gras streets, deserted corridors and—in Deep Throat tradition—underground parking lots. Doesn't Pakula fall asleep doing this stuff?"

Roger Ebert's review was somewhat more favorable. Although Ebert was unimpressed by Grisham's novel, he called Pakula "a skilled craftsman who has done about as much as possible with the material." Still, Ebert found it "depressing to reflect that this shallow exercise in Washington conspiracy has been directed by the same man who made a great film, *All the President's Men*, on the same subject." The public, in its eagerness to see *The Pelican Brief*, was more appreciative.

The satisfaction Pakula derived from the commercial success of *The Pelican Brief* was based primarily on the evidence his work gave that he was still a potent cinematic force as director, producer, and screenwriter, able to attract a sizable audience into the theatre. The experience was less fulfilling artistically, "not as full and rich an experience as his more personal films," as Don Laventhall said, but, withal, a much underrated job of translating a bestselling suspense novel to the screen, and one more example of Pakula's ability to get the best from his actors. Most importantly, perhaps, it gave Pakula reason to believe that he could arrange the financing for another "personal film," one to which he was totally devoted, and would, he hoped, join the ranks of his finest accomplishments.

CHAPTER NINETEEN

A Deal with *The Devil*

"On the first day of shooting *The Devil's Own*, we pulled into the airport
at dawn, about 6:30 in the morning. And Alan's trailer was on fire.
And I thought, 'what an odd, ominous beginning for this project.'"
     —DONALD LAVENTHALL, executive producer of *The Devil's Own*

P AKULA PRODUCTIONS, INCORPORATED IN MAY 1969, was
established to produce films that Pakula would direct in addition to others that he
would not. Don Laventhall, who rose through the ranks at the company, eventually becoming Vice President of Production, searched for material that might
serve as the basis for films he would co-produce with Pakula. Laventhall hoped the
company would "broaden the horizon of what a Pakula production was" by producing films that would be assigned to other directors.

But only the films Pakula directed reached the screen, and several of the films
he intended to direct were eventually abandoned. "We optioned tons of material," Laventhall said. Among them was Donna Tartt's novel of four college students
who murder a classmate, *The Secret History*, for which Pakula wrote a screenplay (after
rejecting Christopher Hampton's script as "too British") and which he intended
to direct. Warner Bros., asked to finance the film, was "a little worried about the
cost because Alan's movies were expensive," Laventhall said, "and they weren't sure
there would be a big enough audience for something like this." They asked Pakula
to give them a detailed budget. "So Alan proceeded to do that, he did a whole
location search and we were about to start committing the script to actors." As this
was occurring, Pakula also become attracted to the possibility of filming an adaptation of Doris Kearns Goodwin's recently published *No Ordinary Time*.

At that point, however (in 1995), Pakula was asked by Columbia Pictures to
direct a film that would feature Harrison Ford and Brad Pitt, *The Devil's Own*.
Initially, he turned it down, preferring to continue his preparations for *The Secret
History*, but Columbia came back, offering a higher salary. Boaty Boatwright sug-

gested that Pakula not accept the project. "I didn't think it was a film that was worthy of his talents," she said, for, at that time, the screenplay suggested nothing more than a conventional melodrama. Twice more Pakula said no to Columbia, and on both occasions the studio increased the salary bid, finally making an offer the director could not refuse: $5 million.

Directing *The Devil's Own* and delaying the production of *The Secret History* seemed to make sense. For one thing, the financing for *The Secret History* was uncertain and a long period of trying to raise the money for the project would probably have ensued. And, on the positive side, *The Devil's Own* appeared to offer a near-guarantee of financial success, for the leading actors were already signed and were two of the most "bankable" stars in Hollywood. Moreover, Ford and Pitt had specifically requested that Pakula direct, so Pakula could anticipate a smooth and stress-free process. Most importantly, perhaps, the $5 million Pakula would receive might make other projects, such as *The Secret History* or *No Ordinary Time*, possible. As Catherine Solt, who often served as Pakula's assistant and who worked at Pakula Productions, said, "I think he thought it could help him make the movies he wanted to make."

Besides, Pakula had other expenses to consider. In Solt's words, he needed money "to keep his company going. It was expensive running it, so he had to work to keep it going." Indeed, although Warner Bros. paid most of the expenses of Pakula Productions, including the employees' salaries, "it didn't cover everything," Laventhall said, "and there definitely were years when there was more money going out than there was coming in."

Only one obstacle had the potential to interfere with a comfortable process, it seemed: word had already circulated that Pitt and Ford were at odds about the script for *The Devil's Own*, but, Solt said, Pakula "thought he could do something with the script and work with those people. That was enticing to him." Indeed, Pakula's stepson, Chris Murray, recalled that Alan, once he had decided to accept the offer, mused, "We'll see what it's like when I'm working with two 200-pound gorillas." Then he smiled and said, "but I think it'll be all right, because I weigh 600 pounds."

Brad Pitt had been eager to appear in *The Devil's Own* since 1992, when Lawrence Gordon, who had been developing the project for nearly ten years, took Kevin Jarre's script to Pitt, not yet firmly established as a major actor whose name could carry a film, but whose star was clearly in the ascendant. The script told a rather simple, action-packed tale about a heroic operative of the Irish Republican Army. Despite Pitt's enthusiasm, Columbia refused to make the film unless a better-known performer was also involved. Finally, Pitt approached Gordon, the producer, and suggested that Harrison Ford be offered a role in the movie.

Soon after sending Ford a copy of the script, Gordon was astonished when Ford accepted, partially because the time the film was scheduled to be made coincided precisely with his availability. "I'd been sending Harrison every script I'd had for twenty years," said Gordon, "so it was to my great pleasure and surprise when he said 'yes' to this one." Ford's participation persuaded Columbia Pictures to finance the film. At the same time, it confirmed Gordon's belief that the script would have to be completely reconceived. Originally, *The Devil's Own* had been designed as a star-making vehicle for Brad Pitt; now, it had to become a film that needed to emphasize equally two characters of different ages. Changes were required to expand Ford's role, give it dimension, and to complicate the relationship between the characters to be played by Ford and Pitt. Gordon was certain that his writers, who now included David Aaron Cohen and Vincent Patrick in addition to Jarre, were up to the job.

Ford and Pitt both had the contractual right of director approval. They drew up a short list of names acceptable to both of them, from which they chose Pakula, primarily because of the warm relationship Ford and Pakula had established during *Presumed Innocent*. On that basis, Ford persuaded Pitt that Pakula would be the best possible choice. "I was delighted to have the chance to work with Alan again," Ford said. "I thought it was material that he would be very good for."

When Pakula was shown the revised script, he was not pleased ("and neither was I," Ford said), so he began to rewrite, attempting to create a character for Ford that was as compelling as the character already created for Pitt. One character in the screenplay by Cohen, Patrick, and Jarre might be given greater prominence, but, as written, the character was not at all viable for Ford. The role of Tom O'Meara was that of "a totally down-on-his-luck, about to retire, overweight cop, who's just passing his time until he can get his retirement check," according to Don Laventhall, the executive producer of *The Devil's Own*. He continued:

Harrison certainly wasn't going to be playing that kind of role, nor would anyone want him to. So from the minute Harrison came on we had to start reconceiving the screenplay. And that meant we were reconceiving the screenplay up until the day the scenes were being shot, because you had two stars who had very different points of view, and very valid ones, and who felt passionately about this film and passionately about their roles.

But that does not necessarily create a smooth working situation, and Alan, who was trying night and day to resolve these different points of view, was stuck in the middle. It was very, very difficult. We were really on the line early on in terms of compromise, in terms of reworking scenes and getting both actors to sign off on them, sometimes the night before the scenes were shot. So Alan's job was a matter of controlling personalities, controlling hundreds of people on the set, people waiting to get answers to things that were being left up in the air because the script was always changing, especially during shooting.

Catherine Solt, Pakula's assistant on the film, felt that a good deal of the conflict came about because "there was a transition in Harrison Ford. He went from appearing youthful to having crossed over into being a middle-aged man in *The Devil's Own*. He looked different. And then he was directly in contrast with a young star. It made it very, very awkward. You had these two stars that wanted different things out of the movie."

Laventhall added, "That required a great deal of rethinking of the script, because Brad had [already] spent a lot of time in Ireland, and was very, very passionate in his own belief about what the script should be about and what his character was, and Harrison has a very strong sense of what the audience expects from him as an actor, and the sort of role he should be playing."

Ford detailed the sort of role he thought was appropriate for him. "The main thing that I was looking for was a character on my side that was as morally compromised as Brad's character," he said, "because originally the character I played was just a jerk, a tool for the [IRA operative], and I thought it would be interesting to develop a moral parallel on my side."

Pitt, however, feared that elaboration of Ford's role would result in a diminution of his own. He felt the revised screenplay was turning him from a heroic figure into a less than admirable one. As Harrison Ford said, "There were questions from Brad's side about the degree to which we deviated from the original script, which I thought of as a sort of apologia for the IRA, which I didn't think would fly, and wasn't very morally defensible."

Pitt continued to champion the original version of the script, because, to quote Ford, "he'd had it for years and it was natural enough that he was obsessed with the idea of trying to play that character in that movie."

Pakula tried to mediate, meeting with both actors regularly to discuss the proposed changes. However, Pakula had his own preferences regarding the rewrites, and his concerns paralleled Ford's. As a filmmaker, he always preferred the complex to the simple, the ambiguous to the overt. As Celia Costas, who had worked with Pakula many times in the past, said, "Alan was always going to try and look at the deeper side of everyone, and turn it into a psychological thriller, because that was what interested him about human behavior. It wasn't guns and it wasn't chasing [that interested him]—that's not what he did. So everybody had a different expectation of what they wanted and the script went into endless rewrites."

Ideally, no shooting would have begun until a satisfactory script had been written. But Mark Canton, the head of Columbia Pictures, insisted that filming commence, regardless of the condition of the screenplay—largely because Ford's participation was based on the shooting schedule already devised. It then became clear that there were not enough hours in the day for Pakula to work on the screenplay at the same time he was attending to the thousand other details involved in preparing and making the film, so he turned the job over to Robert Kamen, an experienced script doctor.

Kamen's task was twofold: to write a screenplay that would give equal weight to the roles played by Ford and Pitt, and to shift the screenplay's focus from action to character. Kamen added scenes that succeeded in giving greater dimension to Ford's part. Then, however, as Ford's role became more complex, Pitt began lobbying Pakula and Kamen to add scenes that would give him the opportunity to play an equally layered character.

Ford and Pitt clashed often during the rewriting process, but their arguments were not trivial and not based on ego. Rather, they "were truly substantive," Don Laventhall said. "They were real issues about character, story, and who these actors felt *they* were and what they should be doing. I'm sure that Brad felt he had to fight for what he believed in. And the script that he signed on to do did not end up being the script that was shot."

The differences between Ford and Pitt created a deep rift between them. Soon, they were not speaking to one another, so Kamen devised a process in which he could communicate with each actor separately. He would meet with Ford, discuss Ford's ideas, then write the scenes according to Ford's conception. He would then confer with Pitt and go through the same process. Eventually he would revise each scene, then "go back and forth between these two camps and negotiate my way through them," Kamen said, until both were satisfied. Then he and Pakula would review the material, Pakula would add his own critical comments, and Kamen would go off to write the new scenes.

Harrison Ford found Kamen's rewrites so much to his liking that he lobbied Columbia to pay Kamen a daily rate reputed to be $30,000. The studio, believing that Kamen's work would be limited to a few days, agreed to Ford's suggestion—but the rewriting process continued for months, much to Columbia's chagrin.

Finally, the four principals—Pakula, Kamen, Ford, and Pitt—went to lunch together one day, agreed on the shape the film was taking, and the tension began to dissipate, only to increase again when Pakula and Kamen realized that all the compromises had resulted in a nearly unintelligible script, and still more scenes had to be added (or existing ones significantly altered) in order to make the new scenes dovetail smoothly together. As a result, new pages continued to pour forth daily from Kamen as filming began in New York in February 1996.

Throughout the shooting, Kamen was ensconced in "his own trailer" on the set, said Laventhall, "and he was sitting in there working night and day to resolve the problems" of the screenplay. Every day the new scenes Kamen created were distributed to the actors, who were expected to film them the following morning. At times, the actors were handed scenes in the morning that they had not yet seen, then asked to memorize them immediately and shoot them before the end of the day. "The problem was that we only came up with the pages hours before we shot," Harrison Ford said. He added, however, "I enjoyed the process, I enjoyed working with the writer [although] I wish we could have done it prior to shooting. It was a huge strain on the relationship between Brad and myself, because he felt that I represented a departure from his original ambitions, but," he added, "he was a gentleman about it. It never affected his work on the set."

Although Kamen's work helped to create a balanced, more coherent film, the process was unnerving to everyone, aggravating an already tense set, delaying the shooting schedule, and increasing the budget.

The stress of making the film under such adverse conditions took its toll upon Pakula. Gordon Willis, reunited with the director for the last time, said, "things were becoming unglued at that point. He [Pakula] isolated himself to point where—it was like he was nailing himself into an office waiting for an Indian attack. He was having a lot of problems, I think, in his relationship with the actors and he just stopped communicating. He just wasn't himself."

Pakula, who seldom shared his on-set problems even with his immediate family, told his niece, Debby Maisel, that *The Devil's Own* was giving him a very rough time. It was, she said, "the only time he spoke to me about how difficult [the process of filmmaking] was." Nor was he able to conceal his feelings about *The Devil's Own* from his stepdaughter, Anna. "Alan was miserable," she said.[59]

One of the few people to whom he revealed his distress was Patricia Anne Doherty, a friend and former assistant to Pakula. She recalls that she "stopped by to visit Alan two or three times" during the shooting in lower Manhattan, "and he said, 'Patty, I'm just not happy. It's really hard.'" It was clear to her that the experience was "a very painful process" for the director.

Some of Pakula's friends thought that the strain of working on *The Devil's Own* took a visible toll on his health. Harrison Ford said, "Alan was damned uncomfortable, and that was what concerned me more than anything else. He was tired.

---

[59]So reluctant was Pakula to discuss details of his films with his friends and family that it caused his friend Peter Jennings to say, "Alan was quite discreet, which was a pity, because on those occasions when you wanted him to tell us a good gossipy story about the film [in this case, The Devil's Own], it was hard to get it out of him." Still, Jennings said, "I knew that Alan was just struggling terribly through this picture." Marilyn Berger said that Pakula never brought his concerns about a film on which he was working to a social occasion. "He did not say, 'Oh, damn that guy.' Never. He would never do that. He was loyal to his actors."

I'd never seen Alan work so hard in order to make it [the film] work." Robert Kamen, too, felt that the film "was physically tough" on Pakula, "because he was trying to stay focused on the picture, and everything else around him was just blowing up all over the place." Pakula's friend Don Hewitt said, "The movie took a lot out of him. He worked at night and frequently came home at daylight."

Hannah Pakula emphatically denied that her husband's schedule differed significantly from the procedure he followed when working on any other film. She recalled that Pakula was home in time for dinner every night and that she didn't detect any undue stress. "You can't get up at seven AM and shoot all day and get home and have a ten-thirty dinner and then go back to work," she said. "You can't do it."

"Yeah," said Robert Kamen, "he was home for dinner, but he and I would talk every night after dinner about what was going to go on the next day. He would say, 'Are the pages in hand?' and I'd say, 'Yeah, they'll be there tomorrow morning.' He only lived three blocks from me [in Manhattan], and I would go up there all the time and go over stuff. I was constantly over at his house. I'd drop off the pages, he'd read them, and he'd make a comment here or a comment there."

Laventhall, who had worked so often on Pakula's films, felt that the director's health was never in danger. "What I saw," he said, "was somebody who was under an enormous amount of pressure and stress, but was fully aware of the pressure and was able, therefore, to manage it very deliberately. He was aware that if he let the stress get to him everything could become undone. He never let that happen. Alan recognized the importance of exercise as a way of alleviating stress. He had a Nordic Track and he'd work out on that whenever he could. He took good care of himself."

If the following description of the plot seems convoluted, it is, because the endless rewrites resulted in a convoluted script.

The final version of the screenplay told the story of Frankie McGuire, whose father is murdered. The experience eventually turns Frankie into an operative for the Irish Republican Army who, on assignment, leaves Belfast for Staten Island, New York, in order to buy missiles for the IRA. An Irish-American judge, sympathetic to the IRA, arranges for Frankie (now calling himself Rory and played by Brad Pitt) to lodge with the family of Tom O'Meara (Ford), a police sergeant in Staten Island. The apolitical O'Meara has no idea that his young boarder, who endears himself to Tom and his family, is a terrorist.

Rory hides a satchel full of money he brought with him from Ireland under the floorboards in his room at Tom's house. He takes a construction job as a cover for his real activities: negotiating with a gangster to buy Stinger missiles and renovating a rundown boat so that he can take the missiles to Ireland.

Tom O'Meara is a cop who, when he feels that his integrity has been compromised, retires from the police force.

The plot becomes incredibly—and, perhaps, needlessly—complicated, when Megan, the sister of a slain IRA operative, who is (for no apparent reason) living in the house of the Irish-American judge, tells Rory that the IRA now wants him to delay the deal for the missiles. She and Rory become romantically involved. The scenes with Rory and Megan (as well as the scenes between Tom and his partner, Eddie) cause the film to veer from its central focus, and—although they may be needed to flesh out Rory's and Tom's characters—distort the story thoroughly.

Obeying the instructions of the IRA, Rory refuses to pay the gangster for the missiles, leading the gangster to attempt, in various sinister ways, to get the money owed him. He sends two hoodlums to Tom's house to look for Rory's money. Rory drives them away when they threaten the lives of Tom and his wife, but when Tom finds Rory's satchel full of money, he realizes that his boarder is an IRA operative.

Rory demands the return of the satchel, but Tom refuses, because, he says, the activities in which Rory is involved will cause many people to die and will prolong the violence in Ireland. Tom (although presumably no longer a member of the police force) arrests Rory. But Rory overcomes Tom, steals his gun, and runs away with his satchel of money. Tom finds Megan and convinces her that Rory is in danger of being killed (by the police, or by the gangster who wants his money, or by the British army). She tells him where Rory is.

At that point, shooting began, the filmmakers still uncertain about how the picture would end.

Don Laventhall recalled the ominous sight that greeted Pakula on the first day of shooting. The director, along with Laventhall and producer Larry Gordon, arrived in a limousine at Newark Airport, where Pakula intended to film the scene in which Rory arrives in the United States. "It was a pretty cold morning," Laventhall recalled, "and we pulled into the airport at dawn, about 6:30 in the morning. And Alan's trailer was on fire. Somehow the heating unit had set the trailer ablaze." Laventhall, who had misgivings about the project from the beginning, could not help but interpret the burning trailer as a portent of further problems—as, indeed, it turned out to be.

During the filming, Pakula was, according to Harrison Ford, "always inventive, supportive, useful, clear," and, although the tensions on the set caused him to lose his temper "once or twice," he was, Ford said, always "the gentleman in the middle of a barroom brawl."

Adding to the stress presented by the continual rewriting and resultant disagreements was the demanding travel schedule. Most of the shooting was done in New York City and New Jersey, but authenticity required that some of the picture be shot in Ireland. Rather than shooting in Belfast, with the possibility of being caught up in a dangerous situation, the filmmakers shot the inner-city Irish scenes on a Dublin set. The last scene to be shot (but the opening scene in the film) was taken on the eastern coast of Ireland, in a fisherman's cottage in an eighteenth-century farmhouse overlooking the sea.

Somehow Pakula managed to shoot enough footage each day so that a coherent film slowly emerged. But filming ground to a halt because no one could agree how the picture should end. Pakula, Kamen, and the actors all made suggestions. Ford proposed an ending in which Pitt's character, Rory, would kill himself. Pitt countered that such an ending would be "idiotic," but the notion that Rory should die at the end of the film appealed to Kamen and Pakula. As Kamen said, "There's more than one way to kill yourself. One way is to take a policeman's bullet," and, since Ford's character, Tom, was an ex-cop who still owned a gun, the notion that Rory would contrive a situation in which Tom would be forced to kill him was not out of the question. But Pakula, although intrigued by the idea, did not commit to it for weeks. "He just kept his options open," Kamen said, "thinking that something else might come up."

But nothing did. Thus, the consensus among the filmmakers was that the most effective ending would be to have Tom shoot Rory. However, as Pakula said, the studio executives "just felt it was too unconventional, too dangerous, to have one great star kill another star." Columbia, Laventhall confirmed, "was terrified. We must have gone through every possible option to not killing Brad Pitt: letting him go, for instance, but how do you let him go? This was such a politically volatile movie." At last, Harrison Ford, in a story conference, said, "Look, either I kill him or I fuck him." As the truth of Ford's ironic comment set in, the filmmakers concluded that indeed the only viable option was to have Tom kill Rory.

As the scene was filmed, Tom arrives at the docks just as Rory (who has killed the gangster and his hoodlums) is about to put out to sea. Tom and Rory exchange gunfire. Rory points his gun at the wounded Tom, apparently about to kill him, but does not fire—because, the filmmakers hoped, it would be seen as an act of redemption (although it could equally be interpreted as Rory's inability to fire because he has no remaining strength, as he slides to the floor). Tom pulls back Rory's jacket and finds a gaping wound in his chest. Rory dies seconds later.

Still, even after the new ending was shot, Pakula was dissatisfied. Two months before the film's scheduled opening, he called the actors and crew together for additional filming. The rewritten scene, originally shot in Greenport, Long Island, New York, was reshot in a studio in California. Pakula felt the relationship between Rory and Tom had been given short shrift in the scene they had filmed. His desire to reshoot the scene was based upon his wish to demonstrate that "these two men still respect and care about each other and recognize that they are basically two good men." Pakula reprised a line for Rory that had been spoken earlier to explain Rory's tragic view of life: "It's not an American story [i.e., with a happy ending]. It's an Irish one."

Because of Pakula's deliberate pace and occasional absent-mindedness (Robert Kamen recalls one day when Pakula got lost on the way from his trailer to the set), Brad Pitt initially believed him to be incompetent. Still, according to Kamen, Pitt eventually came to appreciate the director's "collaborative method." And Ford, who had worked with Pakula before, understood and respected the director from the beginning.

Still, Pitt remained unhappy, although he was less certain whom to blame for what he saw as a chaotic experience. Before a film is shown to the public, the actors invariably describe the process as "great fun" (or a similar complimentary remark) and the film as a groundbreaking achievement, sure to be remembered after many years. In this case, however, Brad Pitt's disdain for the project became known before the film was released. It was, he told a reporter for *Newsweek*, "the most irresponsible bit of filmmaking—if you can even call it that—that I've ever seen." He insisted that "we had a great script but it got tossed for various reasons. To have to make something up as you go along—Jesus, what pressure! It was ridiculous." Pitt blamed Mark Canton, whom he called "this drowning studio head who said, 'I don't care. We're making it. I don't care what you have. Shoot something.'"

Asked why he didn't walk away from the film, Pitt said, "I tried to when there was a week before shooting and we had twenty pages of dogshit. And this script that I had loved was gone. . . . I wanted out and the studio head said, 'All right, we'll let you out. But [we'll sue you for] $63 million for starters.' They sell movies to foreign territories on box-office names and they can sue on what they could have made if you'd stayed in the movie."

Pakula was deeply upset about Pitt's comments. As Don Laventhall said, "it's not done. Actors do not badmouth their own movie. Alan felt it was irresponsible and unprofessional, that it sabotaged the movie. Alan wouldn't have denied Brad the right to those feelings, but he was sorry to see them in print."

I asked Laventhall if he believed there was some way Pakula could have ameliorated the conflicts and tensions engendered by the film. "No," Laventhall answered. "One of the actors would have had to go."

One can sympathize with Pitt's anguish. If the filmmakers have not decided how a film will end (or, for that matter, how a given sequence of events will end), how can the actor proceed intelligently to formulate a characterization? If the actor creates a character based on certain assumptions, only to discover that the character will eventually behave very differently than originally conceived, the actor's performance will inevitably be seen as inconsistent. Thus, Pitt's anguished question, "How can we start a film when we don't have it all lined up?" was not simply a reflection of his temperament, but an indirect statement of the impossibility of performing a role intelligently without knowing the character's destiny.

Ford, too, was, in his words, "a bit unhinged by the failure to come up with more of a script." Therefore, he understood Pitt's outburst, although he would have felt more comfortable had Pitt kept his opinion to himself. However, as Don Laventhall pointed out, many movies have been made exactly the way *The Devil's Own* was made. At least one of them, *Casablanca*, which went through continual rewrites during shooting and in which the actors had no idea how the film would end, is now regarded as a classic.

Pitt's angry outburst led to rumors that he and Ford were feuding about such ego-driven concerns as who had been given the larger trailer (not true, according to those who were present); frantic rewriting (true, as we have seen); lengthy delays in shooting (true, because the continual rewrites made delays inevitable); and a budget that was spiraling out of control (true, because every delay in shooting represented a significant expense).[60] In any case, the derisive comments coming from one of the film's leading actors, damaged—perhaps irreparably—the film's chances for success.

Pakula tried to minimize the damage by denying that Ford and Pitt were feuding, and Ford subsequently added his denial. Even a member of the crew said, "It wasn't the clash of the titans the press made it out to be."

But Kamen told me that the denials were only for public consumption. Actually, he said, something resembling chaos reigned. "There was all the pressure from the studio, and then Brad made the comment about the script being dogshit, and there was the press calling—and there was Alan in the middle of it, trying to keep focused on what was supposed to be done."

Gordon, the producer, said, "There is no secret that we were writing and shooting" simultaneously. "That's a very unpleasant approach to filmmaking. You just slog through it. It's like being in the infantry and fighting in the rain and snow." Still, having recently completed the troubled *Waterworld*, he claimed that the difficulties involved in making *The Devil's Own* were "not that tough."

Kamen, who observed Pakula's attempt to create and preserve a balance between his handling of his two stars, was impressed. "I learned a lot from Alan about actors," he said.

Alan would let the process define itself. He was really smart, really sensitive to actors, and really believed in them. He believed that they had something to say,

---

[60]*The budget was among the disputed items concerning the film. Producer Lawrence Gordon said that the reported budget of $50 million was much lower than the actual figure, but he refused to say what that figure was—although he added that the final cost was lower than $90 million. Most observers felt that the eventual cost was very slightly less than $90 million.*

and he just had to winnow through what came out. He would let things go and let things go and let things go until he felt they were at a point when they were untenable, and then he would nudge them back. It often seemed like he was not directing, but he was keeping the whole thing just in those limits so that the actors could express themselves; and when he felt that it was going over and that it would be counterproductive—or it wouldn't keep the thing on track—he'd just pull it back in.

At first I said, "this guy's not paying attention," but what I realized was, he was allowing everything to come in [i.e., allowing input to come from everyone] and then he was taking from it what he needed and using that. And he was great when somebody'd come up with an idea. He'd never jump on it [by making an instant decision], he would sit with it for however long it was, and a lot of times it would be overnight. He'd come in the next day, and he'd say, almost like a checklist, "Yes, yes, no, yes, no, yes." I remember saying to him one day, "Alan, you don't know the way to the set from your trailer, but you know the way this thing is going, don't you?" And he said, "Yes, I know where the film's going."

You'd see him sometimes, just standing there on the set, he looked like he was lost, but he wasn't lost because he was locked into the movie. A lot of directors have to control every little thing around them. He had to control nothing around him—he just had to keep that story and those characters in his mind. At the end of the day, when that film was put together, I expected it to be a mess, but I went over to the studio and saw the film, and I said, "How did you do this? How did you get all these things to work?" And he said, "You just gotta keep thinking about the film." It was a great lesson.

Don Laventhall's comment supports Kamen's observation. "Alan always felt that there was a way to solve problems, and make things work," he said. "Always. Even in the most complicated filming situation, he felt if he could just stay on track and keep cool, he could always make it happen. He used to say, 'As long as you don't panic, anything is manageable.'"

Unfortunately, all of the frantic rewriting could not conceal some elements of the film that seem utterly out of place. The subplot about Megan is so obscure as to be nearly unintelligible. Who is she? What is she doing in New York and, specifically, in the home of the corrupt judge? Other than to offer a brief romantic interest for Rory, she seems to have no function. Additional questions arise as one views the film. What does the title mean? Was Frankie's father assassinated by the British army or by Protestant militants? And, as Roger Ebert asked in his review in the *Chicago Sun-Times*, "Did [Rory] really plan to sail across the North Atlantic Ocean in a leaky old tugboat?"

It is apparent that there are a great many holes in the film. On the evidence of the movie alone—that is, without any knowledge of the off-screen difficulties—one has the feeling that the filmmakers were frantically including new scenes in order to explain aspects of the plot that would otherwise be unfathomable. The result is incredible complexity—but not the kind of complexity that reflects the ambiguity of life; rather, it is an artificial, contrived complexity designed to explain plot points that would otherwise be unintelligible.

Remarkably, however, despite the inclusion of several scenes that were not fully integrated into the film, *The Devil's Own* is a suspenseful story of two men who, even while opposing one another politically, grow to respect one another. Pakula's friend Keren Saks, while agreeing that the film was difficult for Pakula to make ("I know that he worked very hard and I know it was problematical at times"), said, "I think he was pleased with it when it was finished. I don't know that it was his favorite film, but he was certainly excited about it." Boaty Boatwright said "I think it was an infinitely better film because he did it than if it had been in the hands of a good mechanic," although she would have preferred that he not do it at all.

Pitt's performance, in particular, stands out strongly. Expertly employing a Belfast accent, Pitt plays Rory with intensity and passion. Pakula also evoked fine performances from Ford and from Margaret Colin as Tom's wife.

Don Laventhall felt that the film "probably represented the best work that Brad Pitt has ever done. He was excellent. Alan—in spite of all the bad crap—got two extraordinary performances out of those actors." Laventhall cited particularly the scene "where Brad is in the basement, and Harrison has just found his satchel of money and Brad has tears streaming down his face" as an example of Pitt's outstanding performance.

Ultimately, Robert Kamen said, "when Pitt saw the picture he actually liked it." When the film was completed, Pitt gave Pakula a signed first edition of James Joyce's *Finnegan's Wake*, and inscribed an accompanying card: "To Alan, I would say we've done quite well. Thanks for always hanging in—it's all worth it. Your friend, Brad."

Despite what Harrison Ford described as "a fraught process," he felt that the film turned out remarkably well. "I think the work that Alan did in the editing room made it into a film that I actually feel very strongly about," Ford said. "I was very, very pleased with the result."

Shortly before the film was released, Pitt apologized for his intemperate remarks (under pressure from Columbia, according to rumor), explaining in a letter to *Newsweek* that his comments referred only "to my dilemma before shooting began," and claiming that "it was the belief held by Alan Pakula, Harrison Ford, myself, and others that we could pull off a compelling and personal story.

And that's just what we did." Still, the damage had been done. All those who had followed the controversy concluded that the completed film was certain to be a disaster on the scale of such misbegotten movies as *Ishtar* and *Bonfire of the Vanities*.

Still, Pakula felt—or, at least, said for public consumption—that the ever-changing script had solved the problems. "What's interesting to me is what happens when people with two different senses of what is right and what is wrong meet," he noted. "What's interesting is the fact that these two men can love and respect each other. It makes it more complicated. Much more interesting and much more human." But his unhappiness about the film was clear when, in an interview with the *New York Times* a few days after the picture opened, he referred to *The Devil's Own* as a "disaster." He said, "I can't imagine what it would have been like if it had been my first film." To another reporter, he admitted, "This was one of the most complex movies I have ever made," but praised the performances of Pitt and Ford, whom he called "two quite remarkable actors, possibly the two greatest stars of their generations."

And Pakula insisted, perhaps more than a bit optimistically, that the rewriting had served its purpose. "There's rewriting and there's rewriting," he said. "There's rewriting when you start to make one kind of movie and then everybody panics, or the studio panics and you wind up making another movie. That was never the case here. How to tell the story might have changed; individual plot things might have changed. It was always telling the same story." But, he conceded, the film had taken a much longer-than-anticipated time to complete. "Sometimes," he said, "it takes longer to get there, and sometimes you get there in a shorter time."

When Pakula traveled the country on a Columbia-sponsored tour to promote the film, a series of embarrassing press conferences ensued, in which he was besieged by reporters asking what it was like to work with Ford and Pitt, and why Pitt had criticized the film so severely. Pakula tried valiantly, but often vainly, to return the discussion to its promotional purpose.

The film opened in March 1997 and disappointed at the box office (although it performed better internationally than it did in the U.S.).[61] In the end, the decision to have O'Meara kill Rory *did* disturb filmgoers. As an executive at Columbia said, "Killing Brad Pitt probably cost this movie $20 million."

The critical reception was balanced between negative and positive responses, with more than a few of the reviewers expressing their surprise that the film had

---

[61] *The film took in $140 million worldwide (only $42.9 million in the United States) at the box office; however, as a hoped-for blockbuster, it did not meet expectations.*

[62] *Patricia Anne Doherty, although not a critic, responded precisely in this way. She was prepared for "an atrocious mess," she said, "but thought it turned out very well."*

turned out far better than expected, considering the rumors of disaster.[62] For example, Janet Maslin's *New York Times* review called *The Devil's Own* an "unexpectedly solid thriller," directed by Pakula "in a thoughtful urban style [whose] flair for local color and careful detail make it worth the game." She credited Pitt with "dazzling confidence, showing off all the star power that he usually works overtime to hide," while saying that Ford "does a fine, terse job of playing his father figure. . . . Should the viewer choose not to be an absolute stickler about plot coherence," Maslin added, "*The Devil's Own* delivers two traffic-stopping star turns for the price of one." Given the rumors of chaos and bickering on the set, Maslin noted that "*The Devil's Own* certainly tracks more smoothly than might have been expected." *Variety* offered a similar comment, calling the film "a well-crafted suspenser, [bearing] no signs of the much-reported on-set difficulties."

Ruthe Stein in the *San Francisco Chronicle* found the film a skillful "story of friendship and betrayal." Pakula, she said, recalling *All the President's Men*, "has a feel for expressing male bonding." She also noted that Ford and Pitt "have terrific chemistry." Stanley Kauffmann in the *New Republic* credited Pakula for knowing "how to move things along." Pitt "gives quite a decent account of himself," he added.

Several reviewers noted that the film told two quite different stories without quite meshing. Kenneth Turan was one. In his *Los Angeles Times* review, he said, "Ford has his own half-movie, thank you very much, and Pitt has his, and though they collide at times, they mostly glide by each other like supertankers in the night."

A few critics tore into *The Devil's Own* with a vengeance. Turan said, "No one seeing *The Devil's Own* can miss the fact that its IRA-gunman-meets-N.Y.C.-cop story line feels random, haphazard, even patched together." Colin Brennan in the *London Sunday Times* called the film "a rather grubby action movie," and Desson Howe in the *Washington Post* said it was "epically awful."

By and large, however, the reviews were much more positive than one might have anticipated, considering the chaotic shooting process. I asked Don Laventhall if Pakula felt vindicated by the film's reviews. "I don't think so," Laventhall answered, "simply because the movie was not financially successful. And Alan was a businessman [as well as an artist]. He wanted a movie that succeeded for the studio, for the actors, for everybody."

CHAPTER TWENTY

A Life Cut Short

"[Alan Pakula's] style was more thoughtful, efficient, and adult than most of his flagrantly experimental colleagues, and it wound up having more staying power than most. [Throughout his career] his dignity and intelligence [remained] intact. . . . [He possessed] a respect for audiences, a knack for finding depth in potentially potboiling material (like the thriller *Klute*), and a special flair for encouraging actors to shine. If he was known for creative ambivalence during filmmaking . . . he was just as certain to find precisely the right moments to assemble at editing time. Actors in his films had a way of baring their souls without breast-beating, and he could capture them at their most intimate and appealing."

— JANET MASLIN, summing up Pakula's career after his death

WHEN *THE DEVIL'S OWN* WAS RELEASED IN MARCH 1997, Pakula had only a year and a half of life remaining. Had he known that *The Devil's Own* would be his last film, he would surely have been rueful, to say the least. "I think he very much wanted to finish off his career with something he thought was very meaningful, not *The Devil's Own*," said Catherine Solt.

Early in that year, to commemorate the thirty-fifth anniversary of *To Kill a Mockingbird*, Pakula and director Robert Mulligan laid down a "director and producer's track" for a special DVD edition of a new print of the film.[63] Later, at a party at Gregory Peck's house, Pakula and Mulligan spoke about getting together once again to make another picture. Neither one was fully serious, but, Mulligan thought, the partnership might have resumed had the right property come along. "Months later," Mulligan said, "Alan did send me a new novel by Pete Hamill and asked me to think about doing it as a movie. . . . The thought of working with Alan and Pete did get my attention and I looked forward to reading *Loving Women*. I spent

---

[63]*Pakula also contributed a "director's track" to the DVD of* Sophie's Choice. *And in 1984, he had been interviewed—and appeared on screen—for* George Stevens: A Filmmaker's Journey, *a full-length film directed by Stevens's son, George Jr.*

a couple of weeks trying to break it down to see if it would make a film and decided I couldn't come up with a clear idea how to transfer the book to a screenplay. Alan and I met at his office in NYC and we talked. . . . In the end we agreed and decided to pass on the project. That ended the 'dream' of us doing another movie together. It wasn't sad. Just a reality. We even had some laughs."

Loving Women was not the only project Pakula and Mulligan contemplated but did not film. Years earlier, they had taken options on several projects that did not come to fruition. Among these were a musical adaptation for the stage of *Treasure Island* and such film possibilities as *My Friend Mr. Brown*, *That Others May Live*, and *Flight from Ashiya*. And, over the years, Pakula considered many other projects that he intended to direct but, for one reason or another, abandoned. Some of them have been discussed in these pages. Others included *The Significant Other* (which was to feature Tom Hanks and Debra Winger); *Friday Night Lights*, an adaptation of the book by H. G. Bissinger (which was finally made by another production team and released in 2004); *CDC*, a black comedy about AIDS, for which Pakula intended to collaborate on the screenplay with Garry Trudeau; *Shot in the Heart*, an adaptation of a memoir by the brother of the psychopathic killer, Gary Gilmore; an adaptation of Laura Cunningham's memoir, *Sleeping Arrangements*; and several more.

His plans to produce films at Pakula Productions for other directors never came to fruition. As Don Laventhall explained, "What happened with Alan was that, in developing material that he wasn't going to direct, he would go through the creative process of directing it in his head, and then would no longer be interested in it. He didn't want to spend time producing it for somebody else to direct. Ultimately the decision came down to this: 'Do I really want to spend six months of my time overseeing somebody else doing something? No, I want to spend my time as an artist directing a movie, not producing a movie.'"

Various awards came Pakula's way in his last years. He was decorated by the French government as Commandeur de l'Ordre des Arts et des Lettres, and received the Distinguished Achievement Award at the 1996 Hamptons International Film Festival. ("In a cinematic climate where morality is often discarded in favor of what will sell, Alan J. Pakula's films have always been about compassion in the face of human frailty, and commercialism has not been his concern," the festival's literature declared.) In 1996 he won the Guildhall's Academy of the Arts award for Lifetime Achievement; and in 1997 received a commendation from the City of New York. That same year, another honor, presented by Harrison Ford, was bestowed on Pakula when he won the Irene Diamond Lifetime Achievement Award, given annually to a director "whose life's work demonstrates an outstanding commitment to human rights and film." The citation praised him for "his leadership in introducing mainstream audiences to controversial human rights issues."

Despite turning seventy in April 1998, Pakula had no thoughts of retirement. "He was very healthy," Catherine Solt said, "and he talked over and over again about being able to spend the last ten years of his career doing things he wanted to do." But Pakula did alter his perspective in one meaningful way. "He didn't want to do commercial stuff anymore," Solt said; "I know that for sure."

His much younger colleague, Don Laventhall, confirmed that Pakula had no plans to retire. "He loved working. It was his life's blood," Laventhall said. "He loved working with people and with ideas. He was never going to be a gentleman in East Hampton."

But if, as Hannah Pakula said, "he lost his [directorial] legs eventually," he had plans for other kinds of work. "He had started a novel," she said; "he loved to write, he really liked the process, and he said, 'You never have to worry about me, I want to do this novel,'" and then proceeded to tell her of other projects he hoped to undertake: "all kinds of things he would have been very happy with," she said. They spoke of investigating the possibility of his taking a teaching job "and moving into an academic community."

But after *The Devil's Own*, Pakula was still very much involved in his career. He still might have chosen to direct *The Secret History*. "He had not put it away," Laventhall said. "Alan was very much a spontaneous guy, and he sort of rolled with his emotional flow. So he didn't decide *not* to do it, and he didn't decide that he was going to do it. It was an option that was still available to him if he chose to take it."

But, as he had done throughout his career, Pakula deliberated carefully before he chose a project to direct. "I am slow," he said, because "I know [I'll be spending] a year or a year and a half of my life [on a film] and sometimes more," and if he were to invest so much time on a project, he wanted to make certain the project would be able to sustain his enthusiasm and creativity.

Ultimately his interest in *The Secret History* waned because he grew fascinated by *No Ordinary Time*, Doris Kearns Goodwin's biography of Eleanor Roosevelt and FDR in the years before and during World War II. He became so excited about the prospect of filming an adaptation that he bought the rights to the biography with his own money. As Laventhall explained, "Studios were interested and would have paid for it for him, but he did not want to have a studio in a position to tell him what to do with it. He was definitely planning to move on to something that he *totally* controlled and owned—and he spent quite a lot of money on it, because not only did he option it once, he optioned it a second time. Finally, the option ran out and he had to buy the book for several hundred thousand dollars."

Pakula, a fervent admirer of the Roosevelts and their politics, hoped that his adaptation would be the consummate Alan J. Pakula film: a realization of his belief that movies could handle mature, complex material of a psychological, social, and political nature. Laventhall remarked, "the audience for something like this is a pretty sophisticated, older, educated audience. It's not a date movie. It's going to be an expensive period piece."

Had Pakula lived, *No Ordinary Time* would have taken several years to complete, and might have been his final film. Had that been the case, it would have been a fitting ending to his career, Catherine Solt thought, for "that's what *No Ordinary Time* was about," she said: "something of substance."

As Pakula began extensive researches into the lives and political accomplishments of the Roosevelts, he consulted his cousin Selma Hirsh about her personal recollections, for she had worked for Eleanor Roosevelt during the Second World War. However, most of his five hundred pages of research was based on his readings.

Using the method he had utilized while writing *The Pelican Brief*, Pakula began working on a screenplay of *No Ordinary Time*: taking each page of the biography, adding visuals and dialogue, condensing material here, adding material there. Even though he envisioned dramatizing less than half of Goodwin's book, taking the narrative up to the bombing of Pearl Harbor, he despaired of condensing the screenplay into manageable length, as he told Bob Woodward a few months before his death. Believing that the resultant film would run at least four hours, he considered making two two-hour cable television films, or possibly two separate two-hour (or longer) theatrical films. "He was trying to figure out how he could cut it down, but there was a sense that he shared with me of immense frustration about it," Woodward said.

Horton Foote was certain that Pakula would surmount whatever problems lay ahead. "When he talked about his work on his Roosevelt project, honest and articulate as ever, and modest, always cautioning that he might not be able to fill his vision," Foote said, "I could tell from the depth of his total involvement in the life of the two Roosevelts he so admired and loved that there was no chance of its not being, in whatever form it finally took—a film or miniseries—remarkable. It is a great loss that it wasn't to be completed."

When Pakula was killed, having written about fifty pages of the screenplay, Hannah Pakula (who, as Alan's heir, owns the film rights to the book) turned over her husband's notes to Don Laventhall, suggesting that he complete the script. As of this writing, Laventhall has delivered the third and final draft of the screenplay.

"For me," Hannah Pakula said, "one of the great sadnesses [about Alan's death] was that Alan had finally gotten to a point where he could do that kind of a film and didn't have to worry about not doing a popular thing—but he died before he could do it."

* * *

The task of announcing Pakula's death after the freak accident on the Long Island Expressway fell to Detective Sergeant Brian Traynor, speaking for the Suffolk County Police. Traynor said that police did not know where the seven-foot metal pipe that killed Pakula had come from, but, he said, "We believe the metal pipe was on the road before it struck Mr. Pakula's car," sending it crashing through Pakula's windshield. "I'm trying to find out how the pipe got there," Traynor added.

Alice Siegel, speaking for North Shore University Hospital, said that Pakula was barely alive when the ambulance arrived at the hospital. "He died minutes after," she said, "because he had massive injuries all over."

Hannah, who was not in East Hampton because she was writing a story on Queen Noor of Jordan and had remained in New York City to attend an event at which the queen would be appearing that night, learned about her husband's death when two policemen came to her Manhattan apartment. They were unable to provide details about the accident—where the metal pipe had come from, who drove the car that ran over the pipe, et cetera—and Hannah, after informing her family and her closest friends of Alan's death, called Don Hewitt and Peter Jennings, "because they were close friends and I felt they could both help me find out what had happened." But no one could provide more information, simply because nothing more was known.

Marilyn Berger, a close friend of the Pakulas, whose job at the *New York Times* entailed writing obituaries, among other responsibilities, was taking a piano lesson on the afternoon of November 19, 1998. Suddenly, for no reason she could explain, she stopped and "said to my teacher, 'Can I use the phone? I just want to check to see if anybody died.' And I *never* do that." Later, she remembered her intuition ruefully, for she learned about Pakula's death a few hours afterwards, "when a woman working at our house said, 'Something terrible has happened. Mrs. Pakula called and Mr. Hewitt [Berger's husband] called and said you should call him right away.' Don said, 'It's as bad as it could be.'" Berger went to Hannah's apartment and helped her call the Pakulas' friends.

Debby Maisel, Pakula's niece, recalls that she was in her bedroom at about four o'clock in the afternoon when the telephone rang. It was Hannah. "Alan was killed," she said, "and I wanted to tell you before you hear it on the news." Maisel, in tears when she told me of the phone call, four years after the event, said that Pakula's death was "horrible for everybody" in the family.

Celia Costas spoke for Pakula's friends when she said, "I was devastated by his death in a way that I almost couldn't share with anyone."

Louis Boorstin, Pakula's stepson who, with his family, had celebrated Alan and Hannah's twenty-fifth wedding anniversary nearly a year before Pakula's fatal accident, said, shortly after Alan was killed, "These days, I take lots of comfort from the distractions afforded by two young sons. At the same time, it saddens me deeply that our boys will never get to know Alan. . . . As the boys grow up, I would be more than content to be as good a father to them as Alan was to me."

Several days after the accident, the police announced that they were still looking for the driver from whose truck the pipe had fallen. Attempts to locate the individual were futile, however. Subsequently, Hannah placed a notice in a newspaper and two truckers' journals offering a reward for information. "I certainly wouldn't have done anything about it," she said, "but I wished I'd known. I wished whoever dropped the steel pipe had come forth and said, 'I'm sorry, I dropped it.' I just really was trying to find out what happened."

Pakula was buried in the Green River Cemetery near his home in East Hampton. The facility has been referred to as "the artists' cemetery." Among those who are buried there are painters Jackson Pollock, Lee Krasner, and Elaine de Kooning, and writer A. J. Liebling. The burial site is along a fence at the back of the cemetery, under an oak tree. Prayers in English and Hebrew were spoken as Pakula was laid to rest. Peter Jennings spoke of Pakula as a "spectacular . . . eccentric . . . complicated and extremely modest man . . . who gave a lot of people a lot of happiness and a lot of strength." Don Hewitt said, "I never met anybody in my life who was not a better man or a better woman for having known Alan Pakula."

A memorial service for Pakula was held at the Broadhurst Theatre in New York on February 4, 1999. Among the speakers were his stepchildren Bob Boorstin, Anna Boorstin and Chris Murray, as well as friends Peter Stone, Meryl Streep, Kevin Kline, Horton Foote, and Gregory Peck. Kline, holding back tears, quoted Shakespeare as he summed up his feelings for Pakula: "His life was gentle, and the elements so mixed in him that nature might stand up and say to all the world, 'This was a man.'"

* * *

After his death, Pakula was awarded the Golden Satellite Award for Outstanding Artistic Contribution to the Entertainment Industry. He was posthumously inducted into the Producers Guild Hall of Fame. The Broadcast Film Critics Association arranged for the Alan J. Pakula Award to be given annually "for artistic excellence while illuminating issues of great social and political importance." (The first several winners were *A Civil Action*, *The Insider*, *The Contender*, and *Saving Private Ryan*. Hannah Pakula said she was "particularly proud that [the BFCA] has chosen to honor [Pakula's] initiatives in asking the really important questions of our time.") The National Board of Review of Motion Pictures created an award in Pakula's name.

The American Film Institute began an Alan J. Pakula Memorial Fund.

Along with these honors, critics began to reassess their evaluations of Pakula's lifetime of work. Although many of them had withheld critical approbation of his films when he was alive, praise was lavished upon him in death. For example, Deborah H. Holdstein and R. Barton Palmer wrote in *The St. James Film Directors Encyclopedia* that Pakula "is now considered by many a major cinematic stylist . . . acknowledged within the film industry as an 'actor's director,' eliciting 'richly textured performances.'"

John Anderson, writing in the *Los Angeles Times*, said, "Alan J. Pakula's body of work . . . comprises a monument to their times. And to their maker: They reveal a director and producer whose box-office savvy never precluded his desire for substance, and whose political and social conscience never kept him from making a movie that, as they say, 'worked.'" An article in the *London Daily Telegraph* said that Pakula's "best films achieved great elegance."

Many critics now referred to movies such as *Klute* and *The Parallax View*, that had been dismissed by most reviewers when they first appeared, as classics of American film. Pakula's ability to tell a compelling story without resort to special effects, car crashes, or interstellar warfare was commended. His concentration on adult themes, the psychological depth of his characters, and his perfectionism were all celebrated.

Throughout Pakula's career, the moviegoing public had appreciated his films even when the critical community withheld praise. This might seem less than a ringing endorsement of Pakula's originality and integrity, for one cannot deny that many of the most popular and profitable films in American history have been tasteless, formulaic comedies, action films unsullied by subtleties of plot, bereft of believable characterization, and—especially prior to the 1960s—examples of banal sentimentality. Nevertheless, many artists and substantial works of art won public recognition despite being ignored or berated by the critics. To take a single example from the cinema: Arthur Penn's 1967 *Bonnie and Clyde* was savagely attacked by reviewers nationwide. The film is now recognized as a classic primarily because audiences of the time ignored the critics and formed their own opinions. Outside the world of film, one might point to the critical disdain for the plays of Anton Chekhov in the nineteenth century. Clearly, those critics have been proven wrong.

Perhaps re-evaluations of *Sophie's Choice* and *Starting Over* will, in time, place those films among the finest American motion pictures, just as *Klute* and *The Parallax View* have ascended to that category. No such re-evaluation is called for in the case of *All the President's Men* and *Presumed Innocent*, for both were recognized as outstanding at the time of their release.

Pakula's reputation and achievements would be regarded more highly if he hadn't directed so many films simply because he wanted to work in different styles. Some of his inferior pictures, such as *Comes a Horseman* and *Consenting Adults*, were made simply because he wanted to direct a Western and a Hitchcock-like thriller. Other films had equally questionable derivations. *Dream Lover* seems to have been made, in large part, as a favor to Hannah's nephew (which, most would agree, is not a good reason for making a film); *See You in the Morning* was intended as a highly personal token of love to his wife and her children; and *The Devil's Own* was made simply because the salary was too great to turn down. All of these films are well below Pakula's normal standard. *Rollover*, his most complete failure, is simply inexplicable. But, these missteps aside, Pakula left the world an otherwise remarkably distinguished group of films.

Janet Maslin, in a *New York Times* article entitled "Finding Depth in Society's Shallow End" written shortly after Pakula's death, referred to "his brand of knowing understatement," his "intense attention to detail," and to the fact that, to the very end, he "kept his perspective as sharp as his hauntingly intuitive directorial gifts." She characterized his style as "thoughtful, efficient and adult . . . [allowing] for quiet moments [and] subtle plotting that have all but vanished from more recent films. . . . [P]erformers flourished in the intriguing, multidimensional realm of Mr. Pakula's work."

Pieter Jan Brugge, as Pakula's son-in-law, perhaps cannot be entirely objective in his response to Pakula's movies, but Brugge is also a producer and director in his own right and was a student of film when he grew up in Amsterdam. It is not inappropriate, therefore, to include his assessment. Brugge cited Pakula's "very strong visual style," but described it as a "style of understatement, of extraordinary discipline, and that discipline is characterized by containment and rigorous adherence to point of view. I think that in his own way he was as much a visual stylist—albeit in a much more reserved and contained way—as many other directors who made their mark in the 1970s, like Coppola, Scorsese, Friedkin, and DePalma."

Brugge observed that Pakula never moved his camera unless it was dramatically motivated, "whereas the generation [of directors] after him, like the ones mentioned above, started moving the camera much, much more; it wasn't always dramatically motivated in a classic sense, but they experimented [and] broke new ground. Their cinema was more visceral and kinetic." That, he noted, "was not a style of filmmaking that he [Pakula] subscribed to. He was of a different generation."

* * *

Pakula had some well-considered opinions about filmmaking techniques, and before he died he articulated a number of them. He always planned his shooting schedule meticulously, but, precisely because he could envision several ways of filming a scene, he tended to use a large number of takes, giving him a myriad of choices in the editing room. "You have to be prepared for everything changing at the last second," he said. *Too* much planning, he found, was counterproductive. "I can't work the way Hitchcock works," he said. "I cannot work out and plan everything in advance, and say, 'That's the way it's going to be.' If I did that, my assistant could direct it, and it would be close to the same picture." Instead, he said, "once the planning is done, I then throw an awful lot away while I work. I try to keep one conception in my head, [but] I try to use all the accidents [in rehearsals and during shooting] that happen."

He tended to use close-ups sparingly. "If you use close-ups all the time," he said, "it's like [using] exclamation points, they mean nothing when you use them." Pakula said that "camera movement, cuts, close-ups are the grammar of film, and I happen not to be enthusiastic about writing when there are lots of exclamation points." He advocated using close-ups "with caution and with precision, because if you use them just to keep a scene going, to keep the audience amused, or use them without making a story point, when you *want* to make a story point [it will] mean nothing."

On another occasion, he said, "If you overuse camera movement, it's like screaming, 'Help, help, help,' all the time. . . . If you're looking at the eyes and face of a character, and [the actor is] revealing emotions [effectively], why the hell move the camera, unless that movement makes a statement? I hate camerawork for its own sake. If you don't know what to do with a camera, then don't do anything. . . . When you start imposing something to make it interesting, the whole concentration of the film falls apart. It becomes dishonest and the audience senses it. On the other hand, if I have a woman laughing on the phone, and she gives this huge speech that's wildly funny, and I pan down to her hands, and her fingernails are digging holes into her palms and they're bleeding, there's a reason for that camera movement." Visual style must be "dictated by content," he said. "Otherwise it's just a *tour de force*, and I have no use for that." At another time, he said, "If the design image I have in my mind interferes with the acting—the reality of human behavior—I drop the design image."

A general rule he observed was, "If you show everything in a film, you show nothing. What [the spectators] see is defined by what they don't see."

When Pakula was asked to assess his strengths and weaknesses as a filmmaker, he answered:

I think if I'm passionate about something, I'll get it done. There's a specific concept in what I do, and if I fail, I fail in a specific way. I think that sometimes I become so intensely involved with the material and certain things have such a specific meaning for me that I may be surprised if they don't have that same meaning to the audience. And maybe I become too oblique, although I try to go for very simple narrative pull in my films. . . . They're far from avant-garde, although I experiment with techniques. I'd say I'm from a kind of Charles Dickens school of filmmaking. . . . If we're creative, if we're lucky, we have things that drive us, mysteries that we have to live and relive and act out and reenact. And each time, if you're creative and you're lucky, you get a picture or a book or a story out of it.

Pakula confessed that he was occasionally guilty of "lingering too long on shots, too long on moments of performance." He also felt that he had to take care not to permit sentimentality (which he defined as "when the filmmaker loves his characters more than God does") to creep into his films.

* * *

Many of Pakula's movies seem, at first glance, to be at variance with his personality and experience. Despite his rapid rise to success in Hollywood, his comfortable upbringing in New York, his nearly idyllic relationship with his family, and his ability to make friends and keep them throughout his life, most of the films he directed explored the dark side of humanity. This seeming contradiction was explained by Pakula during a panel discussion in 1983: "The world went through a terrible depression, it went through the rise of Nazism, it went through the Second World War, it went through the Holocaust. I was an American middle-class Jewish boy, blessed by God with this incredibly protected environment. [But] I knew that out beyond my little protected island of a life there was terror." He never ceased to be fascinated by the struggle of individuals to deal with that terror, to begin again even when innocence has been lost.

Loss of innocence offers the thematic material for many of Pakula's films, beginning with *To Kill a Mockingbird*. It may also be said to be at the core of *The Sterile Cuckoo*, *The Parallax View*, *All the President's Men*, *Rollover*, *Sophie's Choice*, and *The Pelican Brief*. Pakula said, shortly before he died, "You look back on your films and you begin to realize that there are things that seem to haunt you as a director, as a filmmaker, whether it's material that you have written or material you have chosen. Somewhere there are these underground rivers that keep pulling you to things." He said that the recurrent theme in his films was expressed by "contrasts between light and dark, between strength and weakness, between the constructive and destructive and self-destructive; those elements existing in one character appear in a lot of my work."

Heroism also assumes a large role in many of Pakula's pictures: the heroism of a small-town lawyer defending a black man in the segregated South; the heroism of a prostitute overcoming the threat of death; the heroism of individuals willing to defy a corrupt government; the heroism of ranchers who resist the efforts of a wealthy man to evict them from their land; the heroism of a woman who is forced to deal with the horrors of the Holocaust.

The mistrust of large and powerful institutions is also evident in many of Pakula's films. Don Laventhall conjectured that Pakula's attitude also reflected a veiled mistrust of the film studio heads who, Pakula feared, wished to wrest control from creative artists such as himself.

Perhaps his finest achievement, and the one that may be best remembered, was his ability to bring so many films dealing with social and political issues to a mass audience. He broke new ground every time he produced a *To Kill a Mockingbird*, directed a *Parallax View*, an *All the President's Men*, a *Sophie's Choice*, a *Presumed Innocent*—for films about racism, political conspiracies, journalistic endeavors leading to uncovering government malfeasance, the Holocaust, and the ignoble underbelly of the American system of justice would hardly have been thought of as films that could appeal to a wide public. Yet most of these films did precisely that.

Concerning Pakula's reputation as a "woman's director": to be sure, he enjoyed the company of women in general and was particularly fond of many of the actresses with whom he worked. But any suggestion that he was unable to achieve first-rate results with men overlooks the excellent performances he evoked from Kevin Kline and Peter MacNicol in *Sophie's Choice*, Harrison Ford in *Presumed Innocent*, Burt Reynolds in *Starting Over* and Robert Redford, Dustin Hoffman, and Jason Robards in *All the President's Men*. It is true, however, that the few weak leading performances given in Pakula's films were given by men, and that he occasionally clashed (quietly, as was his wont) with some of his leading male actors.

Alan Pakula enjoyed every aspect of filmmaking—to such a degree that some thought he preferred working with actors over every other aspect; others thought he derived his greatest satisfaction from post-production; and others, like Boaty Boatwright, felt that the pre-production process was the time he most enjoyed. "He *loved* all of the playing with the costumes and the sets and the lighting, working on the script, casting," she said. "You have a hundred people you're working with, but you're the conductor. No matter what happens in film, it's the director's vision that brings it all together."

Pieter Jan Brugge emphasized Pakula's work on post-production, "in which he was involved in every single area." As an example, he said, "When Alan collaborated with people in sound post-production, it was a genuine discussion about 'how can we get the most out of this scene? What elements of sound truly begin to characterize the dramatic conflict that the scene is about, and how do you best bring that to the fore?'"

Whatever element of filmmaking Pakula most enjoyed, he reserved his greatest enthusiasm for the *process* of making the film, rather than for the ultimate product. "The minute a film is finished I remove everything to do with that film from my office, from my house, and I only have in my office things to do with the next film," he said.

*   *   *

If Pakula's experiences of film were formed in the 1930s and 40s, and if the look of his films, with their meticulous details, was often reflective of the pictures he saw as a child and an adolescent, he was able to surmount the limitations of those films by exploring areas of human interaction that were closed to filmmakers of his youth because of the censorship under which they worked. By contrast, Pakula spent his career defying restriction and dealing with adventurous, previously unexplored subject matter.

His willingness to pass the wisdom and experience he had accumulated on to the next generation of filmmakers is evident from the many occasions he took to speak at universities. He gave a week's seminar at Harvard, for example, and spoke at Yale a number of times. He also served as a resource artist on several occasions at the Sundance Institute, and twice met with students for lengthy discussions at the American Film Institute. In his relationship with students who wished to become filmmakers, but even more in his work with younger artists and craftspeople like Celia Costas, Pieter Jan Brugge, Donald Laventhall, and Dianne Dreyer, Pakula was a mentor. Kevin Kline called Pakula "a mentor, a father figure, a teacher," and Bob Boorstin suggested that Kline's comment represented the feelings of many. Pakula, he said, "was a father figure to any young person who got near him. And that would include people whom he adopted professionally. Alan had this way with young people."

Alan Pakula's legacy, then, is twofold: as a person, he represented decency and sensitivity, and as an artist, he brought his humanity and his professionalism to bear on a significant number of outstanding films. Robert Redford praised Pakula for bringing "sensitivity and intellect to seemingly intractable subjects" such as "the Jim Crow South, Nazism, or Nixon," and making "them into wonderful, and enduring, stories."

In his work with others—actors, co-producers, screenwriters, cinematographers, crew members—Pakula was, in the words of Pieter Jan Brugge, able "to break the tension by not taking himself or the work too seriously. In doing so, he liberated you and created an atmosphere of camaraderie. It was his unique ability to make you feel that your contribution was important to him. [He made you feel that] you were an integral part of the journey. He encouraged you to contribute your very best because he appreciated and understood the collaborative nature of the filmmaking process better than anyone I know."

To the end, directing, writing, and producing motion pictures remained a thrilling adventure for Alan J. Pakula. "My work," he said, has given "[me] a chance to get into worlds I've been protected from, deep into people's souls I would never have understood otherwise, usually souls in chaos, or deep into another kind of world I would never have known."

BIBLIOGRAPHY

I. Books

Anderson, Richard, *William Goldman*, Boston: Twayne Publishers, 1979.

Art Murphy's Box Office Register, Hollywood, California, 1985.

Avisar, Ilan, *Screening the Holocaust: Cinema's Images of the Unimaginable*, Bloomington, Indiana University Press, 1988.

Bernstein, Carl, and Bob Woodward, *All the President's Men*, New York: Simon and Schuster, 1974.

Bobker, Lee R., *Elements of Film*, New York: Harcourt, Brace & World, Inc., 1969.

Box Office Champions 2000: Directors, Producers & Writers, Kagan Moviedata, December, 1999.

Boyum, Joy Gould, *Double Exposure: Fiction into Film*, New York: New American Library, 1989.

Bradlee, Ben, *A Good Life: Newspapering and Other Adventures*, New York: Simon & Schuster, 1995.

Brown, Dennis, *Actors Talk*, New York: Limelight Editions, 1999.

Carnes, Mark C., *Past Imperfect: History According to the Movies*, New York: Henry Holt and Company, 1996.

Ciment, Michel, *Kubrick*, New York: Faber and Faber, Inc., 1999.

Crawford, Cheryl, *One Naked Individual: My Fifty Years in the Theatre*, New York: The Bobbs-Merrill Company, Inc., 1977.

Doneson, Judith E., *The Holocaust in American Film*, Philadelphia: The Jewish Publication Society, 1987.

Draigh, David, *Behind the Screen*, New York: Abbeville Press, 1988.

Emery, Robert J., *The Directors—Take Two: In Their Own Words*, New York: TV Books, 2000.

Eubanks, Georgann, "William Styron: The Confessions of a Southern Writer" (first published in *Duke Magazine*), in James L. W. West III, ed., *Conversations with William Styron*, Jackson: University Press of Mississippi, 1985.

French, Sean, *Jane Fonda*, North Pomfret, Vermont: Trafalgar Square Publishing, 1997.

Gianetti, Louis, *Understanding Movies*, Fifth Edition, Englewood Cliffs, NJ: Prentice Hall, 1990.

Goldman, William, *Adventures in the Screen Trade*, New York: Warner Books, 1983.

Goldman, William, *Which Lie Did I Tell? More Adventures in the Screen Trade*, New York: Pantheon Books, 2000.

Goodwin, Doris Kearns, *No Ordinary Time*, New York: Simon and Schuster, 1994.

Graham, Katharine, *Personal History*, New York: Alfred A. Knopf, Inc., 1997.

Grisham, John, *The Pelican Brief*, New York: Doubleday, 1992.

Harbinson, Allen, *George C. Scott: The Man, the Actor, and the Legend*, New York: Pinnacle Books, 1977.

Hirshberg, Jack, *A Portrait of All the President's Men*, New York: Warner Books, 1976.

Holdstein, Deborah H. and R. Barton Palmer, "Alan J. Pakula" in Andrew Sarris, ed., *The St. James Film Directors Encyclopedia*, Detroit: Visible Ink, 1998.

Insdorf, Annette, *Indelible Shadows: Films and the Holocaust*, Second Edition, Cambridge: Cambridge University Press, 1989.

Kawin, Bruce F., *How Movies Work*, Berkeley: University of California Press, 1992.

Kessler, Lyle, *Orphans*, New York: Samuel French, Inc., 1983.

Kostilibas-Davis, James, and Myrna Loy, *Myrna Loy: Being and Becoming*, New York: Alfred A. Knopf, 1987.

Leuchtenberg, William E., "All the President's Men" in Mark C. Carnes, ed., *Past Imperfect: History According to the Movies*, New York: Henry Holt and Company, 1996.

Lewis, Steven, "William Styron" (transcription of an interview broadcast by the Canadian Broadcasting Corporation in 1983) in James L. W. West III, ed., *Conversations with William Styron*, Jackson: University Press of Mississippi, 1985.

Lupack, Barbara Tepa, *Take Two: Adapting the Contemporary American Novel to Film,* Bowling Green, OH: Bowling Green State University Popular Press, 1994. (Contains the essay, "Sophie's Choice, Pakula's Choices" by Barbara Tepa Lupack.)

Maychick, Diana, *Meryl Streep: The Reluctant Superstar,* New York: St. Martin's Press, 1984.

McBride, Joseph, ed., *Filmmakers on Filmmaking: The American Film Institute Seminars on Motion Pictures and Television,* Volumes One and Two, Los Angeles, J. P. Tarcher, Inc., © 1983, American Film Institute.

Monaco, James, *How to Read a Film,* New York: Oxford University Press, 1977.

Morris, Robert K., with Irving Mailin, eds., *The Achievement of William Styron* (Contains "Interviews with William Styron"), rev. ed., Athens: University of Georgia Press, 1981.

Piersall, Jim, and Al Hirshberg, *Fear Strikes Out,* Boston, Toronto: Little, Brown and Company, 1955.

Rosenstone, Robert A., *Visions of the Past: The Challenge of Film to Our Idea of History,* Cambridge: Harvard University Press, 1995.

Rosenstone, Robert A., ed., *Revisioning History: Film and the Construction of the Past,* Princeton, N. J.: Princeton University Press, 1995.

Sherman, Eric, ed., *Directing the Film: Film Directors on Their Art,* Boston: Little Brown, 1976.

Smith, Liz, *Natural Blonde,* New York: Hyperion, 2000.

Styron, William, *Sophie's Choice,* New York: Random House, 1976.

Toplin, Robert Brent, "All the President's Men: 'The Story That People Know and Remember'" in *History by Hollywood: the Use and Abuse of the American Past,* Urbana: University of Illinois Press, 1996.

II. Periodicals

"Alan J. Pakula, Film Director," *East Hampton Star,* November 26, 1998.

Bobrow, Andrew C., "The Parallax View: An Interview with Alan Pakula," *Filmmakers Newsletter,* September 1974.

Burr, Ty, "An Actor's Director," *Entertainment Weekly,* December 4, 1998.

Carveth, Donald L., "Dead End Kids: Projective Identification and Sacrifice in Orphans," *PsyArt,* June 20, 1998.

Champlin, Charles, "For Pakula, It's Falling in Love With Love and Being in Love," *Los Angeles Times,* March 5, 1989.

Clein, Harry, "Alan J. Pakula, the Gentle Stylist and . . . The Sterile Cuckoo," *Entertainment World,* January 16, 1970.

Combs, Richard, "All the President's Men," *Sight and Sound,* vol. 45, no. 3, Summer, 1976.

Combs, Richard, "World Without Shadows," *Sight and Sound,* vol. 45, no. 3, Summer, 1976.

Culhane, John, "Pakula's Approach," *New York Times Magazine,* November 21, 1982.

"Dialogue on Film: Alan J. Pakula," *American Film,* vol. 4, no. 3, December-January, 1979.

"Dialogue on Film: Alan J. Pakula," *American Film,* vol. 11, no. 2, November 1985.

"Directing All the President's Men: Commentary by Alan J. Pakula," *Action,* vol. 11, no. 2, March-April 1976.

Dunlap, Benjamin, "Pakula's Choice," *Papers on Language and Literature,* vol. 23, no. 4, Summer, 1987.

Fizdale, Robert, and Arthur Gold, "New York State of Mind: Hannah and Alan J. Pakula's Apartment in the Sky," *Architectural Digest,* November 1989.

Gow, Gordon, "Unlikely Elements," *Films and Filming,* vol. 19, no. 3, December 1972.

Gross, Edith Loew, "Wife, Mother, Manager, Remarkable Cook . . . Hannah Pakula," *Vogue,* January 1982.

Hentoff, Nat, "From Woodstein at the Movies," *Columbia Journalism Review,* vol. 40, no. 4, November-December 2001.

Herlihy, David, "Am I a Camera? Other Reflections on Film and History," *The American Historical Review*, Volume 93, No. 5, December 1988.

Jameson, Richard T., "The Pakula Parallax," *Film Comment*, September–October 1976 (Volume 12, No. 5), pp. 8–12.

Kael, Pauline, "The Current Cinema," *The New Yorker*, December 27, 1982. (Review of *Sophie's Choice*)

Kauffmann, Stanley, "Pakula's Choice," *The New Republic*, January 10 and 17, 1983.

Kauffmann, Stanley, Review of The Devil's Own, *The New Republic*, April 21, 1977.

Knight, Deborah, and George McKnight, "The Case of the Disappearing Enigma," *Philosophy and Literature*, 21:1 (1997).

Lyman, Rick, "Watching Movies with Steven Soderbergh," *New York Times*, February 12, 2001.

Mulligan, Robert, "Goodbye," *DGA* [Director's Guild of America] *Magazine*, March 1999.

Music from the Movies, Autumn, 1998 (issue 21): article about the music of Michael Small and about his collaboration with Alan J. Pakula.

New York Times: all references to (and reviews of all the films of) Alan J. Pakula; also all references to Hannah Pakula, 1957–1999.

O'Connor, John E., "History in Images/Images in History: Reflections on the Importance of Film and Television Study for an Understanding of the Past," *The American Historical Review*, Volume 93, No. 5, December 1988.

Pakula, Alan J., "Dialogue on Film," *American Film*, December–January, 1979.

Pakula, Alan J., "Making a Film About Two Reporters," *American Cinematographer*, vol. 57, no. 7, July 1976.

Pizzello, Stephen, "Wrap Shot," *American Cinematographer*, vol. 79, no. 7, July 1998.

Redford, Robert, "Alan J. Pakula: Seeking Truth on the Big Screen," *Newsweek*, November 30, 1998.

Rosenbaum, J., and Alan J. Pakula, "Alan J. Pakula and the Filming of Sophie's Choice: An Interview," *Cahiers du Cinema*, 1982.

Rosenstone, Robert A., "History in Images/Images in Words: Reflections on the Possibility of Really Putting History on to Film," *The American Historical Review*, Volume 93, No. 5, December 1988.

Simon, John, Review of The Devil's Own, *National Review*, vol. 49, May 5, 1997.

Styron, William, "A Wheel of Evil Come Full Circle: The Making of Sophie's Choice," *Sewanee Review*, v. 105, Summer, 1997.

Thompson, Richard, "Mr. Pakula Goes to Washington: Alan J. Pakula on *All the President's Men*," *Film Comment*, September–October 1976 (Volume 12, no. 5), pp. 12–19.

Toplin, Robert Brent, "The Filmmaker as Historian," *The American Historical Review*, Volume 93, No. 5, December 1988.

Toplin, Robert Brent, "Hollywood History: The Historians' Response," *Reviews in American History*, 24:2, 1996.

Turner, II, John S., "Collapsing the Interior/Exterior Distinction: Surveillance, Spectacle, and Suspense in Popular Cinema," *Wide Angle*, 20:4 (1998).

White, Hayden, "Historiography and Historiophoty," *The American Historical Review*, Volume 93, No. 5, December 1988.

Winters, Laura, "Delicately Dissecting the Quiet Life," *New York Times*, November 18, 2001.

III. Unpublished Sources

"Alan J. Pakula Interviewed by Martin Bookspan," Oral History Library Panel Session, William E. Wiener Oral History Library of the American Jewish Committee, Humanities—Jewish Division, New York Public Library, May 14, 1983.

The American Film Institute Seminar with Alan Pakula on November 20, 1974, © 1975 American
Film Institute.

The American Film Institute Seminar with Alan Pakula held May 27, 1976, © 1976 American Film
Institute.

Anson, Jay, *Klute in New York: A Background for Suspense,* documentary on the *Klute* DVD, Warner Bros.,
Inc., 1971.

Bozzola, Lucia, "Alan J. Pakula," Blockbuster web site (www.Blockbuster.com).

Bravo Profiles: *Robert Redford,* Produced and Directed by Toby Beach and Peter Yost,
Traveling East Productions.

Cardillo, Lauren, *Backstory: Sophie's Choice,* American Movie Classics documentary film, 2002.

Directors' Luncheon, March 28, 1977, Academy of Motion Picture Arts and Sciences.

Eleanor Bissinger Papers, Philadelphia, Pennsylvania.

Emery, Robert J., "The Directors," produced by Media Entertainment, Inc.

George Stevens: A Filmmaker's Journey, documentary film produced, written, and directed by George
Stevens, Jr. A production of the Creative Film Center, Inc., SFM Entertainment, 1984.

The Hill School: principal's evaluation (November 15, 1944) and Alan J. Pakula's entry in the
1945 yearbook.

Jacobson, Harlan, "Obituary: Alan J. Pakula," WFUV-FM, November 27, 1998.

Kiselyak, Charles, *Death Dreams of Mourning,* documentary on the DVD of *Sophie's Choice,*
Artisan Home Entertainment.

Kiselyak, Charles, *Fearful Symmetry: The Making of* To Kill a Mockingbird, documentary on the DVD
of *To Kill a Mockingbird,* Universal Home Video, Inc., 1998.

Kiselyak, Charles, "Production Notes" on the *To Kill a Mockingbird* DVD, Universal Home Video, 1998.

Memorial Service for Alan J. Pakula, February 4, 1999.

Nichols, John, "A Personal Tribute to Film Director Alan Pakula," World Socialist web site (wsws.org).

Pakula, Alan J., Director's commentary track on the *Sophie's Choice* DVD, Artisan Home
Entertainment.

Pakula, Alan J., and Robert Mulligan, commentary on the *To Kill a Mockingbird* DVD,
Universal Home Video, 1998.

Pakula, Alan J., *Sophie's Choice* (Screenplay). [New York: GUS Productions, n.d.]

"Reel Pieces," a series of interviews moderated by Annette Insdorf at Manhattan's 92nd Street
"Y." Alan J. Pakula, interviewed by Annette Insdorf, New York City, November 27, 1990.

"Under the Influence Screening of *The Parallax View* [Interview of Alan J. Pakula by Steven
Soderbergh], Directors' Guild of America, Inc.

IV. Interviews

Alexander, Jane	Bradlee, Ben	Dreyer, Dianne	Kamen, Robert
Bacall, Lauren	Brooks, James L.	Fonda, Jane	Kessler, Lyle
Baxter, Rodd	Brugge, Pieter Jan	Foote, Horton	Kline, Kevin
Bergen, Candice	Cioffi, Charles	Ford, Harrison	Lange, David
Berger, Marilyn	Clayburgh, Jill	Gordon, Alixe	Lange [Hollerith],
Bissinger, Annie	Clein, Harry	Gordon, Lawrence	Hope
Bissinger, Buzz	Costas, Celia	Hamlisch, Marvin	Laventhall, Donald
Boatwright, Alice Lee	Creedon, Colleen	Hewitt, Don	Lord, Bette Bao
["Boaty"]	Cronyn, Hume	Hirsh, Selma	Lumet, Sidney
Boorstin, Anna	Davis, Barbara	Insdorf, Annette	Maisel, Debby
Boorstin, Louis	Doherty [Hess],	Jennings, Peter	Manulis, Martin
Boorstin, Bob	Patricia Anne	Justin, George	Mulligan, Robert

Murray, Christopher	Redford, Robert	Smith, Liz	Sutherland, Donald
Newhouse, Donald and Susan	Saks, Gene	Solt, Catherine	Turman, Lawrence
	Saks, Keren	Starger, Martin	Willis, Gordon
Pakula, Hannah	Sargent, Alvin	Streep, Meryl	Woodward, Bob
Pierson, Frank	Small, Michael	Styron, William	

NOTES

(see Bibliography for full citations)

Abbreviations Used in Notes

ACB   Bobrow, Andrew C., *"The Parallax View:* An Interview with Alan Pakula"

AFI1   Alan Pakula: The American Film Institute Seminar with Alan Pakula on November 20, 1974 © 1975 American Film Institute

AFI2   Alan Pakula: The American Film Institute Seminar on His Work, held May 27, 1976, © 1976 American Film Institute

AI   "Reel Pieces," Alan J. Pakula interviewed by Annette Insdorf at the 92nd Street "Y," New York City, November 27, 1990

BRTC   Billy Rose Theatre Collection, Performing Arts Research Center, New York Public Library

DOF1   "Dialogue on Film: Alan J. Pakula," *American Film,* vol. 4, no. 3, December–January, 1979

DOF2   "Dialogue on Film: Alan J. Pakula," *American Film,* vol. 11, no. 2, November 1985

ED   Emery, Robert J., *The Directors,* Produced by Media Entertainment, Inc.

MB   "Alan J. Pakula Interviewed by Martin Bookspan," Oral History Library Panel Session, William E. Wiener Oral History Library of the American Jewish Committee, Humanities—Jewish Division, New York Public Library, May 14, 1983

MS   Memorial Service for Alan J. Pakula, held on February 4, 1999

NYT   *New York Times*

PA   Culhane, John, "Pakula's Approach," *New York Times Magazine,* November 21, 1982

RT   Thompson, Richard, "Mr. Pakula Goes to Washington: Alan J. Pakula on *All the President's Men,"* *Film Comment,* September–October 1976 (Volume 12, no. 5, pp. 12-19)

SCB   Cardillo, Lauren, *Backstory: Sophie's Choice,* American Movie Classics documentary film, 2002

SCD   Pakula, Alan J., Director's commentary track on the *Sophie's Choice* DVD, Artisan Home Entertainment

TT   Emery, Robert J., *The Directors: Take Two*

UE   Gordon Gow, "Unlikely Elements," *Films and Filming,* vol. 19, no. 3, December 1972

PREFACE

"For me, Alan Pakula was one of the . . .": *NYT,* November 18, 2001

CHAPTER ONE

"It's important for filmmakers . . .": Joseph McBride, ed., *Filmmakers on Filmmaking,* © 1983, American Film Institute.

"was a name . . ." [footnote]: Interview with Selma Hirsh

Paul, Ben, and the Bryant Press: Interview with Selma Hirsh

"well-to-do and had . . .": Interview with Alvin Sargent

"My father worked . . ." PA

"some kind of breakdown": Interview with Debby Maisel

"when you would see him . . .": Interview with Debby Maisel

"a good Jewish child" and "because I was terrified": MB

"understood [Alan] more than his father": Interview with Selma Hirsh

"very precise . . .": Interview with a family member who preferred not to be identified

"He always moved carefully . . .": Interview with Alvin Sargent

"even if he had to . . .": Interview with a family member who preferred not to be identified

"a very nice guy . . .": Interview with Rodd Baxter

"were wonderful grandparents . . .": Interview with Debby Maisel

"would be amazed . . .": Interview with Rodd Baxter

"used to fight a lot . . .": Interview with Selma Hirsh

"Alan used to say that my mother . . ." Interview with Debby Maisel

"Our families lived . . .": Interview with Selma Hirsh

"was not very athletic": Interview with Selma Hirsh

Information about life in Long Beach: Interviews with Hannah Pakula, Selma Hirsh,
    individuals in Long Beach

"As a child . . .": *ED*

Pakula's formative film influences: Director's Luncheon, Academy of Motion Picture Arts
    and Sciences

"I wanted him in my business . . .": PA

"Dad, I really wish . . ." [footnote]: Interview with Hannah Pakula

"the resemblance between being . . .": AFI1

"an analytic buff": RT

Bronx High School of Science: transcript

Hill School: transcript

"Hill School was a very starchy place . . .": Interview with Barbara Davis

Anti-Semitism at the Hill School: MB

"a fine, well-balanced youth . . ." and Pakula's I. Q.: Principal's evaluation, the Hill School

"what I was worrying about . . .": PA

Information about the Pipe Club: letter from Denise Spatarella of the Hill School

"Well, Harvard and Yale are . . .": MB

"I didn't. I would take . . .": MB

Courses at Yale: listing of courses from Yale University

"Don't just study films . . .": Interview with Hannah Pakula

"you learn all the rules . . .": AFI1

"I had a great need . . ." MB

"I'll never forget the moment . . .": DOF1

"bounding through the campus . . .": MB

"God through the theatre": AI

"I would hang out in the balcony . . .": MB

"You subsidize me for two years . . .": combined quotation, MB and PA

"Would you be interested in . . ." *TT*, p. 91

"wandering around in his . . ." Interview with Alvin Sargent

"Relax, Sydney, relax" and "You'd see Sydney . . .": AFI1

"stepped in and showed him . . .": DOF1

"directors who use actors . . .": DOF1

"Dad, I'm coming into your business" and following: *NYT*, November 21, 1982.

"Somewhere the insecure . . .": MB

"a close marriage as long . . .": PA

"My grandparents lived . . .": Interview with Debby Maisel

"they got so they had . . ." Interview with Selma Hirsh

"The Pakula family was really . . .": Interview with Debby Maisel

"Everything he said on the phone . . .": PA

"My salary didn't match my title:" clipping, February 26, 1986, BRTC

"When you're assistant to a studio head . . .": Interview with Larry Turman

"It's not that much" and following quotation: AFI2

"I sat in on major meetings": AFI1

"learned the difference between . . .": *TT*

"sort of a hidden workaholic": Interview with Larry Turman

"Everybody underestimated me . . ." and "There was a fierce . . .": Interview with Frank Pierson

CHAPTER TWO

"Once a director's on a set . . .": PA

"Why he did that particular . . .": Interview with Alvin Sargent

"I at one time toyed . . .": MB

"The central theme was . . .": PA

"a kind of mystery . . .": *TT*

"somebody from my generation": *TT*

"I was kind of shattered . . .": combined quotation, UE and Pakula, Alan J., and Robert Mulligan, commentary on the *To Kill a Mockingbird* DVD

"Please, please, please:" combined quotation, UE and *TT*

"took a very deep breath . . ." Robert Mulligan, "Goodbye"

"He was very young . . .": Robert Mulligan, "Goodbye"

"Alan was never on the set . . .": Interview with Robert Mulligan

"protecting the film on release": clipping, BRTC

Importance of Pakula's judgment in *Fear Strikes Out*: Interview with Robert Mulligan

"One of the things . . .": Pakula, Alan J., and Robert Mulligan, commentary on the *To Kill a Mockingbird* DVD

"the breaking out of the chrysalis . . .": DOF1

"so improves upon . . .": *NYT*, March 21, 1957

"Fear Strikes Out rolls Frank . . .": *Time*, March 18, 1957

"should do great business": *Newsweek*, March 25, 1957

"During Fear Strikes Out, we found . . .": Interview with Robert Mulligan

"Neither of us had a dime . . .": Interview with Robert Mulligan

"Alan was absolutely passionate . . .": Interview with Robert Mulligan

"Alan took it particularly hard . . .": Interview with Robert Mulligan

"working with Bob set me back . . .": AFI1

"I do know laughter . . .": Interview with Robert Mulligan

"a girl who is in love . . .": *NYT*, November 7, 1958

"powerful and provocative . . .": quoted by Cheryl Crawford in *One Naked Individual: My Fifty Years in the Theatre*, p. 256

"has theatrical moments . . .": *NYT*, November 7, 1958

"the most exciting actor . . .": quoted by Allen Harbinson in *George C. Scott: The Man, the Actor, and the Legend*

"mechanical . . . the contrived style . . .": *NYT*, November 7, 1958

"he believed I could do it . . .": Interview with Robert Mulligan

"I just didn't feel . . .": Interview with Horton Foote

Pakula's memos to Stanley Young: Eleanor Bissinger Papers, Philadelphia, Pennsylvania

Pakula wishing to cast Robert Redford in Laurette: Interview with Robert Redford

"Luckily, Bob does not . . .": *New York Post*, April 15, 1975

"one of the largest advance sales . . .": Eleanor Bissinger Papers

"unless the cops kick us out" and "We didn't take this seriously . . .": *NYT*, August 27, 1960

"Mr. Griffith and Mr. Prince . . .": *NYT*, August 27, 1960

"I have faith in your intuitions . . .": Eleanor Bissinger Papers

"Laurette is a play in which nothing . . .": *New Haven Evening Register*, September 27, 1960

"droned on . . . stolidly . . .": *New Haven Journal-Courier*, September 27, 1960

"show will not open": Eleanor Bissinger Papers

"I have been waiting to hear from . . .": Eleanor Bissinger Papers

"I am slowly going out of my mind" and "Hate to bring this up . . .": Eleanor Bissinger Papers

"decided that he wanted Myrna . . ." James Kostilibas-Davis and Myrna Loy, *Myrna Loy:
    Being and Becoming*

"very excited about it . . .": Interview with Robert Mulligan

"does not display enough . . .": *Variety*, June 24, 1962

Myrna Loy's belief that the rewrites were ineffective: James Kostilbas-Davis and Myrna Loy,
    Myrna Loy: Being and Becoming

"I have told Jim . . .": Eleanor Bissinger Papers

CHAPTER THREE

"For me, producing a film means . . ." *Movietone News*, October 1973

"A lot of the studios . . .": Charles Kiselyak, *Fearful Symmetry*

"I sensed it would be the role . . .": "Modest Maestro," *People Weekly*, December 7, 1998

"If you want me, I'm your boy": Charles Kiselyak, *Fearful Symmetry*

"Given the fact that we . . .": Interview with Robert Mulligan

"This was only Pakula's and Mulligan's second film . . .": Interview with Horton Foote

"I felt a close . . .": Charles Kiselyak, *Fearful Symmetry*

"breaking it down and . . .": Interview with Robert Mulligan

"I was busy on things . . .": Interview with Horton Foote

"trusted us that the book would . . ." Charles Kiselyak, *Fearful Symmetry*

"was passionately devoted to the novel . . .": Charles Kiselyak, *Fearful Symmetry*

"We'd go over what I was doing . . .": Interview with Horton Foote

"I thought the comparison was . . .": combined quotation, Charles Kiselyak, *Fearful Symmetry*
    and Interview with Horton Foote

"Often we'd discuss . . .": Interview with Horton Foote

"Together, Alan and Horton . . .": Interview with Robert Mulligan

"You know what your problem is . . .": Pakula, Alan J., and Robert Mulligan, commentary
    on the *To Kill a Mockingbird* DVD

"a memory of time that is gone . . .": Charles Kiselyak, *Fearful Symmetry*

"There's a lot of hope . . .": Charles Kiselyak, *Fearful Symmetry*

"The big danger in . . .": Kiselyak, Charles, "Production Notes" from the DVD
    of *To Kill a Mockingbird*

"The tragedy is now . . ." [in footnote]: Pakula, Alan J., and Robert Mulligan, commentary
    on the *To Kill a Mockingbird* DVD

"Let's find kids who are kids . . .": Charles Kiselyak, *Fearful Symmetry*

"Honey, I don't know . . .": Pakula, Alan J., and Robert Mulligan, commentary
    on the *To Kill a Mockingbird* DVD

"He must have liked my . . .": Interview with Boaty Boatwright

"We realized very quickly . . .": Interview with Robert Mulligan

"with their mothers . . .": *New York Herald Tribune*, July 15, 1962

"You couldn't ask them to . . .": Interview with Boaty Boatwright

"I looked at this child . . .": Interview with Boaty Boatwright

"I've found the child . . .": Interview with Boaty Boatwright

"They both had a quality . . .": Charles Kiselyak, *Fearful Symmetry*

"a very unaffected kid . . .": Pakula, Alan J., and Robert Mulligan, commentary
    on the *To Kill a Mockingbird* DVD

"You have to explain . . .": Kiselyak, Charles, "Production Notes" on the *To Kill a Mockingbird* DVD

"In a way became . . .": Pakula, Alan J., and Robert Mulligan, commentary on the *To Kill a*
    Mockingbird DVD

"climb on the equipment . . .": Charles Kiselyak, *Fearful Symmetry*

"sensitive to the fact . . .": Pakula, Alan J., and Robert Mulligan, commentary on the
    To Kill a Mockingbird DVD

"I often saw Mary . . .": Pakula, Alan J., and Robert Mulligan, commentary on the
    To Kill a Mockingbird DVD

"I staged pretty much . . .": Pakula, Alan J., and Robert Mulligan, commentary on the
    To Kill a Mockingbird DVD

"We wanted to retain . . .": *NYT*, May 6, 1962

"I'll never forget the first day . . .": Combined quotation: Charles Kiselyak, *Fearful Symmetry* and
    Pakula, Alan J., and Robert Mulligan, commentary on the *To Kill a Mockingbird* DVD

"That's a lesson . . .": Charles Kiselyak, *Fearful Symmetry*

"That voice was so important . . .": Pakula, Alan J., and Robert Mulligan, commentary
    on the *To Kill a Mockingbird* DVD

"We all went down . . .": *NYT*, May 6, 1962

"and there we were in Maycomb.": Charles Kiselyak, *Fearful Symmetry*

"I know exactly where . . .": Pakula, Alan J., and Robert Mulligan, commentary on the
    To Kill a Mockingbird DVD

"Harper Lee visited the set . . .": Charles Kiselyak, *Fearful Symmetry*

"amused that his tomboy daughter . . .": Charles Kiselyak, *Fearful Symmetry*

"We weren't aware that they . . .": Charles Kiselyak, *Fearful Symmetry*

"a scene where Atticus . . .": Charles Kiselyak, *Fearful Symmetry*

"She did things in that scene . . .": Pakula, Alan J., and Robert Mulligan, commentary
on the *To Kill a Mockingbird* DVD

"There's a shyness in Greg . . .": Pakula, Alan J., and Robert Mulligan, commentary
    on the *To Kill a Mockingbird* DVD

"I had noticed when . . .": Charles Kiselyak, *Fearful Symmetry*

"this film narratively builds . . .": Pakula, Alan J., and Robert Mulligan, commentary
    on the *To Kill a Mockingbird* DVD

"The anger, the frustration . . .": Charles Kiselyak, *Fearful Symmetry*

"the only direction I gave Brock . . .": Pakula, Alan J., and Robert Mulligan, commentary
    on the *To Kill a Mockingbird* DVD

"heroic dimension," a "star quality": Pakula, Alan J., and Robert Mulligan, commentary
    on the *To Kill a Mockingbird* DVD

"Brock gave me a problem . . .": Charles Kiselyak, *Fearful Symmetry*

"One thing I always had to do . . .": Charles Kiselyak, *Fearful Symmetry*

"here is a very attractive . . .": Collin Wilcox, quoted in Charles Kiselyak, *Fearful Symmetry*

"She knows she's lying . . .": Charles Kiselyak, *Fearful Symmetry*

"was a social tragedy . . .": Pakula, Alan J., and Robert Mulligan, commentary on the *To Kill a Mockingbird* DVD

"had been warned that he . . .": Pakula, Alan J., and Robert Mulligan, commentary on the *To Kill a Mockingbird* DVD

"He was a very tough guy . . .": Interview with Robert Mulligan

"he said it in such a way . . ." Pakula, Alan J., and Robert Mulligan, commentary on the *To Kill a Mockingbird* DVD

"I sat him down . . ." combined quotation: Pakula, Alan J., and Robert Mulligan, commentary on the *To Kill a Mockingbird* DVD, and Interview with Robert Mulligan

"I think that seventy-five percent . . .": Pakula, Alan J., and Robert Mulligan, commentary on the *To Kill a Mockingbird* DVD

"just kibitz and free-associate . . .": Pakula, Alan J., and Robert Mulligan, commentary on the *To Kill a Mockingbird* DVD

"Because it was such a . . .": Pakula, Alan J., and Robert Mulligan, commentary on the *To Kill a Mockingbird* DVD

"Alan was younger than I . . .": MS

"would see the dailies. . ." Pakula, Alan J., and Robert Mulligan, commentary on the *To Kill a Mockingbird* DVD

"Gregory Peck is the truest . . .": Dennis Brown, *Actors Talk*

"there could have been a temptation . . ." Pakula, Alan J., and Robert Mulligan, commentary on the *To Kill a Mockingbird* DVD

"is just building the children's world": Pakula, Alan J., and Robert Mulligan, commentary on the *To Kill a Mockingbird* DVD

"They do all come together . . .": Pakula, Alan J., and Robert Mulligan, commentary on the *To Kill a Mockingbird* DVD

"It had to have an individual . . ." Charles Kiselyak, *Fearful Symmetry*

"children love to be scared. . . .": Charles Kiselyak, *Fearful Symmetry*

"the mysterious world of children . . .": Pakula, Alan J., and Robert Mulligan, commentary on the *To Kill a Mockingbird* DVD

"the mysterious world of childhood": Charles Kiselyak, *Fearful Symmetry*

"It caught the spirit . . .": Interview with Robert Mulligan

"print that was just gray . . ." Pakula, Alan J., and Robert Mulligan, commentary on the *To Kill a Mockingbird* DVD

"sure Universal had a great deal . . ." [footnote]: Interview with Robert Mulligan

"For me, Maycomb is there . . .": Kiselyak, Charles, "Production Notes" on the *To Kill a Mockingbird* DVD

"become as much a part . . .": Kiselyak, Charles, *Fearful Symmetry*

"What a number of people resented . . .": UE

"If you deal with a character . . .": UE

"There is so much feeling . . .": *NYT*, February 15, 1963

"portentous airlessness . . .": the *New Yorker*, February 23, 1963

"unsupportable . . .": *Newsweek*, February 18, 1963

"one of the year's most moving . . .": *Time*, February 22, 1963

"most profitable movies made": *NYT*, June 10, 1963

"One of the things . . ." Pakula, Alan J., and Robert Mulligan, commentary
   on the *To Kill a Mockingbird* DVD
"So he took me to Radio City . . .": Interview with Debby Maisel
"He was my best friend . . .": combined quotation, MS and Interview with Horton Foote

CHAPTER FOUR

"Alan was without question . . .": Interview with Robert Mulligan
"Alan and I never discussed . . .": Interview with Robert Mulligan
"not just in moments . . .": Interview with Robert Mulligan
"We made our films together . . .": Interview with Robert Mulligan
"There was a long period . . .:" PA
"they needed to weed through it": Interview with David Lange
"admired him tremendously": Interview with David Lange
"Everybody was sending in material . . .": Interview with David Lange
"Alan liked to have two or three . . .": Interview with David Lange
"He called me in . . .": Interview with Hope Lange
"Alan became emotionally involved . . .": Interview with David Lange
"He was just wonderful . . .": Interview with David Lange
"Now that man has orbited the moon . . .": *NYT*, June 10, 1963
"piles of rocks and desert vistas . . .": *NYT*, June 10, 1963
"was surprisingly small and crammed . . .": Interview with Robert Mulligan
"Our script conference was entirely . . .": Interview with Robert Mulligan
"we were involved with developing . . .": Interview with Robert Mulligan
"a wonderful old house . . .": Interview with Colleen Creedon
"parties with Roddy McDowall . . .": Interview with Robert Redford
"He was crazy about her . . .": Interview with Rodd Baxter
"He really loved her. . . .": Interview with Alvin Sargent
"She had a very strong . . .": Interview with Robert Redford
"I don't think that either Bob or myself . . .": UE
"deserves someone much more substantial . . .": *NYT*, December 26, 1963
"This romantic comedy-drama . . .": *Time*, December 27, 1963
"about all that I can recommend . . .": the *New Yorker*, January 11, 1964
"The great danger of that film . . .": UE
"to drink two large tumblers . . .": Interview with Robert Mulligan
"Cheever smiled a bemused smile . . .": Interview with Robert Mulligan
"a very workable first draft": Interview with Robert Mulligan
"encourage [a major] studio . . .": Interview with Robert Mulligan
"Kate Hepburn greeted us at the front door. . . .": Interview with Robert Mulligan
"Hepburn in slacks . . .": Interview with Robert Mulligan
"reputation for being difficult" and "we often eat directors . . .": Interview with Robert Mulligan
"said something Alan and I . . .": Interview with Robert Mulligan
"just couldn't make a deal" and "It was pretty spread out . . .": Interview with David Lange
"gorgeous music" and "got involved in other things": Interview with David Lange
Placido Domingo and the Gate Theatre: Interview with Hannah Pakula
"You would think. But it wasn't true. . . .": Interview with David Lange
"the character of Georgette . . .": Interview with Horton Foote
"Alan was very anxious to . . .": Interview with Horton Foote
"that's simply a truthful statement . . . [footnote]": Interview with Horton Foote

"dismal dimwit . . .": *Newsweek,* January 26, 1965

"a spectacular failure . . .": the *New Yorker,* January 23, 1965

"a major and totally neglected weakness . . .": *NYT,* January 14, 1965

"We never consciously tried . . . [footnote]": Interview with Horton Foote

"There was a part of Alan . . .": Interview with David Lange

"the character I would be playing . . ." and "When I was in Louisiana . . .": Interview with Robert Redford

"I called Alan and Bob . . .": Interview with Robert Redford

"[I] overproduced it, [I] should have . . .": Alan Pakula, quoted by David Lange

"was his fault" and "got in the way of a simple . . .": Interview with David Lange

"We had a good time making it. . . .": Interview with Robert Mulligan

"There have been [few] pictures . . .": *NYT,* February 18, 1966

"ridiculous . . . fatuous . . . discouraging . . .": *NYT,* February 20, 1966

"By the Hollywood standards of . . .": the *New Yorker,* February 26, 1966

"a wry and entertaining . . .": *Newsweek,* January 28, 1966

"would identify with the struggling . . .": *NYT,* August 20, 1967

"the complex character and . . .": *NYT,* August 18, 1967

"The film has no characters . . .": *Time,* July 31, 1967

"particularly affectless . . .": the *New Republic,* July 15, 1967

"because the script unwittingly makes . . ." and "the oldest of all . . .": the *New Yorker,* August 26, 1967

"I was amazed . . .": Interview with David Lange

"She cared so much about her career . . .": Interview with Martin Manulis

"I hardly saw him": Interview with Hope Lange

"it was essentially two stars . . .": Interview with David Lange

"From the outside, it appeared . . .": Interview with Larry Turman

"His marriage to Hope Lange . . .": Interview with Martin Manulis

"Alan was always fired up . . .": Interview with Colleen Creedon

"They didn't like it. . . .": Interview with Horton Foote

"It was a difficult thing for me . . .": Interview with Horton Foote

"Pakula and Mulligan needed a new script . . .": Interview with Alvin Sargent

"Alan and Bob made it clear . . .": Interview with Alvin Sargent

"It has the simplicity and fascination . . .": clipping from *Life,* BRTC

"a beautiful movie [visually, but] . . .": *NYT,* January 23, 1969

"a factory picture . . .": the *New Yorker,* February 1, 1969

"would have loved to get a good review . . . [footnote]": Interview with David Lange

"Alan told me very early on . . .": Interview with Robert Mulligan

"Alan's decision was a reason . . .": Interview with Robert Mulligan

"Alan and I started out . . .": Interview with Robert Mulligan

"I don't think he was thrilled": Interview with Hope Lange

"When they separated he . . .": Interview with Alvin Sargent

"very despondent, very sad . . .": Interview with Colleen Creedon

"I think Alan was devastated . . .": Interview with Boaty Boatwright

"It was a very difficult . . .": Interview with Martin Manulis

"Well, being married to Alan . . .": Interview with Hope Lange

"You know, Alan didn't like . . .": Interview with Boaty Boatwright

"intense [conversations] with him . . .": Interview with Selma Hirsh

"I heard rumors . . .": Interview with Larry Turman

"she separated right into . . .": Interview with Martin Manulis

"Hope was not the type to . . .": Interview with David Lange

"I have to sort of blame . . .": Interview with Hope Lange

"After two or three weeks . . .": Interview with David Lange

"came over to the house . . .": Interview with Hope Lange

"I think that Hope . . .": Interview with Martin Manulis

"my first wife": Interview with Peter Jennings

"a talented woman": *New York Post,* April 15, 1975

"Alan used to talk about . . .": Interview with Peter Jennings

"He was always very responsible . . .": Interview with Barbara Davis

CHAPTER FIVE

"One thing I think . . .": *ED*

"I always would go into . . .": PA

"felt that it was a difficult step . . .": Interview with Horton Foote

"What the hell are you doing here?" and "While Bob is working . . .": Interview with Sidney Lumet

"It's about time I put up . . .": Directors' Luncheon, March 28, 1977

"He had to be a director . . .": Interview with Alvin Sargent

"And then I thought . . .": combined quotation, PA and AFI1

"Alan would produce and I . . .[footnote]": Interview with Robert Mulligan

"He danced around a lot. . . .": Interview with Alvin Sargent

"got to me, her incredible . . .": *NYT,* December 7, 1969

"just couldn't see it . . .": ACB

"It was the most overly directed . . .": AI

"had them do everything . . .": combined quotation, DOF1, *TT,* and ACB

"were in a state of shock . . .": combined quotation, ACB and AFI2

"Paramount saw the script. . . .": combined quotation, AI and *TT*

"with much trepidation": *TT*

"Evans never said anything . . .": Harry Clein, "Alan J. Pakula, the Gentle Stylist and . . .
   The Sterile Cuckoo"

"If anything, working with . . .": ACB

"waited until after . . .": *TT*

"One of the rules of directing . . .": *TT*

"Liza thought [Pookie] was going to be . . .": DOF1

"It is a story of awakening . . .": Harry Clein, "Alan J. Pakula, the Gentle Stylist and . . .
   The Sterile Cuckoo"

"as if it were a play": PA

"By the time we got up . . .": *NYT,* December 7, 1969

"could have been part of . . .": Harry Clein, "Alan J. Pakula, the Gentle Stylist and . . .
   The Sterile Cuckoo"

"In the chapel . . .": Harry Clein, "Alan J. Pakula, the Gentle Stylist and . . . *The Sterile Cuckoo*"

"It grew out of the fact . . .": Harry Clein, "Alan J. Pakula, the Gentle Stylist and . . .
   The Sterile Cuckoo"

"Who would have thought . . .": Harry Clein, "Alan J. Pakula, the Gentle Stylist and . . .
   The Sterile Cuckoo"

"I wanted to protect . . ." and "I was warned by . . .": Harry Clein, "Alan J. Pakula, the Gentle
   Stylist and . . . *The Sterile Cuckoo*"

"Alan got me together . . .": *NYT,* December 7, 1969

"knew the script . . .": AFI1

"and I said in the most simplistic . . .": combined quotation, MB, AFI1, *TT*, and AFI2

"each one needs different things": MB

"I don't like to be criticized . . .": AFI2

"And I talked. . . .": AFI1

"You get the impression with Otto . . .": *NYT*, December 7, 1969

"forced the film into big . . .": Harry Clein, "Alan J. Pakula, the Gentle Stylist and . . .
    The Sterile Cuckoo"

"doing some easy little . . .": AFI2

"The first take was . . .": Harry Clein, "Alan J. Pakula, the Gentle Stylist and . . . *The Sterile Cuckoo*"

"Liza has a great film face. . . .": Harry Clein, "Alan J. Pakula, the Gentle Stylist and . . .
    The Sterile Cuckoo"

"My concern was that she . . .": Harry Clein, "Alan J. Pakula, the Gentle Stylist and . . .
    The Sterile Cuckoo"

"There was one moment during . . .": *TT*

"The greatest thing was . . .": Interview with Rodd Baxter

"once I've locked the scene in . . .": DOF1

"Thank God there were . . .": AFI1

"this was Alan's first . . .": Interview with Alvin Sargent

"just constantly thrilling": *ED*

"the only relaxed film . . .": AFI2

"I found also that I was very . . .": AFI1

"Naturally I'm concerned with . . .": Harry Clein, "Alan J. Pakula, the Gentle Stylist and . . .
    The Sterile Cuckoo"

"The critical reaction was by and large . . .": UE

"I never liked . . .": UE

"a remarkable piece of work . . .": Harry Clein, "Alan J. Pakula, the Gentle Stylist and . . .
    The Sterile Cuckoo"

"This is the most important . . .": *NYT*, December 7, 1969

"delicate, understated, unobtrusive," clipping, *Motion Picture Exhibitor*, BRTC

"aspires to an unconventional . . .": *NYT*, October 23, 1969

"the relentlessly sentimental . . .": *NYT*, October 23, 1969

CHAPTER SIX

"The best of film . . .": Joseph McBride, ed., *Filmmakers on Filmmaking*, Volume One, © 1983,
    American Film Institute

"I try to come up with . . .": *Music from the Movies*

"From my initial . . .": Interview with Dianne Dreyer

"He loved the idea . . .": Interview with Celia Costas

"In a heartbeat.": Interview with Celia Costas

"It had a lateral quality . . .": DOF2

"ran a lot of old Hitchcock . . .": UE

"the rhythms of melodrama . . .": AFI1

"It's a melodrama in which . . .": AFI2

"*Klute* very much deals . . .": AFI2

"Although *Klute* deals . . . with sadistic . . .": UE

"I wanted to get a sense . . .": AFI1

"I had a rather disturbing . . .": *TT*

"an inhuman scale . . .": AFI1

"a world without sunlight": AFI2

"wanted a very nervous screen:" AFI2

"very vague with lenses . . .": AFI1

"Well, you want it this way . . .": AFI2

"was a huge influence . . .": *TT*

"the Prince of Darkness": Interview with Jane Fonda

"Alan wanted a specific. . .": Interview with Jane Fonda

"We made it into . . .": combined quotation, DOF2, AFI2, and "Alan J. Pakula, Film Director,"
   East Hampton Star, November 26, 1998

"I am fascinated because . . .": DOF2

"I was not involved at . . .": *ED*

"The script, [with its] tabloid quality . . .": AFI2

"We talked for several hours . . .": AFI2

"I was just beginning . . .": Interview with Jane Fonda

"The thing that interested me most . . .": Interview with Jane Fonda

"every picture depends upon casting . . .": *ED*

"Several people turned down . . .": *ED*

"At the time I had . . .": DOF2

"I try to do a lot of planning . . .": AFI1

"I do a certain amount of blocking . . .": AFI2

"Alan, I can't do it . . .": Interview with Jane Fonda

"The first time we sat around . . ." [footnote]: Interview with Jane Fonda

"He laughed! . . .": Interview with Jane Fonda

"I'm not going to let you out . . .": AFI2

"was genuinely scared . . .": combined quotation, AFI1 and MB

"wanted me to tell her . . .": MB

"After talking with . . .": ACB

"the big confrontation scene" and ff: AFI2

"she did walk-bys and little . . .": AFI1

"the kind of research you can only do . . .[footnote]": AFI1

"not sexual. Call girls pride . . .": AFI2

"spent a week with different . . .": Interview with Jane Fonda

"Terrific, I'm going to stage . . ." [footnote]: AFI1

"technical adviser . . ." and ff.: DOF1

"I almost destroyed the scene . . .": AFI1

"I think if I'd said to Jane Fonda . . .": AFI1

"the solutions that you've used . . .": AFI1

"I need to live there. . . .": Interview with Jane Fonda

"I like the actors to live . . .": AI

"she slept in the set . . .": AI

"It was lying in that bed . . .": Interview with Jane Fonda

"we rehearsed rigorously . . .": Interview with Donald Sutherland

"It's one of the few times . . ." combined quotation, AFI2 and Richard Thompson,
   "Mr. Pakula Goes to Washington"

"Jane worked very hard . . .": AFI1

"Alan and I spent many hours . . .": Interview with Jane Fonda

"I was trying to get the dehumanized . . .": AFI2

"when Klute hears somebody . . .": AFI2

"The score can say things . . .": *Music from the Movies*

"key in moments of terror . . .": combined quotation, Interview with Michael Small
   and *Music from the Movies*

"very, very exotic percussion . . .": RT

"I know that Alan guided me . . .": RT

"The scene where the music . . .": *Music from the Movies*

"It was a big risk . . .": RT

"worked on a suspense level . . .": *Music from the Movies*

"was the story of a girl . . .": AFI1

"she has a compulsion . . .": AFI1

"One thing they can't accuse me of . . .": AI

"The major similarity . . .": DOF2

"a middle-class American . . .": combined quotation, DOF2 and AFI1

"a complicated, fascinating man . . .": AFI1

"The character of Peter Cable . . .": Interview with Charles Cioffi

"What made you decide . . .": Interview with Jane Fonda

"It's a brilliant conception, that scene . . .": combined quotation, AFI1 and AFI2

"Gordon, I want that entrance . . .": AFI1

"very middle European erotic": AFI2

"You know, Alan, . . .": combined quotation, Interview with Jane Fonda and *TT*

"made all the difference . . .": *TT*

"Everything changed": Interview with Jane Fonda

"when Bree was inside me . . .": Interview with Jane Fonda

"I never introduced Jane . . .": AFI1

"the only chance for the scenes . . .": AFI1

"And I kept saying . . .": AFI1

"Now [Pakula said], Vivian proceeded . . .": AFI1

"I should've had two cameras . . .": AFI1

"basically an improv": Interview with Charles Cioffi

"And then from that . . .": AFI1

"I had actually gone down to the . . .": Interview with Jane Fonda

"I had a very interesting reaction . . .": Interview with Jane Fonda

"I love when things come out . . .": AFI1

"The murderer came to [Bree's] flat . . .": combined quotation, AFI1 and AFI2

"He's totally cut off . . .": AFI2

"I had the feeling that Bree . . .": Interview with Donald Sutherland

"he allowed you to invent . . .": Interview with Charles Cioffi

"[Good acting] has to do with . . .": Interview with Donald Sutherland

"He gave me the kind of help . . .": Interview with Jane Fonda

"was thrilling. It didn't happen all the time . . .": Interview with Donald Sutherland

"Boy, he was very tough . . .": Interview with Michael Small

"a feminist movie in a strange way . . .": RT

"The actual intentions of *Klute* . . .": *NYT*, June 24, 1971

"no understanding or comprehension . . .": AFI2

"unlikely" and "the film's failure . . .": *NYT*, August 12, 1971

"slick," "hoked up," et cetera.: *Time*, July 12, 1971

"she never stands outside Bree . . .": the *New Yorker*, July 3, 1971

"terminal flaws . . .": *Variety*, June 30, 1971

"relying on her talent . . .": the *New Republic*, September 18, 1971

"enormous advances for me . . .": UE

"across the board": Interview with Charles Cioffi

CHAPTER SEVEN

"were, almost more . . .": MS

"Alan loved London . . .": Interview with Michael Small

"I have an image . . .": AFI1

"How the hell did he . . .": clipping, BRTC

"went around to . . .": clipping, BRTC

"Once I became interested . . .": clipping, BRTC

"a love story of the absurd . . .": Hugh Hebert, "Pakula Switched and Hit Right Track,"
   Louisville Courier-Journal & Times, February 27, 1972

"I'd like you to take out . . .": clipping, BRTC

"We'll finance it if . . ." and "Angela's a very gifted . . .": clipping, BRTC

"a woman of great spine . . .": UE

"has sort of withdrawn . . .": UE

"she finds herself in this very . . .": TT

"a kind of welding problem . . .": UE

"We always had a great . . .": Interview with Michael Small

"Absolutely remarkable": TT

"magnificent (and magnificently funny) . . .": NYT, April 20, 1973

"The movie is at its quiet best . . .": *Time*, May 14, 1973

"is low keyed and totally disarming . . .": *Variety*, April 18, 1973

"roundly rejected": TT

"I have a [belief] that when . . .": ED

"while there were charming . . .": TT

"was a very bizarre . . .": TT

"he had made a tremendous success . . .": Interview with Michael Small

"Jewish geisha": Interview with Barbara Davis

"I was Miss Perfect . . .": combined quotation, Interview with Hannah Pakula and NYT, June 9, 1999

"about everything. Perfect looking . . .": Interview with Barbara Davis

"a man I liked very much . . .": Interview with Barbara Davis

"I realized I was the only person . . .": NYT, June 9, 1999

"I'll call you": Interview with Hannah Pakula

"I did that . . ." [footnote]: Interview with Hannah Pakula

"To go back, after a committed . . .": NYT, April 16, 1989

"If you've been married and [later] divorce . . .": NYT, April 16, 1989

"he was confronted with . . .": Interview with Selma Hirsh

"Alan had been dating my mother . . .": Interview with Louis Boorstin

"was scared of getting married": Interview with Hannah Pakula

"that kids should wake up . . .": Interview with Bob Boorstin

"a member of the family": Interview with Louis Boorstin

"He didn't want to disrupt . . .": Interview with Hannah Pakula

"we might move to New York . . .": Interview with Anna Boorstin

"I was doing what all my friends were . . .": Interview with Anna Boorstin

"I don't want to make a film . . .": Interview with Hannah Pakula

"I loved it and I have never lived . . .": Interview with Hannah Pakula

"short pieces on blue jeans . . .": Interview with Hannah Pakula

"But if I fail . . ." and "Look, I get bad reviews . . .": Interview with Hannah Pakula

"Alan gives support like nobody . . .": PA

"really enabled me to write": Interview with Hannah Pakula

"an enormous gift. . . .": *NYT*, June 9, 1999

"love her desperately . . . he made her whole": Interview with Bob Boorstin

"We would end up having . . .": Interview with Hannah Pakula

"I think he had a horror . . .": Interview with Hannah Pakula

"There were times when I wished . . .": Interview with Bob Boorstin

"Alan had a theory . . .": Interview with Hannah Pakula

"when they were shooting outdoors . . .": Interview with Hannah Pakula

"known in New York social circles . . .": *NYT*, June 9, 1999

"They loved to have people over. . . .": Interview with Marilyn Berger

"Alan wasn't interested in 'society'. . .": Interview with Barbara Davis

"Alan had a talent for friendship . . .": Interview with Larry Turman

"Hannah was great for Alan . . .": Interview with Alvin Sargent

"You know, we don't even bother . . .": Interview with Hannah Pakula

"They were an amazing . . .": Interview with Barbara Davis

"It was the one marriage that . . .": Interview with Keren Saks

"You can never really . . .": Interview with Marilyn Berger

"He was totally fulfilled.": Interview with Selma Hirsh

"To find a woman . . .": MS

"We were enormously happy . . .": Interview with Hannah Pakula

CHAPTER EIGHT

"as it is seen through . . .": ACB

"a kind of despair . . .": Richard Combs, "All the President's Men"

"In America, most films . . .": DOF2

"become a world in which . . .": combined quotation, DOF2 and MB

"was an almost nightmare . . .": Richard Combs, "World Without Shadows"

"sort of an American myth . . .": ACB

"*The Parallax View* was a whole other kind . . .": *ED*

"If the picture works . . .": AFI2

"I wanted to deal with action": AFI1

"wanted a certain surrealism": AFI1

"as it is seen through . . .": ACB

"to deal with a bigger canvas . . .": AFI1

"Every film has some politics . . .": *NYT*, March 17, 1974

"I am always looking for . . .": Kathleen Carroll, *New York Daily News* (clipping, BRTC)

"bold sketches and almost . . .": ACB

"archetypal people, characters . . .": ACB

"made under hair-raising conditions": *ED*

"Talk about improvisation. . . .": AFI1

"jump hundreds of years . . .": AFI1

"made the whole beginning work . . .": AFI1

"Making those observations . . .": AFI1

"I want to start with Americana . . .": AFI1

"the totally rootless modern man": Richard Combs, "All the President's Men"

"much more simple American values . . .": Richard Combs, "All the President's Men"

"distasteful": ACB

"I like to try to solve . . .": AFI1

"One of the problems . . .": AFI1

 "worked on that for at least . . .": AFI1

"starts out with love . . .": AFI1

"the impotent, passive person . . .": AFI1

"You can be destroyed by society . . .": AFI1

"Suddenly you look at swastikas . . .": AFI1

"there's a whole kind of Oedipal thing . . .": AFI1

"I should have had it in": AFI1

"Parallax depended on a certain . . .": AFI1

"designed to whip you . . .": *ED*

"I don't think Alan even heard it . . .": Interview with Michael Small

"He started out with that . . .": AFI1

"Alan, I've got the idea . . .": Interview with Michael Small

"Wow, what an idea": Interview with Michael Small

"both terrifying and very attractive . . .": combined quotation, Interview with Michael Small
    and *Music from the Movies*

"it was empty, and they were putting up . . .": *TT*

"The candidate comes in . . .": combined quotation, AFI1, AFI2, and ACB

"get red, white and blue tablecloths . . .": Richard Thompson, "Mr. Pakula Goes to Washington"

"takes a lot of those American myths . . .": Richard Combs, "World Without Shadows"

"All you hear is this John Philip Sousa . . .": *TT*

"with the third act hanging . . .": AFI2

"was to do *Parallax* in a kind of poster style . . .": AFI1

"He never forgot that . . ." [footnote]: ACB

"That's the old Hitchcock thing . . .": AFI1

"I tried to do a lot of mythic . . .": AFI1

"At the end . . . violence is not fun . . .": AFI1

"a child's fear of darkness . . .": Richard Thompson, "Mr. Pakula Goes to Washington"

"in the sense of people being . . .": ACB

"There were a few major changes . . .": AFI1

"a tough kind of older . . .": AFI2

"It made her death more moving": AFI2

"the classic ex-FBI man . . .": AFI2

"You expect when Parallax comes . . .": AFI1

"That does the work for you . . ." [footnote]: AFI1

"It's Friday, and I work on Monday . . .": AFI1

"Gee, it would be nice to see some pages . . .": AFI1

"the line of the scene": AFI1

"My wife was in the kitchen . . .": AFI1

"Jim, there's nothing to read . . .": AFI1

"He had something in his character . . .": combined quotation, AFI1 and AFI2

"There are sequences where what is best . . .": ACB

"With all the rehearsal . . .": AFI2

"It's a film I'm very glad I made . . .": *ED*

"Novelists are always using the phrase . . .": William Goldman, *Adventures in the Screen Trade*,
    pp. 241-42
"I work very closely with the editor . . .": ACB
"is the sort of suspense melodrama . . .": *NYT*, June 20, 1974
"essentially cheap melodrama": *NYT*, July 28, 1974
"probably the most mindless . . .": *NYT*, August 11, 1974
"*The Parallax View* is too cowardly . . .": *NYT*, August 11, 1974
"He was never well-reviewed in . . .": Interview with Anna Boorstin
"It's interesting . . . film magazine had . . ." [footnote]: *TT*
"the astonishing density of performance . . .": Richard T. Jameson, "The Pakula Parallax"
"Few motion pictures have captured . . .": Stephen Pizzello, "Wrap Shot"
"does not end positively . . .": *Independent* on Sunday, April 22, 2001
"one of the best political thrillers . . .": *Times of London*, April 26, 2001
"perhaps his best film . . .": *London Daily Telegraph*: November 21, 1998
"an excessive fear of the unknown . . .": Richard Thompson, "Mr. Pakula Goes to Washington"

CHAPTER NINE
"How lucky we all were . . .": MS
"It was loving, absolutely loving . . .": Interview with Anna Boorstin
"We all sensed how happy . . .": Interview with Louis Boorstin
"My mother and I had a very, very . . .": Interview with Bob Boorstin
"had intensely historical feelings . . .": Interview with Bob Boorstin
"Alan was brought up . . .": Interview with Hannah Pakula
"When I was sixteen . . .": Interview with Bob Boorstin
"The seminal event in my life . . .": Interview with Bob Boorstin
"The last time I saw Alan before he died . . .": Interview with Bob Boorstin
"Alan never stopped treating my sister . . .": MS
"that Alan didn't have children . . .": Interview with Debby Maisel
"For a man who had no natural . . .": Interview with Louis Boorstin
"it was easier that way . . .": Interview with Bob Boorstin
"I still feel that vacuum . . .": Interview with Bob Boorstin
"He was interested in everybody's children . . .": Interview with Boaty Boatwright
"He really hung out with my . . .": Interview with Anna Boorstin

CHAPTER TEN
"I thought [Alan Pakula, as director . . .]": Interview with Robert Redford
"I know nobody wants to make . . .": DOF2
"absolutely nothing . . . it was just empty": Robert Brent Toplin, "All the President's Men:
    The Story That People Know and Remember," p. 181.
"there was this mix . . .": Interview with Robert Redford
"I said, 'What the hell happened . . .'": Interview with Robert Redford
"completely nuts" and "So that's what journalism's . . ." Interview with Robert Redford
"just sort of laughed it off . . .": Interview with Robert Redford
"a little black-and-white movie . . .": Interview with Robert Redford
"they probably thought . . .": Interview with Robert Redford
"who was very cold on the phone . . .": Interview with Robert Redford
"All of a sudden . . . were vindicated . . .": Interview with Robert Redford
"Woodward. Meet me at the Jefferson . . .": quoted by Robert Redford

"Tell you what, we'll come to your . . .": Interview with Robert Redford

"under surveillance" [footnote]: Interview with Robert Redford

"just got wild with excitement . . .": Interview with Robert Redford

"It's almost like a comic opera": William Goldman, *Adventures in the Screen Trade*

"Look, at the end . . .": quoted by Robert Redford

"Oh, come on. You've got to be . . .": Interview with Robert Redford

"Let us get back to you . . .": quoted by Robert Redford

"The part I'm interested in . . .": Interview with Robert Redford

"The story of Watergate . . .": quoted by Robert Redford

"certainly laid the seeds . . .": "Bravo" network documentary on Robert Redford

"in the meantime . . . while I'm waiting . . .": Interview with Robert Redford

"because the story was so much . . .": Interview with Robert Redford

"I don't think we would have taken him . . . [footnote]": Interview with Bob Woodward

"I cannot overemphasize [Woodward's] importance . . .": William Goldman,
    Adventures in the Screen Trade

"because Goldman writes for cleverness . . .": Interview with Robert Redford

"Throw away the last half . . .": William Goldman, *Adventures in the Screen Trade*

"was extremely turned off by . . .": Interview with Robert Redford

"I knew that this piece . . .": Interview with Robert Redford

"I thought it had a great deal . . .": Interview with Bob Woodward

"Carl, Errol Flynn is dead": Robert Brent Toplin, "The Filmmaker as Historian";
    Interview with Bob Woodward

"that is the reason Bob hired me . . .": AFI2

"If our project was to succeed . . .": *Time,* March 29, 1976

"When I thought about Alan . . .": Interview with Robert Redford

"he was psychologically oriented . . .": Interview with Robert Redford

"*All the President's Men* is a true story . . .": ED

"a lot of problems . . .": AI

"You called at just the right time": AI

"extremely critical of the screenplay . . ." and "If you make this movie . . .":
    Interview with Robert Redford

"The first thing we have to do . . .": Alan J. Pakula, "Dialogue on Film"

"you can't do a whole historical . . .": AFI2

"You know, Bob, . . . I'm not crazy about . . .": *ED*

"Bob, you know, one of the dangers . . .": combined quotation, AFI2, John S. Turner II,
    "Collapsing the Interior/Exterior Distinction: Surveillance, Spectacle, and Suspense in Popular
    Cinema," and Deborah Knight and George McKnight, "The Case of the Disappearing Enigma"

"It doesn't matter that . . .": combined quotation, AFI2 and RT

"you could hear the drums . . .": Alan J. Pakula, "Making a Film About Two Reporters"

"the moment he was on board . . .": Interview with Robert Redford

"sharing phone conversations . . .": Ben Bradlee, *A Good Life*

"he had to go back to work . . .": Interview with Robert Redford

"Look, I can't work with him . . ." quoted during interview with Robert Redford

"holed up in the hotel . . .": Robert Redford, "Alan J. Pakula: Seeking Truth on the Big Screen"

"would meet and discuss . . ." and ff: William Goldman, *Adventures in the Screen Trade*

"Alan did appear indecisive lots of times . . .": Interview with Robert Redford

"I spent my first months . . .": RT

"They were enormously cooperative . . .": Interview with Robert Redford

"In any detective story . . .": RT

"What happened at this point?": Interview with Robert Redford

"Redford was always driving . . .": quoted in Bravo documentary on Robert Redford

"How Woodward and Bernstein will get them . . .": RT

"we couldn't have a Woodward scene . . .": Interview with Robert Redford

"a decision Dustin is unhappy about . . .": RT

"it illustrated a lot about . . .": Interview with Robert Redford

"We spent endless time . . .": AFI2

"all kinds of stuff": Interview with Robert Redford

"Goldman had the structure . . ." [footnote]: Interview with Bob Woodward

"Goldman's script": Interview with Alvin Sargent

"What really blew me away . . .": Interview with Robert Redford

"Oh God . . . this looks like it's some . . .": quoted in *TT*

"What are we going to call it?": Interview with Robert Redford

"Could we at least shoot . . .": Interview with Robert Redford

"remained wary of the whole project": *Time*, March 29, 1976

"We withheld that permission . . .": Interview with Ben Bradlee

"I think Ben was both attracted . . .": Interview with Robert Redford

"Redford kept talking about trust . . .": *Time*, March 29, 1976

"I had promised my daughter . . ." [footnote]: Interview with Ben Bradlee

"they decided it was best to cooperate . . .": "Directing *All the President's Men*:
    Commentary by Alan J. Pakula"

"the old cowboy and . . .": *ED*

"I wanted to pay him back . . .": Interview with Robert Redford

"I look like Ben Bradlee . . .": quoted in MB

"one of the great American . . .": combined quotation, AFI2 and RT

"Ben is a big star . . .": AI

"The major key to that . . .": *ED*

"feel insecure": AFI2

"If you tell me you can do it . . .": AI

"never stopped working . . .": Interview with Ben Bradlee

"I'm going to tell you who I'm casting . . .": *ED*

"I made anybody with a major part . . .": Alan J. Pakula, "Making a Film About Two Reporters"

"of doing a Wax Museum . . .": Alan J. Pakula, "Making a Film About Two Reporters"

Bradlee's astonishment about the authenticity of the newsroom set: Toplin,
    "All the President's Men: The Story That People Know and Remember," p. 189

"When I brought my daughter on to the set . . .": Interview with Ben Bradlee

"was rather difficult for Gordon . . .": AFI2

"I want it hard . . .": RT

"tough poster colors . . .": combined quotation, RT and Alan J. Pakula,
    "Making a Film About Two Reporters"

"incredibly harsh" and "ruthless . . . just marvelous": combined quotation,
    RT and Alan J. Pakula, "Making a Film About Two Reporters"

"To me . . . 'documentary' does not . . .": Alan J. Pakula, "Making a Film About Two Reporters"

"of wanting to see lots of counterpointed . . .": Alan J. Pakula, "Making a Film About Two
    Reporters"

"Gordy is not known for his very bright . . .": AFI2

"It was Alan who thought . . .": Robert Redford, "Alan J. Pakula: Seeking Truth on the Big Screen"

"in scenes showing Woodward . . .": Robert Brent Toplin, "All the President's Men:
    The Story That People Know and Remember," pp. 187-88.
"had a very difficult time . . .": AFI2
"at the height of his power . . .": AFI2
"I don't think there's a more verbal film . . .": RT
"bored with people who say . . .": RT
"a lot of people don't believe me . . .": AFI2
"Oh, isn't it terrific" and ff: AFI2
"My own feeling is . . .": RT
"There would be nights . . .": AFI2

CHAPTER ELEVEN
"is a picture of total . . .": AFI2
"Alan and I were both nuts . . .": Interview with Robert Redford
"this is a story of the power of the word . . .": combined quotation, *ED* and RT
"could be better. . . .": AI
"A lot of filmmakers would have . . .": Rick Lyman, "Watching Movies With Stephen Soderbergh,"
    NYT, February 12, 2001
"Beyond focusing on the foreground . . .": Interview with Robert Redford
"Okay, what are these guys doing . . .": Interview with Robert Redford
"In scenes showing the break-in . . .": Robert Brent Toplin, "All the President's Men:
    The Story People Know and Remember," pp. 189-90.
"I think we feel the reporters' . . .": RT
"One of the people at the *Post* . . .": RT
"likes being seen as bland . . .": Interview with Robert Redford
"a very controlled man . . .": AFI2
"All I can give you in this film . . .": AFI2
"Bob felt, 'there's no part . . .'": AFI2
"I'd say, 'Bob, get your hands . . .'": AFI2
"really a killer underneath": Interview with Robert Redford
"started to get into his scenes in the . . .": AFI2
"Bob has much more range . . .": combined quotation, "Directing All the President's Men:
    Commentary by Alan J. Pakula" and AFI2
"all the telephone calls he makes . . ." and ff: combined quotation, AFI2 and RT
"required using a diopter lens . . .": combined quotation, PA, AFI2, and Alan J. Pakula,
    "Making a Film About Two Reporters"
"It's a major scene . . .": PA
"in my heart I thought . . .": PA
"everybody said it worked . . .": AFI2
"Look, Bob, your work is good. . . ." and ff: PA
"was day and night": AFI2
"a very flashy kind of . . .": Interview with Robert Redford
"Oh oh oh, that's a little Redford . . .": Interview with Robert Redford
"great taste and sensibility . . .": Interview with Robert Redford
"You use things in Bob Redford . . .": Alan J. Pakula, "Making a Film About Two Reporters"
"Dustin loves to talk . . .": AFI2
"There's a part of me . . .": AFI2
"We had our battles": AFI2

"worked very well together": Interview with Robert Redford

"no easy trick to pull off": Interview with Gordon Willis

"magnitude, that these guys . . .": Interview with Pieter Jan Brugge

"Some people say [the sequence] was . . .": RT

"Gordon Willis at his absolute best" and ff: *NYT*, February 12, 2001

"of teacher and acolyte. . . .": Alan J. Pakula, "Making a Film About Two Reporters"

"the essence of investigative reporting . . .": AFI2

"I spent endless time . . .": Alan J. Pakula, "Making a Film About Two Reporters"

"The actor has all that going": Alan J. Pakula, "Making a Film About Two Reporters"

"one of the most exciting weeks . . ." and ff: combined quotation, AFI2 and DOF2

"So he's got to work . . .": AFI2

"He could not break into it . . .": DOF2

"doing a lot of re-wording . . .": Interview with Jane Alexander

"Throughout the whole scene the camera . . .": *NYT*, February 12, 2001

"caught together in time . . .": Richard Combs, "All the President's Men"

"It's brilliant. In that scene . . .": Interview with Jane Alexander

"I would like you to do this . . .": Richard Combs, "All the President's Men"

"in a little blue dress . . .": Interview with Jane Alexander

"It is a long time ago . . .": Interview with Jane Alexander

"I know there have been times . . .": AFI2

"I don't know if they parted this project friends": Interview with Bob Woodward

"and out came Ben Bradlee . . .": AFI2

"Up until he comes on . . .": RT

"had to be cowed by him . . .": AI

"Pakula has Robards walking out . . .": Interview with Ben Bradlee

"His concern is not about . . .": RT

"My God, all the scenes are the same . . .": AFI2

"It was a question of orchestrating . . .": AFI2

"There's sun on the wingchair . . .": RT

"there's something about seeing people on television . . .": Alan J. Pakula, "Making a Film About
 Two Reporters"

"So, we put a TV set way in front . . .": RT

"That is really the David and Goliath image . . .": AFI2

"and the guns boom-boom . . .": *ED*

"Thank God they had the twenty-one-gun salute . . .": RT

"There's never been a film I know of . . .": RT

"how important the story was . . .": *TT*

"One of the things that makes the film work . . .": AFI2

"I liked the irony of ending . . .": RT

"The reason for that notation . . .": AFI2

"a clause in the contract . . .": Alan J. Pakula, "Making a Film About Two Reporters"

"In terms of accusations . . .": RT

"to comment on whether or not . . .": *NYT*, May 23, 1976

"grossly inaccurate . . .": *NYT*, May 23, 1976

"I was bored . . .": *NYT*, May 23, 1976

"the film particularly strains credibility . . .": William E. Leuchtenberg, "All the President's Men"
 in Mark C. Carnes, ed., *Past Imperfect: History According to the Movies*

"it was like the sound of little rats . . .": Alan J. Pakula, "Making a Film About Two Reporters"

"Sound is as much a part of . . .": RT

"Alan used to use an expression . . .": Interview with Michael Small

"trust the actors": AI

"Occasionally, we'd disagree . . .": clipping, BRTC

"The reason that Alan and I got along . . .": Interview with Robert Redford

"nothing to do with their talents": RT

"Now I am convinced . . .": RT

"In presenting stories about the past . . .": Robert Brent Toplin, "All the President's Men:
    The Story That People Know and Remember," p. 20

"realistic, documentary style format . . ." Robert Brent Toplin, "All the President's Men:
    The Story That People Know and Remember," p. 21

"The manners and methods . . .": *NYT*, April 8, 1976

"to miss the point of the movie . . .": *NYT*, April 11, 1976

"the only narrative film . . .": *NYT*, April 11, 1976

"brought about a small near-miracle . . .": Nat Hentoff, "From Woodstein at the Movies,"
    Columbia Journalism Review, vol. 40, no. 1 (November–December 2001)

"the intelligence and seriousness . . .": Robert Brent Toplin, "All the President's Men:
    The Story That People Know and Remember," p. 21

"an inspiring story about . . .": Robert Brent Toplin, "All the President's Men:
    The Story That People Know and Remember," p. 180.

"providing the public policy . . .": William Leuchtenberg, "All the President's Men" in Mark C.
    Carnes, ed., *Past Imperfect: History According to the Movies*

"would have been two-and-a-half . . .": Interview with Ben Bradlee

"The phone always answered . . .": Interview with Ben Bradlee

"We knew the audience . . .": *TT*

"the audience was more on the side of . . .": Alan J. Pakula,
    "Making a Film About Two Reporters"

"much to our amazement we're a great . . .": AFI2

"The realities are that Bob . . .": RT

"the fact is that reporters deal with words. . . .": Alan J. Pakula,
    "Making a Film About Two Reporters"

"This movie just has the perfect balance . . .": *NYT*, February 12, 2001

"thought that it was quite a wonderful genre movie . . .": Interview with Ben Bradlee

"All the President's Men provided a valuable history lesson . . .": Robert Brent Toplin, "All the
    President's Men: The Story That People Know and Remember," p. 193

CHAPTER TWELVE

"Directors make movies at . . .": Interview with Don Laventhall

"have vast differences in style . . ." AFI1

"he made movies he could be proud of . . .": Interview with Marilyn Berger

"always looked a little uncomfortable . . .": Interview with Jane Fonda

"That's so sweet . . .": Interview with Jane Fonda

"You'd go into his trailer . . .": Interview with Jane Fonda

"The idea of an actor . . .": Interview with Martin Manulis

"Dreiserian Western, [dealing] with very specific . . .": AFI2

"an attempt to deal with a classic . . .": DOF1

"great attraction to people . . .": DOF1

"to explore a woman . . .": DOF1

"the obsession with land . . .": combined quotation, *NYT*, June 3, 1977, and DOF1

"the kind of people who built . . .": *NYT*, June 3, 1977

"nineteenth century people. . .": *Women's Wear Daily*, February 28, 1977

"a kind of central character" and ff: DOF2

"the weather kept changing . . .": DOF2

"a piece of clay . . .": Interview with Jane Fonda

"was to write a classic Western score": Interview with Michael Small

"I started playing over some . . .": DOF1

"It deals with classic . . .": DOF1

"there are no emotional or intellectual . . .": *Time*, November 6, 1978

"As usual, though it never comes . . .": *NYT*, November 2, 1978

"It's a fine film, majestic . . .": *Chicago Tribune*, November 1, 1978

"If the [film] doesn't quite jell . . .": *Newsweek*, October 30, 1978

"Take a film that costs . . .": Stanley Kubrick, quoted in Michel Ciment, *Kubrick*, p. 197

"strange combination of artist . . .": Interview with Hannah Pakula

"George gradually, slowly, taking his time . . .": *George Stevens: A Filmmaker's Journey*

"A man and a woman committing themselves . . .": DOF1

"a lot about Alan's . . .": Interview with Jim Brooks

"that's Alan. . . .": Interview with Selma Hirsh

"It became his film": Interview with Jim Brooks

"amazing synergy": Interview with Don Laventhall

"Alan thought of that Christmas finish": Interview with Jim Brooks

"was of a rather ordinary man . . .": *TT*

"an extraordinarily endearing man": *ED*

"It was the first part I read . . .": *ED*

"Under Pakula's handling, Reynolds . . .": *Newsweek*, October 8, 1979

"He's just a terrific director . . .": *ED*

"Jill was nominated, Candice . . .": *ED*

"Burt was tough . . .": Interview with Jim Brooks

"we go up to about take fourteen . . .": *ED*

"every time we'd to a take . . .": *ED*

"room for spontaneous gestures . . .": Interview with Candice Bergen

"It's not that lots of wonderful ideas . . .": Interview with Jill Clayburgh

"I didn't have any of the experience . . .": Interview with Candice Bergen

"Alan came back with her cast . . .": Interview with Jim Brooks

"Alan was shrewd enough . . .": Interview with Candice Bergen

"It's not wonderful singing . . .": *TT*

"One of the most difficult . . .": *ED*

"The crew were holding pillows . . .": Interview with Candice Bergen

"sport that she was . . .": *TT*

"I would never have taken the chances . . .": PA

"someone who was very confident . . .": Interview with Candice Bergen

"Alan really extended himself . . .": Interview with Candice Bergen

"Playing Marilyn in *Starting Over* . . .": *Newsweek*, October 8, 1979

"I have to go back . . ." Alan Pakula, quoted in interview with Jill Clayburgh

"that I just love being . . .": AI

"one of the things about Alan . . ." Interview with Jill Clayburgh

"He never rushed me . . .": Interview with Jill Clayburgh

"He'd dance around like a kid . . .": Interview with Hannah Pakula

"When he takes off his shoes . . .": PA

"boyish, mischievous giggle . . .": Interview with Jill Clayburgh

"I take off my shoes . . .": AI

"when something we did [in *Sophie's Choice*] . . .": MS

"he was more of a responder . . .": Interview with Jill Clayburgh

"was somebody who very much wanted . . .": Interview with Candice Bergen

"because I was making faces . . .": Interview with Jim Brooks

"I know somebody who never directed before . . .": AI

"any initial thoughts I had about directing . . .": Interview with Jim Brooks

"manages to be fast . . .": *NYT*, October 5, 1979

"Pakula gives this fable . . .": *Newsweek*, October 8, 1979

"a perfectly charming movie": *Time*, October 8, 1979

"a delight . . . Audiences may wince . . .": *Variety*, October 3, 1979

"If you make me go . . .": Interview with Debby Maisel

"very, very attentive": Interview with Debby Maisel

"Little is known about modern . . .": Time-Warner videotape notes of *Rollover*

"We went to the premiere . . .": Interview with Don Hewitt

"You can't always get who you want": Interview with Pieter Jan Brugge

"everyone in the production office . . .": Interview with Celia Costas

"He's a Rhodes Scholar . . .": Interview with Jane Fonda

"Some actors get pompous . . .": *NYT*, March 27, 1981

"that we couldn't get the script right . . .": Interview with Jane Fonda

"fundamentally disappointing . . .": *Variety*, December 9, 1981

"the frenzied cacophony . . .": *Newsweek*, December 14, 1981

"is a true stylist . . .": *Time*, December 21, 1981

"The cleverness and proficiency . . .": *NYT*, December 11, 1981

CHAPTER THIRTEEN

"an interesting combination . . .": Interview with Peter Jennings

"funny, witty, enormously perceptive": *Washington Post*, November 20, 1998

"a loyal friend . . .": Interview with Lauren Bacall

"I can't believe it. I not only . . .": *Los Angeles Times*, November 20, 1998

"I loved him. I just thought he . . .": Interview with Jane Alexander

"one of the last gentlemen . . .": combined quotation, *Washington Post*, November 20, 1998,
    and William Goldman, *Adventures in the Screen Trade*

"That's the first thing . . .": Interview with Harrison Ford

"Alan Pakula was a step above . . .": Interview with Charles Cioffi

"because he was the true definition . . .": MS

"Alan Pakula is the one man who, whether . . .": Interview with Gretchen Babarovic

"You could walk down the street . . .": Interview with Don Laventhall

"He was an extraordinary man. . . .": Interview with Louis Boorstin

"an unbelievable person. He was so kind . . .": Interview with Debby Maisel

"He grew more compassionate than ever. . . .": Interview with Selma Hirsh

"a great lover of people. . . .": Interview with Don Laventhall

"had the ability to draw people out. . .": Interview with Hannah Pakula

"he would chat with her until . . .": Interview with Selma Hirsh

"I thought he was Freud reincarnated. . . .": Interview with Ben Bradlee

"even looks like Freud . . .": Ben Bradlee, *A Good Life*

"Alan was a person who, unlike many . . .": Interview with Marilyn Berger

"He was a delicious human being . . .": Interview with Hannah Pakula

"was living proof that working . . .": Interview with Pieter Jan Brugge

"Alan was a very good friend. . . .": Interview with Hume Cronyn

"just a gentle, warm . . .": *ED*

"Alan Pakula was one of the most honorable . . .": *USA Today,* November 23, 1998

"he was complicated. The elements mixed in him . . .": MS

"He liked women a lot. . . .": Interview with Celia Costas

"He was wonderful with women . . .": Interview with Catherine Solt

"He was flirtatious and gentle . . .": Interview with Jill Clayburgh

"was just a guy who liked women. . . .": Interview with Charles Cioffi

"He had a profound empathy for . . .": Interview with Jane Fonda

"I think he was essentially liberal . . .": Interview with Ben Bradlee

"the breadth of his imagination . . .": *ED*

"He liked to nest, you know . . .": Interview with Catherine Solt

"to the light tower . . .": Interview with Chris Murray

"He was natty . . . but he looked like . . .": Interview with Michael Small

"always looked nice, but in a professorial . . .": Interview with Debby Maisel

"Hannah would do the driving . . .": Interview with Debby Maisel

"was absent-minded . . ." [footnote]: Interview with Anna Boorstin

"That's an awfully attractive woman . . .": Interview with Hannah Pakula

"He had all these bizarre brain disconnections . . .": Interview with Anna Boorstin

"One of my favorite Alan moments . . .": Interview with Anna Boorstin

"Each of them was later than the other . . .": MS

"He was often late for all kinds of things . . .": Interview with Robert Mulligan

"he was very tunneled. . . .": Interview with Michael Small

"Alan and I would talk on the phone . . .": Interview with Alvin Sargent

"He could be snarly . . .": Interview with Alvin Sargent

"who could get angry. . . .": Interview with Keren Saks

"It's better to be a short director . . .": *NYT,* March 27, 1981

"chicken salad in the mornings": Interview with Chris Murray

"sort of held in": *ED*

"stiff neck": Interview with Donald Sutherland

"Alan was a very urban man . . .": Interview with Jane Fonda

"I saw him in the pool . . .": Interview with Colleen Creedon

"He liked to ride a bicycle": Interview with Hannah Pakula

"You never heard of Alan doing . . .": Interview with Rodd Baxter

"If you could sing a song . . .": Interview with a relative who prefers not to be identified

"threatened to put a tape recorder . . .": Interview with Hannah Pakula

"Alan was running around telling Hannah . . .": Interview with Michael Small

"when he took me to a Woody Allen film . . .": Interview with Chris Murray

"understood the dark side of human nature . . .": Interview with Bob Woodward

"I think when you do a film . . .": CNN.com, November 19, 1998

"I kept up with him very closely . . .": Interview with Ben Bradlee

"When you're working with wonderful collaborators . . .": *ED*

"Alan would skip as he walked . . .": Interview with Debby Maisel

"Candide-like innocence . . .": Interview with Dennis Brown

"He was young in thinking . . .": Interview with Debby Maisel

"I miss him so terribly. . . .": Interview with Keren Saks

"would sit and talk to me . . .": Interview with Keren Saks

"done not very much except journalism . . .": Interview with Barbara Davis

"Alan as a friend had a tremendous capacity . . .": Interview with Marilyn Berger

"I always knew if I needed anything . . .": MS

"If there was something happening . . .": Interview with Peter Jennings

"such a special person. . . .": combined quotation, Interview with Peter Jennings
    and the *East Hampton Star*, November 26, 1998

"very formal and, therefore, rather cold . . .": Interview with Gene Saks

"Once you had his trust . . .": Interview with Catherine Solt

"something professorial about him": Interview with Catherine Solt

"He was very compassionate. . . .": Interview with Catherine Solt

"He had an amazing life, and it was very broad . . .": Interview with Catherine Solt

"was almost too nice:" Interview with Catherine Solt

"worried too much about offending . . . .": Interview with Boaty Boatwright

"Alan had a quality, the ability . . .": Interview with Larry Turman

"Don't worry. The people who need to know . . .": quoted in interview by Hannah Pakula

"a guy that I would trust with anything . . .": Interview with Don Hewitt

"A lot of it has to do with who you are . . .": MB

"I never knew a better man . . .": Interview with Don Hewitt

"He was as perceptive about the world . . .": *East Hampton Star*, November 26, 1998

"I am very interested in political society . . .": AFI2

"he was kind of a political junkie": Interview with Hannah Pakula

"If something happened in the world . . .": Interview with Peter Jennings

"he had very strong opinions about what we . . .": Interview with Peter Jennings

"watched the talk shows on television . . .": Interview with Hannah Pakula

"His powers of concentration were formidable. . . .": MS

"was created to monitor and protect . . .": www.hrw.org

"Alan was very good on his feet . . .": Interview with Hannah Pakula

"He'd always be late for things . . .": Interview with Catherine Solt

"I think Alan had a real sense of his mortality . . .": Interview with Don Laventhall

CHAPTER FOURTEEN

"was as much a labor of love . . .": SCD

"Nobody loves an adaptation. . . .": Joy Gould Boyum, *Double Exposure: Fiction into Film*

"not all victims [of the Holocaust] . . ." [footnote]: *NYT*, April 17, 1983

"I don't think for an instant . . ." [footnote]: William Styron, quoted in Steven Lewis,
    "William Styron," pp. 259-60

"I always insist that we . . ." [footnote]: William Styron, quoted in Steven Lewis,
    "William Styron," p. 259

"American masterpiece": Paul Fussell, *Washington Post Book World*

"Some readers and critics . . .": Barbara Tepa Lupack, *Take Two: Adapting the Contemporary American Novel
    to Film*

"I don't know of a woman . . .": William Styron, quoted in Barbara Tepa Lupack,
    Take Two: Adapting the Contemporary American Novel to Film

"I want to make this . . .": SCB

"When I read the galleys of Sophie . . .": PA

"when those Jews were going . . .": PA

"the American loss of innocence . . .": Interview with Meryl Streep

"and the adolescent dream I had . . .": SCD

"I seem to have an obsession . . .": SCD

"The final evil that Styron dealt with . . .": *ED*

"I'm so eager to make this . . .": Alan Pakula, quoted in an interview with William Styron

"immediately warmed to [Pakula] . . .": Interview with William Styron

"double suicides are not necessarily . . .": SCD

"If you think I'll change the ending . . .": *NYT*, July 24, 1979

"It won't be an easy motion picture . . .": *NYT*, July 24, 1979

"I suppose I decided to do the picture . . .": *NYT*, July 24, 1979

"Tell me about it" and "Do it": Lew Grade, quoted in an interview with Martin Starger

"I have rarely felt this kind of . . .": *NYT*, May 29, 1979

"was as much a labor of love . . .": SCD

"I think he might have wanted . . .": Interview with William Styron

"I have a great deal of confidence . . .": William Styron, quoted in Robert K. Morris with Irving Mailin, eds., *The Achievement of William Styron*, p. 89

"It's [to be] a mystery film . . .": SCD

"We had several long lunches . . .": Interview with William Styron

"was describing the project . . .": Interview with William Styron

"I can remember hearing Hitler . . .": PA

"If my grandparents had not come . . .": MB

"There's a lot of thematic material . . .": *NYT*, May 9, 1982

"there's something else I strongly relate to . . .": *TT*

"that has an interesting idea . . .": *NYT*, May 9, 1982

"represents the noble spirit . . .": SCD

"arches with great . . ." and "almost a Medieval ceremony . . .": SCD

"something I longed for at Stingo's age . . .": Charles Kiselyak, *Death Dreams of Mourning*

"The structure of the film . . .": SCD

"the balancing act of keeping the audience . . .": Charles Kiselyak, *Death Dreams of Mourning*

"is written in a perfectly . . .": Jonathan Rosenbaum, "Les Choix de Pakula," *Cahiers du Cinema* 23 [April 1982], p. ix

"I remember there was one scene in which . . .": Interview with William Styron

"An example would be when the three . . .": Interview with William Styron

"It was a slow process, but . . .": Interview with Martin Starger

"That always gives a book . . .": *NYT*, July 24, 1979

"there's an audience for this kind of movie . . .": *NYT*, December 17, 1982

Brustein's discussion with Styron about Meryl Streep: *ED*

"Oh, yeah, it's that kid" and "Well, she's grown up" [footnote]: *ED*

"I had just started the screenplay . . .": *TT*

"ten years older than Sophie . . .": *NYT*, July 22, 1981

"he asked her questions about . . .": Interview with Don Laventhall

"fascinating . . . quite a performance:" Interview with Hannah Pakula

"a lovely Czech actress . . .": AI

"there might be someone out there . . .": Interview with Martin Starger

"and was a very important actress . . .": Interview with Martin Starger

"when I was ten, and my mother . . .": Charles Kiselyak, *Death Dreams of Mourning*

"That's the age-old debate . . .": Interview with Martin Starger

"What can you do? . . ." Stan Kamen, quoted in interview with Martin Starger

"Look, I don't want to force anyone . . .": Interview with Martin Starger

"I believe in the subject matter . . .": Interview with Martin Starger

"Just see if you can get me in . . .": Interview with Meryl Streep

"Meryl is embarrassed": combined quotation, Interview with Martin Starger and MB

"Well, who am I not to talk to . . .": MB

"the best thing I'd ever read": Interview with Meryl Streep

"took a great deal of care . . .": Interview with Meryl Streep

"You haven't got a prayer . . ." and ""She was younger than me . . .": SCB

"Has there been a character that interesting . . .": Diana Maychick, *Meryl Streep: The Reluctant Superstar,* p. 141

"You're a very nice actress . . .": combined quotation, Interview with Meryl Streep and MB

"I just want you to know . . .": SCB

"Meryl Streep seemed a woman of great strength . . .": Diana Maychick, *Meryl Streep: The Reluctant Superstar,* p. 134

"I had no idea what she was going to do . . .": ED

"Eventually, there were only two people . . .": *NYT,* July 22, 1981

"Oh, he's amazing . . .": combined quotation, Interview with Meryl Streep and Interview with Kevin Kline

"Meryl Streep came in yesterday . . .": Interview with Kevin Kline

"Marty, I've been thinking . . .": SCB

"went home, slept on it . . .": Diana Maychick, *Meryl Streep: The Reluctant Superstar,* pp. 135-36

"The tragedy of Sophie is her vulnerability . . .": Diana Maychick, *Meryl Streep: The Reluctant Superstar,* p. 135

"Sophie and Nathan were possessed . . .": Steven Lewis, "William Styron," pp. 262-63

"to drive away the memory . . .": Charles Kiselyak, *Death Dreams of Mourning*

"one of the stunning moments . . ." [footnote]: Charles Kiselyak, *Death Dreams of Mourning*

"I'll always go with passion": MB

"He thought the guy was just amazing": Interview with Don Laventhall

"I was dazzled . . .": combined quotation, PA and SCD

"bourgeois Jewishness" and "Nathan's sadomasochistic . . ." and "the charismatic . . .": *NYT,* July 22, 1981

"was such a gentleman. . . ." [footnote]: Interview with Kevin Kline

"insanely athletic and idiotically . . .": PA

"There's a part in here . . .": *NYT,* May 9, 1982

"I'm not going to screen-test you . . .": MS

"I don't need you to audition . . .": Interview with Kevin Kline

"His passion, his heroic qualities . . .": *NYT,* December 12, 1982

"It was the most compelling kind of voice . . .": *NYT,* December 17, 1982

"Peter MacNicol came in yesterday . . .": Interview with Kevin Kline

"a story of the journey of this boy . . .": SCD

"The lady came every day to my house . . .": *Inside the Actors Studio* (Guest: Meryl Streep). A co-production of The Actors Studio and Bravo network

"I was making sounds with my voice . . .": MB

"I had some informational . . .": *NYT,* December 12, 1982

"in his madness, [he] intensifies . . .": Charles Kiselyak, *Death Dreams of Mourning*

"Stingo lives in [Nathan and Sophie's] pauses . . .": *NYT,* December 17, 1982

"Look, this movie is all about you three . . .": Interview with Kevin Kline

"to make sure we understand . . .": PA

"the usual five cups of coffee . . .": AI

"Suddenly Meryl opened her mouth. . . .": combined quotation, MB, AI, and *TT*

"she looked different. . . .": SCD

"everything in Alan relaxed . . .": Interview with Meryl Streep

"He hadn't had a chance . . .": combined quotation, SCD and AI

"was totally content to sit around . . .": AI

"Kevin works through his body . . .": combined quotation, AI and Alan J. Pakula,
   "Dialogue on Film"

"I find it sort of putting the cart . . .": Interview with Meryl Streep

"it took me about halfway through . . .": Interview with Kevin Kline

"Alan loved the discussion . . .": Interview with Meryl Streep

"I always thought of him as a novelist . . .": Interview with Meryl Streep

"it was that time spent together . . .": Interview with Kevin Kline

"I like the actors to live in the set . . .": AI

"because he [had done] all these . . .": AI

"And the blocking practically fell into place . . .": SCD

"One day, we all got around the piano . . .": Interview with Kevin Kline

"I felt nothing but liberty . . .": Interview with Meryl Streep

" a lots-of-Kleenex emotional experience . . .": *NYT*, December 12, 1982

"What I loved about the rehearsals . . .": SCD

Peter MacNicol was "devastated": Interview with Alixe Gordon

"I decided that they should all be done . . .": SCD

CHAPTER FIFTEEN

"The number of questions . . .": Joseph McBride, ed., *Filmmakers on Filmmaking: The American Film
   Institute Seminars on Motion Pictures and Television*

"Some directors take jobs . . .": MS

"broke my heart . . .": SCD

"You've got to know . . .": SCD

"I think it was something . . .": Interview with Meryl Streep

"a perfect way of working. . . .": Diana Maychick, *Meryl Streep: The Reluctant Superstar*, p. 137

"the contrast of seeing her . . .": SCD

"And one of the things that helps you . . .": SCD

"It's an 'eye of God' shot . . .": SCD

"I knew after this that I would kill . . .": SCD

"It was already too far along . . .": Interview with Martin Starger

"In fact, Alan constantly took . . .": Interview with Kevin Kline

"Alan helped me choose a makeup artist . . .": Interview with Kevin Kline

"a safe haven for emotions . . .": *ED*

"When we came in in the morning . . .": Interview with Meryl Streep

"I just want the actors not to be afraid . . .": AFI1

"Alan knew the secret of directing actors . . ." [footnote]: MS

"An atmosphere was created in which . . .": *NYT*, December 12, 1982

"He would hear an electric saw . . .": MS

"Sometimes, someone [on the crew] . . .": Interview with Kevin Kline

"At the end of each day's dailies . . .": Interview with Kevin Kline

"doing a film is like a combination . . .": *NYT*, December 12, 1982

"I can see the reviews now . . .": *NYT*, May 9, 1982

"To be allowed to make suggestions . . .": Interview with Kevin Kline

"the manic, manic quality . . .": SCD

"I'm happy. I've got what I need. . . .": Interview with Kevin Kline

"Well, I'd like to do one more . . .": Interview with Kevin Kline

"Aren't you exhausted? We've covered it . . .": MS

"I've rarely seen that kind of indulgence . . .": Interview with Kevin Kline

"From day one, he indulged our every impulse . . .": Interview with Kevin Kline

"Whatever we've talked about earlier . . .": Interview with Kevin Kline

"whisper things in between takes . . .": Interview with Kevin Kline

"When actually shooting, I will very often . . .": DOF2

"on having the actual actors read . . .": PA

"a scene where Nathan and Sophie . . .": Interview with Kevin Kline

"It was a scene when Nathan runs . . .": Interview with Kevin Kline

"I was happy. I was happy from the first day . . .": SCB

"I would never push Meryl in any direction . . .": Diana Maychick, *Meryl Streep: The Reluctant Superstar*, p. 139

"He knew everything. He was like a rabbi. . . .": Interview with Meryl Streep

"I've never worked with an actor who seemed . . .": *NYT*, May 9, 1982

"I can't do anything wrong . . .": Interview with Meryl Streep

"Alan, she's so different . . .": SCD

"we settled on Stingo [as] the sensitive . . .": Charles Kiselyak, *Death Dreams of Mourning*

"I tried to wreck my voice . . .": *NYT*, May 9, 1982

"It seems strange to say of this tragic film . . .": SCD

"a cover of Life magazine . . .": *NYT*, May 9, 1982

"The Yiddish Art Theatre's . . .": SCD

"I want the present tense . . .": SCD

"will also represent death": SCD

"the saving of Sophie by Nathan . . .": SCD

"with wonderful scenes that just don't . . .": SCD

"I think that people who go through . . .": Charles Kiselyak, *Death Dreams of Mourning*

"the most glorious part of erotic love . . .": MB

"There's no question that Styron's Stingo . . .": SCD

"looked like a boy and his mother . . .": SCD

"Kevin did a wonderful job . . .": SCD

"This is my way of trying to show . . .": SCD

"It seems curiously different in style . . .": SCD

"Peter's wonderful in this scene . . .": SCD

"The caring is here . . .": SCD

"That should have appealed to some . . .": SCD

"What I see in there is hurt . . .": SCD

"where Kevin started to really get [a sense of madness] . . .": SCD

"There are so many ways to play this scene . . .": SCD

"A director is somebody who has to sort of . . .": Interview with Meryl Streep

"We were all lined up in front of the mirror . . .": Interview with Meryl Streep

"that they weren't going to shoot . . .": PA

Polish actors threatened with expulsion from Poland: Steven Lewis, "William Styron," p. 63

"The Polish government's objection . . .": MB

"I did not want to destroy . . ." and "However, all but one . . .": MB

"it's inside that the difference comes . . .": SCD

"almost overripe colors": SCD

"the camera running around the back . . .": SCD

"everything is the inner life . . .": SCD

"like a pig during the whole first part . . .": SCB

"I would never do Auschwitz . . .": PA

"Mr. Pakula, I had my experience at . . .": MB

"stayed by my side at all times": MB

"merely to help her to learn . . .": SCB

"you got stuck in the mud . . .": SCB

"The camera just goes over the . . .": SCD

"as if in some total nightmare . . .": SCD

"like Hollywood Nazis at all. . . .": *NYT,* May 9, 1982

"To see this 'wholesome' . . .": SCD

"are people like ourselves . . .": SCD

"Alan, I don't know that much German . . .": SCD

"The girl's a brilliant actress . . .": SCD

"was very concerned that all of us . . .": SCD

"Well, Jennifer, I hear you can speak Polish. . . .": SCB

"innocence—innocence that we . . .": SCD

"There's a certain kind of pornography . . .": SCD

"I read it once . . . and never read it again . . .": Charles Kiselyak, *Death Dreams of Mourning*

"We have him in there . . .": SCD

"What? She's a little girl . . .": combined quotation, SCD and *TT*

"There goes the scene. . . .": SCD

"didn't do anything cruel . . .": SCD

"I had no idea how I was going to play . . .": SCD

"I thought I was screaming . . .": Charles Kiselyak, *Death Dreams of Mourning*

"more real" and "less conventional": SCD

"It was one of the more barbaric . . .": SCD

"It was one of the most unforgettable nights . . .": SCD

"kind of lyrical, almost . . .": Charles Kiselyak, *Death Dreams of Mourning*

"not only serves as a counterpoint . . .": Annette Insdorf, *Indelible Shadows: Films and the Holocaust,* p. 38

"They were both joined in this . . .": Charles Kiselyak, *Death Dreams of Mourning*

"in some way in death [their] love . . .": Charles Kiselyak, *Death Dreams of Mourning*

"is left feeling kind of ennobled . . .": Charles Kiselyak, *Death Dreams of Mourning*

"was a very good man when it came . . .": Interview with Martin Starger

"with all fondness and respect . . .": Interview with Martin Starger

"is often very good, and often not so good . . .": Interview with Martin Starger

"On the first day of shooting what was the Auschwitz camp . . .": Interview with Martin Starger

"He felt and loved that story . . .": Interview with Martin Starger

"might have been in the areas . . .": Interview with Meryl Streep

"The film is so emotional . . .": DOF2

"ennoble . . . a gentle lovingness . . .": SCD

"to surround and protect": SCD

"people who fail to understand that . . .": Robert K. Morris with Irving Mailin, eds.
The Achievement of William Styron, p. 59

"classical music was Sophie's attempt . . .": Barbara Tepa Lupack, *Take Two: Adapting the Contemporary American Novel to Film*

"astounding . . . was really like a musician. . . .": Interview with Marvin Hamlisch

"The only really tough thing . . .": Diana Maychick, *Meryl Streep: The Reluctant Superstar*, p. 141

"the greatest gift of my career . . .": MS

Cecile Insdorf's tape of Sophie's lines in French: Interview with Annette Insdorf

"was the most wonderful film or acting experience . . .": MS

"spoiled me for all directors after him . . .": Interview with Kevin Kline

"The audience just sat there . . .": SCB

"I think the great virtue of the film . . .": Steven Lewis, "William Styron," p. 261

"I think I was as well served . . .": Steven Lewis, "William Styron," p. 271

"I think that seeing where she does . . .": SCB

"I felt that Peter MacNicol was miscast . . .": Interview with William Styron

"I've worked with some of the most gifted actors . . .": combined quotation, *ED* and Charles Champlin, "For Pakula, It's Falling in Love With Love and Being in Love," *Los Angeles Times*, March 5, 1989

"If I had done that film with [Vasaryova] . . .": AI

"Alan was excellent with Meryl. . . .": Interview with Martin Starger

"I was not aware of any frustration . . .": Interview with Martin Starger

"an infuriatingly bad movie": the *New Yorker*, December 27, 1982

"gummy rhetoric": the *New Republic*, January 10 and January 17, 1983

"its inexorable momentum . . .": *NYT*, December 10, 1982

"a complete woman . . . a woman of the sort . . .": *NYT*, December 12, 1982

"a film that casts a powerful . . .": *New York Daily News*, clipping, BRTC

"the accent and the expressive Polish . . .": *Newsweek*, December 10, 1982

CHAPTER SIXTEEN

"The whole world was the canvas . . .": Interview with Celia Costas

"I just loved him so much . . .": Interview with Celia Costas

"We had a really good relationship . . .": Interview with Gordon Willis

"One of his problems . . .": Interview with Gordon Willis

"very indecisive. He would have problems . . .": Interview with Gordon Willis

"You know, he wasn't the most confident . . .": Interview with Chris Murray

"indecisive is probably the wrong word. . . .": Interview with Anna Boorstin

"I can see twenty-five different . . .": Jack Hirshberg, *A Portrait of All the President's Men*, p. 51

"I don't feel that [he was indecisive] at all. . . .": Interview with Jane Alexander

"No." [about whether Pakula was indecisive]: Interview with Hume Cronyn

"He really wanted actors . . .": Interview with Jill Clayburgh

"It's very important, I find . . ." [footnote]: AFI1

"I would never have called Alan indecisive. . . .": Interview with Dianne Dreyer

"The worst thing to me about making a film . . .": AFI1

"you don't want to make decisions too quickly . . .": Interview with Pieter Jan Brugge

"Procrastination at times . . .": Interview with Pieter Jan Brugge

"One thing about Alan is he never liked . . .": Interview with Don Laventhall

"wanted to have a good time . . .": Interview with Don Laventhall

"I said to him, thinking this was . . .": Interview with Don Laventhall

"I don't think it was control. . . .": Interview with Don Laventhall

"That was the defining moment . . .": Interview with Don Laventhall

"I think he was far more successful with women . . .": Interview with Michael Small

"all different . . . It seems to me . . .": MB

"If I had to summarize Alan . . .": Interview with Robert Redford

"fascinates me . . . because it is an exploration . . .": RT

"is the one I would say I feel closest to . . .": DOF1

"all those films I saw when I was eleven . . .": DOF1

"You can suck up certain techniques . . .": AFI1

"You've got to respect your material . . .": AI

"He could be a little fussy sometimes . . .": Interview with Catherine Solt

"he could be extremely difficult. . . .": Interview with Celia Costas

"than anyone else I've worked for . . .": Interview with Catherine Solt

CHAPTER SEVENTEEN

"Alan had a way of dusting himself off . . .": Interview with Harry Clein

"worthy of his talents": Interview with Boaty Boatwright

"really hated that script": Interview with Alixe Gordon

"were dying to do it . . .": Interview with Boaty Boatwright

"had the same taste in actors": Interview with Alixe Gordon

"If you are working with . . .": DOF2

"for something in the actor . . .": AFI1

"if [she] was emotionally ready . . .": *Movieline*, February 21, 1986

"showcase" and "We just clicked": *Movieline*, February 21, 1986

"a young girl who has spent . . .": *NYT*, March 2, 1984

"another attempt to combine melodrama with character study": *NYT*, March 2, 1984

Intermingling dreams and reality: AFI1

"I think she's one of the most gifted . . .": combined quotation, DOF2 and *ED*

"kind of a disaster in some ways . . .": Interview with Michael Small

"There are a few visual sequences . . .": *ED*

"wasn't up to the level . . .": Interview with Harry Clein

"was very protective about . . ." [footnote]: Interview with Lauren Bacall

"*Dream Lover* is the worst kind of . . .": *Los Angeles Times*, February 21, 1986

"career woman that she is . . .": *NYT*, October 11, 1986

"nervous about his career": Interview with Anna Boorstin

"Alan had a way of dusting himself off . . .": Interview with Harry Clein

"I'd love to work with Alan again. . . .": *Movieline*, February 21, 1986

"a child's fear of darkness . . .": RT

"but, witnessing and in a sense . . ." [footnote]: Donald Carveth, "Dead End Kids: Projective Identification and Sacrifice in Orphans"

"always avoided [using] plays . . .": AI

"was touched and amused by it . . .": AI

"First of all, it is a story about parenting . . .": AI

"the gangster on the lam . . .": AI

"I think there may be a beginning . . .": AI

"deeply respectful": Interview with Lyle Kessler

"open them up . . . they let the air in . . .": AI

"give a sense of the world . . .": AI

"demands a very particular kind of . . .": *NYT*, September 13, 1987

"if Alan asked me to do a scene . . .": *NYT*, September 13, 1987 "he would be so locked into the role . . .": *NYT*, September 13, 1987

"knew where all the laughs were . . .": AI

"difficulty attaining the same . . .": *NYT*, September 13, 1987

"He just started from scratch. . . .": *NYT*, September 13, 1987

"needed an outsize quality . . .": AI

"looked intimidating" and "he made me laugh a lot . . .": *NYT*, September 27, 1987

"kept being haunted by Matthew. . . .": *NYT*, September 27, 1987

"None of the jokes were working . . .": *NYT*, September 27, 1987

"Kevin and Albert were very good . . .": *NYT*, September 27, 1987

"It was in Alan's interest . . .": *NYT*, September 27, 1987

"He worked with them . . .": AI

"Matthew, if you get the speech . . .": AI

"suddenly, everything fell into place": *NYT*, September 27, 1987

"this is a street boy. . . .": AI

"you see the fear on [Modine's] face . . .": AI

"who had no impulse control": Interview with Lyle Kessler

"he invited me to his apartment": Interview with Lyle Kessler

"I looked at it . . .": Interview with Lyle Kessler

"house is Phillip's whole world . . .": *NYT*, September 13, 1987

"Well, Matthew looked all over . . .": *NYT*, September 13, 1987

"I don't necessarily tell them . . .": combined quotation, AFI1 and DOF2

Pakula using Harold's line with his cast and crew: Interview with Celia Costas

"was like going into this . . .": *NYT*, September 27, 1987

"Some people criticized that . . .": Interview with Lyle Kessler

"The unusual accomplishment of Mr. Pakula . . .": *NYT*, September 18, 1987

"top form . . . It's not often that a play . . .": *TV Guide's Movie Guide:* Cinebooks Database

"movies work best when they break . . .": *Chicago Sun-Times*, September 25, 1987

"nothing but amateurish gallery-playing . . .": *Washington Post*, October 23, 1987

"scramble and grapple like demented gerbils . . .": *Washington Post*, October 24, 1987

"a farce . . . and obviously it's not a farce . . .": AI

"we drowned in art. . . .": *Los Angeles Times*, March 5, 1989

"something he wanted to do . . .": Interview with Celia Costas

"true confessions": *NYT*, April 16, 1989

"on the other hand, I couldn't have . . .": *Los Angeles Times*, March 5, 1989

"I guess because . . .": Interview with Boaty Boatwright

"If I do this film, everybody's going . . .": *NYT*, April 16, 1989

"wanted the film to be some kind of . . .": *NYT*, April 16, 1989

"about people who've had other lives . . .": *Los Angeles Times*, March 5, 1989

"Coming out of a bad experience . . .": *NYT*, April 16, 1989

"It means closing the door on ever living . . .": PA

"with a huge roar . . ." [footnote]: Bruce Weber, "Family Ties Bind Pakula To His 'Morning'," *NYT*, April 16, 1989

"terribly twee" [footnote]: *NYT*, April 21, 1989

"glibly elliptical . . .": *Washington Post*, April 21, 1989

"At this point in my life . . .": *Los Angeles Times*, March 5, 1989

"it just didn't happen . . .": Interview with Meryl Streep

"You can't imbue an actor . . .": *Los Angeles Times*, March 5, 1989

"It was a brilliant way . . .": Interview with Michael Small

"a wonderful community for people . . .": www.krige-pate.com/morning/html

"was all improvised. Alan set us all down . . .": Interview with Chris Murray

"It takes a special kind of courage . . .": www.krige-pate.com/morning/html

"because his goal was to entertain people": Interview with Celia Costas

"It was a very special . . .": Interview with Hannah Pakula

"*See You in the Morning* works in the manner of . . .": *NYT*, April 21, 1989

"fairly ghastly . . ." *NYT*, April 21, 1989

"I liked the people in *See You in the Morning* . . .": *Chicago Sun-Times*, April 21, 1989

"I think he was very, very hurt . . .": Interview with Boaty Boatwright

"at the top of lists. . . .": Interview with Harry Clein

"never looked back" [footnote]: Interview with Harry Clein

CHAPTER EIGHTEEN

"When Alan and I . . .": Interview with Harrison Ford

"There are so many ways . . .": Interview with Frank Pierson

"So, I went away and wrote . . .:" Interview with Frank Pierson

"on one condition, and that was that he remain . . .": Interview with Frank Pierson

"all juiced up . . . it opened with a couple making love . . .": AI

"You know, I love the book. . .": Interview with Frank Pierson

"It's about law and it's about order . . .": quoted in interview with Frank Pierson

"It's a completely, absolutely . . .": Interview with Frank Pierson

"Far from being an impressionistic . . .": Interview with Frank Pierson

"a repressed man, controlled man . . .": AI

"a story of a rational, decent . . .": combined quotation, *NYT*, January 27, 1989,
    and *NYT*, July 22, 1990

"gives me a chance to use . . .": *NYT*, January 27, 1989

"*Indiana Jones* may be his . . .": combined quotation, *NYT*, July 22, 1990, and *TT*

"For all his success and great . . .": *Presumed Innocent* Production Notes

"It's one thing to be fascinated . . .": *NYT*, January 27, 1989

"What about *All the President's Men*? . . .": *NYT*, July 22, 1990

"You mean like the screen version . . ." [footnote]: *NYT*, July 22, 1990

"seeing the movie and reading the novel . . .": *NYT*, July 22, 1990

"One of the core problems . . .": Combined quotation, *ED* and *TT*

"It was a very collaborative . . .": Interview with Frank Pierson

"Harrison Ford was always looking to find . . .": Interview with Frank Pierson

"a story about the most unreasonable . . .": *TT*

"would rework it with my computer . . .": Interview with Frank Pierson

"toward the end of it we began to diverge. . . .": Interview with Frank Pierson

"all the little character touches": Interview with Frank Pierson

"When I see the movie I don't understand . . .": Interview with Frank Pierson

"interestingly enough, Alan cut some things . . ." [footnote]: Interview with Frank Pierson

"There were things in it . . .": Interview with Frank Pierson

"Gordy, if you want to do this film . . .": AI

"I [didn't] want a lot of camera movement . . .": *TT*

"I found that [the audience] would concentrate . . .": AI

"was not particularly generous . . .": Interview with Celia Costas

"It was fascinating to sit around the table . . .": *ED*

"this was a tough role . . .": *NYT*, July 22, 1990

"Harrison must sit silently . . .": *NYT,* July 22, 1990

"Those courtroom scenes . . .": *NYT,* July 22, 1990

"Harrison was [playing] a man . . .": AI

"before we got to the stage . . .": Interview with Harrison Ford

"not much of a fan of rehearsal. . . .": Interview with Harrison Ford

"Harrison was very unenthusiastic . . .": AI

"When Alan and I worked together . . .": Interview with Harrison Ford

"a natural guide to inner realms": PA

"To me, the haircut represented a guy . . .": *ED*

"If it helped him give that performance . . .": *TT*

"I see physicalization of character . . .": *Inside the Actors Studio* (Guest: Harrison Ford).
   A co-production of the Actors Studio and Bravo network

"There is a problem . . .": *TT*

"To suddenly cut into a flashback . . .": *TT*

"went through hell": Interview with Frank Pierson

"I cut it because . . .": Alan J. Pakula, quoted during interview with Frank Pierson

"She just knocked me . . .": Alan J. Pakula, quoted during interview with Frank Pierson

"There are directors who feel . . .": *ED*

"an artist—in a community . . .": *ED*

"He was pushing like mad . . .": AI

"You've got to feel that way . . .": AI

"There's a certain amount of tension . . .": AFI1

"can do something that they think . . .": AFI1

"We tried to show how the system works . . .": *NYT,* July 22, 1990

"Warner Bros. and the filmmakers . . .": Warner Bros. Production Notes for *Presumed Innocent*

"spellbinding courtroom novel . . .": *NYT,* July 27, 1990

"Presumed Innocent has at its core . . .": *Chicago Sun-Times,* July 27, 1990

"a solid whodunit . . .": *Washington Post,* July 27, 1990

"Every filmmaker is interested in commercial . . .": Interview with Pieter Jan Brugge

"Alan was always intrigued . . .": Interview with Celia Costas

"There wasn't something that was lined up . . .": Interview with Don Laventhall

"The more I direct, the more I . . .": UE

"Why do you want to make this film?" and "This movie offers me . . .":
   Interview with Pieter Jan Brugge

"worked very hard on the scripts . . .": Interview with Boaty Boatwright

'You'-e going to be the victim . . ." and "I can't believe you could be married . . .":
   Interview with Kevin Kline

'You're ;oing to love working with . . .": Interview with Kevin Kline

'from the first day, it was all about the camera": Interview with Kevin Kline

"This is totally different. . . .": quoted in interview with Kevin Kline

"talking at great length about the color . . .": Interview with Kevin Kline

"No, frankly, I preferred the old way . . .": Interview with Kevin Kline

"a scene in the car with Mary . . .": Interview with Kevin Kline

"that with that film Alan was struggling . . .": Interview with Michael Small

"Disney hoped for . . .": Interview with Pieter Jan Brugge

"to bring a level . . .": Interview with Pieter Jan Brugge

"He can't have that kind of machine gun . . .": Interview with Kevin Kline

"The audience wanted the comfort . . .": Interview with Pieter Jan Brugge

"In terms of his reasons . . .": Interview with Pieter Jan Brugge

"even more far-fetched than most . . .": *NYT*, October 16, 1992

"a great little thriller . . .": *Washington Post*, October 16, 1992

"boneheaded . . . as mindless and sloppy . . .": *Washington Post*, October 16, 1992

"he just tells a wonderful yarn . . .": *TT*

"the relationship between the . . .": RT

"What he did was to take the book . . .": Interview with Don Laventhall

"there were certain things that had to be . . .": Interview with Don Laventhall

"One of my personal favorite scenes in that picture . . .": *ED*

"I gave him tons of material . . .": Interview with Catherine Solt

"No one ever says, 'I love you' . . .": *TT*

"something of a rarity . . .": Interview with Hume Cronyn

"I think at that point he was struggling . . .": Interview with Chris Murray

"He would never have signed on . . .": Interview with Don Laventhall

"I can always tell when you meet with Julia . . .": quoted in *ED*

"time and freedom to find things . . .": *NYT*, November 20, 1998

"She had this containment . . .": *ED*

"She was really, really . . .": *TT*

"I'm telling you, this was a dream": *NYT*, December 12, 1993

"I was blessed with Denzel Washington . . .": *TT*

"Alan's voice was always . . .": Interview with Pieter Jan Brugge

"One thing that Alan was adamant . . ." [footnote]: Interview with Don Laventhall

"we were doing a shot with a crane . . .": Interview with Dianne Dreyer

"enter into that dialogue. . . .": Interview with Pieter Jan Brugge

"genuinely loved collaboration . . .": Interview with Pieter Jan Brugge

"The importance of casting . . .": combined quotation, DOF2, DOF1, and AFI1

"a totally bastardized picture . . .": AFI1

"He interfaced differently . . .": Interview with Patricia Anne Doherty [Hess]

"tremendously significant in my career . . .": Interview with Dianne Dreyer

"We found a way to make her . . .": Notes from the DVD of *The Pelican Brief*

"Alan wanted all of the hotel rooms . . .": Notes from the DVD of *The Pelican Brief*

"Based on financial success . . .": Interview with Don Laventhall

"instant movie material . . .": *NYT*, December 17, 1993

"Visiting aliens wishing to experience . . .": *Washington Post*, December 17, 1993

"a skilled craftsman who has done . . .": *Chicago Sun-Times*, December 17, 1993

"not as full and rich an experience . . .": Interview with Don Laventhall

CHAPTER NINETEEN

"we pulled into the airport . . .": Interview with Don Laventhall

"broaden the horizon . . .": Interview with Don Laventhall

"We optioned tons of material . . .": Interview with Don Laventhall

"So Alan proceeded to do that . . .": Interview with Don Laventhall

"I didn't think it was a film . . .": Interview with Boaty Boatwright

"I think he thought it could help . . .": Interview with Catherine Solt

"to keep his company going. . . .": Interview with Catherine Solt

"it didn't cover everything . . .": Interview with Don Laventhall

"thought he could do something with the script . . .": Interview with Catherine Solt

"We'll see what it's like when I'm . . .": Interview with Chris Murray

Gordon was astonished when Harrison Ford agreed to appear in the film:
Interview with Lawrence Gordon

"I'd been sending Harrison . . .": *Urban Cinefile*

"I was delighted to have the chance . . .": Interview with Harrison Ford

"and neither was I": Interview with Harrison Ford

"a totally down-on-his-luck . . .": Interview with Don Laventhall

"there was a transition in Harrison Ford. . . .": Interview with Catherine Solt

"That required a great deal of rethinking . . .": Interview with Don Laventhall

"The main thing that I was looking for . . .": Interview with Harrison Ford

"There were questions from Brad's side . . .": Interview with Harrison Ford

"he'd had it for years . . .": Interview with Harrison Ford

"Alan was always going to try . . .": Interview with Celia Costas

"were truly substantive . . .": Interview with Don Laventhall

"go back and forth between these two camps . . .": Interview with Robert Kamen

"his own trailer" and "and he was sitting in there . . .": Interview with Don Laventhall

"The problem was that we only came up . . .": Interview with Harrison Ford

"things were becoming unglued . . .": Interview with Gordon Willis

"the only time he spoke to me . . .": Interview with Debby Maisel

"Alan was miserable": Interview with Anna Boorstin

"Alan was quite discreet . . ." [footnote]: Interview with Peter Jennings

"He did not say, 'Oh, damn that guy.' . . ." [footnote]: Interview with Marilyn Berger

"stopped by to visit Alan . . .": Interview with Patricia Anne Doherty [Hess]

"Alan was damned uncomfortable . . .": Interview with Harrison Ford

"was physically tough . . .": Interview with Robert Kamen

"The movie took a lot out of him. . . .": Interview with Don Hewitt

"You can't get up at seven . . .": Interview with Hannah Pakula

"Yeah, he was home for dinner . . .": Interview with Robert Kamen

"What I saw was somebody . . .": Interview with Don Laventhall

"It was a pretty cold morning . . .": Interview with Don Laventhall

"always inventive, supportive . . .": Interview with Harrison Ford

"There's more than one way to kill yourself. . . .": Interview with Robert Kamen

"He just kept his options open . . .": Interview with Robert Kamen

"just felt it was too unconventional . . .": *NYT*, March 30, 1997

"was terrified. We must have gone through . . .": Interview with Don Laventhall

"Look, either I kill him . . .": Harrison Ford, quoted in interview with Don Laventhall

"these two men still respect and care . . .": *NYT*, March 30, 1997

"collaborative method": Interview with Robert Kamen

"the most irresponsible bit of . . .": *Newsweek*, February 3, 1997

"I tried to when there was a week . . .": *Newsweek*, February 3, 1997

"it's not done. Actors do not . . .": Interview with Don Laventhall

"No. One of the actors . . .": Interview with Don Laventhall

"How can we start a film when we don't . . .": *NYT*, March 30, 1997

"a bit unhinged by the failure . . .": *NYT*, March 30, 1997

"It wasn't the clash of the titans . . .": *NYT*, March 30, 1997

"There was all the pressure from the studio . . .": Interview with Robert Kamen

"There is no secret that we were . . .": *NYT*, March 30, 1997

"I learned a lot from Alan about actors. . . .": Interview with Robert Kamen

"Alan always felt that there was a way . . .": Interview with Don Laventhall "did [Rory] really plan to sail . . .": *Chicago Sun-Times*, March 3, 1997

"I know that he worked very hard . . .": Interview with Keren Saks

"I think it was an infinitely better film . . .": Interview with Boaty Boatwright

"probably represented the best work . . .": Interview with Don Laventhall

"when Pitt saw the picture he actually liked it": Interview with Robert Kamen

"To Alan, I would say we've . . .": card from Brad Pitt to Alan Pakula

"a fraught process . . .": Interview with Harrison Ford

"to my dilemma before shooting began . . .": *Newsweek*, February 10, 1997

"What's interesting to me is . . .": *NYT*, March 30, 1997

"disaster . . . I can't imagine what it would have been like . . .": *NYT*, March 30, 1997

"This was one of the most complex . . .": *Urban Cinefile*

"two quite remarkable actors . . .": *Urban Cinefile*

"There's rewriting and there's rewriting . . .": *NYT*, March 30, 1997

"Sometimes it takes longer . . .": *NYT*, March 30, 1997

"Killing Brad Pitt probably . . .": quoted in interview with Don Laventhall

"an atrocious mess . . ." [footnote]: Interview with Patricia Anne Doherty [Hess]

"unexpectedly solid thriller . . .": *NYT*, March 26, 1997

"a well-crafted suspenser . . .": *Variety*, quoted in *NYT*, March 30, 1997

"story of friendship and betrayal . . .": *San Francisco Chronicle*, March 26, 1997

"how to move things along. . . .": the *New Republic*, April 21, 1997

"Ford has his own half-movie . . .": *Los Angeles Times*, March 26, 1997

"No one seeing The Devil's Own can miss . . .": *Los Angeles Times*, March 26, 1997

"a rather grubby action movie": *London Sunday Times*, November 25, 2001

"epically awful": *Washington Post*, March 28, 1997.

"I don't think so, simply because . . .": Interview with Don Laventhall

CHAPTER TWENTY

"style was more thoughtful . . .": *NYT*, November 23, 1998

"I think he very much wanted . . .": Interview with Catherine Solt

"Months later, Alan did send me a new . . .": Interview with Robert Mulligan

"what happened with Alan was that . . .": Interview with Don Laventhall

"He was very healthy . . .": Interview with Catherine Solt

"He didn't want to do commercial stuff . . .": Interview with Catherine Solt

"He loved working. It was his . . .": Interview with Don Laventhall

"he lost his [directorial] legs . . .": Interview with Hannah Pakula

"He had not put it away . . .": Interview with Don Laventhall

"I am slow . . . I know [I'll be spending] . . .": AFI1

"Studios were interested and . . .": Interview with Don Laventhall

"the audience for something like this . . .": Interview with Don Laventhall

"that's what *No Ordinary Time* was about . . .": Interview with Catherine Solt

"He was trying to figure out . . .": Interview with Bob Woodward

"When he talked about his work . . .": MS

"For me . . . one of the great sadnesses . . .": Interview with Hannah Pakula

"We believe the metal pipe . . .": *Newsday*, November 20, 1998

"He died minutes after . . .": *Newsday*, November 20, 1998

"because they were close friends . . .": Interview with Hannah Pakula

"said to my teacher . . .": Interview with Marilyn Berger

"Alan was killed, and I wanted . . .": quoted in interview with Debby Maisel

"I was devastated by his death . . .": Interview with Celia Costas

"These days, I take lots of comfort . . .": Interview with Louis Boorstin

"I certainly wouldn't have done anything . . .": Interview with Hannah Pakula

"spectacular . . . eccentric . . . complicated . . .": clipping, BRTC

"I never met anybody in my life . . .": clipping, BRTC

"His life was gentle . . .": MS

"is now considered by many . . .": Deborah H. Holdstein and R. Barton Palmer, *The St. James Film Directors Encyclopedia*, p. 375

"Alan J. Pakula's body of work . . .": *Los Angeles Times*, November 21, 1998

"best films achieved great elegance": *London Daily Telegraph*, November 21, 1998

"his brand of knowing understatement . . .": *NYT*, November 23, 1998

"very strong visual style . . .": Interview with Pieter Jan Brugge

"You have to be prepared for everything . . .": *TT*

"I can't work the way Hitchcock works. . . .": AFI1

"If you use close-ups all the time . . .": SCD

"camera movement, cuts, close-ups are the . . .": AI

"If you overuse camera movement . . .": combined quotation, DOF2 and RT

"If the design image I have in my mind . . .": PA

"If you show everything in a film . . .": SCD

"I think if I'm passionate about something . . .": DOF2

"lingering too long on shots . . .": DOF2

"when the filmmaker loves his characters . . .": SCD

"The world went through . . .": MB

"You look back on your films . . .": *TT*

"contrasts between light and dark . . .": *TT*

"He loved all of the playing . . .": Interview with Boaty Boatwright

"in which he was involved in every single area. . . .": Interview with Pieter Jan Brugge

"The minute a film is finished . . .": AI

"a mentor, a father figure, a teacher": Interview with Kevin Kline

"was a father figure to any young person . . .": Interview with Bob Boorstin

"sensitivity and intellect to seemingly . . .": Robert Redford, "Alan J. Pakula: Seeking Truth on the Big Screen"

"to break the tension by not taking himself . . .": MS

"My work . . . [me] a chance to get into worlds . . .": MB